A RAGE FOR JUSTICE

JOHN JACOBS

A RAGE FOR JUSTICE

The Passion and Politics of
Phillip Burton

UNIVERSITY OF CALIFORNIA PRESS

BERKELEY   LOS ANGELES   LONDON

University of California Press
Berkeley and Los Angeles, California

University of California Press, Ltd.
London, England

© 1995 by
The Regents of the University of California

Jacobs, John, 1950–
    A rage for justice: the passion and politics of Phillip
Burton / John Jacobs.
            p.   cm.
    Includes bibliographical references and index.
    ISBN 0-520-20076-4 (alk. paper)
    1. Burton, Phillip.   2. Legislators—United States—
Biography.   3. United States. Congress. House—
Biography.   I. Title.
E840.8.B86J33   1995
328.73′092—dc20
    [B]   94-36185
                                                        CIP

Printed in the United States of America
9 8 7 6 5 4 3 2 1

To the memory of my mother,
Leonie Gutman Jacobs, 1915–1993,
to my father, Julius Lloyd Jacobs,
and to Carol, Max, and Maggie

I spent thirty-two years in elective office, and I only met one absolute political genius. That was Phil Burton.

SENATOR GAYLORD NELSON OF WISCONSIN

CONTENTS

AUTHOR'S NOTE
AND ACKNOWLEDGMENTS

One could not grow up in San Francisco reading newspapers in the 1960s, as I did, without knowing that Congressman Phillip Burton dominated the political scene. But it was not until I began writing about politics full-time for the *San Francisco Examiner* in the early and mid-1980s, soon after Burton's death, that I really began to appreciate his remarkable national stature and political skill. Although I only met him once, everywhere I turned, it seemed, I ran up against his legacy. In the mad scramble to succeed his late widow, Sala Burton, in Congress in early 1987, I witnessed his power by observing its absence. For a while, it seemed like almost every politician in the city wanted to run. It was the kind of robust, open competition San Francisco had not seen in years, largely because Phillip Burton had for so long dictated who the candidates would be and single-handedly held political egos in check.

As I looked into Burton's life, I learned the details of his accomplishments in Washington, where he had long been one of the giants of Capitol Hill. It was the difference between knowing that he was powerful and knowing how he exercised that power. The more I discovered for myself his seminal role in national politics and government—from black lung, occupational health and safety, and other labor issues, to congressional reform, House leadership, national parks, and the environment—the more intrigued I became.

Born too late to watch Lyndon Johnson at close hand, I realized that Phillip

Burton was the closest I would likely ever get to observing a political genius. If much of what he did was new and startling to me, I reasoned it would be new to the great majority of other political aficionados not only in California and Washington but around the nation. I found it significant that the most excited responses to my request for interviews came not from his home district of San Francisco, where Burton was known and respected, but from Capitol Hill, where the congressional staffers, political reporters, and operatives had a far deeper and more subtle appreciation of his political talents.

Indeed, it was not until I was well into my research that I learned Burton deliberately sought this anonymity: he distrusted the local press and was reticent about broadcasting his successes, partly out of fear he would alert his adversaries to them. He cared more about getting it done than getting the credit, and if, by letting others claim authorship, he could help a colleague or guarantee another vote on a future Burton project, so much the better.

I reasoned that if I could understand the nature of Burton's political genius—how step-by-step he accomplished what he did—I might then communicate something important about how American politics works. Beyond developing a healthy respect for the pure tactical and strategic brilliance he employed to achieve his goals, I also found Burton to be such a compelling, if often offensive, personality that my interest in him never wavered from the moment of my first interviews in the spring of 1987.

This book is thus an effort to explain the man in his full political dimension and make as explicit as possible how he did what he did. Early in my research, I sought the counsel of noted congressional authority Nelson Polsby, director of the Institute of Governmental Studies at the University of California, Berkeley. Not only was he enthusiastic about a Burton biography, he invited me to research and write the book at his institute as a visiting scholar. It was an offer I eagerly accepted for ten weeks in the summer of 1989 and for nearly fourteen months starting in November 1990. Beyond the obvious—the office, phone, photocopy machine, and impressive IGS library and staff—Polsby supplied something far more valuable: access to a community of scholars and a supporting and civilized environment in which to work, from the afternoon teas with students and faculty to the wide range of scholars, journalists, government officials, and political consultants who were constantly dropping by and sharing their research or discussing their activities.

Over the first of many meals, Polsby observed that most congressional biographies fail because authors understand their subjects either in Washington or in their home districts, but not usually in both places. Intended or not, this was an early warning signal. I became determined to understand my subject in both areas of his life.

Most of the research came from nearly 400 interviews—some as many as fifteen hours long—that I conducted with people from every phase of Burton's life, including forty-seven members or former members of Congress and the last four Democratic House Speakers. The interviews were supplemented by forty-five cartons of his personal papers at UC Berkeley's Bancroft Library. These papers, which I read exhaustively, provided key newspaper and magazine articles, early Burton work product, congressional testimony, occasional correspondence, background on and drafts of his various bills, and new angles to explore. Several sources said they witnessed Burton sitting at his desk, carefully thinning his files, which were extraordinarily well organized when they arrived at the Bancroft.

After several months of going through the files, I began to feel that Burton had maintained them as though he were waiting for a biographer to come along some day and exploit this treasure trove. The markers were there. But as anyone who knew Burton would testify, the deals he cut and the alliances he forged were never written down. It was essential to unravel what he did from extensive interviews with participants. Beyond my own knowledge about local, state, and national politics, I supplemented the interviews and personal papers with extensive reading on state government and Congress.

In most cases, my information came from at least two sources, although often more than two sources provided additional confirmation, backed up by documentation in Burton's papers, in books, or in other written materials. Direct quotations are either from interviews with participants or from written materials that are footnoted or attributed in the text. The more I learned about Burton, the more confident I became in weighing the credibility of sources, particularly in the few instances when I relied on just one.

Three people refused to be interviewed. One was Raymond Sullivan, the former California Supreme Court justice who was once a law partner of Bill Malone, the powerful but now forgotten political boss of San Francisco from the late 1930s to the early 1950s. The other two served in Congress with Burton: David Obey of Wisconsin and former Congressman James Corman of California. The book would have benefited from their contributions.

Beyond Professor Polsby, who read every chapter as it came out of the printer and saved me from errors in fact and interpretation, there are many to thank for their contributions. But a special thanks must go to four other people, without whom this book could not have been written: to Naomi Schneider, my editor at the University of California Press, who solicited this manuscript after reading a magazine excerpt on the 1976 majority leader race and who has been enthusiastic and encouraging throughout this long process; to Tom Leyton, director of the Gerbode Foundation in San Francisco, whose generous early financial support made the book economically feasible; and to Robert and John Burton. This is not an "official" or "authorized" biography, but they made time available whenever I asked to share reminiscences, sometimes painful ones, about their brother and early family life and also came through with family photographs and access to dozens of other friends and colleagues who worked or went to school with Phillip Burton.

At the Institute of Governmental Studies, I also wish to thank Associate Director Bruce Cain, who read and offered comments on an early draft, Assistant Director Adrienne Jamieson, who has moved on to become director of the Stanford in Washington program, former IGS Director Eugene Lee, and Director of Publications Gerald Lubenow. IGS research librarians Terry Dean Langer, Ron Heckart, Mark Levin, and Susan Schneider and staffers Kathy Burgess and Diana Neves were especially helpful in locating obscure monographs and other reference materials. At the Bancroft Library, librarians David Res, Franz Enciso, Alyson Belcher, Jason Pries-Paffner, Walter Bream, Annegret Ogden, Teri Rinne, and William Roberts helped me navigate through the Burton papers and other documents, and Gabrielle Morris of the Bancroft's unsung but invaluable Regional Oral History Office was also generous with her time and oral histories.

I wish to thank five other scholars and activists who carefully read the manuscript, caught errors, and offered useful suggestions: Bill Cavala, a Berkeley Ph.D. in political science who has been one of assembly Speaker Willie Brown's top political consultants for more than a decade and who lived through many of the events recounted here; Tony Quinn, a Republican activist who opposed Burton's reapportionment activities and whose doctoral dissertation in political science on the history of California redistricting was immensely valuable; Norman Ornstein of the American Enterprise Institute in Washington, who has written seminal works on the era of congressional reform in which Burton participated; Larry Berg, director of the Jesse Unruh Institute of Politics at the University of Southern California; and Michael Rogin, a political theorist at UC Berkeley, who read this manuscript no less carefully or thoughtfully than he read my senior thesis twenty-two years earlier. Thanks also to University of California Press project editor Scott Norton, copy editor Steve Gilmartin, and indexer Mary Hughes.

For financial support, I must also thank the May and Stanley Smith Charitable Trust, the Madeleine Haas Russell Fund of the Columbia Foundation,

John Kornacki and the Dirksen Congressional Center, the National Endowment for the Humanities for a summer stipend, and individuals Roland C. Rebele, Lowell Blankfort, and Stanley K. Sheinbaum. Without their help over the years, this book would not have been possible.

Former *San Francisco Examiner* Managing Editor Frank McCulloch not only approved an extended leave of absence, but also read an early book proposal and could not have been more supportive. Thanks also to *Examiner* Librarian Judy Canter; *Examiner* photographer Kim Komenich; Associated Press photographer Rich Pedroncelli; and Peter Schrag, editorial page editor of the *Sacramento Bee*, who was consistently patient, supportive, and indulgent as I sought to finish the manuscript while beginning a new job as political editor and columnist for McClatchy Newspapers based at the *Bee*.

In addition to the Burton brothers, others also made themselves available for multiple interviews, among them: Tom Joe, Gary Sellers, Cleve Pinnix, Dale Crane, Dr. Seymour Farber, Dr. Edgar Wayburn, Congressman George Miller, Agar Jaicks, Judy Lemons, Josiah Beeman, David Cohen, Leroy Hardy, and Michael Berman, who also made available key files and documents.

At my request, a number of psychiatrists and family therapists read key interview transcripts and offered helpful insights into Burton's personality: these were not extended psychiatric workups, and this is not a psychobiography. But their observations permitted me to write with more confidence about family dynamics, although any errors in interpretation are mine, not theirs. I owe a debt of gratitude to Drs. Margaret Singer, Arthur Cain, and Stephen Haig, and to therapists Alan Rinzler and Rosalyn Rifkin.

During my repeated visits to Washington to do research and conduct interviews, friends Kathy Sylvester and Eliot and Blaine Marshall made their extra couches available for extended stays, as did Carol Ostrom in Seattle, and I am grateful to them all, not just for their couches, but for their friendship and encouragement. I am also beholden to Walter Oleszek of the Congressional Research Service, whose meticulous files on Congress should be declared a national treasure. He allowed me the run of his office to read and photocopy hundreds of pages of research material.

For their help along the way, I also wish to thank Susan Rasky and Tom Goldstein of UC Berkeley's Graduate School of Journalism, Duane Garrett, John Mintz, David Kirp, Jay Schroeder, Roberta Cairney, Leo Rennert, Bill Sokol, Cynthia Gorney, Lance Williams, Carol Ness, Tom Rosenstiel, Brian Murphy, Kevin Shelley, Bartley O'Hara, Ed Bayley, Lynn Ludlow, Rick Merrill, Michael Larsen, and Elizabeth Pomada. I am especially grateful to

Scott Miller, who was not only there at a crucial moment with his checkbook, but was there at many other moments to read a chapter, listen to an interpretation, or just offer friendship and support. A special word of thanks to Michael Barone and Grant Ujifusa, editors of the many editions of the *Almanac of American Politics*. Many were the times I found myself writing with six editions spread out on the table behind me. To check a spelling, grab a quick biographical fact, get the essence or history of a congressional district or the seniority on a committee, these volumes were invaluable.

I cannot end without expressing my deepest gratitude to my wife, freelance writer Carol Brydolf, a veteran of the *Oakland Tribune* in its headier days, who permitted me the freedom to pursue this obsession for the better part of seven years. Near the end, she applied her own considerable skills and did a thorough and rigorous final edit of the manuscript.

While I am grateful for many kindnesses that made this book possible, any mistakes or errors in interpretation are entirely my own.

John Jacobs
Davis, California

PROLOGUE

*He was the strategic networker par excellence. You never see a politician
who is nuts and bolts and supremely pragmatic, but then who uses his
tactical and strategic brilliance for idealistic goals. The first two make you
an effective traffic cop. Add the third element and you have a very rare
legislator. No one comes close to Phil Burton. Even now when I go
up to the Hill, I say "Phil, where are you?"*

RALPH NADER

*Phil Burton was the most naturally gifted elected official or politician I
have ever known or run across. All of his habits were tailor-made for
politics. He had an appetite for detail beyond belief on every issue. He had
an unlimited amount of energy. He had supreme confidence, and he was
absolutely devoid of a need to be loved. I think Phil Burton believed that he
could absolutely make a difference in any situation, and he usually did,
and that drove him more than anything else.*

CALIFORNIA ASSEMBLY SPEAKER WILLIE BROWN

ON ONE OF WASHINGTON'S sweltering days in the summer of 1977, several
well-dressed timber company executives crouched down on their knees on
the thick blue carpet of Congressman Phillip Burton's large office in room
2304 of the Rayburn House Office Building, opposite the Capitol, anxiously
studying detailed topographical maps of territory that included their holdings. These men, who ran the firms of Louisiana Pacific, Simpson, and Arcata
were used to getting their way. With an arrogance typical of their rank, they
had exploited the vast forest resources of the Pacific Northwest for decades
and believed it was their right to do so forever. That their land might contain

any value beyond the obvious economic benefit that harvesting trees provides was a foreign concept to them. And they believed they were invincible.

Phillip Burton, their adversary on this day, was coming off the biggest defeat of his political career, a heartbreaking one-vote loss the previous December to Jim Wright of Texas for House Democratic majority leader. Wright's victory made him Speaker Tip O'Neill's chief lieutenant and all but certain successor. Burton thus had something to prove, and as chairman of the House Interior Committee's Subcommittee on Public Lands and National Parks, he was using his committee's jurisdiction over public lands and the environment to do so. His results—preservation of more wilderness than every Congress and president before him combined—have never been rivaled.

Burton was no ordinary adversary. He was a huge burly man with unruly wisps of hair spiraling downward from his scalp. He had fierce brown eyes that always seemed poised to pop out of his head, a rasping voice he could magnify like a howitzer when necessary, the salty vocabulary of the San Francisco dockworkers he represented, and a presence that often left allies fearful and enemies totally terrorized. Burton smoked three packs of unfiltered Chesterfields a day, drank vast quantities of Stolichnaya on the rocks, and never hesitated to explode at friends and enemies alike.

He towered over his fellow politicians in hallway encounters, thumping his finger on their chests, spitting saliva as he shouted, consuming, as one witness put it, "their very oxygen." He ate enormous portions of prime rib, pasta, and Dover sole with such unrepentant gusto that dinner companions said they needed an umbrella to protect their clothes. He did not think twice about spearing the chicken off the plate of a stranger seated next to him at an elegant dinner party, of taking columnist Jack Anderson, a religiously observant Mormon, on a late-night tour of San Francisco's strip joints, of calling Lady Bird Johnson, whom he barely knew, "Babe," or of trailing pillows from meeting to meeting to ease the pain of his hemorrhoids.

As these timber executives looked at the maps and at Burton's latest boundary changes, it dawned on them that Burton was proposing to annex enormous tracts of their land to Redwood National Park in Northern California. When they further discovered that this wild man—there was never any pretense that this was a meeting among friends—seemed to know at least as much as they did about their own timber holdings, labor force, and projected yields, as well as the names of every outcropping, gully, and trail on the maps before them, they could no longer control their alarm.

"We can't accept this, Mr. Chairman," one of them sputtered. "It would put us out of business."

"Fine," replied Burton. "I have an alternative." He pointed to a different stack of maps and drawings on his desk, which sat in a corner of his office that faced Independence Avenue. This one constituted a less extreme vision of his redwood expansion plan.

"Sign off on it by noon tomorrow," he warned, "or this is what you'll get." Not only did these executives agree to his "alternative," Burton went on to fashion a historic compromise that satisfied the usually irreconcilable forces of the federal government, environmentalists, unionized loggers threatened with permanent loss of their livelihood, and powerful timber interests. They all bought the package because Burton threatened far worse if they refused.

"If you show them the depths of hell," Burton told one of his protégés, "everything else looks pretty good."

In doubling the size of Redwood National Park, Burton preserved thousands of acres of irreplaceable and majestic redwood groves. His plan compensated the timber companies and provided loggers with benefits nearly equal to their annual wages for the next four years, some for the next eleven years. And as was true with so much of Burton's legislation over the years, only later did the true cost of the bill finally emerge: in this case, more than a billion dollars. But however big the park or however much it cost, as far as the timber companies were concerned, it was better than the depths of hell.

The tools Burton used so skillfully in the Redwood Park battle typified his approach to policy-making and political persuasion in a career spanning nearly three decades: terror, intimidation, the brute exercise of power, and total mastery of technical detail, all on behalf of labor, minorities, the poor, and the environment. Most people never heard his name pronounced, but his legislation still benefits millions of Americans.

Even though he operated out of the limelight for most of his career, few politicians in American history who held his redistributive and ultraliberal views ever accumulated as much raw power as Phillip Burton in his prime. House colleagues compared him to one other politician: Lyndon Johnson, whom he resembled in style, temperament, earthiness, drive for power, and legislative skill. He once bragged that he could round up 110 votes "to have dog shit declared the national food." A towering behind-the-scenes figure in California and in Washington, Burton used and misused his power in fascinating and sometimes frightening ways. The book of memorial tributes from colleagues that Congress published after Burton's death in 1983 was longer than those published for Lyndon Johnson or Robert Kennedy. That so few people beyond the true Washington cognoscenti knew of him was deliberate. He believed that advertising his successes was counterproductive.

Burton's legislation touched the lives of people everywhere: those who mined coal in Kentucky or West Virginia, who sweated in the broiling sun in lettuce and citrus fields in Florida, Texas, and California, who took a job that paid minimum wage, who worked with dangerous machinery or toxic chemicals, or who collected supplemental social security checks because they were aged, blind, or disabled. Few such beneficiaries lived in his San Francisco district and could repay their debt by returning him to office. But Burton didn't care. He saw the world as his jurisdiction and never forgot whom he cared about or why he was in politics. Personifying a sensibility that has all but disappeared from our modern political life, Burton was completely secure about what drove him—a visceral rage for justice. And unlike many who served with him or have since followed, he never needed a poll taker or an image maker to tell him what to say or think or how a particular vote would "play" with the folks back home.

Burton took the New Deal coalition of Franklin Roosevelt and extended it beyond what anyone thought imaginable. That began in his first successful race for the state assembly in 1956, when he campaigned on behalf of labor unions and San Francisco's Chinatown, a previously unrepresented constituency historically at odds with labor groups in California who long and successfully had pushed anti-Chinese exclusionary laws. He also crusaded for civil rights for blacks at a time when his labor supporters were doing everything possible to keep blacks from joining their unions and competing with them for jobs. In the 1960s, he pushed the coalition to include the burgeoning antiwar movement. In the 1970s, he married, where possible, the conflicting interests of labor and environmentalists. And in the early 1980s, in the final campaign of his life, he united police officers and gay activists.

No one else had ever put together such large and improbable coalitions. He brokered deals among adversaries who by themselves never could have imagined such deals, let alone consummated them. An expert on the inner workings of the House, he routinely delivered blocs of liberal votes to protect cotton, sugar, and tobacco subsidies for appreciative southern conservatives. In return, rural southerners voted for a higher minimum wage, his landmark black lung bill for coal miners, food stamps for striking workers, and other legislation that in earlier eras might have been considered wildly radical. For anyone to assemble such coalitions would be unusual. But for an ultraliberal—coming from a political tradition in the United States that distrusted the unvarnished exercise of power or that avoided wheeling and dealing on such a grand scale—it was almost unprecedented.

In a rare, tape-recorded, and remarkably candid interview with a reporter for a conservation magazine, Burton once crystalized his governing philosophy and style. He was talking only about a particular bill affecting his state, but what he said revealed the essence of how he operated. As far as he was concerned, poor people, workers, and racial minorities needed all the help he could give them. Almost everybody else—especially corporate lobbyists who manipulate legislation for their client's benefit—were his enemies by definition.

> I've got to put the squeeze on the cojónes of the exploitive industries in my state. You'd be shocked how well they'll behave. . . . You have to learn how to terrorize the bastards. . . . If you start *giving* these special interests what they should *end up with*, they don't lose a dime, because they have no limits on their greed or their view of their own self-worth and power. . . . Do not make them figure out how much more they're going to get, but how much they've got that they're going to lose. Most of my colleagues work it the other end: they kiss the asses of everyone.

Burton spent eight years in the California legislature and nineteen years in the House of Representatives, where he became not merely one of its most powerful and influential members, but arguably the most important House liberal of the 1970s. Had he won his 1976 race against Jim Wright, which Ralph Nader called "the most important [in-house] congressional election of the last thirty years," and had he lived long enough to succeed Tip O'Neill, he likely would have become Speaker of the House. Wright himself said at Burton's memorial service on the floor of the House, "Phil Burton was a giant of a man who tended to dominate whatever stage he strode across. . . . He lived and worked and fought with an intensity at which others could but marvel."

Burton's career book-ended an era that began with the resurgence of the California Democratic Party in the early 1950s, after the presidential defeat of Adlai Stevenson, and ended with the presidential election of Ronald Reagan in 1980. First elected to state office in 1956, Burton arrived in Washington in 1964, three months after Lyndon Johnson assumed the presidency following the assassination of John F. Kennedy and ushered in the Great Society.

He soon became the House's expert on welfare and one of organized labor's most effective advocates, prolonging the labor movement's influence at a time when union jobs were disappearing. He shaped important labor bills for minimum wage, coal mine health and welfare, occupational health and safety, and protection of pension rights. Parting with Johnson, he became an early and loud opponent of the Vietnam War, and when the conservative impulses of the House and the seniority system blocked action on important domestic fronts, Burton led the charge to democratize the House, diffuse power to a younger, more liberal group of Democrats and make the House more responsive. He led the Democratic Study Group and the Democratic Caucus as those institutions achieved the most important House reforms of the postwar era. He became the acknowledged master of reapportionment, the high art of drawing political boundary lines to maximum partisan advantage. In his later years, after he lost the majority leader race, he turned to the environment.

That such a man as Phillip Burton, whose friends got caught stuffing the ballot boxes for him when he ran for president of his high school and who was defeated in his first try for public office by an incumbent who had been dead for three weeks, could go on to achieve what he achieved is a story that gets at the essence of American politics, the energy of rage and the nature of power. He was certainly not a typical politician, but he was quintessentially a political animal. Studying his rise, his meticulous planning, his commitment to both social justice and to the accumulation and wielding of power provides a special insight into the American political game as played by a master, a man not born to rule but who nonetheless possessed a genius for making his own success when traditional paths to power were blocked.

His passion for the game and his skill in playing it lifted him above most of his contemporaries. His contribution to American politics involved both process—reapportionment and internal House reform—and substance—his legislation. His genius was that more than any politician of his time, he understood the relationship between the two. Whether making the House more democratic, redrawing congressional districts, or maneuvering to get a favorite liberal ally on a key committee, he never lost sight of his ultimate end: fundamental social and political change.

He was an American original, a unique synthesis of seething outrage, maudlin sentimentality, political craftsmanship, and unwavering dedication to people who needed government help to improve their lives. He told Rian Malan in the November 1981 edition of *California* magazine, "I trust visceral reactions, and I trust workers' reactions. I like people whose balls *roar* when they see justice. . . . I'm determined to make the universe a better place. Not the world, the universe."

Burton had more than his share of human frailties and flaws. His relationships with people and his career suffered for it. But he was above corruption, did not curry favor, refused to accept gifts from corporations seeking good will, even returned the set of cocktail glasses the local bartenders union sent him every Christmas. He died with less than $1,000 in the bank, his only assets the equity in his Capitol Hill townhouse and the funds in his assembly and congressional pension accounts.

He was more comfortable chain-smoking and getting drunk in a darkened cocktail lounge than enjoying the very areas his laws preserved. He lived three blocks from his congressional office but never walked to work. He devoted prodigious amounts of time and energy to improving the welfare of "the people," but, like many reformers, often treated specific people abysmally. He worked like a Tammany ward heeler and rose to be a political boss in a media state famous for its blow-dried celebrity politicians and the political consultants who manufacture them.

Burton's life is also testimony to one other enduring principle of politics: one person, even one as personally obnoxious as Phillip Burton often was, can make a difference. Beyond the force of historical events, beyond the lucky happenstance of being in the right place at the right time, Burton showed by force of personality, self-will, and passion for his point of view that social change could happen. He lived in a world where power was the currency of the realm, and yet he was able to persuade, year after year, hundreds of powerful individuals to follow his lead, even when it was not always in their self-interest. Burton created and moved agendas that without him would not have existed.

Even more arresting than his enduring legislation was his impact on his fellow politicians. To most who encountered him, Phillip Burton was an unforgettable figure, the most compelling personality they ever met, a man whose relentless, day and night politicking, strategic brilliance, and zest for combat distilled the raw essence of their profession. No staff member ever wrote out his questions for him or told him when to cut the deal.

But that very certitude, arrogance, and dominating personality, often made abusive by alcohol, was also his downfall. As his close friend and House colleague Abner Mikva once put it, "Phil had a way of coalescing his enemies." Congress is an institution that prides itself on its collegiality, respect for elders, deference to tradition. It is astonishing in retrospect that Burton blasted his way as far into such an institution as he did. But in the end, in rejecting his bid for leadership, in the most important and tragic moment of his life, his peers opted for someone more safe, known, and predictable.

Although he was only fifty-six when he died in 1983, Burton lived long enough to witness Reagan's counterrevolution. In cutting government and dramatically reducing taxes on the wealthy, Reagan sought, often successfully, to roll back many of the programs to which Burton committed his life. His administration sent labor on a downward spiral by breaking the air controllers union, encouraged reverse discrimination lawsuits on behalf of whites who hated affirmative action, built the defense budget to unprecedented peacetime levels, and appointed an interior secretary specifically to counteract the environmental gains of the 1970s. Yet Burton never stopped fighting.

The special poignance of Burton's life and premature death arises from the collapse of his brand of left-based electoral politics. His was a politics centered on peoples' needs, often desperate needs, for government help without regard to cost. While such an approach is harder to justify in an age of diminished budgets, few remain in Washington who embody that kind of need-based politics, and none who have his abilities. Whether it was the exhaustion of liberalism, frustration with big government approaches, many of which have failed, or social and economic forces that have shaped a contemporary political culture based on fear, resentment, and anxiety, the reality is that but for a few surviving protégés, Burton's politics have virtually died with him. The historic Republican takeover of the House in the 1994 midterm elections dramatically illustrates the point.

The passion in politics these days is on the right, not on the left. Few speak for the powerless, and the way to get elected has less to do with the Burton style of delivering tangible benefits to people who need them or of putting coalitions together. More than ever, getting elected is now about raising large sums of money from political action committees and other interested parties, destroying opponents through thirty-second "attack" ads on television or via direct-mail smears, and paying big fees to consultants who test market cautious bromides and attack lines in focus groups and polls before deciding they are safe for their candidate. Burton found such techniques offensive. His modern-day House counterpart is Republican House Speaker Newt Gingrich of Georgia, whose rebellious temperament, strategic brilliance, and drive for power may equal Burton's, but all on behalf of life's haves, not its have-nots.

"He once said politics was like a bat flying around in a cave, constantly sending and receiving signals, groping now here, now there, until a way was found," Republican Charles Pashayan of California said of Burton in his eulogy. "If politics is an art, no artist painted with a more deft touch. . . . Phillip Burton lived with an intensity and a fury of the sun itself. He was consumed by the fires of his own brilliance."

To explore the seeds of that brillance—and rage—it is helpful to start at the beginning, in Milwaukee in the 1930s, with a Socialist mayor, a Great Depression, and an absentee father.

I

BEGINNINGS

When you grow up, if you can look at yourself in the mirror and smile, you're doing okay.

DR. THOMAS BURTON
Phillip Burton's father

Phillip was always running for something. He always wanted to succeed. He was going to be as good as his father. That was the bottom line.

ROBERT BURTON
Phillip Burton's younger brother

PHILLIP BURTON RARELY spoke of his parents. Friends from early adulthood knew he loved his mother, a gentle, deeply religious woman, and admired his father, a distant, self-absorbed man who could also be gracious and kind. He passed on to Burton and his two younger brothers his ardent liberalism, sense of justice, and concern for the common man. Burton did not analyze his past or talk about it. A friend said it was as though Burton wanted his life to begin anew in law school. Such a reaction is not surprising in a young man whose father was absent during most of his early years. His mother was busy holding the family together during the Depression. She had little time to control her strong-willed eldest son or provide the secure haven and personal affection he craved.

Mildred, Burton's mother, was born in Cincinnati, Ohio, in 1903, the fifth of six children of a second-generation Irish bricklayer named Barney Leonard and his wife Kathleen. Leonard's father—Phillip's maternal great-grandfather—emigrated to the United States during the Great Hunger, the potato blight and famine of the late 1840s. He worked on the canals, according to family tradition, settling in Cincinnati, where his son helped lay its cobblestone sidewalks. A gregarious man, Barney was a sinner in the eyes of his devout wife because he smoked a pipe and drank alcohol. Neither of Phillip's brothers recalled seeing Barney drunk, but Phillip and his brothers all developed substance abuse problems.

Phillip's father Thomas was originally named Berger, but he changed his name to Burton while in his early twenties. He was born of German parentage in Marion, Indiana, in 1900, one of three boys. He was reared in Chicago but at seventeen left home after a dispute with his father. Thomas Burton's sons never met their paternal grandparents or even heard their father talk about them.

By the time he married Mildred Leonard in 1924, Thomas Burton had sold vacuum cleaners in South Dakota, had worked in a Michigan steel mill, had been a drummer in a band, and had played second base in the 3-I League, a Class B baseball league for teams in Iowa, Indiana, and Illinois. As a traveling salesman after his marriage, he became a district manager for the Omaha-based RealSilk Hosiery firm. Later, he sold medical textbooks to hospitals. For a short time, the young couple owned a Pierce Arrow. But these moments of affluence were followed by long periods of poverty.

Phillip Burton was born in 1926 in Cincinnati. Two years later Robert arrived, and John came in 1932. By then, the Depression had hit hard. When John was born, Thomas later told his sons, he was so poor he had to walk several miles to the hospital. Soon thereafter, Thomas moved to Chicago, leaving the family behind to attend a YMCA adult school. He had decided to become a doctor. None of the sons knew why, but Robert recalled years later that a salesman friend convinced Thomas he could do it. A doctor's income could better provide for his family.

The family moved to Detroit in 1934, and two years later, when Phillip was ten, they moved to Milwaukee. The Depression was a grim experience for the Burtons, made more so by Thomas Burton's unusual decision to begin medical school in 1936 in Chicago when he was thirty-six. Again, he chose to live apart from his family, where he could focus on his studies free of the clamor of children. For three young boys already struggling with economic adversity, it meant four more years without their father. His absence placed a great financial and emotional burden on the household.

Enrolled at the University of Illinois, Tom Burton visited on weekends when he could. His studies were demanding. While supporting himself by selling medical texts, he lived at the Garfield Park Hotel. For six dollars a week, he got room and twelve meals. It was there that Thomas got interested in politics, Robert recalled. Franklin Roosevelt was different from the "phonies" he had been brought up to distrust. FDR cared about the common people. Young Phillip also found FDR captivating. When Roosevelt campaigned in Milwaukee in 1936, Phillip heard him speak and traced his interest in politics to that moment. "I do remember this as a touchstone," he said many years later. "Our family were great Roosevelt supporters. My father was a New Dealer."[1]

There were other early political influences. Under socialist Mayor Dan Hoan, Milwaukee was a model for civic welfare programs. The son of an Irish blacksmith, Hoan was mayor from 1916 to 1940. He believed in activist government, and his school recreation and summer parks programs were the envy of the nation. He instituted a merit system, cleaned up city hall, and kept down the price of gas, electricity, and streetcar fares.[2] Phillip saw firsthand that government could make life better for people.

With her husband away, Mildred Burton supported the family by working ten to twelve hours a day for the Catholic diocese, selling ads over the phone for church publications. Unlike Tom, who was not religious, she attended Mass faithfully every day. Robert was an altar boy, but Phillip refused to rise before dawn to kneel on the cold marble floor of the church. Her job paid eighty dollars a month, out of which thirty dollars went for rent on a nine-room upstairs flat. Fern Brown, one of twenty children of a fundamentalist minister, lived with the family and took care of John and the older boys when they were not in school. As the Depression deepened, the boys often saw tramps riding the rails and hungry people raiding garbage cans. Despite their poverty, the Burtons never went hungry. They lived on High Mount and Washington Boulevard, then moved twelve blocks to Forty-eighth and Chambers. It meant leaving a Catholic-Protestant neighborhood for a predominantly Jewish one. But the rent was cheaper and they had a house and garden to themselves.

Burton returned to his old neighborhood with his new playmates one day to play a game. His old friends asked why he was now playing with "kikes." "What are kikes?" Phillip asked. Told they were Jews, he said, "What are Jews?" Many years later he said he could not fathom that his old friends were calling his new ones names. But the Burton family felt at home among their new neighbors. While others in Milwaukee were sympathetic to the new German state, the Burtons worried about Hitler and the rise of fascism. One night in 1938 when Phillip was twelve, they gathered around the radio to hear reports of the faraway Crystal Night, when Nazi storm troopers destroyed Jewish homes, synagogues, and shops all over Germany. Hitler's rabid anti-Semitism and totalitarian tactics and his father's sympathy for the underdog made it easy to divide the world into good guys and bad guys. The Loyalists in Spain were good. The Nazis and Italian Fascists were bad.

Burton worked hard at school, earning A's and getting elected to various class offices. Striving constantly, Phillip wanted to prove, said Robert, that he was as good as his father. Even then, he was domineering and intense, Robert said. The Jewish community's high premium on education and study made the Burton boys proud of their father for bettering himself, training to become a doctor. But if Phillip felt angry or resentful of his father's extended absences, he kept it to himself. Who could be mad at a man who started a medical career so late, worked so hard, and still emerged with decent values?

From the same Milwaukee neighborhood came three other boys who, like Phillip and John Burton, went into politics: liberal Democrats Abner Mikva and Fortney Stark, who went to Congress, and John Schmitz, a conservative Republican elected to the California Senate. They did not know each other. The neighborhood along Center Street between Forty-eighth and Fifty-first Streets consisted of row upon row of solid, two-story frame houses with large, neatly kept yards. Typically, the owners lived downstairs and rented out the upper floor. Activities centered on a shack on a vacant lot at Fiftieth and Center Streets, where the kids pitched pennies and chose sides for games.[3] Phillip, tall and skinny, usually picked sides for his team, which ensured that little brother Bobby would also get picked. On Sundays, the boys sold water for a penny at softball games. Phillip lugged buckets of ice to the field so he could charge two cents.

On a visit home in 1938, Thomas Burton took his boys to the local ballpark to see the Minneapolis Millers and their new hitting sensation, Ted Williams. "If I had his swing," he told them, "I'd have stayed in baseball." But he usually steered the conversation back to Roosevelt and how important it was for the government to help people. His folk wisdom profoundly shaped their social values. "He wears a clean shirt but dirty underwear," Thomas Burton would say, or "them that has, gets" and "the poor always get the short end of the stick."

Mildred Burton had little time for mothering. Between working long hours for the diocese, cooking, cleaning, running the household with Fern's help and attending church, it was an accomplishment simply to survive week to week. A strong proponent of the work ethic, she made sure Phillip always had a paper route or a way to earn extra money. She instilled in the boys a sense of helping the less fortunate and hoped the boys would be doctors or priests.

While Phillip began his first year of high school, his father was finishing his studies. He piled the family into an old Dodge and drove west in 1940 to look at medical internship programs in Seattle, San Francisco, and San Diego. Heading down the coast, they drove through tall redwood forests and later visited the 267-foot General Grant Tree, a sight Phillip never forgot. Franklin Hospital in San Francisco, now the Ralph K. Davies Medical Center, paid thirty dollars a month to its interns, the best offer Tom got. They drove home for his last year of school—stopping in Springfield, Illinois, to borrow money from a classmate to finish the trip—and got ready for a new life in San Francisco.

The Burtons moved into a house on Kirkham Street in the Sunset District, a sleepy, working-class neighborhood on the city's west side in the summer of 1941. Phillip attended George Washington high school, across Golden Gate Park in the Richmond District. He began at Washington in Milwaukee and said he wanted to attend a school with the same name. He was fifteen years old, over six feet tall, skinny, always in a hurry, almost hyperactive. He had an impressive memory. Schoolmates remembered that when he ran into a girl he had not seen for several years, he could recall her phone number instantly.

Young Burton studied hard and set a record for selling more new subscriptions of the *San Francisco News*—eight in one month—than any other paper carrier. He and Bobby also sold papers on street corners. On December 7, 1941, the night every newspaper extra screamed "WAR!" they sold papers until 2 A.M. Motorists coming home from Marin County saw the headlines, stopped their cars, thrust quarters and dollar bills at them, and then drove off without waiting for the change. The boys made $180 that night, more than their father—still an intern—earned in six months.

Tom Burton's internship kept him at the hospital during the week, even to sleep. This put new strains on a marriage already stretched by his frequent absences. The children recalled little intimacy or personal empathy in their household. But Mildred's devout faith made divorce unthinkable. The boys were growing up bright but unbridled. Mildred could not control them, and Tom was often distant even when he was around. When Tom finished his training and began a more normal work schedule, their relationship did not improve. Mildred was used to running things in his absence. Even though they now had more money, he refused her request for a car. She became a legal secretary, saved her money, and bought her own. Later, she coveted a mink coat. Tom thought such things were frivolous. Again, she saved and bought it herself. Eventually, they moved to St. Francis Wood, one of the city's costlier neighborhoods. But when John, the youngest, was old enough to move out, they separated. Dr. Burton confided to his receptionist that he probably never should have married.

Phillip's principal diversion was basketball. As a junior, his basketball ability and leadership captured the attention of some elite seniors, who invited him to join a club called the Falcons. They held most of the important student offices and wore reversible black satin jackets embroidered with the club name. The Falcons met in the basement of one of the members' homes, where they played penny poker and talked about sports and girls. They paid weekly dues of twenty-five cents and went to movies or ice skating rinks together. Burton became especially close to three Falcons—Jack Hanley, Matt Gately, and Doug Brown. Hanley, the center on the varsity squad, remembers that Burton was on his own, answerable to no one. He would arrive home when he felt like it. It was a rule at the Hanley household that everyone had to be home for dinner at 6 P.M.

"What if you're late?" Burton would tease. "I don't want to be late," Hanley would reply, irritated. "Yeah, but what if you are?" Coming from a family that barely lived together, let alone ate dinner together, it was impossible for Burton to conceive that Hanley *wanted* to be home at six, that he desired the family intimacy Burton hardly knew. But Burton loved eating at his friend's house, where he talked about local politics with Hanley's father, a policeman. He was like an adopted son to Doug Brown's mother and always accepted her frequent dinner invitations.

Burton charmed his friends' parents. He was reaching out to families for the affection and comfort he was not getting at home. In the summer, Burton and his friends stacked beer cases at the Acme brewery. After work, he often spent the night at their homes. When they hopped in Matt Gately's 1933 Ford and headed to the Russian River or hitchhiked to Santa Cruz for a weekend, he informed his mother that he was going. He did not ask permission.

On the basketball court, Phillip was known as "Pop-off Burton" because he liked to joke around. He was a great practice shooter, his friends recalled, but the coach never let him start because he wanted to shoot as soon as he got the ball. When Burton was a junior, the coach broke a promise to start Doug Brown in the next game. Brown was so angry he skipped practice, for which the coach told him to turn in his uniform. Burton quit the team in protest. For Brown, this was a supreme act of loyalty. Throughout his political career, loyalty and his word were the qualities Burton valued most.[4]

On the playground he challenged close calls and often got into shoving matches, Hanley recalled. But if an unskilled player or a new kid was hanging around waiting to be picked, Burton would choose him out of compassion. It drove Hanley crazy. As kindhearted as Burton could be, he also had a fierce stare. He was not a physical bully; to get what he wanted he raised his voice or, more effectively, he focused his intense brown eyes. But mostly, Burton was fun to be around, in perpetual motion, a fast talker, full of ideas on everything and eager to voice them.

Hanley thought he was unusually deep. Burton would analyze his friends or talk politics and debate the existence of God with Gately, like him a lapsed Catholic. Gately agreed with Burton that the church could not answer the big questions and had been hypocritical in supporting the Fascists over the Loyalists in Spain—likely an insight derived from his father. Hanley said he thought Burton was more perceptive than most. On their way to a movie one night, a friend came by in a car and offered them a ride. Halfway through the movie, he said, "I gotta go. I phoned home. My aunt is sick." Burton turned to Hanley. "You don't believe him, do you? He probably met some dolly in the lobby." Later that night as they walked home, they saw the boy drive by with a girl in the front seat. "You see that, Hanley!" Burton cried, triumphant. "You're too naive."

Falconers did not think much about the war. The manpower shortage allowed them to compete for dollar-an-hour jobs on the wharf during the summer. But there were few signs of war, other than all the men in uniform moving in and out of the city. Most teachers were women. ROTC classes were large. Gym teachers spent extra time getting the boys in fighting shape, or as the yearbook put it, "Preparing Youth for War." But no one talked about college. That was for later, once their military obligations were fulfilled. Burton wrote in the yearbook that he hoped to become an "aviation cadet."

Going into his senior year, Burton was elected class president and was invited to join the Eagles, a service club for boys who proudly wore caps of alternating scarlet and gray, the school colors. The 1943 yearbook noted that Burton "not only helped his class select their senior sweaters," but as a member of the Executive Council, he was "well known for his powers of persuasion." Most of his friends were six months ahead of him. They were graduating in June 1943. He had to wait until the following February. Even so, they urged him to run for student body president. Burton did not need much prompting. He gave a stirring speech, promising students a bigger voice in running the school.

Two Falconers, Gerard Rhine, a yell leader and ROTC officer, and Stan Perkins, vice president of the Eagles, were ballot counters. When Rhine and

Perkins heard rumors that a teacher was stuffing ballots for Burton's opponent, they decided to do the same for Burton. As they sat by the ballot box erasing names and writing in Burton's, a teacher walked in and caught them. Burton was elected but not allowed to serve. Rhine and Perkins swore he knew nothing about it, unlikely as that may seem to those who later watched him bend the rules of procedure in Sacramento and Washington. Burton said nothing publicly. "Just for the hell of it," he told Hanley, "I'm going to canvass each registry and see how they voted." He had won easily. The ballot stuffing had not been necessary.[5]

Home life was not entirely lacking during Burton's last year of high school. Dr. Burton was around more often. He liked to make spaghetti sauce on Saturday nights and fudge on Sunday. But family activities always seemed to be on his terms, and his stern example was often hard. As a doctor, Tom Burton was permitted two gas ration coupons, a C-sticker for unlimited gasoline, and an A-sticker, good for three gallons a week. He burned the A-stickers, saying he did not want to hinder the war effort. Robert remembers begging him not to. "For Christ's sake, Pop," he would implore, "we want to go to the Russian River." If nothing else, the boys could sell the coupons on the black market for a dollar apiece. But to Dr. Burton, who was setting an exacting standard for his sons, this was not negotiable. Dr. Burton also sent money to the local chapter of the American Civil Liberties Union, which was challenging the order by which Japanese-Americans were sent to internment camps. At a time of acute anti-Japanese feeling, this was another example of his commitment to civil liberties.

An internist, Dr. Burton had a small office downtown and ran a clinic at Franklin Hospital, often treating poor patients for no charge. While on rounds one night, he met David Jenkins, a radical labor organizer for the International Longshoremen's and Warehousemen's Union, the fiery ILWU of Harry Bridges. Jenkins was laid up with a bad knee. At night, when things were quiet, Burton would visit Jenkins and talk. Burton was pro-labor, but not a joiner. He had no use for the Communist Party, Jenkins recalled, and was passionately antifascist. He believed in social justice and in a person's capacity to change—as his own decision to enter medicine late in life testified. Jenkins was so impressed that he recommended Burton be put on a CIO-approved list of physicians.[6] One patient was Mike Quinn, a well-known party member and *Daily People's World* columnist who became a good friend.

The elder Burton was an avid reader who subscribed to *The New Republic, The Nation, The Progressive,* and to a left-wing book club. He wrote a novel about race relations but never found a publisher. He was one of the few white doctors in town willing to make house calls to black homes. He treated a poor black family and refused the fee, Robert recalled, telling the father, "Use the money to buy your kids some shoes." Phillip absorbed the lesson well. As a young lawyer, he represented black clients and often charged little or nothing.

Tom Burton also became friendly with Seymour Farber, a young Harvard-trained physician in the same medical building. He struck Farber as an appealing yet vulnerable man, tall, thin, tastefully dressed. Farber recalled that Burton always had a quiet but politically charged one-liner handy. If a headline said, "Interest rates going up," he would say, "Oh, the bastards are raising the interest rates again and the poor will suffer." When Farber mentioned that his practice was booming, Burton said, "Yes, but in Detroit in the thirties, hundreds of doctors were in dole lines because they had no patients and no incomes."

Farber later became the personal physician to Jesse Unruh, the powerful California Assembly speaker and Phillip Burton's rival in the state legislature. Having known the father so well—Tom confided to Farber about his marital difficulties and subsequent girlfriends after he and Mildred separated—Farber paid special attention to the sons. Tom's sense of injustice, imparted through "those quiet one-liners," Farber said, had "a tremendous impact on his eldest son. I would say it was the most definitive thing that molded Phil."

But as Phillip got older, Farber noticed, some aspects of his personality became the mirror opposite of his father's. Tom was dignified and spoke in a quiet voice. Phillip was always shouting. Tom was meticulous and polite and sat upright. Phillip sprawled. He seemed deliberately boorish, rude, sloppy, and abusive. As an adult, Phillip was often consumed with rage. Angry at injustice—but perhaps also unconsciously furious at a father who abandoned him and failed to provide unconditional love—he learned to channel this rage productively through politics, which became his life's work.[7]

Before Burton graduated from high school in January 1944, army and navy recruiters came to Washington High, as they did to hundreds of high schools, looking for top students interested in becoming officers. Those who passed the exams were admitted into the A-12 or V-12 programs on university campuses. They pursued course work in pre-med or engineering studies, their university expenses paid by the government. Like his father, Phillip wanted to be a doctor. He chose the V-12 program and on March 1, 1944, enlisted as a future navy ensign and enrolled at the University of Southern California.

An apprentice seaman, Burton was assigned to a large barracks on the Los

Angeles campus. He was one of 500 V-12 students. They wore navy uniforms and were subject to military law and discipline, required to stand guard duty and maintain good grades. They drilled and paraded before the captain, a demoted admiral who ran the V-12 program at USC. Flunk-outs were sent off to the fleet. For the first time in his life, Burton, three months shy of his eighteenth birthday, had strict rules to obey, with harsh consequences if he failed. He was up at 5 A.M. every day for calisthenics. His uniforms had to be laundered and neat, his room immaculate. He was paid thirty dollars a month, plus room, board, college fees and tuition. At first, the new students were assigned thirty or forty to a large open room. But after a semester, they shared suites.

USC, a private university with high tuition and origins in the Methodist Church, was known as a haven for the rich, conservative, and well-stationed. Parents may have hoped their children would avoid the radical elements found at the state universities—and make the connections that would serve them later in life. Fraternities and athletics dominated campus life and politics. Even during the war, 50,000 people or more would stream into the Los Angeles Coliseum to watch the USC Trojans play football.

Burton soon met two other V-12 freshman pre-med majors, Siegfried Hesse of Oakland and Robert Peck of Los Angeles, and they became roommates. Hesse and Peck considered themselves radicals and studied hard. Burton told them his father was a doctor with strong political concerns. Hesse knew Mike Quinn, a friend of his mother, was Dr. Burton's patient. But neither ever heard Burton say anything else about his family. Hesse found him intense, earnest, and gregarious, though a bit of the social butterfly.

Burton was less interested in studying than in joining a fraternity, going to parties, dating girls, and becoming a Big Man on Campus. Hesse despised fraternities as elitist and exclusionary. He concluded that Burton was a phony. If Burton wanted to run with the rich ne'er-do-wells, he reasoned, their values must be infecting him. For one who became feared and respected on Capitol Hill for his consuming and no-nonsense liberal politics, Burton's college immaturity may seem odd. But he was still a gawky teenager seeking social acceptance. Burton felt a strong need throughout his life to surround himself with people. Fraternity life provided a comfort and security he otherwise lacked and beat living in a dormitory. As a fraternity man he could walk into any sorority or activity on campus and be accepted immediately.

Burton studied but only in brief, concentrated bursts. After loading up with seventeen units a semester in the hard sciences, he tired of pre-med studies. A year later, he turned to political science and pre-law.[8] Although

Burton's grades were not outstanding, mostly B's, sprinkled with a few A's and C's, several professors recognized his intelligence and hired him to grade essays for their graduate courses.

With the end of World War II approaching, Burton and his roommates knew they would soon be released from duty. Eligible for call-up some time in the future, Burton left the V-12 program in October 1945, halfway through his three-year college career. He moved almost immediately into the Sigma Phi Epsilon house, where his social activities long had centered.

Soon after his discharge, Burton had a major falling out with his father over a trivial incident that revealed their inability to connect. Phillip was nineteen. While he was visiting on a break, Robert recalled, the family was together one Sunday in their book-lined living room. Dr. Burton asked Phillip to pick up some ice cream. It was a two-block walk. Perhaps it was a statement of independence. Perhaps Phillip was tired of his father's intermittent but demanding involvement in his life. Perhaps he just did not feel like going. In any event, he refused. Dr. Burton asked him again and again he refused. In an effort to mediate, Robert offered to go.

"No," Dr. Burton said. "I want Phillip to go."

"I'm not getting it," Phillip said. Mildred tried unsuccessfully to intervene.

"If you don't get the ice cream," his father threatened, "I'm cutting you off. I won't pay for any more of your college education."

"That's fine with me," replied the ever-stubborn son.

Dr. Burton made good his threat, and Phillip never again asked for money. Robert said the pair acted as though the incident had never happened and went to a San Francisco Seals baseball game the next Sunday.[9]

The sudden reversal of fortune had immediate consequences. Phillip returned to USC forced to take odd jobs and scrounge for money. He got help from the GI Bill and spent two years managing the varsity basketball team. But he never seemed to have clothes and was always borrowing from his fraternity brothers. On a campus as affluent as USC, the absence of a car or of spending money was an obstacle to the kind of social life he wanted to pursue.

It did not block his political ambitions, however. In his second year, he won the first of two terms in the student senate, acquiring the nickname "Filiburton." But he was not selected for Theta Nu Epsilon, a secret political fraternity that dominated student life. Nor was he picked for Trojan Knights, the men's honorary society that acted as rally committee and official student hosts. Walter "Buzz" Forward, president of Trojan Knights and member of the secret fraternity, was critical of Burton for always "shooting his mouth off."

When Burton heard that Buzz Forward and his family would be driving to San Francisco, Burton hitched a ride. "I'm so goddam poor, I can't make it home. Can I bum a ride with you?" he asked. Forward's father, a conservative Republican, managed a large manufacturing firm. Mrs. Forward had worked as a volunteer for Governor Earl Warren and Senator William F. Knowland, both Republicans. But Burton spent the the first part of the 400-plus mile ride denouncing corporations and their exploitation of workers. Finally, Mr. Forward exploded.

"Phil, you are riding in a car built by a big corporation," he said. "I am an employee of a big corporation. My son is going to USC because of a big corporation. Shut up!" Burton quieted down, but north of Santa Barbara he started in again. It was dark outside, but Mr. Forward pulled the car to the side of U.S. Highway 101 and said, "Phil, get out."

"I'm sorry, Mr. Forward," Burton said, as he started to get out of the car. "I won't say anything more. I'm very sorry I upset you."

"Phil, I don't want to hear another word from you for the rest of the trip," replied Mr. Forward. "Now get back in and keep quiet." And he did.[10]

Denied membership in the most exclusive clubs on campus, Burton searched for another way to make his mark and put his political talent to work. This was the beginning of a lifelong pattern of sizing up power relationships and figuring out his own way to get where he wanted. Whether it was his personality or political beliefs or both, he recognized early that traditional routes to influence would be denied him. But Burton worked harder and thought more creatively than his peers in devising his alternative path to power.

The first instrument at hand was his fraternity, one of the largest on campus, but considered one of the less desirable houses because many of its brothers were comparatively poor. The president was Joe Holt, a wealthy exception to the rule. His father owned a large dairy and chain of grocery stores. Holt later was elected to Congress as a conservative Republican.

Holt and Burton, the other acknowledged house leader, were intensely competitive. They wanted to win as many student offices and athletic contests as possible. Stationing underclassmen in key spots, such as the bookstore, they would spot talent among the freshmen and then "hotbox" or surround them until they could not move, extolling the virtues of their fraternity. One of their recruits was Gil Ferguson, a Marine who served two years in the

South Pacific during the war. After college, Ferguson returned to the Marine Corps and later was elected to the state assembly as a far-right Republican.

The fraternity met every Monday night. Every month or so, Ferguson recalled, Burton would "rant and rave" about the need to admit Jews and blacks. "But Phil," his brothers typically responded, "the Jews have their own fraternity, ZBT. They don't want to join our house." To consider accepting any of the few blacks on campus was out of the question and, in any case, would have prompted the national fraternity to expel the chapter. But that did not stop Burton. Ferguson could not understand how someone as smart as Burton—he was considered the brightest in the house—could hold such strange views.

Burton also had some bizarre idiosyncrasies. Although handsome and popular, once freed of military discipline he did not much care what his clothes looked like. He never made it out of bed for breakfast and ordered the pledges to forcibly wake him. But one time he heard them coming up the stairs, got out of bed, and hid in the closet. When the pledges, including Ferguson, went into his room and saw the empty bed, they figured he was up and gone. Burton, who had never fully awakened, got back in bed, slept until noon, realized he had missed half a day and screamed at them to do a better job. The pledges learned to tiptoe up the stairs and then force him up.

Ferguson said Burton seemed "spacey," so intense that his eyes bulged. His brain must be pushing them out, Ferguson figured. It made him an easy target for pranks. While he was eating dinner at the fraternity one night, pledges snaked a hose through a window, aimed, and turned it on, drenching him.

Another prank was far more serious and may have reflected the pledges' resentment at Burton's high-handed behavior. Some, like Ferguson, were returning war veterans who had seen combat and who had little patience for upper classmen who were younger and more frivolous. Overpowering him one night, they dressed him in army fatigues and a shirt that said POW, drove him to a train yard, stuck him in a boxcar, and locked it. When the train pulled out, it did not stop until it reached Indio, some 100 miles to the east in the desert past Palm Springs. But it took two days locked inside the boxcar without food or water before Burton made enough noise to alert police. He could have died of heat stroke or dehydration. When they opened the boxcar and Burton climbed out wearing his POW shirt, he had no money or identification. The police called the fraternity house, asking if they knew anyone by the name of Phillip Burton. The pranksters, falling down with laughter, said they had never heard of him.

It took another couple days in police custody before Burton finally found someone at USC to vouch for him. When he returned to the fraternity, Ferguson said, Burton looked forlorn, beaten down, humiliated. He stood under the shower for the longest time, trying to wash out the grime and what must have been the shame and terror of the experience. Then he went to bed and slept for twenty-four hours. He was quiet for days but gradually pulled out of it.[11]

Burton's other campus outlet was Blue Key, a small honor society of about thirty-five students, more important on other campuses than at USC, where Trojan Knights dominated. Burton was soon hard at work turning Blue Key into a group that could rival the Knights. Elected president by one vote, he ran meetings, directed social activities, and recruited new members. When he heard that a student named Chuck Brohammer had been elected president of the Trojan Squires, the junior version of Trojan Knights, Burton asked to meet him.

"If you drop out of the Knights," Burton told him, "I will see that you are made president of the student body and president of Blue Key. You are too good a guy to be involved with those jerks." Brohammer declined. But the offer typified the lengths to which Burton would go, and Brohammer's rejection further motivated Burton to turn Blue Key into a vehicle for his own ambition and ideology. Soon thereafter, Buzz Forward saw Burton and said, "For Christ's sake, Phil, relax. Leave us alone."

"Screw you, Forward," Burton said. "Who appointed you?"

His efforts paid off. Named Blue Key's "Outstanding Man" for 1946, he gave Blue Key the prestige it had lacked. But at a cost. People said Burton was "overpowering."[12]

During the summer of 1946, after he graduated, Burton got a job on a ship headed to Hawaii. The ship also stopped in Guam and Saipan, trust territories over which, decades later, as chairman of House Subcommittee on National Parks and Insular Affairs, he presided as their most forceful and effective advocate. It was during this trip—he had a menial job most likely as a mess man or kitchen assistant—that Burton had his first and most defining experiences with the American labor left. He mixed daily with members of the Marine Cooks and Stewards, the most militant union on the waterfront. MCS members sold subscriptions to Communist newspapers and carried left-wing literature. Four-hour arguments among rival left factions were not unusual.

Those two months at sea equaled a college degree in radicalism. Burton was never a Communist, never would have submitted to party discipline, and believed the party's goals in many ways conflicted with his, even as he fought to protect its civil liberties. But to an impressionable college kid, many of those discussions about social and economic justice and the rights of workers would have had lasting impact. His experience at sea also provided a look at some of labor's most rugged individualists. Phillip grew up poor but there was little that was blue-collar about the way Phillip was reared or the value his family placed on education. Even so, he developed a commitment to working people and labor issues many labor leaders said was straight from the heart.[13]

While Burton was busy with Blue Key, another ambitious, politically astute student arrived at USC from the navy. Jesse Unruh was twenty-four, fat, uneducated, and interested in left-wing politics. Within a decade, Burton and Unruh became the two giants of California Democratic Party politics. Starting in the late 1950s, they began to dominate the political life of the state for the next generation. But they first confronted each other on the seemingly tranquil campus of USC.

The youngest of five children of illiterate Texas sharecroppers, Unruh once said he never wore socks until he was twelve, but his feet were so dirty no one knew the difference.[14] He was smart and liked to read. After Pearl Harbor, he talked his way into the navy, which, like the other services that had rejected him for flat feet, did not want him either. But Unruh persisted. He was assigned to the Aleutian Islands, where he spent the war, bored, cold, and lonely. He repaired airplanes on big carriers and read every book in the ship libraries. Before shipping out, he married Virginia Lemon, a physical education teacher who already had graduated from USC. After the war, they returned to Los Angeles. At Virginia's insistence, Unruh enrolled there on the GI Bill.

USC was transformed by the influx of ex-GIs like Unruh. They were more mature than the younger, less experienced boys, who wore school sweaters and gathered around the statue of Tommy Trojan. The vets had been through a war and some had seen combat. Social rank, water fights, and rah-rah activities did not interest them. Unruh discovered that people not affiliated with the Greek system, the so-called "non-orgs" did not count for much on campus, even though they outnumbered the "orgs" by six to one. The student senate did not want to hear about housing problems for vets or about difficulties with military discharges. Unruh helped form Trovets, a campus group for veterans.

At the same time a vibrant political left began flourishing at USC. Some returning GIs had been radicalized by their experiences in the military. A group called American Youth for Democracy, a successor to the Young Communist League, was active on campus. Unruh was approached by Communist groups and even went so far as to fill out a membership card. He told Larry Margolis, active in the left at UCLA and later his top aide in the state assembly, that he was chasing a girl in the party and actually signed the membership card to impress her.[15] Fortunately for Unruh, nobody ever came to collect it.

But to Gil Ferguson, Unruh's behavior was hard to figure. The U.S. had just won the war, people could buy a house with a refrigerator and washing machine for $100 down, and here was Unruh, distributing left-wing literature at the corner of Jefferson and Howe Streets in his khakis—because those were the only pants he owned.

It might have seemed strange to a conservative like Ferguson, but Trovets was developing a following and compiling an impressive service record. The *Daily Trojan* reported that it organized six dances plus forums and concerts and "helped veterans with housing and terminal leave problems." In 1946, the group elected Unruh its president.[16]

While Unruh was heading Trovets, Burton's old V-12 roommate Sig Hesse was organizing the non-vets and non-orgs. They were known as Barbarians, in contrast to the Greeks. He wanted an atmosphere in which everyone could participate, not just fraternities. Unruh approached Hesse and Bob Peck, Burton's other former roommate. Together they formed the Independent Students Association, which ran a slate of candidates for office and elected Peck senior class president. Student legislators, including Burton, refused to permit a Trovets seat in the senate. Later they reversed themselves, agreeing that veterans could vote for one of their own.

Unruh was a direct threat to Burton's power. They were rivals, not friends, and did not like each other. Moreover, the Hesse-Peck-Unruh alliance was out to break the power of the fraternities. Peck nominated Unruh for the student senate, and Unruh in his brief campaign called for alleviating housing shortages and opposing tuition increases. Even though he was sympathetic to Unruh's political views, Burton worked hard to defeat him. Unruh's opponent was a *Daily Trojan* editorial assistant, nominated by Pat Hillings. Hillings, another campus conservative and fraternity leader, later took Richard Nixon's seat in Congress. (That Burton had worked with Nixonians to defeat Unruh in college was not lost on either when they were in the state assembly and Burton became the most important and powerful figure on Unruh's left.)

Unruh was elected on December 13, 1946. By the time he took office, Burton, after three years at USC, had already graduated and moved home to San Francisco. Still only twenty, Burton had bigger political arenas in mind.

2

BEATEN BY A DEAD MAN

I once asked Ronald Reagan about his parents, and he talked
about his mother for a half hour and never mentioned his father.
I asked Phil Burton what his dad did once, and he changed the subject.
He just didn't want to talk about him. There was a wall there.

LOU CANNON
Ronald Reagan's biographer

THE SAN FRANCISCO IN which Phillip Burton and his family arrived in June
1941 was not the chic, racially diverse, politically sophisticated city for which
it later became famous. Notwithstanding its colorful tourist areas of Fisherman's Wharf, Telegraph Hill, and Chinatown, the city's economy was based
on its status as a major port city and its thriving maritime, printing, construction, and light manufacturing industries. Its downtown was also an important
commercial center for banking, finance, retail trade, and real estate, although
not nearly the financial and service center it would become in subsequent
decades.

The city's 1940 population of 635,000 people was 95 percent white. Most
of its immigrants were Italian or Irish. There were 4,800 blacks, fewer than
1 percent of the population. Asians represented fewer than 4 percent, and
Chinese rarely ventured outside Chinatown.[1] Despite the city's bawdy, Bar-
bary Coast reputation, homosexuality was seldom discussed openly. Homosexuals confined themselves to discreet clubs or bars, where they were
occasionally rousted by the police. The McDonough brothers, known as the
"fountainheads of corruption," paid off the politicians and the police to control prostitution, gambling, and bookmaking.[2]

The city was solidly Democratic and working class. The key power centers
were the downtown business interests, the Catholic Church, and a tightly
knit Irish political machine run by an old-fashioned boss named William
Malone. It was the remnants of his organization that Phillip Burton even-

tually helped dismantle and then replace. Politicians, most of them Irish, responded to the labor unions and to powerful parish priests, from whom it would have been inconceivable to refuse requests for help. If he chose, the archbishop could name the police chief.[3] The church, via Catholic schools that placed graduates, many of them orphans, controlled most jobs in the police and fire departments; Public Works, Parks, and Recreation; the Municipal Railway; and the post office. The most important political jobs were also tightly controlled. As in many other American cities settled by immigrants, the Irish held an important advantage; unlike the Italians and other Europeans, they arrived in the U.S. already knowing the language. Moreover, they seemed to have a genius for political organization.

The man who became the political boss, William Malone, was born in 1900 in Noe Valley, the heart of the city's Irish district. The son of an Irish-born pipelayer, Malone earned his law degree in 1924. He got his start in politics in the mid-1930s during a spat between Mayor Jimmy Rolph and Sheriff Tom Finn, the pro-union Republican boss. Rolph aide Martin Tierney, the superintendent of public buildings, asked Malone to organize a neighborhood club in his St. James parish in Noe Valley and Malone agreed. He did such a good job that the first meeting produced an overflow crowd. Soon, he was asked to organize another club and another. Then Malone decided to run for the county Democratic Party Central Committee. He was elected chairman in 1936.

"What do I do now?" he asked. "Simple," Tierney replied. "Just do what I tell you." Two weeks later Tierney died and Malone was on his own.[4]

Malone learned fast. It was the height of the New Deal and Franklin Roosevelt's popularity, and Democrats were enjoying a resurgence. But as Malone looked around San Francisco, he saw that seven of its eight assemblymen were Republicans, largely because of a practice known as cross-filing. California's Progressive Governor Hiram Johnson twenty-five years earlier had instituted cross-filing to break the back of a corrupt Republican Party, Southern Pacific, and other large corporations that ran the state. Candidates could run in either party's primary without having to declare their party. Because of cross-filing, incumbent Republicans ran in both primaries year after year, without telling anyone they were Republicans. Cross-filing was the key to GOP control of the legislature and most constitutional offices. It virtually destroyed parties and turned elections into personal referenda on incumbents.

In a city as overwhelmingly Democratic as San Francisco, Malone felt that with hard work and organization he could elect Democrats. Another casualty of the Hiram Johnson days was patronage, the glue that holds any political machine together. But Malone found Democratic challengers and built the organization to elect them. One by one, he knocked off Republican incumbents.

Within two years, Malone was state party chairman. Leveraging his influence, Malone eventually controlled local and state judicial appointments as well as directors of the post office, the Mint, the U.S. Attorney's Office, the U.S. Marshall's Office, and the local bureau of the Internal Revenue Service. In a few more years, he controlled most San Francisco representatives to the state legislature and to Congress. Malone never ran a machine like New York's Tammany Hall, Curley's Boston, or Daley's Chicago, where thousands of patronage jobs were dispensed and party discipline was rigidly enforced. Malone at best had only a few dozen jobs to distribute. But for fifteen years he ruled San Francisco and large portions of California. If there was one man a candidate needed to see to get ahead in Democratic politics, Malone was that man.

Malone's role at the 1940 Democratic National Convention typified his method. As chairman of the California delegation, Governor Culbert Olson wanted to appoint Hollywood actor Melvyn Douglas his vice chairman. But Malone wanted San Francisco socialite and oil magnate Edward S. Heller, who had become Malone's main money man. More liberal than Malone, Heller was an early supporter of racial equality and became the patrician Jewish godfather to the tough Irish boss. Malone picked the candidates— whether a reform-minded young district attorney named Edmund G. "Pat" Brown or bakery wagon driver turned union leader Jack Shelley—and Heller wrote the checks.

As vice chairman of the delegation, Heller could serve as Malone's man in the leadership. Malone proposed a deal. If Douglas would step aside as vice chairman for Heller, Malone would select his wife, Helen Gahagan Douglas, as Southern California Democratic committeewoman. Douglas agreed, and Helen Gahagan Douglas's political career was born. Soon thereafter, the woman Richard Nixon later smeared was elected to Congress from Hollywood.[5]

The 1944 Democratic convention in Philadelphia further strengthened Malone's hand. The only major question at the convention was whether FDR would keep Henry Wallace as vice president or replace him. Malone and other pragmatic party leaders like national party chairman Robert Hannegan of St. Louis thought Wallace was too liberal. They believed a more moderate candidate could help Roosevelt win an unprecedented fourth term. Roosevelt left matters vague. He could accept Supreme Court Justice William O. Douglas but said the convention should decide.

Hannegan, Malone, and other big-state party bosses altered Roosevelt's message: they did not tell the delegates that FDR could also accept Justice Douglas, whom they believed no less liberal or electable than Wallace. Instead, they told the convention that FDR could accept either Douglas or the senator from Missouri, Harry Truman. Then Hannegan, Malone, and FDR stalwart Ed Flynn, the New York state party chairman, swung into action. Hannegan controlled a tiny room directly under the speaker's platform inside the convention hall where all the Truman floor leaders met. He, Flynn, and Malone brought key state delegation leaders there and twisted arms. In the end, Malone delivered nearly all of the California votes to Truman.[6]

Less than a year later, FDR was dead and Truman was president. He did not forget how he got there. Bill Malone became President Truman's most trusted ally in the far west, so powerful that when conservative Democratic Senator Pat McCarran of Nevada, chairman of the Senate Judiciary Committee, wanted a federal judge appointed in San Francisco, Malone was able to block it. Truman told McCarran all such appointments had to be cleared through Malone. He set up intimate lunches for Truman in California and got a private White House audience whenever he visited Washington.[7]

Solidifying his power, Malone chaired the state party again from 1944 to 1946 and operated a thriving law practice with Raymond Sullivan, later appointed to the California Supreme Court. Their specialty was tax law. Malone controlled the local tax commissioner, had a direct pipeline to the IRS in Washington, or, failing that, to Truman himself.

Malone also selected most of the state representatives from San Francisco. For a job that paid $100 a month, the pickings were often slim. Malone managed to find and keep in office for years such nonentities as Edward Gaffney, a one-time Shakespearean actor and house painter, whose primary mission was to make sure all eight of his children got through the parish schools. Elected in 1940, Gaffney survived until 1964, when an ambitious and talented young black politician named Willie Brown finally unseated him in the primary. Another Malone pick was Charlie Walter Raymond Meyers. Meyers needed a job and his father, who owned an auto repair shop, was a loyal Malone supporter. Sacramento lobbyists wrote Meyers's bills for him, but he was beloved and good-natured, if dim, and loved to hand out mints. A third member of the San Francisco assembly contingent was William "Cliff" Berry, from Malone's own Twenty-third District.

Malone followed three simple rules: Always have a candidate. Always have a second for a motion. Never tell anyone how you won, because what they imagine always makes you seem more powerful. He also had important financial ties to Chinatown, where he was close to Albert Chow, Chinatown's unofficial "mayor." Because immigration of Chinese was tightly restricted, wealthy Asians from Hong Kong or Taiwan who wanted citizenship quickly learned that Chow could make them legal. Chow would call Malone. Malone would call Congressman Shelley, who would introduce a special bill in Congress. Such favors were always done for the sake of "friendship," although a $5,000 contribution to the party was also helpful.[8] Malone was not considered corrupt. He just played by old rules. Patronage mattered and being the political boss mattered a lot.

When Phillip Burton returned home to San Francisco in early 1947 after graduation from USC, Malone was at the height of his influence. Burton wanted to go to law school but needed to save money first. He worked for three years, selling gas station leases for Time Oil in Richmond, attended Golden Gate Law School at night, and gravitated to local politics. During a union drive, Burton told the chief organizer what management was doing to block the union. When Burton ran for the assembly a few years later, organizer John Sheridan remembered the favor and urged the San Francisco Teamsters to endorse him. Burton "constantly spoke to the drivers weakening under the Bosses' attempt to scare them out of going union," Sheridan wrote. "His efforts were of considerable help [in] obtaining a contract."[9]

While in Richmond, Burton met Democratic activist Bert Coffey, a former Communist Party member and close associate of George Miller, Jr., a liberal young assemblyman who quickly moved up to the state senate. A future Democratic Party chairman, Miller chafed under Malone's top-down control and said the party under Malone was so restrictive that "you need a passport to get in." Miller would play an important role in Burton's early political career.[10]

Miller was not the only young liberal to feel frustrated and excluded from his own party. While Burton walked precincts in Richmond and Berkeley in 1948 to elect Democrats, other young liberals, many of them veterans, also itched to move into politics. But like Miller, they found the path blocked by Malone. Many activists, finishing their college and professional degrees, were like the returning veterans at USC. They had risked their lives for their country overseas and had their own ideas about how things should be run. They resented the old guard who controlled everything and had no use for the handpicked party hacks Malone chose for local offices. This new generation of Democrats, under Burton's later direction, eventually displaced Malone.

Joe Holsinger, for example, had just arrived from Santa Barbara, where he was active with the newly formed Americans for Democratic Action. He and some friends started a Young Democrats chapter as a vehicle for their liberal aims. But there was a problem: a Young Democrats group already existed. It was a phantom organization, however. Most members were over thirty-five, the maximum age permitted under the national bylaws, and it routinely sold its endorsements to Republicans, endorsing Thomas Dewey and Earl Warren in 1948 over Harry Truman.

The insurgent group soon attracted an extraordinary collection of young activists. Besides Holsinger, the club included Yori Wada, a local playground director and war veteran, whose Japanese-American parents were in a relocation camp while he fought for the United States in the South Pacific; a liberal lawyer named Jack Berman, who fought in the Philippines and got his law degree in 1947 (his first wife was a young Stanford graduate named Dianne Goldman, later Dianne Feinstein); and Dr. Carlton Goodlett, a black physician and publisher of the *Sun Reporter* who earned a Ph.D. in child psychology at age twenty-three from the University of California at Berkeley before going to medical school.

Burton soon joined the Young Democrats and rose rapidly to its leadership. War vet Marshall Windmiller joined after a year at the University of Paris. Windmiller eventually became a professor of international relations at San Francisco State University. Listening to Windmiller talk about foreign affairs one day, Burton said, "If I'm ever president, you'll be secretary of state." Neither thought the idea absurd. He also told Windmiller a political advisor was counseling him on his career but never revealed who it was. "I've got a strategy all mapped out," Burton told him.

Burton and Goodlett worked together in the local NAACP chapter and soon became scheming partners at YD meetings, where they huddled in the back of the room. Wada knew Burton from the Booker T. Washington Community Center, where Burton dropped in weekly to shoot baskets with the kids. Wada even got him to coach a basketball team, and at election time Burton returned and asked them to help pass out political leaflets. He was a poor coach, Wada recalled, because he got too excited as the game progressed and was too caught up in winning. But Wada believed Burton really cared about the kids, many of whom were poor, black teenagers, some already school dropouts or petty criminals.

The biggest challenge for the fledgling group was to wrest control of the

YD charter from the conservative group. Holsinger believed the best way to do that was to work with Malone and Elinor Heller, wife of Malone's money man, who helped finance trips to national meetings. Malone tried to co-opt the new group, asking Holsinger and others to help out at party functions. Holsinger kept Malone informed of what the group was doing and appointed Burton to chair the political action committee. Malone in turn helped them retrieve the charter.

Holsinger quickly regretted appointing Burton political action chairman. This chairman was building his own power base. Instead of working only for local Democrats, Burton enlisted some followers to campaign for a state senate candidate. The man lost but appointed Burton to the state central committee.

In 1950, while still in law school, Burton took a job as a janitor in his father's medical building. In a moment that held great significance for his later career, he walked over to 240 Golden Gate Avenue, headquarters for the Building Service Employees union, which represented janitors, and filled out a membership card. Politics, not law, had become his consuming interest. In his work with the Young Democrats, he found he could outthink his rivals just as surely as he had on the playgrounds of Milwaukee and San Francisco and in the councils of Blue Key and Sigma Phi Epsilon. But just as the Trojan Knights and USC's exclusive secret fraternity had blocked his rise to power on campus, Bill Malone and the old guard San Francisco Democrats imposed even tougher restrictions on his political ascent. If George Miller—an elected official—felt he needed a passport to become active in the Democratic Party, Phillip Burton seemed to require a presidential decree.

Burton and Holsinger held sharply different views of the Young Democrats. Burton did not want to work for Malone. He wanted to *be* Malone. He wanted a career in elective office, with San Francisco as his base. He believed he could represent labor unions and racial minorities more effectively than anyone else he saw holding office. Making common cause with other outsiders also suited him temperamentally. So it was no surprise that he did not believe in accommodating himself to Malone or anyone else.

The Young Democrats was for serious, committed liberals, in Burton's view, those who believed in admitting the new Communist regime in China into the United Nations, or who were appalled at the witch hunts and anticommunist hysteria that had seized the nation. These young turks believed the House Un-American Activities Committee was more of a threat to democracy than the Peoples Republic of China. Burton and his allies were not the least bit reluctant to broadcast that point of view, no matter how alienating it might be to rank-and-file Democrats, let alone to Bill Malone. In September 1950, Burton led a contingent of YD activists before the San Francisco Board of Supervisors to testify against approving an ordinance to require all Communists to register at City Hall. Burton's appearance was noted repeatedly in files that the FBI and the Air Force Office of Special Investigations opened on Burton beginning in 1953.

Burton challenged Holsinger for president in 1950, accusing him of "selling out" to Malone. He asked Charlie Warren, a UC Berkeley student, to nominate him. The group met in the back of a bar on upper Market Street. Warren was so nervous speaking in front of the three dozen assembled activists that he had to grasp his chair tightly to keep from shaking. Warren later asked why Burton had chosen him.

"I knew you would be nervous," Burton replied, "but there was a note of sincerity there that I wanted conveyed." Warren was astonished by the degree to which Burton calculated everything. He packed the meeting with his own supporters, some of whom he had signed up as new members. Burton defeated Holsinger that May but alienated colleagues, even though their political philosophies were similar. Yori Wada, a Holsinger supporter, was so angry over Burton's tactics that he never again supported him for any office, even though Wada spent his career as a liberal activist in San Francisco.[11]

While the San Francisco chapter was consumed with internal politics, a rich liberal grape grower in Fresno named Lionel Steinberg formed a statewide Young Democrats organization. Unlike the San Francisco activists, he had credibility with establishment politicians. President Truman, who pulled out a miraculous victory over Dewey, carried California by only 17,000 votes, the margin Steinberg delivered for Truman in Fresno County alone. A last-minute Truman whistle-stop train ride through the Central Valley made the crucial difference. Most people thought Truman would lose to Dewey, but the ever-loyal Malone was one of the few on hand to greet the president when he arrived in Reno the night before the trip began, and he rode with Truman all the way. Impressed with Steinberg's organizational ability, Malone and Elinor Heller offered him directorship of the Mint in San Francisco, but he declined. He wanted eventually to be secretary of agriculture.

After the 1948 election, Steinberg put out feelers to young people he had met all over the state and soon had twelve clubs organized. In addition to the San Francisco chapter, Steinberg contacted Coffey in Richmond and met Burton at their first state convention in Fresno in May 1949. Soon Burton became his closest ally in San Francisco. To Steinberg, Burton seemed an "eager beaver" with flashing brown eyes. He loved to talk, plot, and drink.

Among those who attended that first convention were Malone associates Elinor Heller and state party chairman Oliver Carter, San Francisco District Attorney Pat Brown, and James Roosevelt, left-wing Democrat and son of the former president. Malone worried about where Steinberg was taking the new organization, fearing these young stalwarts would back ultraliberals Roosevelt for governor in 1950 and Helen Gahagan Douglas for the U.S. Senate.

Malone invited Steinberg and his wife over to dinner one night, hoping to keep him out of the Roosevelt and Douglas camps. When he realized that Steinberg could not be dissuaded, he offered some fatherly advice. "Lionel," he said, "I can see a great future for you politically. But don't do what I did. Don't spend your whole life being a power in the party, where you have to deal with all the fights and battles. The road to satisfaction is being in office." With that, Malone rolled up his trousers and showed Steinberg his legs, which were covered with eczema. "This is what you get," he said, "when you have the frustration of party leadership and the need to maintain power. Find something you want to run for and do it quickly."[12]

Malone had never forgiven Douglas for her vote against Truman at the 1944 convention. Worse, however, was her decision after just five years in the House to challenge Malone's friend, two-term Senator Sheridan Downey, in the 1950 Democratic primary. Douglas had voted against the Truman Doctrine of aid to Greece and Turkey and consistently against appropriations to the House Un-American Activities Committee, of which she was a constant critic. Elinor Heller supported Douglas, but Malone worried that Douglas was too liberal to be elected. Her candidacy, he believed, would pave the way for the election of the new favorite of the Republican right—Richard Nixon, late of the Alger Hiss hearings. Nixon could question her patriotism but not Downey's.

When Downey announced he would not seek another term, Malone spent hours trying to dissuade him. He failed to keep Downey in or Douglas out. When Manchester Boddy, the publisher of the *Los Angeles Daily News*, jumped into the primary against Douglas, Malone promptly supported him. Presaging the Nixon smears, Boddy attacked Douglas, saying that she and her supporters constituted a "statewide conspiracy on the part of a small subversive clique of red-hots to capture, through stealth and cunning, the nerve centers of our Democratic Party." But Douglas won, becoming the Democratic nominee.[13]

Unlike Malone, Burton and his friends were thrilled. Helen Douglas embodied his idea of a principled politician. Besides, he was almost in love with this former actress and opera singer who was talented, beautiful, elegant, and left wing. She could articulate all the dreams of this new generation of liberal Democrats. Roz Weiner, a USC activist and driver for Douglas during her 1950 campaign, said Burton followed her around like a puppy. He was so taken with Douglas that when he led her across the dance floor with a moonstruck look on his face one night, he looked as though he would faint from pure happiness. He was so eager and worked so hard that Douglas said to Weiner, "That young man will do anything." Burton asked Weiner out several times during the campaign, talking almost nonstop. When she finally got a word in she said, "You're not interested in me. You're in love with Helen." But as much as Burton admired and believed in Helen Gahagan Douglas, he was also using her campaign to learn how to run for office himself. Soon he would run for the state assembly, and after that for Congress.

In her fight with Nixon, Douglas often gave as good as she got. But between the outbreak of the Korean War, the Chinese invasion of North Korea, and Nixon's skillful attacks, he won easily. Two years later he became vice president on Dwight Eisenhower's ticket. Popular Governor Earl Warren easily defeated James Roosevelt to win a third term. But there was one bright note for state Democrats. San Francisco District Attorney Pat Brown was elected state attorney general. He ran as a moderate, distancing himself from both Roosevelt and Douglas.[14]

The defeats of Roosevelt and Douglas were a bitter blow to the reformers. But Burton developed a new interest to ease his disappointment: Sala Galant Lipschultz, a blond Polish-Jewish divorcée, seven years his senior, whom he met during the Douglas campaign. Born in Bialystok, Poland, Sala Galant emigrated with her family in the late 1930s, just in time to escape the Nazis. Arriving in San Francisco, her parents opened a liquor store and deli. Sala married young and gave birth to a daughter, Joy. The marriage did not last. Glamorous and vivacious, Sala had never shown much interest in politics. But she began attending Young Democrats meetings and soon was a regular. People on the far left of the group assumed she shared their politics and kept Phillip honest about his.

Once Burton was smitten, some friends thought he was pressing Sala to marry quickly. Others, noting her good looks and voluptuous figure, thought Sala overpowered Burton sexually. Ordinarily, he was too busy politicking to chase women. Burton's friend Toby Osos watched as Sala pursued him over several years. In one of the rare discussions she had with Burton about Sala, Osos remarked that Sala was "single-minded on the issues." Burton replied, "I'm afraid I'm one of the issues." Within two years they married, and for the next thirty years, Sala was the most important person in his life.

Every bit as obsessed with politics as her husband, Sala was the perfect political wife. She was his chief strategist and confidante, his eyes and ears, and when he was not around, his most forceful advocate. She never hesitated to barge into YD meetings where her husband's future was being discussed. Yet she possessed a charm and gentle manner that Phillip utterly lacked. She cleaned up his messes, soothing and placating those he insulted or abused. She alone could intervene in a conversation to shut him up. Sometimes just a look or a phrase from Sala could calm him.

Friends joked that the couple's "idea of pillow talk is to go over the latest voter registration figures from Ventura County." There was much truth in that observation. Her utter devotion to politics and to her husband's career explained much of Burton's later success. They did not share the same need for recreation, small talk, family, or other concerns that occupied most couples. This permitted them to focus single-mindedly on their political goals.[15]

As 1952 began, Burton finished law school and threw himself into every political cause he could find. *San Francisco Chronicle* reporter Pierre Salinger reported that the California Federation of Young Democrats at their Stockton meeting voted to favor admitting Red China to the UN. That resolution almost got them thrown out of the Democratic Party. The Young Democrats also voted to repeal the Taft-Hartley Act and a federal law under which Communists could be sent to prison. Osos was elected state president.[16] At a national YD meeting later that year in Reno, Nevada, Senator Hubert Humphrey of Minnesota gave the keynote speech and invited Burton, Steinberg, and a few other leaders to his room afterwards. They talked all night and over breakfast told Humphrey they thought he would make a great president.

Burton became the dominant and unquestioned leader of the San Francisco group, an indefatigable worker, a brilliant tactician and strategist. Whenever a circle of people was hotly debating some issue, Burton was in the middle of it. People were amazed at his single-minded intensity and seeming indifference to anything that was not political. When Mary Louise Allen arrived in San Francisco as a young college graduate from Oregon to visit a friend, she attended a YD meeting in which Charlie Warren succeeded Burton as president. Over drinks after the vote, Burton was still furious because he counted eighteen votes against his position on an issue, and nineteen people opposed him. He was so agitated about who the "traitor" might be that Allen became deeply offended. "My God, he won," she thought. "What's with him?"

But Allen stayed, fascinated by this strange mix of pragmatic tactician and idealist crusader, of Machiavelli and Norman Thomas. She soon became a protégé and eventually state president herself. Even so, she frequently got angry with Burton for trying to dominate everything. It bothered her that some people viewed her as Burton's tool. Yori Wada, for example, often saw Burton scream and swear at his assistants as if they were his paid henchmen for something as simple as failing to line up a vote. Wada was amazed they tolerated such abuse. But Burton was not only domineering, he was "right" on the issues and usually right on the strategy. That made it easier to tolerate his abusive behavior. Burton and his supporters shared the same political vision. When they fought, it was mostly over power and turf, not ideology, disputes fueled by ego and Burton's need to prove he was better than anybody else.

On election night in November 1952 Burton took Mary Louise Allen, Jack Berman, and several other Young Democrats to the ghetto housing projects at Hunters Point to pass out coffee and doughnuts to voters. Because there were only a few precincts, people were waiting in lines a block long to vote. Just as they arrived, a precinct worker came outside and announced that the polls were about to close, shutting out some 150 black voters.

"I'll take care of this," said Burton, who disappeared to make a strategic phone call and scream at the white precinct workers. Moments later, he returned to announce that everyone would be allowed to vote, no matter how long it took. Harvey Matthews, a black longshoreman who witnessed the incident, said Phillip Burton's political base in the black community began that night. Shortly thereafter, Matthews and other activists formed the Twentieth Century Democratic Club, and Burton was a frequent speaker.[17]

In between YD meetings, Burton joined the World Affairs Council, the national and local chapters of the Americans for Democratic Action, the ACLU, the Citizens Political Advisory Board, the American Veterans Committee, the NAACP, the Council for Civic Unity, and even the Junior Chamber of Commerce, where he was named vice chairman of the public affairs committee. Mayor Elmer Robinson selected him as co-chairman of a mayoral commission on voter registration.

Despite the frenetic activity, Burton could never sufficiently impress his father, who did not take his political activities seriously. Dr. Burton's income and social standing had increased dramatically in the years since they arrived almost penniless from the Midwest. Dr. Burton thought his eldest son should be working on his law career, not electoral politics, which he thought demeaning. Burton worked hard and to little avail to keep his father from being upset.

"I try to keep the old man happy," he told Steinberg when his friend asked how things were going at home. To Charlie Warren, who occasionally joined Phillip and his family for dinner on Sunday nights, Dr. Burton showed a populist, almost libertarian distrust of government. But he seemed unimpressed by his son's constant politicking, which he regarded as frivolous. Warren never once had a serious political conversation with him but especially remembered one Thanksgiving dinner at the Burton home. Dr. Burton had attended the ballet the evening before, and the symphony conductor was a dinner guest, as was a Russian ballerina, one of Dr. Burton's patients. While Phillip sat there barely enduring the highbrow conversation, Warren listened fascinated as Dr. Burton, the ballerina, and the conductor debated whether the orchestra had been one beat ahead of the dancers. Who could ever please such a perfectionist?[18]

One morning at breakfast in October 1952, Burton saw the list of those who passed the bar published in the morning newspaper. Wondering whether a young father who sat next to him during the bar exam had passed, he asked Sala to check the list. "He passed, Phillip," Sala said, continuing to scan the newspaper columns. "But I don't see your name."

A less self-confident man might have reacted to such news with acute pain and self-recrimination for failing. Instead, Burton quickly walked to the telephone, dialed the newspaper, and said to the copy boy who answered, "This is Phillip Burton. You published the bar results today. My name must have been omitted by mistake." After holding the phone for what must have seemed like ages, Burton heard the boy come back on. "You're right, Mr. Burton," he said. "Your name was inadvertently left off the list. It will be fixed for the next edition."

But even before he had a chance to practice law, politics intervened again, this time, the Democratic Party's July 1952 nomination of Adlai Stevenson for president. Charismatic, witty, intelligent, and liberal, Stevenson galvanized millions of progressives throughout the U.S. He was also popular with the ultraliberals in California, where state Senator George Miller, Jr., had wrested control of the state party away from the Malone faction. Stevenson helped get Miller elected party chairman.[19]

But many California mainstream Democrats returned home from the convention apathetic about working hard for Stevenson, including Malone. Young activists quickly filled the vacuum across the state. Dick Nevin and Toby Osos in the South, Steinberg and his friends in the Central Valley, and Burton, Charlie Warren, and Berkeley YD president Tom Winnett in the

Bay Area worked long and hard for the Illinois governor. Even Dr. Burton sent a $1,000 check.

Stevenson's California campaign became the catalyst for the rise of the Democratic club movement. A huge outpouring of young, idealistic liberals came into the political system to elect "Adlai." But Stevenson had the misfortune that year to run against war hero Dwight Eisenhower. "The next morning, after Stevenson lost," Winnett later said, "it seemed as if thousands of people went charging out the door, saying, 'it's an outrage that he should be voted down. We're going to organize so that that kind of thing can't happen in America again.'" After Stevenson lost, Helen Myers, chairman of the Los Angeles County Democrats, said nearly 200 people attended a postmortem "wanting to know what they could do to help Stevenson and the party. . . . People felt that if they'd only done more, Stevenson would have won."[20]

George Miller wanted to hang on to the new volunteers. Moving quickly, he called for a January 1953 meeting of Democratic clubs at Asilomar, a serene and beautiful conference center on the Pacific coast near Monterey. Set amid rustic cabins, pine and cypress trees, and the roar of the surf, hundreds of old leaders and new activists, including United World Federalist President Alan Cranston, debated political strategy. Among the chief issues: how to establish an organization to support progressive Democrats in primaries, reinvigorate the state party, and win California back from the Republicans. They would be a counterpart to the California Republican Assembly, an unofficial "club" Earl Warren founded to reassert Republican liberalism after Herbert Hoover's 1932 defeat. The task was formidable. After the November 1952 elections, the Republicans controlled both U.S. Senate seats, nineteen of the thirty congressional seats, 83 of the 120 state legislative seats, and every statewide office except attorney general. Within six years, the Democrats almost completely reversed the numbers.[21]

Between Miller's call for the first Asilomar conference and the formal establishment in November 1953 of the California Democratic Council, Phillip Burton realized he had new military obligations. With the Korean War on, Burton enlisted at the local air force office. He was assigned as a lawyer and first lieutenant to the Judge Advocate General's Office at Camp Parks, Pleasanton, an hour away. When orders came to report to Point Embarcadero, Alaska, he and Sala decided to get married. They kept their plans secret and asked Toby Osos to find a good liberal judge in Los Angeles to marry them. Only a few friends witnessed the wedding in the judge's chambers. Afterwards, they all went to the home of friends, where they ate spaghetti, drank champagne, and argued about politics. The newlyweds shocked Osos that night when they said they probably would not have children. The hostess, a mother of two, said Phillip would love kids. "I guess I'd have to settle down more," the groom replied. The couple honeymooned in Santa Monica.

On his return, a letter arrived informing Burton that all people who had previously served in the military, including in the V-12 program, were discharged from further service. Burton was out. He served in the navy and in the air force for more than three years during two wars and never left California. Afterwards, Charlie Warren said he thought the military and Sala changed Burton. He was thoughtful and affectionate to Sala in a way Warren had never seen. He was mature, confident, serious, and determined to make his mark in politics.

Burton was discharged just in time to attend the next big California Democratic Council meeting in November 1953 in Fresno. More than 500 activists—Stevenson volunteers, Young Democrats, party members, elected officials, and members of the burgeoning club movement—gathered to charter a historic new political movement for California. Tension flared from the very first between elected officials and the more liberal volunteers over which group would set policy and guide the party. That tension lasted throughout the CDC's entire history. But even the elected officials knew how much they needed the thousands of volunteers who could organize in every assembly, senate, and congressional district.

For this conference at least, they put aside differences to establish the organization, adopt rules, and elect leaders. Alan Cranston became the first president. The key figures were Cranston and George Miller. But the most active and liberal contingent were the Young Democrats like Burton, Osos, Winnett, Pasadena lawyer Joe Wyatt, and a young Fresno protégé of Steinberg named Roy Greenaway. Burton urged them to volunteer for everything, from setting up tables and chairs to getting food and taking minutes. By establishing networks everywhere, Burton said, they would know everything that was going on.

CDC activists left Fresno with a new commitment to party building. They established councils in every assembly, senate, and congressional district to work for candidates they had endorsed in the primaries. They vowed to register voters, keep building the club movement, fight cross-filing, raise money for liberals. In his first year's report, Cranston said the CDC contributed more than $21,500 to its candidates, fielded a complete slate of Democrats for every state office for the first time in years, and avoided divisive primary fights.

Following the 1954 elections, the Republicans still held onto the big offices. Voters elected Goodwin Knight governor, who had succeeded Warren, President Eisenhower's pick as chief justice of the United States. But the Democrats picked up five seats in the state senate and six in the assembly, cutting into the huge Republican majorities. The senate went from 29-11 to 24-16, while the assembly Republican margin was chopped from 54-26 to 48-32. Working with the state central committee, CDC activists registered 155,000 new Democrats, the largest gain since the Depression, compared to just 67,000 for the Republicans. Between July 1952—just before Stevenson's nomination—and November 1954, the number of clubs grew from just 75 to 425. For the first time in years, the Democratic Party was on the march.[22]

The same could not be said for Bill Malone. He dodged a direct challenge in 1950, when a former law partner named Elmer Delaney, a crippled and bitter man who often harangued politicians at City Hall, formed a United Democrats ticket to end Malone's "boss rule." Burton and the Young Democrats supported Delaney, but the challenge went nowhere. Indeed, virtually the only press coverage Delaney got was in the Communist Party's *People's World*, in which Delaney said Malone's "machine . . . has treated Negroes and other members of minority groups as second class citizens. It has operated as lord of the manor—holding no regular meetings, profiting financially from its selfish and undemocratic actions."[23]

Malone's troubles soon escalated. In September 1951, in a purge of tax bureaus across the country, President Truman personally suspended and then fired Malone's longtime friend and political ally Jimmy Smyth, collector of internal revenue for the Northern California district, for "incompetence" and alleged manipulation of tax records. Worse, eight of Malone's top aides, including his brother, were implicated in the scandal. The news shocked San Francisco. Smyth was an insider's insider, the 1944 Northern California campaign director for President Roosevelt who was rewarded with the tax post and was said to have a bright political future. Malone's brother took the Fifth Amendment when questioned by a federal grand jury.

The case dragged on for years. Smyth was eventually acquitted of all charges, but the sensational press coverage, which dominated the front pages of San Francisco newspapers for more than a year, destroyed Smyth's career and soured Malone.[24] After sixteen long, tension-filled years as party boss, Malone was ready to get out. But Malone was also worried that Phillip Burton and other insurgent Democrats would unravel his political empire.

"Why is Burton after me?" Malone asked Holsinger. "Because you are where he wants to be," Holsinger replied.

By March 1952, Malone gave up, resigning his posts. "The Malone withdrawal suggests a major upset in the organization that has made things tick in California Democratic politics ever since the first Roosevelt administration," wrote *San Francisco News* political editor Mary Ellen Leary. Malone "wears a fairly glum expression," she said, and has "bitter words" about the investigations of his associates.[25]

Malone's exit was the opportunity for which Phillip Burton spent years preparing. He practiced law intermittently for two years with a black law partner named Joseph Williams, a friend from Golden Gate Law School and Young Democrats. Burton handled a few personal injury and worker compensation cases, but anything other than politics bored him. He asked Williams to look up cases for him. He even let the statute of limitations slide on a case in which his client stepped in a hole and broke his leg. Williams had to convince the client he had no case anyway. As in college, Burton never came alive until late afternoon. By 5 P.M. he was ready to hit a bar to talk politics far into the night.

With the central committee in turmoil over Malone's resignation, the Burtons moved to an old, modestly furnished Victorian flat on Guerrero Street in the Mission District and aimed right at the heart of established Irish power in San Francisco: the Twenty-third Assembly District, Bill Malone's St. James parish, the seat held for ten years by Cliff Berry. Berry, a portly, grandfatherly figure whose attendance record had slipped in recent years, had always been labor's friend. But Burton wanted to take him out, and to the horror of the few Democrats who paid any attention, he declared his candidacy.

Burton organized his first campaign diligently but made his share of mistakes. He was twenty-seven and full of energy. The photo on the cover of his 1954 campaign brochure showed a tall, young, thin, earnest-looking man with smooth skin, a long prominent nose, and a full head of thick black hair, although there were already early signs of a receding hairline. In a letter to Gifford Phillips, publisher of the liberal *Frontier* magazine, he asked for money and laid out some of his progressive views, such as opposition to loyalty oaths and the House Un-American Activities Committee.

"Among my supporters," he wrote, "are numbered almost all of the anti-Malone members of the County Central Committee . . . every Negro leader . . . and promise of endorsement of the Negro newspaper in San Francisco. I will have a decent chance of 'dumping the incumbent' and the more liberal elements of the party support me. This is my maiden venture." In another letter that was both uncharacteristically humble yet revealing about his ultimate ambition, he thanked a local attorney for his ten dollar contribution and wrote: "I expect that I will make a good many mistakes in the months and years ahead, during the formative years of my political life, but they will be those of judgment, not of the heart."[26]

The assembly district contained 50,000 Democrats and 16,000 Republicans. It was blue-collar Irish and intensely loyal to Bill Malone, the local boy made good. A rare exception was a young unemployed reporter just out of the army named Lou Cannon, who lived on Dolores Street. He was between jobs when Bob Burton rang his doorbell and invited him to a meeting at his brother's apartment a block away. Cannon, who was interested in progressive politics, quickly threw himself into the campaign. Another visitor to the Burton household was a UC Berkeley law student from Los Angeles named Frank Mankiewicz. Mankiewicz had run unsuccessfully for the assembly in 1952, and Jesse Unruh had worked in his campaign. Burton argued strenuously with Mankiewicz over the CDC, college rival Unruh, and the role of volunteer activists versus professionals. One evening ended abruptly as Mankiewicz left the Burton apartment, his host leaning over the third-floor balcony shouting down at him: "You whore! You whore!"

Burton, who attended countless labor functions and knew Berry was ill, approached Jack Henning, the director of the state Federation of Labor, for an endorsement. But he had no luck getting the unions to support his insurgent candidacy against a man with a 95 percent labor record.

"You've got a future," Henning said. "But how can you expect us to go against Berry?" Malone stalwarts were appalled. They considered it unseemly to take on any established Democratic incumbent. A young up-and-coming pol was expected to wait his turn. To the political establishment, Burton seemed a brash left-wing upstart, and, worse, he was married to a Jewish foreigner. Even the Holsinger-Wada faction of Young Democrats was angry at Burton's impudence. Holsinger had his own candidate for the seat, but when Berry announced he would seek re-election, Holsinger backed off.

But Burton did not give up. He approached George Hardy, a tough-talking Irish renegade labor leader who later became one of the most important people in Burton's life. Hardy started his Building Service Employees union with five janitors at City Hall in the mid-thirties and through shrewd mergers with Bay Area and East Coast locals eventually built them into the powerful Service Employees International Union (SEIU). He thought his fellow labor leaders were phonies who were not militant enough. After Burton said he worked as a janitor during law school and asked for Hardy's endorsement, Hardy checked his union credentials. Luckily, Burton's dues were current. Hardy was impressed. But even Hardy could not go against his Labor Council's endorsement.

Press coverage of the campaign was almost nonexistent. One small story in a paper called the *News Mirror* said of Burton: "The young barrister is vibrant, well liked and outspoken and frankly for all liberal causes, non-segregation, against the uses of injunctions in labor." Berry, on the other hand, the article said, was a "darling" of the "precinct bosses" and a "dull representative" whose absentee record Burton planned to make an issue. Burton went to every endorsement meeting of every club he could find. Sala canvassed the neighborhood door-to-door.

But when Cyr Copertini, Malone's former secretary, saw Sala on her rounds, she said to herself, "This isn't going to work." An exotic-looking blonde with waist-length hair, a generous bosom, and a foreign accent did not exactly mesh in a neighborhood where most women answered the door in plain house dresses from the National Dollar Store on Mission Street. "Here she comes," they sniffed to Cyr. "Who is he to run against Cliff Berry? We don't know her. We don't like her, and we don't like him."

Burton hit the jazz clubs, ethnic restaurants, homosexual and Negro bars. Whatever the scene, he always had a least one friend, the manager or bartender, who introduced him around. While Berry barely campaigned at all, Burton motivated his troops by demonizing his opponent as an old Irish hack politician. For all his hard work, however, he made little headway.

On May 5, the campaign took a sudden and surprising turn when Cliff Berry died peacefully at his home. It was too late to reprint the ballots. State law gave the county central committee authority to choose an alternative nominee. If Burton won the primary, he was obviously the candidate in November. But if the political lieutenants of State Board of Equalization member George Reilly, who controlled nearly half the committee, and the remnants of Malone's group could turn out a big vote for the late Mr. Berry on election day, they could find somebody else to install in Burton's place.

"Reports are current in political circles," *San Francisco Chronicle*'s political editor Earl "Squire" Behrens wrote on May 17, "of a scheme among a faction of unnamed Democrats to throw the election of a new assemblyman from the twenty-third district by rolling up a majority for a dead man." After Berry's death, Burton got a few labor endorsements, including George Hardy's Building Service Employees union. But Holsinger, who had since moved to Marin County, was still getting calls from the Mission. "We don't like him. What do we do?" they asked. "You can't do anything publicly," Holsinger replied, "but use the back fence." Through Malone word spread all through the parish: stop Burton.

Phillip and Sala Burton, Lou Cannon, and their closest friends met to discuss what to do. No one thought he would lose, but they figured they had better get the word out about Berry. Sala suggested they send a letter with a black border saying they deeply regretted Berry's passing but that Phillip Burton was now the Democratic candidate to succeed him. Even Burton thought that was in poor taste. He turned to a law school classmate named John O'Connell, who was running for the county committee because a friend suggested he had a good Irish name and could get elected on the CDC slate. O'Connell agreed to sign a letter to 10,000 voters that Burton wrote expressing support for Burton and sympathy for Mrs. Berry.

"Dear Fellow Democrats," the letter began. "The tragic and unexpected death of our fellow Democrat, Assemblyman William Cliff Berry, has saddened us all. . . . Mr. Berry's name, for technical reasons, appears on the voting machines; since a vote for him would be a wasted vote, we as fellow Democrats express the hope you will now find it possible to give your unqualified support to Phillip Burton, another Democratic candidate." Burton followed that up with a May 27 letter to Congressman Jack Shelley, asking for his endorsement and noting an "overwhelming shift" of Berry's labor support to him. "There has been some understandable reluctance from some of the Malone group to support me," Burton wrote in perhaps the understatement of the year, "although I have sought out their support." He concluded in a hand-written postscript: "PS: If you feel that intervening would affect your political future (which is damned important to our political future), I'll understand."[27]

Burton was devastated when the votes came in. Always the outsider in the district, he lost to a man in Holy Cross cemetery by more than two to one, 11,677 votes to 5,253. Choosing the successor was now up to the central committee. George Reilly, who wanted to be mayor, controlled ten of the thirty-six votes. In return for making Reilly's son Jim chairman, Reilly delivered his votes along with those of the CDC to John O'Connell, who trounced his Republican opponent by three to one in November.

It was a bitter blow to Burton, although he took some solace in the defeat of the once-mighty Malone machine. He worked hard to elect O'Connell and did not blame O'Connell for getting the job he wanted. But he remained convinced that he, not O'Connell, should be going to Sacramento. He even told O'Connell the only reason O'Connell was elected to the county committee was the name identification he got from sending out the letter on Burton's behalf. Goodlett's *Sun Reporter* editorialized that "Kingmakers in the Democratic Party certainly reflected an active disinterest in the success of Phillip Burton. How long can Democrats expect loyal support and personal sacrifice from young men when they are betrayed from within party ranks?"[28]

Burton recovered quickly, but he never forgot how the county central committee "betrayed" him. He vowed that one day he would control that committee and make sure it never happened again. And he never forgot his first ignominious defeat. Much later, after he was elected to the House of Representatives, a *Congressional Quarterly* questionnaire asked him to describe unsuccessful campaigns for public office.

"1954—for state assembly in 23rd Assembly District," he wrote. "Lost in primaries to a dead man."[29]

3

CHINATOWN AND THE

BATTLE FOR POTRERO HILL

Phil Burton was the precursor of the new politics, scientific, demographic.
He went directly to the people and brought a whole new politics to San
Francisco and California. It wasn't just knocking on doors. It was knowing
what doors to knock on. The 1956 campaign was a frontal assault on
Tommy Maloney and on all of us who were waiting our turn.

JUDGE JOHN ERTOLA
former San Francisco supervisor

PHIL BURTON IS MY NAME. I'm the Democratic candidate running for
assemblyman in this district. I would appreciate it if you would vote for me."
Nearly every night for eight months in 1956, Phillip Burton delivered this
pitch at the doorsteps of some sixty to eighty homes. It had been two years
since his bitter defeat at the hands of San Francisco voters and the Democratic
Party County Central Committee, and he was campaigning door-to-door
with a passion residents found refreshing, if unfamiliar.

"Some suspect he is a bill collector," wrote *San Francisco News* political
editor Sydney Kossen, in one of the few articles that captured the texture of
the race. "Some don't know what an assemblyman is, so he explains. But
most are cordial, and many even invite him in to give him an opportunity
to tell them that he supports increased pensions, more schools, a state prepaid
health insurance plan and job-finding help for persons over forty."[1]

Phillip Burton went into a funk after his humiliation in the 1954 election.
But it lasted only for several days. With a resilience that marked his entire
career, he decided almost immediately to try again in 1956. He then worked
almost as hard to elect John O'Connell to the assembly—the man chosen to
run in place of the late Cliff Berry—as he would have worked on his own
behalf. That clearly showed people Burton was not just fighting for personal

glory. Although O'Connell did not have Burton's intense drive or bulldog personality, he was every inch the pro-labor, California Democratic Council liberal that Burton was. Burton wanted like-minded progressives in the assembly waiting once he finally arrived. And there was no question in his mind that he would, even if it meant taking on the encrusted Irish mafia again. Soon Phillip, Sala, and her daughter Joy moved from their Guerrero Street flat to 845 Pine Street on the downward slope of Nob Hill, which put them in the Twentieth Assembly District. Lou Cannon, who helped in the 1954 campaign, took a job driving a laundry truck and moved to Potrero Hill in Burton's new district. Burton was pleased Cannon could help him organize it. Burton's reason for choosing the new territory to run in was both complicated and yet elegantly simple. It began four years earlier.

Frustrated by continual losses, California Democrats and their labor allies qualified an initiative for the 1952 state ballot that aimed a dagger at the heart of Republican Party rule. The goal: eliminate cross-filing, which perpetuated GOP domination. Not only did cross-filing prevent a candidate from listing his or her political party on the ballot, it permitted candidates to run in both party primaries at once. In effect, most elections were thus decided in the primaries, when incumbents, usually Republicans, won both parties' primaries simultaneously and then ran unopposed in November.

If Republican incumbent Smith, for example, was challenged by Democrat Jones, Smith ran in both the Republican and Democratic primaries. With his superior name identification, Smith defeated Jones in both. Most Democratic voters did not even know they were voting for Republicans, and even though Democrats enjoyed a four-to-three edge in party registration, the GOP dominated. "Under such conditions," Mary Ellen Leary wrote, "party affiliation was practically useless. What good was an organization? Personal politics paid off. A party couldn't tag its men, couldn't weed out the unreliable, the undisciplined. It couldn't even keep its own registered voters faithful to its own candidates. The conservative Republican put on the trappings of a labor advocate in half his campaign literature and discreetly appealed to the merchant's association in the other half."[2]

The Republicans recognized how dangerous the 1952 initiative was and countered with a rival measure. It was designed to confuse people, in the hopes that frustrated voters would reject both measures and maintain the status quo. Instead, the repeal of cross-filing lost, but the GOP measure won. In effect, the Republicans had outwitted themselves and handed the Democrats an important advantage. Merely allowing Democrats to be identified on the ballot starting in 1954 marked the beginning of the end of Republican control. Within two years, they began losing elections. In another four years, they lost control of the state assembly, the state senate, the governor's office, and one U.S. Senate seat.

This ballot change was pivotal to Burton's future. As a rebel and a threat to the Democratic Party establishment in San Francisco, he would never be picked for anything by party bosses. Moreover, he was temperamentally unable to wait "his turn." If Burton wanted an office, he had to get it himself, just as he tried in the Cliff Berry race. As Burton studied the 1954 returns for the Twentieth Assembly District, he spotted something intriguing. Thomas Maloney, the liberal Republican dean of the California legislature, ran as usual in the Republican and Democratic primaries. He won the Republican nomination uncontested. But on the Democratic side, which for years Maloney had also won easily, he barely eked out a victory. His opponent, an unknown, came within 800 votes of forcing Maloney into a November runoff. Only one explanation made sense: for the first time, Maloney's opponent was identified on the ballot as a Democrat. Voters in the most heavily Democratic district in California were starting to wake up.

Burton was almost certain he could defeat any Democratic challengers for Maloney's seat in the primary. But it would be a tremendous upset in November to knock off sixty-seven-year-old "Unbeatable Tommy Maloney," speaker pro tem of the California Assembly, and thirty-two-year veteran of Sacramento. The man was an icon of the San Francisco Irish community. Even so, Burton's course was clear. He was the Democrat, the candidate of the new and changing city. Tens of thousands of blacks who moved to San Francisco to work in the Hunters Point shipyards during World War II had stayed. They were voting but got nothing from the local Democratic organization. The Chinese in Chinatown, all but ignored, were ripe for effective representation. They could not even buy property outside of Chinatown and many were in the country illegally, which made them easy to exploit. Immigrants from Mexico and Latin and Central America were also arriving in the Mission District, just as Irish working-class families began moving to the suburbs. These new arrivals were a potentially important and untapped constituency.

San Francisco was undergoing a demographic sea change. Burton was the first politician with the imagination and intelligence to understand it, seize it, and give it voice. He ignited these disparate, often at-odds groups, creating constituencies, coalitions, and a significant power base that had never before existed. Moreover, representing the disenfranchised also filled a psychological need. Joe Williams, Burton's black law partner, thought Burton identified strongly with blacks and other minorities because he felt emotionally safe among them. He found it deeply satisfying to represent such loyal and deserving voters. His crusading zeal for racial justice was such a rarity among politicians of the era that these groups gave him the unconditional approval he needed and for so long had never gotten from his remote and judgmental father. In a community of whites, he was one among equals, but Williams believed that Burton felt more comfortable around blacks, who lionized him.

And with the explosive growth of the CDC and the Democratic club movement, as well as his Young Democrats, Burton could call on hundreds of issue-oriented white liberals. They canvassed door-to-door, stuffed envelopes, worked the phones, sent mail to carefully selected precincts, and otherwise got the message out that Burton's election represented the dawn of a new age in San Francisco. To Burton and his zealous supporters, this was not just an election, but the triumph of good over evil.

In the two years since his loss, Burton had learned from his mistakes. Looking at the 1954 returns, he saw that "the only places where I had a respectable showing" were places he or allies personally visited. He decided to avoid the calamari clubs and Sons of Italy spaghetti dinners, where endorsements were either meaningless or already stacked for the other guy. Instead, he devoted ten hours a day between April and November going door-to-door meeting voters directly. He estimated that he personally met 30 percent of them.[3]

But it was not just a matter of knocking on doors. One of Burton's innovations in the 1956 election was finding out which doors to knock on. With campaign manager Rudy Nothenberg, a brilliant organizer who joined Young Democrats during the 1952 Stevenson campaign, Burton conducted detailed research on how to win. He approached the task as if he were a political scientist compiling a statistical profile of San Francisco's voting habits. Unlike the social scientist, however, Burton converted every detail into an operational scheme to get elected. He began formulating a series of research-based political strategies that were nothing short of revolutionary in San Francisco. No one had done this sort of political spade work. Cross-filing and nonpartisanship had destroyed political parties in the state. In San Francisco at least, there were no rules for how to run for office, short of being picked by the boss and getting the right endorsements.

So Burton made his own rules. His files from 1956 show hundreds of pages of meticulously prepared data on the district, which was 70 percent Democratic, and which included much of the eastern portion of San Francisco: Chinatown, Downtown, North Beach, Bernal Heights, South of Market, and Potrero Hill. In an early indication of the kind of obsession Burton maintained throughout his life with numbers and details, he compiled voluminous charts comparing the number of Democrats to Republicans in the district for every six month period since December 1948—adjusted for new precincts added after the 1951 reapportionment. He charted census tracts by race. He listed every Catholic church by precinct number (there were twelve in the district). He noted the number of voters who registered and voted in each of the district's 180 precincts in each primary and general election since June 1952. He listed every public housing project, which precinct it was in, and how many units it contained.

He went over precinct lists with colored pencils, underlining all Asian and Jewish names. These groups got specially targeted mail. Burton's data showed, for example, that gubernatorial candidate James Roosevelt and senate candidate Helen Gahagan Douglas lost badly when they ran in 1950. But in his newly reapportioned district, Roosevelt beat Earl Warren by 1,100 votes and Douglas beat Nixon by 5,000 votes. Burton also noticed—and recorded the fact in red and blue ink—that the number of blacks in San Francisco had increased by nearly 900 percent in ten years, from 4,800 in 1940, or 0.8 percent of the population, to 43,500 in 1950, and was still growing. By 1960, he projected there would be nearly 75,000 blacks, 10 percent of the population. His data also showed that whites had a higher death rate and lower birth rate than nonwhites, which told him that the demographic trends would continue.[4]

Burton even sent a letter to the Coro Foundation, a program designed to train young people for leadership in government, asking if any interns would be interested in registering voters for him and seeing "the scientific application of more advanced election principles." The return letter was to the point: "None of this year's interns have chosen to undertake your project."

Armed with this vast array of information, Burton and Nothenberg organized the Young Democrats political action committee and focused on just one assembly district: Maloney's. Then Nothenberg devised a precinct card system. Each card listed the name and address of the registered Democrat and space for entering the voter's response when called or visited at home. Republican voters or Maloney supporters were left alone.[5] In San Francisco in 1956 these techniques were visionary.

The man Burton had chosen to challenge was a San Francisco legend. Born South of Market in 1889, one of eighteen children, Tommy Maloney was a short, feisty, old-style Irish pol. He had worked as a stevedore and semipro baseball player and became president of the Longshoremens' Union in 1919. Republican Sheriff Tom Finn brought Maloney into politics when virtually all the Irish labor leaders were Republicans. He was first elected to the state senate in 1924, served two terms, and won an assembly seat in 1932 after being reapportioned out of the senate. He rose to become speaker pro tem in 1943 and kept the job through four speakers. Maloney was not like other assemblymen from San Francisco, who did little meaningful work. He wrote some of the state's most important laws on worker compensation, benefits for the aged and the blind, housing for veterans, and payments for the sick and disabled. The AFL strongly supported him, as did the "regular" Democrats, with whom he had been friendly for years. He was also close to the legendary Sacramento lobbyist Artie Samish.

Being a Republican had never been a liability in a city where even state Attorney General Pat Brown was a Republican until 1933. But in Phillip Burton, Maloney faced a determined opponent with an explicit strategy to hang his party affiliation around his neck in a three-to-one Democratic district. In the final weeks a worried Maloney hit as many as six political events a night, plus wakes and funerals. "Maloney stands almost alone in the state Capitol as an elderly liberal still wrapped in the mantle of the Grand Old Party," Kossen wrote. "This is no last hurrah," Maloney told him. "I'll never retire from politics."[6]

Maloney garnered more than 100 union endorsements, including the California Federation of Labor, the San Francisco Labor Council, the International Brotherhood of Electrical Workers, and the building trades and hospital workers. For his labor support, Burton turned again to George Hardy, with whom he had developed a close relationship. Hardy was a crucial political ally, but their alliance also fulfilled psychological needs for both the intense young political aspirant and the aging labor leader who had recently lost a son.

Hardy, whose father had also been a union organizer, began working as a janitor at the main branch of the San Francisco Public Library when he was twenty-four. One night his foreman dropped a match behind a radiator. When Hardy missed it, he was fired. It was 1935, the year after San Francisco's famous General Strike. Hardy decided that janitors needed a union. Working with his father and a handful of other Irish immigrant janitors, he organized his union, applying to the mob-run Building Services Union in Chicago for a charter. It took several decades, but he built his janitor's union from nowhere and was grooming his twenty-three-year-old son to succeed him. But in 1955, the son was killed in an automobile accident.

Hardy's son's death opened him up. He began reaching out to younger people, and he grew attached to Burton. The fiery young candidate represented Hardy's idea of what a new, militant generation of political leadership should embody. The fact that Burton had worked as a janitor while in law school cemented the bond. Hardy began sending worker's compensation cases to Burton, who needed the law business. In his dinner visits, Burton seemed to Hardy like an overgrown puppy, so clumsy that he spilled the coffee when he poured it, so intense that he felt compelled to turn off the television set so he could talk without distractions. Hardy had no use for Republicans—even liberals like Maloney—or for labor leaders who got in bed with Republicans in the hopes of gaining clout or appointments. He set up a new group, Labor Committee for Democrats, to wean labor away from the Republicans.

One of the keys to Hardy's strength and effectiveness was his extensive communications network, which kept him in close touch with all his members—whom he bombarded with all manner of bulletins and releases. His union hall basement at 240 Golden Gate Avenue was stocked with mimeographs, typewriters, and huge metal addressograph machines. It was primitive and cumbersome by the standards of late twentieth century political communications, but Hardy's network was effective. In its own way, Hardy's basement operation was also a communications laboratory for Burton. Here he received a hands-on indoctrination in the art of keeping in touch with a constituency and getting the message out. It was a useful complement to the research he was doing with precinct maps and election and demographic analysis.

Whenever Hardy wanted to put out a bulletin, his daughter Joan, another secretary named Susie Kennedy, and usually Hardy himself would troop downstairs and type it on mimeos. Joan and Susie took out the trays of metal plates containing the addresses of every Building Service Employees union member in the city, assembly district by assembly district. They walked them to the addressograph machine—each tray held 500 addresses—slid the tray in and hit the pedal, which printed the address on each stacked and waiting envelope. Without a jam, they could do all 500 envelopes in twenty minutes. Depending on the bulletin—or the election—each mailing could require up to 5,000 envelopes.

Hardy was tough. In the late 1930s when the mob union from Chicago arrived to take control of his Local 87, Hardy and his members used baseball bats to successfully hold them off. But he was also politically sophisticated and could count votes. Of the seven building service locals, he controlled only two and knew the rest did not like Burton. There was no chance for Burton to get endorsed. But labor, in the form of the clunky machines in Hardy's basement, wound up helping Burton without the other union leaders knowing about it. When the Labor Council endorsements came out, Hardy volunteered to mail them to all the locals. The union leaders were oblivious of the real purpose of Hardy's machines and only too happy to let him do so. Daughter Joan's assignment, as she went through the addressograph plates, was to make sure that the 2,000 or so unionists in Burton's district never received the official endorsements. Hardy then got those names to Burton so he could approach them on his own. Meanwhile, Hardy put out his own mailings to those members on Burton's behalf about every ten days.

To the Democratic Party and labor establishment and even the newspapers, which ignored him, Burton was the enemy, the brash upstart who had to be defeated. He was up against the toughest incumbent he could possibly face. But he had a new and hidden weapon: George Hardy was showing him the power of the mimeograph. Years later, people would talk about the "Burton Machine." As the operation got more sophisticated, maps lined the walls listing how many voters needed to be registered in every precinct and who the key leaders were. But no outsider ever truly figured out that the heart of the Burton Machine was located in the basement of 240 Golden Gate Avenue—George Hardy's communications nerve center—and that it began in the 1956 campaign against Tommy Maloney.[7]

In another labor coup, Burton got the coveted ILWU endorsement. Under Australian leader Harry Bridges, a former Wobbly and a subject of repeated FBI investigations and harassment for alleged Communist Party membership, the ILWU was the most important left-wing union in the United States. Bridges, who had been hounded as a radical and repeatedly threatened with deportation by the Truman administration, believed in total independence from both major parties, indeed, from the Labor Council itself. A young pro-labor rebel and threat to the established order like Burton captured his imagination.

Even though Maloney once led an earlier, weaker version of the union, the ILWU had changed dramatically. Blacks now constituted 25 to 30 percent of the membership, and a new generation of militant leaders had taken control. Some, like Bridges, were former Wobblies, some veterans of the radical—and violent—logging battles of the Pacific Northwest. They would have appreciated—many having been there themselves—that Burton attended a reception for famed Communist and singer-actor Paul Robeson at the home of *Daily People's World* editor Al Richmond. And they believed that the energetic Burton could represent them far more aggressively than could tired old Tommy Maloney. Other waterfront unions like the National Maritime Union and the radical Marine Cooks and Stewards—which Burton knew from his 1946 summer cruise—also pitched in. Workers who did not get called at the union hall that morning, and who had a few hours to kill, headed to Burton's campaign headquarters. There, they got instructions on which precincts to canvass and a little "walking around" money.[8]

Most of the disparate elements of Burton's growing constituency were coming together. Carlton Goodlett, the black physician/publisher, gave Burton wildly sympathetic news and editorial coverage in his *Sun Reporter* and introduced him to black church groups and at black social gatherings. Rudy Nothenberg, with Lou Cannon's help, devised the precinct operation, including the all-important Potrero Hill, Maloney's home base. Cannon, who was twenty-three, took a leave from his truck-driving job for several months and went on the payroll. He had read about politics all his life and at one time had been a serious Marxist. Here was a chance to put some of his progressive beliefs into practice. In a novel organizing effort, the campaign sent volunteers to South of Market and Tenderloin pensioner hotels, where retired, often impoverished, seamen, longshoremen, and teamsters lived alone in single rooms. CDC and YD activists registered people to vote who had never been contacted by any political figure. On election day Nothenberg and Cannon repeated the process, dispatching volunteers to make sure everyone voted.

While Burton gathered support among blacks and labor, Chinatown remained a significant untapped constituency. Conventional wisdom said the Chinese did not vote, and there was solid evidence of that. Until the early 1950s, less than half of registered Chinese voters did vote. Those who did tended to vote conservatively, for Republican Thomas Dewey over Truman by 57 to 35 percent in 1948, for example, even as Truman won San Francisco overall, 47 to 45 percent. But the Chinese were a compact community—five precincts contained nearly half of the entire electorate—and Burton was determined to crack it open.[9]

In law school Burton had became friendly with a fellow student named Lim P. Lee, who was born in Hong Kong in 1910 and came to the United States when he was eight months old. Sixteen years older than Burton, Lee grew up in Chinatown, where his father ran a laundry. At a time of profound anti-Chinese sentiment and discrimination in housing, employment, education, and virtually everything else, Lee was a success story. He went to Mission High and got to know Jack Shelley, later a state senator and congressman, and Eugene McAteer, another future state senator. In the early 1930s, Lee earned a scholarship to USC. He studied sociology and became a social worker while writing for the monthly *Chinese Digest*. He spent World War II in the counterintelligence corps assigned to the Philippines and was discharged as a sergeant in 1946.

But politics was in his blood. Even before the war, Lee had gravitated to Albert Chow, Chinatown's unofficial "mayor," and helped him climb to power. Albert and his brother Jack were attorneys, and they had a thriving immigration practice. At a time when federal immigration law restricted the legal immigration to the U.S. of Chinese from all over the world to 105 people a year—a pathetically small number—the Chow brothers constituted one-stop shopping for wealthy Chinese nationals who came to them for "help" in arranging U.S. citizenship. Lee translated into English the letters Chow sent to Bill Malone and to Shelley, his former high school classmate, asking Shelley to take a "congressional interest" in a case. That meant introducing a special immigration bill, just as a congressman in Cleveland might do for a Croatian emigré. The Chows charged a fortune—some said as much as $5,000 a case. But the money never filtered down to Lim P. Lee. Through Malone, Albert Chow met Truman himself—a source of great prestige in Chinatown. Appointed to the Democratic Party State Central Committee, Chow was the man to see in Chinatown for any political favor.

Lee met Burton after his army discharge when he entered Golden Gate Law School on the GI Bill. In 1949, Burton helped elect Lee student body secretary. But Lee never passed the bar. After graduation, he became a probation officer in the San Francisco Superior Court. But he also returned to his old job with the Chows, translating Albert's speeches into English, writing congressional letters, and doing other routine chores. He longed for more responsibilities. As long as he worked for the Chows, he said many years later, he would always be "number three," after Albert and Jack. Just as Lee was arriving at this insight and chafing under his limited role in Chinatown politics, Burton decided to pay a courtesy call on the Chow brothers to talk about his campaign. He asked his old friend to set it up.

The Chow brothers had a sweet arrangement with the powers that ran San Francisco, and they did not want to jeopardize it by encouraging a rival to Tommy Maloney. Nor did they want to share their clout or lucre with an outsider. In Burton's presence, Albert Chow said to Lee in Chinese, "Help him out, but not in any way that will benefit him." At that moment, Lee made a decision that profoundly changed his life.

"I will break with them now," he said to himself, "or I will always be number three. I want to be number one." Lee decided on the spot that Phillip Burton, not the Chow brothers, was his ticket to the top in Chinatown. He would indeed "help him out," but not the way Albert Chow intended. Through Lee, Burton got a unique introduction to the secrets of Chinatown, a view few whites would ever see. Lee showed him where and how to campaign. He explained what the people cared about, what issues moved them and got him special attention.[10] And Burton proved an especially keen student.

Between Lee's connections and Burton's single-minded focus, Burton created a constituency in Chinatown that had never before existed. As he did with labor, blacks, and other constituencies in the district, he set about immersing himself in Chinatown's culture, politics, and unique avenues to power. First, he identified every reporter and editor on every Chinese newspaper and radio station and paid courtesy calls on all of them. Few had ever been stroked by a politician, aspiring or otherwise. Through Lee, he became especially close to Gilbert Woo, editor of the *Chinese Pacific Weekly*, which had more than 10,000 readers and which eventually featured news and photographs of him prominently every week. If the big newspapers, the *Chronicle, Examiner*, and *Call Bulletin* ignored him, Burton went to the media the new San Franciscans were reading, especially the *Chinese Pacific Weekly* and the *Sun Reporter*.

Lee also connected him to the leaders of the Chinese Six Companies, the business group that ran Chinatown. He listed all the members of every important social, business, and political group: the Chinese-American Citizens Alliance, the Cathay Post of the American Legion, the Anti-Communist League of Chinese Six Companies, the Chinese Post of the Veterans of Foreign Wars, the Chinese Chamber of Commerce, the Chinese Optimists, the Chinese Lions, the Chinese YMCA Public Affairs Committee. Next to these groups, he noted the leaders and members of the boards of directors, home and business addresses and phone numbers, party designations, precincts in which they lived, and the dates when their organizations met. He sent Democratic slate cards to Chinese Democrats and "good government" slate cards to Republicans.

And of course he focused on the issues: "1) civil rights, including FEPC [Fair Employment Practices Commission]; 2) McCarran immigration act; 3) firecrackers—religious issue; 4) childcare center Chinatown; 5) mass subpoena; 6) pensions for noncitizens."[11]

Each issue represented a major opportunity to gain votes by taking a stand on something dear to Chinese voters. Every time he appeared before the organizations he so carefully listed, he pressed these points. Any talk of legislation to ban discrimination in jobs or housing found a friendly audience, and, through Woo and other Chinese media, favorable publicity. Immigration, for example, was a huge issue in Chinatown, like civil rights to the black community. Burton promised to introduce assembly resolutions to liberalize the number of people permitted legal entry.

Firecrackers were especially important to the Chinese Six Companies, which imported them from Hong Kong. For years, police arrested people during the two weeks of Chinese New Year. Burton himself hatched the idea to legalize firecrackers by linking them to the "religious" nature of the New Year's celebration, just as Catholics used candles and Jews yarmulkes. He would make it a First Amendment issue.

Pensions for noncitizens spoke directly to the pocketbook. Most Chinese living in the U.S. were noncitizens. That meant they did not qualify for any welfare or pensions, even if they had lived and worked in the United States for twenty-five years. Burton vowed to introduce legislation to correct such "injustices." Chinatown was also among the mostly densely populated areas in the nation. There were virtually no parks or open spaces, no places for children to play while their mothers worked in the district's infamous sweat shops. The need for day-care centers was a surefire issue. No politician had ever proposed programs of such direct benefit to these voters.

But the biggest and most important issue of all was mass subpoenas, which dropped on Chinatown in March 1956 with devastating force. The dirty little secret in Chinatown was that nearly everyone was illegal. Thousands of immigrants arrived every year, despite the legal limit of only 105. The crisis began when an overeager U.S. Attorney's Office decided to wipe out all immigration fraud at once. It arranged to serve a subpoena on all twenty-six Chinese family associations, the Chinese Six Companies, and the Chinese American Citizens Alliance, Chinatown's most prominent political organization. Every Wong, Louie, Lee, Chan, or other Chinese belonged to a family association of that name, which kept detailed records of the extended families. On service of the subpoena, these organizations were given twenty-four hours to turn over all membership lists and photographs for their entire history. As Lim P. Lee wrote in his journal of that year, "March 1956 would go down in the history of the Chinese in California as the most dramatic, demanding, perilous and yet rewarding month of our existence."

The mass subpoenas were so chilling, Lee wrote, that "streets were deserted. Restaurants dropped income. Shoppers avoided Chinatown, and for three weeks it was a ghost town. Worst of all, Chinatown's leadership was paralyzed. Ninety percent of the Chinese came to America under some taint or fraud or illegality, and an investigation by the Grand Jury into the family records will throw the witnesses into jail for fraud, perjury or some other illegality."[12]

Lee told Burton that if he fought the mass subpoenas he would become a hero to the Chinese, and fight it he did. In his first blast Burton called them "shocking," the "shotgun tactics of the Republican administration's Department of Justice." Everywhere he went, Burton hammered on the issue, calling the subpoenas unconstitutional and a violation of civil rights and liberties. He was the only political figure to speak out to the Chinese, and his press releases were carried word for word in *China World* and in *Chinese Pacific Weekly*. Goodlett editorialized in the *Sun Reporter* that the mass subpoenas violated the Fourth Amendment's search and seizure provisions and warned that what the FBI and Justice Department could do in Chinatown it could also do to blacks unless people banded together to stop government persecution of minority communities.

After several weeks, the Chinese community recovered from its paralysis. The Chinese Six Companies hired prominent attorneys, white and Asian, and organized an Immigration Committee comprising its most unassailable representatives: Chinese-American veterans of World War II. Weeks later, Federal Judge Oliver Carter quashed the subpoenas and ended the scare. All the family association records were returned to Chinatown, where, in Lee's words, "we had a hell of a bonfire."

Burton's performance electrified a new generation of Chinese-Americans. Harry Low, for example, another 1952 Adlai Stevenson volunteer, had attended UC Berkeley's prestigious Boalt Hall School of Law, finishing among the top thirty in his class. He was one of three dozen Chinese attorneys in the entire state, but no major law firm had as much as offered him an interview, let alone a job. Eventually, Pat Brown hired him as an assistant state attorney general. Low had watched the traditional pols, including Brown and Mayor Elmer Robinson, dutifully troop through Chinatown, pay homage to Albert Chow, eat at the right Chinese restaurant, and then leave, no wiser or better informed. But Burton's stance on the mass subpoenas issue stirred Low and his contemporaries. They had never before seen a Caucasian champion their issues. As a consequence, they became loyal Burton supporters for life.[13]

Other Burton tactics were less ideological—but effective, nonetheless. He asked virtually every merchant in Chinatown to accept a "snipe," or house sign, but to put it *inside* the store, rather than outside. Any shopper who ventured inside quickly spotted it. But when Tommy Maloney's boys drove around Chinatown looking in vain for Burton signs, they concluded that they did not have to campaign there, either.

Burton refused to cross-file, which meant he ran only in the Democratic primary, while Maloney ran in both. Maloney spent $3,369 in the primary, to Burton's $960. Berkeley YD friend Tom Winnett sent $25 and a note: "If I had $5,000, I would send it and consider it well spent, because if you make this one, you will turn this state upside down within ten years." Burton's mother contributed another $25. "Here is a check, dear, which I know you can put to good use in your campaign," she wrote on May 15, "or whatever you may need it for." Suggesting that he also raffle off an old refrigerator in the basement, Mildred Burton added, "We are addressing the list you gave us and should have it ready for you by the end of the week." Dr. Burton, who by now was separated from Mildred, also contributed to his eldest son's campaign.[14]

On primary day, Burton easily defeated Achille Muschi, his Democratic opponent and Maloney on the Democratic side. Maloney won the Republican nomination. All told, Maloney took 45.2 percent of the vote, compared to 38.9 percent for Burton and 16.4 percent for Muschi. In a congratulatory note, Robert Rohatch, president of the ILWU, Local 10, said of Maloney: "The total opposition vote topped his vote for the first time, which means that the people want a change, and it certainly looks like you are the one they want."

Maloney then mailed campaign literature to every voter in the district featuring photos of him with Jack Shelley and Governor Warren, as Warren signed the "Maloney-Gaffney oleomargarine bill." (During the war, housewives had to dye oleomargarine themselves if they wanted it to look like butter. This law required producers to color it.) Burton's literature, also mailed to all voters, showed him flanked by 1952 Democratic nominees Estes Kefauver and Adlai Stevenson. "Don't be misled by Republican Smears. Elect Burton—Democrat—to Assembly," it said. Another Burton mailer said, "Our district, overwhelmingly Democratic, has for too long been represented by a Republican."

Responding to a League of Women Voters questionnaire, Burton said the most important issues were "greater economic and job security for working people." He wanted bigger pension, unemployment, disability, and worker compensation checks. He called for state health insurance and child-care centers and passage of a Fair Employment Practices Commission. When local chapter CDC President Mary Louise Allen gaveled through an endorsement for Burton, he sent out 30,000 CDC slate cards touting that endorsement. When the California Institute of Social Welfare endorsed him unanimously, he asked for 7,000 copies of their slate card, telling them by telegram, "a large pension vote in district renders victory probable." Burton was pioneering the use of slate cards, cooperative mailings that allowed sympathetic groups to endorse each other's candidates. Local 6 of the ILWU also helped by sending a letter to all Republicans in the district noting that Maloney had been in office for thirty-two years and was entitled to the maximum legislative pension. If he lost, in other words, that pension plus his insurance business "assures him of financial security for the rest of his life."

As the campaign headed into its final weeks, two events shaped the outcome. The first was a fundraising dinner for Burton that was in danger of becoming an embarrassing failure. People were turning him down. Desperate for a headline speaker, Burton called his old friend, Bert Coffey, and asked if Coffey could get George Miller to speak. Coffey was Miller's closest political advisor, and Miller was a star, a former state party chairman who convened the Asilomar conference that launched the CDC. His presence would guarantee a strong labor turnout. Although Miller liked the brash candidate, he had no use for Burton's constant politicking and abrasiveness.

"Get someone else," he told Coffey.

"Phil loves you," Coffey pleaded. "He has tremendous respect for you. This will destroy him if he doesn't have someone prominent." Miller agreed to be master of ceremonies. The event turned out to be a typical South of Market Irish bash. Miller introduced every unionist by his first name, told yarns, charmed everyone, and lauded the assembly candidate as if he were the Second Coming. The dinner lasted until after midnight. Everyone left happy. Burton never forgot that kindness. Miller had helped legitimize his candidacy.

The second key event was a raucous October 4 meeting of the county central committee, the group that had denied Burton the 1954 assembly seat. This time the Democratic establishment outdid even itself. John O'Connell, the man Burton helped elect in 1954, now chaired the county committee. But the remnants of the Malone machine and the George Reilly faction of the local party still controlled it. They could do business with Maloney. Despising everything Burton stood for and arguing that he was not a "good Democrat," they called the meeting to endorse every Democrat on the ballot but him, an illegal ploy. Their real purpose was a red-baiting smear that would have been ugly were it not so inept. His support six years earlier for admission of Red China to the United Nations and his opposition to registering Communists raised questions about his own patriotism, they tried to imply. With a month to go, the party bosses were worried. If Maloney's victory was safe, there was no need for such disreputable tactics. But Maloney was not safe, and it was time to take Burton down.

Gene Marine, a freelance writer for the left-oriented *Frontier* magazine, got wind of the anti-Burton plot. His father-in-law, Jerry Sullivan, sat on the county committee. Sullivan was impressed with Burton's intelligence and commitment to working people. Two days before the meeting, Sullivan got a call. "Reilly and Maloney patched up a beef they had and they're going to dump this punk Burton," the caller said. "Just go along with the vote." Sullivan was so outraged that he called Marine, who tipped off Burton.

Even though he knew what was coming, Burton could not stop it. As word spread, nearly 200 people jammed into the ILWU union hall, crowding the aisles and the back wall. Some were there to boo Burton, some came because they liked Maloney, some were there to do what they were told. As the meeting came to order, an unsuspecting O'Connell recognized a Reilly operative, who moved to endorse every Democrat on the ballot but Burton. O'Connell ruled the motion out of order. He said the state election code required the central committee of each party to support its nominees. O'Connell had appointed a young San Francisco attorney named William Coblentz as his parliamentarian. Coblentz agreed with his ruling. Every time he ruled, the Malone forces appealed the ruling. Every time, Coblentz sided with O'Connell. Hoping to end the discussion, O'Connell said *Robert's Rules of Order* left him no choice.

In a moment that careened between high comedy and complete absurdity, someone moved to suspend *Robert's Rules of Order* and overturn the state election code. Before O'Connell could stop it, the motion carried. But when they went back to the original motion, O'Connell said he still could not recognize it because now there were no rules, in fact, now there could be no meeting. All hell broke loose, with people yelling and screaming for attention.

O'Connell, Coblentz, Sullivan, Marine, and Burton stormed out and headed to a nearby hotel bar, leaving the old guard Irish to do their dirty work in a rump session. Burton was worried. He knew this would make the local newspapers and could harm his campaign. He did not want to be known as the only Democratic candidate to be dis-endorsed by his own party. But O'Connell put the events of the previous hour in perspective. "Hell," he reassured the distraught candidate, "nine out of ten won't read it, and the tenth will say, 'Hey, I saw your name in the paper.'"[15]

Sydney Kossen quickly picked up the story and put it in the *News*, as did *Chronicle* political editor Squire Behrens. In fact, Gene Marine alerted *Chronicle* reporter Jack Morrison to the story. Morrison attended the riotous meeting and described accurately in the paper's first edition what had transpired. But the more conservative Behrens rewrote Morrison's story to highlight the anti-Burton faction's version of events for later editions. Malone loyalist John E. Sullivan, a West Portal attorney, told Kossen that Burton "is not a Democrat," and added in fractured syntax that the party "has principles that are high when it comes to communism and Red China." In response, Burton told Kossen, "I am a member of the American Civil Liberties Union and a civil libertarian and proud of it, and for that reason am opposed to any form of totalitarianism, including communism, fascism or any other."[16]

Maloney released a campaign flyer the next day saying the county committee "dumped attorney Phillip Burton as its candidate" because Burton was not "truly representative of the Democratic Party, its principles and philosophy." Of course, nowhere in Maloney's literature did he mention that he was a Republican. Despite the flap, O'Connell proved to be right. Few people paid attention. But this latest outrage fortified the resolve of the CDC and Young Democrat volunteers to work even harder to elect Burton and rid San Francisco of these reactionaries. Even John Burton, twenty-four, who had ignored his brother's political career until this point, jumped on board. This was personal. They were picking on his brother.

As the campaign entered its final weeks, *Call Bulletin* political editor Jack McDowell, who had paid little attention, suddenly heard that Maloney had taken a poll and thought he could lose. This news shocked McDowell, who assumed, like most of official San Francisco, that Maloney's re-election was as predictable as the Ferry Building clock striking noon. Maloney rushed to shore up support. "I do want to let you know," he wrote Carlton Goodlett on October 18, in a sign of increasing worry, "that during my legislative career, your people have never had any complaints."[17]

Burton took one break from his own campaigning. Presidential candidate Adlai Stevenson was coming to California. Lionel Steinberg had organized a train ride through the Central Valley, Truman style, to connect Stevenson with local officials at every little town and fire them up, and he invited Burton along. At every stop, local officials crowded on board for their moment of glory with the candidate. But Stevenson was so determined to impress the national reporters traveling with him, Steinberg recalled, that he felt compelled to prepare a new speech for every stop. He sat in his compartment writing longhand and refused to see any local politicos. Burton and Steinberg tried in vain to convince him that meeting the locals was more important than dazzling the reporters with each new speech. "Governor," they pleaded, "you've got to meet these people." But Stevenson looked up at them and frowned. "I'm not finished with this speech," he said.[18]

Back in his own district, Burton walked precincts each night, while Nothenberg finished the grass-roots plan to turn out the vote on election day. Between the primary and general elections, the Young Democrats under Nothenberg helped register more than 10,500 new Democratic voters, more than 5,000 alone in the Twentieth District. Because San Francisco regulations prohibited door-to-door voter registration, this was an enormous accomplishment. Having left Chinatown to Burton, Nothenberg and Cannon concentrated on the South of Market area, focusing on 80 precincts out of the district's 180. They sent sixty-three volunteers into nearly a hundred precincts. But the real battleground was Potrero Hill, where Maloney lived, and where, even against the identified Democrat in 1954, Maloney won nearly two-thirds of the vote.[19]

Although it contained some of the best weather and views in the entire city, there was nothing fashionable about Potrero Hill. The gritty, blue-collar neighborhood seemed somehow separate from the rest of the city, self-contained on its own hill, with single-family homes, Victorian two-unit railroad flats, and, on the eastern crest, three gigantic public housing projects built during the war. Unlike the tonier Russian Hill, Potrero Hill housed most of the city's immigrant Russians and other Slavs. Where the hill leveled out on the north was a huge mass of interconnecting Southern Pacific railroad tracks and a sweeping view of the downtown. To the east lay the bayshore and waterfront, San Francisco Bay, and, beyond that, Oakland and Berkeley.

Cannon had twenty precinct workers on Potrero Hill alone, including one Russian immigrant speaker who concentrated on the Russian precincts. Lou Cannon and his pregnant wife Virginia recruited other friends. Alan Cranston, not yet an elected official himself, showed up to walk precincts. Cannon believed that Burton's loss to Cliff Berry in 1954 was an advantage.

"You were beaten by a dead man," Cannon told Burton. "Use it. That means Tommy Maloney won't take you seriously. If it comes up, fine, but the less they think about you, the better." Burton took the advice. Cannon instructed his Potrero Hill precinct workers to say Maloney was a "nice" man and let it go at that. Anyone who seemed confrontational was taken off the hill. They did not want Maloney to know how thorough they were. When kids appeared at a local church one Sunday passing out leaflets calling Burton a Communist and saying he would vote to recognize Red China, Cannon confiscated them.

On election eve, Burton returned to Potrero Hill for one final push. "I had to cut his margin there," Burton said after the election. "On the night before the election, I toured his own district. At ten that night, I wound up across the street from his own house."[20]

When election day arrived, the machinery was in place. In a grass-roots operation unprecedented for modern San Francisco, 250 Young Democrats were dispatched not only to the Market Street headquarters, where they called every pro-Burton voter identified in their precinct cards, but to housing projects, South of Market pensioner hotels, Chinatown, Potrero Hill, and other targeted areas. Burton law partner Joe Williams spent the day ferrying voters between the polling place and the projects on 19th and Carolina Streets on Potrero Hill. Maloney hired several people to do the same. Every time Williams saw these couriers, they were playing cards. They assumed Maloney could not lose.

When the votes were counted, Phillip Burton won a slim but tremendous victory over the man everyone said was unbeatable. The final results were 17,807 votes for Burton to 17,148 for Maloney. Out of almost 35,000 votes cast, Burton won by only 659 votes, less than 2 percent. But he had won. He won 109 precincts to Maloney's 70, with one tied. Of the 50 North of Market precincts, according to Burton's later statistical charts, Maloney won 32. But of the 129 South of Market precincts, Burton swamped Maloney, winning 91. In the primary, Maloney defeated Burton on Potrero Hill by 279 votes. In the general, Burton turned it around. He beat Tommy Maloney on his own turf, winning the battle of Potrero Hill by 164 votes, 2,229 to 2,065 and won 84 percent of all the votes cast in the public housing projects. Even more amazingly, Lim P. Lee's magic also worked. By the same margin, he took 84 percent of the Chinese vote. They did not forget the man who had championed their cause.

Between George Hardy's mimeograph machine, Carlton Goodlett's newspaper, Lim P. Lee's passport to Chinatown, the detail work of Nothenberg, Cannon, and hundreds of volunteers, and the brilliant strategy and unflagging energy of the tall, lanky, indefatigable candidate himself, Phillip Burton, at thirty years of age, was finally launched on the political career he had dreamed about for so long. In the Eisenhower sweep of 1956, he was the only California Democrat to defeat a Republican legislator. He was also to be the youngest member of the assembly, which, despite the Eisenhower tide, had narrowed to a four-vote Republican margin.

Burton was conspicuously absent at the victory celebration that night at Frankie Carter's, a downtown bar near party headquarters. The party was his idea, and hundreds of the volunteers who worked so hard to turn out the vote were celebrating. Burton called and apologized profusely for not being there to celebrate with them, but ordered a round of drinks for everybody on him. Later he said he had spent the early evening with George and Norma Hardy and could not get away. He was in a difficult spot. He could not have won without Hardy or the Young Democrats. But Hardy had got emotional about Burton's victory and talked at length that night about his son's death the year before.

"Do you think you have replaced his son?" a friend asked.

"Well," said Burton, "I've been working on it." The friend was shocked Burton could be that conniving.

Thrilled to have won, Burton hosted another victory party at the San Francisco Rowing Club on the waterfront. But he was drinking heavily—many friends noticed even in the early 1950s that he could take six drinks to every one of theirs—and began verbally abusing a young volunteer named Ann Eliaser, accusing her of conspiring against him. Eliaser had no idea what Burton was talking about, but he continued to berate her until she burst into tears. Eliaser was just getting into politics. Her roots were upper middle class, and her connection was through Roger Kent, the state party chairman from affluent Marin County, and his friend Libbie Gatov, who represented a cerebral, good government approach to politics. The next morning, Sala Burton called Eliaser to apologize for her husband's rude behavior.

"He shouldn't have done it," Sala said. "But what he said was the truth. You're into ivory tower politics. You're the creation of Roger Kent and Libbie Gatov."

"But I'm just coming to know them," Eliaser replied.

"That's true, dear," said Sala, patronizing her. "But they are grooming you for high places, and Phillip is threatened."[21]

4

FIRECRACKERS AND FARM WORKERS

Phil was abrasive. I'd see him at functions and he'd say, "I'd sit down with
you, but you don't have a vote," and I found that refreshing. He knew
exactly what he was about, and he knew exactly what he was doing. He
had an agenda, and he was not lying to himself. He had no illusions, and
he was not afraid to be disliked. That is extraordinary power.

COLEMAN BLEASE
former ACLU lobbyist

PHILLIP BURTON'S UPSET victory over Tommy Maloney, impressive as it was, did not mean Burton knew the first thing about how to govern. Any rookie legislator needs time to learn the game, and Burton was no exception. The capitol had its own culture and traditions. Burton had to learn them, as well as who made things happen, who was trustworthy, who should be avoided.

He had great hopes for his first session. He had an agenda and promises to keep. But the legislature had its priorities and rhythms and no particular incentive to help him along. Indeed, some had every reason to see him fail. Republicans still controlled the assembly and had no use for his left-wing, redistributive philosophy. And his former rival from USC, Jesse Unruh, preceded him by two years and was already moving up fast. Burton's first year was frustrating and unproductive. But he learned quickly and forgot nothing.

Burton was not without allies when he arrived in Sacramento that first week of January 1957 to begin his new job. The 1954 election, besides sending fellow liberal John O'Connell to Sacramento, also sent Unruh to the assembly along with a CDC liberal from Beverly Hills named Tom Rees. Senator George Miller, who had rescued Burton's big testimonial dinner during the campaign, showed the young San Francisco freshman around the capitol. A few GOP reformers, such as Caspar Weinberger, had recently been elected. But Burton was not popular among the legislature's old guard, many of whom resented Burton for knocking off Maloney. His sandpaper personality and steamroller approach to politics did not endear him to many of his new colleagues, either.

But change was coming, albeit fitfully, to a legislature more attuned to a languid, prewar climate than to serving the needs of this rapidly growing industrial and agricultural power. Sacramento, which had slumbered through decades of stale politics and lobbyist-dictated legislation, was still groping for direction after the November 1953 conviction for income tax evasion of famed lobbyist Artie Samish, the self-described "secret boss of California." Were it not the capital of the nation's fastest growing state, Sacramento might be just another dusty farm town in one of the world's richest agricultural valleys. State government, especially since the end of World War II, had transformed the place into a thriving city of 160,000 people, including 30,000 state workers.

Sacramento was a company town, much as Washington was, although it was smaller and more self-contained than the nation's capital. It had the largest state printing plant in the nation and administered the largest welfare program and most expensive school system. Its $1.5 billion budget financed services in a state that anticipated fifteen million people by 1960.[1]

Samish's conviction created a curious power vacuum that took years to fill. He had controlled the legislative process for twenty years by handing out fistfuls of campaign dollars or other boodle in return for votes or the power to dictate committee assignments. There was no one ready or able to take his place. The 300-pound, diamond-studded, cigar-smoking Samish so dominated the legislative scene that in some ways he was the most powerful man in the state. "On matters that affect his clients, Artie unquestionably has more power than the governor," Governor Warren said in 1949.[2]

Beginning as a minor clerk in the state senate, Samish became the state's premier lobbyist, representing the alcohol beverage industry, banks, chemical companies, horse racing interests, the automobile and trucking industry, and other transportation clients. Samish grew so wealthy and powerful that he often helped choose the assembly speaker and designated key committee chairmen. By raising money from other lobbyists and his own wealthy clients and then funneling it to favored politicians and initiative campaigns around the state—an art Samish perfected—he controlled enough votes to pass or kill bills as he saw fit.

No one could stop Samish. Political parties were impoverished and weak. Politicians needed money to get elected and stay elected, and he saw that those who voted his way got what they needed. He ruled from "Samish Alley," across the street from the capitol in the Senator Hotel, where his $3,000 a month rent, not including food, drink, or other expenses, was paid by the State Brewers Institute. Politicians lined up between midnight and 4 A.M. to eat his food and drink his booze. "Shrimp Hour," wrote David Perlman in a 1951 *San Francisco Chronicle* profile, was "Samish's unending cocktail party, where parched assemblymen and senators quaff bourbon by the case and consume pounds of deep-fat-fried shrimp. . . . Samish himself presides at these functions with mammoth bursts of laughter, heavy outpourings of profanity, and—to an occasional backsliding legislator—the warning that 'Artie's gonna get mad, doll. You don't want to act like that, do you?'" Samish had a suite of offices in San Francisco and another at the Biltmore Hotel in Los Angeles. His network of sources and confidants was so well placed that he described them as the "damnedest Gestapo you ever saw."[3]

"We take you, for instance," he told an investigating committee, "and we learn about you, that you're married and got kiddies and who your parents are and what fraternal orders you belong to. . . . We know all about you." Within two weeks, he bragged, he knew what kind of women a new legislator preferred, what kind of booze he drank, and what he liked on his baked potato.[4] But years of high-rolling finally caught up with Samish. It took an out-of-state reporter to blow the whistle. When *Collier's* sent muckraking journalist Lester Velie to California to look at Samish's influence on the legislature, Velie got rare insights and even better quotes.

"If you get a long enough ladder and put it up against the capitol dome, you can take a picture of me unscrewing the gold cupola," Samish told him. He also said, "If you dropped two bucks in the rotunda of the capitol, you'd start a riot." Velie's two articles appeared with a full-page photo of Samish dangling a puppet, which he called, "My legislature." The exposés caused a national sensation and led to Samish's eventual indictment and conviction. When the 1954 session began, Samish Alley was gone. Some observers called the next few years a period of drift; others said it was a rare period of relatively honest government. Samish eventually repaid the federal government more than $900,000 in back taxes and penalties.[5]

Samish was not the only lobbyist, just the most flamboyant and effective. Some 400 other members of the third house who also bought and sold votes did not slink off into the night just because Samish went to jail. They had their spots at the Walnut Room, Bedells, Frank Fats, the El Rancho, or the top of the El Mirador, where they entertained legislators whose pay had risen to a modest $300 a month—a tenth of what Samish paid his top lobbyists.

Every day produced a different free lunch for legislators. The racetrack lobby hosted the steak sandwich on Monday, the California Medical Association had the clambake the next day, and the liquor industry or cattlemen's association a special buffet the third. There was a certain symmetry to the committee system. Each was controlled by the interests over which it had jurisdiction. The railroads owned the Revenue and Taxation Committee, the big agricultural interests dominated the Agriculture Committee. There was even an Oil, Gas, and Mining Committee that the oil, gas, and mining interests ran. For years, the chairman and key members of the Health Committee met with the California Medical Association lobbyist at the Senator Hotel before each session to get their instructions on which bills to pass and which to kill.

In the Sacramento that Burton would come to know, many legislators were an underpaid, underachieving bunch, all too willing to exchange a vote for booze or money. They worked out of tiny cramped offices with virtually no staff. Lobbyists did not just supply wine, women, and song. They happily filled the information vacuum, often drafting legislation and key amendments and offering "helpful" questions during committee hearings. The state constitution limited the legislature's sessions to 120 days in odd-numbered years and just 30 days more to deal with the state budget in even-numbered years. Nobody maintained separate homes in Sacramento, and many rented cheap rooms. San Francisco and Los Angeles legislators often could not afford transportation up and back and hitched rides from reporters.

After the day's session, lawmakers partied into the wee hours and headed home Thursday afternoon for the weekend. Lobbyists treated their favorites to nights on the town, furnished women and hosted card games in spacious hotel suites where the liquor flowed. It beat returning to a room in a seedy hotel. Legislators changed the Ways and Means Committee's regularly scheduled meeting to Wednesday, so "the boys" could play cards all night Monday without Tuesday morning meetings to put a crimp in their style.[6]

Things calmed down after Samish left town. Lobbyists still bought and sold votes, and after the day's session many legislators still acted like fraternity boys. But even as they adjusted to Samish's absence, another huge and unexpected change hit the capital: party designation. The rule that required candidates to declare party affiliation on the ballot—and had helped elect Burton—was beginning to transform state politics. "The significant and strikingly new element in California last year was the resurgence of party fidelity among Republicans and Democrats," wrote Mary Ellen Leary in *The Reporter* a month after Burton's swearing-in. "This was the first genuinely partisan national election California has staged in more than a generation. . . . In just four years—from one presidential election to the next—the climate of politics has been recast in California. Three letters made all the difference: 'Dem' and 'Rep.'"[7]

Years before his election, while Burton was busy learning his politics organizing the Young Democrats in San Francisco and across the state, Jesse Unruh was serving his apprenticeship in Los Angeles. He broke with the left while still at USC, and made a foolhardy run for an assembly seat in 1948, losing badly. He ran and lost again in 1952 and finally was elected in 1954, helped enormously by the letters "Dem" next to his name on the ballot. Initially, Unruh was independent, unwilling to accept any third house money. But he was also broke and the father of five children. The corpulent Unruh, with his huge fleshy features, his double chins and his raw appetites, quickly emerged as the most talented freshman in his class. Democratic Minority Leader William Munnell, another USC graduate who had arrived in Sacramento two years ahead of him, elevated Unruh to a powerful committee known as Finance and Insurance, key to the banking, savings and loan, and insurance industries. After only two years in the assembly, Unruh was appointed chairman. "The business interests needed someone they could trust, someone who had the trust of his fellow Democratic legislators," Lou Cannon, former Burton ally turned journalist wrote years later. "Jesse Unruh, now the chairman of the assembly's most important committee on business legislation, was the only man who seemed to fill the bill on both counts." Unruh began cultivating a close relationship with Howard Ahmanson, owner of the Los Angeles Home Savings and Loan Association and the wealthiest man in California.

By 1957, Unruh was already thinking about how to fill the vacuum left when Samish departed. His idea: move the center of power from the Senator Hotel to the speaker's office. Through Ahmanson, Unruh funneled thousands of campaign dollars to favored legislators. When Unruh directed Pat Brown's 1958 campaign for governor in Southern California, Ahmanson, not the Brown campaign, paid his $10,000 salary. As Unruh moved up the ladder, he enlisted other legislators as trusted lieutenants. Men like Bob Crown, elected from Alameda in 1956, Jerome Waldie from Contra Costa County two years later, and Tom Rees became known as his "Praetorian Guard."[8]

Rees, the Beverly Hills assemblyman, typified the new breed of liberal Democrat whose politics were a blend of idealism and realism born of bitter personal experience. Like others of his generation, he was deeply influenced by the war. In the spring of 1945, when he was twenty, Rees's army battalion was the first to capture a Nazi extermination camp in Germany. After his battalion marched the town's mayor and his wife to see the death camp, the couple went home and committed suicide. Haunted by his experience, Rees, whose district was heavily Jewish, was determined to make the world a little better. The man he beat, former speaker and Samish puppet Charles Lyon, was indicted a month before the election in connection with a major liquor scandal. Rees was not in public life just to take a lobbyist's money and do what he was told. He was in Sacramento to make things happen. If Unruh was where the action was, that's where Rees wanted to be, too. Their strategy was to take over the assembly caucus, make it partisan, and build a strong Democratic Party.[9]

Burton arrived in Sacramento with a legislative package for his first week already prepared. On January, 8, 1957, the second day of session, he introduced his first bill, an American Federation of Labor–supported measure to increase the state minimum wage from $0.75 an hour to $1.25. Acting immediately on his campaign promises, he also introduced bills to legalize firecrackers for Chinese New Year's "religious" celebrations and to increase payments in worker's compensation, disability insurance, and unemployment benefits. His initial hyperactivity earned him some favorable publicity. But getting results proved more elusive. It was one thing to introduce a bill, quite another to get it passed. It took Burton his first two years in Sacramento to understand the difference.

Burton described these bills in a press release he mailed two weeks after he took office. With an attention to detail that marked his entire career, he targeted his first mailing to every "BF" or "Big Family" in the Twentieth District—there were forty-seven such big families, for example, in Precinct 113 where Tommy Maloney lived—to eighteen CDC-affiliated political clubs, to every ethnic newspaper and club and to every AFL and CIO union and labor sheet.

Burton's careful stroking of the ethnic media paid off quickly. A February 1957 editorial in *Young China*, a Chinatown newspaper, saluted Burton as a "friend of Chinese" for three bills: firecrackers, a resolution wishing everyone a happy Chinese New Year, and his co-sponsorship with Assemblyman Augustus Hawkins of the Fair Employment Practices Commission, designed to end job discrimination against minorities, which the assembly passed later in the session. "Mr. Burton is young and capable," the editorial concluded. "He has an unlimited future."

A couple weeks later, Burton proposed a $50 million housing program for the aged and introduced a bill to give eighteen-year-olds the right to vote. When Governor Goodwin Knight delayed signing the FEPC bill, Burton blasted him for "hiding in the cellar." He added, "You can find him there pretty often."[10] In April, Burton and O'Connell, who competed to see which was more liberal, introduced a bill to ban loyalty oaths for all state employees. O'Connell was less intense than Burton, but they were good friends and talked every day.

A California Retail Association yearly report described Burton's AB 338, which would have declared full employment to be state policy, guaranteed by state funds, as "perhaps the most ambitious bill in the labor field." But the report said he had little to show for his efforts. Burton could not get it assigned to the right committee. It languished in the Agriculture Committee, which never bothered to consider it. This was happening to virtually all of Burton's bills.

AB 2940 would have made all county and municipal offices partisan. It died in committee. AB 2939 would have prohibited all applicants for teaching jobs from being asked about political party, religion, race, or color. It died in committee. AB 2941 would have made it a felony to overhear electronic conversations or to install such devices without permission of all parties. It was never taken up. AB 3936 would have created a commission to study the health needs of Californians. It died in committee. AB 243 would have placed the burden on the employer to prove that employee injuries were caused by intoxication or were self-inflicted. It died in committee. AB 453 would have made worker's compensation to agricultural workers mandatory. It died in committee. AB 454, introduced with Hawkins, would have added $5.00 a week in worker compensation cases to the dependent spouse and $2.50 a week for each dependent child. It died in committee. AB 245, his bill to increase the minimum wage to $1.25 an hour was scaled back to $1.00. It survived the assembly but was killed 16-13 in the senate on the final day of the session.

Clearly, Burton had a great deal to learn about the realities of the legislative process. He did get one resolution approved that first year urging the House of Representatives to liberalize immigration laws that restricted the number of Chinese allowed into the U.S. This was symbolically important for his Chinese constituency. But passing a resolution urging the House to do something it had no intention of doing was not much of an accomplishment.

The one bright spot during that first difficult year was AB 1738. On the last night of the 1957 session, both houses passed the bill, which allowed noncitizens who had lived in the United States for at least twenty-five years to get state pensions. In passing this bill, Burton fulfilled an important campaign promise. On June 17, 1957, he sent a letter about this bill to forty-eight ethnic newspapers and local clubs, urging them to write to Governor Knight and demand that he sign the legislation.

Burton was militant, uncompromising, incorruptible, and in the fraternity-party atmosphere of the time, often a stick-in-the-mud. He rarely wanted to talk about anything other than politics or legislative business. He liked to drink, but even drunk he was usually all business, collaring some member in the bar who voted "wrong" or some lobbyist he did not like and jabbing his finger in the poor man's chest. Sala was one of the few wives who accompanied her husband to Sacramento. Her daughter Joy stayed in San Francisco with her father for a time, and Sala was usually in Sacramento by Monday night. She accompanied Phillip on his evening rounds and kept a watchful eye on him.

His behavior on and off the assembly floor alienated colleagues of both parties. Even George Miller was ambivalent about him. He admired Burton's liberalism, commitment, and obvious brains but, like many, was put off by his style. When Jack McDowell, the *Call Bulletin*'s and later the *Examiner*'s political editor, asked Miller about Burton during his first term, he replied, "Jackson, you can't make ice cream out of horse shit."[11]

Burton and Unruh circled each other warily, although they often enjoyed each other's company. Both loved drinking, wielding power, dominating the arena. And both had foul mouths. When they were drunk, the conversation sometimes turned ugly. Unruh would call Sala a "bitch," and question her affection for Burton. Burton would reply, "Well, at least Sala wears a brassiere."

Unruh and many of his lieutenants spent their evenings getting boozed up, chasing women, and then bragging about their exploits in full clinical detail the next morning. Burton was more restrained. But when Sala was not around, Burton's colleagues noticed that he occasionally did a little prowling of his own at the Republican Women's Conference meetings or at hotel tea dances, where he picked up lonely women. Unruh sent his friends into gales of laughter, imitating Republican women in bed with Burton yelling, "I hate you, I hate you, I hate you," as they made love to a man whose politics they must have despised. Although he was utterly devoted to Sala, he successfully chased a number of Democratic women as well when she wasn't around.

Burton was deeply embarrassed when the assembly voted down his firecracker measure, which should have been a noncontroversial bill. One version had it that Republican colleague John Busterud of San Francisco, furious at Burton for not even consulting him about the bill, convinced the San Francisco police and fire chiefs to testify against the bill, thus killing it. Given the San Francisco Irish community's antagonism to Burton, this would not have been hard to set up. It would teach him a lesson about counting votes and working the house, including colleagues in his own city.

But a more cold-blooded analysis interpreted the loss this way: the bill died because he never worked the fireworks kings. If lobbyists got the idea that a legislator could pass a special interest bill (in this case one benefiting the fireworks industry) as a "good government" bill or as one that helped his constituents without getting payoffs from that industry, the whole system could collapse. Burton had failed to "get" something for his vote, and this could not be tolerated. If the fireworks kings did not have to pay cash for their bills, some legislators feared that the liquor industry, the savings and loan, and horse racing interests would also stop paying for the bills they wanted. Perhaps his colleagues were telling Burton to play the game the way it was supposed to be played. Otherwise, hand it off to someone who would. Jesse Unruh had needed no such instructions to pick up that message.[12]

In addition to his legislative duties, Burton continued his outside politicking with the Young Democrats. By the time he was elected to the assembly, he was already a national vice president and plotting to win the presidency at the national convention in Reno in 1957. There was no such thing as down time for Burton. Friends said he was incapable of relaxing or thinking about anything but politics. But there was also a larger purpose. When he was elected to the House of Representatives seven years later, he already knew dozens of House members from his years in the Young Democrats movement.

The Young Democrats were a conservative group nationally, dominated by Southern Dixiecrats. But another liberal, Nelson Lancione, an assistant state attorney general in Ohio, was also running for president, threatening to split the vote. Burton frantically worked the large state delegations. But when the liberal caucuses from the West and Midwest endorsed Lancione over him, Burton pulled out, endorsing Lancione and ensuring the election of the national organization's first liberal. Burton did not walk away empty-handed, however. He made a deal with Lancione that he hoped would guarantee his election two years later and give him immense clout within the organization in the meantime.

Burton had learned something about power. According to a written "understanding" between them, summarized by Burton's Berkeley YD friend Tom Winnett, Burton gave "unqualified" support to Lancione. In return, Burton got authority to select officers and appoint the chairman of the board of regional directors, make all appointments west of the Mississippi, select the credentials committee chairman for the 1959 meeting and fly to any state or regional meeting or convention on a Young Democrats credit card.[13]

In pulling out, Burton also arranged for a young Hawaiian protégé and activist named Patsy Mink to be named a vice president. Mink thanked Burton for the "great sacrifice which you made in order to assure the victory of the liberal movement. The triumph at the convention is yours and yours alone." As for her own elevation, she gushed, "My heart-felt gratitude to you for conjuring up an idea that none of us would have dared to consider, let alone propose." Burton and Mink posed for pictures that appeared in all the Asian newspapers. Years later, she joined Burton as a loyal ally on two House committees.

Burton ran again two years later. He persuaded Governor Brown to write on his behalf to all twenty-two Democratic governors. But Burton embarrassed himself when he tried to turn an expression of good luck from Hubert Humphrey into an endorsement. The flap began when a conversation with the Minnesota senator led him to believe that Humphrey had endorsed him. In fact, the senator had merely written him a thank-you note. Humphrey aide Herbert Waters corrected him, and Burton apologized. "I am particularly distressed that our longstanding friendship should be disturbed by what, apparently, was a misunderstanding on my part," Burton wrote. He lost the election.[14]

Despite these setbacks, Burton dominated the California Young Democrats throughout the late 1950s, putting one protégé after another into office, including his brother John and a friend of John's named Josiah Beeman, who later became a close aide. But even YD and assembly responsibilities were not enough to occupy Burton. He also wanted to firmly establish himself as San Francisco's top elected official, the kingmaker who selected candidates for every office, no matter how seemingly inconsequential.

Burton ran Democratic candidates for every assembly seat in San Francisco, even if they were certain to lose, and ran entire slates for the county central committee. It was routine to find Phillip, John, Sala, Robert, and his wife Shirley all on the ballot. Through the Young Democrats, Burton cultivated a state network of young liberal activists. They developed political, parliamentary, and floor-managing skills by getting resolutions passed, friends elected, rules bypassed. Among the young activists were Henry Waxman, a Los Angeles law student, his friend Howard Berman, and Berman's brother Michael, who was still in high school. Membership in the Young Democrats provided credentials to conventions of the California Democratic Council. Because the CDC endorsed candidates in primaries—which state law precluded the Democratic Party itself from doing—CDC endorsements were valuable and eagerly sought. These endorsements conferred instant legitimacy and committed grass-roots volunteers. Candidates used them in their literature and campaign mail.

As the liberal conscience of the state party, however, the CDC often caused problems for elected Democrats who did not want to have to explain to voters why the group that had endorsed them was also calling for Red China's admission into the United Nations or for the abolition of HUAC. This led to explosions with Unruh, who thought such resolutions bordered on political suicide. These activists took their politics so seriously that during one heated debate at a YD convention at the Roosevelt Hotel in Hollywood, a young Unruh lieutenant from USC named Joe Cerrell grabbed the microphone and began an impassioned speech opposing "leftists" like the Burtons, Toby Osos, and YD President Dick Nevin. Stealing a line from Unruh, Cerrell concluded, "If the Burton brothers aren't Communists, it's only because they are too cheap to pay the dues." Nevin ordered Cerrell ejected, but Cerrell picked up a water pitcher and threatened to hurl it at anyone who wanted to try. Pandemonium broke out. When order was finally restored, the two factions cut a deal: if Cerrell would apologize and put down the water pitcher, he could remain.[15]

When the session resumed in January 1958, Burton was more experienced but still frustrated. Most of his legislation was still too left wing or pro-labor to get past the Republican-dominated legislature, and he did not yet have the skill to manipulate the system as he would in later years. In mid-March he asked Governor Knight to call a special session to deal with the 1958 recession that was putting thousands of Californians out of work. When the governor rejected the request, Burton called Knight's inaction "another indication of the inherent inability of the Republican party to cope with the declining economic situation." California's unemployment rate had doubled, and the economy was a hot topic. Newspapers from all over picked up the story, giving Burton his first major statewide publicity. A month later, Burton and O'Connell introduced a resolution calling for a moratorium on all nuclear weapons. It got nine votes.

Despite his lack of impact, Burton tried valiantly to represent liberal interests during his first term and did a good job publicizing his efforts. As he prepared for re-election, hundreds of labor groups endorsed Burton. The teachers' union was typical: "Dear Phil," its May 22, 1958 letter began, "Your recent query of the California State Federation of Teachers about the forthcoming election is almost unnecessary. There is no doubt whatever that you have been one of the most vocal and active proponents of teachers' interests in either house. Your record is entirely above reproach."

Burton sent out a two-page summary of his legislative activities. It went to big families, nineteen San Francisco club presidents, 216 members of the Democratic State Central Committee and CDC executive committee, all ninety-two members of the local CDC committee from 1952 through 1958 and all "key Potrero Hill helpers." Chinatown leaders held a testimonial lunch and dinner, news and photos of which appeared prominently in the Chinese newspapers. With Harry Low, Lim P. Lee, and his wife Catherine, whom Burton appointed as the first Asian woman to the state party central committee, Burton formed the Chinese-American Democratic Club, which became a major force in Chinatown. He sent a personally engraved copy of the Roster of State Officials to dozens of VIPs and elected officials. He sent a hokey but official-looking Great Seal of California to hundreds of other supporters with their names engraved. Many voters proudly framed the citations and put them on the wall. Burton filed every letter from every constituent, underlining the compliments in blue ink and the address and name of the organization, if there was one, in red.

Burton also began copying what Unruh had been doing on a grand scale for years: funneling money from a big donor to chosen candidates. Burton's political sugar daddy was not Howard Ahmanson, the richest man in California, however, but George Hardy of the janitor's union, and the grand total of $550 was a pittance. But when Hardy sent him the money and a list of candidates it should go to, Burton added his own note with the checks. Hardy was now the "head man" for some forty Building Service Employees locals in California, Burton wrote. He picked key districts and asked candidates to whom he sent money not to mention his name, although he obviously wanted credit and future allegiance from those he helped. After Burton's election, Hardy had begun a statewide Building Services Union newspaper, which publicized Burton as a solid labor vote. It went to every union leader in California.

Burton's 1958 opponent was Achille Muschi, thirty-six, a high school teacher who ran against him in 1956. Muschi chided Burton for his lackluster record saying, "This district needs a representative who can get more than one bill through the legislature." He said he could pass a firecracker bill and hit Burton for supporting admission of Red China to the UN and advocating a ban on nuclear testing. One columnist suggested that Muschi's campaign was being "masterminded" by Tommy Maloney. Muschi never stood a chance.

There was one small snag in what turned out to be an easy re-election. The episode briefly made the newspapers but did not seem to hurt Burton, although it illustrated his volcanic temperament and provided an ominous hint of a character flaw that haunted him throughout his adult life. One day Burton noticed that the Democratic Party office in North Beach had failed to post his sign along with those of all the other Democrats. Twice his workers plastered "Burton for Assembly" signs on the storefront windows at night. Both times they were removed. When Burton heard his signs had come down a second time, he stormed over to a political gathering looking for Gladys Bamberger, the North Beach office volunteer. When he found her, according to the account in the *Call Bulletin*, Burton "berated her in front of fellow Democrats in a sarcastic and insulting fashion." Bamberger demanded an apology and threatened to sue Burton for his abusive behavior.

"Your attitude," she wrote on May 25, "plus the contemptible language you used, makes you unfit to be a public servant. You have caused me distress and emotional concern. You were neither a man nor a mouse to take advantage of a lady." A few days later, a friend of Bamberger followed up, calling his behavior "rude, inhuman and appalling." Unless Burton apologized to this "volunteer of fourteen years in the Democratic Party," they would tell the newspapers about "your terrible attitude" and "denounce you as a political coward." Burton apparently did not respond, because five days after her letter, the story appeared. But nothing ever came of it.[16]

Burton won in a landslide. In his postelection analysis, he scrutinized every precinct (he won Tommy Maloney's 97 to 70) with his usual compulsive zeal. He studied every precinct in which his vote dropped between the primary and the general. What he found comforted him. In Chinatown's Precinct 20, for example, Burton beat Muschi 201 to 27. In Precinct 21 next door, he won 164 to 19.

At the state level, the election was a watershed for Democrats. Pat Brown was elected governor—the first Democrat since Culbert Olson in 1938 and only the second in the twentieth century. Democrat Clair Engle was elected U.S. Senator, and Democrats captured all four State Board of Equalization seats and all but one of the state constitutional offices, including controller, won by former CDC president Alan Cranston. The Democrats took command of both houses of the legislature for the first time since 1891.

It was not political genius that produced such a huge crop of Democrats, however, but a massive Republican blunder. In 1957, powerful Republican U.S. Senator William F. Knowland decided he wanted to return home to California as governor. Knowland was a virulent anti-communist, head of the Senate's "China Lobby" and publisher of the *Oakland Tribune*, one of the three most powerful newspapers in the state. Some said Knowland thought being governor was a better platform from which to launch a presidential campaign. Others said his wife insisted on returning and threatened to make public an alleged affair. But there was one looming problem. California already *had* a Republican governor. His name was Goodwin Knight, and he had every intention of running for re-election. Knowland had to muscle him out of that race.

To avoid a bitter primary that would harm both of them, Knowland forced Knight to swap offices. They would run for each other's job. Voters would ratify the switch in the 1958 election. Knight was helpless to prevent it. He was caught between Knowland's wealthy financial backers and Vice President Nixon, who wanted peace in his home state's party and who won Knowland's support for his 1960 presidential campaign by helping to engineer the switch. To the public, the ploy smacked of the worst kind of cynical, backroom deal—which of course it was—and the whole thing blew up in the GOP's face.

Knowland compounded his blunder by putting a right-to-work initiative on the November ballot, which would have outlawed collective bargaining agreements. That initiative, Proposition 18, gave labor the incentive and the passion to organize as never before to defeat the initiative and every candidate who supported it. George Hardy, for example, set up "No on 18" committees in every assembly district in Los Angeles and San Francisco. That allowed each Democratic assembly candidate to use committee headquarters and phones and to walk precincts with the labor activists. The measure proved wildly unpopular and dragged Republican candidates down with it.[17]

Political pro Don Bradley, who was polling for the Democrats, later said that from the day Knowland pushed Knight out of the governor's race, neither Pat Brown nor Clair Engle ever trailed again. Brown ran a deliberately bland campaign to prevent conservative newspapers from pouncing on any opportunity to criticize him. His campaign manager, Fred Dutton, later said that Squire Behrens of the *San Francisco Chronicle* and Kyle Palmer of the *Los Angeles Times* were so accustomed to helping the Republican Party, that if Brown ever got too partisan or liberal, Behrens and Palmer would write that he could not represent all the people.

Burton, however, was outraged at this cautious approach. He chewed out Dutton twice a week for "muzzling" Brown, for not being liberal enough, for not providing "clarity." But after the election-day victory, Burton conceded that the Dutton-Brown approach had been exactly right, telling Dutton that in "rowing his own boat," as Dutton put it, Brown attracted the widest possible base and brought more assembly and senate candidates into office with him.[18]

The 1958 election was crucial for two reasons. First, the Democrats under Brown could govern California for the first time in nearly seventy years and chair all the key legislative committees. Second, assuming they could hold their majority through 1960, Democrats would have authority to draw the lines for new political boundaries after the 1960 census and thus hold power through strategic redistricting for the next decade. California's congressional delegation would get eight new members, growing from thirty to thirty-eight because of the state's phenomenal population growth. The new majority wanted to ensure they would be Democrats.

Unruh successfully ran Pat Brown's campaign in Southern California. The corpulent legislator now had his pick of jobs in the assembly. Ralph Brown, a popular Democrat from Modesto, was certain to be elected speaker in the January 1959 session. Unruh, with Pat Brown's help, was picked to chair the most powerful committee, Ways and Means. With the Democrats chairing twenty-two of the assembly's twenty-eight committees, John O'Connell persuaded Speaker Brown to appoint Burton chairman of the Committee on Social Welfare. It had jurisdiction over all legislation on mental health and aid to needy children, the aged, and the blind. He also got an interim committee on farm labor.

But his temper and passion for power continued to be a problem. In an angry exchange with Republican John Busterud, Burton shook his finger at his San Francisco colleague and threatened to air some Republican dirty linen.

"Don't go shaking your finger at me," an enraged Busterud replied. "When you tried to defeat me by pushing my opponent, that was all right. He was a Democrat. I'd do the same thing to you. But your running around the capitol trying to keep me off certain committees is something different. We're all up here representing the city of San Francisco and you are hurting your own district and your own city by antics like these."

The incident made the local papers. Jack McDowell reported that Burton sat there "white with anger," but did not deny Busterud's charges. "This, incidentally, isn't Burton's first chewing out of the 1959 legislative session," McDowell added. "He freely admits that Assembly Speaker Ralph Brown called him in and . . . told him he talks and shouts too much and would have far better success if he practiced being quiet."

For a man who vibrated with anger, Burton could be astonishingly sentimental. He continued his regular dinner visits to the Hardy household. Norma Hardy recounted painful stories of her childhood, when her widowed mother and four daughters lived on a seventeen dollar a month welfare check that could not feed the family and endured Thanksgiving dinners where the donated chicken was so scrawny that there was no meat on the bones. Burton listened with tears streaming down his face. Mrs. Hardy thus carried special authority when she asked the new chairman of the welfare committee, as she frequently did, what he had done to help "the widows and the orphans." Burton usually answered, "It's not much better, but it's better." One of his first bills, which took several years to pass, eliminated a residential means test for the aged, blind, or disabled. Before that, people with homes valued over $5,000 were precluded from state aid. Later in his career, he did as much or more for the poor as any Democrat before him.

While the Hardys had become his substitute parents, and he their substitute son, Burton did find time to spend a day with his father in May 1959. Dr. Burton dropped him a note to say how much he enjoyed it. "I am real proud of you for taking a stand and sticking to your convictions," the note said. But ever the withholding and moralistic father, Dr. Burton parceled out his compliments sparingly and could not help adding a reproach:

> As I have often said—in my judgment INTEGRITY is the most important quality a man may have. I am pleased that it is showing in your character. I hope and I am sure it will be carried into all your actions—insofar as it is humanly possible. It was also refreshing to me to note that you are aware and are sorry for some of your sins of omission. In this connection I have written Mother that you regretted being unable to reach her by phone on Mother's Day but that you plan to write her real soon. Hope we can have more days together soon.[19]

Nineteen fifty-nine was a landmark year for California civil rights bills. Under Brown's and Unruh's leadership, the state got a Fair Employment Practices Commission, which made employment discrimination illegal, a Fair Housing Act, which prohibited discrimination in any publicly accessible housing, and an anti-discrimination bill, which increased the fine from $100 to $250 for businesses that violated the law. A Burton press release called the 1959 session the "most productive in history." It cited those bills plus repeal of a law banning interracial marriages and a Burton resolution to Congress urging anti-lynching legislation. The release was sent to "All Minority Press, Chinese, Japanese, Negro, All Negro doctors, All Negro attorneys, All Negro dentists, All Negro ministers," and all Chinese doctors, attorneys, dentists, and ministers.

What must have been especially satisfying to Burton was the June 5, 1959 passage of his firecracker bill. Burton had almost managed to pull a fast one, sticking four words into someone else's bill at the last minute to exempt rockets and missiles from the state fireworks law. When the author spotted the four words, " . . . or for religious ceremonies," he withdrew the bill. Burton convinced the key member—Judiciary Committee Chairman George Wilson of Huntington Park—to approve his bill by engineering a trade. Wilson wanted a bill requiring all judges in California to wear robes. Burton voted for robes and in return, got Wilson's vote for firecrackers. It was an early sign of the pragmatic horse-trading for which he later became known.

In keeping with his commitment to minorities, Burton prevailed on Governor Brown to appoint his Chinese-American allies to the sorts of boards and commissions routinely awarded to Caucasian supporters. Burton's friends began reaping their rewards for galvanizing Chinatown support for Brown and Burton. Lim P. Lee was appointed to the Veterans' Appeals Board. Gilbert Woo, editor and publisher of *Chinese Pacific Weekly*, received a gubernatorial appointment to the White House Conference on Problems of the Aging.

Burton also began focusing on the problems of some of California's newest and most exploited immigrants. As chairman of an interim committee on farm labor, Burton investigated the problems of farm workers and braceros, the Mexicans who were allowed into the state temporarily to work the fields. The law said growers could hire braceros only if there was a shortage of local farm workers. Begun during World War II's labor shortages, the bracero program now was constantly being violated. Growers could pay braceros less and work them harder than American laborers. In the prosperity following World War II, the era of "Okie" migrant workers epitomized by Tom Joad in John Steinbeck's *Grapes of Wrath* had given way to Mexican laborers.

A young lawyer named Coleman Blease proved to be a valuable ally for Burton. Blease had just graduated from UC Berkeley's Boalt Hall and arrived in Sacramento in 1957 as the first paid lobbyist for the Quakers' American Friends Service Committee. He put together what became known as the "Raggedy Ass" lobby, which included the American Civil Liberties Union, the American Federation of Teachers, and the farm workers. They shared what little money and resources they had to lobby a legislature totally dominated by business, commercial, and conservative labor interests. They became prototypes for the kind of public interest lobbying that later opened up Sacramento.

Burton called a hearing in Stockton, but because he knew little about farm worker problems, he arrived a day early and stayed up most of the night debriefing his sources and becoming an instant expert. By the next morning, he knew the issues intimately. More than 200 growers packed the Civic Auditorium that day. One of the "specialists" Burton invited to testify was a young Mexican-American woman from Stockton named Dolores Huerta who worked for Community Services Organization (CSO), a civil rights and social services group that dealt with farm worker problems. CSO had been organized by Fred Ross, a veteran activist who spotted a young Mexican-American worker in San Jose named Cesar Chavez and taught him to be an organizer.

Huerta brought half a dozen farm workers who had been turned down for work that very morning in favor of braceros. They described how they had been told they couldn't work because their hoes were too long or their work boots were not strong enough. When it was the growers' turn to testify, Burton pounded the table and demanded to know what wages they were paying. One grower said he paid seventy-five cents an hour.

"I am going out to your property when this hearing is over," Burton announced at 4 P.M., "and find out exactly what you are paying." Such drama at a committee hearing was rare, to say the least.

As soon as Huerta heard this, she rushed to the work camp that Burton was due to visit. The grower had already sent word of the impending visit, and people were frantically cleaning it up, putting linens on the beds, sweeping out the filth. Huerta rounded up the workers and told them to stay put, so they would be on hand to answer questions when Burton arrived. Burton,

Blease, and officials of the California Department of Employment, which oversaw the bracero program, arrived soon thereafter, and Burton caught the grower altering his books. When he found out that the workers, mostly braceros, were being paid fifty cents an hour, he convinced the embarrassed grower to identify neighboring growers who were also violating the law. On the spot, Burton ordered the growers to fork over full wages with back pay and insisted that the growers in the region hire local workers from then on.

The tactic captured Burton at his best. It combined outrage, bravado, and a moral certainty that overrode procedural niceties. Burton had no authority to do what he did. But he knew the law and he knew the penalties for violating it, and the force of his personality was so strong that his order stood. Farm workers all over the San Joaquin Valley got pay raises that day. To Huerta, a deeply religious Catholic who had never before met Burton, his actions were like "the fire of holiness." She had never before witnessed such a performance, especially not on behalf of poor and voiceless Mexican-American farm workers.

Blease found Burton's performance even more amazing. This was the sort of "intractable" issue on which legislators spent years working, holding hearings, advancing legislation, creating the right moment to take small, incremental steps towards change. But Burton had no time to waste on such ineffectual tactics. He swooped in from Sacramento, learned what he needed to know, exposed the greed and prevarications of the growers and put money in the pockets of exploited workers, all within the space of twenty-four hours.[20]

In Burton's hands, the once-soporific legislative hearings became an effective weapon. He got similar fast results when he held hearings on reducing the cost of prescription drugs to California indigents. The huge pharmaceutical companies were charging California's welfare department full price for the right to sell drugs in the nation's largest market. In announcing the hearings, Burton said the drug companies gave away $15 million worth of drugs free to doctors in one year—a retail value of $46 million. "If the industry can afford to do this massive job of promoting drugs," he said, "couldn't the state get a quantity discount for its indigents?" With the threat of a grand jury investigation into price-fixing looming, Burton then "offered" seven manufacturers the opportunity to testify. Those who did not come voluntarily, he subpoenaed. His hearings revealed that California spent $36 million over three years buying drugs for public assistance, yet got no discounts. A few days later, Burton announced that several major drug companies had agreed to cut the price of drugs sold to the state by 10 percent.

Working essentially alone and without legislation, he accomplished in days what it took other legislators years.

His crusading zeal prompted *San Jose Mercury* political editor Harry Farrell to profile Burton in December 1959 as the most liberal member of the legislature. Burton's "giveaway propensities are such that even the Democratic Assembly Leadership has set up a special Ways and Means subcommittee to second-guess his decisions on welfare," he wrote. Burton told Farrell he ignored mail from constituents on how he should vote and generally supported any bill that "gives something to someone who hasn't got it."[21]

Burton said he supported bills that lowered prices to consumers and opposed "any bill that strengthens law enforcement at the expense of civil liberties." He still explored the outer margins of "acceptable" legislation. One Burton bill went too far: it would have required compulsory health insurance financed by a 3 percent tax on employers. Another would have stopped "greedy night club owners" from forcing hatcheck girls to turn over their tips. In the latter case, Burton charged that more than 100 night clubs in North Beach forced their hatcheck girls into such "kickback" arrangements. Both bills died.

Dolores Huerta worked with Burton again in 1961 when she was sent to Sacramento as CSO's legislative advocate and joined Coleman Blease's "Raggedy Ass" lobby. But the bills she wanted were virtually impossible to pass, including one Burton submitted years earlier to lift the requirement that one had to be a U.S. citizen to be eligible for public assistance. One day, Huerta hung around Burton's office all afternoon to plead her case. When she finally got in to see him, she explained that farm workers had no social security benefits or unemployment insurance and were digging around in garbage cans for food. Burton tried to explain that there was little constituency for such a bill and it would be tough to pass. The legislature had already approved the Fair Employment Practices Commission to deal with racial inequities, Burton said, but Huerta, pregnant with one of her eleven children, burst into tears.

"All right. I'll do it," Burton sighed. "But you have to promise to help me."

Huerta knew nothing about lobbying. Women lobbyists were rare in Sacramento, and she was timid. But over the next several months, Burton transformed her. He taught her how to write letters, who to send them to, and how to organize the constituencies of the legislators she wanted to persuade.

"If legislators get ten letters, they worry," Burton told Huerta, "so get these people to write letters." Cesar Chavez, who was already organizing farm workers, had pioneered a voter registration drive in Madera County, which helped elect Democrat James Cobey to the state senate. Burton taught Huerta how to mobilize Spanish-speaking voters and let Cobey know they wanted old-age assistance for noncitizens. Burton's bill became AB 5. He advised Huerta to bring people to the capitol directly. Even though some who appeared could not speak English, their children served in the armed services, and they sat in the hearing rooms holding photographs of their sons in uniform.

In a minor legislative triumph for Burton and Huerta, Governor Brown signed AB 5 on July 18, 1961, calling it "a significant part of the New Frontier." The news photo showed a smiling Brown signing the bill, surrounded by Burton and CSO officials. It provided $3 million for the first six months of the year for old-age assistance to noncitizens.[22]

Burton also led the battle to increase unemployment insurance, disability benefits, and worker's compensation by $87 million a year. When the money came through, he sent new weekly and hourly benefit schedules for worker's compensation and unemployment to every union in his district. When he heard about an unemployed worker denied his benefits because he was at a funeral and failed to follow up on a job offer, Burton quickly plugged that hole with a bill, known as the Burton Act, which provided flexibility so that jobless residents were not penalized in such emergencies.

Gone now were the days when Burton's bills died ignominiously. Burton, no less liberal than he had ever been, had learned how to legislate. "All I need to function effectively," he told Coleman Blease, "is two people to do what I ask. There will be enough votes on the cusp, and I can manipulate the rest." Many years later, Burton sat down in the House dining room with John Seiberling of Ohio and explained the lesson he had learned.

> One day when I was a young member of the California Assembly, I got a committee chairmanship. I thought this was my great chance to do something for the poor. I was getting all these great bills through the subcommittee and the committee and then to the floor, where they got clobbered. Finally I said to myself, "Burton, you're not helping the poor at all. You're getting all these great bills through your committee but none are getting passed." At that point I sat down and started figuring out who I had to deal with and what concessions I had to make. After that, I started getting them passed. They weren't as good as what I wanted, but at least they were of some help to the poor.[23]

Many years later, looking back over his career, Quaker lobbyist Blease said Burton, more than any politician, shared the concerns of the American Friends. But Burton was different because he took the process so seriously and wanted results. "There is a great problem with people who get into causes in thinking that merely being *identified* with causes is sufficient," Blease said. "My view, and it was Burton's view, too, is that there is no room for that. Which imposes on you a great burden to be absolutely clear about what it is that you are doing and who's affected and why. It imposes an absolute burden on you to become as skillfull as you can."

Blease related a scene he witnessed during those early days in Sacramento that captured Burton's almost obsessive commitment to mastering the legislative game and steeping himself in the history and political inclinations of each of his colleagues. "One night late I was wandering through the building and I came by Burton's office and found him kneeling on the floor," Blease recalled.

> He was putting together hundreds of issues. He kept voluminous scrapbooks on voting behavior of all kinds. He was clipping them out of journals and pasting them in these books, and he was educating himself. I have never seen anyone else do this. He could tell you hundreds and hundreds of details about other members of the legislature. He had mastered the political process in their districts. He knows their political composition . . . the boundaries, the statistical details. . . . Every subject matter area that he got into heavily he mastered. In the welfare area, Phil knew more than anybody, the staff people and otherwise. He combined this enormously detailed knowledge about precise political relations [with] what he knew about issues.[24]

Nor was he above bending the rules to further his agenda. He leaned on Speaker Ralph Brown to put two new Republicans, Bill Bagley of Marin County and Hugh Flournoy of Claremont, on his Social Welfare Committee. Burton planned to roll these newcomers at will. Bagley met Burton in January 1961, when Burton called him and Flournoy to the assembly lounge. For an hour Burton lectured them on the structure of welfare in California, explaining categorical aid programs to the aged, blind, and disabled. These legislators were from suburbia. They did not go to Sacramento to learn welfare politics, but Burton thought they should at least have some background in the unlikely event they decided to enlist in the cause.

Things panned out just as Burton hoped. He passed bill after bill out of committee over their feeble objections. After awhile, they no longer bothered to show up. Burton presided with just three people in the room, reported bills to the floor by proclamation, and became increasingly arrogant. After Unruh became speaker, Burton enraged a young black legislator from Los Angeles named Mervyn Dymally, who also sat on the welfare committee. With characteristic gall, Burton would announce, "This bill is good for Dymally. Dymally votes aye." Dymally joined the Republicans in boycotting the committee hearings.

"What is the purpose of serving on the committee when the chairman votes for you?" Dymally said, when Unruh asked why he had quit.

"You better go back," Unruh said. "He is continuing to vote for you."

Dymally went back. Burton had meant no harm. He figured that once he explained all the intricacies of the specific legislation to Dymally, the man would vote with him anyway. So why waste all that time?[25]

Burton gained his widest notoriety for his involvement in demonstrations protesting the appearance of the House Un-American Activities Committee in San Francisco's City Hall in May 1960. The three days of demonstrations culminated when police dragged and hosed dozens of college students— many from Berkeley—down the steps of City Hall for demonstrating. The "riots," as they were called, were pivotal to the eventual emergence of the New Left. Students were shocked by police beatings and by the subsequent HUAC-endorsed film entitled *Operation Abolition*, which deliberately distorted the events of that week. The experience radicalized some students, who became activists in the civil rights movement in the South and in the Free Speech Movement in Berkeley a few years later.

The hearings and police response to the demonstrations shocked the city. The committee had chosen San Francisco, FBI Director J. Edgar Hoover later wrote, "to inquire into communist activities of educators in Northern California."[26] Hundreds of faculty from the University of California, Berkeley, San Francisco and San Jose State Universities, and Stanford University signed petitions opposing HUAC activities as gross violations of civil liberties and due process. Hundreds more students from all over the Bay Area mobilized to protest. There were few Communists in evidence.

On the first day of the hearings, students began lining up at 7:30 A.M., two hours early, outside the oak-paneled City Hall chambers where the board of supervisors usually met. But when guards began letting in spectators, the students were kept out, wrote Ralph Tyler in *Frontier* magazine. Instead, the committee packed the hearing room with "elderly flower-hatted ladies and soberly suited men from 'patriotic' organizations armed with passes from the Un-American Activities Committee staff itself."

"There were about 150 passes [for some 200 seats]," committee investigator William Wheeler explained to reporters. "I issued them to individuals—to keep the commies from stacking the meeting. We wanted some decent people in here."

The mood turned ugly when the committee began grilling academics, lawyers, and civil libertarians about their alleged "Communist" activities. Over and over witnesses were asked, "Are you now or have you ever been a member of the Communist Party?" Virtually all declined to answer on Fifth Amendment grounds. As Tyler wrote, an elderly woman would put down her knitting needles and hiss to an attorney, "Sit down, Red." To which another spectator would reply, "Shut up, jackal."

On the second day, a thousand people gathered at noon at Union Square, about a mile from City Hall, to protest the hearings and the very existence of the notorious committee. The American Friends Service Committee had invited three speakers to address the protestors: Canon Richard Byfield of San Francisco's famous Grace Episcopal Cathedral, and the assembly's two leading civil libertarians, John O'Connell and Phil Burton, both of whom talked about the sanctity of the Fifth Amendment and the right to invoke it. "I do believe a Communist has a right to hold his political view and to say it aloud in public," O'Connell thundered, "just as I am talking here. This very meeting is a graphic example of what it means to be a free American." Soon thereafter, the crowd marched back to City Hall, where it circled the building, chanted "Abolish the Committee," and carried anti-HUAC signs.[27]

The third day, "Black Friday," was truly ugly. The trouble started when police announced only fifteen spectators would be allowed into the hearing room. By now, nearly 5,000 demonstrators had gathered outside. Some protestors taunted the committee and the police and a few banged on the huge closed doors of the supervisors' chambers, but student monitors worked hard to prevent violence. Even so, both the police and sheriff's departments quickly lost control and moved in with fire hoses. Bay Area residents who watched television news that night saw footage of young women being hosed and dragged down the stairs by their pony tails and police beating other students with nightsticks. Fourteen people were hospitalized, forty-eight men and fifteen women were arrested on charges of participating in a riot, disturbing the peace, and resisting arrest. Word flashed all over the world that "Communists" had disrupted a field hearing of a House committee.

But the worst was yet to come. As *San Francisco News–Call Bulletin* reporters Hadley Roff and Wes Willoughby reported in a week-long series on the demonstrations, HUAC subpoenaed nearly three hours of film from all the local TV stations and gave it to a small commercial studio in Washington. The studio edited the film into a forty-five-minute "documentary" called *Operation Abolition*, which rearranged the week's events to "prove" that opposition to the HUAC hearings was Communist-led and inspired. As Burton and O'Connell spoke, the film's narrator said, "A protest rally attracts nearly 1,000 students and spectators. They listen intently as two San Francisco assemblymen and a prominent clergyman unleash bitter attacks against the House Un-American Activities Committee." The film cut quickly to the "rioters" being hosed down the steps, making it look as if Burton and O'Connell led the charge. In fact, the arrests happened the following day and the two politicians were nowhere near City Hall. But the purported documentary caused a sensation. By January 1961, when the Roff-Willoughby series appeared, the studio had sold 700 prints of the film at $100 apiece.[28]

The movie became so popular that hundreds of patriotic organizations, schools, and church groups around the nation ordered copies to show their members as a warning about the perils of "Communism." But it was so misleading that some religious and civil liberties groups published their own pamphlets rebutting the film point by point.

Burton did not waste time on rebuttals. In fact, back in Sacramento, he enjoyed the celebrity and did not contradict colleagues who assumed he was one of those washed down the marble steps. Later, former Governor Knight hosted a television show that included segments from the movie. In the show, Knight called Burton an "extreme left-wing liberal in the legislature" and went on to recount an alleged encounter with Sala Burton. At a party the Knights hosted for legislators, he said, "Mrs. Phillip Burton walks up to me and says, 'I've been looking over your library and nowhere do I find any copy of Karl Marx's books on communism and socialism.' And I said, 'No, Mrs. Burton, you won't. I have only the friends of America and my beloved country in this room.'"

Those who knew Sala Burton doubted that she ever asked a Republican governor why he did not have any books by Marx in his library. Knight's comments, however, reflected the degree to which Republicans felt they could tag liberal Democrats with a broad red brush and get away with it. But the bigger smear came in the 1962 governor's race between Pat Brown and Richard Nixon. During a debate televised statewide on October 18, 1962, Nixon brought up the HUAC demonstrations, asking a question that enraged Burton.

"I would like to put a question to Governor Brown," Nixon said. "On his ticket . . . are two candidates, O'Connell and Burton, who helped lead the riots against the Committee on Un-American Activities when it met in San Francisco. Does he endorse them?"

Brown sidestepped the question, but Burton threatened to sue Nixon for slander and wrote retraction demands to every television and radio station that carried the debate. The *Chronicle*'s Squire Behrens, who had been furnished an advance text of Nixon's questions, immediately spotted it and told Nixon he should not ask that question because it was inaccurate. But Nixon did it anyway. To his credit, Behrens reported the next day that Nixon's effort to link Brown to Burton and O'Connell and the HUAC violence was "out of bounds" because neither man had been at the scene.[29]

Burton's lifelong interest in civil liberties led him to join Criminal Procedure, a new committee that O'Connell and Blease talked Ralph Brown into setting up with O'Connell as chairman. In return, the liberals delivered their votes to Brown for speaker. The committee's jurisdiction covered everything remotely connected to the Bill of Rights: anti-communism, civil liberties, the death penalty, police powers, pornography, and other land-mine issues for Democrats in a state where such issues often defeated them. The point was to put a few staunch liberals on a committee to kill "bad" legislation early.

By not allowing such legislation to ever get to the floor, the committee protected the rest of the Democrats from ever having to be recorded voting on polarizing issues. In effect, the entire assembly was reduced to four liberals. Brown even let O'Connell name them. Without a fifth vote, the four liberals could not report out their own measures that might embarrass the leadership. But they could block the bills they hated—those that conservative religious groups might bring to ban books, the district attorneys association might bring to expand the death penalty or right-wing groups might bring to curtail free speech in the name of preventing "Communist" agitation. They also killed a lot of crime bills.

For young attorneys like Jerry Waldie and Nick Petris, serving on this committee with stalwarts like O'Connell, Burton, and Crown was an education in constitutional rights and Machiavellian tactics. The Los Angeles Elks Club, for example, pushed a bill requiring capital punishment for drug dealers convicted of selling any amount of drugs, even one marijuana cigarette. The Elks showed up at the Criminal Procedure Committee and dumped petitions containing two million signatures supporting it. The district attorneys association publicly supported the bill, but even this law and order group privately told committee members it would be a disaster. "Please kill this bill," they told O'Connell. "We will never get a conviction. No jury will convict a seventeen-year-old kid of selling one reefer if it means the death penalty." The committee complied.

The committee even sabotaged its own speaker. When Ralph Brown introduced a bill to ban pornography, the liberals watered it down with amendments and reported it to the floor, where it passed. But when it came back from the senate with even more amendments, Brown no longer liked the bill. He asked O'Connell to appoint a conference to work out the differences; Brown didn't care about the details so long as the bill still carried his name. O'Connell stacked the new committee by putting the most liberal members from both houses on it, except for Burton, whom he was saving for a juicier role.

Coleman Blease, meanwhile, now lobbying for the ACLU, found a California Supreme Court case upholding the right to publish Henry Miller's controversial and sexually explicit *Tropic of Cancer*. The court had sustained a California obscenity law by ruling that nothing was obscene unless it was "utterly without redeeming social importance," a stunningly broad definition. Blease brought it to O'Connell's attention, and O'Connell promptly wrote the court's language into the bill. As a consequence, the Brown bill contained onerous penalties, but its broad definition of obscenity virtually guaranteed that few would ever be charged, much less convicted. O'Connell then took the bill—with its unanimous conference report—to the assembly floor.

Here Burton and O'Connell indulged their passion for subterfuge to the hilt. O'Connell would ask for an aye vote, while Burton raged against the bill's penalties. The ensuing furor would distract legislators from recognizing it for the civil libertarian legislation it was. The smokescreen worked perfectly.

"I want you to oppose it and point to the terrible penalties for booksellers," O'Connell told Burton. "If you do that, this bill will sail." Burton happily did what he was told. Lou Francis, who tried without success to get a far tougher anti-pornography bill passed the year before—only to have O'Connell's committee bottle it up—then supported the bill, not realizing what was in it. The legislation passed and went to the governor to sign. Few people ever understood what happened. But the Criminal Procedure Committee, under the guise of passing anti-pornography legislation, worked with the ACLU to fashion one of the most liberal interpretations of obscenity in the nation, and the U.S. Supreme Court cited California's law in several of its later decisions.[30]

. . .

Despite Burton's reputation, it wasn't always partisan politics every waking moment. He often acted out of loyalty and friendship, sometimes even whimsy, and made friends with his opponents. One day, for example, a young Republican senator from Ventura named Robert Lagomarsino came before Criminal Procedure with a dozen bills. There were not enough members for a full hearing, so Burton suggested they meet as a subcommittee and "make recommendations" on his bills. When the senator agreed, Burton shot down every one. That night, Lagomarsino was sitting with George Miller near the dance floor atop the El Mirador Hotel when Burton came over and—seemingly without shame—asked Lagomarsino's wife for several dances. Later, as the Lagomarsinos were leaving, Burton said, "You know, I've been thinking. Two of those bills were pretty good. Come back tomorrow and we'll pass them."

Lagomarsino dutifully trooped back into the committee hearing room the next day, and Burton began giving him a hard time again. "Mr. Burton," he protested. "Last night you said you would vote for two of these bills."

"Yes," Burton said, pausing for a moment and smiling. "But the wrong member of your family is the author." Thinking quickly, Lagomarsino said, "Yes, but the right member of my family is in the back of the room." Everyone turned around to look at his wife.

"Okay," said Burton. "I had two dances. I move two bills."

That was the beginning of a weird friendship between the liberal Democrat from San Francisco and the conservative Republican from Ventura that lasted for the rest of Burton's life. Lagomarsino got elected to Congress in 1974 and was assigned to the House Committee on Interior and Insular Affairs, where he provided key Republican support for Burton's bills, some of the most important environmental legislation of the twentieth century.[31]

5

AB 59

It was a great bill. The scope, the generosity, was so huge. . . .
It was the greatest stunt I ever saw in the California Senate.

FORMER SENATOR JOSEPH RATTIGAN

He was intolerable when drunk, and he was paranoid and he drove you
crazy. The only way to get him to go away was to agree with what he
wanted. He got cooperation by being constantly irritating, but you never
sensed you were giving in to the forces of evil. Maybe to an SOB,
but also to the poor, the disabled, the vulnerable.

HALE CHAMPION
former California finance director

The Burton-Unruh relationship was like the sort that the King of France
tried to maintain with the King or Queen of England. They respected and
enjoyed each other's company. But they discovered that Sacramento was not
big enough for both of them, and each could mean political death to the other.

LEE NICHOLS
former Unruh aide

As DEMOCRATIC LEGISLATIVE majorities widened and Phillip Burton gained valuable on-the-job experience, it was inevitable that he and Jesse Unruh, two giant egos, immensely powerful personalities, and clever politicians would collide in the assembly and in the Democratic Party.

But first they had important business to conduct together: a partisan redistricting of the state following the 1960 elections. Both men had specific career objectives directly related to redistricting. Unruh moved up the assembly ranks carefully, plotting his path to the speakership. Burton, meanwhile, steeped himself in the reform politics of the California Democratic Council, refined and expanded his base in San Francisco as he planned his next career move to Washington, and made himself the undisputed expert on welfare reform in California. That expertise produced the most important and lasting change in state welfare in the entire postwar era—a bill known as AB 59— and Burton repeatedly got the better of Unruh when they clashed.

There was never any question that Unruh would become speaker, the state's second most powerful official after the governor. The only question was when. By the late 1950s, Unruh was supplying campaign money to grateful Democratic challengers. When they arrived in Sacramento, they owed him. He had learned, as he put it later, that "money is the mother's milk of politics." Thousands of campaign dollars came in from savings and loan tycoon Howard Ahmanson, the oil industry, and other business lobbies. Unruh rationalized his reliance on these contributions with another often-quoted aphorism about lobbyists: "If you can't eat their food, drink their booze, screw their women and then vote against them, you don't belong here."

By 1960, Unruh was meeting weekly with his close friends at the El Mirador to plot strategy. He chaired Ways and Means, which originated all state money bills. Tom Rees, the former World War II infantryman, succeeded him as chairman of Finance and Insurance, and Bob Crown chaired Elections and Reapportionment, which helped determine the fate of every state and federal legislator. Those three committees represented an awesome power base. Other members of the Praetorian Guard included Nicholas Petris of Oakland, Tom Bane of the San Fernando Valley, and Majority Leader Bill Munnell. Jack Knox of Richmond joined them after the 1960 elections.

Ralph Brown was speaker, but Unruh was the moving force, the man who was putting Governor Brown's program into law and guiding his budget through the house, while taking care of his corporate donors. With cross-filing eliminated entirely in 1958, the 1960 elections that put John Kennedy in the White House also increased the Democratic majority in the assembly to 47-33 and elevated Unruh to power in national political circles. Governor Brown ran as a favorite son in the 1960 California presidential primary. At the national convention in Los Angeles, he released his delegates, many of them CDC activists who supported Adlai Stevenson, to vote their conscience, a move that enraged the Kennedy forces.

Unruh, meanwhile, worked vigorously to line up delegates for Kennedy. When Kennedy was elected, his White House—angry with Brown's lack of support—quickly decided that Unruh, not Brown, was the man who could get things done in California. Unruh's convention role also cemented the CDC's undying hostility to him. Disgusted by Kennedy's strong-arm tactics at Stevenson's expense, many thought Unruh represented the worst aspects of ruthless, anti-democratic boss rule.

But even as his confidence grew, the normally swaggering Unruh revealed uncharacteristic self doubts. His identity disguised as Assemblyman X, Unruh told Lester Velie, the same reporter who exposed Artie Samish years earlier, that he worried whether he was selling out. In a 1960 *Reader's Digest* article, Unruh said: "This is my dilemma: If I had stayed away from the lobbyists I would have been ineffective. If I take their money and give them nothing for it, I am a cheat. If I do their bidding, I could be cheating the public. I find myself rationalizing what I have done. The tragedy is that I may wind up serving the very elements I set out to beat—yet not even know that I have changed."[1]

Unruh, moreover, was letting his prodigious appetites for food, drink, and sex, much of it supplied by lobbyists, run wild. Like Samish, Unruh ballooned up to nearly 300 pounds, earning the nickname "Big Daddy" after the rotund character in Tennessee Williams's popular play of the period, *Cat on a Hot Tin Roof.* Women were attracted to Unruh because of the aura of power that surrounded him, and it was common for him to bed several in a single night of prowling. He courted high-priced call girls, whom he dispatched to "deserving" assemblymen. When people spotted the long black Lincoln with the phone in the back seat parked at the El Mirador, they knew Jess had invited his friend, a prominent San Francisco hooker, to Sacramento to do some persuading.

The large Democratic majority and the chance to add eight new congressional seats in the 1961 reapportionment gave Unruh a perfect opportunity to convert all of his substantial assets into a bid for the speakership. Reapportionment was the process by which the state legislature every ten years drew new boundaries for the assembly's eighty districts to reflect population growth. As California grew, its share of congressional seats also grew at the expense of other states whose population declined or did not grow as quickly. With Pat Brown guaranteed to sign the bill, the Democrats had their first opportunity in modern times to create a partisan plan or "gerrymander" to maximize their gains. The Republicans had done the same thing to the Democrats following the 1950 census.

Through redistricting, Unruh drew safe districts for Democrat and Republican incumbents alike in return for commitments to vote for him for speaker.[2] While Unruh was redrawing Los Angeles County, Crown did the

East Bay, Bane the San Fernando Valley, Jim Mills San Diego, and Burton San Francisco. One day, committee staffer Lou Angelo spread two maps of Los Angeles County on the floor of Crown's office. One showed all the existing boundaries. The second overlay map showed proposed boundaries. Using a pointer, and padding around in his socks, Unruh said, "Look, Bobby, this is what we're doing in L.A. County." The number of Republican districts Unruh gutted to make new Democratic ones was impressive. "Nice work, Jess," Crown said.[3]

The speakership was almost his. All that remained to cement it for Unruh was to move Ralph Brown out of the job, which turned out to be easy. Brown himself carried the bill establishing a new state Court of Appeal in his home town of Fresno. Brown and Unruh then persuaded Pat Brown to appoint Ralph Brown to the new court. Speaker Pro Tem Carlos Bea—Unruh's only serious opponent—was supposed to assume the office automatically. But Unruh maneuvered to change assembly rules to require a caucus vote. Once Unruh added GOP votes to his total, opposition all but vanished.

On September 30, 1961, Unruh was elected speaker and sworn in by "Justice" Ralph Brown. Despite their rivalry, Burton voted for Unruh and worked closely with Crown and Unruh to fashion the 1961 Democratic gerrymander. He dove into redistricting with such intensity that he soon knew more about the new districts than anyone else, including the technical consultants. They loved to speak in code about reapportionment, which they called "reappo," Burton most of all. During a committee meeting, Burton turned to Crown and said in mock seriousness, "No reappo popo for Reepo oppo," meaning, "No reapportionment population data for the Republican opposition."[4]

Unruh and Burton were not getting in each other's way, at least not in 1961, for each had different plans. Burton ceded Sacramento to Big Daddy and used "reappo" to create a congressional seat for himself. Burton even did some of Unruh's dirty work. He brought members into his office, showed them their new boundaries and said, "I know your district better than you do. Believe me, this is the best you can get, especially if we maximize Democratic numbers." When one member who wanted to chair the Education Committee complained, Burton fixed his glare and said, "If you don't vote for this bill, I don't see you as chairman of Education next year." The man blanched—and voted for it.[5]

"Dear Phil," Unruh wrote Burton on October 13, two weeks after his election. "Just a note to tell you how much I appreciate your unswerving support. . . . As you well know, it began a long way back. You were there all the way."[6]

It was one thing not to get in each other's way, quite another to be close. Burton was never part of Unruh's inner circle. He was not a team player, and Unruh never felt he could be trusted. In April 1961, Burton said he saw nothing wrong with labor unions picketing the homes of assembly members to "express their views" on legislation. Hospital workers—part of George Hardy's growing labor empire—had just done precisely that, which infuriated Unruh and other legislators. They killed a bill, just to show that such tactics were out of bounds, that would have permitted hospital workers to unionize.[7]

Worse from Unruh's point of view, Burton had long been a champion of the CDC, the maverick and progressive arm of the state party. Unruh resisted Burton's efforts to push everything to the left and thought CDC ideologues and their legislative heroes were on suicide missions that could destroy his party's majority. His job was to protect assembly Democrats and thus his speakership. CDC activists might be great at debating left-wing resolutions at conventions, but Unruh believed they alienated moderate-conservative blue-collar Democrats who came from Oklahoma, Texas, or Missouri to find the good life.

But Unruh could not afford to ignore Burton and despaired at his rival's pervasive influence and uncanny ability to sniff out high-level strategy sessions to which he was not invited. If there was a knock on the door, Unruh would say, "It's Phil. He can sense a meeting taking place." Unruh did not believe Burton was a rival for speaker, but he never wanted to let Burton outsmart him. To Larry Margolis, his top aide, Unruh usually began any conversation with, "That fucking Phil Burton did this," or "That goddam Burton wants that."

Margolis, who shielded Unruh from Burton's tirades as much as he could, found Burton obnoxious. "Saliva would pop out of his mouth while he told you what a prick you were and how he would get even, even as he was looking over your shoulder counting the house," Margolis recalled many years later.[8] He got his face so close to people that he totally intimidated them. It was a technique that Lyndon Johnson, another politician who mastered the art of personal persuasion, used often.

Unruh wasted little time consolidating his own power. With a personal slush fund from which he could dispense cash, he took the Samish model and moved it from the third house to his own office. This sometimes caused problems. Unruh almost got into a fistfight on the assembly floor after an especially successful fundraising dinner in Los Angeles. Vernon Kilpatrick, a Southern California assemblyman, attacked Unruh for opposing a legislative pay raise. Referring to the previous night's take, Kilpatrick said, "Certain benefits accrue to the Speaker that don't accrue to other members." Bristling, Unruh said none of that money was for his personal use.

"If you're a good boy, Mr. Kilpatrick," Unruh added, with characteristic swagger, "you might get some of those campaign funds."

"I don't know about that," Kilpatrick responded, "but I'd like to be your treasurer." At that point, the two men had to be separated.[9]

Unruh dispensed perks to keep his members happy. If a legislator wanted to go to Washington, Unruh signed the travel voucher, permitting fifteen cents a mile. A 6,000 mile round trip came to $900. Minus the $300 plane fare, that put $600 in the legislator's pocket. But if someone crossed Unruh, as Republican Bill Bagley occasionally did, he paid the price. Unruh, who could be thoroughly petty, denied Bagley's secretary a new typewriter, even though the keys were broken on hers.

While his loyalists rejoiced at Unruh's climb to power and his ability to get things done, others found Unruh's increasingly autocratic exercise of power threatening. "I won't have that little Nero stomping around on my floor," fumed George Miller, who had risen to chair the powerful senate Finance Committee.

Unruh believed that information and knowledge equaled power, and he set out to ensure that elected officials were able to get the data and expertise they needed to be effective. Information-starved legislators were at a perpetual disadvantage because they were dependent on lobbyists who always supplied facts and figures that benefited their clients. The governor's office, moreover, had an entire executive branch to compile data he needed to make policy. To correct that imbalance, Unruh very deliberately began to professionalize the assembly, hiring more and better trained staff, permitting members larger budgets to hire their own aides, expanding the number of interns.

This was probably Unruh's greatest legacy. There had been a rash of articles about the ineffectiveness of "horse and buggy" state legislatures throughout the nation, anachronisms unable to deal with modern needs and a postwar population explosion. Unruh helped move California into the modern era. Under Governor Brown, California was embarking on major programs for water, schools, higher education, and freeways. Every day some 1,600 new people—one a minute—arrived in the state, equaling in population a city the size of Hanford or Yuba City once a week, Modesto or Ontario once a month, Oakland or San Diego once a year.[10]

Part of Unruh's motivation was empire building. Bigger and better staff gave him a more equal footing with which to compete with the governor and the lobbyists. But it was also undeniably good government to wean legislators from their near-total reliance on lobbyists. Between 1959 and 1966, the number of permanent assembly staff grew by 1,100 percent, from five employees to sixty. They were assigned to committees, to a new Assembly Office of Research, to the Republican staff, to a legislative reference service, and to general management and operation of the house. This number did not count another eighty administrative assistants, one for each member, plus secretaries, who operated offices in the member's district. The new assembly staffers were paid salaries competitive with those of beginning college professors, and, except for the district aides, were usually hired from college teaching, journalism, or private industry.[11] Unruh and Margolis took this task seriously, but Burton thought it was a waste of time. All he wanted was to know which lever to pull. The old legislature was just fine with him, as long as he could manipulate it.

But new staff positions also permitted Burton to hire more people. At a time when legislative staff was almost entirely white, he appointed Lim P. Lee as his district director and hired an Asian woman, Anabel Whang, as his secretary. Burton also accepted a brilliant young UC Berkeley graduate named Tom Joe as his Ford Foundation intern. Joe was a blind Korean-American whose mentor was famed Berkeley professor Jacobus tenBroek. A blind lawyer who chaired the UC Speech Department, tenBroek was a constitutional scholar who was close to Earl Warren and who helped found the National Federation of the Blind. He was chairman of the militantly liberal Welfare Appeals Board, which often embarrassed the Department of Social Welfare by overturning decisions that had denied people welfare benefits. A superb teacher, tenBroek also motivated Coleman Blease to switch from engineering to law.

Fearing Joe was a Berkeley "radical," Margolis shunted him to the Social Welfare Committee, where he mistakenly believed the young intern could not do much damage. But putting Joe together with Burton, Margolis realized later, after their collaboration on AB 59, "was like putting the match to hydrogen."

Burton also wanted a black secretary. A black lawyer on Governor Brown's staff, objecting to what he saw as Burton's tokenism, recommended a young woman named Martha Gorman but did not tell him she was white. Burton hired her by phone. Word quickly spread that Burton had hired a "Negro." Burton was not in Sacramento during Gorman's first few days on the job.

When he arrived, he looked her up and down, went into his office, and slammed the door. Other legislators drifted in, making comments Gorman did not understand. One of the assembly's two blacks, Byron Rumford, went into Burton's office, shook his head and said, "She ain't one of us." Only weeks later, when Burton's law partner Joe Williams asked her some detailed questions did Gorman finally realize she had been recommended partly to teach her boss a lesson.[12]

Burton's efforts to build an extensive San Francisco political operation ran into repeated problems. He wanted to control whatever political apparatus existed, including the county central committee, where he could groom young people for office. The committee had little power, but it almost destroyed Burton's career twice, and he was determined to keep it out of hostile hands. He also had to contend with a new rival Democratic faction led by state Senator Eugene McAteer and his protégé, an energetic young lawyer named Leo McCarthy, who had walked precincts for Burton in 1954 and 1956 while a University of San Francisco law student. Inheritors of the once-formidable Malone machine, they were more progressive than Malone had been, but they were organization Democrats, not CDC-backed reformers. In 1960, they defeated Burton for chairman of the county committee by one vote. The winner, Emmett Hagarty, so feared losing control that he did not convene it for two years.

But working out of Sacramento and San Francisco, Burton became adept at training and encouraging new political talent. Over the next few years, he brought into public office a trio of young, smart, like-minded loyalists, including brother John, who began important careers that would last for decades and significantly shape California politics. One Burton protégé was attorney George Moscone, John Burton's best friend since childhood. While moonlighting as a playground director one weekend, Moscone asked his friend how one got to be a judge. Quoting Phillip, John said politics was the traditional route. Moscone and the elder Burton met for breakfast soon after, Burton firing nonstop questions at him about loyalty oaths, civil rights, and the death penalty. He liked what he heard and ran Moscone in the Twenty-first Assembly District in 1960. Moscone did well, although he lost to a liberal Republican first-termer named Milton Marks. (Moscone was elected to the board of supervisors in 1963.)

Another protégé was Willie Brown, a young black attorney. Arriving from Mineola, Texas, with virtually nothing in 1951, Brown fought his way into San Francisco State College, where he became close to John Burton and worked as a janitor to support himself for two years. Together, they joined the Young Democrats, where Brown met Phil Burton, Joe Williams, Carlton Goodlett, and other activists. After college, Brown attended Hastings College of the Law. He began his law practice in San Francisco's Western Addition, where most of his early clients were hookers or pimps. Brown badly wanted a seat in the assembly. At Burton's urging, he challenged longtime incumbent and Malone holdover Ed Gaffney.[13]

Gaffney, a small man who wore wire-rim glasses and a neatly trimmed mustache, was considered a joke. Between his loss of diction, a touch of senility, and poorly fitting dentures, he sounded like a Greyhound Bus announcer. Gaffney gave only one floor speech a year—on Mother's Day. Whenever Gaffney saw a black person in the back of the assembly, he would rush back, thrust out his hand, and say, "I'm Ed Gaffney. You must be from my district."

Hoping to ease Willie Brown's task, Burton tried to sweet-talk Gaffney, seventy-six, into retiring. He introduced a bill to raise the maximum pension from $375 a month to $475 a month. But Gaffney, first elected in 1940, refused. "Clutching a small black briar between his dentures," Sydney Kossen wrote in the *News*, Gaffney "looked up at Burton and sputtered, 'That bill of yours won't ever get out of committee.'" Gaffney told Kossen, "He thinks he can get me to retire. Well, I won't do it. I'll retire when I'm good and ready."[14]

While his friends Moscone and Brown were running for office, John Burton was running for cover. During the 1962 primary, he was arrested in a downtown parking lot for bookmaking. As noted in the *San Francisco Examiner* account (and carefully placed in the burgeoning FBI file on Phillip Burton), John was busted after phoning in a bet on a horse named Legal Beagle. The twenty-nine-year-old deputy state attorney general had been collecting and paying off bets there for several months, the parking lot attendant told police, who put the lot under surveillance after getting tipped off. "It's all a ghastly mistake. I don't know what this is all about," John told police. Later he told reporters, "It's doomsville on a flick." John Burton was released on $1,050 bail and acquitted when the judge agreed with the Burton defense: the race had been run *before* Burton placed the call. Moscone, his lawyer, reportedly told the arresting officer, "I'm not getting paid for this. The party's making me do it."[15]

While Burton put his acolytes in place, other Democrats hatched their own plans, which often interfered with Burton's effort to control every political move in his city. In one such instance, John O'Connell wanted to go to Washington after eight years in the assembly and decided to challenge GOP incumbent Bill Mailliard. "I don't want to be be playing God on this, but I just don't think you should do it," Burton told him. O'Connell dismissed Burton's "advice," figuring that Burton wanted to get there first.

By vacating his assembly seat, O'Connell touched off a Democratic free-for-all in the primary. Burton had his own candidate, aide Frank Kieliger. But O'Connell supported another liberal Democrat, Bill Carpenter. Many CDC activists, put off by years of Burton's domineering style, were fed up with his bullying and supported Carpenter. But a third candidate, a deputy state attorney general named John Foran, McCarthy's best friend since seminary and USF Law School, represented the McAteer-McCarthy faction.[16] Kieliger and Carpenter split the liberal vote. Foran won the primary and the seat.

In the other assembly primary, the CDC activists were unified and worked hard to elect Willie Brown. But he came up just short, losing to Gaffney by 900 votes out of more than 22,000 votes cast. Hoping to neutralize Burton, the McCarthy faction supported Gaffney. Unruh also sent money to Foran and Gaffney to stop Burton. The now perennial Burton-McCarthy fight for chairman of the county committee played out on the same June 1962 ballot. The candidates were Moscone and a lawyer named Don King, handpicked by Leo McCarthy. An intense fight ensued. King beat Moscone by one vote. Chairmanship of the county committee eluded Burton yet again. After this vote, Unruh attempted to use the committee to destroy Burton a third time. In the congressional race, Mailliard beat O'Connell. In part, O'Connell blamed Burton for his loss, believing that Burton did nothing to help him.

Despite the many obstacles and elements he could not control, Burton's obsession with politics never waned. One night during the 1962 battles, Phil, Sala, John Burton, and Martha Gorman had dinner at a café next to the campaign headquarters. Phillip was trying to read, but Sala kept interrupting, interrogating everyone over how the day's precinct walk had gone. Sala kept nudging him, saying, "You hear that? You hear that?" Finally, he exploded.

"Goddam it, Sala!" he said, slamming his fist on the table. "Would you please shut up and let me enjoy my dinner. All I've done for the last six months is eat, sleep, and breathe politics. I just want to relax and read." With that he turned back to his magazine, which was about the 1960 Kennedy-Nixon campaign.[17]

It was not surprising that Unruh helped Burton's Democratic rivals. Unruh believed Democrats would remain the dominant party in California for many years to come, particularly after Governor Brown trounced Richard Nixon to win a second term in 1962. He also maintained that Brown had promised to support him for governor in 1966—a promise Brown denied ever making. Unruh believed that if he lost weight, cleaned up his "Big Daddy" image and behaved, he could be governor in 1966. Unruh's top aides concluded that only one Democrat—Phil Burton—had the talent to stand between Unruh and that goal. As much as they admired his brilliance, they also hated him for it and for his leadership in CDC, the one statewide organization with the troops to make life difficult. Unruh was not worried that Burton wanted to run for governor himself. But as a tactician and strategist who—like Unruh—wanted to dominate Democratic politics in California, Burton was a rival nonetheless. So Unruh struck first. The first target was CDC. The second was Burton himself.

Unruh went after CDC in two ways. At the August 1962 state party convention, he introduced a resolution requiring the Democratic Party or any group with the name "Democrat" (the CDC, just to name one) to deny membership to any member of the Communist Party, the John Birch Society, "or any other totalitarian group." This was a direct attack on Burton and the party's left wing. Burton objected, but Unruh lieutenant Tom Bane gaveled him down. George Miller argued that a "witch hunt" could destroy the party. The combined strength of Communists and Birchers "couldn't hit a loud foul in a Class D League," he said. After protracted procedural battles, the resolution died for lack of a quorum.

Writing under the pseudonym "Able Dart" in the *liberal democrat*, a monthly magazine published by Burton friends Tom Winnett and Marshall Windmiller, activist Bert Coffey described the fallout from Unruh's attack with bitter invective, making it clear just how much the CDC despised Unruh:

> We had heard that "Big Daddy" went before Resolutions to urge passage of a resolution that would have the effect of setting up his private un-American activities committee. We learned that Unruh placed his personal power as "The Collector" behind this move. . . . The Speaker was going to shape the Democratic Party. He was going to set up an apparatus that could wreck party organization unless it went his way. He has the power to collect money and disburse it. With the filthy rich savings and loan industry in his pocket and many members of the Third House turning money over to him, Big Daddy needed one more thing: organization down below.
>
> With no base outside the Assembly and no mass base among voters,

with the Governor resentful of him, with every constitutional officer in contempt of him, he needs mass organization, a ladder to climb over a lot of bodies into the governor's chair four years hence. The way to do it, he would think, is to buy CDC—or destroy it. And something like CDC is harder to buy than to destroy.

In the same issue of the *liberal democrat*, co-editors Winnett and Windmiller said if Unruh's resolution had passed, "the club movement would have exploded and the fallout would have landed primarily on the governor." That would have weakened Brown and the CDC, who, with Burton, were Unruh's biggest impediments to controlling state politics. "Unruh's power play," they wrote, "may turn out to be Big Daddy's biggest mistake, for his prestige has been damaged and the forces aligned against him have been broadened and strengthened. Unruh has now shown that he . . . can be a loser."[18]

Unruh did lose that round. But he came back early in 1963 with another ploy that made explicit his desire to destroy the CDC and thereby keep Pat Brown from a third term. The means was AB 2922, which became known as the "truth in endorsements" bill. It required any candidate who used primary endorsements from volunteer groups such as the CDC to put a disclaimer on all campaign literature in large type saying the endorsement was "unofficial." The idea was again to weaken the CDC by de-fanging its most potent weapon: the pre-primary endorsement. Unruh pushed the bill through the assembly 45 to 28. This was not easy to do in a body in which many of the members had been elected by virtue of the CDC pre-primary endorsement. It passed the senate by 1 vote. Unruh arrived to twist arms on the senate floor from a formal dinner, still wearing his tuxedo.

Unruh forced Brown to sign the bill by bottling up the governor's bill to outlaw capital punishment. The *liberal democrat* said Unruh's bill could be "the biggest threat to the CDC since its founding." CDC President Tom Carvey told the *Los Angeles Times*, "It was Jesse Unruh who threw down this political gauntlet and dared anyone to challenge his power. It is Unruh—a man driven by an insatiable lust for political power—who gambles recklessly with the future of the Democratic Party faced with a vital 1964 election." Calling on volunteers to resist, Carvey said, "We will not wait or stand by idly and allow Unruh bossism to injure California."[19]

While Unruh was battling the CDC, Burton was giving the assembly leadership fits. A debacle involving DuPont investors typified his antics. It began when a DuPont company plant manager in his district asked Majority

Leader Jerome Waldie to introduce a bill to give tax relief to DuPont stock-holders in California. The request arose out of a Supreme Court antitrust decision that required DuPont to divest itself of its one-fourth interest in General Motors and to distribute that stock to its stockholders. Congress already gave these stockholders a federal tax break. Waldie's AB 652 would have permitted them to treat the dividends as capital gains on their state taxes, a loophole worth $5.75 million. When Waldie tried to sneak it through, Burton killed it, calling the measure "unconscionable tax relief" to DuPont stockholders, whose average holdings in California each amounted to $30,000. In a play on his frequent bills to increase "aid to needy children," Burton asked his colleagues to stop Waldie's "aid to needy DuPont stock-holders" bill.

Burton also infuriated state senators. He was the only Northern California legislator to endorse Proposition 23 on the November 1962 ballot. It would have given substantial power to urban lawmakers at the expense of rural senators. Before "one man, one vote" court rulings, there were huge differences in the number of constituents these senators represented. While Tom Rees of Los Angeles represented nearly seven million voters in his Thirty-eighth District, Stephen Teale represented only 29,000 voters in his three rural counties of Mariposa, Tuolumne, and Calaveras. Yet each had an equal vote.

Rural legislators from the so-called "cow counties" in the north and east dominated the upper body, and they had little incentive to address major urban problems of crime, welfare, transportation, or civil rights. Thirty-four of the forty senators were rural and only six were urban. Those six senators—15 percent of the senate—represented 64 percent of the state's population. To correct this imbalance (which the Supreme Court later found unconstitutional), activists qualified Proposition 23. Had it passed, it would have increased the number of senators from forty to fifty, thus giving the state's urban areas ten more seats.

Liberal Democrats from Southern California had obvious reasons for supporting the initiative (the senate had not been redistricted in thirty years), but so did Burton. In 1961, the upper chamber killed seventy-two labor and civil rights bills. A good number of them were his, including anti-discrimination and minimum wage bills.[20] When the 1963 legislative session began, Senate President Pro Tem Hugh Burns of Fresno decided to pay Burton back for supporting Proposition 23. Burns referred every one of his bills to the ultraconservative Governmental Efficiency Committee, commonly called "the graveyard," because so many bills died there.

It was against this backdrop—the anti-welfare senate angry at him for supporting a measure to curtail its power, Unruh fearing him as his principal political threat in the state, and Waldie furious that he torpedoed Waldie's DuPont bill—that Phil Burton pulled off one of the most astonishing legislative feats of his career. The bill was called AB 59. It began as a minor piece of legislation. But when it finally passed four months later, it contained the most important and costly changes in the history of the state welfare system. Three decades later, people in Sacramento still marveled at Burton's skill in getting it through a legislature determined to kill it. A bill that raised welfare benefits as much as AB 59 did would have been hard enough had Burton been popular with his colleagues. That so many hated him and yet still voted for AB 59 illustrated his legislative brilliance—and a good deal of flat out deceit. It was one man making something happen that never would have happened otherwise.

AB 59 was important for other reasons. It became the prototype for huge, immensely complicated legislation Burton sponsored time and again in Congress, whether for federal welfare programs, black lung benefits, minimum-wage increases, or the most extensive and complex environmental preservation laws of his era. Among legislators, only he had the technical competence and endurance to spend months or years buried in often arcane details, the political know-how to put legislative packages together, and the almost obsessive ability to keep track of all the moving parts.

Such legislation also perfectly suited Burton's temperament. His adult patterns were now firmly established. Whether scheming to take over USC student government or the Young Democrats, push aside Bill Malone and dominate San Francisco politics, or become the most effective and powerful advocate for labor and the poor that Sacramento had ever seen, Burton never deviated from his compulsive, workaholic habits. In his drive to reform the state's welfare system, as in his later legislative schemes, he was aided and abetted by Sala Burton, who was as hardworking and as political an animal as her husband. Phil Burton had no other interests outside of politics—no children, no recreation, no down time. He no longer cared about sports. He never cared about money. He had no interest in friends, other than as allies or a means to his political ends. And he certainly did not care whether people liked him.

His anger was buried just under the surface. He appeared to use alcohol as a form of self-medication, a tranquilizer that allowed him to unwind and relax at the end of one grueling day after another. But when he drank to excess, frequently his custom late at night, the alcohol sometimes let out the inchoate rage—at injustice, at colleagues he believed had "sold out," and perhaps at his absent and withholding father, his emotionally deprived childhood, and difficult family life. Under no circumstances could he permit himself to slow down or even be alone. A quiet or reflective moment might summon the twin demons of hurt and abandonment—and that would be intolerable.

Years later, as he got closer to the pinnacle of power in Washington, Burton's alcohol-induced rages proved devastating to his career. But for now, the rage was mostly tactical. He could channel it for political effect, intimidate people and bend them to his will. And besides, he was always working for the best of causes. Ever the angry outsider, the rebel leftist storming the gates, the man to whom the conventional levers of power would always be denied, Burton was determined to create his own path to power. He had become the perfect blend of his inner needs and political will. He kept his demons at bay through unrelenting work, superior intellect, and sometimes frightening personal force. That combination produced a better life for many people who needed all the help they could get. AB 59 was the first major vehicle.

While Jesse Unruh and his "boys" went prowling in the evenings, Burton usually worked late into the night. Often, he was poring over raw computer data from the State Department of Welfare and processing it into welfare case loads, annual budgets county by county, and estimates of eligible state recipients.

California's welfare program had six components. The first five—Medical Assistance to the Aged (MAA) and Aid to the Aged, Blind, Children, and Disabled—all received different proportions of federal, state, and county tax dollars. The sixth, County General Relief, was paid entirely from county funds. But county welfare costs were soaring and taxpayers were angry. Burton was ahead of almost everybody in figuring out how to shift these programs around to take advantage of new federal laws that, when properly understood, could require the federal government to pay a higher share. That involved getting welfare recipients off county relief and into state and federal programs.

Burton and welfare specialist Tom Joe became experts on how to maximize federal welfare aid and then pass the increases directly to recipients. If, for example, a welfare recipient was getting $100 a month, $55 in state money, $45 in federal money, Burton and Joe wrote legislation (which took advantage of new federal welfare regulations) to recalculate the formulas or the level or type of benefits, forcing the federal government to match the $55 state grant. As a result, the recipient got $110 a month. These tricks infuriated state Finance Director Hale Champion. He wanted the state to keep some of that extra $10 to cover administrative costs. When the Department of Finance tried to take its share, Burton and Joe blocked them. Only a handful of people in the state knew this game was even going on.

"Phil, we're with you," Champion pleaded. "But show some restraint. If you pass it all through [to recipients], you're going to lose political support."[21] But Burton was determined that recipients get every penny. What tax lawyers did for wealthy clients—maximize their income through clever loopholes and manipulation of federal regulations—was exactly what Burton and Joe were doing for welfare recipients. They learned immensely technical regulations and then translated them into new state law for maximum advantage. The difference was that Burton's and Joe's "clients" were the state's poorest residents.

Burton's immersion in the technical details of federal/state welfare matches and categorical aid programs fit his lifelong pattern. With his enormously retentive mind and overpowering style, he mastered a subject and then dominated any situation he could anticipate by knowing more about the politics—and the policy—than anyone else in the room. Unlike other politicians—who carved out broad areas of expertise and left the details to staff—Burton did it all. He knew his own bills down to the minutest detail. But he also studied his colleagues' legislation until he knew more about that than they did. Such knowledge gave him enormous power.

In 1961, while Burton was immersing himself in such details, Pat Brown established a Welfare Study Commission—one of a number of commissions to study state issues—to get a handle on welfare costs, which were climbing at a rate of half a billion dollars a year. The commission included Welfare Director John Wedemeyer—who also understood the federal/state match and who shared Burton's sympathies—several county district attorneys, welfare directors, and probation officers. Tom Joe attended the sessions, which were chaired by Winslow Christian, a Brown-appointed former judge and deputy state attorney general, whom Brown later appointed to head his Department of Health and Welfare. The legislators were Burton, his counterpart in the senate, Social Welfare Committee Chairman James Cobey, and Senator Luther Gibson, the rigidly conservative chairman of Governmental Efficiency (GE). Gibson's committee was dominated by the County Supervisors Association, another conservative, anti-welfare group representing primarily rural counties. The commission's two-year study concluded that the state welfare system was passive and haphazard. With proper direction and coordination, the state could increase federal money and widen eligibility for those who truly needed aid.

Surprisingly, given its political coloration, the commission also concluded that current welfare policies destroyed families. If an unemployed father lived at home with his family, existing law assumed he should be able to earn a living. That poor family was therefore not eligible for welfare (called Aid to Needy Children and later changed to Aid to Families of Dependent Children). The result: fathers left home so their families could eat. Worse, until Coleman Blease sued to stop the practice, county welfare officers sometimes raided homes late at night, looking under beds for errant fathers. The commission also found that under a "relatives responsibility" clause, elderly people could not qualify for welfare benefits unless their grown children contributed money to their parents' upkeep. And counties could file liens against the property of aged, blind, and disabled recipients in hospitals or nursing homes.

Some commission recommendations, including one that permitted needy families with unemployed fathers at home to qualify for aid, were highly controversial. Commissioners figured it would take ten years to write them into law. But Phil Burton decided to do it all in one year. All or nothing. He wanted to go to Congress in 1964 and had no time to waste.

On January 10, 1963, Burton introduced his first version of AB 59. At six pages, it was noncontroversial. For strategic reasons, he planned to sneak the guts of the bill in later. To say welfare was extremely unpopular with most legislators was an understatement. One could support needy children. But it was hard to support putting their able-bodied fathers on the dole. Politicians preferred to deal with almost any other subject. Burton was unpopular with his colleagues in part because he was always pushing welfare in their faces and forcing them to vote on it.

Burton's determination to increase aid to poor families was part of a well-developed political strategy, and he believed strongly that it was the right thing to do. But his campaign to craft and pass AB 59 may also have met some deep psychological need in a man who could empathize with fatherless families. Dr. Burton left his family for medical school, not because the state forced him to flee so his family could eat. Nonetheless, Burton knew firsthand how awful such separations could be. By permitting unemployed fathers to live at home and still collect welfare, a centerpiece of AB 59, Burton ensured that hundreds of thousands of poor children would not suffer the emotional deprivation he experienced. The state would keep families together, not separate them.

Burton had no intention of showing his hand early or pushing the bill he really wanted through an Unruh-led assembly that almost certainly would reject it. His plan was more audacious: keep it nonthreatening and then load it up in the senate—which was even more hostile. By the time it came back to the assembly for concurrence, Burton planned to unite so many constituencies behind the bill that most legislators had to vote for it. The forces he mobilized ranged from Dolores Huerta's farm workers and other unions to a powerful old-age lobbyist named George McClain, from the Catholic Church to disabled quadriplegics who arrived at the capitol in their wheelchairs. More remarkably, for a bill whose costs years later exceeded hundreds of millions dollars a year, it slipped through the assembly without ever being subjected to Ways and Means Committee hearings on its fiscal implications. How he managed all this is a case study of cunning and political intrigue.

Burton began by hiding the unemployed fathers provision in AB 23, a different bill. His strategy was to break this complicated legislation into smaller pieces, get support for the pieces and then blend them into the bigger bill. If they wanted any part of the package, legislators had to support all of it. Burton perfected the technique in his 1978 Omnibus Parks and Recreation Act and in his unabashedly partisan 1981 California reapportionment.

As he steered his package through the legislature, Burton had a major advantage: an archaic bill-writing procedure that made it virtually impossible to track complicated legislation as it evolved draft by draft. The first time a bill added or deleted language to an existing state code, the Legislative Counsel's digest appeared at the bottom of the first page to summarize what the bill would do. But in subsequent versions, the digest disappeared. Only the most conscientious legislators bothered to track down the author to find out how a bill was evolving. Additions to the code appeared in italics. Deletions were shown in strike-over. However—and this is what Burton most exploited—whenever the bill was amended, only the latest change appeared in italics or strike-over. On first reading, the bill might contain hundreds of changes that were immediately obvious. But if the next draft changed just one word, only that change was reflected. Everything else appeared in regular type. It was as if all the proposed changes save the latest were already in effect.

This was an especially neat trick if the author was deleting something controversial from the code, such as the statute that required relatives to contribute their own income to the care of aged parents who wanted state aid. In the first version, the code to be eliminated was in strike-over. In the second, it was simply deleted from the text. The first version of AB 59, for example, added language to the code declaring that welfare recipients could earn extra money without it being deducted from their welfare checks. This repealed Section 1509.6. Appearing in strike-over: "50 percent of the earnings of a needy child under the age of 18 years shall not be considered as income to the family unit in determining the amount of assistance." AB 59 permitted needy families to keep 100 percent of a child's earnings without having their welfare grants cut. But this provision was masked in language that simply said, "Section 1509.6 of said code is repealed." Few had any idea what this referred to.

Burton exploited this repeatedly. The only way anybody could follow precisely what he was doing was to maintain a complete set of every version of the bill in exact sequence and then track the changes. If the paragraphs were roughly the same length, and the words beginning and ending the sentence were also the same, it was impossible to know how Burton was changing the code. Even experts could not follow him. Burton also knew few of his colleagues ever bothered to read bills, let alone the changes. He relied on their underlying laziness and indifference. If legislators asked him what he was doing, he did not lie. But they had to know the precise questions to ask. No one did.

When AB 59 left the assembly for the senate on April 5, it had shrunk to twenty-nine innocuous lines. Now Burton faced an especially difficult obstacle. Because of President Pro Tem Burns's anti-Burton edict at the start of the session, AB 59 was headed to Gibson's committee, the "graveyard." Influencing that committee was going to be tough, given the members' antipathy to him.

Burns was also vice chairman of GE, which operated on consensus, and which usually met for a lobbyist-financed dinner in "executive session" the night before its public sessions. The committee arranged its business in secret, even orchestrated roll call votes. If Burton could get AB 59 out of the graveyard, it would go to Senate Finance, where Burton's one friend, Finance Chairman George Miller, would help him. But GE existed precisely to kill such wild-eyed legislation. Needing a friendly ally, Burton approached Dugald Gillies, Gibson's powerful committee consultant, and casually asked for a small favor.

"Look, I know I'm going to get a haircut over here," Burton told Gillies, knowing that virtually all of his bills would go nowhere. "But I'd like to get one bill." Gillies said he would talk to the committee about Burton's request. What he did not realize was that hidden in Burton's seemingly innocuous "one bill" would eventually be almost the entire ten-year agenda of the Welfare Study Commission and would change welfare policy in California for decades.

Gillies also told Burton he would check the bill's provisions with Bill McDougall, head of the powerful County Supervisors Association, whose members were complaining loudest about skyrocketing county welfare costs. Surprisingly, McDougall had no problem with it as long as the feds, rather than the counties, paid the hospital bills for the aged for the first thirty days. That was just part of what AB 59 did.

Among AB 59's most important provisions was "presumptive eligibility." If someone showed up at a welfare office, he was presumed eligible and would get payments immediately rather than waiting sixty days for an investigation. AB 59 also liberalized the definition of disability and broadened eligibility for tens of thousands of other people. It reunited families so that unemployed fathers could live at home while looking for work and still get AFDC payments. It eliminated relatives' responsibility. It increased monthly welfare payments to all categories of blind, aged, needy, and disabled people by exploiting the federal "match."

Federal law made welfare an entitlement, meaning anyone who met eligibility requirements was entitled to it, and the government was legally obligated to pay it. AB 59 extended this entitlement to state and county assistance as well. The bill also prohibited counties from taking liens on the property of the aged, blind, and disabled who were getting medical care in county hospitals. Each of these elements was expensive and controversial, just the sort of do-good bill that legislators hated to vote for. It subjected them to intense criticism from constituents, especially in conservative rural districts. Most voters did not want their tax dollars paying for somebody else's upkeep.

But by exploiting federal matching provisions so that the federal government really did pay for the first thirty days in the hospital for the aged, Burton, Governor Brown, and the legislature could claim the bill was actually saving the counties $50 million in the first year. Moreover, they argued, AB 59 would cost the state only $4.2 million the first year and $17 million a year after that. It was an entirely specious argument. In fact, in establishing California's modern welfare system, Burton knowingly set in motion a sequence of events that saw caseloads skyrocket and budgets explode. He also set in motion the 1966 gubernatorial election of a conservative Hollywood actor named Ronald Reagan, who was elected in part to clean up the "welfare mess."

Just when things looked bleakest, Burton found an ally on GE, the one token liberal. Dr. Stephen Teale had treated poor people as patients. In his first senate assignment, Teale had served as vice chairman of Social Welfare, where he had two years to learn the intricacies of welfare regulations, financing, and politics. He was also on Senate Finance, close to Miller, and friendly with Gibson. Teale believed in the bill. At the height of the Depression in 1932, when he was sixteen and the eldest of four children, he and his father earned six dollars the entire year. They traded labor for food, gasoline, and other necessities. He understood what it meant to not have enough to put on the table. "The kids were hungry," he said many years later. "That was what it was about. Not whether fathers should be there or not."

GE alone subjected Burton's bill to six weeks of constant negotiation and amendment. At Teale's suggestion, Burton was uncharacteristically diplomatic. He knew he was despised, but he kept his goal in mind every time he said, "Yes, Mr. Chairman. We'll work on it some more." Gibson appreciated the concessions on the county hospitals, and Teale was probably the only member who understood what the bill actually did, according to notes Gillies took at the time (though even Teale had no idea how much it ultimately would cost). McAteer, he wrote, was "often disdainful of Phil Burton, but ambitious and could not offend a power in San Francisco politics. He went along."

While Burton was working the GE committee, he also pioneered new lobbying tactics in Sacramento, organizing groups to support the bill that had never come to Sacramento before. Burton understood his colleagues' districts so well that he knew which interest groups should lobby individual members. He sent their leaders to Sacramento. The corridors of power belonged to all the people, he told them, not just to the officials and the lobbyists. In effect, he was saying, "Use the capitol, organize, agitate, lobby. I will hold the door open."

Burton knew, for example, that the Catholic Church opposed welfare rules denying aid to unemployed fathers. Such rules disrupted families. On the day of big votes, important monsignors and archbishops from key districts called their legislators off the floor and urged them to vote to keep families together. And a dozen years before the "disabled" movement burst onto the national scene in 1975 by occupying San Francisco's Federal Building for wheelchair access and other rights, Burton invited six severely disabled quadriplegics and their wives to a beer party at San Francisco's Ocean Beach. He taught them how to lobby, write letters, and agitate at home and in Sacramento just as he had taught Huerta years earlier. Tom Joe advised them on what to say, and together they created the sense they were a major organization. They were precursors to Berkeley's internationally known Center for Independent Living.

Burton's labor allies from the ILWU also lobbied for AB 59. One aide saw Burton himself grab legislators by their coats, shove them against the wall and literally thrust fistfuls of George Hardy's cash at them. "Take this money, and don't you dare vote against this bill," he warned. Such on-the-spot cash donations were not new in Sacramento. But no one had ever before enlisted them in the cause of increased welfare benefits for poor people. Burton turned again to Huerta, with whom he worked to secure passage of old-age pensions for noncitizens. Because farm workers lacked unemployment benefits, she began lobbying for AB 59 full time. Burton pushed relentlessly.

"What are you doing this weekend?" he asked Huerta, who was seven months pregnant and tending to a dying mother. "You've got to get down to Madera and write letters." Huerta spent her weekends galvanizing support. She would leave Sacramento on a Thursday night and head down Highway 99 to Central Valley farm country. She organized letter-writing parties, supplying paper and pens to dozens of farm workers who wrote hundreds of letters. She collected signatures on unsigned letters of support in grocery stores and barber shops. Exhausted, she would arrive back in Sacramento early Monday with 2,000 letters. She slept on a couch in Burton's office or at Tom Joe's apartment. In that way, they produced thousands of letters from voters in the districts of Cobey, Burns, and Gibson.

At one final GE meeting, Gibson turned to Teale. "Is this bill okay or not?" he asked. "Luther," replied Teale, "this is a good bill. It takes care of our problem, and it doesn't give away the store." Little did he know.

Combining grass-roots lobbying and his own restraint, Burton escaped from the graveyard. On April 17, Gibson provided the critical sixth vote and AB 59 was headed to Senate Finance, seven of whose eleven members also served on GE. But first, Burton had to cut a deal. Cobey, an influential welfare study commissioner whose support was crucial, wanted to kill the liberal Welfare Appeals Board headed by Berkeley speech professor Jacobus ten-Broek. If Burton agreed, Cobey would support his bill. Burton called tenBroek and left the choice to him. He would have to give up a powerful job, but tenBroek said it was worth the price.

George Miller usually got what he wanted in his committee, where Burton's bill underwent three more series of amendments. It was here that Burton, with Miller's assent, put in—and took out—some of his most controversial sections. In the May 7 version, Burton slipped in language calling for aid to families in these circumstances:

(a)   The death, physical or mental incapacity, or incarceration of a parent;

(b)   The divorce, separation or desertion of his parent or parents and re-sultant continued absence of a parent from the home for these or other reasons; or

(c)   The unemployment of his parent or parents.

This last was the key provision that would help so many families, yet bring so much fiscal grief to counties down the line. Burton went even further, adding Section 1523.7, which defined the terms by which the unemployed could refuse jobs and still get welfare. This section also explained in part why Hardy and the ILWU were lobbying so hard for the bill: "Good cause for refusal of employment shall be deemed to exist, when: The job is available because of a bona-fide labor dispute, the existence of which has been estab-lished by the State Department of Employment."

In other words, not only could unemployed parents get welfare for the first time, they could refuse a job and still collect welfare because they did not want to break a strike. They could also turn down jobs that were low-paying or that required a move. The California Taxpayers' Association, which consistently opposed the bill, argued months later that by subsidizing striking workers, this provision could prolong labor disputes. Had legislators truly read and understood this passage, it is unlikely they would have voted for this bill. But neither the legislators nor advocacy groups like CAL-TAX really grasped the full implications and potential costs. In fact, only three people fully understood the bill: Burton, Tom Joe, and Ed Percell, the attorney in the Legislative Council's office who helped draft it. Percell described drafting legislation for Burton that year as "nightmarish" because the man never left him a quiet moment.

Now action moved to the senate floor. While most senate Democrats merely despised Burton, senate Republicans found him utterly intolerable. Some hated him so much that they would not speak to him under any circumstances. John Murdy, an Orange County conservative, refused to vote for any Burton bill, even on the rare occasion when he agreed with its policy aims. He thought Burton was radical, obnoxious, profane, and un-American. He told liberal Senator Joseph Rattigan he could not vote for the Rattigan-Burton Act, which increased federal funds for medical care to the aged, even though Murdy thought the bill was necessary. Burton turned to Rattigan to lobby such senators, and Rattigan worked them carefully. He stuck to the merits: AB 59 was compassionate and humane and the money was there. While Rattigan rounded up Republicans, Miller twisted Democratic arms.

The night before the senate vote, Tom Joe was so nervous that when he ran into Rattigan at a restaurant, Joe offered to brief him again on the spot and fortify him for the next day. "Don't worry, Tom," Rattigan told him. "I'll carry it." Rattigan delivered what Tom Joe, Jerome Waldie, and Winslow Christian all said was one of the finest political speeches they ever heard, a "cry to conscience," in Christian's words, on why AB 59 was necessary. Then the senate did the unthinkable. On May 15, on a vote of 30 to 9, it passed a Phil Burton big-money welfare bill.[22]

Burton still needed a two-thirds assembly vote for concurrence in the senate amendments. Governor Brown wanted the bill approved too, and Tom Joe and Tom Moore in the governor's office kept Unruh and the leadership informed of the bill's progress.[23] Despite his personal antipathy to Burton, Unruh could not kill this bill even if he wanted to. It had become bigger than both of them. To try to stop it now would unmask Unruh's political motives, and Unruh was smart enough not to try. He also had a pressing personal problem the bill would resolve. For years, Unruh moaned that it cost him a fortune to pay his mother's nursing home costs. If the section on relatives' responsibility was eliminated, he no longer would have to pay, as Burton no doubt reminded him. Besides, Unruh, too, agreed with the overall objectives.

Even so, there were huge objections to the way the bill moved through the house. During the ninety-minute debate, Republicans complained that even though the ultimate price could reach $100 million a year, they never got to debate the senate amendments—really, Burton's amendments—in assembly committees. GOP objections went nowhere. Indeed, five of the eight Republicans voting for the bill were committee chairmen appointed by Unruh and beholden to him. Unruh and Burton wired the house, and the bill was approved on May 20 by a vote of 56-19, 2 more than the required two-thirds.

Anticipating the negative political fallout likely to hit some supporters, Democratic leaders tried to line up only as many "yes" votes as necessary. One assemblyman, Myron Frew of Hanford, gave his word he would vote for the bill. Once they had the votes, Burton and Unruh tried to convince Frew to abandon his pledge and protect himself. But Frew was determined to stick by his original commitment. He lost his seat in the next election largely because of that vote.

"Good morning," Governor Brown said at his press conference the next day to announce he would sign the bill. "I have one announcement to make. California's county government stands to save $21 million under the terms of this Assembly Bill 59 . . . the most important piece of welfare legislation which has been adopted during my administration, and I think it shows the effect of a good executive-legislative commission working together."

There was more than a little hypocrisy here. Brown and several of his top aides had to be dragged kicking and screaming into supporting some of the most controversial elements of AB 59. But as long as he could hide the true costs with fog-shrouded replies, the governor was happy to take the credit.

REPORTER: Governor, all through this bill we have been unable to get any cost factor. Do you have any figure on it?

BROWN: Yes, we have. I haven't them with me this morning. I can't give them to you, but I'm sure this bill has been priced out completely.

REPORTER: Burton can't give them to us. Nobody seems to have any figures.

BROWN: Have you asked the Department of Finance?

REPORTER: Asked just about everyone.

BROWN: Well, I'm sure you can get them. We know exactly what each one of these programs costs. Whatever I put in the budget, we know exactly what it costs and provided revenue for it.

In fact, Brown had no idea how much this bill would cost, and neither did the Department of Finance. Burton knew but he was not about to tell anybody. In the grand tradition of politicians everywhere, Brown retreated to safer ground:

BROWN: But the fact is, as I talk to you this morning, the State of California is in excellent fiscal condition, and we'll come out of this session, come out of this fiscal year with a very substantial surplus, despite all the demands that are made on a growing state like this.

REPORTER: In saving the counties that money, aren't we just taking it out of another pocket, when we get federal aid?

BROWN: That's right. The people pay for this. There's no use of kidding about it. But, of course, the federal government has a broader tax base.[24]

An honest response at last. Taxpayers, including those in California, would foot the bill. The stork was not delivering free welfare checks. Although the story led both the *Los Angeles Times* and the *San Francisco News–Call Bulletin* the following day, reporters emphasized Burton's legislative tricks and accepted without question the figures handed them. Jack McDowell said Burton's "legislative gymnastics were awarded the capital decathlon medal" for producing "a twenty-two page bill with financial and policy changes in nearly every phase of California social welfare, many put in as author's amendments, without any hearings by any committee." The turning point, McDowell wrote, was an amendment to exploit federal dollars for the first month of hospitalization for the aged. This would save $21 million in the 1963–64 fiscal year, $27 million the next year, and $32 million the year after that. This amendment helped convince some legislators the bill would save money.[25]

But *CAL-TAX News*, the newsletter of the California Taxpayers' Association, was not fooled. "By allowing counties to transfer some of their county-financed general relief load to other state-federal financed programs," *CAL-TAX News* wrote, "savings to counties are estimated at $21 million. As the new foundation is laid by the new law for other county welfare cost increases, doubt exists on how much, if any, of this wishful estimate will become available to the taxpayer." The following month, the same publication estimated that San Bernardino County would need an extra $500,000 to pay for welfare costs for unemployed parents at home. Fresno County estimated it would need to hire up to sixty more case workers to handle the expected "flood of welfare applicants." Aid to unemployed parents was expected to cost an additional $2 million for the first five months. Orange County also predicted a $1.5 million increase in welfare costs just for the remainder of 1963.[26]

It took a year before any publication tried to calculate the true costs of the far-ranging bill. And it wasn't one of the state's elite newspapers, either. The *California Farm Bureau Monthly* finally documented what AB 59 had done to California counties, especially rural ones. "We did not know 'saving' money could cost so much," began Farm Bureau Research Director Don Collin. AB 59 was supposed to save the counties $27 million in 1964–65, he said. But the state had to spend an extra $17 million and the federal government an extra $53 million. The net increase to the state was at least $43 million. Despite the cost shifts, Collin reported, there were catches in every provision of the bill requiring the counties to spend more money, not less.[27]

But even the Farm Bureau underreported the true costs by 50 percent the first year. Shortly after passage, Phil Burton and Tom Joe were having a congratulatory drink at the El Mirador when Mervyn Dymally said, "Come on, Phil. How much does it really cost? Never mind the county cost or the state cost or the federal cost. What is the overall total?"

Burton turned to Joe, took out a note pad, jotted a few figures down and then replied, "About $88 million, the first year."[28]

Despite complaints from conservative sources, Democratic legislators were awed by what Burton accomplished and how he did it. "AB 59 has taught a lot of us how a committee bill should be written," Bob Crown wrote Burton on July 3, 1963, "and how to shepherd one through the house. AB 59 is a fitting tribute to an impressive legislative career."

Freshman Assemblyman John Quimby of San Bernardino was equally awed. When he arrived that January, Unruh was the "gargantuan presence that dominated everything, the big hog," he recalled. But at the same time, there was "this other thing," this lurking, frightening presence named Phil Burton, "who was really doing things, and doing them under Jess's nose, and Jess didn't like him, and he was a real threat, and Jess was worried." An Unruh supporter, who was himself confined to a wheelchair and thus sympathetic to the need for more aid to the disabled, Quimby signed on as an AB 59 co-sponsor even though he had no clue what was really in the bill. As it went through the process, Quimby said, "It was like watching Phil Burton weave together a gorgeous tapestry thread by thread. Only he knew what it looked like. Then he gets done with the tapestry, pulls back the curtain, turns on the lights for everyone to see, and it's your mother fucking a rhinoceros."

Jealous of Burton's success with the bill, Unruh wasted little time trying to take Burton out once and for all. Several weeks later, Unruh enlisted Rules Committee Chairman Tom Bane in a complicated ploy to do just that. Bane introduced AB 3042, promptly dubbed the "Get Burton" bill. Egregiously anti-democratic, the bill was another attempt to destroy Burton and the CDC at the same time. Everyone knew Jack Shelley was coming home to run for mayor of San Francisco in November and Burton wanted to succeed him in Congress. Moreover, Burton was grooming his brother John to succeed him in Sacramento. Unruh also knew that Burton did not control the county Democratic central committee, which Moscone had lost by one vote in 1962.

The Unruh-Bane bill required that in the event of a special election—to fill a congressional seat, for example—the county Democratic and Republican central committees could each choose a candidate to face one another. Because Leo McCarthy supporters on the San Francisco committee hated

Burton, Unruh envisioned that they would surely name some Democrat besides him. But the stratagem backfired. The bill was too raw even for Unruh supporters. Burton called it a "gross perversion of the democratic process." Alan Cranston said AB 3042 would destroy volunteer participation by allowing party bosses to name their own candidates rather than give voters a choice. The *San Francisco Chronicle* called for its defeat, "even though it puts us in the unwelcome position of making common cause with Phil Burton."[29]

In a Democratic Caucus vote, Unruh lost badly. Then the caucus added insult to injury and gave his bill to Burton to rewrite. What emerged was a solution to a problem that had plagued Democrats for years in winner-take-all special elections. Democrats often lost these elections because so many jumped into the race, splitting the vote and handing the election to the opposition. The more disciplined GOP, by clearing out the field for one candidate, took seats in Democratic districts they had no business winning. Burton's rewritten bill instituted a primary and general for special elections. The top vote-getter from each party would advance to the general, just as in regularly scheduled elections, unless one candidate got more than 50 percent, in which case, that candidate was elected outright.

This solution, not surprisingly, also helped Burton. He knew he could defeat any San Francisco Republican one-on-one in a special election to succeed Shelley. Without this bill, however, the hostile McAteer-McCarthy faction could throw up a candidate and split the Democratic vote. Now, even if the Republican finished first, Burton as top Democratic finisher, was guaranteed to be in a runoff he could easily win.

After Unruh's uncharacteristically rare defeat, Martha Gorman asked him why he wanted to keep Burton from going to Washington. Wouldn't he be better off to get Burton as far from Sacramento as possible? "He'll be replaced by Johnny, who'd be worse," Unruh snapped. Unruh's flippant response masked a power play that failed. Unruh did not always think clearly. He thought he could block Burton from going to Washington and also keep him out of the assembly, because Phillip had already anointed John. But he miscalculated. Unruh was still speaker, still the dominant political bull in the state. He got most of what he wanted most of the time. Except in his dealings with Burton.

Having embarrassed Unruh before his own caucus, Burton waited for the session to end before ripping the entire legislature in language that politicians rarely used when speaking about colleagues: "Assemblyman Phillip Burton of San Francisco blistered his fellow Democrats Friday night for the 'worst legislative session in a decade,'" began a September 15 *Chronicle* story in which Burton blamed the poor session on "heavy financial contributions to my own colleagues" from powerful business lobbies who killed any bill they did not like. "They called the tune, they had their way completely, and I'd like my colleagues to explain why," Burton told the San Francisco Labor Council. He said lobbyist contributions to legislators "paid off in the millions" in the defeat of pro-labor bills. His colleagues, he said, "got boondoggled by having drinks with bank vice presidents. They either ought to shape up or be replaced."

"Many of the fellows have contacted me wondering if you were quoted accurately," Majority Leader Waldie wrote Burton. "I would appreciate an opportunity to discuss the situation with you at your earliest convenience."

But Burton had no interest in that. He was turning his full attention to getting Jack Shelley elected mayor. And he had bigger things in faraway places to think about. "I already bankrupted one budget," he quipped to Martha Gorman. "I need a bigger one to play with."[30]

6

THE COCKATOO'S HEAD

Looking East

*If they think I've been a controversial assemblyman,
they haven't seen anything yet.*

NEWLY ELECTED CONGRESSMAN PHILLIP BURTON

PHIL BURTON HAD GONE about as far as he could go in Sacramento, as long as Jesse Unruh remained speaker. Even though he bested Unruh repeatedly in 1962 and 1963 and became the champion of all the anti-Unruh Democratic reformers in the state, he knew that with his personality and his politics he could never be elected speaker. Besides, he wanted access to the national stage and, as he joked to Martha Gorman, the national budget. He had accomplished important things in Sacramento, including his welfare reform package. But it was time to jump from Triple A to the Major Leagues. Indeed, Burton was planning a career in Washington even before he was elected to the assembly.

Just as Unruh fixed the speakership as his goal early, so Burton meticulously prepared his route to Congress. But a politician as serious and professional as Burton left nothing to chance. His future was far too important to jeopardize by actually losing an election. The trick was to reduce that possibility to near zero. The means was reapportionment.

Burton's first exposure to that arcane but powerful world came in 1952, when he showed up to walk precincts on election day for Adlai Stevenson and Frank Havenner. Burton was shocked to discover that the seven-term Democratic congressman from San Francisco had been reapportioned out of his once-safe district. Havenner had been an assistant to Hiram Johnson, California's Progressive Era reformer and a committed New Dealer. That mattered not at all to the Republicans who were determined to take back control of the House, starting with the seven new seats California was slated to get following the 1950 census.

In the first ever partisan reapportionment of the state, Republicans so weakened Havenner's district by redrawing his boundaries that Republican William Mailliard defeated him in 1952, making Havenner the only California member to lose his seat that year. GOP map-makers moved heavily Republican precincts into his district, apparently with the blessing of Democratic boss Bill Malone, whose main concern was to strengthen the other San Francisco congressman, protégé Jack Shelley, first elected in 1949. By now, Havenner was old and no longer in his prime, but his defeat shook Burton. How, he wondered, could a hardworking, scandal-free politician with all the advantages of incumbency suddenly find his career cut short? There was only one answer. Burton saw firsthand how powerful a weapon reapportionment could be. The next time around, he vowed, the Democrats would control the maps.[1]

Once in Sacramento, Burton gravitated to the Elections and Reapportionment Committee. As his third term began, its task was to draw new lines following the 1960 census. At a December 15, 1960 committee hearing, Burton brought up the 1950 GOP gerrymander and cited statistics showing just how the Republicans had stacked the process. In Los Angeles County, for example, five congressional Democrats each represented an average of 642,000 people. The seven Republicans, meanwhile, represented just 393,000 people each, 250,000 fewer people per district. That difference was what allowed the Republicans to hold more seats. Burton also brought up Havenner's case, accusing the Republicans of having committed "butchery" the previous decade. "We had a congressman who was on House Armed Services," he said. "We wanted all the experienced men we could have thinking in terms of the defense of our country. Yet Congressman Havenner's head was lopped off as neatly as you please [even though] he was the senior Democrat west of the Mississippi, the third ranking member of the Committee."

Burton wanted badly to chair the committee. But Speaker Ralph Brown, fearful of his rough edges, ultraliberalism and partisan slant, gave the chairmanship to Bob Crown. Crown was a safer choice. But he was close to Burton, who had his own not-so-hidden agenda: a specially drawn congressional district Burton was a cinch to win. The present district belonged to Shelley, a solid, pro-labor Democrat who hated Burton from the moment Burton took over Malone's operation in 1954. Thinking years in advance, Burton set out to draw a district so favorable to himself that he could even beat Shelley in a primary, a district so liberal it might push Shelley into running for mayor in 1963—which Shelley was already inclined to do.[2]

But Shelley was not easy to muscle or intimidate. Born "south of the slot" in San Francisco's Mission District in 1905, the eldest of nine kids, Shelley had been a merchant seaman and bakery wagon driver for eight years while putting himself through night law school. He earned his law degree in 1932 but turned down a job working in Hiram Johnson's law office to continue driving the bakery wagon. He said labor needed educated men.

Shelley was a large, blustery, red-faced man who could tell a ripe story and wasn't afraid of strong drink. In 1937, at the age of thirty-one, he was the youngest president of the San Francisco Labor Council ever elected. Malone quickly spotted him and ran him successfully for state senator in 1938. In 1948, he chaired the California delegation to the national convention, and soon after, while he was president of the California Labor Federation, he was elected to Congress and re-elected easily ever since. An intelligent man, he nevertheless often got by more on his Irish charm than by hard work. Shelley heard the rumors that Burton was meddling with his district lines. Throughout 1960 and early 1961 he regularly called reporter Jack McDowell from Washington "just to check on what that SOB is doing to my district," McDowell recalled.

Burton was doing plenty, exhaustively searching out every demographic and technical detail that could help him manipulate the district to his advantage, as well as preserve Democratic gains statewide. His file, bulging with data from all over the country, showed which states would win and lose seats in the 1961 redistricting. California's unabated growth increased the state's House delegation by eight to thirty-eight members, which Burton turned to his advantage in ways that were too complicated for his colleagues to understand.

The state constitution said it was illegal to split an assembly district into more than one congressional district. That meant Crown's committee had to put at least two full assembly districts into each congressional district. But because thirty-eight congressional districts times two equaled only seventy-six (of eighty) assembly districts, that left four extras, which meant that four congressional districts would consist of three assembly districts each—the leftovers—and would thus contain populations roughly 50 percent larger than the rest.

Coming into the 1960 reapportionment, San Francisco had six assembly districts. Declining population dictated that it shrink to four. This was quite a comedown. In 1922, the city had thirteen assemblymen, reducing to nine in 1932, eight in 1942, six in 1952. In fact, the city's precise entitlement was not even a full four districts, but 3.73. Burton, however, needed San Francisco to have five assembly districts for his plan to work. With four, each of the two congressional districts would consist of two assembly districts, roughly equal in population. But with a fifth assembly district, Burton could draw one of the most left-wing congressional districts in the U.S. for himself by bunching the city's most liberal voters together.

Here's how it worked: Burton, working with staff aide Frank Kieliger, put two assembly districts from the liberal and minority-dominated east side of San Francisco, including his own, into Shelley's new district. The other three—the rest of San Francisco and all of the city's conservative areas—he put into Mailliard's new district. When he succeeded Shelley—there was no question in his mind about if—the new district would allow him to be as ultraliberal as he wanted to be.

Once his congressional career unfolded, this fact of life became pivotal. He would never have to justify a vote to his constituents. He would never have to explain himself. Unlike most of his colleagues in the California delegation, he would not have to take the red-eye from Washington to California and back twice a month to maintain contact with people who already saw him as their champion. He would be free to devote himself virtually full time to his Washington legislation and to his political maneuverings.

But the immediate political problem at hand was formidable: when the city had six assembly districts but barely qualified for four, how on earth could Burton ensure that San Francisco would get five?

Burton's strategy became explicit during a November 22, 1960 hearing in San Francisco. He would annex the fractions of other cities' entitlements to build San Francisco's fifth assembly seat. "We have a lot of odds and ends," Burton noted. "Santa Clara has three-tenths of a district [extra], 3.3. Obviously, they're not going to get four [districts], and if there are enough of these odds and ends around . . . it is conceivable that we [San Francisco] may only lose one seat." Quickly spotting the ploy, Crown replied, "Our committee has many representatives from all over California. I think I can speak for them [by saying] they're not abdicating all the odds and ends."[3]

But Crown gave Burton authority to draw the San Francisco lines. Burton's first goal was to maximize the census count. Critics later charged that in his bid to pump up his city's population, he counted everyone on board ship in harbor on the day the census was taken—military and civilian—and all the federal prisoners on Alcatraz Island. In a pre-computer age, Burton also devoted enormous amounts of time to compiling finely detailed demographic and statistical charts and then transferring them onto color-coded maps. CDC volunteers helped with the task. These maps illustrated how each precinct voted for each of the preceding ten years for governor, senator, legislative, and other partisan offices. A red precinct meant high Democratic loyalty. Orange was less so, yellow marginal, blue leaning Republican and purple represented the most Republican precincts. By studying the maps, Burton thus learned the precise voting history of every precinct in San Francisco.

All this detail merely confused Assemblyman Charlie Meyers, a big-hearted but profoundly limited man who once introduced a bill making it a misdemeanor to jump off the Golden Gate Bridge. In addition to handing out mints to anyone he saw, Meyers was also known for waiting until the last day of session to introduce all his lobbyist-written bills ("he gets stage fright," one friend explained).[4] Meyers objected at first. He wanted his district lines to conform to his parish lines so that every time he went to a wake or to church on Sunday he would see "my people." Crown repeatedly tried to tell Meyers that many of those churches were now in Republican precincts. But Meyers never understood that GOP votes, even Catholic ones, could kill him. He reluctantly went along. He served in the assembly for twenty years, until Leo McCarthy pushed him aside in the 1968 primary, a bittersweet relic of a bygone era.

To hear Burton and his aides tell the story, Burton was willing to do everything necessary to keep that crucial fifth district in San Francisco, including deliberately feeding misleading information to the staff, in particular to Dr. Leroy Hardy, a political scientist from California State College at Long Beach, and to Lou Angelo, Crown's intern. Acting on bad data, staff drew the new map, the story went, and discovered in a last-minute panic that they had drawn only seventy-nine districts. But Burton, who with staffer Frank Kieliger had drawn his own map of San Francisco, came to the rescue. He supplied the eightieth seat, which saved the plan. That eightieth district happened also to be San Francisco's fifth seat.

Burton loved to tell this story, because it boosted his reputation for technical wizardry. Most likely it did not happen exactly that way, however. There is no doubt that San Francisco did get a fifth seat and that Burton was responsible. He made no secret of wanting it or of using "odds and ends" from other regions. Moreover, said Angelo and Hardy, Burton argued persuasively to justify that seat: San Francisco was the commercial, cultural, and geographic hub of the Bay Area. It deserved extra representation because hundreds of thousands of people commuted into the city every day to work, significantly boosting the population, even if only for eight hours. It is more probable that Burton simply wore everyone out with his single-minded persistence. Repeatedly, Angelo heard him say to Crown, "But Bobby, look what happens if you do this. Just take these fractions and assign them to San Francisco, and you'll have a safe Democratic district. Isn't there a logic to this?"[5]

That fifth seat belonged to the hapless Ed Gaffney, who was incapable of stopping Burton, even if he had the foggiest notion of what Burton was doing, which he did not. Burton altered Gaffney's district to include more of the heavily black Western Addition, thus designing it for protégé Willie Brown. After his bitter loss in 1962, Brown won in 1964. Burton worked so hard on Brown's behalf that he even manipulated the score card by which organized labor judged legislators. Gaffney prided himself on his perfect labor record. But Burton rejiggered the rating. No matter how Gaffney voted, he could not achieve 100 percent, which enraged him.

Gaffney's anger was mild compared to the justifiable fury the Republicans felt when the Democrats unveiled their plan in May 1961. In a foreshadowing of the contentious reapportionment battles of 1971, 1981, and 1991, Republicans were not allowed to see the maps in advance. They could offer no amendments to a plan that saw Democrats gain eight new seats in Congress and eliminate three GOP incumbents. At a May 18, 1961 hearing, Republican Minority Leader Joseph Shell called the new congressional districts "unconscionable, . . . a very definite indication that the plan is deliberately aimed at eliminating the Republican Party as any kind of influence in the state of California." Shell added, "The results of this picture, very much like ten years ago, are the results of work of a few men. . . . I don't believe he [Crown] always had his druthers. I think very often he had to acquiesce and get the permission of Mr. Unruh and Mr. Burton."

"I'm willing to accept Mr. Shell's compliment," replied Unruh. "I get very few of them."[6]

Burton said nothing. He didn't have to. His plan for San Francisco spoke louder than anything he could possibly say. San Francisco, with 742,855 people, got five assembly districts for the next ten years even though it was losing population. Ultraconservative Orange County, the hotbed of the John Birch Society, with 703,905 people, got three districts. Santa Clara County, with 642,315 people, also got three seats. The latter two counties were not only Republican but the fastest growing counties in the United States.

Burton designed the new Fifth Congressional District to include his assembly district—to which he added more of the solidly working class and bohemian North Beach, Chinatown, increasingly Latino Mission, and black

Hunters Point districts, and Gaffney's new, heavily black district. The total population came to 296,000 people, the smallest in the state. Most of his future constituents were poor and minorities. Mailliard's district got everyone else, for a total population of 437,000.[7] Shelley's new district was 68 percent Democratic. Nearly 18 percent were black, 9 percent Chinese, and 9 percent Spanish-speaking. Less than 15 percent owned their own homes, and 43 percent had incomes of less than $5,000 a year.

In a January 1964 article in *San Francisco* magazine entitled, "The Cockatoo Squawks," former *Chronicle* city hall reporter Richard Reinhardt described the new Fifth District as a

> minor masterpiece of gerrymandering, shaped roughly like the head of a cockatoo. Its neck is down at Hunters Point; its beak touches (but does not nibble) Forest Hill [with its] eucalyptus trees, Republicans, and Anglo-Saxon attitudes; its top knot is up in North Beach. . . . [These] amiably incoherent boundaries, encompass most of San Francisco's Negroes, Mexicans, Puerto Ricans and Orientals: the burgeoning black families in 'housing' on the windy ridge above the naval shipyard; the spirited Latins of the Mission district; the Chinese of Grant Avenue, Nob Hill and Ping Yuen; the Japanese along the raveled edges of the Western Addition. . . . [The district was also home to] solitary gray-haired pensioners in hot-plate housekeeping rooms on Howard Street; to Old Believers and young sculptors on Potrero Hill; to bachelor girls in overheated flats off Larkin Street; to shrewd, conservative Irish-American carpenters on the steeps above Eureka Valley. By comparison, Congressman Bill Mailliard's Sixth district, with twice as much territory (all the rest of San Francisco) and almost twice as many registered voters, is a bland and pale-faced land of singular monotony.

Reinhardt even discovered the "Ertola Triangle," the site of an old family home on Greenwich Street in North Beach that San Francisco Supervisor Charles Ertola owned with his two politically ambitious anti-Burton sons, John and Chadwick. As Burton drew the district lines down Columbus Avenue, they suddenly veered east and south creating a "wedge-shaped notch" or triangle that eliminated the Ertolas from the district and thus from challenging either Phillip or John Burton. The Ertola Triangle was put into the Twenty-first Assembly District, which Republicans Marks and Mailliard represented.[8]

None of the political insiders were oblivious to what Burton was doing.

He and his labor allies believed he could do so much more in Washington. Shelley was always a good labor vote. But he did not have the youth, energy, imagination, or total determination Burton had to move the political and labor agenda to the left. Shelley would not go any higher in Congress. Burton, some of them believed, could be Speaker some day.

Tension between the two men was palpable, and their relationship was tempestuous. One morning, as they shared a breakfast booth at a 1962 CDC meeting in Fresno, Shelley began screaming at Burton so loudly that acquaintances nearby began discussing in whispers whether Burton was "trying to give Shelley a heart attack right now so he can take his seat?" That year both men happened to take the same flight home from Washington. After a few drinks, Shelley indicated he might run for mayor. Burton threatened that if Shelley did not run, then he—Burton—would challenge Shelley in the 1964 congressional primary and beat him. Shelley would be out of office completely.[9] Shelley denied that conversation ever took place, but he hurriedly called a council of war with advisors Morris Bernstein, James Rudden, and Bill Malone, and decided to run for mayor.

Despite his public declaration of candidacy, Shelley was ambivalent. He loved being in Congress and was accumulating seniority on the powerful Appropriations Committee. But Burton called on his labor supporters to pressure Shelley to come home. Friends also urged him to run both for his sake and to stop state Senator Eugene McAteer, who had already announced his intention to run for the job. The two men shared the same labor base and had been jockeying with each other for months. Shelley's wife Thelma was also pushing him to leave Washington. They had two small children, and she was tired of dragging them back and forth across the country. But Malone turned out to be Shelley's most persuasive advisor and important operative. After leaving the county central committee in 1952, Malone had faded into the background, surfacing occasionally to raise money for Shelley or Pat Brown.

After eight years of Eisenhower, Malone re-emerged in a conspicuous way for Irish-Catholic presidential candidate John Kennedy, raising more than one million dollars for him in 1960. Kennedy and Shelley, moreover, were good friends from their days together in the House. Malone badly wanted his one-time protégé Shelley to be mayor. With the kind of access a million dollars in fundraising can produce, he called the White House and asked Kennedy to intervene on behalf of their mutual good friend Jack Shelley. Unless McAteer could be persuaded to drop out, he and Shelley—two like-minded Democrats—would split the vote, and a third candidate, Republican lawyer Harold Dobbs, could win, Malone explained. A Dobbs victory could make it harder for Kennedy to capture California in 1964. Kennedy or somebody speaking for him made the phone call. McAteer reluctantly agreed to step aside.

Had McAteer stayed in, their battle would have split the Democratic establishment in half. Like Shelley, McAteer's roots were also San Francisco Irish, Mission High School, and organized labor. After serving on the board of supervisors, he was elected to the state senate in 1958 and re-elected in 1962. More than anything, Gene McAteer wanted to be mayor. He promised the top staff job to Leo McCarthy, who spent 1962 lining up support for him.

Without warning one day in February 1963, McAteer invited his young protégé into his office and told McCarthy he was not going to run for mayor. To McCarthy, McAteer seemed confident he could beat Shelley or Dobbs and traumatized by his own pull-out. It was a bitter personal blow to a man who dreamed of being mayor. McCarthy, who looked upon McAteer as a father, was deeply hurt that he had neither been consulted about the decision nor told why McAteer made it. A few days later, he heard about openings on the board of supervisors. If McAteer was not running for mayor, then he would run for supervisor. Now it was McAteer's turn to be hurt. Thirty days later, McCarthy resigned. They never healed their breach.

San Francisco antitrust attorney Joseph Alioto, one of McAteer's campaign co-chairmen, was trying a case in Salt Lake City when McAteer called. "I've had a request from the president to withdraw in favor of Shelley, and I'm accommodating him," McAteer told Alioto. But Malone, who launched Shelley's career in 1938, may never have told Shelley all the strings he pulled to force McAteer out. Thelma Shelley was in Washington when she heard the news of McAteer's withdrawal, and her husband was en route to San Francisco. She was the one who told her husband what had happened.

"Oh, shit," Shelley replied. "Now I have to run."[10]

No one outside of Malone's or McAteer's tight circle ever got wind of the White House phone call. Writing in the *San Francisco Examiner*, Sydney Kossen quoted Malone as saying there was "no deal whatsoever" to force McAteer out. "Family, physical and business considerations—not a backroom power play—dictated his decision," Kossen wrote. Malone confirmed, however, that "there had been much talk and deep concern among party leaders [who] had feared old political alliances and personal friendships would be ruptured if Shelley and McAteer fought for the same office."[11]

Dobbs, Shelley's remaining opponent, was a three-term supervisor and a prominent Jewish Republican lawyer who represented what was known as the "Downtown" interests. Co-owner of a chain of restaurants, Dobbs had also employed a young law student named Phillip Burton for three months in 1951, just before he ran for the board for the first time. Each had been impressed with the other, but Dobbs said they never discussed politics.

The Shelley-Dobbs campaign was a standard liberal-conservative battle, with both sides trading predictable charges. Typical of the media's continuing hostility to Burton, the *Examiner* listed three reasons to vote for Dobbs: "1. Let's Keep Dobbs in City hall. 2. Let's keep Jack Shelley in Congress. 3. Let's keep Phil Burton out of Congress."

Bad blood between Shelley and Burton was no secret. But for the sake of their mutual ambition, they had what Burton thought was an understanding. Burton drafted Shelley's mayoral welfare program and loaned Josiah Beeman to Shelley to coordinate his get-out-the-vote effort. Beeman was the high-profile president of the state Young Democrats. In return, Shelley was supposed to endorse Burton to succeed him in Congress.

One night Burton appeared at his twentieth Washington high school reunion. As he began to speak, Burton noted the presence of his Falcon Club friend Gerard Rhine. "Twenty years ago," he said, telling the story for the first time, "Gerard was caught stuffing the ballot box, and I wasn't able to be president. This year, if Shelley is elected mayor, I will run for his seat. But my very good friend Gerard is working for Harold Dobbs."[12]

On the last weekend before the vote, the campaign suddenly caught fire. A group of civil rights protesters, many from the Congress of Racial Equality (CORE) and the radical W. E. B. Du Bois Club in Berkeley, had been picketing Dobbs's restaurants to protest what they said was his poor record in hiring minorities. Dobbs disputed the charges. Led by a fiery young radical named Terrence "Kayo" Hallinan, the son of prominent leftist attorney Vincent Hallinan, the protesters escalated their tactics. As they began a mass picket line at Mel's Drive-In, one of Dobbs's restaurants, they angered customers, who began throwing food at them. The picketers went inside the restaurant and fought back, and nearly 200 were arrested.

Dobbs lost his composure. "We all know San Francisco is not a city of racial violence," he told the newspapers. "But at the last minute, violence has been brought into the campaign in an ugly way. . . . Mr. Shelley must share the onus for this disgraceful performance. Mr. Shelley has spoken in defense of these demonstrators. Mr. Shelley should hang his head in shame."

Shelley deplored the protests. "On Friday," he responded, "I warned the voters that one of my opponents might resort to improper tactics—the Big

Lie. When Harold Dobbs said I was responsible for picketing his home and restaurants, he lied."[13]

The race looked too close to call. On November 2, retired Registrar Thomas Toomey predicted Dobbs would win by 15,000 votes and said the picketing of his restaurants would help Dobbs, who would win the "so-called silent vote." Many labor leaders privately blasted the young radicals, telling them their tactic could cost Shelley the election.

Going about their business quietly, Burton and Beeman mobilized the largest grass-roots citywide precinct operation San Francisco had ever seen, as different political currents converged to work for Shelley's election. Hallinan and his friends went almost directly from their jail cells to Shelley's headquarters for their precinct kits, most of them feeling guilty for damaging Shelley's campaign.

Even though San Francisco was a Democratic town, the local offices were nonpartisan—another remnant of the Hiram Johnson Progressive Era reforms. The city had not elected a Democratic mayor in sixty-seven years. Support for Shelley ranged from Bill Malone and the most conservative, anticommunist Democrats to Phil Burton and the W. E. B. Du Bois Club, which included Communists and young, white civil rights activists. On election day, close to 1,200 Young Democrats, CDC volunteers, and other activists from all over the Bay Area showed up in San Francisco to turn out voters.

Many walked precincts because they really wanted Shelley to win; others merely wanted Shelley out of the way so they could put their real champion—Burton—in Congress. Taking his cues from Burton's 1956 campaign against Tommy Maloney and subsequent CDC-styled volunteer efforts throughout the state, Beeman assembled the most advanced precinct operation in local history.

The election was a triumph for Shelley. In defeating Dobbs by 28,000 votes, he became the first Democrat elected mayor since James Phelan in 1896. Despite his temporary accommodation with Burton, his impressive victory and the significant role Burton played in achieving it, Shelley still detested and distrusted Burton. When the polls closed, an aide ordered Shelley's campaign workers to pack up all their precinct lists so Burton's people could not use them. But Joe Beeman was one step ahead: all the card files and precinct lists had been duplicated and taken out of the office by 5 P.M.

Burton, meanwhile, had already printed and addressed his official announcement for Congress. Before midnight on Tuesday, November 5, the night Jack Shelley was elected mayor, Burton mailed it to more than 5,000 residents. The same night, Burton protégé George Moscone and Burton enemy Leo McCarthy were elected to the board of supervisors.

It only took a day for the Shelley-Burton bad blood to surface publicly. Shelley welched on his promise and began searching for a candidate to run for Congress against Burton. His first choice was Jack Henning, who had once served with him as executive director of the California Labor Federation. Henning was in Washington as undersecretary of labor. At a press conference to announce his support for Henning, Shelley said Burton "is enamored of the idea of succeeding me, and has been for some time, but it's no secret there's no love lost between us." In a letter he wrote that day, Burton constituent Orin Cassmore urged Henning to back off. "If you think Phil's ultra-liberalism offends his constituency in the 20th Assembly district, you are profoundly mistaken," Cassmore wrote. "Desperately poor people, pensioners, working men, minorities, eat it up. For them, the New Frontier does not exist. The fights along the old frontier, which were won for most of us in the Thirties, are the ones important to them, for they have not participated in the gains we have won. The situation in the 18th District is even more favorable to him."[14]

On November 7, Burton called a press conference at the *Sun Reporter*—Dr. Goodlett's influential black newspaper—to officially announce his candidacy for Shelley's seat. "I intend to conduct my campaign as I have in the past," Burton said, "by meeting voters in their homes. I expect several hundred active volunteers will help me. I called this conference at the *Sun Reporter* because in my judgment, it is symbolic of the nature of the campaign I will wage. This is the heart of the district." Burton added that the two biggest issues would be civil rights and Medicare. Then he opened it to questions but refused to be baited into attacking Shelley.

REPORTER: What is your reaction to Shelley's support of Henning?

BURTON: I did not attend the press conference. I think Shelley's support is an important factor. I do not know what Shelley will do. There are a number of interested prospective candidates, and I welcome them one and all. . . . I intend to run as a fighting, liberal, Kennedy Democrat.

REPORTER: Did you campaign for Shelley?

BURTON: Yes.

REPORTER: Are you upset that Shelley is apparently not supporting you?

BURTON: I do not know what Shelley will do. I intend to seek the support of all who live in the district, of which Congressman Shelley is an important vote.

Moving on to other topics, Burton was asked how he could bring government contracts and jobs to San Francisco. "I hope the fact that I am personally acquainted with eighty to 100 members of the House," he said, "and fifteen members of the Senate . . . will help get California its fair share of work."[15]

Shelley kept searching for another candidate. He approached John Ertola, even though Burton had eliminated Ertola's home from the district. Still, under the law, a candidate need not live in the district to run in a special election. Burton and Ertola had once been friends, and Burton paid him a visit, armed with polling and precinct data that spelled out why Ertola could not beat him. Then Shelley left on a two-week Hawaiian vacation.

The *Examiner* published a front-page story about a prospective Ertola candidacy in its first edition on November 22, 1963. That was a bad day to try and make news. Within hours, President Kennedy was shot and killed in Dallas, and the Ertola story was reduced to a tiny squib on the back page. For weeks the Kennedy assassination stopped everything. People were too grief-stricken to pay attention to politics. There had also been a sense that Shelley's close friendship with Kennedy would make him a strong mayor, and San Francisco would have a good friend in the White House. No longer. Shelley cut short his vacation to return to Washington for the Kennedy funeral. "No one will ever know how close I was to that man," a shaken Shelley told a reporter in his Washington home. After a period of mourning, Shelley kept looking for a candidate and even tried to enlist Kennedy press secretary Pierre Salinger, a former *Chronicle* reporter. But Salinger was registered to vote in Virginia.[16]

In a rare journalistic departure, Herb Caen, San Francisco's highly read short-item columnist, devoted an entire column to the stormy Shelley-Burton relationship, quoting Burton extensively and at his most diplomatic. "I have no idea what Shelley has against me," Burton told Caen. "I always thought we were friends. During the campaign I promised that if he lost, I wouldn't run against him for Congress. Maybe he's sore because one of the papers suggested I could beat him. . . . I guess that would burn me up a little, too." Burton was being disingenuous. He knew exactly what Shelley had against him. He had threatened Shelley and had altered his district in a successful effort to push Shelley out of Congress and grab his job.

Perhaps reacting to questions about his patriotism, Burton tempered his leftward slant in his interview with Caen and said he now opposed admission of Red China to the United Nations because "their reaction to the assassination of the president was horrifying." Burton described himself as a "New Deal Democrat who believes in the Constitution." But some principles he would not compromise. "Certainly I'm against HUAC. Everybody knows that. It's not a legislative body. It tries people in the newspaper headlines—innocent people walk around with 'guilty' stamped on their foreheads just because they were called—with nothing proved yet. I don't think the Committee will be voted out just yet. But there's a growing feeling in Congress that it's not a healthy thing. It'll be whittled away, its funds cut down gradually."

On December 10, Shelley's efforts to find another candidate came to a crashing halt when Governor Brown endorsed Burton. He did so after exacting a promise that Burton would not rock the boat in his first term and would support President Johnson, whose nomination Brown later seconded at the 1964 convention. "I want one commitment," Brown said. "If I'm going to support you, keep your mouth shut for two years. Listen and learn. And lay off Vietnam."[17] Burton agreed. "If I lived in his district, I'd vote for him," Brown told the *Chronicle*. "Mr. Burton assured me he supports the programs of the late President Kennedy and President Johnson, particularly in foreign policy."

Brown's endorsement ended any major challenge. Three days later, Shelley said he was ready to endorse Burton and Ertola withdrew. Only minor candidates remained, the most vigorous of whom was Dobbs supporter Ed Heavey. In desperate attempts to discredit Burton, Heavey dredged up Burton's speech the day before the 1960 HUAC demonstrations, but he got little press attention. In a letter to Burton, Heavey even said he doubted Burton's "grief over the killing of John Kennedy" was real. Burton's "maneuverings" against Kennedy at the 1960 convention, Heavey said, made him "strongly suspect that such grief as you are capable [of] is reserved for the Communist who shot him." Then he proposed a debate topic: "That the election of Phillip Burton would materially aid the subversive program of the Communist Party, USA."[18]

Burton ignored Heavey, but Heavey's assertions reflected a concern shared by many conservative Democrats. Several newspaper stories hinted at Burton's supposed ties to left-wing groups, and the commotion prompted Governor Brown to back away from lending his name to a $25-a-person Burton dinner at the Fairmont Hotel. It was not the governor's finest moment.

Burton had used Brown's name on the invitation. "I have whole-heartedly given my support to this affair," Brown wrote in the invitation, "because Phil is an able, responsible and effective legislator. He has consistently fought for and helped to enact a liberal, progressive and sound legislative agenda."

Within days, Brown was backpedaling furiously, accusing Burton of using his name without his permission. Burton was too professional to have done that—having learned his lesson years earlier in the incident with Humphrey and the Young Democrats. He called the incident "a breakdown in communications." But Brown said, "The only breakdown in communications was that Phil Burton didn't get my signature, and so far as I know, didn't ask me for it." He said he had planned to attend but changed his mind. Burton let Brown off the hook.

There had been no misunderstanding. The governor turned and ran at the first hint of red-baiting.[19] George Miller came to the rescue again. He, Bert Coffey, and Jack Knox made a special show of supporting Burton, and the unions turned out in full force. But coming just a few months after Burton's blast at the legislature for "the worst session in a decade," many people begged off.

Burton had a strong incentive to campaign hard. If he won more than 50 percent of the vote, he could skip the general election and go directly to Washington. It was during this campaign that Burton stumbled across the issue that would turn out to be one of the cornerstones of his political career. One night environmentalist Margot Patterson Doss gave a fundraising party for him at her Russian Hill townhouse with 200 guests. Burton pulled her aside. "What do you want from me, Margot?" he asked.

"Parks, Phil," she said. "Parks."

"Hell, that's a rich man's game," he replied. "I'm a labor candidate."

"Who do you think uses parks," said Doss. "The working stiff, that's who. The rich man has two acres of his own at Lake Tahoe and another house at Pajaro Dunes."

"You're right," he said. "You'll get your parks." Burton had no inkling then that conservation and environmental protection would constitute one of his most impressive legacies.[20]

Writing about Burton's candidacy in the *liberal democrat*, publisher Tom Winnett described the evolution of Burton's legislative style. At first, "the regulars did not let him get any bills of any consequence to the governor's desk," Winnett wrote. By the end of his eight-year tenure, however, he passed AB 59, "the most far-reaching bill in the field of welfare since the Federal Social Security Act of 1935." What changed? "I've learned the players, the legislative mentality," Burton told him, "the way to oppose a man's bill while incurring the least possible animosity from him. I've done my homework. And I'm out from under [Tommy] Maloney's shadow—his name is no longer known to many assemblymen." Asked what he would do in Congress, Burton replied, "I hope to have an impact on the development of issues. One can't have much right away. . . . I think my state legislative experience will be immensely valuable."

Winnett said Burton "looks like the winner." The CDC endorsed him 107 to 0 over Heavey, "a reactionary attorney who somehow registers Democratic." When Heavey asked the delegates, "Do you want to be represented by a man who would abolish the Un-American Activities Committee?" the cheers lasted for two minutes.[21]

As election day approached, Burton readied his grass-roots volunteers again. Taking nothing for granted, he sent a letter to every minister in the Fifth District. "If you could touch upon the responsibility to vote in your sermon on Sunday," he wrote, "it would be greatly appreciated."[22]

The *Christian Science Monitor* described February 18, 1964—election day—as "a sparkling warm day with pink plum blossoms and gold clouds of acacia peeking around the corners of the wartime residential barracks at Hunters Point, the shipyard area Democrats call Burtonville because of the new congressman's strong 'in' with neighborhood minority groups."

There was no suspense. Running against seven little-known candidates, Burton won 52 percent of the vote. Heavey placed fourth, with just 1,225 votes. Burton lost a few Republican precincts, but in some precincts he won overwhelmingly; in one, he took 301 of 304 votes cast; in another, 180 of 207. The next day, as Burton basked in the glow of his victory, John Burton filed papers to succeed him in Sacramento.

Burton's triumph gave him his first burst of national publicity. An AP wirephoto in the February 20 *New York Times* showed a happy Burton clutching a telephone to one ear, as a smiling Sala looked on, her forehead pressed to her husband's cheek. In the same edition, *Times* correspondent Wallace Turner profiled Burton to an East Coast audience that had never heard of him. While Burton said he supported President Johnson's foreign policy, he also supported lifting travel restrictions to Cuba. Burton said he favored trade with Communist China—though not recognition—on the same terms as with the Soviet Union and said he would base defense spending on legitimate defense needs, not employment needs. Burton said there should be free medical care for anyone who needed it, noting his physician father "doesn't approve of my stand."

Some people, Turner wrote, "have thought Mr. Burton to be a dangerous radical. . . . One of Mr. Burton's great blocks of support comes from the highly organized Negro civil rights groups. He goes to Washington fully committed to support civil rights legislation." A UPI story in the *Washington Post* observed that Burton "is expected to be one of the nation's most liberal lawmakers," citing his opposition to HUAC, his support for free travel to Cuba, and his description of defense spending as "the WPA of the Sixties."

The *San Francisco Chronicle*'s Michael Harris profiled a confident Burton. "In the last two sessions," Burton said, "I passed as much meaningful legislation as any member of either house." But he added, "As a freshman congressman, I'm going to do a lot of listening and learning, as any freshman with a brain in his head would do. They've been running that shop for a long time without me." As for Unruh and others happy to see him leave, Burton said, "Unruh and I met four times in the last session, and I beat him three times. There's a grand myth that some newspapers have generated—the idea that I have no party support and can't get legislation through. But other legislators have voted for my bills because they were convinced of their merit."[23]

The *Times* and the *Post* were not the only national organizations to track Burton's progress. His FBI file, growing thicker by the month, was being circulated at the highest levels of the bureau. The San Francisco office forwarded to Washington every scrap of information it could find on Burton, on the W. E. B. Du Bois Club and other civil rights groups and on the latest in the Burton-Shelley-Pat Brown saga. A February 19, 1964 cable from the San Francisco office to Director J. Edgar Hoover and to Assistant Directors William Sullivan of the Domestic Intelligence Branch and Cartha DeLoach of the Crime Records Division included a recitation of all the FBI's previously obtained raw data about Burton and his association with groups the FBI believed to be Communist or Communist-infiltrated. "It is suggested by the San Francisco Office that BURTON not receive a letter of congratulations from the Director in view of his past activities," the memo said. A memo the next day to DeLoach said Burton was a member of the Young Democrats, the NAACP, the ACLU, the Americans for Democratic Action and the American Veterans Committee. "The AVC falls in the Communist-dominated class," it said. "Burton has advocated the repeal of two sections of the Smith Act, which make it unlawful to teach or advocate the violent overthrow of the government."[24]

FBI snoopers notwithstanding, Phillip Burton's election gave him his life's dream. At thirty-seven he was headed to Washington. He would honor his pledge to Pat Brown and keep his mouth shut—for a little while. But as always, he had an agenda and a desperately poor constituency to serve. He also had advance billing. Scores of members knew him, and most described him the same way: as a wild man.

Burton started at the bottom: last in seniority in an institution that valued seniority above all else. But he was to shake up Congress just as he rocked the California legislature, rising so fast over the next half dozen years that colleagues shook their heads in amazement at the speed of his ascent. Burton was going to Washington to make waves. He began making them his first week on the job.

7

CAPITOL HILL AT LAST

I remember lots of conversations about him coming to town.
The guys were worried. He had quite a reputation. I remember the words:
"wild man." At the first meeting of the California delegation
he sat quietly like a mouse. That was the last time.

IRVING SPRAGUE
former California lobbyist in Washington

WHEN PHILLIP BURTON ARRIVED in February 1964, the House of Representatives could not have been more different than the California Assembly, where men of talent and ambition moved quickly to the top. Jesse Unruh became chairman of Finance and Insurance after one term, headed Ways and Means after two, and ascended to speaker after three. Even Burton, not the most popular man among his peers, became chairman of Social Welfare after just one term.

But in the House, seniority was the key to upward mobility, and most members paid careful attention to Speaker Sam Rayburn's sage advice that "to get along, go along." Junior members, even those who had served a dozen years or more, were frustrated by their inability to achieve power and influence. But by and large they kept quiet. While the United States was poised to enter one of its most liberal eras—Lyndon Johnson's Great Society—its most representative body was controlled by reactionary farmers from one-party southern states, lawyers with small, lily-white constituencies in Mississippi, South Carolina, or Virginia. Not every chairman was a reactionary, but most ascended the ladder of seniority because they had the right genes and no competition at home. The House was far more conservative than either the White House or the Senate.

But Burton, promises to Governor Brown notwithstanding, had no intention of getting along or going along. There was nothing in his personality or background to suggest that he would suddenly bow to established authority and become a good soldier. His powerful drive to make things happen, indeed, shake up the established order, ensured that he would not stand by quietly, year by year, waiting for his elders to retire or lose an election or die so he could move up a notch on a committee.

Within months, Burton threw himself into the hottest issues of the day. By summer he was visiting civil rights organizers in Mississippi. By early 1965 he was taking on his president over the Vietnam War. By the end of his first term he had emerged as one of the leaders of a lonely band of House liberals determined to end U.S. intervention in Southeast Asia. By his second term, Burton was in the thick of the fight that involved embattled Harlem Congressman Adam Clayton Powell.

In the Eighty-eighth Congress, Burton became the 259th Democrat. There were 176 Republicans. The average age was fifty-two, forty-three for freshmen. The typical House member was a native-born Protestant in his fifties, a lawyer and veteran with a military reserve commission. Nearly 300 members were war vets. Just 11 of 435 members—fewer than 3 percent—were women.

According to data compiled by influential Rules Committee member Richard Bolling of Missouri and published in his controversial 1966 book, *House Out of Order*, there were 175 liberals, including 15 Republicans, and 185 hardcore conservatives, including 45 Dixiecrats. Depending on the issue, Bolling estimated liberals could assemble from 200 to 230 votes, while conservatives could muster 200 to 220 votes. There were four main groupings: liberal Democrats, big-city organization Democrats, Dixiecrats, and mainstream Republicans. In most instances, the Dixiecrats and Republicans, aided by the committee chairmen, beat back the liberals and big-city Democrats.

The chairmen of fourteen of the House's twenty committees were from rural areas, ten from the South. Among Democrats, most ranking members were southern or rural. Sixteen of twenty ranking Republicans were rural. On the all-important Ways and Means Committee, most Democrats were from southern or border states. Five of ten Democrats on the powerful Rules Committee were southern. Only three key committee chairmen, including Ways and Means Chairman Wilbur Mills of Arkansas and Education and Labor Chairman Adam Clayton Powell, were even born in the twentieth century. Four chairmen opposed Kennedy on eight of twelve key votes his first year, even though a House majority supported Kennedy in ten of them.[1]

Faced with such a hidebound institution as the House, it was no surprise that liberal legislation encountered major difficulties. Men like Howard

Worth Smith of Virginia, chairman of the Rules Committee, bottled up bills they did not like, especially if they pertained to civil rights. Smith was rumored to retreat to his farm for weeks at a time to avoid scheduling hearings on issues he did not want to deal with. The ranking Democrat on Rules, segregationist William Colmer of Mississippi, publicly opposed the 1960 Kennedy-Johnson ticket. Chairmen with plantation values who shuttled between their Deep South districts and Washington, itself just emerging from a long history as a sleepy, segregated southern town, were determined to block civil rights bills.

They kept junior members in line through an elaborate system of rewards and punishment. Those who went along got water contracts, military bases, highways, post offices, and other federal boondoggle for their districts. It was no wonder John Kennedy was frustrated. No one seemed in charge. Rayburn's powerful Speakership "obscured" the need for reform, Bolling wrote.

> But since his death, the state of the House has been revealed—it is a shambles. The Speakership as an institution has become atrophied. Power is dissipated among senior Democratic committee chairmen whose views often do not accord with those of the party majority. The Democratic leadership does not have the allegiance of its sub-leaders. . . . It allows key posts to fall to extreme conservatives who use them to block party programs. Key posts are also permitted to go to incompetents. . . . On occasion even a Member both arrogant and erratic rises to a committee chairmanship where he gleefully thumbs his nose at President, Speaker and his own party's majorities.[2]

Change seemed unlikely, however, as long as House liberals were too timid to challenge the status quo. What Bolling wrote of the typical House liberal would not have been so scathing were it not so true:

> He distrusts power, indeed, he treats it as some sort of dirty weapon. Some liberals give evidence of possessing a legislative will-to-lose, a sort of death-wish. If more than a dozen votes show up for a bill he favors, he begins to wonder, like the fastidious literary critic confronted with sudden popularity of a hitherto obscure novel, that perhaps there is something "wrong" with the bill. . . . "Good ideas" in domestic welfare and in foreign policy tend to remain just that as long as the liberals refuse to take the time and the infinite pains necessary to transform them into legislation.[3]

Things deteriorated after Rayburn's death, but even the powerful Speaker had problems getting around the old guard. Rayburn had to do something to curb the power of Howard Smith and his Rules Committee in 1961 or Kennedy could not pass his programs. Except for unanimous consent items, moves to suspend the rules—which required a two-thirds vote—and rarely used "discharge petitions," all bills needed a rule from the Rules Committee before they went to the floor. That committee maintained absolute control over how a given bill could be debated and how and whether it could be amended. To kill or modify legislation hostile to segregationist Democrats and conservative Republicans, the Rules Committee could simply refuse to issue a rule for how a bill would be debated, thus killing it. It could issue rules to limit amendments or the time allocated for debate. Or it could hold a bill hostage by threatening not to issue a rule unless the bill was substantially changed.

Working with Bolling, Frank Thompson of New Jersey, and other reformers in what became an epic battle, Rayburn succeeded in January 1961 in expanding the Rules Committee from twelve to fifteen members, enough to get around Smith's obstructionism. That expansion broke a 6-6 deadlock by which conservatives killed, delayed, or changed bills they did not like.[4] Rayburn died that November. He was succeeded by Majority Leader John McCormack of Massachusetts, a devout Catholic first elected in 1928, who lacked Rayburn's strategic brilliance or total devotion to the House.

In the race to succeed the colorless McCormack as majority leader, Bolling challenged Majority Whip Carl Albert of Oklahoma. One of the brightest intellects in American politics, Bolling was first elected in 1948, representing President Truman's home district. A former aide to General Douglas MacArthur, Bolling grew close to Truman and to Rayburn, the legendary Speaker from Texas. He prided himself on being an insider's insider, but his inability to tolerate lesser intellects did not endear him to colleagues. Indeed, his arrogance, abrasiveness, and inability to mount an effective "inside" campaign among members forced him to withdraw, political scientist Nelson Polsby later wrote. Considered a "hatchet man" for Rayburn, Bolling seemed incapable of asking colleagues for their votes, and tried to mobilize support through pressure from interest groups and editorial writers. He demonstrated the same problem fourteen years later in his leadership race against Phillip Burton and Jim Wright. The popular Albert won, converting a career based on personal relationships into firm commitments.[5]

Such was the House that Burton entered. Speaker Thomas Foley of Washington recalled his first day in January 1965, ten months after Burton's, when

McCormack gave a cautionary welcome to the entering freshmen: "It was a very polite, warm greeting, then suddenly turned kind of chilly," Foley recalled. "He said the leadership had found over the years that many new members were elected by accident. . . . But he said the judgment also was that members were seldom re-elected by accident. Message: Come back in two years time, after your first re-election, and we'll know that you're not one of the accidental ones. It was a rather sharp slap across the face."[6]

The Burtons arrived in Washington on February 24. McCormack swore him in the next day. Burton had no idea how to assemble an office, pay his staff, or introduce a bill, and no one was around to explain it. He told his staff—Joe Beeman, Frank Kieliger, Lim P. Lee, and Doris Thomas, a black woman who worked for him in the assembly—that he would pay "Peace Corps" wages. But Beeman said he would "unionize" the office unless salaries were raised from $700 a month to $900. A profile of Burton in the February 26 issue of *Roll Call*, the weekly paper that covers Capitol Hill, described him as "to the far left," and said he was planning to "keep his mouth shut and earn his place in the House."

But Burton's reputation preceded him. Irving Sprague, Pat Brown's Washington lobbyist, knew the California congressional delegation well because he took minutes at its weekly meetings. He knew from dozens of conversations that some members worried about Burton's leftist politics. Some of the old-timers, like Cecil King, Chet Holifield, Harold "Bizz" Johnson, and Bernie Sisk were pro-defense and anti-communist legislators and not at all happy about Burton's arrival. One liberal from Berkeley knew Burton intimately. Jeffrey Cohelan was married to the sister of Robert Burton's wife.

Many knew him, and some resented him, for having drawn their congressional districts in the 1961 reapportionment. Through CDC, the Young Democrats, and of course the assembly, Burton had been a fixture in state Democratic politics for years. And because of his intensive national campaigning to become president of the Young Democrats in the late 1950s, Burton had developed extensive contacts with many other Democrats outside California who were already in the House or on their way there.

Even Bolling knew who Burton was. He followed politics around the country and feared that Unruh's steamroller tactics and generous allocation of campaign money might be a harbinger of what was coming to national politics. Bolling believed fervently in the democratic process. Unruh and Burton, he feared, did not understand or seem to care about process. They would do anything to win. Because no rule appeared too sacred to be bent or violated, Bolling, too, viewed Burton's arrival with trepidation.

But devoted liberals like Robert Kastenmeier of Wisconsin, first elected in 1958, were delighted at the arrival of that "young wild man from San Francisco." He felt an immediate kinship with the new legislator, and they became fast friends and drinking companions at the Democratic Club. Kastenmeier said that because of Burton's extensive legislative grounding in California, "he never felt like he had to learn the ropes. That came naturally. He was not awed by the institution and had a tremendous network of associations through his work with the national Young Democrats. He was far better prepared to serve here than almost anyone I ever saw."[7]

Burton's opening move in the House was auspicious. On March 4, the week after he was seated, he blocked for thirty seconds a unanimous consent approval of HUAC's 1964 $300,000 budget. "Speaker John McCormack first declared the budget approved before he spied Burton on his feet," reported UPI, whose dispatch was printed in the *Chronicle* and *Examiner* and clipped for the FBI files. "McCormack then rescinded the declaration and put the question in the form of a motion for voice vote." It passed "without audible opposition."[8] Left-wing journalist I. F. Stone described the incident in his *I. F. Stone's Weekly* of March 16, calling it a "fitting congressional debut." In an interview with Gilbert Woo, editor of the *Chinese Pacific Weekly*, Burton explained what had happened.

> When the budget hearing for the Un-American Activities Committee was brought up, [Woo wrote,] he planned to follow James Roosevelt and others by casting a negative vote. But . . . Roosevelt and others disappeared. When it appeared that the bill was about to be passed unanimously, he stood up and asked for permission to speak (he did not actually know whether or not it was the proper thing to do). The Chairman [sic] did not see him, so he stepped forward to the microphone. By the time he was ready to speak, the bill was already passed. . . . He felt strange that for political reasons they all cast favorable votes.

Burton told Woo there was a "progressive block" of thirty-seven House Democrats. "Not only is Mr. Burton a member of this block, he is also its secretary and treasurer."[9]

Burton was sending powerful signals that he was not like the other "liberals" whom Bolling had described so contemptuously. He would not run for cover when a tough vote came. And he was certainly not suspicious of exerting power or worried that one of his measures would attract too much support.

Given his priorities and agenda, Burton's assignment to the Committee on Interior and Insular Affairs was puzzling. Because of the way the committee system worked, Burton would have no standing to carry bills on issues or problems not directly connected to his committee's jurisdiction. For a hard-charging urban liberal interested in labor, welfare, and civil rights, a committee with jurisdiction over western lands and resource management had about as much relevance as one on national weights and measures. It is not clear how Burton landed there, whether he chose this committee himself or whether his foes parked him there thinking it would effectively neutralize him.

William Thomas, who later worked for Burton and briefly was Shelley's mayoral press secretary, maintained that Shelley, still in a snit over Burton's election, called his good friend John McCormack and suggested that the Speaker assign Burton a dead-end committee. Others said Shelley—a strong labor advocate—would not have punished a fellow liberal just to exact personal revenge. Cecil King, dean of the delegation, would have been key to determining Burton's assignment. He also had little reason to help Burton. But in a 1975 magazine profile, Burton acquaintance Ralph Dewey said Burton may have actually sought the seemingly irrelevant assignment himself. "Phil could rattle off the ages and assess the re-election chances of the senior members of virtually every committee," Dewey said. "He chose Interior because he could gain seniority there faster than any place else."[10]

Despite his general sense of impatience and need to accomplish things quickly, Burton was not crazy. He knew the norms of the House well enough to know he should not attempt to attract too much attention at first. Whatever big splash he might make could be more than offset by making permanent enemies of powerful members who could keep him in his place for years. Kastenmeier said Burton was content at first to "broaden his perspective, especially on foreign policy." Some insiders, nevertheless, held him to a very tough standard. Writing from Washington in the *Examiner* of March 31, 1964, Jack McDowell reported that "scuttlebutt under the big national Capitol dome says Burton was not greeted with the majority party's biggest welcome mat." While Republican Bill Mailliard extended the civility expected of a new arrival from his home town, McDowell wrote, "the Democratic brass didn't fire a 21-gun salute. . . . Being low man on a tall totem pole at the moment, the [Interior] committee gives him little in the way of a big voice that will be heard and/or recognized in terms of San Francisco problems." Meanwhile, "old legislative hands are blunt in their comparison: Jack Shelley, they remind you pointedly, was on the House Appropriations Committee."[11] This was an unfair comparison—freshmen rarely got appointed to such power committees, especially when they were sworn in after the session had begun and assignments made. Shelley had no such power committee his first term, either. But it represented the kind of coverage Burton received from the conservative hometown newspapers. His critics turned out to be dead wrong, and the potential significance of Burton's first committee assignment was not lost on local or national environmentalists.

One night soon after McDowell's article ran, Burton happened to be at the same restaurant where physician Edgar Wayburn, president of the San Francisco–based Sierra Club, was dining with his Washington lobbyist. Wayburn had paid a welcome call to Burton at his office that afternoon and Burton eventually joined him at his table. Burton listened closely while the men talked at length about conservation matters, including legislation for a park in Northern California to save the giant redwood forests. Wayburn said it would be nearly impossible to get anything past the autocratic and powerful Interior chairman, Wayne Aspinall of Colorado.

"We'll get rid of him," Burton blurted. Coming from a new member, that bold statement struck Wayburn as extraordinary. Years later, Burton made good on his blustery promise, helping to break Aspinall's iron grip on the committee. That dinner was the beginning of a special relationship between Burton and Wayburn that held immense significance for the future of the American conservation movement.[12]

On July 2, Burton gave his first speech on the House floor, supporting final passage of President Johnson's landmark Civil Rights Act. The next day, he began a trip to Mississippi that not only prompted elaborate FBI surveillance but signaled his intention to become a national player on civil rights issues and a public advocate for activists who were organizing blacks to vote in the South, often at great personal risk. Burton accompanied fellow members Don Edwards of San Jose, a young liberal and former FBI agent who became a close friend and who had preceded Burton in the House by two years, Gus Hawkins of Los Angeles, Burton's former assembly colleague, and William Fitts Ryan of New York. The purpose of the trip was to observe voter registration efforts by the Student Nonviolent Coordinating Committee, CORE, and other groups. Blacks made up 40 percent of Mississippi's population and a majority in more than one-third of the state's counties. But between 1961 and 1963, only 4,700 or 5 percent of the 70,000 blacks who tried to register to vote had actually voted. Violence and intimidation were widespread.[13] The congressmen arrived just as the FBI began searching for the bodies of civil rights workers Mickey Schwerner, James Chaney, and Andrew Goodman, believed to have been murdered near the small town of Philadelphia.

In Rulesville, Mississippi, the delta home of segregationist Senator James Eastland, where Don Edwards's son was working with black voter rights activist Fanny Lou Hamer, Deputy Attorney General Nicholas Katzenbach briefed them on the safety of volunteers for the Mississippi Freedom Democratic Party. At a rally there Burton said, "It will be a long hot summer for all, but it is going to be a lot hotter for the segregationists." Governor Paul Johnson responded that their visit "cannot do our people, both Negro and white, any good" and said the Yankee congressmen were grandstanding for re-election.[14] One of the homes Edwards stayed in was blown up the day after he left.

Even before his election, the FBI furnished raw intelligence files on Burton to Walter Jenkins, a special assistant to President Johnson. The trip South prompted a new flurry of internal memos and confirmed the bureau's previous spying and efforts to discredit Burton. On May 14, Cartha DeLoach wrote Assistant FBI Director John Mohr that "Governor Brown of California presumably endorsed Burton on the condition that the latter not 'rock the boat' during his first term.... Derogatory data on Burton has been furnished to Mr. Jenkins at the White House by letter dated 2/6/64."

A July 2 FBI memo from DeLoach to Mohr noted Burton's travel schedule to Mississippi, including the airline and moment of arrival. "Since being in Congress," DeLoach noted, "Burton has showed a great deal of interest in civil rights matters. . . . It is recommended that Mr. Rosen and the other men on this matter be alerted about this visit and that if they are contacted by these congressmen they should receive them politely, explain our jurisdiction but give no details as to our investigative steps and investigative actions in this regard."

The FBI investigation concerned the missing civil rights workers, whose disappearance prompted intense national interest. On July 5, Burton praised FBI diligence in searching for the bodies. He even sent a copy to the FBI, which must have caused no end of confusion. How could a man who received "strong support from Communist-front groups" support the FBI? "His background is so strongly liberal," another FBI memo said, "that President Johnson inquired of Governor Brown as to his background at the time of his election, and Burton allegedly promised that he would behave in his first term."[15]

Burton did manage briefly to keep his promise to Governor Brown, passing up his first chance to jump into the growing debate over the war in Vietnam. Between his return to Washington and his party's national convention in mid-August in Atlantic City came a momentous event: the Gulf of Tonkin resolution. Acting quickly to shore up congressional support for a wider war in Southeast Asia, including the bombing of North Vietnam, President Johnson pushed through Congress a resolution allowing him to take "all necessary measures" to protect American troops and "prevent further aggression," even though critics argued that much of the aggression that precipitated the resolution had been provoked, if not imagined or faked. Only two men, Senators Ernest Gruening of Alaska and Wayne Morse of Oregon, voted no. In the House, the resolution passed unanimously. In voting for Johnson's Tonkin resolution, Burton honored his pledge to Pat Brown. He would support his president, especially on foreign policy, for his first term, however personally painful it might be. For the rest of his life, he said it was the one vote he most regretted. Never again did he support any measure to prolong that war.

While still in his first months in Congress, Burton became heavily involved in the controversies at the 1964 Atlantic City convention. Two weeks after the Tonkin vote, the Democratic Party met to nominate LBJ. Joining them were activists from the Mississippi Freedom Democratic Party, including Fanny Lou Hamer, who arrived hoping to force the national party to seat them over the segregationist—in some cases pro-Goldwater—official state party.

In sensational testimony, Hamer told the Credentials Committee and a live national television audience how police beat her bloody in a Rulesville jail while she was registering voters. Her group's attorney, longtime liberal activist Joseph Rauh, was trying to round up votes to seat the new delegation, but President Johnson would have none of it. Burton and Beeman loaned their delegate badges to Freedom Party delegates so they could wander the convention floor and lobby for votes, and Burton was in the thick of strategy meetings to get them seated.[16] But after Johnson and running mate Hubert Humphrey offered a deal allowing just two of them official status, the Mississippi activists rejected it as a liberal betrayal and walked out.

Hamer, Rauh, and the rest of the Mississippi activists lost the battle. But as things turned out, the party took a bigger loss as the Vietnam War deepened. "Committed to the welfare-warfare beneficence of his hero FDR," sociologist and New Left activist Todd Gitlin wrote in his book on the sixties, "Johnson hadn't the faintest idea that his war also passed a death sentence on his Great Society and killed his chance for a full second term."[17]

But while the New Left turned resolutely against the liberals, Burton was an incrementalist to the core, both in the Democratic Party and in congressional politics. Some opponents of the government expressed their anger through demonstrations and later through violence. But Burton stayed on the inside, in many ways no less committed a rebel, but by all accounts a far more pragmatic one. In a different society, even close friends like Agar Jaicks maintained, he might have been a dictator. But in the United States, he learned to manipulate the levers of power. He turned his attention to global and individual instances of injustice, attacking both with equal fervor. In one small example soon after his election, Burton discovered that black barbers in the Capitol were paid a dollar an hour less than white barbers. Outraged, he complained to McCormack, who corrected the wage imbalance. Within a few years, he was making deals with the same southern reactionaries whose civil rights policies appalled him.

On district matters, Burton sent an early signal home he would operate differently. No longer would he tolerate the corrupt practice of "buying" citizenship for wealthy Chinese via private bills, as Shelley had done for years through Malone and Albert Chow. In another interview with Gilbert Woo, he said every request for private bills "must be accompanied by affidavits stating that no money is to be paid to legislators, attorneys or any other persons who have assisted." Woo said Burton was doing this to prevent "private profiteering."[18]

The rest of Burton's first term produced little controversy to match that of the first six months. But he actually accomplished a good deal for a brand-new freshman, especially by establishing an early reputation for liberal activism. In a departure from the cautious tradition of most first-term legislators, Burton took some unpopular stands. In June 1965, when the House approved a bill requiring the death penalty for assassinating a president or vice president, for example, Burton was the only member to vote against it. And an August 1965 "Merry Go-Round" column by Washington columnist Drew Pearson described a "Burton deal"—the first of many. Burton urged California urban members to support LBJ's wheat and cotton subsidy bill. In return, conservatives would support repeal of Section 14-b of the Taft-Hartley Act, which permitted states to pass right-to-work laws. The provision was repealed and the subsidy passed. Voting for repeal were Central Valley Democrats Bizz Johnson, John Moss, John McFall, Bernie Sisk, and Harlen Hagen, not exactly Burton allies. But over the next nearly two decades, ideological opposites would cooperate with him time and again to achieve benefits that otherwise might have been unthinkable.

Before his first term ended and in what must have been an enormously satisfying moment, Burton paid off a political debt and completed a circle at the same time. When he learned that San Francisco Postmaster John Fixa was retiring in 1965, Burton selected Lim P. Lee for the job. Lee, Burton's San Francisco field representative, became the first ever Chinese-American postmaster. He presided over one of the nation's busiest postal districts, with 7,000 employees and $100 million a year volume. Wire services carried Lee's appointment all over the world. It took nine long years, but Lim P. Lee finally achieved the dream he envisioned back in 1956 when Burton walked into Albert Chow's office in Chinatown and asked for help defeating Tommy Maloney. In breaking with Chow that day and aligning himself with Burton, Lee became not merely "number one" in Chinatown. He was now the highest-ranking Chinese-American in the entire federal government.

The FBI also watched the Lee appointment, forwarding a news story about it to Washington "in order that the Bureau will be aware of the type of individual who is being proposed." A December 6, 1965 memo from the San Francisco office to J. Edgar Hoover recommended that if Hoover had not already sent this information to the White House, "it is suggested that such be done at this time in the event the President has another candidate in mind . . . but it is not believed that, under any circumstances, BURTON should become aware of the Bureau's interest in this."[19]

Burton's "wild man" reputation was also known to the labor movement, which had a way of handpicking members of the House Education and Labor Committee and which saw Burton as far too independent to reliably count on. Nevertheless, Burton wanted to join that committee for the jurisdiction it would give him over issues he cared deepest about. On October 28, 1965, Speaker McCormack appointed Burton to the Education and Labor Committee, upon the resignation of James Roosevelt. Few considered Ed and Labor, as it was called, a desirable committee. Republicans were always fighting with Democrats over big-spending labor programs. Democrats often felt the yoke of the AFL-CIO and its powerful chief lobbyist, Andrew Biemiller, a former member from Wisconsin who tried to block Burton's appointment.[20]

"He's too liberal, and we can't control him," Biemiller told Dick Murphy, George Hardy's Washington lobbyist. "He wants to get on Ed and Labor, and we're going to prevent it." His failure to stop Burton was a rare loss for Biemiller.

And in besting him, Burton demonstrated some deft moves early. He spent a good deal of time stroking McCormack. Burton also cultivated the chairman of the committee, the flamboyant Adam Clayton Powell. Powell knew of Burton not because of any labor issues but because of his close association with black civil rights activists like Carlton Goodlett in San Francisco. Once Powell learned of Burton's interest, he insisted on Burton joining the committee. It was a perfect assignment for Burton. Finally he had a forum in which to push for pro-labor legislation. Under Powell, he had a like-minded, if lazy, chairman.

But many committee liberals—notably fourth-ranking Frank Thompson or "Thompy," as he was known, John Brademas of Indiana, and Jim O'Hara of Michigan also tried to convince McCormack not to put Burton on the committee. They considered themselves intellectuals. They believed in decorum, and like Bolling, in process. Burton was too crude, seemed too much in a hurry. He was also close to Powell, whom they hated and believed brought disgrace to the House through his inattention to business, constant flouting of House rules, high living, and junkets with gorgeous secretaries. Ken Young, who lobbied the Education and Labor Committee for the AFL-CIO, was told his organization should have no relationship with Powell, because there was a price for everything. AFL-CIO President George Meany refused to operate that way.[21]

Thompson, Bolling, and Biemiller were also close. Thompson managed Bolling's abortive 1962 run for majority leader against Albert, telling Bolling to withdraw when the votes were not there. First elected in 1954, he was a protégé of Senator Eugene McCarthy of Minnesota, who helped found the Democratic Study Group, a small but respected group of reform-minded House liberals. An assistant minority leader in the New Jersey legislature, Thompson was wise-cracking and irreverent when he arrived in Washington. But he was quickly summoned to "Mr. Sam's" office and lectured for shooting his mouth off. Later he said it was the best thing that ever happened to him, because if the Speaker had not cared about him, Rayburn never would have called him in. Thompson liked to study each new class and pick out future stars. He singled out Brademas, O'Hara, and William Ford of Michigan, all of whom joined him on Ed and Labor. He did not single out Burton.[22]

Burton lived up to his reputation—and did not endear himself to the high-minded liberals on the Ed and Labor Committee—when he became embroiled in the long-simmering controversy over Powell. Just two years into his House career, Burton emerged as one of Powell's few staunch defenders during his sustained battle to retain his chairmanship.

Powell was born in 1908. His father, Adam Clayton Powell, Sr., built the Abyssinian Baptist Church into one of New York's largest Protestant denominations. The son was educated at Colgate and Columbia. He got his Doctor of Divinity degree from Shaw and succeeded his father at Abyssinian Baptist in 1937. Always the "playboy," as his chief aide C. Clement "Chuck" Stone once wrote of him, Powell plunged into civil rights activities in Harlem and was elected the state's first black congressman in 1944 and only the second black House member. He became a leading civil rights figure, although when Martin Luther King, Jr., and others emerged, they soon surpassed him in effectiveness and dedication.

Powell's highly publicized marriages to a succession of beautiful and controversial women brought him notoriety and eventual dishonor, although his Harlem constituents loved him for poking his finger in the white man's eye. During one campaign in Harlem, Stone wrote, an opponent began listing all of his infidelities and extravagances but was interrupted by a supporter who said, "Aw quit it, man. The cat's livin'." In 1961, Powell assumed the chairmanship of Ed and Labor over Meany's objections. He was close to Rayburn and was a surprisingly early supporter of Rayburn's 1960 candidate for president, Lyndon Johnson. Perhaps, Stone suggested, that was a payoff for Rayburn's support of his chairmanship.[23] Powell relied heavily on his subcommittee chairs to do the substantive work.

The Powell crisis boiled over soon after Burton joined the committee, but it had been heating up for years. His attendance record even while chairman in the early 1960s averaged about 50 percent on roll call votes—compared to 80 to 90 percent for the average member. In the middle of the 1962 session, Powell took a taxpayer-financed six-week trip to Europe, where newspaper accounts recorded him at glamorous night spots accompanied by two attractive women on the committee staff. His wife was also on the payroll for more than $20,000 a year, even though she lived in Puerto Rico and did no work. During the twenty months of the Eighty-ninth Congress, he billed the committee for some sixty-five trips to Puerto Rico and to Miami—from which it was just a short jaunt to his Bimini vacation home in the Bahamas.

When members criticized Powell, he charged they were singling him out because of his race. He said his behavior was no different than that of white chairmen. In fact, Powell's behavior often seemed deliberately outrageous. Stone wrote, "Adam Powell not only defied the great American conception of black people as submissive and speak-only-when-spoken-to 'house niggers,' fawning and shuffling when the white plantation master has given permission, he ungraciously destroyed it."[24]

What hastened the crisis, however, was Powell's habit of ransoming major labor bills in exchange for anti-discrimination riders, known as "Powell amendments," some of which even NAACP lobbyists opposed. This practice incensed the AFL-CIO and the committee. He held up antipoverty bills and voted against both the 1965 Voting Rights Act and the 1966 civil rights bill, calling them a "phony carrot stick" for the black middle class. On September 15, 1966, Sam Gibbons, a Florida Democrat, said Powell missed 75 percent of the roll and quorum calls that year. Powell called him a racist. The following week, led by Gibbons and Thompson, the committee voted 27-1 to adopt new rules to substantially curb the chairman's power.[25]

The new rules allowed the six subcommittee chairmen or the full committee to "take the necessary steps" to bring a bill to the floor if the chairman failed to act. They forced Powell to prepare a committee budget for each session—to be approved by the majority members—and a detailed monthly accounting of all committee expenses, as well as majority party veto over hiring and firing of staff members under Powell's jurisdiction. Given the wide discretion and power committee chairmen routinely and sometimes arbitrarily exercised, this was an extraordinary curtailing of his powers. But Powell took credit for passing the new rules, calling them some of the most important reforms in the history of the House. One Republican voted against the new rules and three Democrats voted present: Powell, Hawkins, and Phil Burton.

"There weren't too many who stood firm with me during the crisis of the last few days concerning my Chairmanship," Powell wrote Burton on September 26, his public bravado notwithstanding, "but your strong and unyielding support of me was that tower of strength which sustained me. . . . Negroes all over the country will never forget that when the chips were down, Phil Burton stood shoulder to shoulder with Adam Clayton Powell."

But soon the news turned worse for Powell. On the same day he wrote Burton, a House Administration subcommittee chaired by Ohio Democrat Wayne Hays began investigating Powell's use of congressional funds. In response, Powell charged that in 1963 Hays took the House dining room headwaiter with him to Europe for a meeting of the North Atlantic Treaty Alliance.[26] The subcommittee invited Powell—vacationing on Bimini—to testify, but Powell said he would testify only if the investigation also included a "comparative analysis of travel vouchers of staff members of other full committees and subcommittees, including your own."

This was a valid point. Hays was corrupt in much the same way Powell was. The Administration Committee reported on January 2, 1967, that Powell and some staff members had used assumed names on airline flights to cover up committee-paid trips to Florida, that there was "strong presumption" that his wife had done no work to earn her salary, and that all travel regulations should be tightened up. Another investigation showed he had taken ten committee-paid trips to Miami with his $19,000-a-year secretary.

The following week, liberals approved a Democratic Caucus move to strip Powell of his chairmanship, the first such action since 1925, and seat him conditionally, while yet another committee investigated whether he was fit to serve. That investigation ended February 23 with a recommendation that Powell be seated, but censured, stripped of his seniority, and fined $40,000 as partial recompense for committee funds he had misused.

But the House went against the leadership of both parties and voted overwhelmingly to prevent him from being seated at all. A huge volume of anti-Powell mail prompted Elmer Holland, a Democrat of Pennsylvania, to say that he had no doubt "that it was largely motivated by the notion that a Negro congressman ought to be more circumspect, more humble and more 'grateful' than his white colleagues need be. I submit, Mr. Speaker, that . . . the effort to exclude the gentleman from New York could not have succeeded, and might not even have been attempted, had Adam C. Powell done everything he is accused of doing, but had he been—to coin a phrase— 'less colorful.'"[27]

In a January 14, 1967 letter to the *Sun Reporter*, Burton said the refusal to seat Powell "will be recorded as one of the darkest hours in the history of the House." He said the voters of Harlem were being denied a voice. "One does not have to condone all of Adam Clayton Powell's adventures in order to believe 400,000 Americans residing in Powell's district have the undeniable right under our Constitution to select a representative in Congress of their own choosing." Burton said the seniority system had never been "sacrosanct" to him, but if it was good enough "to keep Howard Smith of Virginia as Chairman of the Rules Committee and now Bill Colmer of Mississippi," it was good enough to retain Powell. "When an exception to the seniority rule is made in the instance where the chairman is a Negro American," Burton wrote, "this action invites justifiable speculation as to the real reasons behind it."

In a letter to the newspaper six months later, Powell aide Chuck Stone praised the "tremendous job" Burton did "to prevent the political emasculation of one of the most powerful 'brothers' in America." No congressman fought harder, Stone wrote, "or more militantly on the House floor for Adam or spent more time talking and buttonholing other congressmen on Adam's behalf . . . this guy has got more soul than nine-tenths of the Negroes walking around the Urban League offices telling 'Mr. Charlie' what he wants to hear."[28]

Because of a criminal contempt citation in an unrelated libel case, Powell faced arrest if he set foot in New York. During the special election to fill his seat that April, Powell remained in Bimini but still won with 86 percent of the vote. "Delighted but not surprised," Burton cabled. "Harlem kept the faith, baby," a play on Powell's trademark saying. The House continued to exclude him, however. He remained in Bimini and pursued a lawsuit—which he eventually won—challenging the constitutionality of the House action.

Powell returned for the 1969 session. He was seated after a five-hour debate, but Congress stripped him of his seniority and required him to pay a $25,000 fine, in addition to the $55,000 in pay he had forfeited. On June 16, 1969, the Supreme Court ruled 7 to 1 that Congress had violated Powell's constitutional rights by refusing to seat him in 1967. The Court said Powell met the Constitution's sole standards to be seated: age, citizenship, and residence. But by then, the long and costly battle and Powell's own human failings had destroyed his career. In the 1970 primary, he was defeated by Charles Rangel.

While still enmeshed in the Powell controversy, Burton returned to the issue that consumed him for most of his career: reapportionment. On the day before he was elected to Congress, the Supreme Court handed down an important reapportionment opinion. Building on its famous 1962 *Baker v. Carr* decision requiring equal representation, the court in *Reynolds v. Sims* said the Constitution required both houses in a bicameral state legislature to create districts on the basis of equal population. In California, that meant grossly unfair senate boundaries, skewed to protect Northern California water from thirsty Southern Californians, would have to be redrawn. Los Angeles County alone would get fourteen senators, instead of one.

Burton, who had the smallest district in the state, knew its days were numbered, too. In early 1965, he called reapportionment expert Leroy Hardy at Cal State Long Beach, and asked him to fly back to Washington. "We've got to start thinking about realigning the congressional districts," Burton told Hardy. "We want to be ready." Burton talked his California colleagues in Washington into creating a new plan, and Hardy talked about how to equalize the population of the districts. Many left the issue to Burton because his work in 1961 helped bring six of them to Congress. They did not have the time or interest to plunge back into the technical aspects of redistricting.

Hardy was constantly amazed at Burton's ability to absorb all of the professor's details and analysis and then dazzle his colleagues with his knowledge of their districts, their demographics, their voting patterns, their geography. "He knew he was going to talk to Congressman Jones," Hardy recalled, and would "pump me for all the information I knew about Jones's district. . . . Then he would go and make his case with the congressman [who] would just be awestruck, I mean, speechless."[29]

Despite Burton's enthusiasm, Unruh and Bob Crown did not want to redistrict in 1965 unless they had to. That changed with a 1967 California Supreme Court case. The court stated that unless the legislature passed a new congressional plan by December, the court would adopt one itself. In the interim, Ronald Reagan was elected governor, however, which guaranteed a sweetheart or "incumbent protection" act. The only way a Republican governor would sign a redistricting plan drawn up by Democrats, in other words, was if incumbents of both parties were protected.

In Washington, the California delegation met to consider what to do. Judging by the petty concerns the members raised, however, it was clear they had no idea how the 1967 court case threatened their existence, which drove Burton to distraction. Dean of the delegation Cecil King said he wanted to keep the Seventeenth District but did not want to live in it. George Miller of Alameda (no relation to the chairman of the state senate Finance Committee) said he wanted his grandparents' graves to remain in his district. Bizz Johnson said he wanted to keep the jumping frogs of Calaveras County in his district, because he loved judging the famous contest every year.

"Goddam it! This is bullshit!" Burton exploded, having heard all he could tolerate. "This is bullshit. We're not going to survive with this bullshit. Goddam son of a bitch! Don't you understand?" With that, he stormed out.

After the meeting abruptly ended, George Gould was in his office when the phone rang. An Unruh operative who helped elect Los Angeles Democrat Charlie Wilson to Congress, Gould remained in Washington as his aide. Wilson was on the line saying Phil Burton wanted Gould to work with him on a new plan. "Charlie, he's not in charge," Gould protested. "Jim Corman [a Los Angeles congressman] is in charge."

"I think he ought to be in charge," Wilson replied.

"Jess is not going to like this," Gould said.

"Goddam it!" Wilson said. "We're not going to survive in this delegation unless somebody takes charge to hold it together."

A few weeks later, Burton was asked to write the new plan. Corman's district was becoming more Republican. One of Burton's jobs was to give him a safer one. The delegation had turned to one of its most junior members in desperation, fear, love, and hate. They did not have the skill to save their own skins. Burton did. He could draw districts to meet new court standards of compactness and equal population and still preserve incumbent seats. They appreciated his brilliance but hated delegating the task to him. They wanted to be in charge of their own future but did not know how. It gnawed at them that Burton was now controlling their political fortunes. And he wouldn't let them forget it.[30]

Over the next few months, Burton did exactly what was asked of him. His plan united the fractious thirty-eight-member delegation on the new district lines. And for good reason. He guaranteed all of their re-elections for at least the next four years, some for a lot longer than that. Democrats and Republicans alike found their districts strengthened. Burton negotiated one-on-one with members, finding out what they wanted. Then he gave it to them or threatened to take it away. During one "negotiation" with Charlie Wilson, Burton said, "The trouble with you, Charlie, is you want me to take 100,000 blacks out of your district for the primary and then put them back in for the general, and even I can't do that." In another conversation, somebody observed, "Phil, it looks like you're starting every plan with the Fifth District" (Burton's). "You gotta start somewhere," he replied. "This is where the domino effect really applies, not Vietnam. You take 10,000 people out of one district, you gotta put them somewhere else."[31]

While he did the negotiating, Hardy did the technical work. Corman's Democratic registration increased from 53.8 percent to 57.2 percent (he remained in Congress another thirteen years as his district gradually turned Republican again). Richard Hanna, the only Democrat in Orange County, unloaded so many Republican constituents that Democratic registration dropped from 60 to 50 percent in neighbor Charles Wiggins's district, enough for Hanna to hang on for another couple of terms in that conservative GOP bastion. Both men were delighted with the changes.[32]

Burton's work captured everyone's attention, including the *Wall Street Journal*'s, which on November 9, 1967, said it produced "what may be the greatest bipartisan gerrymander in U.S. history." On December 18, 1967, the state supreme court approved Burton's plan. While his district gained more than 130,000 voters, all in San Francisco in what had formerly been Mailliard's district, Mailliard hopped across the Golden Gate Bridge into southern Marin County.

Vietnam and the domino effect were much on Burton's mind. Even before he left Sacramento, Burton was concerned about Vietnam. As early as September 5, 1963, he expressed his "deep concern over the rising tide of violence and suppression of religious freedom in South Vietnam." While he said ultimate decisions rested with President Kennedy and Secretary of State Dean Rusk, "most Americans cannot help but be appalled by the widespread violence and callous harshness of statements by those close to the Diem government."

Despite his misgivings, Burton voted for the Tonkin resolution because he had given his word to Governor Brown. But on May 5, 1965, Burton was one of only three members to vote against a $700 million appropriation to continue the war. Taking on a powerful, popular incumbent president of his own party who had won a landslide victory over Barry Goldwater was no easy thing for anyone to do. Lyndon Johnson's political skills and powers of persuasion were legend. But Burton was willing to stand up and become one of the antiwar leaders in the House. On March 1, 1966, Burton again voted against a military appropriation bill. "I do this with sadness," he said, "for I do not like to oppose the president who, no less than myself or any other member of this House, is acting out of conscience and a profound desire to serve the best interests of this nation." Nor, Burton said, did he lack appreciation for the "terrible sacrifices" that American soldiers were making each day.

"I oppose this bill," he said, "as a futile attempt to achieve, by additional force of arms, solutions to problems which are not primarily military, but essentially political, economic and social." Burton said the country was "sinking deeper and deeper into a land war in Asia for goals which become increasingly obscure and at costs which we dare not fully assess."

The next day John Burton wrote him a letter. "Dear Phil," he said, "I have never been as proud of my big brother since 'Bud Burton' hustled in two buckets and a free throw to win high point honors for Washington in the game with Lowell." "Bud" was the mangled name one of the local papers used to record Burton's basketball heroics that day. A month later, Burton got a letter from Robert Peck, his "radical" navy and USC roommate, now a Los Angeles physician.

> It's 4:30 A.M. My friends ask me why I get up so early. The answer seems to belabor the obvious—to get ahead of the Fascists. For your part, as I remember, you always stay up late—for the same purpose, I'm sure. I just

read in *I. F. Stone's Weekly* for March 7 that you voted against the $4.8 billion supplemental to the Vietnam War bill. I wasn't surprised you were one of just four dissenters. But it occurred to me I haven't written to tell you I take you for granted for a long time. It is marvelous work you are doing.

Dr. Burton was not so easily impressed. "Phil, why don't you just do something about that war in Vietnam," he said over breakfast with his son and Chuck Hurley, a new aide and former *Fresno Bee* reporter. "Just take care of it. And when was the last time you saw a dentist about your teeth?"[33]

After his vote, Burton met with President Johnson in the White House. He told Kastenmeier that Johnson pulled him aside, reached into his pocket and let Burton read a secret cable from his field generals saying the prognosis was good. Burton was impressed. "Phil, he pulls out that dog-eared telegram for everybody," Kastenmeier said. "That has no relevance at all as to whether we should be in that war." Burton thought about that for a moment and agreed. But for a brief moment, LBJ had convinced him.[34]

In September 1967, Burton was invited on a Potomac cruise and had a long conversation about Vietnam with a Johnson aide, who recorded what Burton said in a memo to Johnson. Burton was probably well tanked by the time he began fulminating. Despite the alcohol, his mind was not dulled. There was no hint that LBJ would not seek another term, that Eugene McCarthy would do well in early presidential primaries in 1968, or that Robert Kennedy would jump in. But Burton had an uncanny sense of what the war could cost in political, as well as in human, terms.

"Vietnam will destroy the Democratic Party," Burton began.

> We will lose five to eight California House seats, probably the California legislature. It makes no difference whether the president is re-elected or not, because we will be so badly off in the Congress that we can all just sit there for four years and watch the country slowly go to hell. . . . Every time the president lashes out at dissenters and pickets, he is applauded by people who would vote for a dead dog rather than *any* Democrat—and he loses 10,000 votes from people who are trying to stay with him in spite of everything.

Burton said that even he stopped listening to Johnson's speeches, because the more he heard the less likely he would support the president.

What I think about Vietnam is spelled out very well by [Vermont Senator George] Aiken. We ought to structure things over the next few months so that we can say, "We won"—and then get the hell out of there. We won't do this because Johnson has become a True Believer on Vietnam. His ego is so tied up in this thing that he will never let history say he failed to win "his" war. His greatest virtue always was not being a True Believer—and he isn't a True Believer now on anything else. But he is throwing it all away on Vietnam. . . . The president is leading our Party right down the hole—and it is *all* Vietnam. . . . Everybody on the Hill knows that the only smart thing to tell the White House is what it wants to hear. I don't like to do that because this is not how you win elections. But then sometimes I say to myself, "Why not?" Everybody knows by now that the White House isn't *in* politics anymore, anyhow.[35]

Burton exaggerated slightly. The Democrats kept their substantial congressional majorities, but Richard Nixon captured the White House over Hubert Humphrey, and the California Assembly did go Republican in 1968 for the first time in twelve years. Worse for the Democrats, however, was the debacle at their national convention in Chicago. Torn by the war, the party nearly self-destructed while the nation watched on national television. Riots, tear gas, and violence inside and outside the convention hall provided a scary portrait of a party that could no longer contain itself, that was about to lose the confidence of mainstream voters—Nixon's "silent majority"—and five of the next six presidential elections.

As American and Vietnamese death tolls mounted and students across the U.S. protested with increasing vehemence, the House remained loyal to Johnson and supportive of his war policies. But with each election cycle, the number of antiwar liberals slowly grew and formed a small, informal organization known as "the Group." The other members besides Burton were Kastenmeier, Don Edwards, and George Brown of California; Don Fraser of Minnesota; Ben Rosenthal, Ed Koch, John Dow, and Bill Fitts Ryan of New York; John Conyers of Michigan; Father Robert Drinan of Massachusetts; Abner Mikva of Illinois; and Bob Eckhardt of Texas.

The Group included chairs and former chairs of the Democratic Study Group and of ADA. They were social friends as well as political allies and met intermittently to discuss tactics to end the war, reform the House, and achieve other liberal goals. The Group published a book entitled *Anatomy of an Undeclared War: Congressional Conference on the Pentagon Papers*, edited by staff aide Pat Kraus. When the all-male Group expanded, freshman hellraiser Bella Abzug of New York joined, but one of the founders said they found her so obnoxious they disbanded after one more meeting.[36]

As opposition to the war spread in early 1968, Burton was torn over whether to support Johnson—out of loyalty to his old friend Hubert Humphrey—or Eugene McCarthy's insurgent candidacy. He asked a staffer to call McCarthy, but never got a call back. When he heard that his brother had endorsed McCarthy in California, he decided to try again. But Robert Kennedy called first. They took a long walk around the Capitol grounds, during which Kennedy asked for and got Burton's support. That endorsement led to a rapprochement in Sacramento with Jesse Unruh, who was directing Robert Kennedy's California campaign. Burton helped with the Northern California portion.

It was already an extraordinary political year by the time the June 1968 California primary arrived, with its winner-take-all system of allocating 174 delegates, the most of any state. In late March, LBJ shocked the nation by announcing he would not seek another term. The following month, Martin Luther King, Jr., was assassinated in Memphis, where he had gone to lead a strike of garbage workers. His death touched off riots in black ghettos in more than 120 cities. During the first six months, meanwhile, 9,557 Americans were killed in Vietnam, more than the number killed in all of 1967.[37]

Amid these grim events, it looked as though the California primary would determine the nomination. Humphrey, trapped by his commitment to an unpopular, lame-duck president and to an even more unpopular war, was so far ahead in the delegate hunt that he was within reach of clinching it. Capitalizing on years of contacts among labor and party regulars, Humphrey, however, had avoided all the primaries, including California's. But if Kennedy could beat McCarthy in California, he could challenge Humphrey going in to the Chicago convention on the grounds that Humphrey had not submitted himself to the voters. Wherever Kennedy went in Northern California, Burton was at his side.

Shortly after midnight on June 5, as Robert Kennedy walked through the pantry at the Hotel Ambassador, he knew he had won a close but critically important victory over Gene McCarthy. Most people around the country had gone to bed when Kennedy headed downstairs to the victory party in the hotel ballroom. He had hit his stride in this state, offering hope to traumatized and deeply disillusioned liberals, angry, working-class, socially conservative whites, and blacks and Hispanics, including his friend Cesar Chavez, whose United Farm Workers union worked hard for Kennedy's victory. As Kennedy looked out over the celebrants, he said, "On to Chicago, and let's win there."

"What happened next, at approximately 12:20 A.M.," Nelson Polsby wrote fifteen years later, "was one of the most extraordinary and consequential events in modern American political history. On the night of his victory in the California primary, Robert Kennedy was shot and killed. It was widely and immediately assumed that Vice President Humphrey was the obvious beneficiary of this dreadful act. Events were presently to reveal, however, that nothing could have been further from the truth."[38]

Phillip Burton was celebrating Kennedy's victory in San Francisco with brother Ted when the horrifying news came that Robert Kennedy had been shot. Burton immediately called the Presidio Army Base nearby to order a plane to fly Ted to Los Angeles, but a hesitant army major seemed unwilling to bend the rules without higher authorization. "This is Congressman Phillip Burton," Burton bellowed. "I am standing here with Senator Edward Kennedy, whose brother has just been shot and who may be the next president of the United States. You are at a point I call a career decision, Major. Either you get that plane now or your career is over."[39] Kennedy got his plane. Unruh, meanwhile, chose the delegates for Kennedy.

The assassination set the stage for the looming disaster in Mayor Richard Daley's Chicago, where antiwar protestors prepared to battle what many considered a bankrupt party. Many Kennedy activists were so grief-stricken they did not participate, leaving a less acceptable McCarthy to carry the antiwar banner to party regulars committed to Humphrey. The same southerners who walked out of the convention in 1948 during Humphrey's famous civil rights speech to form a segregationist third-party candidacy for then-Democrat Strom Thurmond, now accepted Humphrey as the least objectionable nominee.

The biggest fight inside the hall, once it became clear that Humphrey would be nominated, was the platform plank over Vietnam. Unruh controlled the California delegation, but Burton led the charge for a peace plank on behalf of the McCarthy forces and what was left of the Kennedy campaign, some of whom were moving to Senator George McGovern of South Dakota, and for a brief moment, to Ted Kennedy. The California delegation, almost entirely opposed to Humphrey, was subjected to petty indignities and annoyances in order to minimize its influence from the moment it arrived. The delegation was housed at a hotel far from the action, and delegates were constantly hassled on their way into the hall and onto the floor. Before the real violence at the convention began, California delegates even threatened to nominate Unruh for president unless the delegation was given better treatment.

The conflict over the Vietnam plank began on August 15, before the convention opened, when McCarthy told a huge rally at Madison Square Garden that he would demand "forcefully and without compromise" a platform that admitted errors in Vietnam policy and that called for "a new government in Saigon open to the participation of the National Liberation Front." The fight continued on August 19 in Washington, where the Platform Committee, chaired by soon-to-be Majority Leader Hale Boggs of Louisiana, opened hearings. Burton, the only other House member on the committee, pressed for a peace plank. He also wanted planks supporting Cesar Chavez's drive to organize farm workers and endorsing the recent Kerner Commission report on urban riots and race relations.

"It would be a mistake to assume that alienation goes no deeper into the society than a few thousand hippies, yippies, beatniks and kooks," Burton told the committee. "There are many signs that ordinary, serious young people feel alienated from the American political system." Burton urged the committee to "say something meaningful" or "say nothing." Something meaningful meant a guaranteed minimum annual income for all citizens, opposition to an anti-ballistic missile system, reform of congressional rules and an end to "knee-jerk" opposition to every revolution the world over, from Russia to Cuba to Vietnam. "A much wiser policy would be one that does not interfere in the revolutionary process abroad," Burton said. "It would be a policy which recognized that in some cases revolutions are necessary and good, just as the revolution of 1776 in this country was necessary and good."

"If this is the guy they sent to help me out," Boggs told aide Gary Hymel, "good Lord."

As Secretary Rusk began testifying to the Platform Committee on Vietnam the following day, Burton stood at the microphone, poised to attack. But aides hurriedly swept in bearing urgent notes: Soviets tanks had just rolled into Czechoslovakia to quash the Prague Spring of Czech leader Alexander Dubcek. "These are momentous events, Mr. Secretary," Boggs told Rusk. "We will understand if you have to rush back to your office." For one of the few times in his life, Burton was left open-mouthed.[40] The next morning, in his first address since his brother's death, Ted Kennedy called Vietnam "the tragedy of our generation" and urged a bombing halt in North Vietnam, mutual withdrawal from the South, and renewed effort to create a legitimate government in Saigon.

By the time the Democrats moved to Chicago, events were already unraveling as antiwar protesters, hippies, and yippies converged on the city. Each night the street violence escalated, culminating on August 28, when police used nightsticks, mace, tear gas, and rifle butts against surging crowds of thousands of demonstrators, who chanted, "The whole world is watching" to the waiting TV cameras. Inside the hall, delegates and journalists alike were hauled off the floor by beefy security guards or arrested for such petty violations as having the wrong credentials. Set amid this poisonous atmosphere, Burton addressed the convention to argue for the Vietnam peace plank, knowing the other side had the votes. CBS News anchor Walter Cronkite introduced Burton as a forty-two-year-old lawyer and World War II veteran.

"If we continue our effort in Vietnam," Burton said, "I fear that many more Vietnamese will be killed, many more brave Americans will perish, many mothers and fathers will weep, and this great nation will be cast over by a shadow that only the passing of time will dispel." Most of his speech was telecast. Occasionally the cameras cut to an earnest-looking nun or delegates draping newspapers over empty chairs to read the convention coverage. "History will judge this nation and this convention harshly," Burton went on, "if we fail to act or contribute in any manner to the prolongation of this war or its escalation. Mr. Chairman, the war in Vietnam continues, and we find ourselves committed to more money expended in any given month to destroy the countryside some 10,000 miles away than we spend in a full year in our war on poverty at home. . . . This is not acceptable."[41]

The minority plank called for an immediate bombing halt, a mutual withdrawal of troops, and negotiation with the National Liberation Front to form a new government in the South. The majority plank said: "We reject as unacceptable a unilateral withdrawal" and called for support of the Paris peace talks and "the initiative of President Johnson which brought the North Vietnamese to the peace table."

Under no circumstances would Lyndon Johnson accept a peace plank. It lost by more than 500 votes. "It was a debate that had no parallel in American convention politics," wrote *Congressional Quarterly* in its 1968 almanac, "and the vote was a record of party opinion that could not help but influence the party's eventual nominee, Hubert Humphrey. That forty percent of the delegates had voted against his position was a signal that he would have grave difficulty in holding his party's vote in November."

With hindsight, 1960s chronicler and New Left activist Todd Gitlin was harsher: "What exploded in Chicago that week," he wrote, "was the product of pressures that had been building up for almost a decade: the exhaustion of liberalism, the marauding vengefulness of the authorities, the resolve and recklessness of the movement, the disintegration of the Democratic Party. But Chicago threw all the elements into chemical reaction. . . . Chicago confirmed that no centers were going to hold, no wisdom was going to prevail."[42]

As images of violence and chaos from the convention and the streets were televised to a nation wondering if it was coming apart at the seams, one small scene briefly stood out. It held enormous implications for the future leadership of the House and eventually for Phillip Burton. Lyndon Johnson was watching on television as the convention chairman, Majority Leader Carl Albert, lost control. Johnson called Daley—who already had been televised making an obscene gesture to Senator Abraham Ribicoff of Connecticut when Ribicoff criticized Daley and the Chicago police's "Gestapo tactics"—and ordered Daley to take control.

Daley signaled his man, Dan Rostenkowski, who, at six feet five inches, towered over the tiny Albert, to seize the gavel. Albert never forgave Rostenkowski for what he considered a slight on national TV. In his autobiography, Albert said he "gave" the gavel to Rostenkowski as a favor to the hometown congressman. Nobody believed that. Later he punished Rostenkowski by refusing to name him whip, even though he was the choice of the new majority leader, Thomas P. "Tip" O'Neill of Massachusetts. Rostenkowski earned his way back into the good graces of the House leadership by supporting Burton's Texas opponent for majority leader eight years later.[43]

8

THE "BURTON MACHINE"

The people around him would jump if Phil gave the order, because they
would think that was marching orders and they had to follow.

CASPAR WEINBERGER
former California Republican Party chairman

PHILLIP BURTON WANTED it all. He wanted rapid advancement in Washington, both to exercise power and to push his agenda. He also wanted to
dominate the political life of San Francisco from the county committee to
the mayor's office. But as he gained influence on Capitol Hill and finally
even seized control of the county committee at home, he ran into a major
roadblock on the way to city hall. His overpowering personality gave opponents a target around which to unify. As Mayor Jack Shelley stumbled
through his term, as the newspapers began writing ominously of Burton's
growing clout, a new political rival suddenly emerged in San Francisco named
Joseph Alioto who battled Burton on his home turf. Their fights became
legendary in local political circles.

When Burton was elected to his first full term in Congress in November
1964, brother John was re-elected to Phillip's former assembly seat (after
winning a special election earlier in the year). To sweeten their victory, Willie
Brown prevailed in his second attempt to defeat the seventy-eight-year-old
Ed Gaffney. The combined results produced the closest thing to a coalition
of like-minded politicians that California had seen in years, if ever. Jesse
Unruh put together a similar operation of Southern California assemblymen
based almost entirely on personal loyalty to him. Burton's group was based
not just on loyalty but on ideological commitment to the full range of liberal
concerns: civil rights, civil liberties, and support for labor, peace, welfare,
and the poor. He had a dozen votes on the county committee, or just under
half, counting friends, relatives, and protégés. But Leo McCarthy's rival fac-

tion still outnumbered them, and McCarthy ally Don King held onto his county chairmanship in 1964, despite challenges from pro-Burton forces.

At a 1964 breakfast with King, Bill Malone, Mayor Shelley, and a large, powerfully built man in a Stetson named Don Silverthorne, president of a local bank, Burton was his typical overpowering self, screaming, bullying, manipulating, doing whatever it took to be named chairman of the "unity" committee to pull Democrats together for LBJ. They worked out a compromise: Burton and the local district attorney would co-chair the committee.

"Young man, I've been around a long time," Silverthorne said to Burton during a pause. "I've seen a lot of things. You're riding high right now. Some day you're going to take a fall. You are driving people away from you. But you'll need them later." In fact, it was Silverthorne, who liked to hand out diamond cufflinks to San Francisco officials (Burton sent his back), who fell soon thereafter, when his bank collapsed, causing a scandal. But he was one of the few who ever had the guts to talk to Burton like that, even early in Burton's career.[1]

Unlike Burton, Mayor Shelley, a creature of the more collegial Congress, had no interest in building a political machine. He never got tough with the board of supervisors or even leaned on them heavily for a vote. But he was also capable of temper and strong language. When Burton visited City Hall for an ill-fated attempt at reconciliation with Shelley after Burton's election to Congress, the shouting could be heard through two layers of heavy wooden doors. On later trips to City Hall, Shelley would get wind of his approach. "Jesus Christ, I don't want to meet with that son of a bitch," he would tell aide Peter Trimble. "Don't let him in here." At times, Burton got so infuriated at Shelley's dodges that he literally kicked the doors of the mayor's office before storming out.[2]

Burton could not keep from interfering in all manner of political deal making. He even helped Republicans, as long as their opponents were worse. Extremist supporters of Arizona Senator Barry Goldwater, for example, many of them members of the John Birch Society, embarked on a plan to take over the California Republican Party. The plan involved running ultraconservative candidates in fifteen congressional races, five senate races, and thirty-eight assembly races, knowing they would lose all of them to well-entrenched Democratic incumbents. But simply by winning the Republican nomination, they automatically were put on the Republican State Central Committee and could each name three more members. At a time when there were few Republican incumbents in either house, they eventually could control the entire state party.

Assemblyman Bill Bagley, a Rockefeller Republican and friend of Burton from the assembly Social Welfare Committee, got a taste of the right wing's political agenda at the 1964 state convention, where incumbents were outnumbered by ultraconservative insurgents two to one. While many delegates were at dinner, a resolution suddenly appeared that called for adopting a provision of the 1878 GOP platform to send blacks "back to Africa." Only by lack of a quorum could Bagley and fellow moderates adjourn without adopting any platform and thus stave off catastrophe.

He told Burton about what happened, and Burton jumped into the fray, convincing assembly Rules Chairman Tom Bane to accept a Republican amendment to a bill that until then had concerned only Democrats. The amendment permitted GOP incumbents—the moderates—to make eight selections to the state central committee, rather than three, and thus deny the Birchers their majority.

Recounting the incident in a letter to Sala Burton years later, Bagley said Burton's intervention had long-lasting impact on the party: "Thus was the California Republican Party saved from destructive and disastrous far-right, neo-fascist domination from 1965 forward. And, not by coincidence, the Ronald Reagan forces began to arise from the ashes of 1964, but without the Birch taint that had helped bury Goldwater. The party and the Reagan for Governor campaign could now claim credit to be constructively conservative."[3]

The Burton "machine," as it soon came to be called, finally came together in 1966. Notwithstanding an often rocky relationship with Unruh, John Burton and Willie Brown became leading figures on the Democratic left in the Bay Area as the free speech movement dawned in Berkeley and the antiwar movement and counterculture took root in San Francisco. At the same time, the court-prompted reapportionment entitled San Francisco to one more senator. On the same 1966 ballot that saw Reagan crush Pat Brown to become governor, George Moscone defeated Leo McCarthy for that second seat. Just as satisfying, longtime Burton confidant Agar Jaicks was elected chairman of the county committee. His election meant Burton now controlled nearly all the key offices and the local committee that had repeatedly sought to destroy him.

Jaicks came to San Francisco from Illinois in 1950 from a staunchly Republican family, but his wife was a niece of Eleanor Roosevelt. A gentle, soft-spoken man, Jaicks had flirted with the far left while a University of Chicago student. He met Burton in 1952 in the Young Democrats. Appalled at Burton's personal manner, he nevertheless was attracted because he saw in Burton an "uncompromising progressive." He took three weeks off from work in 1956 to walk precincts for Burton and was a loyal friend and supporter from then on. Because of Burton's commitment and total disregard for personal enrichment—Burton never had more than $700 in the bank—Jaicks was willing to excuse Burton's arrogance, rudeness, or insensitivity to others.

Burton also had a strong following among liberal college students and minority activists. Marty Eber, president of the Hastings College of the Law Young Democrats, could turn out 250 volunteers to walk precincts or get out the vote at places like Laguna Honda, a city-run rest home for hundreds of impoverished and sick elderly. The rest home had its own polling place. Eber and his volunteers would show up on election day, help the patients fill out their ballots, and, if necessary, carry them downstairs to vote.

Other supporters manned the tables in the basement of 240 Golden Gate Avenue, where George Hardy regularly turned his union's basement into the headquarters for whatever political campaigns interested him. By the early 1960s, Burton's entire political operation was centered in Hardy's basement. In addition to extensive mailing lists, mimeos, and giant addressograph machines, the basement contained maps and statistics for every city precinct, as well as names of key leaders and those registered to vote. Activists concentrated on areas like the Tenderloin, where most residents were poor, minorities, retired people, or immigrants. The Burtons and their friends walked the Tenderloin or the hot-plate South of Market rooming houses themselves. Using early direct-mail letters and in-person visits, Burton forged a real connection with some of the city's loneliest and most disenfranchised residents.

One day during the McCarthy-Moscone senate campaign, Burton walked by a pensioner hotel on Sixth and Mission Streets near skid row, turned to aide Chuck Hurley and said, "Watch this." A dozen people were in the lobby. When Burton entered, the place suddenly came alive. Clamoring for his attention, the residents told Burton they were planning to vote for Moscone. By the time Burton got halfway around the lobby, people were coming out of their rooms on the upper floors. "Hi, Mr. Burton," they all said. "I got your letter." Later he said to Hurley, "Most direct-mail advertising doesn't care about these people. They appreciate getting a letter. Aren't you glad you did that letter?"

He didn't always do as well with the rich and powerful. The same year, Burton got a call from Jim McClatchy, whose family owned McClatchy Newspapers, published in Sacramento, Fresno, and Modesto. Jim had just purchased a small San Francisco newspaper called the *Daily Commercial*. He had stitched together all the union contracts he needed to run the paper, save one, a small Teamster local that was giving him problems. McClatchy called Burton and asked if he could intercede. Burton said it would be difficult but helped straighten out the problem. When he tried to call in the chit, however, he got nowhere. Burton asked Hurley, a former McClatchy reporter, to call Jim McClatchy and ask for an endorsement. McClatchy balked, telling Hurley that Burton did not need it. "Yes," Hurley replied, "but he wants it, and it would mean a lot coming from you."

That night, Burton took his entourage to dinner. There were only a handful of restaurants in San Francisco where Burton regularly ate, and the House of Prime Rib on Van Ness Avenue was his favorite. Management reserved a booth for him and knew his habits well. They served his vodka in water tumblers and brought tall glasses of milk, platters piled high with giant slabs of prime rib, and creamed spinach on the side. Burton decided who sat where, and thought nothing of spearing food off other peoples' plates. At the end of a huge dinner, he liked to walk around the block, checking apartment mailboxes as he went, to see if the demographics were changing.

After dinner, Burton instructed Hurley to walk around the block with him. Once alone, Burton wanted to know every detail of Hurley's conversation with McClatchy. When Hurley explained why McClatchy would not endorse him, Burton became enraged. It seemed to him that once again the establishment was thumbing its nose at him. "Goddam it! This is the story of my whole career," he shouted. "I've had to scratch and claw and fight for everything I've gotten."[4]

While Burton and his allies were turning out white votes, black activists like Joan Brann were going door-to-door in the Western Addition. Brann, an Oakland native, first got active in politics through Carlton Goodlett in the late 1950s. Goodlett believed that if politicians wanted to court the black vote, they should come into the black community and ask for it directly. Brann helped Goodlett set up a speakers forum that allowed white politicians to do just that. Through Goodlett she met Phil and Sala Burton and worked hard in Willie Brown's 1962 and 1964 campaigns. Through Brann's political activism, she eventually met and married Frank Brann, who had known Burton since they were students and fellow Falconers at Washington High. The son of a liberal attorney, Frank Brann showed an early interest in politics. Of the two, their classmates believed Brann was the more natural politician. But his political career never took off. Burton ran him unsuccessfully in several assembly campaigns against Republican incumbents.

Burton taught Joan Brann and many of her friends how the system worked, how to to be issue-oriented, how to use modern campaign techniques. She became an adept canvasser. As Brann walked through the black housing projects on election day, she met people who were ambivalent about voting, handed them slate cards and in some cases did everything but vote for them. When a woman complained that she could not leave her apartment to vote— she had a child asleep and a meal on the stove—Brann offered to take over.

"I'll watch the baby, and I'll stir the pot," said Brann. "Well, if you'll do that, I'll go vote," the woman laughed. If she trusted Brann enough to watch her baby, she trusted her enough to vote for her candidate. Brann gave her a slate card and a copy of the *Sun Reporter*, whose endorsements matched the names on the slate card and those endorsed by the Black Ministerial Alliance. As Brann described it years later, "You had the black ministers, the black newspaper, the local black Democratic club, a black candidate, and a black person on your doorstep willing to watch your baby. That's a powerful message."[5]

Unfortunately for Jack Shelley, being mayor was not the crowning achievement of his career, as he had hoped. Shelley's first six months in office produced one crisis after the next. As the civil rights movement gained steam in early 1964, Shelley met with labor leaders to get support for local equal opportunity programs. They were hostile, telling Shelley they would refuse to participate in "any civil rights program that involves putting whites out of work to give Negroes jobs." The next month, civil rights activists from the Congress of Racial Equality and the W. E. B. Du Bois Club, began picketing a supermarket chain to protest discriminatory hiring policies. In March, more than 1,000 demonstrators with the same complaint picketed the Sheraton Palace; 600 invaded the hotel lobby and sat in for several hours. Nearly 200 were arrested.

With each incident, pressure on Shelley grew. As he tried to settle that confrontation, hundreds more activists sat in at "Auto Row," site of the large, all-white auto dealerships on Van Ness Avenue. Shelley was getting it from all sides: civil rights activists were angry that he was not doing enough. Others complained he was being too lenient with the protesters.

On March 11, Shelley announced that further demonstrations would not be tolerated and appealed to "responsible Negro leaders" to calm their community and end the protests. In the midst of all this, Phil Burton arrived from Washington and met with demonstrators. He drove by Auto Row with his friend Bert Coffey the day after the police arrested more than a hundred activists. People were still gathering and some rocks were thrown. Many of the showrooms were boarded up in anticipation of more disorder.

"Let me close the window," Coffey said as they drove past.

"Absolutely not," said Burton. "These are my people." Then he headed over to a federal poverty program. The local director had complained to Burton that they had not received their weekly paychecks. Burton grabbed the phone and screamed at a bank officer, who said the bank would deliver the checks the following Monday. "I want them now," Burton yelled. "These kids are not going to starve over the weekend. You don't push people around like that." The checks arrived that day.

Shelley tried to negotiate a solution. After a four-hour meeting with civil rights groups, he announced a "cease fire" by demonstrators. In return, he appointed a commission to study job discrimination. But a few months later, Shelley was in trouble again when judges began sentencing those who had been convicted to months in jail. The long jail terms prompted protests from longtime Socialist presidential candidate Norman Thomas and black civil rights leader A. Phillip Randolph. In July, NAACP leader Dr. Thomas Burbridge, a black physician and professor of pharmacology at UC San Francisco, was sentenced to nine months in prison by a judge who said that, despite the nature and purpose of the arrest, no civil rights issue was involved.

Shelley's ordeal continued. In August 1965, he was hospitalized for severe abdominal pains while watching the Watts ghetto explode on television. Then a citywide poll showed Shelley in third place among leading contenders for his office, trailing McAteer, who had stepped aside for him once before, and Republican Harold Dobbs, whom he beat. A week later, the Human Rights Commission, which Shelley created, reported that although 22 percent of all city employees were minorities, all of the twenty-four employees who worked directly under Shelley were white.

In a January 1966 *Examiner* poll, a majority of supervisors said privately that McAteer could beat Shelley in 1967. In February, McAteer all but announced his candidacy. In June, Shelley placed third in another poll, and in September, Hunters Point blew up. Full-scale rioting broke out after a police officer shot and killed a sixteen-year-old black youth. Shelley, who usually had trouble making decisions, was by now considered ineffectual. But he rose to the occasion during this crisis. Hoping to cool down the city in the riot's aftermath, Shelley spoke from his heart about the need to end racism, even as he declared a state of emergency and asked for a voluntary curfew. "I fully realize that I am placing in jeopardy my entire public career," he said, taking on labor, his biggest constituency. "Nevertheless, I wish to state with complete candor that in my opinion the medieval practice of discrimination by some labor unions is just as sorrowful and just as unfair as the archaic attitudes expressed by some . . . management groups."[6] Shelley toured Hunters Point, where he dodged a brick, but calmed frayed nerves, and local residents gave him credit for settling the outbreak quickly.

Shelley moved up in the polls but was still considered weak. By January 1967, McAteer was making inroads among Republicans and labor unions, and Mexican-American leaders blasted Shelley for failing to appoint more Mexican Americans to boards and commissions. Burton at first had sought to build bridges to Shelley's troubled administration. Later, he tried to help re-elect him, and, when that failed, to choose his successor. In his time of political crisis, the mayor reached out to his old enemy. In what was widely interpreted as a deal, Shelley appointed Burton aide Joe Beeman to the board of supervisors, but it was not clear that Burton was in turn endorsing Shelley. "The Burton machine has not moved into City Hall, but there is a friendly relationship," Shelley said.

That was the first printed description of Burton's political operation as a "machine." Soon there were many. As the 1967 campaign heated up, the *Examiner* ran an extraordinary five-part series about the "Burton Machine," written by Hubert Bernhard. The first article, "Phillip Burton's Political Mystique," observed that no other politician was as universally loved or hated—depending on which city block a person lived. It quoted opponents who viewed him "darkly as 'controlling' not only his own seat, but two in the Assembly, one in the Senate and at least one on the Board of Supervisors." Bernhard said Burton "is now being wooed" by mayoral candidates Shelley and McAteer. The second article described the web of family and friends that constituted the "'Burton Bloc,' the 'Congressman's Coalition,' or—more grimly—the 'Burton Machine.'"

"Because of their avowed liberal stance," Bernhard wrote, "they are viewed with alarm in some quarters. 'Dangerous' is a word occasionally applied to their usually united front; 'threatening' is another. The adjectives come, respectively, from some who view the bloc as a reincarnation of the 'Red Menace,' and from a few rival politicians to whom they are, indeed, threatening in a survival sense." Part three, "A Machine with 'Balky' Cylinders," conceded that Burton's organization could split over the mayor's race and that it sometimes broke ranks over other candidates as well. "If we back someone unanimously, we're a machine," John Burton said bitterly. "If we divide in our support, we have a foot in both camps." Part four, "Ballot Paradox Is Clue to Burton Bloc Success," explained where Burton's support came from. It was based on four groups, said Supervisor Jack Morrison: "the minorities, the elderly poor, the labor unions, and the Democratic clubs."

The final article was even more negative. It used words like "sinister," "ruthless," and "threatening" to describe how Burton operated, and it quoted longtime opponent Don King as saying, "Any tactic needed to win, Phil Burton will use." Burton was asked directly if he would "stop at nothing."

"That is absolutely untrue," Burton said. "I'm an opponent of the school which thinks that the end justifies the means. That is the vital difference between a free and totalitarian society." A quote from George Hardy in part four provided some balance: "People who are working every day say, 'I understand poverty: I went through the Depression,'" Hardy said. "That is malarkey. They have forgotten. They don't know what it means to support a family on $1.30 an hour, and when they lose that job what a tragedy that is. A dollar means three loaves of bread on the table. Phil understands that." Because he did, Hardy said, Hardy could rally 2,000 campaign workers "merely on the word that Phil needs you."[7]

The *Examiner* had finally awakened to Burton's power and influence. But the series, with its repeated innuendos that there was something deeply troubling, indeed subversive, about him, reaffirmed Burton's view that the city's established institutions would never accept him. Yet it was also clear that these institutions recognized him as a powerful force. The *Chronicle* and *Examiner* discovered that again the following year when they asked him to help obtain federal approval for a joint operating agreement so they could merge business and production facilities while operating two separate daily newspapers. Burton did intervene on their behalf with the Justice Department, and the newspaper JOA was approved.

Burton often was unpleasant. He used threats and intimidated people, and that was news. But nowhere did the series define a political machine or say specifically why Burton was seen as a sinister force. Unlike politicians in the old days, Burton did not take bribes or pass out jobs, other than a few staff jobs and one that went to Lim P. Lee. No one was fired for breaking ranks. There were no ward heelers or bagmen collecting payoffs. Nonetheless, the series left readers with an ominous sense that bad guys were taking over.

Commenting on the *Examiner* series, *Sun Reporter* Managing Editor Thomas Fleming said the Burton brothers

> have been denounced by the Hearst organization every election day as a force that would bring no good to the city. But each time, despite such denunciations, the two Burtons have managed to capture the imagination

of enough voters to retain the real or imaginary power which the papers freely donate to them. . . . [The Hearst papers, the *Los Angeles Times*, the] Knowland-owned *Oakland Tribune* and the *Chronicle* have resisted all of the changes the population explosion brought to California. Negroes, in particular, have felt the resentment their presence brought to the state. Burton, who has yet to show that his interest in Negro welfare is politically staged, quickly stepped into the breach as a real friend of the Negro in the Negro's drive to become a vital part of the mainstream. . . . The *Examiner*, well aware that the city must choose a new mayor this year, is caught in its own indifference to the emergence of the multiracial complexion of the voters of the city. In its own dilemma, the *Examiner* is asking just who the so-called Burton machine will support for mayor.[8]

. . .

On May 2, 1967, Shelley announced for re-election. Two days later, Bill Malone said he raised $184,000 from Shelley's friends in less than an hour. On May 23, the Chamber of Commerce leaked a poll showing McAteer had more support than Shelley and Dobbs combined.

But three days later, the vibrant and athletic McAteer keeled over and died of a heart attack while playing handball at the Olympic Club. His death turned San Francisco's already topsy-turvy politics into an uproar. Writing in the *Examiner*, Sydney Kossen said political insiders not only expected McAteer to be elected mayor, they also predicted his November victory would have made McAteer a strong contender for governor in 1970. "Now Shelley is expected to regain much of the Democratic support McAteer had lured away. And Republican hopes of recapturing City Hall must now be reassessed."[9]

McAteer's death also stopped a stunner of a deal: the Burtons and Willie Brown were about to throw their support to longtime adversary McAteer because they concluded Shelley could not win. Carlton Goodlett laid out the rest of the plan to labor organizer Dave Jenkins: Phil Burton would run for the U.S. Senate in 1970, while Willie Brown took his congressional seat.[10]

Predictions that Shelley would gain from McAteer's untimely death proved wrong. By July, polls showed Dobbs leading Shelley by twenty points, and some of the city's leading Democratic money men met to ease Shelley out in favor of a stronger candidate. At the same time, in what became San Francisco's wildest political season in many years, a special election was called to succeed McAteer in the state senate. John Burton announced he was running, as did Milton Marks, who had lost his assembly seat in the 1967 reapportionment. Governor Brown appointed him to the municipal court, but seven months later, the liberal Republican was back in politics.

The Burton-Marks race had state and national implications. In the first special election following Reagan's landslide gubernatorial victory, people were watching to see if Reagan's magic extended to liberal San Francisco. Moreover, Democrats controlled the senate by the slimmest of margins, 20-19, and a Marks win would give Republicans a working majority. Lieutenant Governor Robert Finch, elected with Reagan, could break the tie. Phil Burton threw everything he could into this election. At a time when nobody had yet produced computerized campaign mailings, he brought in consultants to design them. They were primitive and volunteers had to sort the mailers by zip code, stuff and seal them by hand. Burton was so excited by the results that he took samples back to Washington to show off the wave of the future.

But Burton went overboard. Even though Shelley was likely to endorse his brother over a Republican, Burton took law partner Joe Williams to see Shelley and Malone. Almost immediately, Burton began threatening them. Shelley, who had a bad hip and used a walking stick, got so angry that he stood up, hobbled over, and said, "I don't give a fuck what you do or what you think. As far as I'm concerned, you can kiss my Irish ass." Williams, the Burton loyalist, nearly fell over laughing. Burton, he recalled, kept talking but more quietly.[11]

Burton engineered a late mailing with endorsements from Humphrey and Robert Kennedy, but even they were no match for GOP money, a nonthreatening Republican candidate, and the temper of the times. The election turned on John Burton's opposition to loyalty oaths, fears about the Burton "machine," and such "soft on crime" votes as John's opposition to crackdowns following the Watts riots. On August 15, Marks defeated him by 6,000 votes out of more than 200,000, becoming the first Republican to win a senate seat in San Francisco in thirty-two years. The Burtons were disappointed, but tried to put a positive spin on the loss, saying the defeat proved there was no such thing as a "Burton machine."

Attention quickly shifted back to the mayor's race, just in time for another shock. "Mayor John F. Shelley will not run for re-election, an unimpeachable source told the *Examiner* today," began a September 7 story, which said the sixty-two-year-old Shelley's physician "ordered him to quit the race." Shelley was not in good health and he was tired. Wealthy and influential insiders Ben Swig, Cyril Magnin, Walter Shorenstein, Morris Bernstein, and Bill Malone, Shelley's closest political associate, were convinced he would lose. They talked Shelley into withdrawing in favor of fifty-one-year-old antitrust attorney Joseph Alioto. After thirty years in politics, engineering this switch was Malone's last hurrah. In return, Shelley was given a low-stress, $25,000-a-year job as Sacramento lobbyist for the city. His political career was over. He had had nothing but trouble ever since Burton helped muscle him out of Congress.[12]

Alioto was a brilliant and wealthy lawyer who could quote Dante as easily as case law. A former school board member, he had been close to McAteer for years, most recently as his finance chairman. Part of an extended Italian clan that helped establish the fishing industry at Fisherman's Wharf, Alioto was a New Deal Democrat educated at Catholic University Law School in Washington. "Bored" with making money, Alioto was between cases and said he did not want to give Dobbs "a free ride." The election was two months away.

The next day Shelley announced from his hospital bed that for health reasons he would not run. He denied there had been any deal. It was "a matter of life or of death," he said. His doctors were "afraid that I might win." Alioto held his press conference ninety minutes later, and hotelier Swig followed shortly after with a "fundraiser" in his Fairmont Hotel suite that brought in pledges of $237,000 in twenty-two minutes. Meanwhile, Supervisor Jack Morrison decided he too would enter the race to carry the liberal mantle.

Phil Burton arrived from Washington in the middle of all this. Furious that no one from the Alioto camp had checked with him first or got his "permission," he called his own press conference. As the *Chronicle* reported it, Burton questioned the "murky circumstances" of Alioto's sudden emergence. "It looks a lot more like a deal of some kind," he said, "because I've never seen a full-blown candidate emerge within hours after an incumbent announced he would withdraw. . . . I don't believe I've ever met Joe Alioto [but] he must be a man of some talent" to amass such sudden support.

Just then, Burton's phone rang. "Hi, Joe," he said, grinning to reporters and TV cameras. "Joe, I'm in the middle of a press conference and you might prefer not to discuss anything now. But I'll give you a call before the end of the day." Then he turned back to the reporters: "That was Mr. Alioto."[13]

Alioto was furious. He had called to ask for Burton's support. Instead, the phone call was shown on the local news, with Burton lambasting him for making deals to run for mayor. He told Burton on the phone that in 1956, he supported Burton over Tommy Maloney, sent him a $100 check, and took heat for it. But he swallowed his anger and invited Burton to his exclusive Presidio Terrace mansion to discuss the race privately.[14]

Burton and his "machine" were totally flummoxed by the week's events, which were mucking up all his plans. He quickly called a meeting at Agar Jaicks's house to plot a counterstrategy. Those who gathered included Morrison, Jaicks, Beeman, neighborhood activist Sue Bierman, and ILWU political fixer Dave Jenkins, whose union was about to endorse Alioto. Alioto was president of the California Rice Growers' Association. The ILWU represented 500 rice workers. Jenkins was set to manage Alioto's campaign, and Alioto later appointed ILWU president Harry Bridges to the San Francisco Port Commission. Burton, who saw Alioto's rapid emergence as a major threat to his domain, began by turning to Jenkins and saying in Morrison's presence, "We're going to shove Jack Morrison's bald head up Joe Alioto's ass." Morrison gulped at the vulgar reference to his own pate but otherwise sat quietly. His candidacy was nowhere without Burton, who was furious with the ILWU for supporting Alioto, screaming at Jenkins that it had stopped being a "progressive union." Jenkins said the union could not go with sure loser Morrison.

Burton ultimately endorsed Morrison, even though he, too, knew Morrison could not win. Morrison was not really part of Burton's team and resented it when the newspapers included him. He defied Burton several times, supplying the crucial vote in 1962 to deny Moscone chairmanship of the county committee, and supporting another Democrat over John Burton in 1964. But Burton wanted to show Alioto's powerful supporters they could not ignore him.

Burton took Jaicks to the meeting with Alioto. It was a foggy, almost eerie night, and Alioto's home struck Jaicks as huge but austere, a Roman palace with no warmth, inside or out. They were ushered into a study, furnished sparely with one large chair, a leopard-skin couch and leopard-skin rug on the floor. As Alioto and Burton circled each other like two bulls, Jaicks watched closely to see who would get the chair. Alioto darted for it and positioned himself so that no one else could sit there. Burton was left with the couch. Alioto took brandy orders, and after a brisk knock, one of his sons quickly appeared with snifters.

As Jaicks recounted the conversation, Burton began with pleasantries and then asked Alioto why he wanted to be mayor. Offended at being questioned in what he regarded as a patronizing manner, Alioto almost jumped out of his chair. "Look, Phil, I'm not a Boy Scout," he said. "I have a successful law firm. I can be a good mayor. I need your help. I've reached the stage where I want it. I can turn the practice over to my son." Jaicks was impressed by Alioto's sincerity, but Burton refused to commit, drawing him out further. Alioto promised to consult with Burton on appointments, a promise Burton interpreted later to mean that Alioto would give Burton appointment powers. When Jaicks reminded Alioto that he had not supported John Burton over Marks a few months earlier, Alioto said, "Well, you can fault me on that."

Jaicks knew Burton could never support Alioto. He represented the institutions Burton opposed all his life: downtown financial interests, Malone, and the city's political establishment that had tried repeatedly to destroy Burton's career. Moreover, Burton seemed incapable of treating him as an equal, and Alioto was not about to play the subordinate.

Alioto recalled the conversation differently. Arriving in a "hyper" mood, Burton began by saying, "I slowed your train."

"What train?" said Alioto.

"Your train," replied Burton.

"You can't deal with me that way," Alioto exploded. "I'm Sicilian."

Alioto reminded Burton again that he was the only "significant" Catholic to support Burton over Maloney eleven years earlier. Getting even angrier as he saw ash from Burton's cigarette burning a hole in his leopard-skin rug, Alioto snapped, "I didn't know I was supposed to get your permission to run."

When Burton told Alioto he was going to support Morrison, Alioto exploded again. "You'd better be sure I don't win," he snarled. The conversation was over.[15] Alioto believed Burton was supporting Morrison to divide the Democratic vote and elect Dobbs. Burton could live with a Republican in City Hall if he could still control the Democrats.

As expected, Alioto romped to an easy victory. Burton was right to worry. Alioto swept into office with massive labor support and quickly demonstrated concern for civil rights. He made exactly the inroads into Burton's labor and minority base that Burton feared. Alioto appointed blacks to boards and commissions in record numbers. When a Hollywood film company wanted to make a movie in San Francisco, Alioto extracted the promise that in return the company would pay for construction of a swimming pool for disadvantaged black youth in Hunters Point.

Alioto was less than deferential to the man who tried to play kingmaker. Two weeks after his election, Alioto ran into Carlton Goodlett, who proclaimed that he was the "philosopher of the Burton movement." Alioto repeated the line in an after-dinner speech soon thereafter. "I didn't know Burton had a movement, and if he did, I didn't know it had a philosophy," Alioto deadpanned. "The only time I knew he had a movement was when he got a strange look on his face." The audience roared. When word got back, Burton was furious.[16]

Most of the time, however, Alioto worked around Burton rather than with him. He kept Burton informed of what he was doing, but as a moderate pro-war Democrat, Alioto grew close to President Johnson and even gave a speech nominating Hubert Humphrey for president in Chicago in 1968 during that disastrous convention. Through his rice grower connections, Alioto knew House Ways and Means Chairman Wilbur Mills and Senate Finance Chairman Russell Long. When he needed anything in Washington, Alioto went through them or to the cabinet.

Tensions were never far from the surface. One night in Washington, Alioto dined with Burton and friends and brought up the possibility of appointing the city's first Hispanic supervisor, Robert Gonzales, a young lawyer and president of a local Mexican-American organization. Drinking heavily, Burton told Alioto he didn't like "that SOB Gonzales."

"One thing you can't do is appoint him," Burton blustered. Angered, Alioto replied cooly, "You just did."

For a year that started out with such promise, 1967 ended with the much vaunted "machine," such as it was, in near tatters. Phillip, John, Moscone, and Willie Brown still had their offices, but they had been bloodied. Marks took the senate seat. Alioto came out of nowhere to lay claim to city hall, and he was likely to keep the job for the next eight years, driving a wedge between Burton and the ILWU. Even Burton stalwart Joe Beeman lost his supervisorial seat.

With city hall gone, Burton turned back to Washington. He hired former Shelley aide Bill Thomas in part to prepare for a possible 1970 U.S. Senate race. In the meantime, Cecil King, California's representative on the Ways and Means Committee, announced his retirement. With its enormous jurisdiction over welfare, Social Security, Medicare, and Medicaid, Ways and Means would have been Burton's dream committee. But Jim Corman wanted it, too, and he had four years more seniority. Corman easily won delegation support for the California slot. But to Corman's chagrin, that did not stop Burton from acting as if he was on the committee.

Indeed, after five years of learning the ropes, Burton finally seized an opportunity to play for keeps on the House floor. The incident brought him national attention and notoriety and confirmed what most of his colleagues had already observed: he was a tough, irascible legislator who would not let anybody intimidate him and who would not hesitate to disrupt the orderly and routine workings of the House to get his way. On June 25, 1969, Hale Boggs, Chairman of Ways and Means in Mills's temporary absence, asked for unanimous consent to approve Senate amendments to HR 4229, a bill to make permanent what had been a temporary suspension of duties on hetanoic acid, or crude chicory roots. Without the unanimous consent procedure, former President Johnson's 10 percent surtax on income taxes to pay for the Vietnam War would expire five days later. Contained in the Senate amendments to the chickory roots bill was a new provision to provide authority for the nation's employers to continue withholding the surtax from their employees' wages. Congress wanted the taxes deducted another month while it debated whether to continue the surtax.

It seemed a routine request. But Burton was on his feet, ready to object. He had been seething for months about congressional inaction on a matter dear to him—aid to dependent children—and he was about to teach his fellow liberals a lesson in hardball politics. On June 30, five days later, when the wage surtax was scheduled to end, a long delayed "freeze" on federal funds for AFDC programs was also scheduled to begin. In other words, unless the states made up the difference, thousands of needy children might be wiped off the welfare rolls. Suddenly, by virtue of his willingness to buck the House leadership and block the unanimous consent request, Burton had leverage. If he "objected" to this routine item, Boggs would not get the vote on his chicory roots bill. More importantly, the employee surtax would end. If the House agreed to repeal the freeze on federal funds for welfare, he would withdraw his objection.

"Mr. Speaker," Burton said, "I merely want to pin down while we are in this more favorable context, whether or not the House is going to fish or cut bait on this matter that is of such great concern to my own local community."

Boggs replied that while he opposed the AFDC freeze, too, Chairman Mills had authorized no such action. Ranking Republican John Byrnes of Wisconsin said he supported "lifting" the freeze for a year but did not know what the House leadership wanted. Burton was insistent. He did not want the freeze lifted. He wanted it repealed. In what was later called "as fine a mixture of metaphor as ever found expression, even in the House of Representatives," Burton held firm: "Before acceding to the unanimous consent request, I believe I have a right as one Member to give the firmest of assurances at least to the people of my community . . . that we are not going to have this sword of Damocles hanging over their head, while we contemplate, if you will pardon the expression, this legislative navel."[17]

After some momentary confusion, Boggs agreed to appoint a conference committee to take up the matter and resolve any differences between the House and Senate versions of the bill. As the ranking Republican, Byrnes would be a conferee. Burton was on his feet again. Appointing a conference was not enough. He wanted a guarantee that the conference would repeal the freeze. What was Byrnes's intention: lift the freeze or repeal it outright? "Before I make my objection to this unanimous consent request, I will pose the question one more time," Burton said. "I would merely like to have the gentleman's view as to whether or not he will support his administration's position that the freeze be repealed. That lends itself to a 'yes' or 'no' answer. If this gentleman feels this is not the proper forum for such a response, it would be my intention, as I have told the gentleman privately, to withhold consent."

Byrnes was not amused. "In the first place," he replied, "I do not intend to be threatened." Moreover, he added, "I think it is completely inappropriate to suggest what one can or cannot do in a conference. . . . I do not intend to be browbeaten or blackmailed by having it suggested that I have to take a position that conforms with that of the gentleman from California as a conferee."

The dialogue, such as it was, continued. Byrnes said it was "appropriate" for Burton to have pointed out that no conference had been appointed. "But why we have to be threatened with creating chaos for the workers of this country and the employers of this country in making out their payroll next week is beyond me," Byrnes said. "That we should be threatened . . . unless we agree ahead of time on what as conferees we are going to do and what i's will be dotted and what t's crossed I think is absolutely unreasonable and preposterous." Perhaps it was, but Burton had no use for legislative niceties when it came to the poor, and he couldn't care less whether Byrnes or anyone else liked him.

When the Speaker asked for unanimous consent, Burton executed his threat and objected. The next day, the newly appointed conference committee met and agreed to support the chickory roots bill and full repeal of the freeze on welfare payments. Two days later, the House voted 250-65 to accept the conference report. Burton had won. The following week, *New York Times* columnist Tom Wicker devoted an entire column to the saga, highlighting Burton's role in blocking Boggs's bill until he got the freeze repealed. The moral, Wicker concluded: "Around here, it sometimes requires browbeating, blackmail, mixed metaphors and guts to feed poor children."[18]

Wicker's column was reprinted in newspapers around the nation, including the *San Francisco Chronicle.* Burton got hundreds of letters congratulating him on his victory. Now the nation—or at least important segments of the East Coast intelligentsia—knew what Congress already had learned. After five years in the House, Phillip Burton had arrived.

9

"EATING ITALIAN" AND THE
POLITICS OF BLACK LUNG

Of all the legislators I was exposed to over fifteen years, Phillip Burton
may have been the most remarkable and effective. He had a devastating
intellect. He got it right away, in one flash, message sent, message
received. He was as good as any legislator could ever be.

ROBERT VAGLEY
former staff director of the Labor Subcommittee of the
House Committee on Education and Labor

His skill was born out of his enormous desire to win and prove he was
smarter than anybody else and of his commitment to equality. He had a
rage at inequality and a rage at his own inadequacies.

GARY SELLERS
former general counsel to Ralph Nader

IN THE EARLY HOURS OF November 20, 1968, ninety-nine men on the
"cateye" shift entered Mine Number Nine of the Consolidation Coal Company's Farmington, West Virginia, mine to begin the life-threatening business of extracting coal. As a byproduct of extraction, the mine also produced
eight million cubic feet a day of methane gas, enough to heat a small city. A
cold front that day lowered the barometric pressure, which liberates the colorless and odorless gas. Methane is so lethal a single spark can spell catastrophe. That mine, it was later revealed, had been cited repeatedly for safety
violations.

At 5:20 A.M., something—a cigarette, an exposed wire, or a spark from a
machine striking rock—ignited the methane. The explosion was massive and
devastating. People in buildings twelve miles away felt the blast. Tons of

debris from the mine shaft were hurled into the air, followed by a 150-foot plume of ash and smoke that lasted for days. Some miners quickly emerged, but seventy-eight miners were trapped below. Television cameras rushed to the scene of the disaster and broadcast searing images to a nation settling in for the Thanksgiving holiday. The footage showed grief-stricken families hovering aboveground, hoping their men would be found alive, or failing that, found at all. As with the bloody Tet offensive, the assassinations of Dr. King and Robert Kennedy, the Chicago riots, and the tanks rolling into Czechoslovakia, network news brought gripping drama and tragedy into American living rooms again.

Rescue efforts proved futile. Nine days and sixteen explosions later, as most of the mine shafts continued to burn and gas filled the rest, company officials ordered the mine sealed. When they tried again to recover bodies, another explosion ripped apart two fifteen-ton slabs of concrete used to seal it. Eventually, fifty-nine bodies were recovered, but the bodies of nineteen miners remained buried underground. In a twist that Charles Dickens or Upton Sinclair would have appreciated, some of the dead designated the company whose mine had killed them as the beneficiary of their life insurance policies.[1]

At the time of the tragedy, Phillip Burton had given little thought to the plight of the nation's coal miners, although their working conditions would soon obsess him. But after flirting with a 1970 U.S. Senate race and then discarding the idea, he was looking for an issue. The era of big-money media campaigns and blow-dried politicians had dawned, and when he failed to earn even the California Democratic Council's Senate endorsement, Burton must have known that he was not mediagenic enough to make it as a media darling. He refused corporate campaign money, and he was far more liberal than most California voters. CDC ally Alan Cranston was elected to the Senate in 1968, but that had been something of a fluke. As in 1958, when Senator Knowland and Governor Knight sought to swap jobs, the Republicans had fallen on their swords again. Cranston's opponent, an ultra-right-wing ideologue named Max Rafferty, defeated a highly regarded moderate incumbent, Senate Minority Leader Thomas Kuchel, in the June GOP primary. Rafferty was easier for Cranston to beat in November than Kuchel would have been.

The Democrat who won the seat Burton wanted, who beat GOP incumbent and former Hollywood actor George Murphy in 1970, however, was the quintessential politician of the new media age: John Tunney, a Los Angeles congressman about whom the film *The Candidate* was loosely based. Tunney, the son of former boxing champion Gene Tunney, was vaguely liberal but seemed motivated more by glamor and ambition than any need to do good.

Once Burton gave up his Senate ambitions, he set his sights on joining the elite ranks of House leadership, confiding to a few friends that he would be Speaker some day. On core issues he never abandoned his liberal views, but he picked his fights more carefully. Whether it was a growing pragmatism or simply political maturation, Burton decided he could not afford to squander his reputation on lost causes or meaningless symbols. In February 1970, for example, former assembly colleague Jerome Waldie forced a vote of confidence in Speaker McCormack to protest his pro–Vietnam War views. Waldie got only twenty-three votes, Burton's not among them. Waldie said years later he found it "historically interesting" that Burton, regarded as "the principal bomb-thrower" in the House, "was not there to throw that bomb" with him. Future House leaders did not seek to humiliate current ones.

By 1969, Burton wanted something big, challenging, worthy of his legislative talent. He needed an issue that would impress colleagues and bring him into the orbit of mainstream House Democrats, where he could prove he could speak their language, understand their needs, work with them in responsible ways. Even though many still regarded him as a wild man from the nation's kook capital, after just five years Burton had already compiled an impressive list of accomplishments. In late 1966, in only his third year the House, he added significantly to the largest extension of the minimum wage program since its inception in the mid-1930s. Working with Labor Subcommittee Chairman John Dent of Pennsylvania, Burton pushed through new provisions that extended minimum wage guarantees to some 8 million previously uncovered workers, including farm workers, federal workers, and 1.5 million hospital and nursing home workers, now represented by George Hardy's fast-growing Service Employees International Union.[2]

Burton, moreover, was also a national expert on welfare, a leading opponent of the Vietnam War, and fast becoming a power in the Democratic Study Group, where efforts to reform House rules were underway. Despite his achievements, however, he had done nothing comparable to AB 59, his revision of California's welfare code. That was about to change.

One day after Tom Wicker's *New York Times* column about chicory roots and poor kids was published, the big issue Burton was seeking walked through the door in the person of Gary Sellers, a short, intense, thirty-two-year-old attorney whose visit to Burton's office was not accidental. After compiling data on coal mines and worker safety for years, Sellers approached Morris Udall of Arizona. "Who do you know on the Hill I can talk to about this?" Sellers asked. Udall referred him to Burton, who served on a mining subcommittee with him. "He's got the personality of a brillo pad," Udall said, "but he gets a lot done."

Udall's tip proved fateful. Just as Tom Joe teamed up with Burton to change welfare in California, Gary Sellers directed Burton to his next crusade and then worked with him to fashion a historic—and expensive—black lung bill for hundreds of thousands of disabled coal miners and their families.

A 1963 graduate of the University of Michigan Law School, Sellers soon joined the blue-chip Washington law firm of Covington and Burling. In 1965, he moved to the Johnson administration's Bureau of the Budget (later the Office of Management and Budget), where he spent the next four years learning occupational health and safety issues in order to write coal mine legislation. Sellers, whose father was a surgeon, came from a conservative Republican family in Michigan. But like many young professionals of the era, his own politics were changing rapidly. Sellers became friendly with consumer advocate Ralph Nader, who was best man at his wedding and who was turning to occupational health and safety issues after taking on the auto industry. Worried that Nixon's election would dampen domestic initiatives, Sellers joined another law firm whose Washington office was headed by Tom Kuchel, the man Rafferty had just defeated. After a week, Sellers quit in disgust when Kuchel asked him to literally retrieve his Senate chair.

"Come work for me," Nader said. "I'm just getting started." Sellers became Nader's first general counsel, one of five associates who laid the foundation for his public interest "Nader's Raiders" lobbying network. In a 1972 book called *Citizen Nader*, writer Charles McCarry described Sellers as Nader's "Patton," a true believer who "carries the brain of a Florentine courtier and the instincts of a revolutionary in the body of a flyweight boxer."

While Sellers was planning his approach, Burton aide Bill Thomas was planning a Fourth of July escape. But Thomas realized with horror that his boss would be home all weekend with nothing to do. When Sellers called and asked to come by, Thomas welcomed him eagerly, figuring the young zealot would distract his issue-hungry boss and thus guarantee Thomas's long weekend off.

Burton was working in his Rayburn Building office that Saturday when Sellers arrived. "You're on Ed and Labor," Sellers began. "I've got twenty things I want to talk to you about." Burton listened carefully for ninety minutes, especially to what Sellers said about pneumoconiosis or "black lung," a crippling disease coal miners contracted after years of working underground breathing coal dust. Burton had heard testimony on a coal mine safety bill. The subject was not entirely new, but it was intriguing.

Sellers and Burton spent the entire weekend together and then the following week. Over the next eighteen months, Sellers devoted so many twenty-hour days to this and follow-up legislation that it cost him his marriage. Thomas was only partially joking when he said he did not see Burton again for three months. Sala Burton was more tolerant of her husband's workaholic pace. She knew he finally had his issue: greedy coal companies versus exploited miners who got sick and died because of deplorable working conditions. Impressed with Burton's diligence, ability to listen, and quick mind, Sellers brought him ideas from some of Nader's student interns who had been researching new legislative approaches. Together, they drafted the most important occupational safety and health bill organized labor had ever seen.[3]

Coal mine safety and miner deaths had been a national disgrace for more than a century. Writing about it in the *New York Times Magazine* early in 1969—after the Farmington mine disaster—reporter Ben A. Franklin described the industry's horrors in grim detail. He documented its flagrant disregard for worker safety. Congress, the White House, and the United Mine Workers looked the other way. The UMW had once been a proud and militant union under legendary founder John L. Lewis. But under Lewis's hand-picked successor Tony Boyle, it opted for bigger paychecks and a fatalistic "accidents will always be a part of mining" attitude, rather than forcing coal companies to make the mines safe. "It is hard to tell which is more gripping," Franklin wrote, "the penny-pinching, corner-cutting and profiteering waste of human life in mines still operated today," or the "callous result, the history of human carnage. . . . In the 100 years that partial records of fatal mine accidents have been kept, more than 120,000 men have died violently in coal mines, an average of 100 every month for a century."

Worse even than the accidents, however, was the occupational illness, what Franklin called the "progressive, gasping breathlessness" that plagued some 100,000 active and retired miners who suffered from black lung. A debilitating disease that over time so clogs a miner's lungs that he must stop and gasp for air after just a few steps, black lung resulted from years of inhaling abrasive but fine-grained particles of coal dust. Coal dust was not a major problem until the onset of huge, automatic 100-bit electric drilling machines, some of them, Franklin wrote, with "rotary bits the size of railroad wheels." These machines increased the amount of coal dust almost exponentially.[4]

Unfortunately for miners, the federal government did not restrict the level of coal dust permitted in mines. The union was bankrupt on the issue. A

UMW spokesman told Robert Sherrill, a reporter for *The Nation*, that the union had never sought compensation for black lung or even to eliminate the conditions that caused it until 1969, because "we didn't know the disease existed."[5] Yet Great Britain had recognized it as an occupational disease since 1943 and even Alabama—no bastion of labor laws—was compensating some miners as early as 1952. Most of the West Virginia medical establishment denied there was a problem. A few even suggested that black lung was a "healthy condition." But three West Virginia physicians, one of them the son-in-law of Congressman Harley Staggers of West Virginia, began traveling the state speaking of its dangers. To underscore his point, Dr. Hawley Wells would show his audience a piece of blackened lung, crumble it in his hand and say, "You're crazy if you let them do this to you." The UMW's "safety and health division" in Washington consisted of a single staffer.

Workers who often descended hundreds of feet underground to begin their shifts were well paid by the standards of dirt-poor Appalachia. But their working conditions were dreadful. In a typical eight-hour shift at the Farmington mine, each worker mined nearly nineteen tons of coal. In most instances, the only illumination was cast by their own head lamps. Besides coal dust, the air contained dangerous levels of methane. Sometimes, when methane combined with coal dust, which acted like gunpowder, no spark was needed to set it off. Another danger was the rock dust sprayed on the coal to counteract the methane. It contained silica, which causes silicosis, similar to pneumoconiosis.

Many miners worked in a crouch or in puddles of water. Some had to crawl on their knees for a quarter mile to get to the next coal face. Those who did not succumb to disease were in constant danger that collapsing support roofs would crush them. Ventilation was so poor miners were lucky if the air they breathed, circulated by large fans, moved at the languid rate of 50 cubic feet a minute. Later federal standards required movement of air at 3,000 cubic feet a minute. Some got dizzy or suffered headaches from the carbon monoxide in the stale air. Once the giant machines came, dust was so thick that many miners never saw further than a few feet from where they worked. Miners were sometimes advised to wear respirators with filters over their mouths and noses. Many refused because they could not chew tobacco. Besides, they were told, there was no real harm breathing coal dust.[6]

In the spring of 1969, a few months after the Farmington explosion—the worst mining disaster in seventeen years—more than 40,000 miners began the largest wildcat strike in modern history, shutting down the industry for three weeks. It ended only after the West Virginia legislature approved a law to compensate victims of black lung without requiring medical proof of disability. "Speaking in terms of corporate resistance to change," wrote Sherrill, "it is no exaggeration to call this law a miracle. About a month ago West Virginia miners had no economic protection against losing their livelihood. . . . Today they are protected by the best workmen's compensation law in the world."[7] But the new law would work only if it was administered correctly, and it wasn't. With little funding and no enforcement, the problems continued.

The Farmington tragedy did spur the government to action in the waning days of the Johnson administration, shamed by the disclosures of what passed for mine safety. Interior Secretary Stewart Udall convened a conference on mining and said, "We have accepted, even condoned, an attitude of fatalism that belongs to an age darker than the deepest recess of any coal mine." Soon thereafter, the federal government, under Bureau of Mines Director John O'Leary, issued new instructions. His inspectors no longer could give mine operators advance notice of inspections. They should shut down mines in imminent danger of explosion, rather than write a report and then do nothing.[8]

Six weeks after his inauguration, President Nixon submitted proposals for coal mine safety, although they did not include money to compensate victims of black lung. For too long, Nixon told Congress on March 3, 1969, miners had "endured the constant threat and often sudden reality of disaster, disease and death." It was time to "replace this fatalism with hope by substituting action for words. Catastrophes in the coal mines are not inevitable."[9]

The following day, Dent's House subcommittee began hearings. Under Chairman Harrison Williams of New Jersey, the Senate Labor and Public Welfare Committee began its hearings a week earlier. Among those testifying were the West Virginia physicians who brought the issue to prominence. Dr. Donald Rasmussen, chief of the pulmonary section of the Appalachian Regional Hospital, testified that he found pneumoconiosis in 80 percent of 202 miners on whom he had performed autopsies. Dr. I. E. Buff presented a slide show demonstrating what happens to black lung victims and said: "You live fifteen and twenty years and you choke to death as if one takes a string and ties it around your neck, day by day, tighter and tighter [while you are] begging for a little air, just a little air." The two subcommittees held nineteen days of hearings and accumulated several thousand pages of testimony.

The biggest point of contention involved detecting the presence of pneumoconiosis. Buff and Rasmussen said black lung did not need to appear on X rays to be present. They said the disease obstructed or diminished the capacity of blood vessels inside the lung, which made it hard to get enough oxygen to breathe. With this new definition, virtually any lung disease in miners could be job-related. Many other physicians strongly disagreed, maintaining that Britain and the World Health Organization required X ray proof to document its existence. X rays had to show "radiological opacities," or white dots. Even a miner so disabled he could barely walk was suffering from something else if there were no white dots on the X rays, these experts maintained. Nevertheless, Education and Labor Committee Chairman Carl Perkins, who represented Kentucky miners, wanted compensation in the bill. So did Senator Jennings Randolph of West Virginia.

By the time Sellers walked into Burton's office that first Saturday, the hearings were in full swing. The bill Sellers once worked on for President Johnson still existed and was sitting in a House committee. Burton and Sellers quickly seized on it as the vehicle for the sweeping provisions they contemplated: strict limits on coal dust, which would require unprecedented changes in air quality and ventilation; limits on the silica content of the rock dust used to counteract methane; mandatory lighting and guaranteed health and welfare provisions with twenty-seven specifically timed deadlines; and, most important of all, money for black lung victims.

The money was by far the most controversial element. It represented the first time the federal government would step into the sticky area of worker compensation matters, ordinarily reserved to the states. It was the first time (one year before the landmark bill establishing the National Institute of Occupational Safety and Health) that the federal government would recognize not just injury but on-the-job illness as something for which a worker could be compensated. More important from labor's perspective, proving the causal link between disease and the workplace was often extremely difficult. The Burton-Sellers bill gave coal miners a "rebuttable presumption" that their illness was job-related.

The Nixon administration's rival bill, on the other hand, contained no compensation program, but Burton made clear what he wanted when he told Under Secretary of Labor James Hodgson that if Nixon's bill did not provide money for miners who contracted lung disease because of their job, then, "this bill is an absolute fraud."[10]

Not a single coal miner or retired miner lived in his district. But Burton worked on the bill with a tenacity and an intensity unusual even for him. Even Bob Kastenmeier, his close friend and fellow liberal, eventually grew tired of Burton's endless descriptions every night over drinks at the Democratic Club of all the intricacies of his legislative maneuvering. As usual, there was a political component to his mania. Burton had another constituency to impress: more than three dozen congressional "coal rats" to whom he could build bridges. These men, including very conservative southerners, represented districts with coal miners in such states as West Virginia, Virginia, Kentucky, Ohio, Pennsylvania, Illinois, Montana, Colorado, and Alabama. Ordinarily, his chance of establishing rapport with them was remote. But if he gave them something concrete to take home to their constituents—something they had been unable to get themselves—his stock would go up. And he would need these conservative colleagues for future deal making and his own leadership ambitions.

The coal rats were practical, working pols. They were men like Wayne Hays, a twenty-one-year House veteran and an intimidating power on the Administration Committee. Hays, who grew up in a small Ohio town, detested antiwar protesters and called them "dirty hippies." Ordinarily, he would have little to say to the likes of Burton. But during the floor debate on this bill, Hays said the first funerals he ever attended as a child were for the fathers of two first-grade classmates killed in the mines. The entire class went. Another coal rat was Dan Flood, a former Shakespearean actor with a waxed mustache, who represented coal miners in Wilkes Barre, Pennsylvania. He was a senior member of Appropriations. A third was Subcommittee Chairman Dent, a one-time coal mine operator. His district, just east of Pittsburgh, was Italian and heavily unionized. Its industry was steel, and the area was known as "black country" for its bituminous coal deposits. These members were "organization" Democrats, like Tip O'Neill, Dan Rostenkowski, and Hale Boggs.[11]

The coal rats differed from the erudite liberals on the Ed and Labor Committee, men like Frank Thompson, whose district included Princeton University, and John Brademas, a Rhodes scholar who helped create the National Endowment for the Humanities and the National Endowment for the Arts. To staffers who observed the chemistry of personal relationships, it was obvious that these men found Burton uncouth and obnoxious. His barely controlled fury, intimidating manner, and take-no-prisoners style repelled them.

Although the Thompson-Brademas contingent were able legislators, Burton regarded them and their allies as philosophical liberals only and had little respect for their policy-making skills. To Burton, these men knew how to introduce bills but could not pass them. They valued process over results. In some ways, they were not unlike his father, the genteel, cerebral liberal, impeccably groomed, correct in his thinking. At the same time moralistic, withholding, unwilling to abandon high-minded principles to get things done.

Much of their criticism of Burton was valid. Fueled by vast quantities of alcohol, three packs a day of unfiltered Chesterfield Kings, and anger at the world, injustice, exploiters and politicians who did their bidding, Burton was rarely pleasant to be around. But amid the bluster and shouting, staffers saw countless personal courtesies. Many reveled in his energy, ultraliberal views, and tough-minded brilliance. He could move swiftly from idea to legislation.

Success with this black lung bill would do more than dazzle the coal rats. If it passed, it would enhance Burton's reputation among the leaders of the nation's most powerful labor unions. They were based in Washington and were watching the outcome closely, often from white marble buildings that rivaled the grand structures of the government bodies they lobbied. Major credit would go to Carl Perkins, who made the coal mine health and safety bill his top priority. But the insiders and the labor lobbyists saw who was really getting it done. Burton was becoming one of organized labor's most important congressional allies. He told Jack Sheehan of the Steelworkers Union that, in Martin Luther King, Jr.'s words, he was going to bring labor "up to the mountaintop."

Beyond the obvious political benefits of the black lung campaign—and there were many—Burton had a genuine passion for the issue. The tough advocate sometimes wept when he heard the stories of deprivation and death that miners and their families endured. Their problems cried out for precisely his kind of expertise. Just as he had been deeply moved in George and Norma Hardy's living room when she described her desperately poor childhood, Burton empathized deeply with miners who made their way to Washington to testify, although some could scarcely draw a breath.

A former majority leader in the Pennsylvania Senate, John Dent was accustomed to cutting deals with Republicans. At first, like many of his colleagues, he thought Burton was nothing more than a screaming ideologue and despaired when he thought about actually working with him. During one critical juncture, Burton was pushing to drastically limit coal dust, the cause of pneumoconiosis. The argument in the subcommittee was over what the permissible levels should be. The House was considering 3 milligrams per cubic meter. The Nixon administration was holding out for 4.5 milligrams. Burton turned to Dent and said, "Why shouldn't it be zero? Why not eliminate it altogether?" Yeah, agreed Bill Ford of Michigan, also on the subcommittee.

Dent was shaken. How could he negotiate with the Republicans and still please these extremists? Burton, meanwhile, assumed that Dent was easily bought and would sell out to the coal industry. He figured subcommittee Staff Director Bob Vagley, twenty-six and new to Washington, would help his boss water down the safety regulations. With Vagley on the receiving end of four phone calls a day from the "junior" member, it did not take long for Burton's overbearing manner to irritate him. Vagley went to Dent and said, "How much of this do I have to put up with?" Dent must have told him to do what he had to do. Soon thereafter, Burton traced Vagley to the Legislative Counsel's Office and began berating him over the phone. Vagley had reached his limit.

"Congressman, why don't you go fuck yourself. I'm not going to take this shit anymore," he shouted back and hung up. Five minutes later, the door burst open and Burton appeared. Vagley was terrified. But Vagley's outburst had impressed Burton, a master at using bombast to intimidate staffers, and Vagley, immensely relieved, found that Burton had calmed down. He even apologized for his initial outburst and the pair spent the next hour discussing the merits of the bill. In standing up to Burton, Vagley altered the relationship. From then on, Burton trusted him. After pushing Vagley as far as he could, they became, as Vagley put it, "joined at the hip." Vagley found himself working as much for Burton as Dent. Burton would drop by late at night, summoning the younger man by phone from the lobby of his own apartment building. Only the frequently invoked excuse of entertaining a female companion could keep Burton away.

Burton cultivated Dent, spending hours in his office almost every night talking about the bill or the events of the day. Many evenings, Dent tried to go home at a reasonable hour, but then Burton would drop by with an armload of papers and tie him down. The strategy worked. Vagley one day overheard a conversation between Dent and Flood, in which Dent said, "Now, Dan, take another look at this Burton. He's not a bad guy. He's thoughtful, he's bright, he's an effective legislator. Give him a chance." The coal mine safety bill also gave Burton a pretext to visit Hays and others in their offices.

Legislators like Dent and Perkins were content to let their staff do the detail work and represent them at key meetings, but Burton insisted on being at the table. When controversial elements of the bill made Vagley nervous, Burton called in Bureau of Mines Director Jack O'Leary to give the legislation an appearance of authority. O'Leary advised whether particular provisions were feasible. Often, these sessions were held at Burton's Capitol Hill townhouse at 332 Constitution Avenue. The working group consisted of Burton,

Vagley, O'Leary, and Sellers, who was also working to elect UMW insurgent Joseph "Jock" Yablonsky over entrenched union president Tony Boyle.

Burton choreographed these supposedly spontaneous meetings to an extraordinary degree, and he had the senior mines administrator, the government's voice of supposed impartial reason, in his corner. Each morning he checked in with Sellers. "What's on the agenda?" he asked. "How many provisions are radical? How many are difficult?" During one meeting, Burton folded a note and passed it to O'Leary. When Burton left to use the bathroom, Sellers retrieved the note from the trash can. He was dying to read it.

"Jack," Burton had written, "on this next item, I want you to say yes." It would have been difficult, even for a senior bureaucrat, to cross a member of Congress staring at him across a table, let alone one as intimidating as Burton.

"Do you know why we're going to win?" Burton often said to Sellers or Vagley at 2 A.M. "Because we're going to outwork the bastards. They're in bed asleep. We're still working." Tom Joe heard the identical lines when Burton was in the throes of putting together AB 59.

Sellers wondered who "they" were. He got at least a partial answer one morning at 4 A.M. when Burton revealed that Sala lost a baby early in her pregnancy during his 1954 assembly race. The Burtons had received hostile phone calls late at night. Burton blamed the stress of those calls for his wife's miscarriage. "*They* killed my baby," he seethed. Looking at Burton's face, Sellers said, was like looking into a volcano up close.[12] In the deepest part of his soul, Burton saw the world as "us versus them," good versus evil, and this internalized view often gave his actions an intensely personal edge.

Sellers found working with Burton exhilarating. With no children, an understanding and equally political wife, and no other interests, Burton took the time to anticipate and plan for any scenario. Most members made decisions on one percent of the available facts, he told Sellers. If he knew one and a half percent, he knew fifty percent more than they did. Of course it might take him half the night, including blustery midnight phone calls to hapless bureaucrats, to dig up the extra information. Then he overwhelmed his colleagues with paper and plotted every conceivable tactical and strategic advantage.

To Sellers, who looked on Burton almost like a father, and other staffers like Vagley and Tom Joe, working with Burton was the legislative experience of a lifetime, the political equivalent of devising and executing a perfect military campaign or a successful high-stakes business merger. It was not until years later, when he worked for other members of both houses, that

Sellers saw how lazy, careless, and inattentive some legislators could be, and how much responsibility they routinely dumped on their staff.

Burton did not tell his subcommittee chairman about some of the most controversial and potentially expensive elements in the legislation, such as mandatory lighting in the mines, a provision based on the plausible argument that coal miners sometimes behaved inexplicably because they worked in the dark. Nor did he specify that he and Sellers also wrote in mandatory health and welfare provisions with deadlines specifically timed to ensure compliance. Such provisions could have been negotiated through collective bargaining. But Burton did not trust the UMW to fight for its own workers. And he had no faith in the agencies whose job it was to regulate the industry. Dent already had decided to leave the details to Burton, with Vagley there to stand guard.

On September 18, 1969, the full committee reported the bill out. Burton, who knew Dent loved Italian food, briefed Sellers on their next move. "We're going to eat Italian every night for two weeks," he said. "This is when the lobbyists come out of the woodwork, and Dent will want to make concessions."

For two weeks, Burton and Sellers babysat John Dent in his sweltering apartment in the Congressional Hotel. Shirts off, they played poker and "ate Italian." Dent had no idea they were babysitting him. He thought they liked his company. Burton knew the lobbyists would arrive with proposals for "modest" compromises that could affect thousands of workers. To be nice, Dent might go along. When they came, Burton and Dent listened courteously.

"John and I will talk about it," Burton would say, dismissing them. Dent said the concessions seemed reasonable, but Burton stiffened his resolve. "No, John," Burton said. "You can't do that." Burton was the last to leave every night before Dent went to sleep. When Sellers heard Dent might be ready to buckle, he suggested a truly devious strategy. What if Ken Hechler of West Virginia, a former speechwriter for Adlai Stevenson, called a press conference and accused Dent of selling out?

"Go ahead, but don't leave any fingerprints," Burton told Sellers, who enlisted the sympathetic Hechler as a co-conspirator. The press conference was news, and Hechler's charges got wide coverage. The ploy worked. "I can't give them a thing," an infuriated Dent said of the coal companies he might have been inclined to help.

Meanwhile, Burton was working on John Corcoran, president of Consolidation Coal Company and chairman of the National Coal Association Board of Directors. Corcoran was the smartest of the dozen or so coal operators closely watching the bill. His company also owned the Farmington mine. A realist, he knew the coal industry could not stop a safety bill that year.

"If you don't accept this," Burton said, "we'll fucking socialize your industry." Corcoran could not be sure the congressman wouldn't. Burton also brought union insurgent Yablonsky to Capitol Hill to convince people like Wayne Hays that the far-reaching provisions in the bill were necessary. Then he played Yablonsky off against rival Boyle, getting them to compete with each other to do more for their members. "Here's your opportunity to look good, Tony," Burton told Boyle. "You can't let Yablonsky get the jump on you." Burton wore down the unions and the mine operators, who finally agreed not to oppose the bill as long as the federal government paid for the compensation program.

One morning at 2 A.M. Vagley was trying to decide how to set compensation rates for miners. "Look," said Burton. "I want it to be 50 percent of what we pay GS-2 employees. Are you interested in why?"

"Why, Phil."

"There are two reasons. Don't you understand?"

"No, Phil. I'm still learning from you."

"The first reason is that no one on the floor will vote against a guy with black lung who gets 50 percent of what we pay our lowest government workers. And number two, government raises are automatic. We'll never have to raise the benefits again."[13]

It was another elegantly simple ploy. They set the rate at $136 a month and increased it to $272 for a miner with a wife and three dependents. Burton understood something fundamental, which he used again and again in his battles to increase welfare payments and minimum wage: if he built into the legislation an automatic pay or benefit escalator, it was as good as a guaranteed cost-of-living adjustment. Burton and his colleagues never had to take the political heat for asking for more money or even risk losing the vote. Ten years later, when the black lung law was in disfavor, it would have been impossible to increase benefits. But by then, because of the huge inflation of the 1970s, the monthly payments had more than tripled, just as GS-2 salaries had.

Burton knew getting this bill approved would be tough. He was not only obligating coal companies to establish dramatically new health and safety standards inside their mines, he was creating a brand-new entitlement— although, as with AB 59, few legislators knew it at the time. The black lung bill was as generous to miners as it was costly to the federal treasury. Burton was ready to deal.

The opportunity came on October 9 when the House faced a vote on whether to insist on retaining a $20,000 ceiling on agricultural subsidies to individual farms in a House-Senate conference report. The sponsor was Silvio Conte, a liberal Republican from Massachusetts. It was the kind of progressive issue Burton always supported. The alternative was the existing system, which allowed wealthy, often corporate farmers to pocket millions of dollars a year not to grow such crops as cotton. Opposition to these tax subsidies to rich farmers had been a staple of Young Democrat and CDC resolutions for years.

But these subsidies were also what the reactionary "King Cotton" lords of the House lived for, especially Appropriations Chairman George Mahon of Texas. Mahon, sixty-nine, was first elected in 1934 and had as much power over the budget as anyone in Congress. A fiscal conservative, he was a hawk on Vietnam and fervently for states' rights. He had about as much in common with Burton as he did with Stokely Carmichael. But Burton took the time to bridge these differences. He spent months in the House dining room with the southerners, getting to know them, learning what mattered in their districts. He was such a quick study that after a few minutes he could talk intelligently about peanut, tobacco, or cotton subsidies. They were astonished. No big-city northern liberal had ever sat down with them like that.

As the roll call on Conte's $20,000 ceiling progressed, the vote was so close that it looked as though Mahon and ally Jamie Whitten of Mississippi, chairman of the subcommittee on agricultural appropriations, would lose. If they did, Burton knew Mahon would likely kill the ceiling later. In other words, the House would have made a symbolic statement but achieved nothing. In a quick calculation that distinguished him from almost every other liberal of his generation, Burton saved Mahon the trouble and took the first steps toward guaranteeing passage of his own bill. He persuaded Dent and several other liberals to vote with the southerners against the bill. The bill lost by four votes, 177–181. Intrigued, *Sacramento Bee* Washington correspondent Leo Rennert hunted Burton down to find out why he voted for subsidies to big agriculture. Burton said nothing.[14]

Before the coal mine vote, Burton held court at the Democratic Club, explaining how he was going to put the votes together to pass the bill. Freshman David Obey of Wisconsin did not follow him.

"How can you talk to Mahon and get him to do anything?" Obey asked.

"I will do it, David. Don't worry about it," Burton replied. Obey kept pressing him for answers, trying to draw Burton out. But Burton answered indirectly: "I make it my business to understand this man. I know his district and what is important to him."

When Obey persisted, Burton finally lost his temper. He turned to the hapless freshman. "David, you are a fucking mechanic," he bellowed in a voice that could be heard across the room. "You will never understand how to deal with people. You will never understand how this place operates." Sellers, who witnessed the conversation, wanted to disappear under a table. It was so unnecessarily cruel, he thought.[15]

The Senate passed its coal mine bill unanimously on October 3. On October 29, the House took up its version. Burton had prepared well, carefully courting a large bloc of southerners over leisurely meals, telling them he had protected their cotton subsidies, and "now you owe me." Several Republicans objected to creating an unprecedented federal worker's compensation program for coal miners. But Mahon and the southerners stayed with Burton.

The vote was 389-4, but Burton's work was far from done. Both the Senate and House bills provided money to miners "totally disabled" from "complicated pneumoconiosis" or to their widows. In the Senate version, the miner had to be so disabled he could not work elsewhere. In the House version, if the miner was totally disabled and had worked in the mines at least ten years, there would be a "rebuttable presumption" that he contracted the disease on the job. A House-Senate conference committee was needed to resolve differences.

The conference coincided with the first anniversary of the Farmington mine disaster. Both bills called for aid only to victims of the most disabling stage. But those victims were just 5 percent of the miners, not the 100,000 or more many had estimated. Nevertheless, miners were being told the solution was at hand. If they were disappointed, a huge wildcat strike seemed likely.

Conferee John Erlenborn of Illinois, the ranking Republican on Dent's subcommittee, supported the House version because he thought it was the humane thing to do: compensate miners in the advanced stages of the disease and encourage the states to change their laws and eventually take over the program. Other members of the conference committee included Dent, Burton, and Senator Randolph, all of whom wanted payment to the widest number of coal miners. Erlenborn soon got the shock of his political life.

The conferees finished their work late at night, and Perkins asked staff to draft the final report. When he passed around a signature sheet in advance of its completion, everyone signed, including Erlenborn. Because of Burton's expertise in other income transfer programs, such as welfare and food stamps, conferees who wanted more than 5 percent of the miners compensated turned to him to rewrite the legislation. In other words, they gave Burton authority to go far beyond what both houses had agreed to. This violated the rules governing conference committees. It was not unusual as long as both sides approved the changes and both houses voted again. But both sides did not agree. They did not tell Erlenborn what Burton was doing.

When Burton finished three days later, the results were striking. Just as he loaded up the most expensive and politically charged portions of AB 59 in the state senate and then brought it home to the assembly, bypassing its most important committees, Burton now covertly inserted the most controversial and costly elements of the bill after the conferees signed off. By removing the word "complicated" from the bill wherever applicable, Burton permitted every miner who claimed black lung and had ten years work in underground coal mines to be presumed eligible.

In his important study of the black lung provisions of the bill, John R. Nelson, Jr., explained the difference between "simple" and "complicated" pneumoconiosis. "There was basic agreement," Nelson wrote, "that coal dust exposure might over time cause nodules (hard lumps of tissue) to encase the dust particles. As these nodules increased in number and concentration, they could coalesce (fibrosis) to inhibit lung function. Ultimately, this fibrosis, if progressive and massive, might result in heart failure and death. The nodule stage of the disease was labeled simple pneumoconiosis, the advanced stage, complicated pneumoconiosis, or progressive massive fibrosis." Beyond changing the original bill's definition, Nelson wrote, Burton also replaced the original with "a categorical, federally-financed and administered program."[16]

Having tricked Erlenborn once, Perkins tried to bypass him again. He snuck the conference report as Burton wrote it to the floor for final approval early the next morning, December 17. He called it the "greatest step forward taken in any industry to assure safe working conditions" and said it should be "construed liberally in providing benefits." Erlenborn got wind of the Democrats' attempted subterfuge and showed up ready to contest every change Burton made.

Erlenborn called for a point of order as House debate opened. "Mr. Speaker," he said, "there was no disagreement between the House and the Senate as to complicated pneumoconiosis being the sole basis that is compensable. . . . But in the report of the conference, simple pneumoconiosis was made compensable."[17] Dent defended the procedure, saying he "gave wide latitude to the staff." Erlenborn continued to object but was overruled again and again. The House leadership was determined to pass this bill.

Having lost his point of order, Erlenborn accused Perkins of deceiving him. Urging that the report be sent back to conference, he produced a hastily written letter from Labor Secretary George Shultz opposing the new provisions. Then he pulled his trump card: "I am authorized to say that if this conference report is approved and if this bill becomes law . . . the President may be required to veto the bill." Erlenborn said the original cost was estimated at $40 million a year. With Burton's liberalized definitions, he said, it would rise nearly ten times that much, to $385 million. In fact, he was not even close to estimating the bill's ultimate cost.

Erlenborn refused to yield to Burton. "This is a travesty," he insisted. "Unless we send this bill back to conference . . . this will have been a black day for the House of Representatives and the legislative process." Dent dismissed Erlenborn's new estimates. "If you took every miner in these United States, paid him $5,000 a year and bought his wife a chinchilla coat," Dent said, "you would not spend that much money."

The floor debate continued for hours. Speaker McCormack himself settled it: "I am very happy to be a member of this House today while this bill is in its final passage. I am confident that the clear majority of the members will reject [Erlenborn's] motion to recommit." It was time to vote. The motion was defeated by a veto-proof 258 to 83, and the bill then passed overwhelmingly. Mahon and his southerners held firm again.[18]

Erlenborn cited Dent's comments about the chinchilla coats when the costs of the black lung program exceeded $2 billion. And he never again signed a conference report without reading every word of it first.

On December 30, 1969, President Nixon signed the Federal Coal Mine Health and Safety Act of 1969. He was prepared to veto the "pioneering occupational hazards measure," the *New York Times* reported, because the black lung provision was a potential "budget buster." But 1,200 West Virginia miners had begun a wildcat strike the previous midnight to protest Nixon's delay and threatened veto. The government feared it could spread quickly and "pose a serious threat to fuel supplies, particularly for the power industry." The *Times* article, which made no mention of Burton, said 50,000 miners, retired miners, and widows would begin receiving payments within ninety days. The new law also limited permissible coal dust particles to no more than three milligrams per cubic meter, two milligrams by December 20, 1972. The stricter standard was expected to cut new cases of pneumoconiosis in half.[19]

The battle was over and Burton had triumphed. But instead of being elated, he seemed let down. The relentless pace, the total absorption in the legislative complexities served their purpose. The bill was historic and it accomplished many of Burton's political objectives. He allowed himself to revel briefly in that victory. Colleagues accorded him new respect and status. Hundreds of thousands of miners and their families were destined to live better lives. But he needed to get busy again fast to keep a step ahead of his demons.

As Burton headed over to Vagley's office every night for a week afterwards, he seemed to Vagley a depressed and lonely figure. He had nothing to do, and it drove him crazy. Burton just sat and reminisced. He needed Vagley to remind him how excellent the bill was and how good his performance had been. Vagley helped him re-live the tough negotiating points.

While Burton rested and prepared for his next challenge, reporter Leo Rennert figured out the story behind Burton's vote on the cotton subsidies. He called the Burton-Mahon deal "one of the best-kept secrets" of the Ninety-first Congress. It would not do "to let the folks back home—or even colleagues on Capitol Hill—know that a conservative Southerner and a flaming Northern liberal were working the same side of the street," Rennert wrote. He said Mahon rejected any notion of a deal but did concede that there was "some relationship" between the bills.

"I was interested in the coal mine safety bill as a result of conversations I had with people like Mr. Burton," Mahon told Rennert in that way politicians have of describing a done deal as though it were some wonderful idea that just popped into both men's heads simultaneously. "I assured him I would be in favor of it after he explained it to me," Mahon said. "But there was no trade. I just wanted to be as helpful as possible to Mr. Burton. And he indicated that he had a sympathetic interest in my position. I thought his provision for 'black lung' compensation was a bit far out—but worth trying." Sellers was more explicit. The deal worked perfectly, he told Rennert, because "Southerners really are honorable people and if they make a pledge, they keep their word."[20]

But the story of the black lung bill did not end there. Two years later, because of an oversight, the legislation required amendments. That opening gave Burton a chance to expand the benefits of the already costly bill even further and extend payments to greater numbers of miners and their families. By December 1971, two years after the law passed, more than $500 million had been paid to 239,000 coal miners and their widows, $28 million a month. Seventy percent went to the residents of just three states: Pennsylvania, West Virginia, and Kentucky. Even so, the Social Security Administration denied for cause 31 percent of the claims from Pennsylvania, 52 percent from West Virginia, and 72 percent from Kentucky, none of which pleased their powerful representatives in Congress.[21] Rather than accept these figures, Congress reopened hearings. Carl Perkins took the unusual step of testifying about his unhappiness with the high denial rate before his own committee. This provided political support for liberalizing the program.

In the original bill, a dependent child was entitled to benefits of a deceased parent. Because of a quirk in the law, however, if the dependent was an orphan, that child was not entitled to the benefits of either parent. There was no disagreement about fixing this provision. The fix was made in the first title of the new bill. Burton, however, seized the opportunity to reopen Titles II through VI and expand the benefits for everyone else. Not only would doubts get resolved "in favor of the disabled miner or his survivors," the new legislation called for "prompt and vigorous processing of the large backlog of claims consistent with the language and intent of these amendments." In other words, the revised law required the government to pay claims to miners that had been previously denied.[22] At Burton's insistence, however, Vagley was instructed to describe in the legislative summary only Title I: "a bill to provide compensation for double orphans of victims of coal miner's pneumoconiosis."

As members filed in to vote, Burton stationed himself at the House entrance. "This is a bill for coal-miners' orphans," he announced. Vagley said he looked like a carnival barker.[23] Over the objections of John Erlenborn, the Social Security Administration, HEW, and OMB, the new bill was approved. President Nixon signed it because Senate Minority Leader Hugh Scott of Pennsylvania told domestic policy advisor John Ehrlichman that without it Nixon would lose his state in the 1972 election.

More than half of the 190,000 claims that had been denied were subsequently approved, pushing the cost of the bill to more than $1 billion for 1973 alone. Between 1969 when the first bill was signed and 1981 when the Reagan administration curtailed the program, the government paid more than $9 billion to nearly 400,000 coal miners or their families—nearly 75 percent of those who applied.[24] Burton never cared how much it cost. He never considered it his job to limit federal spending or save money for the taxpayers. There was no shortage of politicians to do that. His job was to spend money, particularly on behalf of people who did not have much.

10

THE LEGISLATOR

*Phil uses power for better ends than 99 percent of the people
in this institution, even when he makes his shabby little deals.
He can't be bought, and there's only one constituency he gives a
damn about: the poor, the elderly, the black, and the disabled.*

FORMER CONGRESSMAN JEROME WALDIE

PHILLIP BURTON SPENT HIS adult life detesting everything Richard Nixon
stood for. But while many Democrats chafed under Nixon's centrist Republican policies and House liberals agonized over how to exert influence, Burton
spent the late 1960s and early 1970s producing some of the most important
social legislation of his career. Burton quickly followed up his black lung
victory by working on additional landmark legislation in occupational safety
and health.

He also worked to set higher benefit levels for recipients of welfare and
food stamps, calling on the southern coalition that worked so well with coal
miners. In return for continued agricultural subsidies, antiunion southerners
at Burton's behest approved food stamps for striking farm workers. From his
other committee, Interior and Insular Affairs, Burton worked to bring equal
benefits to residents of American trusts and territories—from Guam to
Puerto Rico—and to fashion his first major park, the Golden Gate National
Recreation Area, which became the most spectacular urban park in the
United States.

Burton played pivotal but backstage roles in many areas of social policy.
His ego, though large, did not require public adulation. His constituents
returned him to Washington again and again because they knew he was
fighting for them and because they felt he could not be bought. He no longer
bombarded voters with self-serving press releases to "big families" and never
engaged in the kind of preening and image-building that characterizes so

many politicians. By making sure through reapportionment that his district was always safe, of course, he never had to behave as though he was always campaigning for re-election. Most of his colleagues from districts that were more competitive or at least less ideologically attuned to the member did not have this luxury.

But beyond his safe district, Burton was also shrewd enough and goal-oriented enough to know that by avoiding the limelight and sharing credit with his colleagues, lawmakers would seek him out because his hard work and expertise made them look good. His colleagues could be remarkably "flexible" about key points, Burton found, as long as their name went on the bill or at least were spared public embarrassment if he beat them. When he celebrated, he often did so privately. In part, he did not want to alert colleagues to his many successes. More often, he was on to the next battle before his opponents from the last one knew what hit them.

Just as when Coleman Blease found him compiling legislative "profiles" of his assembly colleagues late one night in Sacramento, Burton continued to immerse himself in the details of House districts once he got to Washington. He studied not just the geography and demographics of a district, but who voted where, what issues mattered to the local representative, what groups he wanted to please or avoid. All such information proved useful when persuading the member to vote a certain way. Even members outside California were flabbergasted to find that he could draw the shape of their district on a cocktail napkin from memory. Many said he knew their district better than they did. "Phil will establish an immediate rapport with a new member by asking him how he expects to do next time in the North Ward above 225th Street, which he only won by 150 votes," Tom Foley said.[1]

Burton got to Appropriations Chairman George Mahon through cotton subsidies. He discovered which buttons to push with other legislators in the same methodical way. His black lung performance demonstrated to anyone who still needed convincing that Burton had arrived as a legislator. In winning respect, keeping his word, and delivering what he promised, he pursued his own agenda for change while establishing himself as an important player, one who could get things done and sway large blocks of votes. Not caring who he offended proved costly in the long run, but it gave him enormous power. "Phil was like a white Adam Clayton Powell," recalled chief AFL-CIO lobbyist Ken Young. "He didn't give a damn what people thought of him."

Because of the success of the black lung legislation and the precedent it established, Nader attorney Gary Sellers suggested that Burton turn his attention next to broader occupational health and safety issues. Thus began a new period of hyperactivity for Sellers, with Burton protecting him at every step. Despite opposition from predictable business interests and from entrenched union leaders threatened by Sellers's "intrusion" into their turf, Burton helped guide a landmark occupational safety and health bill into existence even though he wasn't in the right place to do so.

"Jesus, I'm not even on that subcommittee," Burton said when Sellers first broached the idea. But he walked Sellers over to the office of Dominick Daniels of New Jersey, chairman of the Select Labor Subcommittee, which was working on a less ambitious occupational health and safety bill. "Gary will give you some good ideas," Burton told Daniels. "Do I have your authority to have him talk to your staff person?" When Daniels agreed, Burton then walked Sellers over to committee counsel Dan Krivit. "You can trust him," Burton said of Sellers.

Every year, some 14,500 workers were killed on the job and 2.2 million workers were injured, according to the Bureau of Labor Statistics. There were also 390,000 cases of occupational disease, resulting in a loss of 250 million days of work, $1.5 billion in wages, and an estimated $8 billion a year from the Gross National Product. Wearing his Ralph Nader hat, Sellers worked closely with Krivit. He was armed with thousands of responses on worker safety from United Auto Workers union questionnaires, the results of which Sellers said "radicalized" Krivit about the need for a serious bill with tough enforcement mechanisms. They spent months writing legislation, which went through seven drafts, and converted an eight-page bill left over from the Johnson administration into a forty-two-page bill to increase on-the-job safety for sixty-seven million industrial, farm, and construction workers and more than four million work sites.

Specifying hundreds of mandates on worker safety, the bill gave the Secretary of Labor authority to set safety and health standards to protect workers and required employers to furnish workplaces free of "recognized hazards." It authorized federal inspections and investigations of workplace conditions. It said an employer could be cited and fined if the workplace created "serious dangers" to employees, and it authorized the government to close a plant and levy $10,000 fines for each willful or repeated violation. It also established a National Institute for Occupational Safety and Health to conduct research on job safety.

Not surprisingly, the bill faced intense opposition. The U.S. Chamber of Commerce and the National Association of Manufacturers fought the bill with everything they could summon, knowing full well how expensive it would be to make workplaces safer and comply with the new regulations. But even Nixon said that an OSHA bill "ought to have become federal law three generations ago. This was not done and three generations of American workers have paid for it." Some union leaders did not want to support a bill they had not helped create, even if it would benefit their members. Except for Jack Sheehan, a lobbyist with the steelworkers union, AFL-CIO officials were "disinterested and absurdly passive" about the legislation, Nader recalled.[2]

Biemiller in particular was furious because Sellers had not consulted with the AFL-CIO before drafting the bill. Several officials marched into Burton's office demanding that Sellers be fired, but Burton refused. He was paying Sellers the congressional minimum of $1,600 a year, anyway, and he enjoyed their discomfort. While Nader was agitating for the bill on the outside, getting journalists interested in doing stories about worker safety scandals, for instance, Sellers was fending off attacks on each draft and using Burton to plot strategy on how to make the various drafts acceptable to the Republicans and to recalcitrant Democrats following orders from the AFL-CIO.

"This was a battle," said Nader, "where the inside maneuvering was critical. Burton wasn't even on the subcommittee, but he was our main person. When the Chamber of Commerce and NAM [National Association of Manufacturers] came in to gut the provisions, we went to Burton to steer the strategy step by step."

Nowhere does Burton's name appear on the bill. But he put together unlikely coalitions of dissimilar lawmakers to get the bill passed. Aside from the main participants and a few labor historians, few people know Burton's behind-the-scenes maneuvering ensured that this tremendously important bill survived. Nixon signed it one year after he signed the coal mine bill.[3]

In the same way, Burton played a key role in ERISA, the 1974 Employment Retirement Income Security Act, one of the most important bills of the Ninety-third Congress. ERISA established vesting rights for some twenty-three to thirty-five million workers enrolled in pension plans, union and nonunion. It subjected pension funds to federal regulation, financial reporting, and arm's length financial transactions by trustees. Most important from labor's point of view, it ensured that the unfunded portion of worker pensions would be protected by a quasi-public agency, the Pension Benefit Guaranty Corporation, if a pension fund was terminated or a company went out of business.

Labor wanted such "re-insurance" to be a federal responsibility. Envisioning a sudden windfall, however, private insurance companies clamored for the business. When Burton learned that Labor Subcommittee Chairman Dent changed the wording of an important provision of the bill to give the insurance industry its chance at the lucrative re-insurance business, he went through the roof.

Burton agreed with labor that protecting pensions was the obligation of government and should not be subject to the economic whims of a for-profit insurance industry. He became enraged when he heard that a business lob-byist had got to Dent and was determined to buck these powerful interests, who never before had expressed any interest in protecting worker pensions. Burton called a quaking committee staffer into his office late on a Friday night and ordered him to rewrite the bill by Monday morning to reflect the "sentiment of the committee" and "to give the steelworkers and [union president] Mr. I. W. Abel what they want," according to a key labor lobbyist who witnessed the meeting. "He used his volcanic temper to terrify this guy and get it done for the good of the cause," the lobbyist recalled. "Dent got pretty mad when he came in Monday, but there was overwhelming popular appeal for the legislation."[4]

Burton played a bigger and more public role in the most ambitious do-mestic program of Nixon's presidency, a proposal to federalize welfare in the United States, called the Family Assistance Plan (FAP). Although the guts of the program never emerged from Congress, Burton alone salvaged what he could from the wreckage: a program called SSI or Supplemental Security Income. It provided monthly cash payments, starting in 1974, to more than six million aged, blind, and disabled Americans. It has since become a crucial form of public assistance for many who otherwise might not have been able to live independently or afford basic amenities. But even Burton could not get the revolutionary program passed in its entirety.

On August 8, 1969, while Burton was still immersed in the black lung bill, President Nixon unveiled his Family Assistance Plan, engineered in large part by Daniel Patrick Moynihan, the Harvard political scientist (and Democrat) turned counselor to the president. It was a stunning proposal coming from a Republican administration, far more daring than anything the Democrats had come up with in the Great Society. Nixon called FAP the most significant legislation since enactment of Social Security in 1935. Had the Senate Finance Committee not killed it in 1970, Moynihan wrote in a book on FAP years later, it might have been regarded as one of the "half dozen or dozen most important pieces of social legislation in American history."[5]

The plan would have guaranteed annual federal payments of $1,600 to every family of four in the U.S. that qualified. That amounted to $134 a month, compared to the $61.55 a month a family of four in Alabama with no other income got from combined federal-state aid in June 1970, and the $264.25 a month a similarly situated family of four in New York received. FAP was designed to replace and equalize virtually all state welfare programs, whose costs were skyrocketing, and to make welfare a federal entitlement. Under FAP, the working poor could earn up to $3,920 a year before completely losing their federal income supplement. Blind, aged, and disabled people with no other income would get a minimum monthly payment of $110.

Under FAP, for the first time there would have been one federal standard for welfare payments. The program would have extended eligibility to families headed by an unemployed male living at home as well as to families headed by a full-time employed parent. FAP also would have ensured that unemployed men and women with children over six would get job training or be required to look for employment. This provision alone convinced many tight-fisted Republicans that FAP was a better alternative than the present welfare system, which they said encouraged dependency.

In adding as many as twelve million Americans to welfare rolls, FAP was expected to increase costs by some $4.4 billion a year, according to administration estimates. Those most knowledgeable knew it would cost far more. The poor, aged, blind, and disabled would be entitled to cash grants, free of wasteful bureaucratic regulations. Until this program came along, no federal analyst had even attempted to calculate the minimum amount of money poor and otherwise needy people required to make ends meet. Those questions always had been left to the states. No longer would the poor be dependent on a reactionary legislature in Mississippi or South Carolina to appropriate meager state funds year after year for its poor, many of them black.

Almost nobody, not even Moynihan, knew how much the poor got each month or where the money came from. But the need for reform was obvious. The federal cost of AFDC reached one billion dollars by 1960. Seven years later it had doubled. In 1968 alone, it grew another half billion dollars. Welfare assistance was an incoherent and disorganized patchwork that varied greatly from state to state. While the program would not have put more money in the pockets of the poor in New York City, Moynihan estimated that many states in the South would have benefited greatly. In Mississippi alone, nearly half the population would have been eligible for some portion of an FAP grant.[6]

If some of these provisions resembled Burton's California welfare bill, AB

59, there was good reason. One of Nixon's top advisors was Robert Finch, California's former lieutenant governor. With Nixon's election, Finch was given his choice of cabinet jobs. Close friend John Veneman, a Modesto assemblyman, convinced Finch to take over the Department of Health, Education and Welfare rather than become attorney general.[7] When Burton was still in the assembly, the Republicans designated Veneman, Burton's seatmate, to keep up with Burton to the extent he could on welfare issues.

In doing so, Veneman became an expert in his own right. He followed Finch to Washington and then dominated him as Under Secretary of HEW and brought with him Burton's favorite staff analyst, Tom Joe, his AB 59 co-architect. Joe was the master of exploiting the state-federal welfare match and one of the FAP masterminds. In fact, it was Joe who suggested to Veneman that as long as the government was going to federalize welfare, why not federalize aid to the aged, blind, and disabled at the same time? It was a little "add on" they put together one afternoon at the White House, Joe recalled. This add-on is what became the SSI program.

Burton, meanwhile, devised a creative strategy for being involved in Ways and Means issues even though he was not on the committee. He established a fifteen-member Democratic Study Group (DSG) Welfare Task Force and got himself made chairman. He spent so much time around Wilbur Mills and Senate Finance Chairman Russell Long that he became known as an "ex-officio" member of both committees and as the 101st senator. He even showed how, exploiting the state-federal welfare match, Mills could save Arkansas taxpayers $10 million a year.

Because Burton was considered the most knowledgeable liberal in the House on social insurance programs, Mills and Long asked him to help draft welfare legislation. Long even asked Burton to attend his committee's executive sessions, almost unheard of for anyone not on the committee. It was just the sort of situation he loved. By mastering arcane subject matter, Burton converted his superior knowledge into power, ran over opponents, and served poor people all at the same time. It was precisely such careful monitoring of benefit levels that enabled him in 1968 to hold up the chicory roots duty bill until Congress repealed the freeze on AFDC payments to the poor.

Burton was playing the same game now on a national level that he played in California, maximizing federal grants to the states to increase the dollars that poor, disabled, and elderly people got each month. Working with Tom Joe, Burton plunged into the tables, charts, and statistics all over again. No single congressman, with the possible exception of Wilbur Mills, and few staff could keep up with him. As in California, Burton specialized in passing on increases to recipients. If an elderly person received $100 a month in Social Security payments, for example, and $50 in aid to the elderly, and the Social Security payment increased by $5, it was standard for the other check to shrink by $5 to keep the overall payment at $150. But Burton found some vehicle in the Senate Finance Committee, a shoe import bill, for example, onto which he could graft an amendment to increase the benefit. Then Burton would browbeat Senator Alan Cranston—who was terrified of him but who needed his San Francisco base—into introducing an amendment to "pass through" the extra $5 to ensure the recipient would get $155. Burton didn't always succeed.

During one battle, Burton stormed onto the Senate floor, looking to strong-arm Cranston into introducing some amendments. Burton knew the FAP proposal would go to conference, and he wanted leverage. Cranston aide Pam Duffy had been designated to watch this legislation and take the heat for Cranston's refusal to introduce amendments that were sure losers. Duffy had experienced Burton's wrath when one weekend he traced her to the Capitol Hill apartment she shared. While she hid in the kitchen, having instructed her roommates to tell him she was not at home, Burton stuck his foot in the door, screaming, "I know she's in there," before leaving in frustration.

Cranston spotted Burton coming. Thinking quickly, he jumped to the podium to take the gavel from Vance Hartke of Indiana, who loved presiding over the Senate. Senate rules precluded Burton from getting to Cranston there.

"Burton's coming through the Senate doors and he's after me," Cranston told Duffy. "I'm going to take over the chair. You stop Phil till I get there." Duffy, a petite five feet three inches, got between Burton and Cranston, who had to argue with Hartke to get him to relinquish the gavel. In one glance, Burton saw exactly what Cranston was doing and became livid. Duffy somehow managed to get him into an anteroom off the Senate floor. Still steaming, he put his hands around her throat and lifted her off the ground by her jaw, berating her for her treachery, real or imagined. "My little feet were dangling," she recalled.

"You might consider putting her back on the ground," a Senate sergeant at arms suggested meekly. Eventually, Burton calmed down.[8]

Liberal Democrats were bewildered by Nixon's plan because it ran contrary to Republican dogma. Many Republicans, including Nixon, spent their careers campaigning against welfare cheats and a system that "sapped individual enterprise." Now they were proposing something far more generous than anything the Democrats had ever put forward. Moynihan's later explanation was intriguing: Nixon was incapable emotionally or intellectually of pandering to "bleeding heart liberals" by making largely symbolic if headline-grabbing gestures to reduce poverty, as the Democrats often did.

"With symbolic politics barred," wrote Moynihan, who was pushing him to the left from within the White House, "Nixon was led—it could be said he was forced—to put forth substantive legislative proposals of unprecedented magnitude for the abolition of poverty and inequality. In a steady succession of legislative messages, he proposed to spend more money for the direct provision of the needs of low income groups than any president in history."[9] But the Democrats did not trust a Republican administration to do the right thing—or want Nixon to get the credit if it worked—and $1,600 a year seemed a pitifully small yearly stipend for a family of four, even if it was more than what many southern states paid.

Burton never hesitated. He understood the implications of the Moynihan-Nixon proposal immediately. As he read it "comma for comma," he said, he was surprised by its generosity. Not only was the principle sound, he believed the $1,600 level was irrelevant. He criticized it for political reasons as inadequate. But to Rick Merrill, a DSG staffer assigned to his Welfare Task Force, Burton said repeatedly, "I don't care if it's a dime." In establishing the principle of a federal entitlement, he knew he could always manipulate the figures upward as he had with so many other programs. "If we enact FAP," he told Merrill, "I'll bust the federal government within two years."

Even before Ways and Means reported FAP out of committee, Burton's DSG task force endorsed it. "It is my objective," he told the *Los Angeles Times*, "that the product we end up with will [lend] support to Mr. Nixon's family assistance plan." Anticipating opposition from liberals who wanted more than $1,600, Burton added, "I don't intend to become so dazzled by the notion of constructing a perfect bill that I lose sight of the chance that we have to make meaningful improvements in the welfare program this year." Too liberal a program, he said, would scare off Republican votes.[10] Between Wilbur Mills's skillful floor management and Burton's leadership of nearly one hundred DSG liberals, House Democrats overcame their resistance and easily approved the legislation on April 17, 1970.

But a number of House liberals, including Burton's enemies on House Education and Labor, opposed the bill. They included Frank Thompson, John Brademas, Jim O'Hara, and William Ford. In part, they were stampeded by a group then reaching the height of its power, the National Welfare Rights Organization, led by a charismatic young social worker named George

Wiley. He convinced key Senate Democrats and a number of House Democrats that $1,600 a year was insulting. He organized a march on Washington by welfare recipients demanding a minimum of $5,500 a year. As the battle heated up, Wiley's NWRO called FAP the "Family Annihilation Plan."

On a deeper level, Tom Joe and Rick Merrill said the very idea of a new entitlement program profoundly scared these House liberals. They believed in funding Great Society categorical aid: benevolent, government-knows-best programs, in education, day care, job training, or other areas, financed a year or two at a time. Their committees wrote the guidelines and regulations. Entitlement programs, on the other hand, narrowed rather than expanded their jurisdiction. If the programs were automatic, they had nothing to do.

Burton had no patience for such reasoning. The best way to put money in poor people's pockets, he told Merrill and Joe, was to cash out as many categorical programs as possible, including food stamps. "Mills, Long, and Nixon said cash out the money and give it to the poor," said Joe. "Phil Burton said yes, and the Education and Labor people found this incredibly threatening."[11]

After House passage, FAP moved to the Senate. But the bill ran into opposition from liberals and conservatives alike, including Russell Long, George McGovern, and Herman Talmadge. In a retrospective series of reminiscences on Burton collected by Washington reporter Michael D. Green, Green himself described Burton's encounter with Talmadge, just as Talmadge was exiting the Senate's private dining room, patting his belly and lighting a large cigar:

> He was suddenly blocked by Phil's huge frame and backed up against the wall. Without introducing himself or engaging in any kind of preliminary amenities, Phil started yelling at Talmadge in that foghorn voice of his and thumping Talmadge in the chest for punctuation. Phil launched into a ten-minute, non-stop lecture on the intricacies of welfare reform legislation. Talmadge's eyes got wider and wider. His cigar began to droop. Phil roared on about five percent set aside reduction formulas for state administrative costs under Title III, subsection (a), or something or other, and about other clauses and paragraphs and semicolons, all from memory. Talmadge's cigar by now was just hanging lifelessly. Finally, after a few more minutes of this, Phil finished and jabbed Talmadge in the chest one more time. Then he wheeled and stormed back towards the House, undoubtedly satisfied that his message had been safely delivered. And Talmadge, with a glassy look in his eyes was murmuring after him, "Yes . . . well . . .

thank you . . . yes . . . " Then, when Phil had completely disappeared, he turned to the rest of us who had been standing in the corridor watching all of this and inquired, "Who was that?"[12]

On November 26, the Finance Committee killed the bill for the year. The administration brought it back in 1971 with a new name, HR 1, and included new Social Security amendments. Again it passed the House, but President Nixon requested a year's delay to save money. In April 1972, it ran into heated opposition from Senate liberals again, and the Senate deleted the FAP provisions.

After two years, FAP was dead. But Burton was the only legislator in either house with the perseverance to rescue what he could. When Congress finally did pass HR 1, it included SSI, a new entitlement, which would have died were it not for Burton's efforts. What had started out as Tom Joe's simple "add-on" was now all that remained of FAP. If they could not reform an archaic and unjust welfare system for needy children and poor people, at least they could set minimal federal standards and cash out welfare for everyone else. As Jodie Allen, then a staffer in HEW's Office of Planning and Evaluation put it, "Burton looked at the part [of HR 1] that no one else was looking at, which set a floor of payments for the aged, blind, and disabled. He knew that if he could get that into law and add indexing, it would be a hell of a thing for old people. SSI is in the law as a monument to Phil Burton. He was indefatigable."[13]

Of the 6.2 million Americans eligible when SSI began in 1974, 4.6 million were elderly. They received these payments in addition to monthly Social Security checks. The other 1.6 million were blind or disabled. Because of this law, the majority of elderly poor would never have to be destitute again. By July of 1974, minimal SSI income levels were $146 a month per person and $219 per couple. By contrast, minimum state payment to the aged or disabled in Mississippi had been half that, $75 a month, $85 in Missouri, $90 in South Carolina, $96 in Maryland, $97 in Tennessee.[14] Since 1974, tens of millions of Americans have benefited and continue to benefit every month from SSI payments. Few ever heard of Phillip Burton.

Even while grappling with Nixon's welfare proposals, Burton made time to fulfill a 1964 campaign promise to San Francisco environmental writer Margot Patterson Doss that he would do what he could to create new parks. What she had said at her fundraising party that night years earlier had been true: rich people did not need parks as much as poor and working people did. They had their own spacious grounds and beachfront property. But to get anything done, Burton always had to work around Interior Committee Chairman Wayne Aspinall, who blocked most of the conservation movement's agenda. Aspinall believed that natural resources should be exploited—minerals, timber, water, oil, and gas—and that the Departments of Interior and Agriculture should be given wide discretion in administering national parks and forests.

A frustrated Sierra Club constantly battled Aspinall, especially over his successful efforts to bottle up and then emasculate legislation to create a Redwood National Park in Northern California. The park was envisioned to preserve historic groves of the world's largest trees and oldest living things. Berkeley Democrat Jeffrey Cohelan's bill called for a 90,000-acre park. But after years of delay, it emerged a pale shadow from Interior. Aspinall had stripped it to less than 50,000 acres, more than half of which was already preserved in state parks. Northern California timber interests opposed any park, and Aspinall represented like-minded timber companies in his Colorado district. The awesome trees were preserved along Redwood Creek, but half a mile away, on the ridgetops above the creek, timber companies clearcut other redwoods, causing such serious erosion that the protected groves were soon endangered.

Burton co-sponsored Cohelan's bill, but there was nothing environmental about his life. His idea of a nature experience would have been to look out the car window as he was being driven through Washington's Rock Creek Park. Nevertheless, the conservation issue struck a chord. Burton's district included the Sierra Club's national office and a growing number of people who called themselves environmentalists. It was a term just coming into popular use in the aftermath of Rachel Carson's *Silent Spring*, Paul Erhlich's *The Population Bomb*, Aldo Leopold's *Sand County Almanac*, and other books that celebrated nature or exposed the man-made perils that threatened it.

The Sierra Club ultimately supported the stripped-down redwood park bill because club president Edgar Wayburn, the physician who later became Burton's chief environmental advisor, was convinced it was the best they could get. But Burton was furious at what he considered Aspinall's highhanded tactics. With uncharacteristic vehemence for a junior member, Burton took the floor on July 15, 1968, to protest his chairman's behavior, in particular Aspinall's assertion that there had been no time to get a rule from the Rules Committee. Aspinall had called the bill to the floor by suspending the rules. Under House procedure, that meant it needed a two-thirds vote.

But it also meant members could not amend the bill, which of course was the point. It was a tactic that Burton himself later perfected.

To be stuck with a "woefully inadequate bill" was outrageous, Burton said. "We are told that if we do not vote for this puny version, enactment of any legislation will be imperiled. This borders on the abuse of the committee process and rules of the House." Maybe so, but Aspinall's tactic worked.[15]

That bitter redwood park experience and the political advantages that would flow from championing parks gave Burton special reason to use his spot on Interior to advance environmental legislation. Just as Nixon's FAP proposal launched Burton on national welfare reform, the Nixon administration also provided the impetus for the creation of Burton's first great park, the Bay Area's Golden Gate National Recreation Area. Soon after Nixon appointed former Alaska Governor Walter Hickel Secretary of Interior, Hickel announced an ambitious "parks to the people" plan, including large urban recreation areas for New York, New Jersey, the Golden Gate, the Santa Monica Mountains, and the Cuyahoga Valley outside Cleveland. At a time when Congress was approving few parks bills and those that were approved took six to eight years, Burton rammed GGNRA through Congress in less than three. The experience showed him how popular parks could be, especially with Republicans.

The idea for the Bay Area park began in the early 1950s in the fertile imagination of famed photographer and conservationist Ansel Adams. Until he moved to Carmel in 1962, Adams lived in San Francisco's West Clay Park in the home his parents built. Every day he looked out at the Golden Gate Bridge and the Marin Headlands. The view inspired him to want to create a Headlands park as a symbol of the West, just as the Statue of Liberty symbolized New York. A member of the Sierra Club Board of Directors, Adams wrote to state park officials, to newspaper and magazine editors, and eventually to the National Park Service. Already known as the "great man" of the Sierra Club for his spectacular photographs of Yosemite, the High Sierra and Big Sur, Adams began talking to army generals about how to preserve surplus military land around the bay. His idea began to catch on. Wayburn, meanwhile, was working with state park officials to preserve portions of the Marin Hills, Mount Tamalpais, and what eventually became Point Reyes National Seashore.

Hickel's announcement rekindled interest in these ideas. But part of his motivation was the November 20, 1969 occupation of Alcatraz Island by militant Native American activists. Refusing to leave the former federal prison on San Francisco Bay, they demanded the island as compensation for previous lands "stolen" from Indian tribes across America.

"Get those goddam Indians off Alcatraz," Nixon told Hickel, whose department had jurisdiction. Hickel's solution seemed ingenious: make Alcatraz part of a national recreation area. Republican Don Clausen, who represented parts of Marin County and who was close to Nixon, also touted the idea as a way to bring parks closer to where people lived. A Hickel staffer called Burton aide Bill Thomas and asked if Burton was interested in pursuing the park. Thomas said yes. Soon thereafter, Thomas noticed that Republican colleague Bill Mailliard introduced a bill to create a national recreation area from Bay Area surplus lands. Thomas thought it was ill-defined and took the idea to Burton.

"Look what that son of a bitch did," Thomas said. "Let's do it right." They found a Standard Oil map, assigned an intern to check boundaries and then began drafting legislation. Their first park plan included all government-owned and surplus land bordering the bay and nearly all the open space along the bay. In what must have been especially galling to Nixon, the bill transferred Alcatraz to the Indians for twenty-four dollars, equivalent to the beads that Peter Minuit gave the Canarsee Indians for Manhattan Island in 1692.

Unknown to Burton, a group of San Francisco neighborhood activists were also crusading for a major headlands park about the same time on an entirely different track. Their efforts began when they read that the General Services Administration was thinking about constructing a federal archives building as big as a football field at Fort Miley overlooking San Francisco Bay. John Jacobs, head of a planning group called San Francisco Planning and Urban Renewal (SPUR) was appalled. He said the building was completely inappropriate for the nearly pristine area with the spectacular bay views.

Richmond District activists who lived near Fort Miley met a few days later to discuss how to block the GSA building. Led by an artist named Amy Meyer, they established a network connecting SPUR, the Sierra Club, the city Planning Department, and the Outer Richmond Neighborhood Association. It did not take long for them to move beyond stopping the project and begin lobbying for a Headlands National Park, similar to what Hickel proposed and Ansel Adams first conceived. Eventually, Amy Meyer and Bill Thomas hooked up.

Wayburn, meanwhile, had already formed a group called Headlands Inc. to pressure the government to preserve surplus federal properties, including miles of coastline and beaches, in Marin. In April 1970 he flew to Washington and presented his proposals to Mailliard. "You're asking for an awful lot,"

Mailliard said. After Wayburn persuaded Mailliard that the plans were feasible and worthy, they took them to Senators Cranston and Tunney, who introduced legislation in the Senate.

Soon they all joined forces. Wayburn and Amy Meyer formed another group, People for a Golden Gate National Recreation Area, to lobby every environmental group, planning agency, local governmental body and politician they could find. PFGGNRA (Wayburn said he thought the acronym, pronounced "piffganera," sounded like a social disease) was backed by sixty organizations, including business and labor. Their urban park proposal provided what Burton called "a remarkable opportunity to establish a unique national park reserve that will save for the people of the United States and the world a magnificent open space immediately adjacent to one of the major metropolitan regions of the United States."

After several more months of planning and map drawing, Wayburn took a new plan to Burton, who studied the maps long and hard. "Is this what you want?" Burton asked. Wayburn said it wasn't entirely what he wanted.

"What do you want?"

Wayburn said he wanted 8,000 more acres in Marin's Olema Valley. This would connect Point Reyes National Seashore with 17,000 acres in the Marin Municipal Water District that were already open space and thus would not have to be counted as part of the park. But it would block commercial or residential development in between.

"Why didn't you present *that* to me?" Burton said.

"I didn't think it was politically feasible," said Wayburn.

"Get the hell out of here," Burton exploded. "You tell me what you want, not what's politically feasible, and I'll get it through Congress."

No one liked it when Burton screamed. But Wayburn was delighted. Burton's outburst provided the impetus for him to spend two more months with Meyer adding more land. Burton introduced the new bill on June 16, 1971, five days after marshals forcibly removed the Indians from Alcatraz after their nineteen-month occupation. In a statement Thomas wrote for August field hearings, Burton said there was an urgent need to combine open space from surplus military installations with city and state parks and private land to preserve coastlines and valleys. "Here a man can walk and be lost in peace, hearing the sea, feeling the wind, touching the land," said Burton, for whom such activities were about as likely as his taking LSD in a Berkeley commune.

The Burton-Wayburn-Meyer plan was audacious. In Marin, the land included Forts Barry, Baker, and Cronkhite; the Olema Valley; Marin Headlands State Park; and Angel Island State Park. On the San Francisco side, land included historic Fort Funston; Forts Miley, Mason, and Point; 700 acres of the Presidio; Baker, Phelan, and Ocean Beaches; and most of Lincoln Park. Burton also included Marincello, a spectacular area overlooking the bay on the Marin side. Gulf Oil owned it and planned to build expensive homes and apartments. The real estate firm Coldwell Banker listed 2,138 acres for sale at $9 million or $42,000 an acre for a "major residential development" of some 5,000 units. But the mayor of Sausalito got wind of the plan and tipped Burton, who replied by return mail that his legislation allowed no occupancy of homes built after July 1, 1971, thus killing the development.

Burton and Thomas also lined up Olema Valley ranchers, who, to the surprise of subcommittee members, supported the bill. One rancher advised them to sell their land to the government—they got $750 a acre—then lease it back for grazing and avoid property taxes. Altogether, the GGNRA proposal totaled 34,000 acres and cost $118 million—$58 million for facilities, protection, and preservation; $60 million for land acquisition.[16]

Burton's bill also removed authority from the military for future development of the Presidio—which included some of the most spectacularly scenic and valuable undeveloped urban real estate in the world. It was located in the heart of San Francisco and served as headquarters for the U.S. Sixth Army. The Presidio was established by the Spanish in 1776 and taken over by Mexico in 1822. It became a U.S. military outpost after marines from the USS *Portsmouth* captured it in 1846. In removing the military's authority, Burton sought to prevent the Pentagon or anyone else from subdividing or otherwise developing the land if the base ever closed, as it inevitably would. The bill also gave the Department of Interior veto power over new construction. In an especially shrewd move, Burton added the Presidio Golf Course, which overlooked the Golden Gate Bridge and the Marin Headlands and was considered one of the most beautiful courses in the world, to the GGNRA. Army brass who coveted the chance to play there, howled in protest, as Burton knew they would. So Burton, the very model of reason, amicably agreed to give the golf course back to the brass in exchange for an air field—the land he had really wanted all along.[17]

Burton's bill went far beyond Mailliard's, and political jockeying over the proposed urban park became intense. Horrified by the Wayburn map, the army wanted to reduce the park by 10,000 acres to 24,000 acres, and opposed transfer of the Presidio and consultation with Interior over new construction. Mayor Alioto supported the army's position. When the board of supervisors approved a resolution to add the Presido to the GGNRA, Alioto vetoed it.

Cranston, however, supported Burton's bill. Even though 99 percent of federally owned recreational land was in rural areas, Cranston said, 73 percent of the population was urban, and there was a "special responsibility" to "bring parks to the people, especially in the inner city."

Burton's bill, which Mailliard ultimately supported, emerged from committee in mid-August 1972 and headed to the House floor. "You have shepherded the bill through the House Interior Committee with rare expertise and onto the floor virtually intact," Wayburn wrote Burton. "[It] is literally all we could ask for." Amy Meyer added, "I am so pleased . . . the land area is there, the controls on the Presidio are strong."

But problems remained in the Senate, where Alan Bible of Nevada, chairman of the Subcommittee on Parks and Recreation, delayed hearings. Frustrated and seeking advice, Meyer called her counterparts, activists lobbying for a Gateway National Recreation Area in New York. They said nothing happened there until Nixon personally flew over the area. By now it was summer and Nixon's re-election effort was in full swing. When a staffer for the Committee to Re-Elect the President visited Jacobs of SPUR, a leading local Republican, and asked how best to get news coverage, Jacobs suggested Nixon tour the proposed GGNRA by boat and endorse it. It would make great footage for TV.

Bill Thomas, meanwhile, left Burton's office to rejoin the *Chronicle* as a reporter, where he had worked off and on for many years. His beat was to report on progress of the GGNRA, even though he just spent eighteen months drafting it. The only person to comment on the obvious journalistic conflict was Burton. He complained that Thomas was giving too much coverage to Mailliard.

"I have to be fair," Thomas said.

"Bill Mailliard never did a fucking thing," Burton replied.

Thomas's story of Nixon's visit ran on top of page one on Labor Day under the headline: "Nixon to Dedicate an Uncreated Park." His lead paragraph said Nixon would arrive to dedicate what Congress had not yet created, the "greatest urban park in the nation." A project of "immense ambition," Thomas said, it included all the coastline from Aquatic Park around the Presidio and Lands End to the San Mateo County line, as well as Fort Mason, the Maritime Building, the Marina Green, and the San Francisco Yacht Harbor.

Nixon arrived the next day and boarded a ferry boat for a forty-five minute ride around the bay with national parks enthusiast Laurence Rockefeller. He met Wayburn, Meyer, and other PFGGNRA officials at a receiving line on an old coast guard fishing pier, where he endorsed the park.

"The president just endorsed your bill," Thomas told Burton.

"You know that extra land in Marin that Ed and Amy want to add?" Burton replied. "Put it in. He can't oppose it now." Two days later, Senator Bible scheduled hearings.

One major snag remained. Armed Services Chairman Edward Hebert threw a fit when he discovered that the Burton bill, which transferred military land, had not gone through his committee. "I am seriously distressed," he wrote on September 21 to Speaker Albert, "that a precipitous action of this kind could be taken by a committee of the House without consultation with the committee which has primary jurisdiction." He said the land was "urgently required for continuing military missions," an absurd claim.

The original Burton bill had gone to his committee. Hebert could have blocked it, but no one knew it was there. Attaching a letter from Army Secretary Robert Froehlke calling Burton's Presidio maneuvers "gerrymandering," Hebert concluded, "I wish to register the strongest possible objection to any action by the Leadership to bring this bill before the House for consideration."

But between Nixon's support, the obvious environmental appeal, and the typically thorough job Burton performed in rounding up House votes, Hebert lost. It was a rare defeat for a committee chairman, especially at the hands at so junior a colleague, and one that foreshadowed a much bigger loss for Hebert a few years hence. Burton met with the Speaker, who said the bill would be debated. Within hours, Hebert sent an "urgent" letter to all members demanding its defeat. The army sent a dozen brass dressed in civilian clothes to lobby against it. The *Chronicle* editorialized that the army was behaving "like a dog in the manger" and called the army's resistance "unconscionable." On October 11, the House passed the bill. The Senate followed the next day. To Wayburn's and Meyer's surprise, Burton got nearly everything they wanted. In her thank-you letter, Meyer said, "I can't believe we ate the whole thing," but the proper Wayburn crossed it out.

The night the bill passed, Amy Meyer got a drunken call from Burton and Thomas congratulating her for her work. "You're a great broad, Amy," Burton screamed into the phone. On October 27, a few days before the election, Nixon signed the bill. Socialite Charlotte Mailliard put on a luncheon at the St. Francis Hotel to celebrate the bill and to honor her brother-in-law, Bill. Burton selected a characteristically plebeian menu: hamburgers, popsicles, and beer. The charge was $6.50 a person. Despite his ringing endorsement and the scenic photo opportunity on the bay, Nixon lost San Francisco.

Phil Burton never let up on the GGNRA. For the next decade he returned to it again and again, adding amendments in a variety of bills to increase its size, budget, and funds for acquisition. The original legislation, for example, included Fort Mason, located on San Francisco Bay. Attorney General John Mitchell came up with the ludicrous idea of building a prison there for youthful offenders, prompting Burton to suggest in a letter to Mitchell that the best comparison he could make would be if "the government decided to build such a facility next to the Watergate apartment complex in the District of Columbia," where Mitchell lived ("I know you would like that.")[18]

But what could easily have been sold to private developers to build luxury high-rise condominiums with the best views in San Francisco remained open to the public by virtue of Burton's legislation. A private, nonprofit Fort Mason Foundation transformed the base. What once had been a parking lot for GSA's auto fleet became a cultural and ethnic hub for San Francisco, with theaters, shops, and an internationally known gourmet vegetarian restaurant called Greens, owned by the San Francisco Zen Center. Other nonprofit groups that rented space at the ridiculously low price of fifty-five cents a square foot included Greenpeace, Western Public Radio, the San Francisco Children's Art Center, Media Alliance, and the Oceanic Society.

Bill Thomas, a lifelong enthusiast of old ships, convinced Burton to include in the park land that would incorporate the Balclutha, a square-rigged Cape Horn sailing vessel built in Scotland in 1886 and berthed as a tourist attraction near Fisherman's Wharf. In 1977, the National Park Service added to GGNRA what became the National Maritime Museum, devoted to West Coast seafaring, whaling, and Gold Rush history at Aquatic Park. The museum acts as caretaker for eight historic ships, six built between 1886 and 1915, at the Hyde Street Pier, Fort Mason, and Pier 45.[19]

11

THE PATH TO POWER

Phil Burton was always planning his agenda for power. As soon as he got to the House, he knew exactly what to do. That's one reason why he was so powerful. When progressive reformers took over the Democratic majority in the House, Burton was the only one with an agenda.

ABNER MIKVA
White House counsel and former chairman of the Democratic Study Group

We used to gather at the DSG offices in the late afternoon, and Phil Burton would hold forth. . . . Phil didn't originate the notion, but he certainly adopted the idea of slicing the salami year by year so that instead of major, threatening, confrontational change that brought out the do-or-die resistance of the establishment of the House, they'd take a slice or two every Congress and make important but incremental changes.

FORMER HOUSE SPEAKER THOMAS FOLEY

The two brightest individuals I ever saw in Congress were Richard Bolling and Wilbur Mills for sheer ability. The next three were Foley, Burton, and Brademas for knowledge and depth on issues and legislation. They were masters. The most abiding Democrat, the one for whom the Democratic Party was most in his heart and in his mind, was Phil.

FORMER HOUSE SPEAKER THOMAS P. "TIP" O'NEILL, JR.

IF THERE WAS ANY HOUSE chairman guaranteed to frustrate the freewheeling Phillip Burton, it was one of his own, the crusty and autocratic Wayne Aspinall of Colorado. Aspinall, a hated foe of environmentalists, ran the Committee on Interior and Insular Affairs with a rigid hand. Fifty-two when he entered Congress in 1949 for the first of twelve terms, Aspinall moved quickly up the seniority ladder, becoming chairman a decade later.

A former teacher, peach farmer, and speaker of the Colorado legislature, Aspinall took attendance, required absolute decorum, and sat next to his subcommittee chairmen, no matter how senior, as they conducted hearings he scheduled. He decided who served on which subcommittee and where each bill went. If his colleagues deviated from his script, he rebuked them like errant children. He controlled their budgets, staff and travel, and until his secretaries convinced him otherwise, he scheduled appointments in two-minute allotments. He created a subcommittee on the environment that Tom Foley later recalled as a "place of detention for bills he did not wish to move. Once committed, a bill was in for twenty, if not life."[1] Environmentalist and longtime adversary David Brower told the *Wall Street Journal,* "We have seen dream after dream dashed on the stony countenance of Wayne Aspinall."[2]

Aspinall's conduct was not unusual. Many chairmen acted like little dictators within the confines of their committees and sometimes beyond, as Edward Hebert's temper tantrum over Burton's GGNRA bill made clear. But Burton had not come this far to be frustrated by petty tyrants. The progressive changes he envisioned—in Congress and in the U.S.—could not happen in the House as it existed. If he were to move into the leadership, and there was no doubt that was his aim, the House had to be democratized and the virtually absolute authority of the committee chairmen curtailed.

The conventional route to leadership involved playing along, performing routine political chores, not alienating important people. Gradually, in this way, a few of the chosen were accepted into the inner circle. One man, especially skilled and blessed, was personally selected when the time came to be House majority whip and serve under the Speaker and majority leader.

Burton could play this game up to a point. He had gotten close to Majority Leader Carl Albert and to Wilbur Mills. He invited them to San Francisco and led them (separately) on tours of bawdy North Beach strip joints, including the Condor Club on Broadway, where Carol Doda performed. (He even led a reluctant Jack Anderson, the muckraking columnist and a religiously observant Mormon, on the tour, after which Anderson said, "I think he wanted to watch me sweat.") Burton's father was the personal physician to Doda, who helped create the topless craze in San Francisco with her forty-four-inch silicone-injected breasts, spotlighted by the giant profile of her body on the sign outside the Condor, the nipples blinking in red neon.

One night Burton dragged Sala and Carl Albert to Doda's show. Doda knew Burton through his father and joined their table after her "dance." One can imagine the effect this must have had on the diminutive Albert. Apparently at a loss for an opening conversational gambit, Albert volunteered to Doda that Israeli President Golda Meir was a good friend of his. Unimpressed, Doda gave him a withering look, turned to Sala and said, "Who is this little man and why is he talking to me about Golda Meir?"

North Beach strip joints and alcohol aside, Burton was temperamentally unable to wait his turn in the House, as if it would ever come, or accommodate himself to the old-boy system. He showed he could horse-trade with the best of them on specific legislation, but Burton's politics were often far to the left of what constituted Democratic Party consensus.

With the traditional means thus barred, Burton had to create his own path to power, an alternative route up the ladder. Building on currents of change already swirling around the House to reform the seniority system and make the committee chairmen more accountable, Burton ascended by winning chairmanship of the Democratic Study Group and later the House Democratic Caucus. The caucus was an inert body that other reformers as well as Burton hoped to resuscitate and use as a rival base from which to challenge all-powerful committee chairmen. From there, Burton could blast directly onto the top rungs of a House leadership that had its own candidates.

This was the recurring pattern of Phillip Burton's life. If the Trojan Knights or Theta Nu Epsilon rejected him at USC, he took over Blue Key and by force of personality made it important. If Bill Malone's San Francisco machine would never tap him for office, he found his own way, taking on the established order directly and eventually replacing it with his own. And if Jesse Unruh viewed Burton as his primary rival in the California Assembly, Burton still found ways of beating him at his own game, even assuring Unruh's support of AB 59 by authorizing the state to pay for Unruh's mother's nursing home costs via a change in the law on relatives' responsibilities.

Now the task was yet more formidable. The stakes were higher and his opponents were more skilled. Burton began agitating on his own committee, where his first target was Aspinall. Both committees on which Burton served produced major challenges to their chairmen. On Education and Labor, Adam Clayton Powell's flagrant abuse of rules and perquisites produced new rules that diffused his power to the subcommittee chairmen. Aspinall was no

Powell, but in the same way, Burton began to loosen the Coloradan's grip on Interior.

One day, after he had been on the committee for a few years, Burton made it clear he was not willing to bow and scrape in deference to the rigid chairman. Arriving late to a committee hearing, Burton burst into the hearing room, talking loudly, slapping spectators on the back as he made his way to the dais, where members sat at the horseshoe-shaped table. By rudely interrupting the meticulous Aspinall in mid-question and blowing his nose loudly at inopportune moments, he showed his colleagues they did not have to sit like terrified school boys quivering in fear of their stern headmaster.

Burton also began working the committee system, still controlled by the Ways and Means Committee, to import reform-minded liberals onto a committee where any challenge to the chairman was considered near suicidal. He was not the only member who chafed under Aspinall's rule, although allies Mo Udall of Arizona and Lloyd Meeds and Tom Foley of Washington were more respectful of their chairman's prerogatives. Burton's manipulations paid off. His closest friend, Robert Kastenmeier, a liberal Wisconsin environmentalist, joined Interior, followed by Jonathan Bingham of New York and Patsy Mink of Hawaii, whom Burton helped elect vice president of the Young Democrats a decade earlier.

After liberalizing the committee with these new members, Burton then expanded it. As chairman of the Subcommittee on Trusts and Territories, he proposed legislation to give offshore territories like Guam and the Virgin Islands representation in Congress. Puerto Rico already had a nonvoting "delegate." Over Aspinall's objections, Burton's bill was approved and enacted into law. These delegates could not vote on the floor, but they could vote in committee and in the caucus. Burton told the delegates they should seek appointments to Interior. It was the only meaningful committee to serve on, he advised them, because it had jurisdiction over their territories. This was how they could bring federal dollars home, and with his help, some became absolute masters of pork. Once Burton got them assigned to Interior, these delegates were his for life. Years later, when American Samoa got its delegate, Burton began with four votes on virtually any issue. He converted enough of the rest of the committee to have his own majority without ever being chairman.

Aspinall mistakenly believed he could dominate these Democratic Study Group liberals, whom committee conservatives nicknamed the "Crazies." Working with Foley and Meeds, Burton plotted revolution. He figured out what needed to be done, then used Meeds to make the speeches while he rounded up votes. Indeed, over the next few years, when the machinery was put in place to democratize the entire House, Foley and Meeds later said it got its first test in the Interior Committee. Committee Republicans, it turned out, were also chafing under Aspinall's iron rule. Burton approached them, too, about curtailing the chairman's power.[3]

By 1971, they were ready to strike. As Republican Sam Steiger of Arizona described it in a February 19, 1971 newsletter to his constituents, what happened next was "genuine rebellion," which Steiger called "unreported and apparently unnoticed, but in my limited experience a totally refreshing renewal of hope that the rigidity of precedence is not unbreakable." For six years, Steiger said, the "ultra-liberal Democratic Study Group has been loading the Interior Committee with some of its wildest-eyed members. They have been at almost constant odds with the chairman, and he has made no secret of his concern that they represent potential harm to the orderly process of the committee." But Meeds and Burton, "a genuine, rug-chewing liberal activist," Steiger wrote, drew up written rules—which required a committee vote—to force Aspinall to be more responsive. First, subcommittee chairmen, including Burton, could hire their own professional staff.

"Really meaty, heroic stuff," Steiger wrote, tongue partly in cheek. "Not to you, perhaps, but tantamount to flag despoiling to the chairman." Burton and Meeds then offered them a deal.

> If we, the Republicans, would support the DSG people, they would permit us to hire our own staff at a ratio of one minority staffer for every two majority staffers. Since we currently have only one staffer, this was great. Most of the Republicans thus joined with the DSG people and over the shocked disbelief and chillingly clear threats of retribution of the chairman, passed the staffing amendment. This improbable alignment of bitter philosophical enemies had so much fun spanking the chairman, they kept it up for another full day and changed a whole series of rules.[4]

Aspinall was furious, but there was little he could do. Against his will, the committee he dominated was being democratized and decentralized, his authority dispersed to subcommittee chairmen. In 1970, the full committee employed fourteen people, with no separate subcommittee staff. Four years later, the full committee staff had doubled to twenty-eight, and the seven subcommittees employed twenty-five more.[5]

Burton was not working in a vacuum. Calls to reform House rules and procedures were coming from many quarters, especially as cities burned,

Vietnam opposition mounted, and the House did little to address either issue. Lyndon Johnson's 1964 landslide gave him such a huge margin in the House that he worked around reactionary chairmen. But in the 1966 elections, the balance of power shifted with the defeat of forty-seven Democrats. With Nixon's victory two years later, the Republican-Dixiecrat alliance, which flourished during the Eisenhower years, was poised to re-emerge.

While Nixon was putting his government together, panicked liberals met to discuss strategy and their fears of just such a development with DSG Chairman Jim O'Hara. Begun in 1959 by a cautious band of liberals who wanted to pass civil rights and labor legislation, the Democratic Study Group had grown to more than 100 members. But they were badly split over Vietnam and now faced what promised to be a tough-minded GOP administration. Participants in the O'Hara meetings included the executive board, many of whom came from Education and Labor: O'Hara, Brademas, DSG founder Frank Thompson, plus Udall, Henry Reuss of Wisconsin, Donald Fraser of Minnesota, Burton, and new DSG Executive Director Richard Conlon.

Conlon was soon to become one of the most important House staffers of the postwar era, a man who played a more significant role in reforming the House than almost every elected representative. Conlon worked for newspapers in Duluth and Minneapolis before winning a prestigious American Political Science Association fellowship. Upon arrival in Washington, he was assigned to work for Frank Thompson and later for Senator Walter Mondale. Thompson got him the job at DSG in March 1968.

The other key participant in the O'Hara meetings, although originally hostile to DSG, was Richard Bolling, whose 1966 book, *House Out of Order*, was extremely influential. Bolling wanted to invigorate the Democratic Caucus, which had fallen into disrepute in the nearly six decades since all-powerful Speaker Joe Cannon and his "King Caucus."

To break the power of the committee chairmen, Bolling also believed in recreating a strong Speaker, whose authority had been dramatically curtailed ever since the 1910–11 House revolt against Cannon's near-absolute rule. Cannon was stripped of his authority to appoint committee chairmen and chair the Rules Committee himself. The seniority system became institutionalized only since Cannon's fall. But Bolling believed the pendulum had swung too far.

A strong Speaker—the job to which Bolling still aspired—should appoint the chairman and members of the Rules Committee, thus converting Rules into an instrument of the leadership, rather than what it was, a reactionary obstacle. The Speaker's other instrument, Bolling believed, should be the House Democratic Caucus, which included every elected Democrat. There, a majority of the majority could vote on policy that would bind all Democrats to follow suit and thereby diminish the GOP-Dixiecrat alliance, as well as tame or at least counter the committee chairmen.

None of this had happened in decades in the caucus, but the power was there to use. If the caucus issued a resolution on how all Democrats should vote on a bill or a procedure, in other words, committee chairs and other Dixiecrats could ignore it only at their peril. But ever since Cannon's fall, the Democratic Caucus had been weak. It met once every two years at the start of each session to elect leaders and ratify new committee assignments made by the Committee on Committees, which in fact was the House Ways and Means Committee acting in its other capacity.[6]

Bolling also wanted to use the caucus to strip some Dixiecrat chairmen of their committees, including Mendel Rivers of South Carolina, the hawkish and autocratic chairman of Armed Services. There was precedent for using the caucus to unseat uncooperative chairmen and to keep errant Democrats in line. Several Dixiecrats broke ranks and supported Nixon for president in 1960 and suffered no harm. But Bolling and others warned the Dixiecrats not to do so again. They should not get the benefits of the seniority system, including chairmanships of major committees, and then endorse the rival party's presidential candidate. Despite the warnings, southerners John Bell Williams of Mississippi and Albert Watson of South Carolina supported Goldwater over Johnson in 1964. Afterward, the caucus made good its threat and stripped them of their seniority, and thus their chairmanships. Williams resigned, precipitating a special election, changed parties and was re-elected as a Republican. Watson resigned several years later.

In the DSG strategy sessions, Don Fraser proposed a frontal assault: a direct challenge to the seniority system. The caucus should vote on whether to extend every committee chairman's tenure. But when O'Hara floated the idea to colleagues outside DSG in early 1969, he found little enthusiasm. Progress would have to be made "an inch at a time," O'Hara reported back. Most House members believed the seniority system was too entrenched to give way.[7] One modest suggestion did prevail, however. The caucus would be permitted to meet once a month with a set agenda.

McCormack and Albert reluctantly went along, because in January 1969, just a few months after the DSG executive board meetings began, Udall challenged the seventy-seven-year-old McCormack for Speaker. McCormack easily won, but his concession to insurgent liberals was his promise to let the caucus hold monthly meetings. Over the next two years, many were canceled for lack of a quorum. But the caucus did meet eight times to discuss reform issues and Vietnam.[8]

Because of deep divisions over Vietnam, some liberals considered walking out and forming another organization. But to everyone's surprise, Don Fraser, one of their own, was elected DSG chairman. The son of a college professor, Fraser was cerebral and scholarly. He grew up in Minnesota's good government tradition and was a staunch progressive. While Burton leaned on him from the executive board, he in turn pushed the entire membership to become more aggressive.

New director Conlon, meanwhile, increased the staff and DSG's usefulness and prestige. DSG turned out fact sheets and dispassionate analyses that soon became required reading in advance of key votes. DSG was saying, in effect, the leadership's weekly one-page Whip notice of pending legislation was not good enough. DSG was providing a supplemental analysis of all bills and putting it on every member's desk first thing Monday morning. These supplements helped the members do their jobs better, gained credibility for DSG, and educated members about reform issues. With an old and passive Speaker and a weak majority leader, there was an emerging sense that the reformers, Burton among them, were moving gradually to fill the power vacuum.

In March 1969, DSG published a study on how DSG members and Democratic nonmembers differed on thirty key votes. The results were startling. DSG members voted with the Democratic Party's official position 91 percent of the time, versus 31 percent for non-DSG Democrats, not much more than the 24 percent figure for House Republicans. Moreover, the alliance of GOP and non-DSG Democrats led to twelve of the seventeen defeats the Democrats suffered. One-third of all chairmen voted with the Republicans more often than with their own party. Twenty-eight subcommittee chairmen and six full committee chairmen voted against Democratic positions 92 percent of the time. Even the Republicans could not match that record.[9]

As an example of the deep schisms, when Bolling tried to get a lottery for draft-age men established to create a more equitable draft, Mendel Rivers blocked it. "I do not know what makes a man like Mendel Rivers think the way he does," Bolling told Walter Cronkite on CBS News. With surpassing arrogance (and a surfeit of classical allusions), Rivers replied: "We've never gotten 150 votes against us. Caesar in all his glory cannot make that statement. I'm the chairman of the Committee on Armed Services, elected by the House. I don't plan to give that toga to anyone else. Any time any of these people want to take us on in the caucus, come on in, the water's fine." Conlon reproduced Rivers's remarks and distributed them to all his members.

The next DSG challenge involved changing teller voting, the practice by which members voted on amendments to major bills without recording their vote. It was contrived in part so that House proceedings would not be slowed by time-consuming roll calls. But teller voting happened so quickly that reporters and lobbyists could seldom see how more than a handful of members voted. The secrecy allowed many to escape the consequences of tough votes on issues of intense interest to their constituents, such as the Vietnam War or the debate over the SST, the supersonic transport plane that many environmentalists opposed.

Burton was not a major player in this drama, but at Conlon's urging, DSG pressed forward. Working with a savvy activist named David Cohen, who was lobbying for a new public interest group called Common Cause, they convinced Tip O'Neill of Massachusetts, a respected member on Rules who was close to McCormack, to lead the fight against this stealth voting. Bolling had already turned them down. DSG President Fraser sent hundreds of letters to editorial page editors and columnists around the country to get outside support for this "anti-secrecy" legislation. After eleven days of debate, the reformers won.[10] A year later, the House reversed itself and defeated funding for the SST by eleven votes. Sidney Yates of Illinois, who wrote the amendment, said he believed that forcing members to have their vote recorded "made a difference."[11]

An emboldened DSG continued its search for ways to attack the seniority system. Conlon suggested creating a committee to discuss reforms, including seniority, and report back to the caucus. Thus was born the Committee on Organization, Study, and Review, chaired by Julia Butler Hansen of Washington, a respected nine-year House veteran. Working with the leadership, Democratic Caucus Chairman Dan Rostenkowski picked the members, including Burton, who represented major Democratic groups: northern DSG liberals, moderates, and southern conservatives. Thompson and O'Hara joined Burton as the DSG contingent.[12]

Burton's maneuvers on this key committee took him a giant step closer to realizing his leadership ambitions. Having impressed the coal rats with his work on black lung, he was now about to show other moderates and conservatives he could work within the system.

Two key recommendations emerged from the Hansen Committee, both of which were accepted. The first permitted any ten caucus members to demand a vote on whether to retain individual chairmen. Moreover, in selecting a chairman, the committee recommended that the caucus "need not necessarily follow seniority." This rule was a slowly ticking time bomb that exploded a few years later. Liberals on the committee wanted a caucus secret ballot to automatically vote "up or down" on every chairman's continued tenure, but Burton and the southerners opposed it. Under cover of anonymity, they said, caucus members could gang up on unpopular chairmen. Burton proposed a compromise: permit a vote when ten members requested it publicly.[13]

Thompson made the second recommendation: no one should chair more than one subcommittee. Powerful chairmen often consolidated power by also dominating key subcommittees. By eliminating this practice, this proposal would "spread the action" to more than thirty younger members who now got to chair their first subcommittee and hire their own staff. Unlike the first reform, the effects were immediate and dramatic, and the southern stranglehold—southerners still held half the chairmanships—began to ease.

The Democratic Caucus approved the two proposals in January 1971, the same time that Burton, Foley, Meeds, and the Republicans were "spanking" Aspinall. In the course of pushing for institutional reform, Burton was quietly amassing influence. "Unquestionably a moving force in the [Hansen] Committee's activities," congressional scholar Norman Ornstein concluded, "Burton also managed to bring about a major change in the attitudes of some non-DSG members towards him. Previously considered to be an 'ultraliberal,' Burton was highly praised by moderates and conservatives for his openmindedness, ability to compromise, and integrity. Burton's desire to become part of the leadership was no secret, and his participation on the Hansen Committee figured in his overall 'plan.'"[14]

While the Hansen Committee was meeting, McCormack announced he would retire at the end of his term and support Carl Albert to succeed him. Reverberations from the internal jockeying for power that ensued rippled through the House for the next two decades. What with reformers seeking to oust committee chairmen and erode the seniority system, the Democratic Caucus about to grow powerful beyond almost anyone's imagining, and a near free-for-all among Democrats fighting for leadership posts, this was a particularly volatile era. Burton appeared at the right time in the right place to capitalize on the ferment and enlist these powerful congressional players, wittingly or not, in his own end-run strategy of building a power base from the outside.

Albert's sole opponent was John Conyers of Michigan, who had no chance of winning. But one important delegation—Illinois, led by Dan Rostenkowski—did not line up behind the Speaker-to-be. Rostenkowski made matters worse when he bragged publicly that he might run against Albert himself. It was a boast for which he soon would pay dearly and for which Burton later would suffer as Rostenkowski struggled to work his own way back into the good graces of a new House leadership.

Remembering the debacle at the 1968 convention, neither Rostenkowski nor his patron, Mayor Daley, wanted Albert to be Speaker. They preferred Majority Whip Hale Boggs, like them a Catholic, big-city organization Democrat from New Orleans. Three Illinois members told Albert the delegation moved as a single unit, and Rostenkowski "won't let us go."[15] Rostenkowski's delays notwithstanding, the caucus elected Albert overwhelmingly in January 1971. Boggs won the intense fight to succeed Albert as majority leader, besting four other candidates: Mo Udall, B. F. Sisk of California, Jim O'Hara, and Wayne Hays. A few months later, on March 31, 1971, the caucus voted for the first time to withdraw all troops from Indochina.

Having selected Albert and Boggs as its new leaders and approved the Hansen Committee reforms, the Democratic Caucus had one more task: to elect a new chairman. For the first time since 1910, the job would actually mean something if the reformers were serious about making the caucus matter. Rostenkowski had served two terms already, and it was widely assumed he would be re-elected without opposition. But Tiger Teague of Texas, chairman of the Veterans' Affairs Committee and an amiable old war hero with no political enemies, was suddenly thrust forward as a candidate.

Many people saw Carl Albert's hidden hand in Teague's candidacy. Observers could see for themselves that the new Speaker wouldn't at all mind taking Rostenkowski out. But Jim Wright said Teague was thrown into the race involuntarily. When their delegation met to decide committee assignments, Wright said, somebody asked why no Texan was challenging Rosty. Teague was "volunteered" because he was the only Texan absent from the meeting, and no one else wanted the job. No one said out loud that Albert would be pleased if Rostenkowski were dumped, but even Wright conceded years later that some members may have known what Albert wanted. At any rate, Teague was an unlikely candidate. Angry that he was nominated without his permission, Teague said publicly he would vote for Rostenkowski and apparently did. But between the Texans, many liberals still angry at Rostenkowski over Chicago, and Albert's known hostility, Teague won.

Burton was shocked by the defeat, particularly after Rostenkowski had worked so hard to get the Hansen Committee started. "Jesus, Danny, what a tragedy, after all you did, to be turned away by the very liberals you were working for," Burton told him. "We've got to find you a platform." Rosten-kowski figured Burton did not want him to "fall into the shadows of gov-ernment."[16] Teague called his victory "the damnedest fluke you ever saw."

Boggs wanted to name Rostenkowski majority whip and bring him into the leadership. Rosty was his friend from Ways and Means. But Albert re-fused. "I have to go talk about the Whip. I will mention Rostenkowski again, but I know he won't go for it," Boggs told aide Gary Hymel on his way to a meeting with Albert. That narrowed the choices to Hugh Carey of New York or Tip O'Neill.

It was an easy choice. O'Neill, chairman of the Democratic Congressional Campaign Committee and a twenty-year veteran, had also considered run-ning for majority leader but dropped his plans when he heard that his room-mate and friend Ed Boland planned to run. But Boland eventually withdrew. Hymel said the only time he saw Boggs smile during the entire leadership fight was when O'Neill called and said, "I'm with you, and I'm bringing eighteen guys with me from New England."

O'Neill's call cemented Boggs's victory. If he could not get Rosty for the whip's job, O'Neill was an easy second choice.[17] But Rostenkowski still had to tell Daley that his man in Washington had lost everything. He was not caucus chairman or majority whip. It was his lowest point. Observers said that Rostenkowski, an emotional and expressive man, wept at these bitter defeats.

With the leadership fights out of the way, the caucus turned next to the committee system and seniority, scheduling a vote on the committee chair-men for February 3. In anticipation, DSG issued a study on the "age and tenure" of these chairmen. The study seemed designed to set the younger generation against its elders. While the average age of committee chairman from 1911 to 1920 was fifty-two and their average tenure as chair was 1.4 years, the study found, the average age had increased fifteen years to sixty-six during the 1960s. The average tenure had increased five-fold to 7.5 years. "Chairmen over seventy," the DSG report said, "used to be rare, while chair-men in their thirties and forties were commonplace. Today, the situation is just the reverse. Chairmen over seventy are commonplace, while chairmen in their thirties and forties have been nearly extinct for the past two de-cades."[18]

The big test vote was on whether to oust John McMillan of South Carolina as chairman of the District of Columbia Committee. A seventy-seven-year-old obstructionist who opposed home rule for the District, opposed civil rights, and represented the worst of the seniority system, McMillan was an obvious target. Even so, the reformers lost. The vote to retain him was 126-96. But it was close enough to signal other chairmen to be more responsive and accountable. Next time, a McMillan might not be so lucky. (In fact, he was defeated in the 1972 primary, as was Aspinall, whose Colorado district had been weakened by reapportionment.)

A few weeks after the caucus vote, Burton made his move. He announced his candidacy to succeed Fraser as DSG chairman. His announcement galvanized his liberal DSG enemies to find another candidate. The man they came up with was Jim Corman, a fellow liberal from California who had used his seniority to best Burton a few years earlier for California's spot on Ways and Means. Corman likely resented Burton's intrusion onto his welfare and social security turf via his DSG Welfare Task Force and Burton's leading role in pushing for the Nixon-Moynihan FAP program. He probably did not appreciate Burton showing up at hearings as an honored guest of Wilbur Mills, either. Corman had neither Burton's toughness nor shrewd intelligence, but Richard Bolling and the Thompson-O'Hara-Brademas faction figured they could work better with a man who was more "reasonable" and less personally threatening. Conlon, still finding his way as DSG director, believed Burton would overpower him and opposed his candidacy. Conlon also owed his job to Thompson.

For the first time, the DSG chairmanship was contested. To many, that seemed a sign of health: DSG finally mattered enough that people would battle to lead it. Burton began his campaign by expanding DSG, recruiting new members who were certain to support him. He instructed Mark Gersh, whom Conlon had hired the year before as a political aide fresh from the University of Maryland, to ask nonmembers, particularly in the South, to join and pay the $100 annual dues. DSG was irrelevant to them, but if they could do a favor now for Phil Burton, that was a small price to pay for a political reward down the line. Meanwhile, the fourteen-member DSG executive board split, seven for Burton, seven for Corman. But in the enlarged DSG, fattened with his handpicked recruits, Burton won easily.

DSG became important, Bolling said later, from the moment Burton took it over. In a story from the Washington news bureau of Knight-Ridder, where he now worked, reporter Lou Cannon, who had helped Burton defeat Tommy Maloney fifteen years earlier, quickly grasped the significance of Burton's election. "While his driving ambition repels many of his colleagues," Cannon wrote, "his willingness to accept a bill rather than the credit for it attracts the most committed among them. He knows more about the welfare system than any other congressman. Despite his ultraliberalism, he is a close friend of [Carl] Albert and of . . . Wilbur Mills."

Burton is "the most creative congressman I know," colleague Don Edwards told Cannon, with "an absolute genius for getting things done within the system while holding fundamentally different views from the leadership." Cannon noted that no ex-DSG chairman had endorsed him, and called it a "curious irony" that Burton could work so well with the leadership but apparently not with the DSG establishment.

On a more prophetic note, Cannon concluded: "The energy and application that won Burton the chairmanship will almost certainly characterize DSG efforts during the next two years, and this should give conservatives pause. Conservatives have always benefited from the natural distrust between DSG-Democrats and those outside the fold, a distrust that Burton's working relationship with Albert and Mills will go a long way to erase. A new day may be dawning for liberals in the House."[19]

Cannon was correct, although it took a few more years for the "new day" to fully dawn. Abner Mikva, an anti-Daley liberal from Chicago and a former law clerk to Supreme Court Justice Felix Frankfurter, said he knew of no other House reformer who seized power with a specific agenda. The DSG originally called itself a "study group" so as not to be threatening. Burton *wanted* DSG to be threatening, Mikva said, and once he got used to the idea, so did Conlon.

Almost overnight, DSG became an important center of House activities, the engine of reform and the instrument of Burton's power. Indeed, just as a twenty-four-year-old congressional staffer and budding power broker named Lyndon Johnson took over an ineffectual group of House aides called the Little Congress and made it his in 1933 (also by packing that house, according to Johnson biographer Robert Caro), Phillip Burton was about to put his own indelible stamp on DSG.

Previous leaders were respected men of substance. None, however, possessed Burton's power drive or combination of extreme liberalism, uncanny operational abilities, and hardball tactics. But his remained a difficult brilliance. He could be an ugly drunk, spewing saliva as he screamed vulgarities or berated colleagues in front of staff or peers. Mikva, Foley, Kastenmeier, and Edwards willingly accepted that aspect of his personality because they knew he was incorruptible, could accomplish things few others could, and never deviated from his mission to help the poor, even as he accumulated personal power. But not everyone forgave him his flaws. Liberals such as Corman, Thompson, Brademas, and, later, Tip O'Neill were so offended by his crudeness and almost willful lack of social grace that they could not stand to be in the same room with him, let alone on the same side.

Late every afternoon, Burton, Conlon, Gersh, Foley, Mikva, David Cohen, another Common Cause advocate named Fred Wertheimer, and a rotating band of other House liberals and friends gathered at the DSG office to discuss strategy. In Sacramento, Burton opened the legislature to the "Raggedy Ass" lobby of fledgling public interest groups, such as the ACLU, the American Friends Service Committee, and the United Farm Workers union. Now in Washington, Burton was inviting similar groups into DSG, including Common Cause, ADA, the National Committee for an Effective Congress and some of Ralph Nader's spin-off groups, all of which knew that without congressional reform, liberal social legislation was unattainable.

Every afternoon at six, Burton brought out the vodka and whiskey, and the DSG mutineers plotted their next moves. As Foley recalled the meetings, Conlon laid out the technical aspects of the reforms they wanted to accomplish, Burton assessed the politics of what was possible and defined the strategy to get them done, and Mikva and Bob Eckhardt of Texas analyzed each issue carefully with their sharp legal minds.

Nader's top assistant, Joan Claybrook, profiled Burton for *Congress Watch*, which compiled such profiles on all members. He would not see her alone, so Gary Sellers and Dick Conlon sat in on the three-hour interview. Claybrook found Burton "totally fascinating," but incomprehensible because he spoke in a kind of code. She had to interrupt and ask Conlon or Sellers to translate what Burton had said. "California's burly, beefy Phillip Burton," her twenty-six-page profile began, "has a voice like a sonic boom, the charge of a bull in a congressional committee room, and a mission in politics. The 46-year-old San Franciscan is the political Pied Piper for America's alienated poor and mistreated workers. He has two kinds of fervent supporters—those who are wealthy and liberal enough to champion an iconoclast, and those who are too desperately poor to find any other advocate for their cause."

Devoting most of her profile to his role in DSG reforms, black lung, and the occupational safety and health legislation of 1970, Claybrook concluded:

> He has been described as crude and abrasive, a man who mixes legal jargon with blue-movie aphorisms. . . . The most fascinating side of the California legislator is the manner by which he adapts congressional rules and colleague complaints to create his own legislative triumphs—and it is rarely if ever visible to the media or the public. The method is a combination of behind-the-scenes maneuvers and "confrontation" politics with either

small groups of powerful members or with members in a position to cast determining votes. . . . He lives, eats and drinks politics. His concentration on the subject and the intensity of his interest sometimes exhausts those around him. And his sometimes overbearing manner tires even his friends.

A later, updated *Congress Watch* profile called Burton a "raging alcoholic," but the reference was removed because the author said there was no evidence his drinking affected his work. Even so, Sellers brought the rough draft to Burton to read. "Phil, I want you to see this so you know what people are saying about you," Sellers told him. He stood there while Burton read paragraph after paragraph of convincing descriptions of what he was like when he was drunk. Burton thanked Sellers but said nothing further.

Even as he became the leader of the liberals in the House, Burton maintained important relationships with powerful enemies of reform, including Mills, Louisiana conservative Joe Waggonner, and the much-feared Wayne Hays, whom most colleagues regarded as an obnoxious bully. These three men could not have disagreed more with Burton on most issues, but they were fellow power brokers and respected each other's abilities. Burton finagled an appointment to the North Atlantic Alliance, which Hays chaired. The assignment gave Burton another opportunity to mix and bond with members he might not otherwise have befriended, including Hays and Texan Jack Brooks, a tough and wily liberal, the ranking member on the Government Operations Committee.

The assignment also gave Burton and Sala a yearly junket to Europe. Burton worked hard and often politicked among his European colleagues just as he did everywhere else. But these trips also afforded opportunities for wild bouts of carousing, particularly on the rare occasions when Sala could not make the trip. An Education and Labor colleague recounted later that he once saw Burton leave his London hotel with a prostitute on each arm.

On the eve of a week-long NATO Alliance conference, an aide to another member spent two days with Burton that he never forgot "drinking, gambling and whoring." The weekend began with drinks at the Playboy Club in London, where they each picked up several women, headed to a country inn outside London, stopping at every pub along the way. They spent the night, headed back to London, where they each picked up another three women and repeated the scene. After the following Monday's full load of briefings and hearings, during which the aide said Burton "never missed a beat," Burton said, "You want to go out again?" The aide, twelve years Burton's junior, said, "Phil, I can't do it. I'm going to bed."

But sex, like food and alcohol, seemed to be an essential release to a man of Burton's prodigious appetites and passions. Tom Rees, who joined him in Congress, saw Burton as a giant "blast furnace," who required vast quantities of fuel to keep him stoked. He ate with such gusto that friends joked they needed an umbrella to protect their clothes from flying debris. Others were appalled at his manners. At one elegant dinner party, Burton was seated next to NBC White House correspondent Judy Woodruff, whom he had not met before. That did not stop him from reaching over and spearing a piece of chicken off her plate with his fork. Another time, when he slathered huge chunks of butter on a piece of sourdough, Joe Beeman said, "Phil, why don't you just inject the cholesterol directly into your veins?"

Conlon recalled to reporter Mike Green what it was like one Sunday when Sala was out of town and he invited Burton over for dinner, which included flank steak, potato salad, and fresh corn:

> Phil started eating corn on the cob, and it was like a corn on the cob eating machine! He didn't say a word. He didn't touch another bit of food. He did nothing for about five or ten minutes but eat corn on the cob. He literally went through five ears . . . and corn is flying all over the place. And he's got—the kids are sitting there with their mouths hanging open. I mean, here's Daddy's boss home, you know, for dinner and the whole thing, and all of a sudden corn is flying all over. He's got corn all over him! He's got it all over his shirt; he's in a short-sleeved shirt. He's got it on his face. He's got it in his hair.[20]

Mikva said the "overwhelming aspects of his personality" drove Burton to "drink so hard, screw so hard, and work so hard." Mikva, Edwards, and Rees worried about his health and tried to get him to the House gym for some exercise, but to no avail. Edwards once brought Burton as far as the steam room, where he drank several cups of coffee and chain-smoked Chesterfields before storming off to do something "useful."

Despite the occasional philandering, Sala Burton remained the enduring love of his life. She was his best friend—indeed, possibly his only true friend—his most trusted advisor, and hardest worker. Most of the time he was utterly lost without her. She cleaned up his messes and calmed him when no one else could. She laid out his clothes for him in the morning, because, left to his own devices, he would wear different-colored socks or ties that clashed horribly. He never noticed. Burton was once photographed in the Oval Office with Jimmy Carter, a piece of toilet paper clinging to his cheek where he had cut himself shaving that morning. A small dark stain was visible at its center. Burton was likely one of the few men in politics—or anywhere else, for that matter—who could walk into the White House to meet the president wearing toilet paper on his face and either not realize it or not care.

Sala hated to cook and wasn't good in the kitchen, but she understood the need for working dinners at home with aides and colleagues or more intimate gatherings in which her husband could be seen in relaxed settings. When the Group, the collection of antiwar House liberals, came over for dinner one night, she cooked pasta that was all stuck together, "really dreadful stuff," one participant recalled. But she believed in him and in his progressive agenda every bit as much as he did, which helped justify her long nights at home alone, night after night, while Phil was working on a new bill or a new scheme. When she called, Burton became a changed man. He might be on two phones at once, chewing out a White House bureaucrat or House colleague on one line, even as he was on another line terrorizing a hapless Census official for not getting him the right data. But when word came that Sala was on the phone, his demeanor changed instantly to that of gentle, soothing husband. "Yes, 'heart," he would say in a calm and solicitous voice. "Yes, 'heart. I'll be home soon, 'heart. Thirty minutes, 'heart." Putting down one phone, he would resume his screaming match almost in mid-sentence, until, forty-five minutes later, Sala was on the line again.[21]

Burton had big goals for DSG. He did not want just an information and referral service, nor even merely a place to center reform efforts. He wanted DSG intimately involved in electing like-minded Democrats to Congress. Mark Gersh, whose detailed demographic knowledge of every congressional district in the country nearly rivaled Burton's, prepared election strategies with Burton, almost as if DSG was an arm of the Democratic Congressional Campaign Committee. Then Burton rounded up money from his allies in organized labor and doled it out to promising challengers. All told, DSG under Burton and Conlon raised $200,000 in 1972 for its candidates and lent essential aid to Democrats otherwise shunned by the party establishment. A number of them went on to major House careers.

One day in 1972, for example, a young North Carolina challenger named Charlie Rose was startled to get a check for $2,000 from the Democratic Study Group, Chairman Phillip Burton. Rose had never heard of the group or of Burton and had not even won his primary. A protégé of former Governor Terry Sanford, Rose asked his staff whether he should accept the money. They urged him to do so and to explain to anyone who asked that DSG was a "research organization." When the newly elected Rose showed up in Washington, he looked up Burton at the DSG office to thank him and seek his counsel. Rose wanted a spot on the Agriculture Committee, where he could work to preserve North Carolina tobacco subsidies. Because he had an interest in computerizing House operations, he also wanted assignment to the Administration Committee. Burton told him who to lobby to get on Agriculture and which tactics to use. As for Administration, Burton suggested he get himself appointed to the North Atlantic Assembly, where he could get to know Wayne Hays. Rose followed his advice to the letter on both counts. He made it onto Agriculture and traveled to Europe with the assembly in 1974, where he persuaded Hays to support him for Administration the following session. (In 1990, Rose became chairman of House Administration and in that capacity president of the North Atlantic Assembly. He said he owed both jobs to Phillip Burton. He also ranked fourth on Agriculture and chaired a subcommittee.)

In Colorado, the Democrats were virtually ignoring another promising liberal, treating underdog Patricia Schroeder, a thirty-two-year-old antiwar candidate, "like I had the plague." She was challenging a vulnerable one-term Republican. Told that Burton would be arriving soon to campaign for her, she was still wondering who he was when Sala called and asked if Phillip needed to bring his overcoat. Burton roared into Denver, checked her donor list, asked countless questions, offered his advice, and roared off. She won and when she arrived in Washington she also looked up her benefactor. Burton helped get Schroeder onto Armed Services, over the objections of ultraconservative chairman Edward Hebert, who succeeded Mendel Rivers. She promptly voted to cut off American military aid to Cambodia.[22]

On March 13, 1972, a year into his chairmanship and in a move uncharacteristic of the once passive DSG, Burton blocked for two days a House-Senate conference report to raise the national debt. The point, Burton said in a DSG press release, was to "impress on the Nixon administration the urgency" of making tax reform recommendations to the Congress. "While our domestic problems fester and our cities and states fight off fiscal disaster," Burton said, "we can no longer tolerate the fact that high-income corporations and individuals pay little or no tax and much-needed monies are siphoned into private pockets. As long as the rich are able to evade paying their fair share while many middle and lower income Americans feel the sharp bite of the federal tax system, there will be no true tax justice." But Nixon, not

Burton or the DSG, held the cards. Wilbur Mills wrote Nixon and requested tax reform proposals, but Nixon indicated he would not submit any, and although DSG made its point, the Democrats were helpless.[23]

A few weeks later, however, on April 20, 1972, DSG accomplished something historic, forcing the House to deal more substantively than ever before with the Vietnam War and empowering the Democratic Caucus to assert its authority over recalcitrant chairmen. Working with Cohen of Common Cause and Father Robert Drinan, an antiwar congressman and Catholic priest from Massachusetts, Burton guided the caucus to direct Foreign Affairs Chairman Thomas Morgan to report a bill out of his committee. It wasn't just any bill. It set a date terminating the Vietnam War, subject only to release of American POWs. This sort of direct intervention in the authority and prerogatives of a committee chairman just was not done, and other chairmen besides Morgan were furious but also put on notice. Burton was helped enormously by Majority Whip O'Neill's decision to sponsor the resolution.

The campaign began a year earlier when Cohen convinced O'Neill and four other mainstream Democrats to sign a letter opposing further funding of the war. After grass-roots lobbying by Common Cause, 160 Democrats voted for an amendment to cut off funds. The mechanism Bolling had long envisioned was finally beginning to work. The caucus had directed a committee chairman to send out a bill against his will. Burton, Conlon, and Common Cause had significantly raised the stakes in this battle for power.

"Adoption of the O'Neill resolution by this morning's Democratic Caucus by an overwhelming margin," Burton wrote that day, "is a magnificent victory for the American people. I am proud of the Democratic Study Group and its members who provided almost all the votes to pass this resolution and worked tirelessly to get this issue before the caucus. For the first time, we in DSG have broken through the parliamentary barricades erected by the Republican/Dixiecrat conservative coalition and forcefully condemned the Nixon administration's unnecessary prolongation of this bloody war."

Besides sending a powerful message to Nixon, Burton added, "The Democratic Caucus has in addition taken the historic step of establishing its authority over the committees of the House and their chairmen. For the first time, the caucus has *directed*—not 'urged' or 'recommended'—that a chairman and his committee report legislation to accomplish the will of the caucus. We have instructed the Democratic members of the Foreign Affairs Committee to bring legislation to the floor of the House within thirty days to get our troops, planes and ships out of Indochina before the end of this Congress."[24]

In a memo to Burton four days later, Conlon wrote that adoption of the Indochina resolution presented "a major problem and an unprecedented opportunity." Conlon's memo laid out how the caucus should proceed:

> Party discipline must be maintained. If it is not, dissenting Democrats on the [Foreign Affairs] Committee will join with Republican committee members to prevent a bill from being reported or to report a bill putting national Democrats in a disadvantageous position on the floor. The end result will be that many DSG members will be hurt politically and House Democrats will again come off looking hopelessly divided, leaderless and foolishly ineffectual. If this effort fails, the caucus will lose credibility among many members as an effective instrument. If, on the other hand, we can maintain discipline and get a half-decent bill to the floor, we will have achieved a major breakthrough. Thus we should make an all-out effort to make the handling of this resolution a model of how the national Democratic "majority of the majority" can work through the caucus to overcome the decentralization of power which hobbles Democratic leadership and prevents effective legislative action.

Conlon's strategy called for enlisting the Speaker's help because it represented a major opportunity for Albert to "take charge and strengthen his leadership." He also suggested that "Bolling could help tremendously in this respect, and I think he would be willing—even though he voted against the resolution—because he has long advocated caucus action as the way of strengthening the leadership."[25]

The strategy made sense, but Conlon misread the politics. They got the bill to the floor, but Albert, Boggs, and Bolling worked with the administration to defeat it. Despite Conlon's fears of looking "foolishly ineffectual," however, DSG and the caucus demonstrated newfound power.[26]

For every two steps forward, Burton also stumbled backwards. At a time when he was consolidating power, achieving breakthrough successes with DSG and the caucus and serving notice that he was marching inexorably up his own ladder to leadership, Burton made the blunder of his career. He didn't realize it at the time, but a drunken encounter with an influential colleague at a political event cost him dearly for the rest of his life.

In the early fall of 1972, Tip O'Neill attended a Beverly Hills fundraising dinner in his role as chairman of the Democratic Congressional Campaign Committee. After the event, he adjourned to a cocktail lounge in the Beverly

Hills Hotel with Phil and Sala Burton and John and Betty Stephens. Stephens, a wealthy Santa Barbara contributor, made his fortune in the kitty litter business and dabbled in politics. Burton had been drinking. As was his wont when lubricated, he became aggressive and profane, using "fuck" in every sentence. Burton usually got away with such behavior because he intimidated people and deferred to no one. The alcohol, which cooled his hyperactive personality, also loosened his tongue and sometimes made him a mean drunk.

But O'Neill, ever the polite, old-school gentleman, was also the Majority Whip. He had no reason to fear Burton and found his behavior offensive. Irritated, O'Neill said, "Phil, we're in mixed company. You shouldn't talk that way in front of your wife and my friend Betty." That tactic did not work. Burton grew more profane until finally O'Neill snapped, "Curb your tongue."

Incensed, Burton stood up and challenged O'Neill to a fight.

"That's the silliest thing I ever heard," O'Neill said. "Two leaders fighting. We'd both be defeated."

As Burton started to reach across the table to O'Neill, Betty Stephens, a tall woman, jumped up, put her hand on Burton's chest to hold him back, and said, "You touch him and I'll knock your goddam head off." Burton seemed momentarily stunned. "This is crazy," O'Neill muttered. "This is not the way people in the public eye behave."

Before Sala could calm her husband, he repeated several times to O'Neill, "I'll never forgive you for this. I'll run against you for majority leader."

Phil Burton lost control at the wrong time in front of the wrong man. O'Neill decided that night that he could never support Burton for a top leadership position. If Burton lost control like that again, O'Neill feared he would embarrass and dishonor the Democratic Party. From that moment on, Burton would have much to overcome to get back in O'Neill's good graces.

"There should have been a close affiliation between Phil and myself," O'Neill recalled years later, describing the rupture for the first time.

> We were friends to a degree. I had knowledge of him. He had knowledge of me. But that night we broke apart completely. I don't know if Phil thought I could interfere with him and his rise to power. I was ambitious as well as he was. Did we all have a couple? Sure. I was never a drinker. This was just a social occasion, but when I used the words, "Curb your tongue," that was the opportunity to really pounce on me. He was going

to take me out of the leadership. That's where the break came, and [then] there was a terrific coolness.[27]

Sooner than anyone imagined, O'Neill saw whether Burton would carry out his threat. On October 16, 1972, while he was campaigning with freshman Nick Begich in Alaska, Majority Leader Hale Boggs's plane disappeared and was never recovered, despite a massive search for the man expected to succeed Carl Albert as Speaker. After waiting a respectful period and getting widow Lindy Boggs's permission, O'Neill announced his candidacy to succeed Boggs. He was elected without opposition when the caucus met in January.

Burton did not challenge him. He knew he would lose to the affable and popular Cambridge pol, who maintained friendly relations with everyone. But Burton had another scheme, another stealth path to power. His term as DSG chairman was ending, and it was against DSG tradition to run again. Traditionally, the Speaker and majority leader selected the whip. Burton knew that if there had been any chance of being selected—and that chance was at best dim—it disappeared entirely after the drunken encounter with O'Neill in Beverly Hills. But Burton seized on a strategy first tried in 1971: to make the whip's job elective. He already showed he could win one election in the caucus: DSG chairman. If he could get the caucus to make the whip elective, he would win the post himself and continue his upward climb, despite O'Neill.

Burton pursued his new strategy with characteristic maniacal zeal, spending weeks before the January 1973 caucus contacting 85 percent of the House Democrats. He gave Nancy Larsen, a staffer he hired for the Interior Committee, a list of members to lobby. Larsen kept a color-coded set of four-by-six-inch index cards with a member's name, seniority, and committees. One color meant the member supported electing the whip and specifically Burton; another meant yes on elective whip, no or undecided on Burton, and so on. "Jesus Christ," Conlon said when he saw her cards. "Does this guy ever let up?"

Burton also convinced the easy-going Albert to support his plan. Albert was apparently oblivious to the fact that this was a direct attack on O'Neill's prerogatives. But O'Neill quickly set him straight. "You can't do that," O'Neill exploded. "He's a revolutionary. He's crazy. We can't work with him on a leadership team." Albert backed off.[28]

O'Neill later wrote in his memoirs that he opposed the change because the whip's job was to count votes for policy already determined, not to make policy. O'Neill believed the whip should therefore reflect the views of the Speaker and majority leader. But clearly more was going on. Burton was very much a threat. Moreover, O'Neill believed the whip should be totally loyal. An appointed whip guaranteed that loyalty. Burton was a loose cannon whose loyalty would be questionable at best.

In what for Burton was an agonizingly close vote on January 2, 1973, the caucus denied Burton's bid for power by nine votes. Burton had secured more than enough to win. But O'Neill, seeing what was happening on the floor, called a recess and lobbied Burton's southern base, members who had worked with Burton on preserving cotton and tobacco subsidies.[29]

The caucus reconvened after lunch. O'Neill did his job well and switched the five votes he needed to change the outcome. Burton, who knew exactly what was going on but was not about to say so publicly, blamed the loss on "unexpected defections" among southern Democrats. "I think, frankly, that the Southerners were a little bit more for the election until today. Then they changed. Don't ask me why," Burton said after the vote. He said J. J. Pickle of Texas told a closed meeting of the caucus that changing the way the whip was elected was a DSG effort to put one of their own in the leadership. Pickle, of course, was correct. The bad blood between Burton and O'Neill would cost Burton an even bigger prize a few years later.[30]

It was often the custom to promote the deputy whip to whip, but it must have given O'Neill special pleasure to pass over Burton and elevate John McFall, another Californian, instead. "I have had twenty-six people say they would be interested in the whip's job," O'Neill told CBS before the appointment. "John McFall has been floor whip through the past two years and has done a magnificent job." As for Burton, O'Neill said, "Phil Burton and I— our philosophies seem to bend the same way. I think very highly of Phil." He stopped short of saying anything critical. The real inside story behind leadership battles and internal rivalries such as theirs was closely held within the House Democratic family. Neither Burton nor O'Neill was willing to clear the air in public or even confide to close aides or most of their colleagues.[31]

But the fact that O'Neill was lifting up another Californian was more than a happy accident. Any Burton move to vault over McFall would be complicated by a split in his home state, which boasted the largest delegation in the House. Albert and O'Neill selected John Brademas, another Burton opponent, as deputy whip, and after getting a phone call from ex-Speaker McCormack, they appointed one more. "The party has always had a special Boston-Austin connection," McCormack told O'Neill. "There was Rayburn and myself. There was Kennedy and Johnson. Now that you're in the leadership, I'd like you to tell Carl Albert that I would appreciate it if he would keep it going." McCormack's candidate was Texan Jim Wright, and Tip O'Neill obliged him.[32]

Phillip Burton, as his brother Robert said, never let defeat stop him. In his final two months as chairman of DSG, he pushed through the most important internal House reforms since the 1910–11 revolt against Speaker Cannon. A week after the whip vote, fifty DSG activists approved a package of reforms that Burton drafted. They included: an automatic secret caucus vote on every chairman; a new rule guaranteeing all freshmen Democrats one major committee assignment; and a rule prohibiting members of Ways and Means, Appropriations, and Rules from serving on other committees because of their heavy work load. These reforms shocked and dazzled the Washington pundits. With help from Conlon and friends, including Udall, Foley, Mikva, Eckhardt, and Dante Fascell, Burton used the caucus, the leadership, the Hansen Committee—even the threatened committee chairmen—when he thought necessary.

More than forty outside groups also lobbied. They formed an umbrella organization, the Committee for Congressional Reform, financed by liberal philanthropist Stewart Mott, which included the ADA, the UAW, the League of Women Voters, the United Methodist Church, Common Cause, and the Friends Committee on National Legislation. Burton had enlarged DSG by more than a third, to 165 members, which gave it more clout. Some, like Pat Schroeder, the freshman on the executive board, fit the DSG mold. Others were conservative southerners who did not even want their membership advertised.

"If some conservative can help us get out a decent environment or health bill," Burton told *Congressional Quarterly,* "that's as good as anybody else helping. We don't tell people that if they don't vote with us on the war, we won't want their help on minimum wage." Common Cause lobbyist David Cohen added, "In the old days, the DSG was viewed as a band of Young Turks. Now its leaders are matured legislators with a sense of how power relationships work."

In making DSG more "operational," one of Burton's favorite words, he kept it from chasing hopeless causes. "We made a conscious effort a couple of years ago," he said, "not to fill up the Caucus with losing ideas, even if they were good ones." Setting a withdrawal date from Vietnam and forcing that bill out of committee and blocking an anti-busing constitutional amendment, Burton said, were two examples of how DSG had learned to pick winners.[33]

Over Conlon's initial objections, Burton earlier suggested reconvening the Hansen Committee to review more reforms. DSG proposals the Hansen Committee did not get around to involved modifying the "closed rule" by which Wilbur Mills and other powerful chairmen could bring legislation to the floor without amendments, reforming committee secrecy and reviving a Democratic Steering and Policy Committee as a vehicle for leadership to hash out policy before taking it to the caucus. Soon, they were all implemented.

When the caucus met on January 22 to consider automatic voting on every chairman, there was furious maneuvering over whether the vote would be secret or open. The method was important; would junior members have the nerve to vote against senior chairmen if they were identified? Breaking a logjam, Benjamin Rosenthal of New York worked out a deal with O'Neill. The caucus would vote secretly on each chairman as long as 20 percent of the caucus requested the vote, an easy number to round up. Even though no chairman lost—none was as unpopular as John McMillan had been two years earlier—the process was now firmly established for how to dump chairmen.

"I'm wildly happy at what we've done," Burton told the *New York Times.* "We're finally getting somewhere." O'Neill supported these reforms for a simple reason: if the majority leader had to face election by his peers, why shouldn't the committee chairmen? Moreover, if their power was trimmed, that would help O'Neill once he became Speaker.[34]

"May I express my deepest appreciation and admiration for your work on the Organization, Study and Review Committee," Hansen wrote Burton on February 2. "Your work on the floor of the Caucus has been terrific. Words can't even begin to express my appreciation for your great job."

Amid all the hoopla over the chairmen, the reformers also sneaked in a "subcommittee bill of rights" that proved tremendously important. Originally conceived by House staffer Peter Barash, Burton and Thompson pushed it through the Hansen Committee and then the caucus. Whenever a vacancy arose, Democrats on each committee would caucus and vote on subcommittee vacancies, based on seniority. Each subcommittee would have its own fixed jurisdiction, budget, and staff. Each member of the full committee would get at least one prime assignment. These reforms continued to erode the power of hitherto all-powerful chairmen, much as the revolt on Interior several years earlier had weakened Wayne Aspinall, and they spread power to several dozen new subcommittee chairmen.[35]

But the work was not yet complete. Meeting a month later on February 21, they implemented the rest of the DSG reforms. The groundwork laid, these reforms now seemed reasonable, even logical. The caucus voted to open committee sessions to the public unless a majority voted to close a particular session. This allowed the public, primarily lobbyists and journalists, into "markup" sessions for the first time, where the essence of the legislative process took place, where bills were drafted line by line, clause by clause. Moreover, the caucus also modified the "closed rule" that had been a key to power for chairmen like Wilbur Mills, whose bills were voted on without a word changed.

Supporters of the closed rule argued that members of Ways and Means often spent months listening to expert testimony on extremely complicated subjects including Medicare, welfare, Social Security, taxes, and trade. Their bill reflected those long months of work. They did not want it altered on the floor by parochial or special interests that had not been part of that process (as opposed to parochial and special interests that had been) and that could do major mischief quickly. The modification of the closed rule respected that concern: it permitted a specific amendment to a specific bill only when fifty or more House Democrats proposed one. If the caucus approved the amendment, the bill would go to the floor but the House could vote only on that amendment.

This was a direct assault on Mills's power, but Burton said he consulted Mills beforehand. "Wilbur told me this is a procedure he can live with," Burton told the *New York Times*. He said it was designed to prevent "every wing-ding tax proposal in the world from reaching the floor."[36] The following day, with Albert's blessing, the caucus created a Steering and Policy Committee to set policy and legislative strategy. Members included Albert, O'Neill, Teague, five whips, twelve members elected regionally, and three more appointed by Albert.

Taken together, these changes were stunning. Writing in his prime spot on the op-ed page of the *Washington Post*, political columnist David Broder said the reforms "merit that overused adjective, 'historic.'" Noting that there were still "feudal baronies in some House committees and subcommittees," Broder said the House "has come an enormous distance in the five or six years since a handful of young Republicans and Democratic Study Group liberals began agitating, much to their elders' distress, for reforms. . . . It is the most heartening development in Washington."

Ten days later, on the same page, syndicated columnists Evans and Novak left little doubt what they thought about these "do-gooding reforms," which "pose a threat that coming battles over tax reform and foreign trade will become orgies of legislative excess." Conlon told *The New Republic* that a decade earlier, former Rules Committee Chairman Howard Smith "could go milk cows if he wanted," and "Wilbur Mills could sit on Medicare for six years, and everyone accepted it. You'll see much less of that now."[37]

Burton and Conlon received their loudest praise from *Congressional Quarterly*. In a six-page analysis that appeared that June, *Congressional Quarterly* said DSG was "getting a reputation it has never had before. It is beginning to look like a winner." Iowa Democrat John Culver succeeded Burton as chairman, but in looking back over the preceding few years, *Congressional Quarterly* attributed the group's success to Burton and Conlon. "It was Conlon who drafted and redrafted the reform proposals to make them acceptable to a majority of the Democrats in the House. And it was Burton who served as chief lobbyist and tactician for the ideas, compromising in many places, but insisting that the end product was still a long step toward basic reform of the House." The magazine said Burton and Conlon "were the most effective leadership team the organization has had in the years it has been pushing for House reform and liberal legislation."[38]

Richard Bolling watched these reforms roll through the House with great interest. What Burton did with DSG "suited me," he said many years later. Burton and Conlon were fundamentally weakening the seniority system, and that was valuable. But Burton was also confirming his worst fears. With his decades on the Rules Committee, process, rules, and order meant everything to Bolling. He was horrified to find that to Burton they were simply instruments to achieve other ends. "Burton was just like Lyndon Johnson," Bolling said. "He had the damn fool idea that getting something done was more important than making the process of democracy real to people. It's a legislative trick. If you do that, you destroy process and faith in process and government of laws. And that's how Hitler gets to be Hitler." Bolling's dislike of Burton turned into deep jealousy and hatred. Burton had no use for Bolling, either, calling him a "white collar liberal," who cared more about rules than helping poor people.[39]

Bolling wondered whether, once set loose, the reform movement would explode uncontrollably. He worried that new rules the caucus approved with each new Congress were encroaching on his Rules Committee turf. One of Bolling's key reform proposals was coming true, however: Burton was turning the House Democratic Caucus into a policy instrument of the majority of the majority. Another goal—strengthening the Speakership—had not yet been achieved, partly because Albert did not want to seize the moment.

But Bolling prevailed on Albert and O'Neill to approach reform from yet another angle: establish a new select committee to examine the House committee structure itself and streamline unwieldy practices to eliminate cumbersome, overlapping jurisdictions. Bolling wanted to structure committees to correspond to the executive branch: separate committees for energy, education, labor, and the like, rather than the chaotic system by which five or more committees, for example, could each claim jurisdiction over environmental issues. Minority Leader Gerald Ford of Michigan consented, in part because the ten-member committee was strictly bipartisan—five Democrats and five Republicans—and a budget of $1.5 million was set aside.[40]

This was Bolling's effort to make his mark on the House. He made it bipartisan because he believed reform was valid only if it came from consensus. It seemed to staff member Linda Kamm that Bolling viewed his efforts to rationalize the House as an "intellectual exercise." He put like-minded intellectuals on the committee, people Burton dismissed as "Boy Scouts," his derisive term for good-government types who would rather make the right speech and lose than exercise power and win. Everyone assumed Bolling would cut deals to get the reforms through, but he never did. But it was also clear that Bolling wasn't above going after old enemies, among them Wilbur Mills, Wayne Hays, and Phil Burton, in the process.

Sixty-three members and dozens more outsiders testified before Bolling's committee. After nearly a year of meetings and staff reports, it proposed these major changes: eliminate the Merchant Marine and Fisheries and the Post Office and Civil Service committees; divide the Education and Labor Committee in two; hit Mills by transferring jurisdiction over foreign trade, health insurance, and currency agreements from Ways and Means to other committees; create a new Energy and the Environment Committee to replace Interior and absorb all other energy-related matters; transfer federal campaign spending authority from Hays's Administration Committee to an Ethics Committee; and expand Rules Committee power by giving it authority to transfer all bills—which led to charges that Bolling was trying to increase his own power. Finally, under these recommendations, members could serve on just one committee.[41]

Burton saw the plan as a personal attack on his power. He would have to relinquish one of his two committees, Interior, where he already chaired the Subcommittee on Trusts and Territories, or Education and Labor. If he stayed with the latter, he would have to give up half the committee's jurisdiction. Burton was also troubled by the one-committee limit, because any member stuck with a hostile chairman would have no recourse if that were his or her only committee.

It took Burton and Conlon about twenty minutes to decide how to torpedo the Bolling recommendations, although finessing the politics was more time consuming. First, Burton said the House should wait until after the November elections. President Nixon's Watergate troubles were mounting, crowding almost everything else off the agenda. When that play for time did not hold off Bolling, Burton decided in a moment of exquisite irony that they should refer his rival's plan to the caucus, where no Republicans could participate, for a vote. Bolling, who crusaded for years to make the caucus more powerful, would be hoist with his own petard. Once there, opponents could refer Bolling's recommendations to the Hansen Committee, where nine of eleven members opposed it, to kill or modify. It looked bad, however, to be seen as opposing "reform," especially for those with reform credentials. Moreover, other reformers supported it, including Culver, Meeds, Fraser, Fascell, and New York liberals Bella Abzug and Jonathan Bingham.

But Burton had plenty of help, including the Thompson-O'Hara-Ford-Brademas contingent. Virtually every committee chairman hated the Bolling plan, as did most of the members on Education and Labor, Ways and Means, and Interior, and of course those on committees slated to be abolished. Moreover, now that the "action" had been spread to some three dozen new chairmen, they, too, worried that they would lose their subcommittees. AFL-CIO chief lobbyist Biemiller gave his tentative okay to longtime friend Bolling, but organized labor opposition quickly overwhelmed him, especially the maritime and public employee unions. They objected to separating one committee they dominated and eliminating two others on which they had major influence.

While groups like Common Cause and ADA supported the reforms, Nader opposed them. He feared the oil companies could easily dominate one committee, where all energy and environmental matters would be centered, preferring the present system, where jurisdiction was more diffused. John Dingell of Michigan, a power on Interstate and Foreign Commerce, reflected widespread sentiment when he said, "The only good thing about [Bolling's report] is that it is written on disposable paper." He added, "The most charitable thing is to inter it gracefully with some kind words for the author."[42]

On May 9, 1974, as the Watergate crisis was entering its most decisive phases, Phil Burton moved to have the caucus refer the Bolling plan to the Hansen Committee, for a report in sixty days. William Ford then moved for a secret vote. "It was the secret vote that killed the Bolling reform," reported the ADA's *Legislative Newsletter*, "for without a secret vote, House members would have been reluctant to oppose a measure to improve the operation of Congress—something the American public clearly wants."[43]

Bolling objected, but amid the parliamentary confusion, caucus Chairman Teague incorrectly ruled against him. The secret vote was 111-95 to refer. The Bolling reforms were dead. In leading the fight against Bolling, Burton endeared himself to the very chairmen whose power he had previously curtailed. In Bolling himself, he infuriated an even more implacable enemy.

"The name of the game is power," O'Neill said after the vote, "and the boys don't want to give it up." There was some suggestion that O'Neill did not support the Bolling reforms. He served on Rules with Bolling and respected Bolling's intelligence enormously. But he also saw Bolling as a potential rival for Speaker and did not want to give a potential adversary a major victory.

The Hansen Committee, as expected, restored most of the cuts that Bolling's plan would have inflicted on the committee system. Education and Labor was reunited, the abolished committees were reconstituted, Ways and Means was given back most of its jurisdiction. Some Hansen Committee members thought Burton wanted to create a supercommittee he could control with jurisdiction over health, welfare, and labor. In other words, Ways and Means would raise the money, and he would spend it, a chilling thought to any but the most free-spending liberal. But Bolling staffer Bill Cable said Burton showed "rational restraint." Even though he wanted to disburse power throughout the House, and add to that which he already had accumulated, Burton also supported Hansen reforms to increase the Speaker's power.

After delays, hearings, and six intense days of floor debate, Bolling finally demanded a roll-call vote on his original reform package. O'Neill was right; Bolling's plan gored too many powerful interests. The new Hansen Committee recommendations were adopted as a substitute for the Bolling plan 203-165. After that, they were adopted overwhelmingly 359-7. Wayne Hays likened the Bolling plan to a "drunk at the county fair." The drunk said he "could knock the block off any man in the city," said Hays. "No one said anything. Then he said he could punch out any man in the county. Still, no one said anything. Finally, he said he could beat any man in the whole state. Suddenly, a man stepped forward and flattened the drunk. The problem was that he took in too much territory. That was the Bolling Committee's problem. They took in too much territory."[44]

Burton was the man who flattened the drunk. He would pay later.

12

REVOLUTION IN THE HOUSE

We had a real sense of urgency. We came here to take the Bastille.

GEORGE MILLER OF CALIFORNIA
"Watergate baby"

Phil Burton had no jurisdiction. The House was his jurisdiction.
Ever since the democratization of the House, no one has been able to control
it except Phil Burton. He wasn't Speaker, he wasn't Majority Leader,
he wasn't Whip, but he could manipulate the House.

JOAN CLAYBROOK
director of Ralph Nader's Public Citizen

THE FIRST EVENT THAT profoundly changed the House of Representatives and catapulted Phillip Burton to the pinnacle of power in 1974 was the resignation of a president. The second was the 2 A.M. discovery near the Washington Tidal Basin by park police of Ways and Means Committee Chairman Wilbur Mills, drunk, bleeding, and in the company of a stripper named Annabella Battistella, also known as Fanne Fox, the "Argentina Firecracker." The third was the midterm election of November 5, when seventy-five freshmen Democrats were elected to the House, for a net Democratic gain of forty-nine seats and a two to one Democratic majority.

President Nixon's demise disgraced his party and his profession and helped elect the new Democrats. Mills's pathetic fall hastened reforms that irretrievably changed the House. The new reform-minded class—which through its youth, numbers, and mandate for change implemented those reforms—became the shock troops in Burton's assault on the citadels of power.

At 9 P.M. on August 8, 1974, Richard Nixon addressed the nation as president for the last time. "I have never been a quitter," Nixon said, speaking from his desk in the Oval Office and looking grim and somber in a dark suit, dark tie, and white shirt. "To leave office before my term is completed is abhorrent to every instinct in my body." But the Watergate scandal had so overwhelmed his administration that for Nixon to continue in the face of certain impeachment in the House and conviction in the Senate, "would almost totally absorb the time and attention of both the President and the Congress. . . . Therefore, I shall resign the Presidency, effective at noon tomorrow."

Newly sworn-in President Gerald Ford, the House Republican minority leader before his selection as vice president, quickly assured the country that "our long national nightmare is over." The worst scandal and the greatest fall in American political history was complete. But the repercussions from Nixon's disgraceful conduct lingered. For eighteen months, talk of cover-ups, hush money, secret tapes, and smoking guns dominated the nation's capital and much of the rest of the country as nothing else had. Voters were repulsed.

What started as a seemingly petty break-in to the Democratic Party's Washington headquarters at the Watergate complex in June 1972 became, in White House Counselor John Dean's infamous phrase, "a cancer on the presidency" and a constitutional crisis of the first order. Two months of televised hearings in the summer of 1973 made Senator Sam Ervin of North Carolina a folk hero, joining Federal Judge John Sirica and *Washington Post* reporters Bob Woodward and Carl Bernstein as the men who brought down a president.

The year before Nixon's resignation had been traumatic. October 1973 alone saw a new "Yom Kippur" war in the Middle East, the resignation of Vice President Spiro Agnew for accepting bribes as governor of Maryland and as vice president, and the "Saturday Night Massacre." Attorney General Eliot Richardson and deputy William Ruckelshaus resigned rather than fire Special Prosecutor Archibald Cox, as Nixon ordered. On October 23, the Judiciary Committee decided to hold hearings to consider impeaching Nixon. Nine months later, after the televised impeachment hearings, the U.S. Supreme Court unanimously ordered Nixon to turn over secret tape recordings of meetings in his own office. One tape proved obstruction of justice and showed Nixon had been lying for more than two years.[1] Ford's pardon of Nixon a few months later brought it all back, further undermining the Republican Party as it headed to the November elections.

Long before the Watergate scandal began to unfold, House reformers tried unsuccessfully to curb Wilbur Mills's awesome power. A Rayburn protégé and Harvard Law School graduate, Mills was regarded as one of the shining intellects on Capitol Hill, so immersed in the technical details of his committee's special jurisdiction that people said only half in jest that he took the tax code to bed with him. First elected from a rural district in Arkansas in 1938, Mills served in the House for more than half of his sixty-five years. When he took over the committee in 1958, he abolished all subcommittees to better concentrate power in his hands, and he often excluded staff from meetings, which gave him even more leverage over less knowledgeable members.

Mills's power also derived from his ability to send complicated and extremely important bills to the floor under a closed rule, which permitted no amendments. Not until the LBJ sweep of 1964 produced a majority of pro-Medicare supporters on his committee did Mills change his position on Medicare, which he had blocked for years. Mills also presided over Ways and Means's other function, one that reformers were also aiming to curtail: determining committee assignments for every House Democrat. This was a key source of power that kept reformers away from such areas as the oil depletion allowance. By carefully choosing the composition of his own committee, as well as others, he blocked access for liberals to jurisdiction over such sweetheart tax breaks for the oil industry and other large interests. When people urged Mills to run for president, he quipped, "What, and give up being chairman of Ways and Means?" In 1972, he succumbed to the bug of presidential fever, but his campaign went nowhere.

In February 1973, the House Democratic Caucus, going along with Burton's DSG reform proposals, modified the closed rule. In May 1974, the caucus acted on it for the first time, launching a direct challenge to Mills's power. It voted to permit the House to consider an immediate and retroactive end to the oil depletion allowance. That tax break, by which oil and gas interests exempted the first 22 percent of gross income from taxes, would have cost the oil industry $1.8 billion in 1974 alone in extra taxes. Excess oil profits were an attractive target for many politicians following the first Arab oil embargo of 1973–74, which sent gas prices soaring and created hours-long gas lines. Mills consented to a three-year phase out of the depletion allowance, but Ways and Means member William Green of Pennsylvania wanted to end it retroactive to January 1. Under the new caucus rules, he needed fifty votes to bring the amendment to the floor. He got 128, half the 257 House Democrats.

Despite the encroachment on his power, Mills stayed one step ahead of the posse. He told the Rules Committee he preferred no rule at all to a modified closed rule. He would take the bill directly to the House floor and dare anyone to amend it, in effect scuttling it. Mills knew Democrats could not restrain themselves if presented with such a rare and inviting target. Chaos likely would ensue. Bolling, who agreed with Burton on this issue, said the chairman's tactic was like offering a drink of water to a person coming out of the desert and then immersing him in a tub of water. Such "open" rules, Bolling said, "made the House look idiotic and totally ineffective." Bolling despised Mills, who in turn regarded Bolling as a "damn ingrate." Mills put him on the Rules Committee twenty years earlier at Rayburn's request, "and he always opposed me."[2]

"Mills is engaged in a desperate battle," wrote *Washington Star-News* columnist Milton Viorst, "to retain what he can of the autocratic power he once exercised." The outcome, he wrote, "could go far toward determining whether Congress will continue as the diffuse and inept body it has been for decades—or transform itself . . . into an institution with direction and purpose, reflecting the will of its majority."[3]

Mills won that round, although his fall was coming soon. The leadership let him off the hook. Albert, from oil- and gas-producing Oklahoma, had no interest in forcing the issue. No bill emerged, thus no rule, open or closed. But soon, the caucus was after Mills again. This time, the fight was over how to pick fourteen Democrats for a new House Budget Committee, ordinarily a job Ways and Means performed. Liberals worried, however, that Mills would appoint like-minded conservatives to the new committee, which would make important decisions on federal spending priorities. The caucus ultimately decided Mills could select only the three members from Ways and Means. Mahon of Appropriations also could pick three and Albert would pick the other eight.

The prospect of liberal Democrats regularly exercising such newfound discipline scared the Republicans to death. Third-ranking House Republican John Anderson of Illinois warned that "King Caucus" had returned. If the Democrats made major gains in the 1974 elections, Anderson said, a "majority of the majority" could ride roughshod over outgunned House Republicans. Ringleader Phil Burton denied such fears were valid, although that was precisely the role he envisioned for the caucus.

"The Caucus could serve as an instrument for a more thoughtful process in decision-making," Burton told the *Washington Post*. "But I don't view it as a monolith, running over dissenting views." The caucus had been used only four times since the 1920s, either to bind a member to a particular vote or to instruct a committee procedurally. But in the past three years, the caucus was activated five times, three times in the previous two months.

"Since giving up the chairmanship of the DSG last year," the *Post* wrote, "Burton has maintained his influence through his close ties with its savvy staff director, Dick Conlon." Burton denied reports that he wanted to succeed Tiger Teague as caucus chairman after the November 1974 elections. But that was his plan. Now that the caucus was finally becoming a power in the House, Burton wanted to make it dominant. (After close friend Foley took over chairmanship of DSG, Burton said to Common Cause President Fred Wertheimer, "I will keep him [Foley] very close to me. He is the one person capable of being Speaker, rather than me."[4]

Burton also maintained close ties to conservatives Mills, Waggonner, and Wayne Hays, who was chairman of the Democratic Congressional Campaign Committee (DCCC). Hays was hated, feared, and seen as a vindictive bully. In taking over the House Administration Committee, he converted a minor committee whose jurisdiction involved housekeeping matters into a major source of power and irritation. He awarded favors to friends and punished those who crossed him. He deprived enemies of favored parking places or exiled them to tiny offices far from the action. He badgered elevator operators who did not stand up fast enough to suit him. Frank Thompson, the ranking member of Administration and chairman of a subcommittee that oversaw budgets for all House committees, hated Hays with a passion. So did O'Neill and Bolling.

Hays was useful to Burton, although associating with him had its downside, indeed later proved costly at exactly the wrong moment. Burton cultivated Hays. As the new DCCC chairman, Hays had more than $200,000 to hand out in congressional campaign funds. As the first Democrat to fully realize how to exploit the electoral implications of Watergate, Burton helped Hays decide where the money should go. Hays in turn knew how useful Burton and the large number of votes he controlled could be. Hays was also ambitious to move up.

Burton realized early on that voters were disgusted with Nixon, Agnew, the infamous "plumbers" unit in the White House basement, and everything else associated with the Watergate scandal. As voter outrage grew, campaign year 1974 represented a rare opportunity for challengers to make huge gains in Congress. If Burton could get to them first with campaign money, he could win their loyalty once they got to Washington.

Burton took the principle Jesse Unruh established in California—using campaign money to fund candidates who would support him once elected—and applied it nationally. Lyndon Johnson did it on a smaller scale when he chaired the DCCC in the early 1940s. Tip O'Neill spent $80,000 on House races in 1974. But no one before ever even envisioned the systematic effort Burton put forth that year. He was running for caucus chairman the way Unruh ran for assembly speaker or the way Nixon ran for the GOP nomination in 1968, campaigning for candidates all across the U.S., earning votes chit by chit.

Working again with Mark Gersh, with the DSG bankroll, with Hays at DCCC, and with his labor union friends, Burton schemed and plotted constantly for Democratic challengers all over the country. Sometimes on his word alone, labor sent money to challengers. He talked constantly with Ken Young at the AFL-CIO, Bill Holayter at the Machinists, Dick Murphy at SEIU, Dick Warden at the United Auto Workers, and Jack Sheehan at the Steelworkers. They went over every contested race in the country, district by district. When Burton found out that a union was planning to contribute to a candidate, he often beat the labor rep to the phone to call the candidate with the good news.

"Jesus, Phil," Ken Young teased. "Did you even have the decency to call the union first to check or did you just hear about the contribution and call the candidate up?" Burton would laugh. He took great glee in calling Young just to gloat that he had got to the candidate before the union donating the money did.

Hays let Burton do the same thing with the DCCC's money. There was nothing an obscure challenger in Michigan, Long Island, Colorado, or Indiana liked better than getting a call from an important congressman to announce that money was on the way. Together, Burton and Hays gave nearly as much money to challengers in 1974 as incumbents, a fact that angered many incumbents who felt they should get it all since they helped raise it. Of the DCCC's $200,000, $87,000 went to sixty-nine challengers, an average of $1,260 each. Every Monday from the summer of 1974 on, Burton met with Hays, Doug Frost, his political aide, Al Barkham of the AFL-CIO's Committee on Political Education, and Democratic National Committee Chairman Robert Strauss, to discuss House races. Burton alone campaigned in forty districts.

Back home, brother John had been elected to Congress in a special election earlier that year. Burton had nearly a half dozen other protégés running in the state, starting with Henry Waxman from Beverly Hills and George Miller III from Contra Costa. Waxman was a longtime ally from the Young Democrats and worked closely with Burton on the 1971 state reapportionment. Miller was the son of the late chairman of the state senate Finance Committee who meant so much to Burton when he arrived in Sacramento as a rookie legislator in 1957.

When the elder Miller died suddenly of a heart attack in 1969, Burton tried to save his seat for his son. Working a room of labor lobbyists at a San Francisco political event, Burton extolled the virtues of the twenty-three-year-old Miller to all who would listen as he hit them up for money. Turning to one new face, he demanded, "You, what are you going to do for young Miller?"

"But Congressman Burton," the young man stammered, "I *am* George Miller." Miller lost but went to work in Sacramento for George Moscone. Still only twenty-eight in 1974, he was moving up. "We joked that a 'Burton dollar' was worth ten times that much," Miller said later. "It was the fastest circulating dollar in politics. Candidates did not hear much from Washington in those days. But Burton calls to tell you he can get you money. Then he calls to tell you he got you money. Then he calls to tell you the money is on its way. Then he calls to tell you how you should spend it. Then he sends you a note saying he was able to do all that for you."

Waxman had to laugh when Burton took credit for getting $1,000 for him from the Retail Clerks. Waxman's father worked for that union for thirty years.[5] Burton also nurtured John Krebs, a German-born county supervisor from Fresno. Krebs was challenging GOP incumbent Bob Mathias, a former Olympic decathlon gold medalist whose district shifted after the last reapportionment to include large parts of Democratic Fresno County. Similar stories existed all over the U.S.: Jim Blanchard and Bob Carr in Michigan, Stephen Solarz in New York, Toby Moffett in Connecticut, Jim Santini in Nevada, on whose behalf Burton made three visits, and dozens more were getting phone calls and checks, just as Pat Schroeder and Charlie Rose had two years earlier.

Although happy to dispense labor money, Burton also wanted to clean up Watergate-style excesses. Concerned that members of Congress were often beholden to conservative business interests who funded their campaigns, he pressed for a bill for public financing of congressional as well as presidential campaigns. That meant taking on his friend Wayne Hays, who was opposed to using tax money for congressional elections. Burton narrowly lost the battle. Fred Wertheimer said many years later he was "still sick" about how close they came. Had Burton succeeded, the system might have been cleaned up, but Hays would have benefited from the bill as it eventually developed.

That possibility outraged Tip O'Neill and further convinced him that Burton and Hays could not be trusted.

Congress had already passed a bill to publicly fund presidential campaigns and set up a Federal Election Commission to administer the new law. But a Supreme Court decision struck down part of it. Only the president, not Congress, the Court said, could make executive appointments to the new FEC. A new House bill, a version of which the Senate already passed, was Common Cause's top priority in 1974. But Hays was bottling it up in his committee. He despised the reformist group, which he called "Common Curse." The group, begun in 1970 as the "Peoples' Lobby," had grown to 323,000 members by March 1974, with a $6.3 million annual budget.

Extending public financing to congressional campaigns was not popular with incumbents. Even Tip O'Neill opposed it, telling Wertheimer and David Cohen, "I'm not going to subsidize my opponent." It was a view he regretted once he became Speaker and eventually saw how the tremendous infusion of political action committee money limited his ability to move legislation.

While Common Cause argued with Hays, Mo Udall and John Anderson were pushing an amendment for matching public funds for congressional campaigns by voluntary taxpayer checkoff. But with O'Neill and Hays opposed, the amendment had no chance of success. Burton worked on the bill with Wertheimer, then took the proposed changes to Hays. Wertheimer spent one entire weekend at Burton's townhouse going over the bill line by line.

In August, as the Watergate crisis sped toward resolution, Burton brokered the deal that almost worked. The pending bill covered presidential elections but did not include congressional funding. The Senate version contained both. Hoping to break the impasse, Burton put Hays, Wertheimer, and an O'Neill emissary in a room near the House floor and proposed the following: Common Cause would not oppose the bill Hays wanted. Frank Annunzio, a machine Democrat from Chicago who was close to Mayor Daley and Hays, would then introduce the Udall-Anderson amendment, which would permit public funding and designate the DCCC and the Republican counterpart, the RNCC, as the appropriate bodies to dole it out. Hays would keep quiet. He had good reason; as DCCC chairman he would have a whole new pot of money to dispense as he saw fit. Wertheimer bought the idea because it put money back in the hands of political parties, thus strengthening them, which he thought was worthwhile.

Burton got everyone to agree. Then, as required under new caucus rules,

Burton put a notice in the *Congressional Record* two days in advance of the vote announcing Annunzio's amendment. Annunzio was no reformer, however, and his name on a piece of reform legislation smelled fishy. Once people discovered that the public funds would be controlled by none other than the despised Wayne Hays, everything fell apart.

The brilliance of Burton's ploy was to repackage the amendment, substituting machine Democrat Annunzio for reformers Udall and Anderson, and giving Hays the power of the purse in order to buy his assent. But it was just too raw. What seemed to Burton a reasonable compromise to get public funding (after all, Hays would not run the DCCC forever) looked to others more like slush funds and placement of one more weapon in Hays's already too formidable arsenal. When O'Neill realized what was going on, he hit the roof. So did Bolling, who supported public financing and who was Common Cause's chief ally on Rules. Everything collapsed on Annunzio, who retreated fast.

On the day before Nixon resigned, the bill went to the floor. Anderson and Udall introduced their amendment. Hays led the fight against it, calling it a "scheme to break down the two-party system." It lost by 41 votes, 187-228. The rest of the bill, which established public funding of presidential campaigns in time for the 1976 elections and political action committees, was approved.[6] Had Burton's deal gone through, Congress might have been a different place in the 1980s. The Democrats in particular might have been neither addicted to special interest PAC money nor as beholden as they became to corporate lobbyists and shady savings and loan operators whose ubiquitous campaign funds compromised them and led to one of the worst financial scandals in U.S. history.

About 4 P.M. on election day 1974, Burton phoned Lionel Van Deerlin, a San Diego congressman, and said his phone banks were ready. He was planning to call all the winners that night all over the U.S., especially the freshmen, as soon as the results were known. "Here I was worrying whether I'd covered all my precincts," Van Deerlin said, "and he was already running for chairman."[7] This was yet another example of how Burton's district liberated him. Not only did his district not constrain his votes, it was so supportive that it permitted Burton to devote his full attention to national and internal House politics. Burton believed he didn't have to campaign at home, which became less true as the years wore on.

As Burton went to work in his hotel suite at the Del Webb in San Francisco that night, he resembled nothing so much as a corporate raider leveraging the deal of his life, grabbing frantically for one of at least six telephones arranged before three TV sets broadcasting the returns. Nearly all of the news was good. In many cases, Burton was the first to congratulate the candidate; in a few cases, where he had early information from registrars, Burton was the first to tell them they won.

Paul Rosenberg, a local activist who color-coded precincts maps for Burton as a hobby, watched him in awe. After Burton called John Krebs in Fresno to congratulate him for beating incumbent Bob Mathias, he wanted to speak to the campaign manager. "Let me talk to Irv," Rosenberg heard Burton bark. "Yes, I know. Let me talk to Irv. Yes, John, you'll be a great congressman. Let me talk to Irv. John, PUT IRV ON THE PHONE." Then the real questions began. "How did he do in Dinuba? What was his margin?"[8]

Of all the Democratic victories that year, Burton was especially pleased to hear that his friend Abner Mikva was returning to Congress after a two-year absence. The Daley machine had redistricted him out of his South Side seat, but he ran again from the North Side and was elected.

Coming on top of big Democratic classes in 1970 and 1972, the huge new class of 1974 had a mandate to clean up Washington following the Watergate scandal. That required more reforms. What made it easier was that half the Democrats in the caucus now had less than six years of service, which gave them a compelling motive to take on the seniority system.

Shortly after the election, Burton announced his candidacy for caucus chairman. And when the freshmen legislators arrived in Washington a few weeks later for orientation sessions, Phil and Sala Burton were everywhere. The Burtons became the glue that held them together, in many cases the only two people at the reception who knew all of them, who could walk one across the room and introduce him or her by name to another.

Burton quickly set up a "buddy" system. Mikva, John Burton, George Miller, Henry Waxman, and others were assigned to meet specific classmates, engage in conversation, and find out how they thought and what they were interested in. Miller, who Burton always called "the kid," learned only years later that he was just one of a team of freshman allies gathering data for Phil Burton, and he never knew how many others Burton had enlisted. But the tactic was vintage Burton. He kept things so tightly controlled that no one else ever fully knew what was going on.[9]

It was soon apparent that this was no ordinary class. It was not just the class size, but the type of elected official within it. These were younger, more reform-minded Democrats, many from marginal districts who defeated Republicans largely because of the public revulsion over Watergate. Traditional

Democratic constituencies, such as organized labor, meant little to them. They seemed more interested in expertise and getting the right answers than in unquestioningly representing interest groups. To Joe Crapa, staff director of the new members' caucus, the most important thing about the "Watergate Babies," as they came to be known, was their own conviction that they were reformers.

> They had a sense that the people had elected a different kind of Congress. Their reputation as a class was therefore to do things differently. . . . They were children of the sixties, activists who came up in politics by working outside the system. For the most part, they were not party people, but outsiders, ministers or Ph.D.s and even one house painter. There were fewer lawyers and state legislators than usual in entering classes. Many had won their races via the media, so they were fairly sophisticated about using television. They were not out of the old labor background. They were suburban, well educated in good schools, and they thought as long as they kept the image of being reformers, they would be okay. They were clannish and self supportive and not dependent on anyone.[10]

Looking back, political analyst William Schneider wrote: "The class of '74 was dominated by politicians whose inclinations were anti-establishment, whose careers were independent of political party, and who had to survive in unfriendly political territory."[11] Gary Hart, McGovern's 1972 campaign manager elected to the Senate from Colorado that year, was more succinct: "We are not a bunch of little Hubert Humphreys," he said.

Other newcomers included Tim Wirth of Colorado; Norman Mineta, the mayor of San Jose, California, who became one of the class presidents; Tom Downey of Long Island, who was barely twenty-five; and Paul Tsongas of Massachusetts. One of their heroes was Phillip Burton. Another was Richard Bolling. Around the nation, anti-incumbent voters also elected Jerry Brown governor of California, Richard Lamm governor of Colorado, and Michael Dukakis governor of Massachusetts.[12]

They did not know it yet, but the class of '74 provided the bodies for the last major bombardment on House tradition. Many believed afterwards that they overturned the seniority system all by themselves. But the mechanism was carefully designed years earlier in the DSG offices. Under O'Hara, Fraser, Burton, Culver, Foley, and Conlon, reformers made steady, incremental change. They restored the power of the caucus and weakened the seniority system. The Watergate Babies were there to finish the job. Between sixty-five and seventy of them voted for Burton for caucus chairman.

Burton's opponent was B. F. Sisk, at sixty-three, sixteen years older than Burton. A Texas native, Sisk represented Fresno and the Central Valley. Many of his constituents were transplants from Oklahoma, Texas, and Arkansas who migrated to California during the dust bowl era. They remained Democrats but were conservative. Sisk, an influential member of the Rules Committee (first put there when Rayburn expanded the committee in 1961), was the choice of both the leadership and the House establishment. With twenty years of service, he had double Burton's seniority. A founding member of DSG, Sisk moved to the right over the years and became a vigorous supporter of the Vietnam War. In 1966, his vote on the Rules Committee killed home rule for Washington, D.C.

Assisted by an able young aide named Tony Coelho, Sisk ran for majority leader in 1971, placing a distant third to Boggs and Udall. Two years later, he founded the United Democrats, designed to counter DSG, but it never went anywhere. Sisk was also part of the troika of powerful rural California members who built dams and perpetuated dirt-cheap federal water subsidies to large California farm interests. Sisk, along with Bizz Johnson on Interior and Public Works and John McFall on Appropriations, kept California agribusiness as well as smaller farmers well represented. Over the years, Burton fought with him over the water subsidies, Vietnam, grape boycotts, and Cesar Chavez and the farm workers, who were picketing some of the growers Sisk represented.

One of Sisk's supporters was Deputy Whip Jim Wright. Like other moderates in the House, Wright "resented the manner in which Phil Burton sought that office," he said many years later, and resented "the very fact that he made a fight and contacted all these new members. That had never been done before. People saw this as unbecoming. This should be an office that was bestowed rather than sought."[13]

One major issue that separated the two candidates was Burton's support for transferring Ways and Means's power to make committee assignments to the new Steering and Policy Committee. Reformers also wanted to expand Ways and Means from twenty-five to thirty-seven in the hopes of getting more liberals on the committee.

As the likely winner, Burton became the subject of for him unprecedented publicity. One colleague told the *Washington Star-News* that Burton was "one of the weirdest people I've ever met," yet "one of the most sagacious minds I've ever encountered." Another member, describing Burton's low boiling point, said, "He has a disconcerting way of walking away from you in mid-sentence—yours." But Burton was aware of all this, reporter James Dickinson concluded. "Last week he was extolling his wife's virtues—beauty, charm, intelligence and political savvy. 'I don't know how she puts up with me,' he said."

As so often happens in Washington, where power is calibrated constantly and where insiders never tire of analyzing who is up and who is down, the cognoscenti soon had a new and lively topic of conversation. Assuming Burton won his new post, would he challenge O'Neill for Speaker, perhaps even as caucus chairman "usurp" Carl Albert's job? Noting Burton's attachment to Hays, the *Washington Post* said some suspected Hays would support Burton if Burton supported Hays for Speaker two years hence. The *Star-News* also noted fears that a Burton-Hays alliance might prove "too formidable." By mid-November, Burton had contacted 220 of the 291 Democrats, asking them to support him for caucus chairman.[14]

On the eve of the vote, the *Wall Street Journal* began a long profile of Burton by telling how, earlier that year, House and Senate conferees met secretly in a hideaway office belonging to Harrison Williams to finish work on a minimum wage bill. They met there for just one reason: to escape Phil Burton, whose presence at earlier meetings had ruined efforts at compromise.

"A few minutes into the meeting," the *Journal* reported, "the door burst open and in walked Burton, uninvited and unwelcome. He marched straight to Williams' liquor cabinet, poured himself a glass of vodka, complained about the absence of ice, and as an afterthought, asked whether anyone else wanted a drink. 'Phil Burton has no shame,' said one who was present that day."

If Burton won, *Journal* reporter John Pierson predicted, "it will be the first time . . . that a real liberal with a taste for power and ability to exercise it will have gained a position of leadership in the House. Some say that Majority Leader Thomas O'Neill of Massachusetts already fits that description. But liberal pressure groups like the Americans for Democratic Action rate Phil Burton higher than Tip O'Neill." Predicting that "some day, he could be Speaker," Pierson observed, "There is something almost scary about the sheer animal energy that Burton brings to any task." Would he use the caucus to force Democrats into voting certain ways on the floor? "Burton rolls his big, dark eyes heavenward. 'I would never support anything that required a member to vote against his conscience.'"[15]

Burton won the secret ballot election, 162 to Sisk's 111. He was now launched, elected by his peers to chair a body whose power he was about to expand dramatically. Had he merely split the vote of the class of '74, rather than taken more than 90 percent of it, Burton would have lost. All that effort had paid off. "The winds of change have arrived at the U.S. House of Representatives," he told reporters after the vote. He said his agenda for the new Congress included "meaningful tax reform, an adequate health-care bill, adequate consumer legislation." He said he would not challenge Albert in 1976 or "leapfrog" O'Neill if Albert stepped down. But Dan Rostenkowski, who seconded Sisk's nomination, pointed to Albert's office and said, "Phil Burton will try to set the pace and probably take giant steps toward that door."[16]

In news that overshadowed Burton's election, the caucus with Albert's reluctant support also transferred the task of making Democratic committee assignments from Ways and Means to Steering and Policy. "I didn't mind losing it," Mills said years later. "I was glad to get rid of it. You appoint one ingrate and all the rest of them are mad at you." But his staff thought Mills should keep it, because it gave members leverage when their bills were up for a vote.[17]

As a member of the new Steering and Policy Committee, Burton was always scheming to get the best assignments for his liberal allies, knowing that activists like himself, given the right jurisdiction, could wield power far beyond their numbers. That morning, December 2, he engineered Fortney Stark's selection as the new California representative to Ways and Means. Stark beat senior members George Brown and Glenn Anderson in a contest that hitherto had been decided exclusively on seniority. Stark was an antiwar banker who gained publicity by putting a giant peace sign on his Walnut Creek bank building.

The next day Burton helped Yvonne Brathwaite Burke, who nominated Burton for caucus chairman, obtain the California spot on Appropriations, even though the young black legislator, like Stark, was just beginning her second term. Burton also took care of his California freshmen. He got George Miller on both of his committees, Interior and Education and Labor, Krebs on Agriculture, and Waxman on the coveted Interstate and Foreign Commerce Committee.

"It was a given that Phil Burton would get it for me," Waxman recalled. "I never knew how difficult it could be to get on a committee. Now I know. People go through their whole careers not getting on the committees they want. But he took care of me and George Miller and put us where we thought and he thought would be best." Waxman said Burton traded to get liberals on Ways and Means, Appropriations, and Interstate and Foreign Commerce. In return, he helped southerners get on Armed Services and Agriculture, "which were throwaways to him because they were so conservative that liberals were outvoted."[18]

The vote to strip Ways and Means of its committee-assigning power got easier after Wilbur Mills's bizarre and widely publicized Tidal Basin incident with Fanne Fox. In the early hours of October 9, park police pulled over a speeding Lincoln. When the car stopped, Fox jumped out and ran to the Tidal Basin, leaving Mills inside, drunk and bleeding from facial cuts. People close to him knew for years that Mills was a serious alcoholic, but this was the first public sign that he was anything other than staid and straight as an arrow. He returned to Arkansas to campaign, joking to constituents that they should never drink with foreigners, and was easily re-elected.

But on November 30, two days before the caucus vote, Mills flew to Boston and appeared on a burlesque stage where Fox was performing, billed as "The Tidal Basin Bombshell." His walk-on lasted no longer than five seconds, "an interlude of no more than passing audience interest between the live acts and the porn flicks," *Newsweek* reported. Then he held an impromptu press conference in her dressing room. Appearing unsteady, he referred to Fox as "my little ole Argentine hillbilly," and promised to help her get into the movies, as he had other young actresses, including Shirley MacLaine. MacLaine said she never met him. Someone in the audience had a camera. The photograph of the august chairman at a strip joint congratulating Fox after her act was published in the *Washington Post.*

The publicity toppled a Washington giant almost overnight. "We could overlook the Tidal Basin incident," Ways and Means member Sam Gibbons of Florida told *Congressional Quarterly.* "But not Mills's antics in Boston. He's flipped." There was talk of relieving Mills of his duties when the caucus voted the following month on every chairman. Mills seemed certain to lose.

"I'm tired. I'm tired of all this," Mills said as he returned on a plane he spent $800 to charter to Boston. He told reporters he made the trip "to be seen" and to end talk of anything improper between him and the Argentine stripper. As the caucus voted unanimously to expand Ways and Means by twelve, Mills checked into Bethesda Naval Hospital, suffering from exhaustion. Albert and Burton said they would not support a move to remove Mills as chairman. "I feel sorry for him," Albert said. "He was one of the greatest congressmen of my generation, but he is a sick man."

The next day, December 3, Albert confirmed that Mills would resign his chairmanship and was considering retirement. Now that Mills was out, stories surfaced of the "tyrannical" way in which he ran the committee. One member said Mills had been "drinking heavily for years." *Newsweek* reported that in 1972, Mills had to be restrained from climbing on stage with another stripper at the "Body Shop" in Los Angeles. On December 4, the third day of caucus meetings, Burton and David Obey of Wisconsin moved to block Ways and Means—under orders to create four subcommittees—from jumping the gun. Heir apparent Al Ullman of Oregon wanted to establish them immediately to monopolize the power slots before the dozen new members joined.

Burton was less than diplomatic in describing what happened. "I heard about it and went to Tip O'Neill with the AFL-CIO guy in tow," Burton told the *Washington Post*. "O'Neill said he'd talk to Ullman and tell them to unscramble the plan or we'd whack their ass at 6:01 P.M. [when the caucus was to reconvene]. We don't want a confrontation, but if they try it, they'll get creamed."

Ullman quickly backed off. "We're not stupid," he said. "We get the message. Half our discussion was how to protect the new members and their assignments."[19] Burton's crudeness offended many people, not least of them O'Neill. The next day, a one-paragraph brief on the front page of the *Wall Street Journal* said O'Neill had urged Albert to announce that this would be his last term. This would free O'Neill to seek votes for Speaker and get the jump on Burton. "If Phil mellows a bit, there's no limit on how far he can go," Van Deerlin said. "But the House won't stand for anyone who's going around whacking asses" (or who threatens to in public).[20]

Mills "lost his chairmanship so rapidly," *Washington Post* congressional correspondent Mary Russell wrote, because Democrats had to produce an economic turnaround or face defeat in 1976. "The basics of that program— tax reform, curtailing of excess profits by the oil companies, unemployment compensation, were in the Ways and Means Committee," Russell wrote. "It could cost Democrats their political life to let Mills run the committee on which so much of the Democratic record depended."

Less than a week later, on December 10, 1974, Mills resigned his chairmanship, conveying the news to Albert through his close friend Joe Waggonner, who visited Mills in his hospital room. "I'm bone tired. I'm worn out. I'm in no condition to serve. . . . I want out," Mills told Waggonner. The next day Steering and Policy announced the new Democrats for Ways and Means. Ten of the twelve were considered moderates or liberals.[21]

In a year-ending analysis, Evans and Novak said the real loser was Tip O'Neill. Burton, not O'Neill, they wrote, "now becomes the potential successor—probably within four years—to Speaker Carl Albert. . . . Indeed,

Burton is the true successor to Mills as the uncrowned king of the House."[22]
O'Neill could not have been happy to see that bold prediction in print.

As Congress adjourned for Christmas, Phillip Burton could pause and take stock. In an institution that valued seniority, decorum, collegiality, respect for elders, and a wait-your-turn mentality, he had violated, if not obliterated, all of those values. Yet he was number four in the leadership after just ten years and poised to move higher. Number one was weak, number two was looking over his shoulder, number three—McFall—was a creature of numbers one and two. Number four was getting all the attention. No one with Burton's extreme liberal and redistributive views ever rose so high or so fast or held such power in the U.S. House of Representatives. Now he would use it.

In *The Nation*, longtime Burton observer Mary Ellen Leary called his rise

> a chronicle of breaking down barred doors, throwing open customarily closed institutions and forcing grudging or even hostile colleagues to make way for his bumptious but purposeful presence. Burton is a rare man in politics: he does not need to be loved. Since 1950 he has moved through state Democratic circles, the state legislature and into Congress, so singularly intent upon mastery of the political game, at which he is phenomenally adept, that he has had no time for such niceties as cultivating the media, placating rivals or being diplomatic with allies. As a result, what is known about him focuses upon his abrasive manner, his perfectly apparent ambition. His ability has been overlooked.[23]

As the Ninety-fourth Congress convened in January 1975, Burton scheduled three more days of caucus meetings to set rules for the new session and to vote on committee chairmen. But first he had a score to settle with an institution he and many on the left considered a blight on American politics and culture for decades: the House Un-American Activities Committee. Chairman Richard Ichord of Missouri, recognizing its notoriety and declining base of support, had got the name changed to HISC, the less threatening-sounding House Committee on Internal Security.

Burton first heard about HUAC's abuses from his civil libertarian father, who believed like many that the committee recklessly ruined the lives and reputations of intellectuals, liberals, and unionists under the guise of anti-communism. Burton spent his adult life fighting HUAC, as a Young Democrat in the early 1950s and in the state legislature. He spoke in opposition when the committee appeared in San Francisco in 1960—for which Richard Nixon later smeared him. His first act in Congress was to hold up funding for HUAC, if only for thirty seconds. Every year after he opposed funding it. Now that he had real power, Burton was not after cheap headlines. He wanted to kill outright this committee that he had hated for so long. Like most of his quiet maneuvers, his strategy was methodically planned and brilliantly executed.

In one very fast and very deft action at the start of the first day of caucus meetings, Burton recognized his friend Don Edwards, chairman of the Judiciary's Subcommittee on Civil Rights and Constitutional Rights. Edwards, the former FBI agent who was permitted to examine the inaccurate files the committee maintained on him, moved to transfer HISC to his subcommittee's jurisdiction. Burton called for a voice vote and pounded the gavel so quickly that few people understood what happened: Burton and Edwards had just abolished the most infamous and anti-democratic committee of the postwar era. They kept it low-key so as not to alert conservative Republicans.

HUAC was first established as a select committee in 1938 to investigate activities of the German Bund in the United States. In 1945, the House voted narrowly to make it a permanent standing committee. HUAC shifted its investigatory focus from fascism to communism, just in time to coincide with the postwar anti-communist fever sweeping America. The dramatic HUAC testimony to the committee of Whittaker Chambers, who denounced State Department official Alger Hiss as a traitor who passed secrets to the Soviets, gave the formerly obscure Nixon a platform from which he began his climb to prominence.

By the late 1960s, even most members of Congress conceded privately that HUAC had outlived whatever usefulness it might have had. But few wanted to be seen voting against it. During one debate, Burton submitted a 1965 study from the Library of Congress showing that the $851,000 budgeted for HUAC, or nearly $95,000 per member, was more than double the average of the next most expensively staffed committee, Government Operations, which spent $42,000 per member, and quadruple the $24,000 that Education and Labor spent per member. Burton's other committee, Interior and Insular Affairs, had a staff of ten, compared to HUAC's fifty-seven.

Father Drinan joined the committee expressly to abolish it, and every year argued against its existence. Its legislative output was pathetic, he said. In its entire history, only six bills were ever enacted into law (supporters said it was primarily an investigative, not a legislative committee). But by 1975 it had issued 174 contempt citations—ten times more than all other House committees combined. Almost all of them were thrown out by the courts. Even so, the committee possessed more than 750,000 cards on individuals, and Drinan said that in 1970 alone, federal agents made 1,348 visits to the files.[24]

Drinan urged every freshman to vote against funding the committee. But Burton, with his genius for using procedural tactics to accomplish substantive reforms, formulated a sneak attack. "We've got to do this in the caucus," he told Mikva, Drinan, and Edwards. "We could never do it on the floor."

Every year the caucus establishes or continues governing rules for every committee. No one had ever before thought of simply not continuing the rules for this one. But what to do with HISC members? Burton convinced every member but Chairman Ichord to resign. He did so by creating spots for them on better committees, and created vacancies there by promising those members even better spots. Using his position on Steering and Policy, Burton produced a musical chairs effect that rippled throughout the House.

"I don't even recall making a speech," said Edwards. "I said, 'Mr. Chairman, I have an amendment to the rules at the desk.' I could hear, 'All in favor? All opposed?' It was the fastest gavel since Gary Cooper in *High Noon*."

Committee members Drinan and Richardson Preyer of North Carolina went to Government Operations. Mendel Davis, a conservative from South Carolina and key member of Burton's southern base, moved to Administration. Claude Pepper of Florida had no choice but to step down under a new caucus rule forbidding members of Rules from serving on any other committee. Then, Steering and Policy recommended no new Democratic members take their place, even though freshman Larry McDonald of Georgia, a John Bircher, requested HISC. All the Republican members sought other committees as well.

"Liberal ideologues opposed to HUAC normally did not think through these things," recalled Kastenmeier, who, in 1961, was one of only six members to oppose HUAC. "Phil found better assignments so the members would not fight it. He negotiated it away. . . . It was one of the most astute operations ever achieved. It's almost impossible to put a committee out of business, especially *that* committee. It was a master stroke, one of the great things he did."

Resolutions to cut funding for HUAC had always been "a marvelous high profile loser," recalled Mikva. "But now seventy-five freshmen were being told the hot issue in the caucus was to abolish HUAC. Ichord was frustrated. There was nothing he could do. His committee was evaporating out from under him completely. By the time the caucus met, it was a done deal. This was such a great event that we wanted to trumpet it. But Phil wanted to move on. We had a party to celebrate at Edwards's office, and Burton came, but he was already onto the next crusade."

The next day, the full House ratified the change. There was no debate. Among the Washington press corps, only columnist Mary McGrory reported what really happened—and that was several weeks later. In a column headlined, "The Old Terror Is Gone," McGrory wrote that the Burton-Drinan "cloak and dagger operation" was probably the only way to kill off the committee. "Burton began a series of delicate parliamentary maneuvers," she wrote. "His object was to pick off Democratic members of HISC. . . . By skillful evocation of old House practice and new House rules, Burton was able to remove them at a rate that left Ichord standing alone."[25]

One reason why the abolition of HUAC got so little attention was because it was overwhelmed by other caucus news. In voting to dump three entrenched southern committee chairmen, the class of 1974 earned itself a permanent place in the history of the House. The "revolution," as many called it, was led by Phil Burton. Nearly two decades later, participants described this upending of the seniority system almost as though they still could not believe they had pulled off such a shocking challenge to the established order.

The freshman class served notice early that it was no ordinary group when it opened its own office two blocks from the Capitol and hired its own staff. Over four days in mid-January, every chairman was invited to address the class. This alone was an astonishing turnaround from previous years, when meek freshmen inquired politely about committee assignments. The new leaders were Tim Wirth, Toby Moffett, and Norman Mineta. At first, Mineta recalled, the chairmen were "too busy." Mineta delivered the message that the class would vote en masse against anyone who refused to meet with them. "When would it be convenient?" they wrote back.

Up to and during these closed sessions, Burton counseled the class on how to use its collective strength. When Armed Services Chairman Edward Hebert showed up, Gladys Spellman of Maryland was prepared. The previous summer, Carl Albert had appointed Pat Schroeder his representative to a NATO meeting in Europe, the first woman to be so honored. Hebert tried to block her appointment, refusing even to sign her voucher to travel. "Mr. Chairman," Spellman said, "I'd like to ask you about your attempt to prevent Representative Schroeder from being the Speaker's representative to the NATO meeting."

At that point, Mineta said, "you could see red flames" emerging. Hebert clearly didn't yet feel any heat but his own. With a condescending air, he stood up, leaned over and said, "Okay, boys and girls. Let me tell you what it's like around here." With that comment, Hebert was history. Albert came out of a similar meeting, saying, "They don't want a leader. They want a bouncer."[26]

In a well-timed release, Common Cause added to the volatile atmosphere by issuing a major report on House chairmen. Using three standards—compliance with House, caucus, and committee rules; use of power; and fairness—the report concluded that Hebert "flagrantly violates all three." Three more chairmen, Mahon of Appropriations, W. R. Poage of Agriculture, and Hays of Administration, "show a pattern of serious abuse." The report quickly became the hottest document in Washington.[27] The machine was primed, the crew was in place, and Common Cause had just loaded the fuel.

When the twenty-four-member Steering and Policy Committee convened on January 15, 1975, to vote on chairmen, O'Neill moved that all of them be nominated by voice vote. But new rules required separate votes on each chairman, which the committee proceeded to do alphabetically. The first three chairmen, Hebert, Poage, and Mahon, were narrowly approved, 14 to 10. But when it got to Banking and Currency, the committee for the first time rejected seniority and voted against longtime populist Wright Patman, 11 to 13. In his place, it recommended fourth-ranking Henry Reuss of Wisconsin. It was the job of the caucus to ratify or reject these recommendations.

Not only did the new caucus, aided by the Watergate Babies, not rubber-stamp the Steering and Policy recommendations, it dumped two more chairmen besides Patman, substituting Tom Foley for Poage as chairman of Agriculture and Melvin Price of Illinois for Hebert on Armed Services.[28] Two of the three deposed chairmen, Poage and Patman, were Texans.

This was the most significant power shake-up since the 1910 revolt against Cannon. It put every chairman on notice again that unless he was fair and responsive to his members, the same fate might befall him. With his black manservant, superhawk Hebert, seventy-four, seemed like a remnant from the nineteenth century. He was first elected in 1940, served loyally for thirty years until he succeeded Mendel Rivers as chairman.

"We got him. We got him. Man, oh man," rejoiced Les Aspin of Wisconsin. Poage, seventy-five, was first elected to the House in 1936. He had an ADA rating of 6 out of 100 and consistently opposed efforts to feed the poor through surplus food programs at a time when liberals had spotlighted hunger in America. "It's going to make a big difference," Mikva said of the changes. "During the Vietnam War, the most divisive issue in the country, we couldn't get a committee to hold hearings. Now I think we will be able to confront the issues of the country."[29]

As hard as he tried, Burton couldn't orchestrate all the changes that shook Congress that year. He did not know it, but when he walked into that same Steering and Policy Committee meeting, Phil Burton also walked into an exquisitely set trap laid by Richard Bolling, Frank Thompson, John Brademas, and possibly Tip O'Neill, although all of them later denied it. When it was time to vote on the chairman of House Administration, the room quieted. Wayne Hays was expected to be a shoo-in. A few at most wanted to reinforce the message the Common Cause report laid out.

In its explosive report, Common Cause took revenge on Hays for the campaign financing bill and other sins, writing that he "abused his power by threatening to cut congressional staff off the payroll to settle purely personal scores." It said Hays had refused to release the paycheck for an aide to Don Fraser who lined up witnesses for a bill Hays opposed. "In addition," the report said, "during the impeachment investigation, Hays threatened to cut the Judiciary Committee's impeachment staff after he got into an argument with two interns in an elevator." In the four years of his chairmanship, Hays expanded his committee's jurisdiction to include federal elections, parking, and information systems. He also controlled office staff, expenses and fringe benefits, and committee budgets. His first principle of politics seemed to be retribution, and he never hesitated to use even the most mundane request as a club.

"How shall we vote on this one, Thompy," someone yelled to Thompson, next in line to succeed Hays. "Vote your conscience," he replied. They did. The vote was 12 to 12. People were stunned. This was not some senile dictator they were taking on, but one of the most feared men in the House.

"You should have seen the expression on Phil Burton's face," Bolling said afterwards. Dawson Mathis of Georgia, a conservative Burton loyalist who heard Bolling's comment, believed Burton had been sandbagged. "Why would Bolling even be looking at Burton's face unless he knew what was going to happen," Mathis wondered. The vote remained deadlocked through a second round and a third. On the fourth and final ballot, one vote changed, and Hays was rejected, 11 to 13. Then the Committee voted 20 to 4 to recommend Thompson to succeed Hays.

The attack on Hays was one of the most Byzantine and closely guarded secrets of the House leadership. O'Neill and Albert hated Hays and believed his autocratic bullying and corrupt use of government funds on overseas shopping trips brought disrepute to the House. Hays had even threatened to run against Albert for Speaker but then called him from London to say he would not do so in 1974 but would make no promises for 1976. Thompson, an aide said, considered Hays an "arrogant prick" who picked on defenseless people. Thompson had been waiting years for a chairmanship. Deputy Whip Brademas was close to O'Neill and Thompson. Bolling hated Hays but hated Burton even more, and with this ploy, he could hammer both men at once.

All of them believed Burton was planning to move up the ladder. If they could take out Hays now and force Burton to defend Hays before the caucus, and especially before seventy-five reform-minded freshmen, Burton's own reform credentials would be questioned. Moreover, Burton allies Fraser, Rosenthal, Mikva, and Conlon despised Hays and supported Thompson. Burton's own DSG power base was thus sorely divided.

"This was pure, raw House caucus politics," recalled Hays aide Doug Frost. "Tip led the fight. You could not be majority leader and not be in on this. It was a watershed. It had never been done before. They could kill two birds with one stone, Hays and Burton."[30]

It wasn't so easy. Three hours after the vote, Hays convened a meeting with Burton, Frost, Bill Stanton of Ohio, fellow coal rat John Dent, and the Hays-Burton southern faction led by Dawson Mathis, Mendel Davis, and Charlie Rose. Some had formed their alliances over the black lung bill. Most were on House Administration. They were with Burton because he had helped preserve their agricultural subsidies and kept his word. On any given issue, Mathis estimated they could deliver fifty votes, but not always the same fifty. Burton never told them explicitly that he was going to run for majority leader, "but those of us who hitched our wagons assumed he would make a move and were comfortable with that," Mathis recalled. "I wanted to be among the fifty or so who controlled things in the House, and I saw an opportunity with Phil Burton."

Hays was downcast. "I'm beat. Screw it," he said at the meeting, which witnesses described as "half wake, half resurrection." But his allies decided to take the fight to the caucus. What had happened in Steering and Policy had been, in Burton's words, "a stiletto job." But before the caucus could vote on Hays, it first had to reject Thompson as chairman. If that happened, the caucus could choose a week later between Thompson and Hays. A vote against Thompson was therefore not necessarily a vote for Hays.

Thus was born the "fairness doctrine." It went like this: because Hays got knifed in Steering and Policy, the entire caucus should have a chance to consider his chairmanship. The only way to do that was to first reject Thompson. Armed with this strategy, Hays partisans hit the phones. With less than a day, the operation took on the intensity of a political convention. "Word went out," Frost said. "No one needed a sandwich board. This was a serious personality clash between Hays and Thompson." One characterization that "Hays had a working set of balls and [Thompson] didn't," particularly infuriated Thompson.

The Hays-Burton strategy worked. Many freshmen, in addition to feeling grateful to Burton for helping elect them, also felt obliged to Hays. Moreover, the *New York Times* reported, several said Hays and Burton made a deal to provide them with funds and office space. Hays won a decisive victory when the caucus rejected Thompson 176-109. It was still possible for Thompson to beat Hays in a head-to-head contest a week later, but Thompson was torn.

Not until the last minute did Thompson decide to run—and only then when he heard rumors that Hays was promising a $35 per diem allowance to all members if he kept his job, a pay raise of several thousand dollars a year. At that point, Thompson said members called, urging him to run. He was undecided until a "close ally of Mr. Hays," called and said, "You had better rethink your position. You are in danger of losing your [subcommittee] chairmanship if you run against Mr. Hays and lose." Thompson refused to name the caller, but said he had no doubt this was a "direct threat" from Hays.[31]

The *Washington Post* and *New York Times* editorialized against Hays. The *Times* was especially harsh, calling him "a disgrace to Ohio, the Democratic Party and the House of Representatives and [one who] plays the crassest kind of old-fashioned politics." As for Burton, the *Times* said, "Practicality is one thing and cynicism is another. Representative Burton seems not to know the difference." But Hays triumphed again, defeating Thompson 161-111.

"If you promise not to use my name," one veteran liberal confided to Mary McGrory, "I'll tell you I voted for Hays. I barely speak to the guy, but you've got to remember he talks back to Common Cause and Ralph Nader, who screech every time we get a new allowance and call our recesses 'vacations.' He takes a lot of heat for us, and we appreciate it. He stands up to the press, too. It's like having your own hit man." When Joe Williams, Burton's former law partner, asked why Burton led the fight for Hays, Burton replied, "He gave me everything I needed, here and in Washington, all the perks, all the money [for staff]. I couldn't vote against him."[32]

Burton had every reason to celebrate what the caucus accomplished, especially in overturning the sanctity of the seniority system. But he was outraged at the attempted ouster of Hays. Burton had scripted almost everything, from abolition of HISC to the revolt against the chairmen. He led the fight for procedural reforms in the caucus, then financed and helped elect the class to push them through. But the Hays episode was not part of his script, and it took precious political capital to fix it.

With internal House and caucus business complete, people wondered what Burton would do next. "Obey fears Burton might use the [caucus] chairmanship for his own purposes, for the pure joy of exercising power," wrote the *Chicago Tribune*. "Kastenmeier says he is convinced Burton will use it only to advance liberal legislation, while Mikva says both will happen."[33]

Burton's previous news coverage was nothing compared to the avalanche that followed. Almost all the action was in the House, and he was leading it. The *Democratic Review* ran a lengthy interview with Burton that asked the question on everyone's mind: what was the next rung for Burton, majority leader or Speaker? How powerful was he? How fast would he move? Burton was judicious, if not entirely believable.

Q: What's the relationship of the Caucus to the leadership? Who's in charge, you or Albert?

BURTON: The Speaker's in charge. Tip next. I preside over the Caucus.

Q: But isn't the Caucus going to be the tail that swings the dog?

BURTON: If the majority of the Caucus feels strongly about something . . . they have a way of making those views known. But the Number One man is Carl Albert, and the Number Two man is Tip O'Neill.

Q: Will you be checking with them before doing things like setting up agendas?

BURTON: Certainly, oh certainly, certainly.

Q: You won't be moving out on your own?

BURTON: Oh, heavens no. We elected Carl Albert as our Speaker, our Number One man. We elected Tip O'Neill as our Number Two man, and it would be a usurpation of function if I didn't work with and under them.

Q: Do you plan to run for Speaker in four years?

BURTON: I have my hands full with the job I have just been elected to. Let's just see how that works out.

Q: . . . If Albert did step down as he has indicated, and if Tip wanted the top job, you would support Tip?

BURTON: I would anticipate I would run for Majority Leader. I *would* run for Majority Leader.[34]

His comments notwithstanding, Burton wasted little time before demonstrating his independence. On February 25, 1975, the caucus voted 152-99 to require a House vote on attaching repeal of the oil depletion allowance to a $21 billion antirecession tax-cut bill. The House leadership opposed the effort to force a vote. Burton supported it. A few days later, the full House voted 248-163 to end the oil depletion allowance. James Naughton was prompted to write in the *New York Times* that the House leadership seemed unable to control events. "Mr. O'Neill, who has waited patiently, traditionally, for two dozen years to succeed to the Speaker's position," he wrote, "has been told so often by Mr. Burton that no challenge is intended that, Mr. O'Neill's associates say, he is beginning to expect one."

Burton used *Boston Globe* Washington bureau chief Martin Nolan to put that rumor to bed quickly. Nolan got to know Burton when they wound up on the same plane to San Francisco in 1972 and Burton invited him on a tour of his district. Nolan found it "as phenomenal a political experience as I had had in a very long time. I never saw a guy who knew his district so well." People in the East figured California was *only* a media state, but Nolan witnessed an old-fashioned political boss, a man who was using power all the time and never even thought about the media. Nolan made a point of staying in touch.

To squelch the rumors, Burton invited Nolan to a lunch at the Women's National Democratic Club, where he was to introduce O'Neill. With Nolan there taking notes, Burton said he wished to "end press speculation that our Democratic unity is going to bust apart" by introducing "not only the next speaker at our luncheon, but the next Speaker of the House of Representatives, the Honorable Thomas P. O'Neill of Massachusetts."[35]

A week later, as President Lon Nol's Cambodian government was falling, the caucus voted overwhelmingly, 189-49, to cut off all further military aid to Cambodia and Vietnam. Freshman Bob Carr sponsored the resolution and Burton supported it, despite leadership opposition at first. The vote "clearly spells the end to any further military aid for Cambodia and South Vietnam for the balance of the fiscal year," Burton told reporters. It was the lead story in the next day's *New York Times*.

With this vote, however, conservatives and moderates began to rebel. This was policy—not procedure—and some felt the caucus had no business dictating to the House International Relations Committee what policy it should follow the day before it was to hear from administration officials. "If this is the way we're going to operate," exploded Chairman Thomas Morgan during the closed caucus debate, "let's abolish the committee system, open up the Caucus and call witnesses." O'Neill eventually voted for the resolution, but this was the second time in a month he stuck up for a chairman and lost. Frustrated conservatives circulated a petition to make caucus meetings public.[36]

Traditionalists hated Burton's aggressive leadership. For an institution that moves slowly when it moves at all, Burton was moving the House awfully fast, threatening entrenched power centers. It was one thing to make chairmen accountable or spread power among younger subcommittee chairs. It was quite another to bypass the committee system entirely and use the caucus to make policy. If this was a harbinger of how Burton might behave given even more power, say majority leader or Speaker, the signs were disturbing.

Vice President Nelson Rockefeller recognized Burton's new stature by asking Burton to make out the guest list for his first political dinner at his enormous Foxhall Road mansion on March 19. The idea came out of a long Burton-Rockefeller conversation at a British embassy party several weeks earlier. During a three-course candlelit dinner that included Burton, Mikva, Foley, Fraser, and Republicans Albert Quie of Minnesota, John Anderson and Robert Michel of Illinois, and Barber Conable of New York, the new caucus chairman asked for "cooperation" from the White House on the antirecession bills moving through Congress."

Without such cooperation, Burton warned Rockefeller, he had the votes to override any vetoes. Moreover, he threatened, the Democrats on the Hill would savage President Ford and the country could be damaged by ferocious partisan fighting. The days of cutting deals with Wilbur Mills or George Mahon were over, Burton told Rockefeller, and Ford should stop taking "cheap shots" at the Democrats. Columnists Evans and Novak wrote that Rockefeller's decision to "build his first intimate political dinner around Burton shows where the power is on Capitol Hill." A Republican who was present said he was "offended" by Burton's manner, which he described as his usual "Burtonish self." His ultimatum: "Play ball, or we will crush you like a pea."[37]

In another sign of his growing notoriety, *New York Times* columnist William Safire devoted a column to explaining why Burton was now the most important man in Congress: besides running the caucus, he also held the biggest "I.O.U. in Washington." During negotiations on campaign reform the previous summer, Wayne Hays slipped an amendment into the bill reducing from five years to three the statute of limitations on violations of the Campaign Spending Act. Republican Bill Frenzel of Minnesota told Safire it was Burton's amendment, and it passed. Several months later, it became known that Ashland Oil Company had given DNC Chairman Robert Strauss two cash payments totaling $55,000 in 1970, which Strauss allegedly laundered to disguise the source. It was a personal, legal gift, Strauss said.

Two days before the new law took effect, Safire wrote, Ashland pleaded guilty to illegal contributions to Nixon campaign officials but not to Strauss. Under Burton's amendment, that four-year-old gift was outside the new statute of limitations. "Phillip Burton," Safire concluded, "King Caucus himself—holds a big I.O.U. from his party's chairman. One day he will cash that in, while the rest of us behold in wonderment all that can be accommodated in the name of 'campaign spending reform.'"[38]

But the ink on Safire's column was barely dry before Burton and Hays teamed up again. In return for Burton's help in saving his chairmanship, Hays submitted a resolution providing formal recognition and staffing for the first time to the Democratic Caucus. Burton got $66,000 a year for clerical help and a staff employee. To make this more palatable, salaries and office expenses were also raised for the Speaker, majority and minority whips, majority and minority leaders and House Republican Conference. It came to $486,000 a year and was approved on a voice vote. In a wide-ranging session with the *Washington Star-News*, Burton was asked about his relationship with Hays.

"Well, Wayne and I are personal friends," Burton said. "He's a tough-minded legislator, and I learned the hard way it's a little easier to work things out with Wayne in advance than it is to ignore his point of view. We have found over the years that we had been able to accommodate our respective points of view quite well on most occasions." When asked if he considered Hays and himself "the most powerful people in the House," Burton replied, "No. I think there are a great number of very powerful members of the House."[39]

More Burton profiles soon appeared. In an article entitled, "The Most Powerful Man in Congress?" *Dun's Review*, a business magazine, devoted four pages to answering that question in the affirmative while raising questions about how antibusiness Burton might prove. "'I can't pinpoint how I stand on tax reform,' insists Burton, puffing on an ever-present Chesterfield, 'because I have no expertise here. In fact, I don't know what the hell I'm talking about. I will take a look at the issue when it actually firms up in committee.'"

In late May, the *New York Times* ran its first profile, which began with Secretary of State Henry Kissinger finding time for a "leisurely, two-hour chat" with Burton even as South Vietnam was collapsing. Kissinger's action, the *Times* concluded, "underscored a growing feeling within the Ford Administration that Representative Phillip Burton of California, with whom Mr. Kissinger met, may be one of the few Democrats in Congress who can deliver votes on any issue." In language that for overloaded adjectives alone rivaled the *San Francisco Examiner*'s 1967 series on the Burton Machine, the *Times* went on: "He is often abrasive, sometimes overbearing, frequently volatile. Some colleagues regard him as a wild-eyed radical; others consider him power mad."[40]

Despite his notoriety and the success of the caucus in overriding the leadership and the committee chairmen, a backlash was setting in. After the caucus passed the resolution cutting off military aid to Indochina, Burton said to Carr, "Some people were steamed. We have to lay off using the caucus for a while." Former ally Joe Waggonner, meanwhile, was so offended by Burton's tactics that he joined the effort to make caucus sessions public.

Even reformers Foley and Obey said they were upset over using the caucus to stop funding the war before the appropriate committee had even met. "The Caucus shouldn't be overused to take positions on substantive issues," said Fraser. The alternative, they said, was to use Steering and Policy as a place where issues could be tried out first. But Conlon defended the caucus, saying, "Cambodia, because of the Vietnam legacy, was an extraordinary situation. There are no other suggestions that the Caucus be used that way."

Burton told *Congressional Quarterly* he was pleased with what the caucus did. "First, we had to democratize the process," Burton said, "which we did. We had to encourage newer members in the process. That's happened. We had to make the effort to attach the oil depletion amendments to the tax bill to get meaningful tax reform and take up the Cambodia resolution to clear the air." The Republicans helped conservative Democrats who wanted to open the Democratic Caucus by voting to open their House Republican Conference. But Burton was opposed. "We've just adopted the most important House reforms in sixty years," he said, "and we're getting fuller, freer, and franker communications in the closed Caucus."[41]

By mid-June, frustration, discord, and finger-pointing set in, not over the growing clout of the caucus or Phil Burton's political "nymphomania," as one critic put it, but over the caucus's failure to stand up to President Ford, who consistently vetoed Democratic programs passed by huge majorities. This was supposed to be the veto-proof Congress. And yet, as the recession deepened, the House passed an emergency farm bill, a strip mining bill, a jobs package, and an emergency housing program, and Ford vetoed each one. In each case, the House failed to override.

Republican and conservative Democratic votes gave Ford his margin. Burton's threats to Rockefeller in March had been hollow, but the blame fell on the leadership, especially Carl Albert. Burton went to Albert and O'Neill and suggested tying the farm bill, jobs bill, and housing bill into one giant package that either Ford could not veto or the House could override, having amassed votes from so many affected interests. But nothing came of his suggestion.

Soon, the blasts were coming daily. Tom Wicker said the Democrats were "in disarray," with neither the "will, nor the courage—nor perhaps the leadership" to solve major problems in energy, the environment, and the economy. O'Neill told *New York Times* reporter David Rosenbaum that if the Democrats could not override Ford on a bill as important as creating new jobs in a recession, "then we cannot win on any vote." *Newsweek* captioned its story, "Capitol Marshmallows." Said Bolling, "We're looking like a bunch of idiots."

At a meeting of Democrats, several freshmen complained that Eastern, big-city Democrats voted to sustain Ford's veto of the farm bill, while southern conservatives voted with the president's veto of the jobs bill. Why couldn't the leadership have pulled the dissenters on each bill into a room and explained to them that if they voted for each other's bills they would all get what they wanted? Burton had already suggested that, but to no avail.[42]

It fell to Richard Conlon to make the defense. Writing months later in the *Harvard Political Review*, Conlon said Congress had received poor marks because "it has not lived up to the overblown expectations of the press, the public and members themselves, especially many of the freshmen." Conlon argued that the Ninety-fourth Congress was faced with an unprecedented political situation: a president who had never been elected by the people. In worrying whether he would win his own party's nomination, Ford had to appease his party's right wing. "Instead of working with Congress to find solutions to national problems," Conlon wrote, "he has adopted a strategy of running against Congress and sought confrontation in an effort to project an image of Horatio at the bridge fighting off a horde of irresponsible big-spenders in Congress. He has used the veto to kill programs initiated by

Congress and at the same time exploited presidential access to the media to attack Congress for 'do-nothingism' and 'reckless spending.'"

To really be veto-proof, Conlon argued, the Democrats needed a three-to-one majority, not the two-to-one majority it had. He said Ford was using the veto in a way the Founding Fathers never intended while initiating nothing new himself. At the same time, Conlon said, reforms in the House, election of committee chairmen, revival of the caucus, and election of a new generation of issue-oriented members "unwilling to vegetate for fifteen or twenty years" had all dispersed power. "Congress was not meant to be efficient any more than it was meant to 'lead' the nation," Conlon concluded. "A political body of 535 members can do neither. Instead, it was designed to be difficult and slow, to represent the total diversity of the nation, and to enact legislation that reflected a national consensus. . . . Congress may not be doing as good a job as we would like. It never does. But neither is it the failure its critics have contended."[43]

Phil Burton wanted to end the drift. He could put competing Democratic factions in a room and hammer out a deal. That was the hallmark of his legislative style. He made no secret of wanting to be the next majority leader. In fact, he later told an interviewer, he decided in 1973, the day his resolution to make the whip elective lost, that he would run for the post.

By summer, Albert was hinting to intimates that he would retire at the end of his term, amid reports that his drinking was excessive, that he was the object of ridicule among members, and that he sometimes seemed oblivious to House developments. Other reports indicated that from a dinner in San Francisco Burton already had amassed more than $50,000 that he planned to use in 1976 House elections, and he planned another dinner in Beverly Hills.

But Bolling strongly believed that as majority leader Burton would destroy his beloved House. Bolling still wanted to be Speaker. But he had another compelling reason: to stop Burton. Bolling had made the first move once before, declaring his candidacy for Majority Leader on November 19, 1962, the day after Sam Rayburn had been buried. In September 1975, he said he would announce again, "when Carl Albert leaves the Speakership."[44]

Soon after Bolling made his plans explicit, Burton overreached in the caucus. When the conservatives launched their effort to open caucus meetings to the public, Burton ruled the resolution approved on a voice vote. Waggonner had won, but demanded a roll call, shouting, "Mr. Chairman, Mr. Chairman." Burton ignored him, even though witnesses said Burton clearly saw and heard him. He moved on to other business while Waggonner continued shouting. When Burton finally recognized him, he said Waggonner's demand was not timely.

"It was clearly a case of Waggonner and Burton being on opposite sides," Bolling happily told reporters, "and Burton just arbitrarily ignoring Joe. If there is one thing that Burton should have learned by now, it is that fairness transcends ideological disputes. I just couldn't believe what was happening." Others dismissed the incident, saying that by opening the caucus, Waggonner had made his point. Now he was just trying to rub it in. But some of Burton's freshman supporters were perturbed. "What we wanted and what we still want is leadership that has ears, can listen, can react fairly," said Robert Edgar of Pennsylvania. "We want leaders who are a little more democratic, a little less arbitrary."[45] Score one for Bolling.

After visiting San Francisco in early November, Phil Burton returned to Washington feeling extremely fatigued. He called a doctor, whom he later said examined him and found nothing wrong. But when he did not improve, the physician advised him to enter Bethesda Naval Hospital. A reporter called his office to find out why Burton had been missing from the floor for several days but was given a runaround. Minutes later, John Burton called the reporter to say Phillip was home with an "intestinal flu-type ailment." But the reporter kept checking and discovered Burton had been admitted to Bethesda with a possible heart ailment. At that point, Burton called the reporter himself.

"I have had a series of tests," Burton confirmed. The doctors told me I am right on the edge of whether or not I had a slight heart incident." It turned out that Burton had been admitted to the same hospital a year before, and there had been rumors then of a minor heart problem, which Burton had said was intestinal.

"I have cut down from three packs a day to two, and I am drinking maybe one gallon of coffee rather than two," Burton said. "But I have made a private vow that after I get out of the hospital, I will cut down to a pack a day. After a certain number of cigarettes, you don't enjoy them, anyway." But he added it would be tough to get him to slow down. "I am not built to loaf or to jog. If I didn't have more to do in a given day than there is time to do it, I couldn't stand it."[46]

Between Waggonner's slap and his own health problems, it was not the most auspicious way to begin the most important political campaign of his life. But there was plenty of time, and Phil Burton, more than ever before, was operating from strength. Events were moving his way. Or so he thought.

13

TRIUMPH AT HOME

*To me, the Moscone election symbolized the achievement of
political change and leadership that capped twenty years of struggle,
beginning with Phillip Burton's first election in 1956.
It ratified what we thought: that San Francisco would have,
should have, younger, vibrant, multiracial leadership.*

CALIFORNIA ASSEMBLY SPEAKER WILLIE BROWN

WHILE PHILLIP BURTON was focusing his considerable energy on ascending rapidly in the House of Representatives, California was fitfully groping through the post-1970 reapportionment process, the results of which determined who controlled California for the next decade. San Francisco also was changing as the eight years of the Joseph Alioto administration drew to a close. The results of all this political ferment were more pleasing than even Burton could have hoped: a remap that benefited his family, friends, and allies; an end to the rancorous and time-consuming two-decade war with the Democratic faction controlled by Leo McCarthy; and the ultimate local triumph, the election of Burton protégé George Moscone as mayor of San Francisco in 1975.

Just as Burton had predicted during his 1967 Potomac cruise on the "Honey Fitz," Lyndon Johnson's Vietnam policies had both hurt and deeply divided California Democrats. The liberal California Democratic Council, for example, and much of the Democratic club movement as well, collapsed and died over divisions created by the war. Despite Alan Cranston's Senate victory over an even more divided Republican Party in 1968, the Republicans took control of the state assembly that year, deposing Jesse Unruh as speaker after eight years, the longest reign in California history.

With popular Governor Ronald Reagan preparing for re-election in 1970, the outlook looked bleak for the Democrats, just when the state was slated to get five new congressional seats, for a total of forty-three. The Republicans were eagerly poised to carve up California with a partisan redistricting plan, to do to the Democrats after 1970 what Unruh, Burton, and Robert Crown did to them after 1960 (they were paying back the Republicans for 1950). *New York Times* reporter R. W. Apple was just passing on accepted wisdom when he wrote in September 1970 that although the Democrats had twenty-one of the state's thirty-eight seats, the Republicans likely would control the delegation within a few years. Some Republicans, Apple noted, predicted a turnover of twelve seats in California for a "shift of considerable national importance."[1]

But 1970 turned out to be another bad year for California Republicans. Reagan defeated former Speaker Unruh in the governor's race, but Unruh cut Reagan's 1966 margin over Pat Brown in half. Democrat John Tunney, son of the former heavyweight champ, won the other U.S. Senate seat, defeating Republican George Murphy, a political lightweight seeking a second term. A newcomer named Edmund G. "Jerry" Brown, the thirty-two-year-old son of the former governor, was elected secretary of state on the strength of his name. Democrats won back control of the assembly and the senate.

Los Angeles Democrat Bob Moretti became the new speaker. Like his mentor Unruh, Moretti passed out bags of campaign money during the 1970 election cycle to assembly challengers—$20,000 to one candidate in Berkeley alone. Moretti's closest associates were Willie Brown, whom he named to chair Ways and Means, and state Democratic Party Chairman John Burton, whom he appointed chairman of the Rules Committee. Moretti named another Burton loyalist, Henry Waxman, whose friend and campaign manager, Howard Berman, joined him in the assembly in 1972, to chair the important Elections and Reapportionment Committee.

As all these pieces fell into place, the stage was set for another Burton-style incumbent-protection plan. Howard Berman's younger brother Michael, meanwhile, joined Waxman's committee as a consultant. Nearly all of these people—Waxman, Howard and Michael Berman, Phillip and John Burton, and Willie Brown—would play pivotal roles in the politics, public policy, leadership wars, and redistricting of California for much of the next two decades.

Next to Sala, Howard Berman was Phillip Burton's favorite person on earth, someone he looked upon almost as the son he never had. A committed liberal and civil libertarian, the son of an Orthodox Jewish immigrant from Poland who sold textiles door-to-door, Berman was first attracted to Burton via the movie *Operation Abolition*, the pro-HUAC propaganda film that featured Burton speaking out against HUAC at the 1960 Union Square rally in San Francisco. He met Burton through Young Democrats conventions and slept on Sala's and Phil's living room floor while a college intern in Washington. Berman never forgot working a Hunters Point precinct in 1966, where voters filed into the voting booth with their Burton slate cards in hand. In the Reagan sweep, Berman recalled, Pat Brown lost just four votes in that entire precinct, while Burton received every single vote cast. In 1968, Berman was elected president of the California Young Democrats. He was a Robert Kennedy supporter and active in the antiwar movement.

Brother Michael attended the affluent and liberal Hamilton High School in West Los Angeles in the early 1960s, where the local Young Democrats chapter had 400 members. Phillip Burton was the chapter's patron saint. Soon Michael was driving Burton around Los Angeles on his periodic visits. Phillip and Sala vacationed for a week every year at the Miramar Hotel in Santa Monica, where they had honeymooned, and Burton loved to play hearts with Michael. A brilliant rebel, Michael was kicked out of three schools for poor grades: UC Berkeley, UCLA, and USC. Like his mentor, Michael Berman lived and breathed politics.

As reapportionment heated up, Burton, with five new seats to play with, worked the Washington end to protect incumbents. The deal was two seats for Democrats, two for Republicans, and the fifth a toss-up. George Gould, Unruh's former aide from Southern California, became staff director of the Census and Statistics Subcommittee of the Post Office and Civil Service Committee. At Governor Reagan's request, the Nixon administration held up release of census data for key states in order to keep the Democrats in the dark as long as possible. But Gould leaned on the deputy census director— a Democrat—to get him early data, which Gould fed to Burton. Members of the delegation resented Burton as they had in 1967 for his power over their political futures, but his work on the state plan was the talk of Congress, Gould said, because it was so effective. As in 1967, state and congressional Democrats gave Burton authority to draw up the congressional plan, which protected every incumbent. Then the Democrat-controlled state legislature approved it.

Even as he created safe districts for his colleagues, he never hesitated to rip them if they voted wrong on some issue. "He controlled his rage, but he was angry all the time," Gould recalled. "He felt he had a duty to kick ass, to shake things up, to be tough and smart, because in his mind so many people were sellouts. 'They don't freelance here, George. They got elected by somebody,' he'd say, "and if they don't represent somebody, they don't belong here.'" When Matt Gately, Burton's old Falcon Club friend from high school, visited, Burton told him, "Every day they're trying to buy me, and I won't sell."[2]

As part of the redistricting plan, Burton created one new seat just south of San Francisco for a moderate assembly Democrat named Leo Ryan. To do so, he moved Republican Pete McCloskey further south. He created a black seat in central Los Angeles for Yvonne Brathwaite. (She later married and took Burke as her last name.) Not only did Democrats Ryan and Brathwaite win, but all thirty-eight incumbents were re-elected. A third Democratic seat at the intersection of Los Angeles, Riverside, and San Bernardino Counties went to ex-Congressman George Brown, a close Burton ally. Brown, an antiwar Democrat, served with Burton in the assembly and went to Congress in 1962. He gave up his seat in 1970 to challenge John Tunney in the primary but lost. With Burton's help, he got a new district.[3]

House Republicans were happy with Burton's congressional lines, for obvious reasons, but state Republicans who were shut out were furious and challenged the plan. In a critique submitted to the state supreme court, Republican congressional candidate Gordon Knapp argued, for example, that conservative Orange County was entitled to three House seats. Under Burton's plan, it got one. The only criterion Burton used, he argued, was partisan or incumbent advantage. It unnecessarily divided counties and minority communities and was neither "contiguous" nor "compact." The Thirty-sixth District was Burton's compromise, the fifth seat that Republican William Ketchum won. But state Republicans like Knapp seized on it as an example of everything that was wrong. Among other things, Burton added the liberal UC Santa Barbara campus to the southernmost portions of the conservative Central Valley.

"The mind boggles," Knapp wrote, "at the blatant cynicism it took to create the long and virtually empty arm down the Santa Barbara Coast, without even a highway running the length of it, reaching just far enough to UC Santa Barbara . . . and adding it to this basically agricultural Central Valley district." But Knapp's favorite example was the Forty-second District, which comprised most of San Diego. It added a "long, irregular arm" eighty miles up the coast to Orange County to take in 29,000 people, 60 percent of Newport Beach. "This creates the anomalous situation," Knapp wrote, "where in an urban area, a citizen can reach his representative's office more quickly on a regularly scheduled commercial airliner than by driving to it."

Reagan had agreed to sign Burton's plan as long as the five seats were divided evenly, with the fifth a toss-up. But Burton went too far in pleasing

Charles Teague, an old GOP warhorse, whose new district included Santa Barbara, but not the student enclave of Isla Vista, and Ventura, but not the Latino enclave of Oxnard. That Burton gave to Barry Goldwater, Jr. Goldwater complained to his father, who complained to Reagan about how his son had been treated, and Reagan vetoed the plan. Burton later said it was a mistake to get "the old man" riled up. But the state supreme court permitted his plan to remain in place for the 1972 elections. The five new members of Congress had to run from somewhere, and the court judged his plan to be bipartisan.[4]

Most of the Democratic combatants took a break from the redistricting wars for the 1972 Democratic National Convention in Miami that nominated antiwar candidate George McGovern for president. Willie Brown and the Burtons were key participants. At the same time that DSG was beginning its push to reform the House, the McGovern-Fraser Commission—created after the 1968 debacle in Chicago—re-wrote the rules by which Democratic presidential candidates were nominated. It was no accident that the candidate who best understood the new rules—McGovern—could best take advantage of them. But the reformers were so oblivious to the electoral ramifications of the new rules that they eliminated whatever small chance McGovern might have otherwise had to defeat Nixon. They threw out Mayor Daley's entire Illinois delegation of machine regulars, for example, thus writing off Illinois in the general election, and adopted a busing plank that wrote off Michigan, where Democratic McComb County, a working-class white suburb of Detroit, had opposed busing in a 1971 referendum by fourteen to one.

Wayne Hays said the new rules "reformed us out of the presidency, and now they're trying to reform us out of a party." Added fellow coal rat John Dent, "It's the damnedest mess. You've got quotas for everything—blacks, Chicanos, eighteen-year-olds. Pretty soon they'll want quotas for draft dodgers."

McGovern's victory in the June California primary clinched his nomination. But a combination of organized labor, Hubert Humphrey, Henry "Scoop" Jackson, and other mainstream Democrats opposed to McGovern, the reformers and the cultural liberalism of "acid, amnesty, and abortion," as party conservatives sought to paint their adversaries' platform, conspired to take it away. The means was a decision by a Humphrey-stacked Credentials Committee to change California's winner-take-all system of apportioning delegates, even though that primary had already taken place. The ruling meant McGovern should be entitled to only 44 percent of his 271 California delegates, the same percentage of votes he won in the primary. The effect would have been to strip McGovern of 120 delegates—enough to deny him the nomination.

McGovern's nomination thus came down to California, whose delegation was co-chaired by Willie Brown, John Burton, and farm worker organizer Dolores Huerta. Brown gained widespread exposure for an impassioned "Give Me Back My Delegation" speech on national television. But in his mind he and John Burton were "rookies" playing on a national stage for the first time. They looked to Phillip for guidance and credibility with key inside players. A strong McGovern supporter—he could not support Humphrey because of the war—Burton was ubiquitous, attending most of the key strategy sessions that saved McGovern's nomination. Through remarkable anticipation and floor discipline, the McGovernites held off the credentials challenge.[5]

Amid the chaos over California's role in McGovern's nomination, Burton challenged Tunney's credentials as a McGovern delegate from California because Tunney had voted against farm workers and because he had previously endorsed Ed Muskie, an early front-runner. In fact, early on, when McGovern campaign manager Frank Mankiewicz heard about Tunney's impending endorsement of Muskie, he called Willie Brown and said he needed Brown's endorsement of McGovern to offset Tunney's.

"Did your father ever do any boxing?" Mankiewicz asked him.

"Yeah, he did a little fighting in the navy," Brown replied.

"Did he win anything?"

"Yeah," Brown said. "I think he won a few tournaments on his ship."

"What did he weigh? Can I call him a lightweight?" Mankiewicz pressed.

"You can call him whatever you want," Brown said.

At the next day's press conference, Mankiewicz introduced Brown, described his father's boxing triumphs and said he would rather have "the heavyweight son of a lightweight champion than . . ." The reporters broke into laughter and Mankiewicz did not have to finish the sentence.[6]

Burton's attempt to keep Tunney off the delegation was guaranteed to infuriate a U.S. senator, but it was entirely consistent with Burton's approach to politics. Tunney cast bad votes in Congress. Now it was payback time. Win or lose, Tunney would always remember what it might mean next time to cross Burton on issues close to his heart. Huerta helped Burton line up the votes to dump him. But Mankiewicz blanched at the prospect of alienating not just Tunney, but his friends, the Kennedys. He got McGovern to implore the California delegates by phone to keep Tunney in the delegation. On the first ballot, Tunney actually lost. Huerta and Phillip had done their job well. But there was no way Tunney could not be seated. In a rare moment in which he worked against his brother, delegation co-chairman John Burton, Bob Crown, and aide Bill Cavala advised Willie Brown to make a "real stem-winder." This would give them another twenty minutes to scrounge votes for Tunney. On the next ballot, Tunney sneaked in by two votes—but only because the ballots were stuffed.

As expected, President Nixon crushed McGovern in November. After the McGovern debacle and another year of turmoil over reapportionment in California, Governor Reagan on June 27, 1973, again vetoed the state legislature's reapportionment bills. This forced the matter into the California Supreme Court, which appointed special masters, staffed by a University of San Francisco law professor named Paul McKaskle. Reagan and his Republican advisors figured that a nonpolitical staff could only help the GOP after Burton's partisan effort. Not only was Reagan wrong, but one consequence of his miscalculation meant another Burton went to Congress.

In releasing a new plan, the court said: "Masters have concluded that the factor of overriding importance in each plan (that Reagan vetoed) was the good of incumbent re-election. . . . The objective of reapportionment should not be the political survival or comfort of those already in office."

One of the incumbents about to be discomfited, however, was San Francisco Republican William Mailliard, a twenty-two-year House veteran. Mailliard wrote an angry letter accusing the masters of "arbitrarily exchanging 150,000 people now represented by me for 150,000 now represented by Mr. Burton." In disturbing the "historic relationship" of Mailliard to his constituents, the masters also "seriously reduced the possibility of the re-election of a senior member of two important House committees," Mailliard protested, adding that if the Republicans controlled the House, he would be chairman of the Foreign Relations Committee. His complaints went nowhere.

When the court approved the masters' plan on November 28, 1973, John Burton, speaking as state party chairman, could barely contain his glee. "It insures Democratic control of the legislature and may even improve it," Burton said. "Thanks to Governor Reagan for vetoing the reapportionment bills." The Democrats had feared that the masters would do far more damage that they did to Democratic legislative and congressional hegemony. In possibly the worst prognostication of the decade, Putnam Livermore, chairman of the GOP's Reapportionment Committee, called the court's approval of the masters' plan "the death knell of gerrymandering in California."[7] The masters did make the congressional districts more competitive, which should have helped the Republicans, who held just nineteen of the forty-three seats. In the November 1974 midterm election, the first one using the masters' new districts, however, the GOP lost four more House seats and ended up with fifteen to the Democrats' twenty-eight. The masters were not the villains, however. The Watergate scandal did in the Republicans that year.

The Burtons had special reason to celebrate the court decision. Because it ratified the changes in Mailliard's district, Mailliard accepted a Nixon appointment as ambassador to the Organization of American States. This cleared the way for John Burton to join Phillip in Congress, representing a district that had become Democratic. In leaving Sacramento, John Burton was giving up key positions to be a first-termer in Washington, where he would be Phil's little brother. But he could provide his brother with a unique window into the class of '74, the Watergate Babies who became the elder Burton's power base. "Everyone says I'll be in Phillip's shadow," John said. "There are worse shadows to be in." Even so, it was wrenching to leave Sacramento, where he was happy and a major player.

A skilled politician in his own right, John did not have his brother's ferocious temper or intensity. He could be just as rude but was far more likable and lighthearted. When Reagan called him a "nut," John Burton called a press conference on the Capitol grounds and fed the squirrels. But as chairman of Rules, he also led the only successful override of a Reagan veto, an action that kept open the state mental hospitals. And working with his brother on Capitol Hill, he kept his eye on California's welfare recipients, who were under constant threat of losing benefits as long as Reagan was governor.

John Burton negotiated directly with Reagan for three weeks in 1971 and produced a deal that allowed Reagan to proclaim he had cleaned up the state's welfare system. Every major provision Reagan changed, however, was later invalidated by the courts as unconstitutional, as the Burtons and Ralph Abascal, one of the public-interest lawyers working with him, predicted. Before that happened, though, and in return for these Reagan "reforms," the food stamp program was made mandatory in every county, and cost-of-living adjustments, or COLAs, were made automatic, which eventually produced billions of dollars for California's poor and disabled. Reagan's political cover: the COLAs did not take effect until Reagan left office.[8]

Following the 1972 elections, Assembly Speaker Bob Moretti began planning to run for governor in 1974. That touched off a two-year war to succeed him between rival San Franciscans: Moretti loyalist Willie Brown and Burton nemesis Leo McCarthy. As it was happening, redistricting compelled San Francisco to reduce its assembly contingent from four to three.

Of the four—John Burton, Brown, McCarthy, and McCarthy law partner John Foran—Foran was the weakest link. Moretti protected Burton and Brown by making it clear he would approve no assembly plan that weakened their districts. That left Foran and McCarthy to fight over the third seat. Foran knew McCarthy could beat him if it ever came to that. Foran had been in the job for ten years and wanted to run for the state senate.

But before the Democrats knew for certain that Reagan would veto the remap, they needed Foran's vote to pass the plan that eliminated his seat. Asking a career pol to eliminate his own district—without guarantee of something better—is like asking a surgeon to cut off his hand. The approach is tricky at best. Phil Burton put his big paw on Foran's shoulder and said that if Foran would vote for the plan, Burton would take care of him. Burton could not predict the future, of course, but something good was bound to come along.

In fact, something did. Because of the logjam over redistricting, all legislators ran in their old districts for two more years, which guaranteed Foran's survival until 1974. Then they cut the deal: when John Burton went to Congress, Foran ran for *his* assembly seat. In return, the McCarthy forces agreed not to run a rival candidate against John. But the battle for speaker continued unabated.

While McCarthy and his top aide, a young staffer named Art Agnos, quietly lined up votes for speaker, Brown was making enemies as the flashy chairman of Ways and Means. Dressed in thousand-dollar Brioni suits, Brown demeaned colleagues who came before his committee. Most were not quick enough to keep up with him, a fact he seemed to relish pointing out. For every member he alienated, particularly Hispanics and blacks, McCarthy and Agnos soothed them with big promises.

Berman and Waxman should have been natural allies of Willie Brown. Instead, they said they were disappointed in Brown's performance as Moretti's top lieutenant. In Moretti's consuming need for special-interest money to finance his campaign for governor, Moretti and Brown were thwarting the liberal Waxman-Berman legislative agenda. And while McCarthy romanced Berman for his vote, Brown assumed he had it. Berman said Brown never specifically asked Berman to vote for him for speaker. Over a game of hearts at the Miramar Hotel in August 1973, Howard Berman told Phil Burton he was irritated with Brown. Burton nodded sympathetically, and

Berman assumed—incorrectly—that Burton would not mind if Berman supported McCarthy.

In the spring of 1974—while Burton was in Washington plotting the election and capture of the Watergate Babies—Berman and McCarthy made the deal in California that delivered the speakership to Leo McCarthy. Berman and Waxman would bring a half dozen members with them, including Julian Dixon of Los Angeles. In return, Berman would become McCarthy's majority leader and Dixon the caucus chairman. In a further act of "betrayal," they also endorsed Jerry Brown for governor over Moretti, even though Moretti had made Waxman chairman of Elections and Reapportionment. John Burton was livid, and Willie Brown was stunned. Phil Burton stayed out of it.

With his superior name identification and a strong media campaign, Jerry Brown won the June primary, defeating an impressive field of candidates, including Moretti, Joe Alioto, and Jerome Waldie. Even though Moretti was a lame duck, he hoped to hold the speakership through November, and then hand it over to designated heir Willie Brown. But helped by the Waxman-Berman switch and by assembly blacks and Hispanics who felt abused by Brown's arrogance, Leo McCarthy had the votes. A group of moderate Republicans, led by Ken Maddy of Fresno, who were close to Moretti and Brown, also voted for McCarthy. When they learned that Brown was making promises to some of the conservatives in the GOP caucus while taking the moderates' votes for granted, they bolted.

"I state flatly that I have a majority of both caucuses," McCarthy told reporters the day after the primary. "The Speaker stated at least three times last month that he would step down in June. I take him to be a man of his word. I will ask him in the name of caucus unity not to attempt to manipulate the Speakership by the timing of the election simply because the candidacy of his candidate—Willie Brown—is collapsing." Brown maintained that he, too, had the votes but wanted to wait until the legislature passed the state budget in mid-June. McCarthy agreed to give Moretti a five-day face-saving period, one of the few civilized acts among any of these fierce rivals. On June 14, Brown was reported "near tears" after making an appeal to his colleagues in the Democratic Caucus.[9]

McCarthy won by four votes. Four of six blacks and four of five Hispanics supported him. "Only racial minorities have found it convenient to leave me, for some reason," Brown said. His longtime rival, John Miller of Oakland, the first black to back McCarthy, said, "I'm not going to inflict Willie on black people." In possibly the second worst prognostication of the decade,

Miller added, "In six months, Willie Brown will either fade into the woodwork, become a model for Wilkes Bashford [a glitzy San Francisco clothier whose pricey suits Brown favored] or join some big law firm."

McCarthy won over nine of the thirteen freshmen, none of whom held power under Moretti. "But under McCarthy," wrote *Examiner* correspondent Dennis Opatrny, "they could see their careers soar to lofty chairmanships, key leadership posts and access to the inner circle." *California Journal* editor Ed Salzman added: "Almost every politician has a huge ego. But many, including McCarthy, conceal it. Brown lets it all hang out, and some people find this offensive." John Miller's endorsement of McCarthy, he wrote, "made it easier for a liberal to support McCarthy without looking like a bigot."[10]

Five weeks later, while Brown continued to seek votes for a December challenge to McCarthy, McCarthy announced he was replacing Willie Brown as Ways and Means Chairman with boyhood friend John Foran. A few days after that, McCarthy dropped him from the committee altogether, saying he had offered Brown another committee to chair, but Brown had refused it. An infuriated Brown called McCarthy and shouted, "You never offered it, Leo. You did not offer it. I do not want to be sandbagged! You make me look like some cat who sits around and mopes in his beer, and that is unfair."

McCarthy beat back Brown's final challenge in December. "I think it is a sickening spectacle," McCarthy said of Brown's efforts to round up votes. "I am astonished that any man's ego could be so consuming [as] to allow him to drown in his own self pity."[11]

Willie Brown's recollection of events was considerably different. He lost the speakership that year, he recalled, because blacks double-crossed him and McCarthy rewarded Howard Berman's consuming ambition. Black legislators John Miller, Julian Dixon, and Leon Ralph, "said they could do better under a white leader," said Brown. "Because of my standards and personality, they could not achieve as much under me. Ralph wanted chairmanship of Rules and got it. Dixon wanted the caucus chairmanship and got it, and Miller wanted the Judiciary chairmanship and got it." Berman would have supported Brown in return for being named majority leader, even though he was in his first term. Brown said he was unwilling to go that far. Seniority mattered, and he had senior Democrats already committed to him he could not pass over for Berman. McCarthy had no such inhibitions. But he paid dearly for it five years later.[12]

After a decade in the assembly, three years of which was spent pursuing the speakership, Willie Brown was now about as far out of the loop as it was possible to get. McCarthy exiled him to a tiny, closet-sized office in the state capitol and stripped him of staff.

With his two closest friends—Moretti and John Burton—leaving the assembly, there was little reason to hang around, although Brown was not ready to give up his seat. He retreated to San Francisco to bide his time and expand his law practice. As the San Francisco skyline soared with high-rise office towers, and big out-of-town department stores wanted a piece of the lucrative Union Square carriage trade, Brown spent more time representing wealthy developers and retailers at the county Planning Commission than constituents at the capitol. He would arrive in Sacramento on Monday morning and leave at noon. He would return on Thursday and head home an hour later.

McCarthy, on the other hand, made so many promises to become speaker that he was constantly afraid he would lose the powerful office. Two years into McCarthy's speakership, rebel Ken Meade of Berkeley, a Moretti lieutenant who supported Brown and never made his peace with McCarthy, announced he was leaving the legislature. "McCarthy had to buy the Speakership and gave everything away," a bitter Meade told *California Journal* in a parting shot. "That's why this place is languishing. The new Speakership was put together on a shoestring, and he can't do anything to offend people."[13]

While the Burtons and Brown were preoccupied with their struggles, Senate Majority Leader George Moscone was quietly making his own big plans. Moscone was popular and respected in Sacramento and carefully considered running for governor himself in 1974. But after agonizing for months, he decided to come home and run for mayor in 1975. Joe Alioto, who froze the Burton team out of most of the local action for eight years, was leaving office. Moscone discovered that the city had profoundly changed.

The club movement was dormant. White ethnics were leaving the city as manufacturing jobs disappeared and as San Francisco's once preeminent maritime industry shut down or moved across the bay to Oakland's shiny new containerized port. Meanwhile, the always tolerant San Francisco was gaining a reputation as a mecca for gay liberation. Gays were migrating from small towns and big cities all across America, even as Asian, Mexican, and Central American immigrants continued to arrive. A neighborhood and environmental movement also arose to protest the high-rise office buildings that Alioto had championed with the happy acquiescence of the business community and the building trade unions.

Alioto brought Model Cities and other federal poverty funds to San Francisco, and a new generation of minority activists grew up administering them in local neighborhoods. But most were excluded from city hall and they wanted in. All this ferment changed the city's politics. It was now a city more sharply divided than ever between left and right, east side and west. The east side of town, Phil Burton's congressional district, included many of the newly emerging minority activists, gays, and white progressives. The west side, Republicans and moderate-conservative Democrats, represented much of old San Francisco, the wealthy enclaves of Pacific Heights, Sea Cliff, the Marina, and St. Francis Wood, and what was left of the Irish and Italian middle-class burghers in the Richmond and Sunset districts.

In his quest for power in Washington, however, Burton was losing touch with both sides of town. Each faction represented a different reaction to the eight years of Alioto. The liberal neighborhood response was to demand an end to rampant growth and inclusion on the city's important boards and commissions, which were dominated by pro-growth trade unions, conservative minorities, and business. The conservative neighborhood response was to say that San Francisco's problems were caused by all the "new people," the gays and the immigrants, and the excessive power of the public sector and craft unions.

As Moscone came home and walked the city's neighborhoods, he began to understand for the first time what the new San Francisco was about. He liked what he saw and became its champion. The polls showed Moscone to be the front-runner in the city's first-ever election that required a runoff between the top two vote-getters. Moscone had four opponents: John Ertola, a moderate Democrat, superior court judge, and former president of the San Francisco Board of Supervisors; Dianne Feinstein, first elected to the board in 1969 and twice its president; Republican Supervisor John Barbagelata, a popular, right-wing, anti-labor realtor; and moderate Republican Milton Marks, who had defeated John Burton for the state senate in 1967.

Ertola and Marks competed for the same base of upper-middle-class homeowners; neither turned out to be a major factor. Barbagelata represented conservative homeowners who felt Alioto had given everything away to the unions and who were still furious over a strike that year by police and firefighters. Feinstein, who ran for mayor in 1971 and was crushed by Alioto, was the centrist, good-government candidate expected to place second and challenge Moscone again in the runoff.

In 1969 when she first ran for office, Feinstein saw Burton law partner Joe Williams at a fund-raiser and asked how she could get on Burton's slate card. She said she was embarrassed to ask directly because she didn't know him.

Mildred Burton with her three boys. Phillip is standing with his hand on Robert's shoulder. Johnny is in his mother's lap. (Courtesy of Burton family)

Above: Phillip Burton on his graduation day from the
University of Southern California. (Courtesy of Burton family)

Opposite, above: Mildred Burton with her three grown sons.
Phillip at left, John middle, Robert right. (Courtesy of Burton family)

Opposite, below: Phillip and Sala Burton with his parents,
Mildred and Dr. Thomas Burton. (Courtesy of Burton family)

Above: Phil Burton and Jesse Unruh look over maps of the 1961 state reapportionment.
Seated is Unruh aide Larry Margolis. Standing is Unruh aide Jack Crose.
(Reprinted by permission of the Bancroft Library, University of California, Berkeley)

Opposite, above: Assemblyman Phil Burton presents Assembly Resolution
to U.S. Supreme Court Chief Justice Earl Warren honoring him on the
tenth anniversary of his leadership of the Court. (Courtesy of Burton family)

Opposite, below: California Governor Pat Brown signs Burton's landmark welfare
reform bill, AB 59, with Burton and state Senator George Miller looking on,
May 21, 1963. (Courtesy of Congressman George Miller III)

Phillip and Sala Burton with volunteers at his campaign headquarters.
(Photo by Marshall Windmiller; courtesy of Marshall Windmiller)

Front page of Dr. Carlton Goodlett's *San Francisco Sun Reporter*, the entire issue of which is devoted to electing Burton to Congress in February 1964. Note photo in upper left of Burton with attorney Willie Brown, who later that year is elected to the state assembly. (Photo of newspaper by Rich Pedroncelli)

Above: House Speaker John McCormack administers the oath of office
to newly elected Congressman Phillip Burton, February 25, 1964.
(Courtesy of Burton family)

Opposite, above: Robert Kennedy (back to camera) at an Oakland rally
before the June 1968 California primary. With him are Willie Brown,
Burton, and Jesse Unruh. (Reprinted by permission of the
Bancroft Library, University of California, Berkeley)

Opposite, below: Burton with a young George Miller III (right) and
Ted Risenhoover, Democratic Congressman from Oklahoma.
(Photo by Dev O'Neill; courtesy of Burton family)

Opposite, above: Phil and Sala Burton with House Speaker Carl Albert. (Photo by Dev O'Neill; courtesy of Burton family)

Opposite, below: Burton with House Majority Leader Tip O'Neill and Speaker Carl Albert. (Photo by Dev O'Neill; courtesy of Burton family)

Above: Burton with President Jimmy Carter. Burton may be the only man in America who either doesn't know or doesn't care that he has walked into the Oval Office to see the president with toilet paper on his face. (Reprinted by permission of Bancroft Library, University of California, Berkeley)

Opposite, above: Burton with San Francisco Mayor George Moscone.
(Courtesy of Burton family)

Opposite, below: Congressional brothers John (licking the spoon) and
Phil Burton at ceremony for the Golden Gate National Recreation Area.
(National Park Service, photo by Richard Frear; courtesy of Burton family)

Above: Burton speaks at GGNRA ceremony.
(National Park Service, photo by Richard Frear; courtesy of Burton family)

Opposite, above: Burton cooking up something with
AFL-CIO President Lane Kirkland, July 1982. (Courtesy of Burton family)

Opposite, below: Phil and Sala Burton with Golden Gate Bridge
in background. Taken during and used for his 1982 re-election campaign.
(Courtesy of Burton family)

Above: Phillip Burton statue at Fort Mason headquarters of GGNRA.
Sculpture is by Wendy Ross. (Photo by J. L. Bierne; courtesy of Burton family)

Burton's Last Hurrah, the 1982 campaign. (Courtesy of Burton family)

"You're a nice lady," said Williams. "I can't get you on, but he'd support a liberal like you for the board of supervisors. I'll set up a meeting."

Soon Burton himself arrived at the gathering, and Williams went over to ask him. "Dianne Feinstein, you know her?" Burton nodded. "She wants to get on your slate mailer, and I said I'd set up a meeting."

"I asked that bitch to support John for the senate," Burton said angrily, "and she told me no twice." When Williams got back to his table, feeling burned by Feinstein for not having imparted that crucial piece of information, Feinstein wanted to know what Burton said. Williams repeated it word for word.

"Is that true, Dianne?" he asked.

"I just didn't know John that well," she replied weakly.[14]

Barbagelata wisely focused on Feinstein, rather than Moscone, and to everyone's shock squeezed past her by 1,300 votes to make the runoff. He was helped enormously by his own ballot initiatives to eliminate some of the special privileges public safety workers had gotten into the city charter, which passed easily. Barbagelata organized a volunteer phone campaign, which he ran from a converted roller skating rink. In a hard-fought, five-week runoff, Barbagelata narrowed the gap, painting Moscone as a free-spending liberal.

Moscone managed to hold on and won by just 4,400 votes out of some 200,000 cast. It was a narrow victory. But the photo in the next day's *Examiner* showed a triumphant Moscone, surrounded by Willie Brown and Phil and Sala Burton, looking out over an ecstatic crowd of gays, blacks, Asians, Hispanics, and white progressives—Moscone's new coalition. At long last, the Burton "machine," such as it was, had finally captured city hall.

Moscone's election also led finally to a peaceful resolution of the Democratic wars between the Burton and McCarthy factions that had ripped San Francisco politics apart for nearly twenty years. In his role as assembly majority leader, Howard Berman became a bridge between the two factions and helped broker the deal: Burton, Foran, and McCarthy had earlier made their own agreement, which put Foran in John Burton's assembly seat. Now Moscone was vacating his senate seat, and Foran would move to the upper chamber, which he had long wanted to do. McCarthy chief aide Art Agnos would run for Foran's assembly seat, with the Burtons' support. Moreover, John Burton leaned on McCarthy to rehabilitate Willie Brown, eventually elevating him to chair the important Revenue and Taxation Committee.

Such "deals" left ordinary Democrats wondering how any outsider could ever break into the inner circle. Was there really any difference in the way old-time boss Bill Malone and Phil Burton operated? Burton had a more progressive and activist agenda than Malone ever had, and he was determined to include minorities. But he was also far more ruthless and authoritarian in his control of San Francisco politics than Malone had ever been.

A gay grass-roots activist named Harvey Milk, who was running against Agnos for Foran's seat, found that out the hard way. Milk had a real base in the emerging gay enclave of the Castro District, where he owned a camera shop, and was a natural organizer and coalition builder. But he was a threat to the Burton-brokered deal, and they left him to dangle in the wind. As San Francisco political consultant David Looman said years later of the Burton-McCarthy rapprochement: "They buried the hatchet in Harvey Milk's head." Even so, Milk ran a spirited campaign against "the machine" and almost beat Agnos.

"They decided to sit down and divvy up the spoils," recalled Looman. "Harvey Milk almost upset their apple cart. That the election was close was an indication of how much the town was changing. It had been years since any of these guys had run a campaign. Had Moscone not put a whole bunch of new forces together in 1975, God knows what would have happened."[15]

It took some doing for Phil Burton to accept Agnos. It required John Burton to help legitimize Agnos to his brother. John's wife and Art's wife Sherry Agnos were best friends in Sacramento. Agnos still had to seek Phillip Burton's endorsement in person. McCarthy briefed him for hours the day before on issues and politics. "He's going to ask you for appointments to the county committee," McCarthy told Agnos. "Whatever he asks for, give it to him."

The next morning Agnos trudged over to the Del Webb, where Burton was staying. Burton opened the door wearing an undershirt and said, "Come in, kid. I don't know you very well, but my brother says you're my kind of guy. You should have been with us a long time ago. You're loyal, a liberal, a progressive. So I'm going to endorse you. My brother told me you'll do all right on the issues. This district is very important to us. We've represented it for a long time and we care about it. I'm going to ask you one thing. If anything happens to me, I want you to take care of my wife. Nothing is going to happen to me. I'm in perfect health. But I don't have anything in this world."

"Should that ever be necessary," Agnos replied, "I will go see John, and he will tell me what to do."

"You Greeks always have the perfect answer," Burton said. "Let's see how we can win this election."

Burton's health was not "perfect," however. He had recently been hospitalized with heart trouble. He was a walking collection of risk factors. He drank too much. He smoked too much. He never exercised. He worked all the time. He always seemed on the verge of blowing a fuse. If most politicians were type A personalities, Burton was type A+. But it was also true that he had nothing in the world but his salary and house on Capitol Hill. Even though he was only forty-nine, mortality was on his mind. His father died in 1974 after a long illness. Burton had been in such a foul mood on the flight home to San Francisco after his father's death that he had crudely insulted the president of Stanford University. He was worried about what might happen to Sala if he died. And though he never took care of his own body, he made arrangements for her in his own fashion.

"That was one question Leo never prepped me for," said Agnos.[16]

With the election over and the senate and assembly seats as well as San Francisco's city hall in friendly hands, Burton returned to Washington to prepare for the biggest fight of his life.

14

ONE VOTE

From the outset it looked like Phil was a cinch. No one was lying in the weeds. . . . A lot of the boys said I was the one who voted against him. A dozen guys voted against him because he and Tip were cool. But I didn't campaign against *him. No way did I campaign against him.*

FORMER HOUSE SPEAKER TIP O'NEILL

The conservatives were afraid of Burton because he was too liberal. The moderates were afraid of him because he was uncontrollable. The vested interests hated him because he was not on the take, and the liberal establishment was threatened by him and did not like his style. Other people thought he would be the strongest Speaker since Rayburn.

MARK GERSH
former Burton aide

He might have made a lousy Speaker, but as majority leader he would have made Tip O'Neill the greatest Speaker in American history.

MICHAEL BERMAN
former Burton associate

FRANK THOMPSON WAS IN Europe when the Wayne Hays scandal broke. He must have permitted himself at least a small smile. "This is God getting even," he told aides later. News that the feared chairman of the House Administration Committee was using committee funds to pay a "secretary" $14,000 a year to have sex with him hit Washington like an exploding rocket shell.

The scandal broke on the front page of the *Washington Post* on May 23,

1976. "I can't type. I can't file. I can't even answer the phone," Elizabeth Ray told reporters Rudy Maxa and Marian Clark. The well-endowed secretary, who later posed nude for *Playboy*, told the reporters she showed up at her private office on the fifth floor of the Longworth House Office Building once or twice a week for a couple of hours.

For Phil Burton, the timing of the scandal could not have been worse. Just weeks earlier, Burton announced what everyone knew since the day he was elected Democratic Caucus chairman: when Carl Albert stepped down and Tip O'Neill moved up to Speaker, Burton would run for majority leader.

It was equally well known that Burton was close to Hays and had interceded in the caucus to save his chairmanship in January 1975. Burton had been confident he could withstand any controversy over his efforts on Hays's behalf. But this scandal threatened to turn up the heat. People would question whether Burton had cooked up one deal too many. Enemies could use his Hays "problem" to pry loose wavering liberals or to solidify hostility to Burton from moderates and conservatives.

Even without the Hays debacle, Burton's candidacy was certain to be controversial. Plenty of conservative members had reason to feel threatened by the prospect of a liberal Speaker from Massachusetts and an ultraliberal majority leader from San Francisco, who could easily dismiss their kind of politics and regional issues. Those in Texas, Arkansas, and Oklahoma, moreover, where oil and gas interests had a direct line into the highest reaches of the House leadership for decades, and where Burton's efforts to kill the oil depletion allowance had not gone unnoticed, were uneasy. They had just lost two committee chairmanships—Poage on Agriculture and Mills on Ways and Means. With Albert's retirement, they would lose the Speakership itself.

What ensued over the next seven months, as political scientists Robert Peabody and Bruce Oppenheimer later described, was the "closest, most volatile and least predictable contest for the office of House Majority Leader in the 200-year history of Congress." It was also one of the most important.

The Hays scandal that created such problems for Burton at the outset of his majority leader campaign came to light almost by chance. Hays at first denied the Elizabeth Ray story, then said he "misspoke" to protect his new bride, a longtime Hays aide and companion named Patricia Peak, who ran his Ohio district office. When a *Post* reporter asked before the scandal broke if and when he was planning to marry Peak, Hays replied, "I'm waiting until Ben Bradlee marries Sally Quinn. We'll have a double ring ceremony." Hays was so proud of his quip about the *Post*'s editor and his girlfriend, the con-

troversial feature writer Quinn, with whom Bradlee was living, that he repeated it all over Washington.

The *Post*'s Marian Clark met Liz Ray by chance. They shared a first-class
cabin on the New York to Washington Metroliner one night. Clark, who
had just been jilted by her fiancé, happened to remark on how "lousy" men
were.

"Men, the stories I could tell you," nodded Ray, sympathetically. She said
just enough to intrigue Clark. They met again, and then with Maxa, like
Clark, a writer for the newspaper's Sunday magazine. Maxa traced Ray's
employment to Hays's office. After Hays announced his marriage to Peak,
Ray called Clark and sobbed into the phone that she wanted to meet immediately. She was so upset about not being invited to the wedding, even
though everyone else in the office was invited, even the "colored girls," that
she threw a fit, just as Peak walked in. Hays called the Capitol Police and
had her thrown out.[1]

Two days after the *Post* story was published, twenty-five members of Congress called for a House Ethics Committee investigation. In an angry June 1
meeting, Tip O'Neill told Hays to resign his chairmanships of Administration and the DCCC immediately. Hays refused. New DSG chairman Abner
Mikva, along with Dick Conlon and Fred Wertheimer of Common Cause,
drafted a "sense of the Caucus" resolution that Hays should voluntarily step
down. Then they called Burton and asked him to pass the word to Hays.
Burton negotiated Hays's resignation with Mikva on one phone and Hays
on the other.

Burton found himself in the awkward position of mediating between Hays
and O'Neill, who despised Hays and had wanted him out of the job the
previous year. Two days after his stormy meeting with O'Neill, Hays resigned
his DCCC post. A week later, Hays was admitted to an Ohio hospital un-
conscious from an overdose of sleeping pills. He won re-election in his primary, but just barely. Unlike Adam Powell's Harlem constituents, Hays's
Buckeye voters did not consider him a hero.

Still hospitalized on June 18, Hays resigned his other chairmanship. Conlon and Burton drafted the letter. But O'Neill thought Burton was pleading
for lesser punishment for Hays and resented it. David Cohen, Wertheimer's
colleague, heard from O'Neill's office that Burton was trying to plea bargain
for Hays and was appalled. Whether Burton was or whether O'Neill wanted
people to believe he was, or both, is unclear. What is clear is that Burton's
association with Hays badly damaged him in his own race later that year and
lent an unsavory aura to his otherwise impeccable reform credentials.[2]

O'Neill tells his version of the Hays incident in his memoirs. His account reveals how he was filling the power vacuum that Albert's weak Speakership created. "I've been to see the Speaker," Hays told O'Neill, "and he says we can forget about this thing, and that the leadership can let me off with a warning."

"No way," O'Neill replied. "You've disgraced the Congress and you've got to resign from your chairmanships."

"But Carl said it would be all right."

"It may be all right with the Speaker," O'Neill said. "But it's not all right with me. If you don't resign, I'm going to bring this business before the Caucus, and we'll strip you of your chairmanships on the spot."[3]

Burton wasn't the only one who paid a political price for his ties with Hays. The sex scandal tarnished everyone, especially freshmen, just gearing up for their first re-election effort. Many, at Burton's urging, had voted to retain Hays as chairman the year before and now appeared compromised. Some, including freshman Jim Lloyd of California, were in marginal districts they won from Watergate-weakened Republicans. Less than a week after the story broke, Lloyd's opponent charged that he was "bought by Hays in 1974 and they've been trading favors ever since." This was a gross exaggeration. As DCCC chairman, Hays sent Lloyd $1,500 for his first campaign. Lloyd voted for Hays over Thompson but barely knew him. Even if untrue, the charges were hard to disprove. The *San Gabriel Valley Tribune*, the largest newspaper in Lloyd's district, headlined its story: "GOP Candidate Charges Lloyd with Ties to Hays." Lloyd and others were bound to resent Burton for the trouble their support of Hays was now causing them.[4]

On June 7, two weeks after the Hays scandal broke, Carl Albert said he would retire, effective at the end of the session. O'Neill, who had been biding his time, promised to be an activist Speaker, the first since Rayburn. If the Democrats could defeat accidental President Gerald Ford in November, a Democratic Congress could work with a president of its own party for the first time in years. Albert's announcement made explicit what the *Post* called the "guerrilla war" that had been raging for nine months to succeed O'Neill. There were now three candidates: Bolling, Majority Whip John McFall, and Burton.

Despite his Hays tarnish, Burton was presumed the front-runner, a dangerous position for anyone in politics. His supporters said he had the race "locked up," but McFall was skeptical. "That's an old tactic of Burton's," he observed, "to say, 'I've got all the votes. Everyone can go home.'" Other candidates described as interested included Brademas, Brock Adams of Washington, and Deputy Whip Jim Wright of Texas.

Burton's relationship with Hays brought O'Neill's "antipathy" to Burton to the surface. A *Post* story predicted "war" if Burton were O'Neill's second in command. O'Neill told reporters Burton lobbied him in an effort to save Hays's chairmanship, but Burton said he went to O'Neill only to discuss how the matter should be handled in the caucus.

"I can work with O'Neill. Ask him if he can work with me," Burton said.

"I can work with anybody," O'Neill snapped.

Burton's most formidable opponent was Bolling, who, trying to overcome his reputation for aloofness, began holding small catered dinner parties at his home to cultivate supporters. One member said he liked Bolling but found him arrogant, self-important, and too quick to play the know-it-all. "If I told him they just discovered an atom bomb under the Capitol, he'd say, 'Yes, I knew it was there all the time,'" this member said. When Thompson asked a Pennsylvania member to vote for Bolling, he replied, "Why should I vote for that son of a bitch. He's never even said hello to me."[5]

O'Neill was unhappy with the choices. He feared and distrusted Burton. He served on Rules for years with Bolling and could not tolerate his arrogance. "Jesus, Dick made a lot of enemies," O'Neill said, recalling how, when people came to the Rules Committee to get a rule for their bill, Bolling cut them to shreds. "You have the nerve to come here and waste our time and not be knowledgeable," Bolling would typically tell some committee chairman. "I move this meeting be postponed until such time that the chairman or advocate of this legislation be better prepared." McFall, on the other hand, would have been a fine choice, a pliant man O'Neill could work with. But he could not win. O'Neill needed a new candidate.

After Burton announced, he called Rostenkowski and asked to see Mayor Daley. The most powerful mayor in America, the head of Chicago's Democratic machine and the man who ordered police attacks on antiwar protesters in Chicago in 1968 could be a valuable ally, lining up votes and bestowing legitimacy to a candidate some still saw as a dangerous radical. Burton was surprised when Rostenkowski agreed to the request. After the three men talked, Daley was impressed, particularly with Burton's commitment to the needs of the big cities. "Geez, that Burton is a helluva guy," Daley said. "Slow down, Dick," Rostenkowski replied. "Let's see who else is in the field."

Rostenkowski had his own reasons to be cautious. O'Neill was moving into the job that by rights should have been his. But Albert ruined his chances when he prevented Hale Boggs from appointing Rostenkowski whip. He, not O'Neill, would then have moved up on Boggs's death to majority leader and again to Speaker with Albert's retirement. Like Bolling and Burton, Rostenkowski was a large, physical man. He was a product of the rough and tumble of Chicago ward politics and retained his position as alderman even while in Congress. He relished using power but had precious little left. He knew there was small chance of Burton or Bolling sharing any of theirs with him.

Rostenkowski and Burton had tangled in years past, and Rostenkowski told O'Neill he feared Burton would win. Backing a new horse with O'Neill's covert blessing would be a way to ensure good relations with the new leadership. He could be included again in the small meetings where powerful men made decisions that moved the House and the nation.

Soon after the Daley meeting, Rostenkowski was boarding the underground subway between the Capitol and the Rayburn House Office Building when he bumped into Bolling.

"I'm in the race for majority leader," Bolling said. "You have no problem with me, do you?" Rostenkowski was noncommittal.

"You don't think that son of a bitch Burton will be majority leader, do you?" Bolling pressed. Again, Rostenkowski did not commit. He was no Burton fan, but he had even less use for Bolling's "superior attitude." He said Bolling acted like "Socrates" and treated everyone else like supplicants waiting to receive his wisdom. Personality aside, Bolling could not beat Burton, either.[6]

O'Neill did not want to work openly against Burton. If Burton were to win, and it looked as though he would, O'Neill's active opposition would just make matters worse. But he could not stomach the idea of Burton as his chief deputy. After five loyal years of protecting Albert's back, O'Neill did not want to spend his Speakership watching his own. Nor did he relish the prospect of breakfast every morning with a man who, in one aide's evocative phrase, "would reach over and rip your lungs out" if he did not approve of some strategy or decision. Burton would constantly be on him to push the dialogue to the left, engineer some deal, or force the members to take a stand they did not want to take. Or just make him work harder.

Despite what the members said about wanting "strong leadership," many of them wanted no such thing. They wanted to skirt controversy and hide under rocks whenever possible. In forcing his issues to the top of the agenda, Burton could make O'Neill's life miserable. Tip was not ready to retire, but he liked a round of golf now and then. Burton, on the other hand, stopped working only to sleep. And O'Neill still harbored bitter memories of Burton's drunken and abusive behavior in Beverly Hills. Who knew when Burton would go off again and embarrass him or the party? It was only a matter of time before Burton's crudeness and sloppy drinking habits would spill over into public view.

For his part, Burton insisted that he would be loyal to Tip O'Neill. Ben Palumbo, Burton's caucus aide, heard Phil and Sala argue about Tip. Sala, who had been there that night in Beverly Hills, said she thought O'Neill was working against him. Burton disagreed, saying he never caught the majority leader doing anything overt. Burton thought they could work together, even though Burton's first move as majority leader would have been to name Abner Mikva whip and Charlie Rose deputy whip. O'Neill would have fought him on it, preferring Brademas to Mikva, and would have thought it outrageous that the new majority leader would choose someone he didn't want, Mikva recalled. If Burton won, Mikva and Rose figured that would be just the beginning of their battles. Tom Foley, whom Burton convinced to run for caucus chairman, saw the Burton-O'Neill tension up close. He once found himself in an increasingly argumentative meeting, during which Burton and O'Neill became so combative that they could not stop shouting long enough to figure out they were saying the same thing. Foley had to intervene to point it out. Burton may have felt he had the votes, with or without O'Neill, and once he was elected, O'Neill would come around.

Desperate for an alternative to Burton, O'Neill designated his closest friend and aide, Leo Diehl, to work with Rostenkowski and several other members to find another candidate. The group included Jim Howard of New Jersey, who chaired a subcommittee on Jim Wright's Public Works Committee; Bernie Sisk, whom Burton defeated two years earlier; and Bill Alexander, a moderate-conservative from Arkansas. They decided the only man who could stop Burton was Wright, one of the best orators and floor managers in the House. He spent a career doing favors for colleagues on Public Works, which he was in line to chair. Except for the two most liberal members, Jack Brooks and Bob Eckhardt, both of whom endorsed Burton early, Wright would have the entire Texas delegation on his side. He was not a leader in any of the House reforms, but to some, that was a decided advantage.

The first time Jim Wright said anything out loud about running for majority leader was in March, to his closest aide and best friend Craig Raupe. During a four-hour drive back to Washington after campaigning for Harley Staggers, chairman of Interstate and Foreign Commerce, Wright turned to Raupe and said, "What would you think if I were to run for majority leader?"

It seemed a long shot, but Wright believed he could win. "I was not a reluctant candidate," Wright recalled. "I found the thought of being majority leader very appealing. I had wanted for some years to have a little more forceful and effective hand in determining what might happen in Congress."[7]

After Wright's name had been floating for weeks, Rostenkowski approached Wright, who was still vacillating. "I'll give you two weeks," Rostenkowski said. He did so, in Bolling's view, because, "Rostenkowski hated me. He had to find someone else. He came up with Wright."

Wright worried that Burton and Bolling had too much of a head start. But other friends, mostly from Texas or Public Works, who did not like the current field of candidates also urged him to run. Some, committed to McFall, told Wright they were bound to McFall only on the first ballot. After that, they were free to vote for Wright. One after another said they admired Burton's political skills but feared this ultraliberal crusader would use power to punish his enemies. Others hated Bolling so much they would vote for anyone else simply to stop him. "I was accepting all of those pledges and writing them down," said Wright. In a system where the rules dictated that the person with the fewest votes would drop out after every round of balloting, Burton and Wright talked candidly about what might happen to their supporters if either was eliminated on the second round. Each wanted the other's support for the crucial third round.[8]

Burton and Wright attended the Democratic National Convention in New York, where former Georgia Governor Jimmy Carter was nominated for president. Burton had a hospitality suite where congressional challengers dropped by. David Harris, a former antiwar activist and Stanford student president in the late 1960s, was challenging Republican Pete McCloskey, himself a staunch Vietnam opponent, in McCloskey's suburban Palo Alto district. After waiting to see Burton, Harris was ushered in, like so many other challengers that year, to "kiss the Pope's ring," as he recalled.

Wright's operation was distinctly lower key. He had a small room off Central Park, where the Texas delegation was billeted, and colleagues brought challengers in one by one for informal chats. They told him what committees they wanted and what public works projects they sought for their districts. Among the visitors were Barbara Mikulski, a liberal from Maryland, and Allen Ertel of Pennsylvania. Both invited him to campaign for them. Mikulski hoped Wright, either the next majority leader or the next chairman of Public Works, could help her with the business community, which had great interest in improving Baltimore Harbor. Ertel's district had been devastated by recent floods. Wright made twenty-three appearances in one day for him.

Wright announced his candidacy on July 27. The role of the majority leader, Wright said, was to be "advocate, conciliator, occasional innovator, part evangelist, part parish priest, and every now and then, part prophet." It would be a close race but he could win. A close friend of Wright assessed the race this way: McFall was "beatable." Burton had a "significant constituency, but we felt it had a cap on it. He'd been after the job for two years, but still hadn't locked it up." And Bolling was the "child prodigy of Sam Rayburn, but you can't be that forever. . . . He was sixty years old. We just felt he'd worn out his welcome."[9]

Wright did not worry Mikva. He was "an afterthought, put up by the power brokers who didn't want Burton or Bolling. None of us took him seriously. . . . He was drafted. Phil had a way of coalescing his enemies. No one thought Wright could win." Thompson described the field years later this way: McFall was an "amiable nonentity." Wright was "an unctuous evangelical with a pocketful of chits from the Chicago and New York City guys." Bolling was "the hortatory Monday morning quarterback, an extremely bright, good looking fellow who had a kind of snippy air about him." Burton was "incandescently bright. A lot of people were afraid of him. A tremendous number of my friends said, 'This guy is almost invariably right, but vociferous as hell, and I don't know what would happen if we disagreed with him.' He was not a bully. Wayne Hays was a bully. He was just sort of overwhelming."[10]

The field was finally set. On the ideological scale, Wright was the most conservative and Burton the most liberal. Wright had an ADA rating of 30 out of 100, compared to 65 for McFall, 75 for Bolling, and 90 for Burton. Their labor rating from the AFL-CIO's Committee on Political Education was closer. All were between 86 and 96. Wright voted with the Democratic Party 62 percent of the time, compared to 82 percent for Bolling, 84 percent for McFall, and 88 percent for Burton.[11] Burton's long and steadfast opposition to the Vietnam War was worth a dozen votes, estimated Peabody and Oppenheimer. Wright's resolution in the early seventies to support Nixon "in his efforts to negotiate a just peace in Vietnam," on the other hand, infuriated liberals, especially those in DSG. But issues and ideology were not the only criteria, or even the most important.

"Voting for majority leader," said Charlie Rose, "is like picking your wife. You [the candidate] have got to have a personal relationship to get them to vote for you." In such a race, "a new sort of chemistry sets in in this place, and people lie to their mothers about their true intentions."

McFall had some leadership and California support. He was, after all, in the customary spot to move up. But virtually everyone saw McFall as the weakest. McFall did not know how to ask for votes. As one participant recalled, McFall would walk up to a member and say, "Hey, Bill, I guess you heard I'm running for majority leader, and I'd like to count on you." The member would reply, "John, you'd make a helluva leader." And McFall thought he had his vote. That was a mistake neither Wright nor Burton made. Each nailed down the vote directly—for each ballot. Bolling's campaign manager was the respected Gillis Long of Louisiana. Bolling also had an executive committee of about thirty people, including the AFL-CIO's Biemiller, who enraged Burton by throwing a party for Bolling. Washington pundits with whom Bolling socialized were quick to broadcast his accomplishments or denigrate his opponents.

Bolling's base was the Missouri delegation, with eight votes, the Rules Committee, with ten, and the Joint Economic Council, which he chaired. A hero to many in the class of '74 because of his books, *House Out of Order* and *Power in the House,* both of which diagnosed what was wrong with the seniority system, Bolling hoped to peel away reformers put off by Burton's connection to Hays. But his main reason for running was negative: to block Burton. His wife wanted him to be majority leader. He wanted to be Speaker.

Wright had a bigger built-in constituency than Bolling or McFall. In addition to the nearly unified Texas delegation, he served with twenty-six members on Public Works and twenty-eight on Government Operations. Public Works crafted omnibus bills that dispensed pork to congressional districts all over the country. Wright was instrumental in delivering the goods to specific members. As deputy whip, he served with Brademas and McFall. He was also chairman of the Speakers Committee of the Democratic National Committee, which became important when he cultivated 1976 Democratic challengers.

But at the beginning of this extraordinary campaign, none of these formidable assets could rival Burton's. He was ahead because he was the only candidate who already had won two elections among House Democrats: DSG and caucus chairman, in which he carried 90 percent of the class of '74. Despite his wheeler-dealer reputation, no one questioned his effectiveness or honesty. After twelve years on the Hill, important people considered him the most powerful man in Congress. Even O'Neill conceded that he knew how to put coalitions together quickly. "When you have that ability," O'Neill recalled, "you really have talent. Not many people can do that."

Bolling wrote about how to change the House. Burton did it. More than any other Democrat, Burton was responsible for reforming the seniority system and spreading power, especially subcommittee chairmanships, to dozens of junior members. Moreover, California's twenty-nine Democrats represented 10 percent of all the House Democrats. Burton figured he could claim nearly twenty, virtually the same number Wright claimed from Texas. He assumed most of the rest would come over once McFall dropped out. Like Wright, he also served on large committees. Interior had twenty-eight members and Education and Labor twenty-six. They were not "power" committees like Public Works or Rules, but Burton had momentum. He derived some power simply because so many people assumed he would be the next majority leader.[12]

Burton also had a powerful base of southern support, men whom he dealt with for years, protecting cotton, tobacco, or peanut subsidies in exchange for their votes on liberal social welfare issues.

"There were dwindling votes for these subsidies," recalled Dawson Mathis of Georgia. "They were always in danger. We had to create alliances to keep them going. Phil Burton brought the most to the table. No one else had the imagination to see [deals] like that. I thought I'd have a better chance of being protected with a left-wing liberal like Phil who honored his word and was committed to me than with a southern moderate-conservative like Jim Wright who owed his election to northern liberals and who was not obligated to me."

To Charlie Rose, Burton was never explicit about tradeoffs. It was more subtle.

> We all knew that Phil was running for majority leader, and that helping him was part of what getting there was all about. I had no compunction about voting for his programs. We often laughed about it, and some of his more far-out labor proposals I simply couldn't vote for. But no one had ever given a more effective boost to the southern agricultural problem than Phil Burton. I felt very justified in telling my people back home that we have made a pact with these Californians. We were going to have to vote for some of their proposals, but in turn, they were going to help us, and he did.[13]

Unfortunately for Burton, for every Dawson Mathis and Charlie Rose, there was a Frank Thompson, Joe Waggonner, Frank Annunzio, Ike Skelton, or Leo Ryan who seethed at some gratuitous Burton insult or betrayal. Thompson's and Waggonner's opposition were well known. In Annunzio's case, Burton abruptly removed him from the Hansen Committee one day.

"I get the impression this is personal," said Annunzio. As a Sicilian and a machine pol from Chicago, he was not one to forget an insult.

"You got it, Frank," Burton replied.

"No, you don't understand," said Annunzio. "I get the impression that this is a personal insult to me."

"That's right," said Burton, who should have known better.

In another incident, when Democrat Ike Skelton, one of whose arms hung lifelessly from his shoulder, the result of a navy wound, walked onto the floor one day, an overeager lobbyist grabbed his sleeve. Skelton had just been elected, and the lobbyist likely did not know about his arm. But Skelton was enraged and went to the DSG with a proposal to prevent lobbyists from standing near the members when they entered. Because the proposed ban affected labor lobbyists more than others, Burton dismantled Skelton in front of his colleagues. As a Missourian, Skelton supported Bolling in any event, but after that performance, Skelton would never give Burton the time of day.

Finally, there was Leo Ryan, elected to Congress in 1972, after Burton helped design his district for him in San Mateo, just south of San Francisco. Ryan came out of the McAteer-Leo McCarthy faction of the party. Soon after his arrival in Washington, Ryan worked to get the House Banking and Currency Committee expanded by one. He wanted that committee and assumed the seat would be his. Instead, Burton maneuvered to give it to banker Pete Stark, elected the same year as Ryan. Ryan never forgave him.

People figured Burton was behind everything that happened. He was like Mayor Daley, said Mikva, who became Burton's campaign manager. He "gets credit for things he never went near and blamed for things he never touched."[14]

Shortly after Wright announced, Burton gave Jay Power, then the chief lobbyist for the Carpenters' union, a taste of what he wanted to do as majority leader. "When I beat Jim Wright, there will be a cornucopia of the greatest labor legislation this country has ever seen," Burton vowed. "I'm going to make Adam Clayton Powell seem like he was asleep at the switch." Power, a labor brat who had worked on Capitol Hill since he was a teenager (his father was a union president), could put up with all of Burton's vulgarities for that. Power believed Burton cared more deeply about workers than any politician he had ever met.

Even so, Power was not prepared for the scene Burton made one night that summer at the Monocle, a darkly shaded Capitol Hill restaurant, whose walls were lined with photos of politicians. Burton dined there often with staffers or other pols. The waiters were used to his behavior, which included ordering them around, taking off his shoes, and being loud and abusive. On this night, Burton had already consumed about seven vodkas and was eating rare steak with his fingers, when a tall Texan in a cowboy hat recognized Burton and ambled over to his table, only to regret it deeply. He was from Fort Worth, Jim Wright's district. Even though he was a Wright supporter, he just wanted to say he really respected Mr. Burton and hoped their contest would be "friendly."

Burton cast a withering look his way. "Why are you here?"

"I'm here for the farm bill," the man said. "We have some farm subsidies and Jim Wright has promised to help maintain them." This was the wrong thing to say.

"Fuck Jim Wright. Fuck the farm bill. I will single-handedly sink all this redneck Texas special interest SHIT," Burton screamed, rising to his feet. "I'll make sure there is no farm bill and that you are out of FUCKING BUSINESS!" At that, the man silently crept away. But unlike the incident with Tip O'Neill or other episodes in which a well-lubricated Burton had utterly lost control of himself, this time Burton's rage was purely tactical.

"Phil, why the hell did you do that to him?" Power asked after the man left. "Jay," Burton replied, "I don't even want Jim Wright to have a meeting with a favored constituent without feeling me breathing down his fucking neck."[15]

Wright, meanwhile, worried about Burton's advantage with the incoming class, on whose behalf Burton was sending money and campaigning extensively, just as he had in earlier years. It angered Wright that Burton's promise of DCCC money to challengers made it seem as if all the money that House Democrats raised Burton alone was responsible for. To counteract that advantage, Wright decided to imitate Burton's system of personally allocating funds to Democratic challengers. Wright sent Raupe, another aide named Marshall Lynam, and Texas state Senator Don Kennard to visit a friend in Texas named Arthur Temple. Temple was a multimillionaire and former chairman of Time, Inc. When they asked him for help, Temple wrote a check for $500.

"Arthur, that isn't exactly what we had in mind," they said. "Jim doesn't need money, but he has a lot of colleagues and young people running for open seats who do need money. So instead of giving $500 to him, how about $100 to each of them, and Jim will send it to them."

"That's an interesting idea," Temple said, "but I don't know any of those people." They might also be a bit too "liberal." But he agreed to take three names. "How about eight names?" said Lynam. Just then a friend of Temple's phoned. "Hey, listen, you got any political money?" Temple asked. "Okay, you got a pen? Write out a $500 check to Barbara Mikulski." Then back to the phone. "You don't need to know what it's for. Hell, I don't know whether she's liberal or not. All right, send it to me, not to her. Okay?"

"It's going to be kind of costly for my friends to call me for a while," he said with a grin. But it was so easy that Temple enjoyed doing it and asked five or six of his other friends to do the same thing. Pretty soon Jim Wright had bunches of checks to send out. He included a cover note explaining that some of his Texas friends wanted to help. Raupe and Lynam estimated that Wright raised $50,000 this way to spread around. He appeared in twenty-three districts for Democratic challengers, Burton in twenty, Bolling in ten. McFall limited his appearances to districts in California.[16]

Rostenkowski invited Wright to Chicago to meet with Mayor Daley. After breakfast, Daley turned to his man in Washington. "What do I do, Danny? Phil Burton really impressed me."

"Let's look at what Jim Wright has done for us on Public Works," Rostenkowski replied. "I'm for Jim Wright with both feet." Daley went along. At Rostenkowski's behest, the most powerful big-city mayor in America called other big-city mayors, urging them to support Wright and lean on their congressional delegations to vote for him. Daley called New York City Mayor Abe Beame and reminded him that Wright had rounded up the votes to prevent New York from going bankrupt. Wright had persuaded conservative Texans who did not want to appropriate money for the evil big city up north that nine cents out of every tax dollar came from New York City, money that was used for reclamation and flood control projects in Texas. Beame did not forget that, and Governor Hugh Carey, a former House colleague, leaned on others in the New York delegation.[17]

Burton, who had trouble delegating anything, firmly believed that the only way to campaign for a secret ballot election was member to member. Caucus aide Palumbo thought Burton needed to designate lieutenants, such as John Burton, Miller, Rose, or Mikva, to talk to members. Burton trusted no one else to do that. Consequently, no one else could deliver messages to Burton that people did not want to deliver to him face to face. His own brother felt excluded.

"He was so goddam brilliant he didn't need a brain trust to bring in ideas," said John Burton. "He needed a leveler. But he kept everything to himself. What hurt him was that the people who really cared did not feel like they were part of an operation. It was a one-man show."

One person whose support Burton needed was Mo Udall, his colleague on Interior, who spent the first half of 1976 running for president. Had Udall not been a presidential candidate, he likely would have run for majority leader, as he had once before. Udall took a bad fall while painting his house and was walking around with both arms in casts when Burton called. His opening gambit to Udall was characteristic of the man: "Mo," he began, "I've been sitting here wondering how you wipe your ass." A few minutes later he put down the phone and told Palumbo he had Udall's vote. And Burton didn't ask, "will you vote for me?" but "will you vote for me on every ballot?"

With Jimmy Carter's narrow victory came forty-eight new House Democrats. All but three Democrats from the class of '74 were re-elected. Together, the two classes equaled 122 members, 40 percent of all the House Democrats. But the new class was more conservative than the Watergate Babies. Many already held elective office, whereas Congress was the first office for many in the previous class. Moreover, the geographic spread was completely different. In 1974, Peabody and Oppenheimer calculated, California and New York together sent nineteen new members to Congress. In 1976, they sent three. The South sent 28 percent of the new class, compared to 12 percent in 1974. The shift South helped Jim Wright.[18]

A few days after the election, the *Washington Post* reported that McFall had accepted $4,000 from Korean lobbyist Tongsun Park, who passed out large sums of money to buy influence in Washington and who was being investigated by the Justice Department. McFall said he put the money in his office account and that accepting it was not illegal. Nevertheless, the revelation damaged him. He also resented the fact that Burton had escaped any damage, indeed, had made a point of returning an expensive gift that Park had left at his office.

As the freshmen began arriving for the December caucus meetings, the Burtons were there to greet them, as they had the class of '74. Sala Burton even helped find homes for new members and made their wives feel comfortable. But Bolling had made inroads with some members of the class of '74, who were disgusted by the Hays scandal and burned by Burton's friendship with Hays. They called new members saying, "Don't be taken in by Burton's solicitude, as we were." Dale Kildee, a new member from Michigan and a former state senator, told the *Post* he had been to Burton's home for dinner.

"Phil impressed me," he said. "We have a lot in common." But, he added, he took no money from anyone. "I've seen leadership races in my statehouse. We're a little less impressed by such things." Freshmen were not the only ones being romanced. Pat Schroeder never got so many phone calls as during those last weeks. When they called and asked how she was, she said, "Fine. About the same as I was at six o'clock yesterday when I last talked to you."[19]

On November 16, Burton became the only candidate to release his tax returns and finances, going back to 1971. His estimated income for 1976 was $47,200, of which $44,600 was his salary. He earned $2,500 in honoraria that year: $1,000 from USC, where he was named graduate of the year, $1,000 from the Rural Electric Cooperative, and $500 from the National Automatic Merchandising Association. This was more than he ever earned before. But what he told Art Agnos earlier that year was correct. If he died, Sala would have little. His records showed less than $3,800 in his assembly retirement fund, and about $37,000 in his federal retirement fund. Other assets included a savings account of $3,025, a checking account with less than $1,000, and a $150 State of Israel Bond. Half of his home, valued at $50,000, was paid off at $404 a month. His only other asset was a coin collection of annual mint editions, which he valued at $450. His only liabilities were "current household bills."[20]

The contest for majority leader captivated Washington as few others had. The competitors were so interesting, the rivalries so intense, the stakes so high. McFall would drop after the first ballot. Where would his votes go? Who would drop next? If Bolling were eliminated on the second round, would his votes go to fellow liberal Burton or to Wright? If Wright were eliminated on the second round, where would his votes go? Who did Burton believe was easier to beat, and would he throw votes to one to eliminate the other?

This was fast becoming Washington's favorite parlor game. Columnist David Broder called it the "second most important election of 1976," because the House, rather than the more individualistic Senate, would likely be "the arena of the major legislative-executive struggles of the next four years." He called Burton a man of "intellectual brilliance, an indefatigable worker whose maneuverings for power are a wonder to some and a fright to others."

Rostenkowski resumed meeting with Leo Diehl, O'Neill's emissary. They carefully selected people to call every afternoon. Rostenkowski gave lists of names to Diehl, and Diehl made the calls for Wright. A call from Diehl was as good as from the next Speaker himself. Diehl called nearly twenty people. Burton never knew about it, although he and Rostenkowski shared their vote counts, but not the actual names, with each other. In fact, even Wright was surprised fifteen years later to hear about Diehl's phone calls on his behalf.

Burton was also friendly with Diehl, a small man crippled by polio, who used crutches to move around. Every opportunity he got, Burton passed the message through Diehl to O'Neill that he would be a loyal majority leader and had no interest in usurping O'Neill's role as Speaker. The two men were too far apart to communicate directly. Even though both understood power, they spoke a different language. And no matter how many reassuring messages Burton sent, O'Neill was never reassured.

Four days before the vote, the Burton campaign received a jolt: a Herblock cartoon in the *Washington Post.* It showed a flashy-looking Burton standing by a sign saying, "Wheeler Dealer Phil Burton's Used Congressional Cars." He was trying to sell a car marked, "The Burton Leadership Deal," to a battered accident victim labeled "House Democrats." The victim had a huge throbbing bump on his head and was holding a severed steering wheel. Just outside the car lot was his old car, a battered, useless wreck labeled "The Wayne Hays." On the fender was a bumper sticker: "A Burton Special."

There were many theories in Washington about how that cartoon by the *Post*'s prize-winning cartoonist came to be. One had it that Brademas, a friend of Bradlee, planted the idea during a dinner party. In another version Bolling did it. But even allowing for the most likely explanation—that Herblock didn't need anyone's help—Burton, Mikva, and other allies considered it below the belt, especially devastating to impressionable freshmen who had just arrived and who took the *Washington Post* very seriously. A letter to the editor dispatched that day and signed by Joan Claybrook of Nader's Public Citizen, Carol Tucker Foreman of the Consumer Federation of America, Louise Dunlap of the Environmental Policy Center, and Marian Edey, chairwoman of the League of Conservation Voters, called the cartoon a smear.

"Herblock usually hits the mark," they wrote, "but he missed the boat on Phillip Burton. What he should have portrayed is a man who has fought the special interests in Congress, who has been the most influential leader in democratizing the House, who has repeatedly pressed his colleagues to vote for the public interest on tax reform, antitrust improvements, consumer and environmental protection. . . . To picture Burton as a Wayne Hays used car salesman is a smear tactic." Although Burton supported Hays in his 1974 chairmanship fight, he also "successfully pressed a very reluctant Hays, at the request of Common Cause and others, to act on campaign finance reform."

To control the damage, a "Dear Colleague" letter also went out the same day to every Democrat, signed by fourteen members, among them, Edwards, Kastenmeier, Eckhardt, Mikva, George Miller, Norman Mineta, Toby Moffett, a reform freshman from Connecticut, Richard Ottinger of New York,

Charlie Rose, John Seiberling of Ohio, and James Florio of New Jersey. Their letter said Burton's ability to "build broad coalitions for causes as diverse as farm programs and black lung benefits" caused some to refer to him as "wheeler-dealer." Such phrases, they said, connoted one who was engaged in personal gain, which was clearly not the case here.

> It is true that Phil has developed working relationships with colleagues of varying philosophical points of view. From such relationships came the Election Law Reform Bill. For it was Phil Burton, with his ability to work with disparate forces such as Wayne Hays, Common Cause and organized labor, that saved the new Federal Election Law. . . . Rather than "wheeling and dealing," this is the kind of coalition building that is one of the key ingredients in the legislative process. . . . As much as any other member, Phil Burton has helped bring about the sharing of power in the House.[21]

Wright got another lucky break and quickly capitalized. Nicholas Masters, a political scientist, Wright supporter, and senior staffer on the Budget Committee, happened to run into Bolling one day as the vote approached. To Masters's delight, Bolling was arrogant enough to tell Masters why he believed Wright could not win. Indeed, Bolling told Masters exactly what Wright's problems were and how his opponents were exploiting them. First was Wright's vote against the 1964 Civil Rights Act. Next, Wright had an oil and gas lobbyist working actively on his behalf, which allowed Burton and Bolling to charge that Wright would be in the industry's hip pocket. Third, he did not have the Texas delegation solidly behind him.

Masters quickly sought out Wright aide Marshall Lynam and repeated the conversation. The Wright staff moved immediately to fix the problems. To counteract the civil rights vote, Wright supporters phoned members to describe how Wright had refused to sign the "Southern Manifesto," which denounced the 1954 Supreme Court case declaring school segregation unconstitutional. Next, Wright circulated a letter of support signed by every member of the Texas delegation except Brooks and Eckhardt and put out word they would have supported him too had he declared his candidacy earlier. That was certainly true with Brooks, Wright's closest friend in the House—some said his only friend. But he had committed early to Burton, and Wright never would have considered asking him to switch. Finally, the Wright campaign moved the oil and gas lobbyist out of sight, defusing that issue.[22]

A few days before the vote, Michael Berman arrived from Los Angeles to help out and stayed with former Burton aide Joe Beeman, who was also lending a hand. Berman immediately spotted a major problem: there was no floor operation, no plan to lobby key legislators between ballots. Mikva and Toby Moffett pleaded for a whip operation on the day of the vote, but Burton refused. They wanted a system that would tell Burton supporters where to go for additional votes once Wright or Bolling was eliminated. Burton vetoed the idea. He believed he already had the votes. His colleagues told him so privately. Because he kept his word, he could not imagine fellow lawmakers not keeping their word on a matter of such personal urgency. Moreover, after the bruises he got for his association with Hays, he did not want to look like a bully. Bolling's aides, meanwhile, converted the House Republican cloakroom—no Republicans would be on the floor that day—into a boiler room operation. Wright was also well organized.

"Why am I here?" said Michael Berman, frustrated at being shut out of the process. "I hate this place." After a full day of waiting around, Burton finally gave Berman an accurate vote count. When Berman asked to be on the floor during the vote, Burton said only one staffer was allowed.

"Fine," said Berman. "This is what I know. I spent my life in Young Democrats."

"How can I do that to Palumbo?" said Burton.

"So let two staffers on the floor."

"No," replied Burton. "It looks bad." Berman and Beeman had to watch from the House Gallery.[23]

"Burton may be the more technically competent of the viables," concluded former Wright-staffer-turned-playright Larry L. King in the December 5 *Washington Star*, "and Bolling the more brilliant, but when Jimmy Carter is looking for a friendly face in what will soon prove to be a hostile crowd, it stands to reason he'd prefer one more nearly his own kind." This plug for Wright and southern brotherhood was quickly scooped off the news stands by Wright aides and delivered to the offices of every House Democrat. A special stamp said, "Inside: Larry L. King on the House Leadership Struggle." Members saw it first thing Monday, if they missed the Sunday paper.[24]

Wright talked often with President-Elect Carter, but the question of Carter's explicit support never came up. "He was prudent enough to know," Wright recalled, "that his opinion had not been requested." Nevertheless, some labor lobbyists firmly believed that the oil industry supported Carter because Big Oil thought Carter would not prevent huge price increases for domestic oil and gas. The price of gas had already shot up over a dollar because of the Arab oil embargo. The industry wanted to push it even higher and supported Wright, knowing Burton was distinctly unsympathetic. Any overt moves to meddle in an internal election would have been counterproductive, but many Democrats did not need to be told what Big Oil preferred.

His close ties to Hays continued to dog Burton, especially during that Sunday's "Meet the Press" news show with all four candidates. "Mr. Burton," said panelist Linda Ellerbee, "why should the Democrats elect a man who has a reputation as being a back-room wheeler-dealer, who doesn't get along very well with Tip O'Neill, but who got along very well with Wayne Hays?"

"I would like to think that my role has been one of marrying the diverse elements in the House," Burton replied, "reconciling the various points of view to a common solution. . . ." Moments later, Daniel Rapoport of *National Journal* came back to the topic:

"Congressman Burton, two years ago at this time some of your fellow House Democrats tried to depose Wayne Hays as Chairman of the House Administration Committee, feeling he had become too powerful. You helped him fight off that challenge. Now some of your opponents are using that against you. Do you regret your association with Hays?"

Burton said he worked hard to develop relationships throughout the House and worked "very closely with Wayne" on the federal election bill. "I think primarily because of my efforts in that respect we came out with election law legislation that was a great deal better than most reformers hoped for. . . . The events of the past six months were unknown to all of us—certainly to me—at the time the judgment was made on retaining him in his position."

David Broder: "Do you think it will hurt tomorrow?"

Burton: "I have seen no discernible impact on my candidacy. I think everybody stipulates I am well ahead. I agree with that conclusion. I believe I will win tomorrow."

Ellerbee asked Burton if it was possible his colleagues were lying to him about who they would vote for. "I like to think my relationships with my colleagues are noted for their candor and directness," Burton said. "I don't think my colleagues lie to any of us who are candidates. . . . I do believe I am ahead. I don't think there is any dispute about that."

Neil McNeil of *Newsweek* asked Bolling why Tip O'Neill and Jimmy Carter were not working for any of the candidates, particularly not for him. "You entered the race more than a year ago," McNeil said, "with the avowed purpose of blocking Mr. Burton who—it is no secret—you regard as not good news for the House leadership."

Bolling: "That is no secret. That is certainly true, but I haven't got anything to do with what Mr. O'Neill does or what the President-Elect does. That is their business, and I hope they will pursue it."[25]

After "Meet the Press," the candidates moved on to a luncheon with the freshman class that Wright had organized. Wright later said the lunch had an important impact on the vote. It was the only event where all the freshmen could see all the candidates at once. Wright made sure to invite his competitors and then was generous in introducing them. McFall and Bolling each gave short talks. Then it was Burton's turn. Only he had worked the crowd beforehand. Asked how he would get on with O'Neill, Burton said, "Tip is running for number one. I'm running for number two. I'd be a good and loyal majority leader." He suggested that the class should organize itself, as the class of '74 had done. This gave Wright the opening he was looking for. He introduced Carroll Hubbard of Kentucky, who succeeded Mineta as the class of '74 president. Hubbard stood up and said, "I'm for Jim Wright." It looked to Wright at least as though Burton's grip on the election was beginning to slip.[26]

On Monday morning, the candidates made their final preparations. Bolling met with his executive committee, gave each of them color-coded index cards of who to contact on the second ballot and handed out buttons with Bolling's name on them. Wright got surprise calls of support from members that he never expected. He too had campaign buttons. Burton went over his lists for the final time with Mikva, Rose, John Burton, Beeman, and Berman.

Some of Burton's votes "smelled" wrong. People who said they were for him did not seem the kind of people who logically would be. As they went over individual names, Mikva or Rose would say, "I can talk to him," but Burton usually snapped, "Leave him alone," and Rose and Mikva exchanged looks as if to say, "Which part of the United States has been traded off here?" The agenda for the caucus was decided days earlier. First, Rostenkowski, substituting for Burton, would conduct the election for a new caucus chairman. Then came Speaker and finally majority leader.

Burton and Rostenkowski continued to exchange vote tallies. Burton was counting on 117 votes on the first ballot. He needed 148 to win. Rostenkowski counted 111 for Burton, with 78 definites for Wright and 20 maybes. His strategy was simple: peel off as many McFall votes as possible, especially in California. As they walked onto the floor, Rosty turned to Burton.

"How we gonna do?" he said.

"I'm going to win this goddam thing. I'm going to haul your ashes."

"If it ain't us, I hope it's you," replied Rostenkowski. The two men shook hands. Members filtered onto the floor. Burton ran into Wright at the back rail.

"Well, Phil," he asked. "You got the horses in and the barn door locked."

"Yeah, Jim. I think so," said Burton. The two men also shook hands and wished each other luck. They were tough adversaries and they had fought hard. But they respected each other and neither had uttered a harsh word publicly against the other. There was no such camaraderie with Bolling, who was counting on 100 first ballot votes and who had circulated nasty rumors about Burton. Burton resigned as chairman and handed the gavel to Rostenkowski. In the election to succeed Burton, Foley easily defeated New Yorker Shirley Chisholm. O'Neill was unopposed for Speaker and was soon installed.

Now came the biggest single moment of Phillip Burton's political life. He had come so much further and had worked so much harder than his rivals, who lacked the burdens of his militantly liberal politics and often offensive personality. Peter Rodino of New Jersey, who presided over the widely watched Watergate impeachment hearings as chairman of the Judiciary Committee, nominated Bolling. They had arrived in the House on the same day twenty-eight years before. His seconders were Gillis Long, Bolling's colleague on the Rules Committee, Andrew Young of Georgia, the former aide to Martin Luther King, Jr., who did so much to legitimize Jimmy Carter to blacks and white liberals that year, and Tim Wirth, one of the influential leaders of the Watergate class. "When I was a new member last year," Wirth said, "Dick Bolling was for me teacher and leader and colleague. He knows the rules and knows how to help others understand them. He has been the point man on the tough issues."

Next was McFall. Colleague and friend B. F. Sisk nominated him. Seconders were Tom Steed of Oklahoma, his colleague on Appropriations, John Murtha of Pennsylvania, who called him "the most helpful person I have met in this House," and Harold "Bizz" Johnson, like Sisk a Burton opponent and Californian. Johnson was in line to chair Public Works if Wright were elected and could be counted on to vote for Wright if McFall were eliminated early.

Yvonne Brathwaite Burke nominated Burton. Jim Florio of New Jersey, Rose, and Mikva seconded the nomination. "Several years ago," Rose said, "the Carnation Milk Company built a great plant in the South and they hung a large sign out in front of it that said, 'Milk from contented cows.' One local farmer refused to sell his milk to that company. . . . He put a sign on the side of his milk cart that read, 'My cows are not contented; they are constantly striving to do better.' Phil Burton is not contented; he wants you and me to make this place do better."

"We have an agenda to make government work better," said Mikva. "That is why I think Phil Burton is the right candidate. . . . He is a doer. Phil looks for ways of getting the problem solved. Phil is a coalitionist. He puts people together. Sometimes odd couples, but that is the way this process works."

Jim Wright came last. The man nominating him was Charles Wilson of Texas, who said Phil Burton was his closest friend of all four candidates and the man to whom he personally owed the most. "So why Jim Wright? Jim Wright because of courage." Hoping one last time to defuse Wright's civil rights record, Wilson said: "He has voted for the Civil Rights Act of 1957, 1959, and 1960. He has consistently supported home rule for the District of Columbia. He has supported every anti-sex discrimination act in his tenure. He spoke from this very well for the Voting Rights Act of 1965, which was about as popular in Fort Worth as terminal cancer, and it was that voting rights act that gave Jimmy Carter his victory in Florida, South Carolina, Alabama, Mississippi, and certainly my state of Texas." In rounding up the votes for aid to New York City, Wright was also a southerner who could deliver for the North, said Wilson. Jim Howard of New Jersey—part of Rostenkowski's team of Wright backers, Allen Ertel of Pennsylvania, the freshman for whom Wright made twenty-three appearances in one day, and Rostenkowski himself seconded Wright's nomination.[27]

With the nominations complete, tellers for each candidate walked up to the well of the House to stand before the three wooden boxes where members deposited their paper ballots, according to the first letter of their last name. Burton had never been sure of Mineta. The San Jose legislator was on Wright's committee and stood to chair a transportation subcommittee if Wright moved up. Moreover, although new in the House, Mineta was spotted as a comer. He could not rise as fast if another Californian—Burton was only fifty—was ahead of him on the leadership chain. Mineta swore loyalty to Burton, indeed, signed the "Dear Colleague" letter complaining about the Herblock cartoon. But Burton did not trust him. "Watch Norm," he told Mikva. "Get behind him."

"That's crazy," said Mikva. "I can't see his ballot if he wants to hide it." But Mineta knew why Mikva suddenly appeared behind him in line. He took out his ballot, showed Mikva that it was marked "Burton" and said, "Tell Uncle Phil." O'Neill let McFall look over his shoulder while he wrote McFall's name down.

When the results of the first ballot were counted, Burton was comfortably ahead with 106 votes, to 81 for Bolling, 77 for Wright and 31 for McFall. But the total was troubling; those 106 votes were eleven fewer than Burton expected, five fewer than Rostenkowski's count showed. With McFall out of the running, it was down to the big three. Wright and Rostenkowski counted on winning the majority of McFall's votes to eliminate Bolling. Burton wanted a two-man final with Wright. As the remaining liberal, he figured he would get Bolling's liberal votes. O'Neill retreated to the far corner of the floor to cast his vote in secrecy. About then, Dawson Mathis came up to Burton.

"Should we throw some votes to Wright?" Mathis asked.

"Are you crazy?" Burton said. "If that gets around in this chamber, there will be so many people thinking I want them to vote for Wright that I won't be able to control it. No. We play straight football."

Then the second ballot results: Burton 107, Wright 95, Bolling 93. Bolling was eliminated by two votes. Dawson Mathis and Charlie Rose admitted many years later that they threw their own votes to Wright on the second ballot. At least two more Burton supporters did the same thing. Every Burton aide, including John Burton, denied that throwing any votes was part of the strategy. But Mathis and Rose were clever and discreet enough to have secretly worked it out in advance. Intentional or not, it worked. Bolling was gone. But Burton's total grew by only one vote. Up in the gallery Beeman and Berman looked at each other nervously.

"Uh oh," Beeman thought. "This isn't going well. Phil isn't getting the surge he should." Bolling and his supporters were shocked. They never expected to be eliminated. Some, including Bolling, believed Burton threw votes to Wright. The second ballot tally did not make sense otherwise. How could Burton gain only one vote from McFall's thirty-one votes unless he was being cute? And if he was playing games, didn't that just reinforce all their concerns about him? In their anger, some Bolling supporters may have switched to Wright just to pay Burton back.

The atmosphere was unbearably tense. Burton paced like a caged tiger. Bolling and other Burton enemies fanned out to persuade Bolling voters to switch to Wright. Bill Cable, a Thompson aide who was manning Bolling's boiler room operation in the Republican cloakroom, passed Burton on the floor and congratulated him. Most people now assumed he would win. Then Cable spotted Thompson and asked him which way he was going—Burton or Wright?

Thompson, who had never forgiven Burton for his role in the battle with

Hays, turned to Cable and glared. "Fuck Burton," he growled. "We're going to show him what it means to fight us. Shut up and watch."

Thompson headed directly to his New Jersey colleagues, where he personally switched three Burton votes to Wright. "This guy worked me over and I want to teach him a lesson," he told everyone he could find. "It's a Hobson's choice. Go my way." Thompson was not excited about Wright. But Wright had little to do with it. Frank Annunzio, waiting to get even for more than a year, walked up to Burton, waved his ballot in Burton's face and said, "See this? This is the vote that's going to kill you." Joe Waggonner, still angry over Burton's refusal to recognize him in the caucus eighteen months earlier, worked the southerners for Wright, especially the freshmen. Mineta sought out Moffett to show that he voted for Burton again. But some of Burton's close friends figured Mineta had switched to Wright on the pivotal third ballot. "He probably had another ballot marked "Wright" inside his coat," one said, still bitter years later.

The House floor was ringed with intense concentrations of normally friendly people arguing among themselves. Members sensed the historic importance of what they were deciding. This was not just routine House business. With such a stark choice between Burton and Wright, they were deciding the future direction of the Democratic Party in Congress and possibly beyond for years to come. The air was electric, politics at its highest pitch, equivalent perhaps to a full-scale floor fight at a national presidential convention with the nomination hinging on the outcome.

There were also some genuine shockers. Ben Palumbo stood next to Burton at the back rail when a member approached and showed him his ballot. "I want you to know," said Larry McDonald of Georgia, possibly the most conservative man in the entire House, "that I'm going to vote for you. You're the only one of the bunch who's ever been fair to me." Burton nodded and McDonald walked away. "If you ever say a word about this, I will kill you," Burton told Palumbo. (McDonald died in 1983 when the Soviets shot an off-course Korean airplane out of the sky over Sakalin Island, killing him and all other 268 passengers and crew.)

Mikva greeted Tip O'Neill, who stared at his Burton button. Tip looked around to make sure no one was listening. "You know," he said. "We've never used those buttons before. I'm not sure it's a good idea." One should respect the secret ballot enough not to pressure people into publicly displaying their preferences. The button was confrontational. If Burton won, O'Neill was suggesting, he should be careful not to override the minority.

As the balloting wound down, Rostenkowski saw Lud Ashley of Ohio heading to the well. Peering over Ashley's shoulder, Rostenkowski also saw that his ballot was marked Burton.

"What the hell are you doing?" Rostenkowski said, stopping Ashley.

"Is this important to you?" replied Ashley, surprised by the question. O'Neill and Burton were both liberals. Pledged to Bolling but now free, Ashley figured O'Neill wanted to work with a fellow liberal. Burton's office was also across the hall from his and they were friends. But Burton had made a rare slip, according to Ashley, had violated one of the cardinal rules of politics: if you want a vote, you've got to ask for it. Ashley maintained that Burton never had. When Rostenkowski explained that O'Neill wanted Wright, Ashley crossed Burton's name out and wrote in Wright's. He did it because Rostenkowski was standing there asking him for a personal favor. In the internal politics of the House, such requests were exceedingly hard to ignore. "Don't ever tell anyone," Ashley said. "Phil Burton would kill me."[28]

With Bolling out and even with only half of Bolling's votes, Mikva was still confident Burton had an easy win. Burton, however, was pacing the corridors, adrenaline surging, while Mikva kept an eye on the boxes. The count from the first box was announced.

"What is it? What is it?" Burton demanded, sweating profusely.

"Two votes, you're up by two votes."

"Is that all?"

"Yeah," said Mikva, "but at least you're up."

As Charlie Wilson finished counting the third box, Burton was up by five. Then Wilson heard somebody say Wright won the second box by five. They were dead even with one ballot left to count. "I reached out my hand like it was dead weight and turned up the last card," said Wilson. "It was Jim Wright."[29]

Most people were certain Burton had won. But then the rumble began from the well and rapidly moved to the back, growing louder with each row, swelling to a roar. Just one word. wright. Wright. WRIGHT. WRIGHT! People gasped. He had achieved the impossible, defeated Burton, 148 to 147. Their votes really had counted. More than fifty of Bolling's ninety-three supporters went to Wright. When he heard, Leo Ryan thrust his fist into the air in triumph. Then he saw that John Burton had spotted him and knew that a fellow Democrat from the Bay Area had just derailed his brother's career. Ben Palumbo was the man who had to tell Burton. He walked over and said, "Phil, I'm sorry. You lost."

"Don't feel sorry for me," said Burton. "Now we have to protect the guys who supported me." Hiding his crushing defeat from public view, Burton looked up at Sala in the gallery and nodded slightly.

Wright got the news a different way. "Two fellows came in the door holding up one finger with smiles on their faces," Wright recalled. "It dawned on others before it did me, I think, because I was suddenly surrounded by people reaching over, shaking hands, congratulating me. I was overwhelmed by a tide of emotion and then when the announcement was made, I was still in a state of euphoria." One of the first to congratulate him was Tip O'Neill.

"Come on down to the office," he said. "Let's have a drink." O'Neill had won two battles that day. He was elected Speaker and he got the team player he wanted. Mikva, who said he learned to curb his temper in high school, almost lost it when he heard Bolling say just a few minutes after the vote was announced, "Well, I lost the battle, but I won the war." Bolling later said he went home and had two drinks, one in condolence, the other in celebration.

Foley brought all three men to the podium to announce the vote officially. Before doing so, he said he would on his own authority order a recount. This was too important to have any question about. Foley wanted absolute certainty. Most of Burton's supporters agreed. Their careers were riding on that vote, too. But Burton refused. "If you don't announce it," he told Foley, "I'm going to take the microphone right now and concede." Foley thought it odd but felt he had no choice but comply. "You would think that for ten years he devoted most of his waking hours to that moment, and then he makes that decision," said Foley. "It was amazing to me he handled it with the grace he did."[30]

Wright embraced both men and offered thanks and congratulations to his competitors on a well-fought contest. Then Burton began to speak. "Jim," he said, "first of all, you have proven one thing to me. You count a lot better than I do. I want to thank those who helped me. I want to commend those who competed for this position and pledge my support to our new elected leadership, Tip O'Neill, Jim Wright and Tom Foley. We have a lot to do. If we work together as I know we will, we will get it done. Thank you very much."[31]

As people milled after the speeches, Burton stood talking with Mikva and another supporter when Rostenkowski approached and burst into tears. "I never dreamed we could do this. I never thought you'd lose," he said, overcome by the emotion of Wright's victory. Burton thought Rostenkowski secretly hoped Burton would win. Even if that happened, Wright would still be indebted to him and Chicago and better still would be the new Public Works chairman. But Rostenkowski later said Burton's analysis was wrong.

He never would have worked as hard for Wright, never would have turned Lud Ashley's vote around, he said, if he really wanted Burton to win.

Before he left the chamber, Burton took a phone call in the House cloakroom from Agar Jaicks in San Francisco, who called to express his disappointment and to try to boost Burton's spirits. Burton interrupted him. "My good friend," he said, "my good friend. Just relax. It's all over. Sala and I are going on vacation. It's okay. I'm not disheartened."

But he was. It was a devastating loss from which he never fully recovered. For the rest of his life he viewed his colleagues through a prism. Had they voted with him or against him? But he also never gave up trying to recover his base to challenge Jim Wright again.

Some Burton partisans later called the House leadership contest a turning point in postwar American politics, certainly a turning point for the Democratic Party. Never before had anyone of the left combined Burton's ideological commitment, love of combat, and operational ability to get things done. Had he become Tip O'Neill's majority leader, these partisans argued, the Democratic Party might have given President Jimmy Carter a legislative record to run on for re-election in 1980. Given the profound economic problems of that time, including double-digit inflation and interest rates, the Iran hostage crisis, and the failure of Carter's helicopter rescue mission in the Iranian desert, it is doubtful any legislative record could have saved Carter that year.

But failing that, with Burton as majority leader, congressional Democrats might not have given such easy approval to Ronald Reagan's 1981 package of tax cuts and spending cuts, might not so easily have approved the massive defense buildups of the 1980s, might not have tolerated the military adventures in Central America or the nearly wholesale purchase of so many Democratic members of Congress via corporate honoraria and campaign contributions.

At the "party" in the caucus offices that night, Mikva said Burton was in "deep trauma." Mercifully, the party ended early. While Burton talked with the Foleys, Mikva, and other supporters, caucus staffer Pat Kraus said she just kept moving from room to room to keep from breaking into sobs. They all felt they somehow had let him down. George Miller was almost in tears. Mikva fretted because he was convinced that the one person who abstained all day was Illinois colleague Paul Simon, who was dismayed by Burton's drinking. Mikva felt he should have made a stronger effort to turn Simon. He also believed Sid Yates of Illinois voted for Wright, and he had let Yates get away, too. The agony of a one-vote loss was so many "what ifs?" It was not just that Phil Burton had been so dramatically yanked off the leadership track. To Burton, it must have seemed that after a half dozen years of amazing legislative and procedural victories for him and for his brand of liberalism, the enemy had triumphed.

Burton was not so traumatized that he could not pull himself out of bed at six the next morning—an ungodly hour for him—for a breakfast meeting to choose California's representative on the Steering and Policy Committee. The contest was between Glenn Anderson and Henry Waxman. Burton knew Anderson voted against him. He made sure that Waxman got the slot. That was an easy payback, a first step on the long march to revenge. But Burton was also protecting "my people" from whatever retribution might be in store.[32]

Over the next few days the newspapers were full of postmortems, more over how Burton lost than how Wright won. The contest turned into an "anyone-but-Burton" race, concluded the *Post*. "In the final analysis," Mary Russell wrote, "Burton was seen as too driven, too ambitious, too manipulative, too contentious—despite the fact that his liberal credentials are impeccable, he had support from some in labor and environmentalists, and his reputation as a 'reformer' is good." One top Democrat said, "Look, we've been through the war, we've been through Watergate, we've been through fighting with two presidents. We're tired of confrontation. The thought of infighting between O'Neill and Burton and divisiveness among House Democrats now was just too much."[33]

As the caucus met over the next few days, O'Neill and Wright got virtually everything they wanted. The caucus voted down another attempt to make the whip's job elective. Some said if that proposal had won, Burton would have got the job, and Burton supporters took to wearing buttons that said, "147," to signify the number of votes he got. Instead, O'Neill and Wright appointed John Brademas as whip to succeed John McFall. The new deputy whip was Rostenkowski. Only forty-eight, Rostenkowski had backed the right horse and as a reward had earned his way back into the leadership. To underscore the finality of Burton's defeat, the curtain came down on most House reform efforts. Burton argued to permit the caucus to elect Ways and Means subcommittee chairman. He said the change was "imperative" to make them "more responsive." It lost 98 to 22. Many felt "democratization" had gone far enough.

San Francisco Chronicle correspondent John Fogarty interviewed Burton a few days after the vote. Burton told him he did not want to run for chairman of the Budget Committee, as some suggested, because, "I have never needed a platform in the past, and I don't need one now." With defeat of the latest batch of reforms, Burton added, "I was not the candidate of the establishment here, and I think many liberals—including those who did not support me—are a little sick right now." Burton conceded that his own intensity frightened people, but "that's the way I am. When I feel strongly about something, I work hard to get things done about it." Burton appeared to take solace from how close he had come. "If you had predicted two years ago that I'd be the Majority Leader, someone would have taken you off to an institution. But I came within one vote, and I did it without waiting around to become the consensus candidate who spent years in one appointed House post after another, waiting for my turn to lead."[34]

Any analysis of why Burton lost has to start with California, which, unlike the large eastern and midwestern delegations or Texas, was rarely unified about anything. California was just too diverse, had too many competing interests to expect unanimity, and the absence of strong political parties usually meant candidates ran for office and were elected on their own. Once in Washington, they owed little to anyone other than their own constituents. There was no one to crack the whip, no formal party organization, unlike in Illinois, Texas, New York, or other states, where politicians had incentives to act in concert and consequences if they didn't. Phil Burton came closer than anyone to cracking the whip, but did so only by moral suasion and force of personality.

For that he paid dearly. Burton lost between ten and as many as fourteen California votes out of twenty-nine on the final ballot. How people voted that day is still such a tightly held secret that, nearly two decades later, people could only guess how others voted. Mineta, who is widely thought to have voted for Wright on the critical third ballot, grew visibly agitated in a 1991 interview when he saw that Burton listed him as "undecided" on Burton's own postelection vote tally. Again, he denied emphatically ever voting for Wright.

Some of the people who knew Burton best lied to him most convincingly. It was no secret that McFall, Johnson, and Sisk voted against him on every ballot. Nor that Jim Corman, with whom Burton had a bitter rivalry, would also choose Wright. Leo Ryan was another anti-Burton vote. "Was it [losing the slot on] Banking and Currency that did it?" an aide asked Ryan. "No. Just put it down to the fact that I don't like the way he operates," Ryan replied. "If Burton were elected Speaker, he'd be ruthless, and I don't want to be a member of a House that works like that." A top House staffer said

Ed Roybal, Charlie Wilson, and Robert Leggett were all ready to vote for Burton provided he apologize to them for one slight or another he had committed over the years. When this news was communicated to Burton before the vote, the staffer said, Burton said he would take care of it. Instead, they said John Burton called and apologized for him. That just made them angrier.[35]

Glenn Anderson also resented Burton. Over dinner with Burton in San Francisco not long before the vote, prominent San Francisco fund-raiser Mo Bernstein, who had been close to Anderson for years, said he would call Anderson and nail down his vote if Burton wanted. But Bernstein said Burton was so confident he declined the offer. If all four—Roybal, Wilson, Leggett and Anderson—voted for Wright, that made nine votes against, ten counting Mineta.

A few Burton supporters believed freshman Tony Beilenson of Beverly Hills, no friend of Waxman or Berman, voted for Wright. Subsequent behavior gave them more grist for their suspicions. Beilenson approached Bolling and O'Neill directly and won a coveted spot on the Rules Committee after the 1980 elections, and Burton "rearranged" Beilenson's district following the 1980 census. Like Mineta, Beilenson vehemently denied voting for anyone but Burton on all ballots. He liked and respected Bolling, he said, and "told him flat out who I voted for." When Bolling chose him for the Rules Committee, Beilenson said, he did so because he wanted "thoughtful people" on it.[36]

Burton himself put Gus Hawkins on his list as having voted for Wright. Eleven. Various sources mentioned two more possibilities—Jim Lloyd and John Moss, but there is no evidence. If all of these members voted for Wright, that would have amounted to thirteen votes, fourteen if Beilenson is counted, half the California delegation. But in a one-vote loss, only one was necessary. "I've thought a hundred times since then, how would you correct the problem in the delegation," said George Miller. "I'm not sure you could have, but it was serious. Those closest to Phil Burton sometimes took the brunt of the force. He saved them. They resented it. That's where the heat was most intense."

There were similar "what if" stories in other states. Wayne Hays resigned from Congress on September 1. Democrat Douglas Applegate took his place. Hays would have voted for Burton. Applegate voted for Wright. He was put on Public Works. In Utah, Allen Howe was one of only three Watergate Babies to lose his seat. A friend since their days in the Young Democrats in the 1950s, Howe likely would have voted for Burton. But he was caught soliciting a prostitute in Salt Lake City who turned out to be a police decoy. In Louisiana, Burton supporter and conservative power Otto Passman was indicted for extorting lucrative foreign aid and shipping contracts from foreign governments. He was eventually acquitted, but he was beaten in the 1976 primary by Democrat Jerry Huckaby, who won the seat and voted for Wright. In West Virginia, Nick Joe Rahall defeated incumbent Ken Hechler, a likely Burton supporter, given their work together on black lung. Burton assured Jim Abourezk of South Dakota that he had Rahall's vote. But Abourezk, whose parents came from the same Lebanese village as Rahall's parents, doubted that. Wright campaigned for Rahall. Abourezk told Burton he could get Rahall's vote easily. Burton said that would not be necessary.

Despite the agonizing and endless "what if" mind games, Burton was correct in what he told reporter Fogarty. In many ways the shock was not that Burton was defeated. It was that a man who was so threatening—to corporate interests, to the House establishment, to fellow liberals, not to mention moderates and conservatives, to all the people he had offended or insulted over the years—could come within one vote of being elected majority leader. He made it that far in spite of everyone, especially in spite of fellow liberals. The only appointment he ever got was to the Hansen Committee.

Viewed that way, it was astonishing Burton came so close. Patrick Tobin, the ILWU's Washington representative, believed Burton was "so good at what he did that he overestimated how good Congress was. He lost sight of the fact that Congress was largely run by corporations, not by the people, and he got caught up in thinking how much could really be accomplished."[37]

"Burton is dead," an anonymous House staffer told the *Washington Post* a few days into the new year. "But I'm not putting any money on it."

15

COMBACKS AND TALL TREES

It is a rare thing to have a productive life in the House after a defeat.
You become a walking dead man, a pariah with colleagues
who have rejected you. It's different than voters rejecting you.
These are the people who know you best.

DAVID BRODER
Washington Post *columnist*

No one ever took a loss as beautifully as he did. Another fellow would have
been disappointed. Or a fellow of his nature, you would have thought he
would have been disdainful and bitter, but he wasn't. He grew strong after
that. He became a real factor. . . . He brought us ideas that were brilliant.
All the environmental stuff.

FORMER HOUSE SPEAKER TIP O'NEILL

FOR THE REST OF HIS LIFE, Phillip Burton was haunted by his one-vote loss. Gone not only were the perks of power—the extra staff, large offices, and reporters clamoring for interviews—but more importantly, the sense of upward movement. From the moment he decided not to run for the U.S. Senate in 1969, and probably even before that, Burton set his sights on becoming Speaker. He created the wave and then rode it. But in an instant it had crashed over him. Half of his power was simply the notion—or the fear—that this already tremendously powerful man was going to have a great deal more power. Once that was gone, Burton had to find other ways to satisfy his need to accomplish, to outsmart the establishment. Slowly, one step at a time, he set about to reassemble his political base for another run at power.

But fearing precisely that, the House leadership was hostile to Burton. Of the five men in the leadership—Tip O'Neill, Jim Wright, John Brademas,

Dan Rostenkowski, and Tom Foley—only Foley was his friend. The rest were determined he should not rise again. "They kept seeing him behind every stone," said Foley aide George Kundanis, whose first day on the job was the day of the vote. "Wright fully expected Burton to run against him two years later. There were two visions of reality. Foley knew his good friend Phil Burton was trying to recover. The other side thought Mephistopheles was loose, full power, full cylinders, still omniscient."[1]

Shortly after his defeat, Burton sent a letter to all House Democrats urging unity and pledging to work hard with President Carter and the new leadership. On December 30, Speaker O'Neill replied, adding in his own hand at the bottom: "Phil, many thanks, my door is open, I am looking for your support and advice at all times." O'Neill then gave Burton a minor plum: chairmanship of the House delegation to the North Atlantic Assembly, NATO's parliamentary body, succeeding Wayne Hays. Clement Zablocki of Wisconsin, new chairman of the International Relations Committee, was furious and told O'Neill he would resign unless he took over the delegation. O'Neill held firm. "Phil's been on that committee for six years," O'Neill said. "Zablocki's been on it for three months."

While this hardly constituted political rehabilitation, it was a gracious gesture on O'Neill's part. Burton took the European meetings seriously, even if he used his off-hours to carouse. Most colleagues saw it as just another junket. The House sent up to eighteen members each year, twelve chosen by the Speaker. Burton selected the rest, as well as those who would serve on the NATO body's various economic, scientific, political, and defense committees.[2]

Burton spent several weeks recuperating from his loss, part of that time in Hawaii with Sala. When he returned to Washington in January 1977 for the start of the Ninety-fifth Congress, some who knew him well saw a changed man, a man for whom life in the House would never be the same. He did not talk about his defeat, but knowing he was in line to chair a subcommittee on national parks, he quickly plunged into an almost entirely new arena: the environment.

At fifty, he was still young. He could give up and fade away, nursing his bitterness in alcohol, as others had done. But Phillip Burton was unable to relax or slow down. If anything, the defeat intensified an already burning rage. He had come so tantalizingly close, only to have the prize yanked away at the last moment. The outsider hurling grenades was at the gate, on the verge of storming through, when another, heavier, barrier descended, shutting him off. Now he had to change direction fast, turn his prodigious energy elsewhere. As Charlie Rose said later, "If Phil Burton got out in the street, he would organize a parade just to have something to do. That was basic instinct. The fact that it did not have an immediate objective was sort of irrelevant."

These two assignments in January 1977—chairmanship of the North Atlantic Assembly and of the National Parks and Insular Affairs subcommittee—were not much of a base from which to launch a comeback, especially for one with Phil Burton's reputation and list of enemies. But that is precisely what he had in mind. Beginning the long process of political rehabilitation, he set out to prove to his peers that they had made a mistake. He was not just a wheeler-dealer, not just somebody interested in power for its own sake. With what little power he could muster in a subject about which he knew little, he would show his colleagues that he could pass important, substantive legislation, which, not incidentally, would also help them in their districts. He would accumulate a record he could match against anybody, including Jim Wright and Tip O'Neill.

"It burned in his soul that he lost by one vote," Udall later recalled. "After the announcement that day, he began to see who did it. Then he decided he was going to go somewhere. The vehicle he chose was parks."[3]

Between Burton's seniority on Interior and his friendship with Udall, a new route to power began to emerge: he could easily step into a leadership role in an environmental movement he saw as politically inept but potentially powerful. With a Democrat in the White House, a window was opening on conservation matters, affording Burton the opportunity to grab everything he could. Jim Wright's ascension to majority leader opened up the chairmanship of the Public Works and Transportation Committee. Interior and Insular Affairs was also open. James Haley of Florida, who succeeded Wayne Aspinall, was, if anything, to Aspinall's right. But he was a weak chairman and chose to retire.

The ranking Democrat on both committees was Californian Bizz Johnson. The choice of which committee to head was his. The seniority system was still very much alive; the caucus changes had simply introduced an important mechanism by which members could vote to remove chairmen who were autocratic, inept, or out of touch. If Johnson, who was none of those, chose Public Works, the far more liberal Udall would get Interior. After Udall, Burton was next in seniority.

Burton and Udall cooked up a plan to secure the chairmanship for Udall. If Johnson wanted Interior, they would not fight him in the caucus for it, they told him. They would, however, fight him constantly on policy once he was chairman. Had they threatened to run against him, on the other hand, Johnson might have got his back up and taken the committee. But Johnson was more interested in building dams than fighting environmentalists on his own committee. The next day, Johnson called Udall. "I've decided I'm taking Public Works," he said. "Congratulations, Mr. Chairman." Burton never again had to worry about the chairman of Interior being hostile to him.[4]

Udall and Burton then divvied up the subcommittees. Udall took over Energy and the Environment and created a special new subcommittee on Alaska Lands, to which he named John Seiberling as chairman. The mission: pass the largest land preservation bill in American history—a hundred million acres in the huge Alaskan wilderness. Burton took over National Parks, succeeding a courtly North Carolinian named Roy Taylor. He already chaired Trusts and Territories, with jurisdiction over such offshore possessions as Micronesia, Guam, Puerto Rico, the Virgin Islands, and American Samoa, nearly two thousand islands and nearly four million people. In what some called an "annexation," Burton combined the two subcommittees and became chairman of the Subcommittee on National Parks and Insular Affairs. The national parks would never be the same.

Counting his own vote, Burton always had four reliable votes on the trusts subcommittee—the delegates from Guam, the Virgin Islands, and Puerto Rico (his legislation to give American Samoa a non-floor-voting delegate came a few years later). Burton thus started out on any issue with one-sixth of the votes he needed to pass anything. On the new subcommittee, those votes became leverage to effect parks legislation. Burton was also emotionally attached to the territories, having fought to bring them health, education, and welfare benefits far beyond what anyone in Congress had ever done. If Burton couldn't run the United States, he told subcommittee aide Jeff Farrow, at least he could run the territories, which had their own military and social policies. If he could not be on Ways and Means, he could still determine taxes, health, welfare, and other policies in these faraway regions.

Burton took the welfare of these islands as seriously as any of his other issues. His authority to help mold social policy and deliver government aid gave him opportunities to promote the same welfare and benefit packages he had engineered for residents of California, for miners in Appalachia and other coal mining areas, and for the aged, blind, and disabled throughout the country. He took his responsibilities so seriously that he routinely called people at home on weekends to make sure the latest welfare bill included the offshore islands.

Gaylord Nelson of Wisconsin, who was on the Senate Finance Committee, got so tired of listening to Burton's tirades that he made up stories to get off the phone. On one Saturday morning, Burton phoned just as Nelson put some eggs on to boil. When the eggs were done, Nelson put down the phone, walked from his study into the kitchen, retrieved them, ran them under cold water, shelled them, and walked back into the study. When he picked up the phone a few minutes later, Burton was still talking.

Burton was the key player in getting a historic Northern Mariana Islands Covenant through the Congress. The people of the Marianas, first colonized by the Spanish, then by the Germans, were later occupied by the Japanese. In bloody World War II battles, the U.S. took back most of these islands, including the Marshalls and Micronesia, and administered them as UN Trust Territories. It was from Tinian in the Northern Marianas that U.S. bombers left for Nagasaki and Hiroshima with their deadly payloads of atom bombs. After the war, the people of the Northern Marianas said they wanted to become a self-governing U.S. Commonwealth. Reaching that point, however, involved years of diplomatic talks with Dr. Haydn Williams, president of the Asia Foundation, whom President Ford named as his negotiator.

Working closely with Williams, Burton rammed approval of this covenant—the most advanced the U.S. has with any island state—through the House in three days. In the Senate, it took more than a year. Burton made sure the covenant extended Supplemental Security Income benefits to all citizens. In nearby islands, where the U.S. had conducted extensive nuclear testing, Burton's legislation ensured that the inhabitants got the best care possible, including free lifelong medical care for radiation victims, and hospitals for the Northern Marshalls and Bikini atoll.

When he discovered that the CIA had spied on the representatives from the Trust Territories during the negotiations, Burton sent a blistering letter to CIA Director George Bush. "I can only say that my concern exceeded even my shock and disbelief," Burton wrote Bush on January 3, 1977. "Certainly it must have been understood by the CIA that the United States Government was not negotiating with a foreign country. . . . The [U.S.] is responsible to the United Nations for the performance of its responsibility. . . . We were, therefore, negotiating with a people to whom we have had a particular and unique responsibility and obligation. . . . I am forced to express my outrage."[5]

Burton's first task was to acquaint himself with his new subcommittee's staff and jurisdiction. After years of focusing intensely on House reform, national issues, and his own upward climb to leadership, parks were about the furthest thing from his mind. But in January 1977, Burton found himself the ranking member on Interior and chairman of a backwater subcommittee that had been run in desultory, if gentlemanly, manner by Roy Taylor. Taylor's top aide was a fellow North Carolinian named Cleve Pinnix, a former park ranger until the National Park Service tapped him for a management program and sent him to Washington in 1974. Pinnix landed on Taylor's subcommittee, where he saw little of Burton, who was devoting most of his time to the majority leader race.

Like most people on Capitol Hill, Pinnix assumed Burton would win. Instead, Burton became his boss. In mid-January, Burton told Pinnix that Sierra Club President Ed Wayburn liked him. Burton wanted Pinnix to stay on for a while. In the meantime, Burton wanted to know the subcommittee's history. What had it done? What should it do? What had been a waste of time? Pinnix, who saw no visible sign that Burton was affected by his loss to Jim Wright a month earlier, found the questions intriguing. Maybe Burton could inject some life and energy.

Burton also said he was frustrated over Redwood National Park, whose creation he had opposed in 1968. Congress did "a really stupid thing" by passing that bill, he told Pinnix. Aspinall had kept the park so small that it wasn't protecting redwoods. Burton was no expert, but he was going to fix that and expand the park if it took whatever political capital he had left. Moreover, he would give the subcommittee an activist agenda. Pinnix's hopes rose with every conversation. "We'll pull the environmental community into the late twentieth century," Burton said. "We'll do things no one has ever thought possible." Already the political wheels were turning. Parks were good. People liked them. He could deliver more. Members would owe him. That would give him power.

Expanding the Redwoods National Park would not be easy, however. This was not even remotely similar to establishing Golden Gate National Recreation Area five years earlier. It was not a "motherhood" issue on which everyone was in agreement, for there were enormous political forces stacked against Burton. After creating the most expensive national park in American history nine years earlier, Congress was not even likely to revisit the issue. By 1977, costs had climbed to nearly $200 million. Worse, labor objected to expansion. Thousands of logging jobs were at risk if the lumber mills closed. For Burton to take on this issue meant directly challenging his most important constituency. Organized labor often joined with business to protect jobs and economic growth. The timber industry opposed losing thousands more acres of highly profitable, redwood-rich groves, as did Republican Don Clausen, who represented the area in Congress.

Regardless of the political difficulties, however, massive timber industry clear-cutting immediately above Redwood Creek was destroying the park. Like Burton, environmentalists were unhappy with the 1968 legislation, but unlike him they believed it was the best they could get. Because of Aspinall's maneuvers that year, the world's tallest trees were protected only in a narrow, twelve-mile strip along Redwood Creek known as the "worm." But clear-cutting along the ridge tops, just a quarter-mile above Redwood Creek and in one of the most geologically unstable watersheds in the world, created huge problems of erosion, timber slash (massive debris from trimmed tree limbs), and destruction of scenery. After felling the trees, the timber companies used large tractors to haul the logs down to roads. The tractors stripped the hills bare of all vegetation and ground cover. In an area with 80 to 100 inches of rain a year, the runoff rushed down the denuded hillsides, creating enormous landslides and filling the streambeds, which rose by twelve feet. Burton had introduced a park expansion bill every year since 1970. But neither Aspinall nor Haley would ever schedule a hearing, and despite Burton's clout in the caucus, he did not have the seniority to go around them.[6]

A National Park Service study concluded in 1971 that "without a buffer zone comprising about 10,000 acres" and more benign logging methods, old-growth redwoods within the park were threatened. The report was made public years later, only because a conservation group forced its release under the Freedom of Information Act. With continued bulldozer logging, clear-cutting, and road construction, the report warned, "there is nothing to prevent the tributaries in the Park from becoming the nightmarish tangle of debris and downed trees as were observed along some of the tributaries above the park."[7]

The Sierra Club, meanwhile, sued the secretary of interior in federal court for abuse of responsibility. In 1975, Federal Court Judge William Sweigert ruled that Interior and the National Park Service failed to protect the park from harm. The world's tallest trees—the tallest was 367 feet—could be wiped out by the next big storm. But there was nothing else Sweigert could do. Redwood National Park was failing. It was up to Congress to save it. In 1976, Cleve Pinnix got letters from the secretary of interior on down calling the situation "desperate." A Government Operations subcommittee sharply criticized Interior's handling of the situation. Campaigning in California in October 1976, Jimmy Carter said that if he became president, he would push to expand park boundaries.

Recognizing the urgency, Burton took matters into his own hands. At the very first meeting of his subcommittee, Burton declared that no legislation would move until a redwoods expansion bill was approved. On a flight home to San Francisco soon thereafter, an environmental lobbyist saw Burton spreading large topographical maps all around his seating area. "Phil," the man said. "I didn't know you knew anything about the environment."

"I don't," he said. "But when I get done, I'll know more than anyone."

Burton personalized the issue. Anyone who had a problem with his bill had a problem with him. He educated himself, learning not just the background and history of the park, but the economics of the timber industry. He developed his own data on the holdings of the three main timber companies in the area: Arcata, Louisiana Pacific, and Simpson. He learned how many workers each company employed, how many acres were under cultivation, where the watersheds were, and which companies were taking extra precautions to cut around the stream areas. He learned which companies used old-growth redwood as a cash cow to finance the rest of their conglomerate, thus cutting as fast as possible, and which logged at a more responsible rate that maintained jobs yet sustained the forests. When timber executives appeared before the subcommittee, he knew more about their land holdings than they did.

Burton was also armed with a detailed study on redwood harvesting from the Congressional Research Service, which concluded that the redwoods—like oil reserves—were a "non-renewable resource." The study said the original redwood habitat of 10 million acres—450 miles long by about 35 miles wide—contained 1.5 million acres of redwood forests. Their location was determined by the atmospheric moisture contained in the Coastal Zone. Whenever mountains or climactic conditions cut off the ocean fog, redwoods disappeared. This study said one tree alone, 1,800 years old, yielded 480,000 board feet of lumber. Their value as lumber was their unique resistance to rot and decay—but that was only true for trees more than 100 years old. Current plans all called for 50-year rotations. "There is little doubt," the study said, "that the current rates of harvesting, if unchanged, will substantially liquidate most of the current operable old growth stands of redwood by the year 2000." After that, it would take "rotations based on two or three centuries to regrow trees that have the qualities of those we have mined."

Because the environment that sustained redwoods was shrinking and because they were being cut at a rate and in a manner "that far exceeds the opportunity to replace them in kind," the study concluded that "redwoods are an endangered species." The unmistakable political implication was that jobs would be lost whether or not the park expanded. Indeed, an attractive, decent-sized park that could attract tourists might do more for the local economy than an industry that, while profitable in the short run, would soon disappear. A *Los Angeles Times* article quoting forestry professors and a Forest Service study predicted that the California North Coast would experience "precipitous declines" in timber production over the next ten years, regardless of expansion, and could drop by two-thirds by 1985. Such a decline would have "calamitous results" in an area where the unemployment rate was already 14 percent.

Burton invited National Park Service and Interior officials, including Dick Curry, NPS's associate director of legislation, to help draft the legislation. Burton's first draft called for a 74,000-acre expansion. But working closely with the Carter administration, he eventually agreed on 48,000 acres. There were twenty early drafts of the bill, which Burton tracked by marking a small dot on page two of each version. He restricted distribution. One night, just to see what might happen, Curry wrote #19 on a draft that was supposed to be #18 and shipped it over. When he got to Burton's office, Burton was in a fury.

"Goddam it," he bellowed. "Where the fuck is number 18?" It took Curry a half hour to assure Burton he was just kidding.[8]

While they wrote the bill, the trees continued to fall. In March, Interior Secretary Cecil Andrus and Burton called on the three timber companies to observe a six-month moratorium on clear-cutting. The companies refused, citing the "economic disruption" such a move would cause. "One moratorium would simply lead to another," Louisiana Pacific President Harry Merlo wrote Burton. "It is premature to talk about expanding the present park when some of the companies have still not been fully compensated for the original park created in 1968." In other words, bug off. They would continue to clear-cut immediately adjacent to the park.

Burton called their refusal "unconscionable" and said his subcommittee "will accelerate its timetable" on expansion. "We are looking into all possible actions—including legal action," an angry Andrus said. Udall agreed. "The tone and temper of their response indicates a narrow and selfish view of the national interest," Udall said. Park supporters were thrilled. Intransigence in the face of such obvious environmental damage would create a backlash.[9]

After hearings in March in Washington, Burton scheduled a field hearing in Eureka, California, the following month. This hearing, he knew, would be explosive. Timber companies, loggers, unions, and businesses were already aroused. The mills closed that day so that "everyone" could attend. Local stores delayed opening until eleven to encourage protests. Flying in from Washington, Burton stopped at San Francisco International Airport to change planes for Eureka. He was met there by twenty-seven-year-old John Amodio, who had dropped out of nearby Humboldt State University to direct a small nonprofit group called the North Coast Environmental Center. Amodio first learned about the park problems from a forestry professor and now worked full-time for the Sierra Club. Wayburn introduced Burton to Amodio, who called him Mr. Burton.

"Goddam it, kid, call me Phil," Burton said. Amodio was so intimidated he stammered in reply, "Okay, Mr. Phil."

Because the flight north was delayed, the young lobbyist found himself with a rare opportunity to brief Burton for two hours, while Burton ordered double scotches at the bar. Amodio said the three timber companies were not only destroying the park but falsely scapegoating environmentalists for all the problems their clear-cutting created. Burton probed him carefully about the impact of park expansion on the local economy. When their plane touched down in Eureka, television reporters besieged Burton for comment. Amodio was amazed that Burton had retained and synthesized every piece of information Amodio had given him.

Yes, they would expand the park, Burton said. It was "imperative" because of the mismanagement and callous practices of the timber companies. They, not the environmentalists, were responsible for the economic conditions there. Timber and union officials said expansion would endanger 4,800 jobs. Burton said "at most," 2,800 workers would have "varying degrees of difficulty," but it was "excessive" even to say 800 jobs would be lost. He promised to include a major provision to help train displaced workers.

The next day Burton, Clausen, and Keith Sebelius of Kansas, the ranking Republican on the subcommittee, toured the groves and flew over the park in an army helicopter. Clausen, who argued the timber industry's case, directed the pilot to fly over land where logging had devastated the landscape twenty years earlier, to show how it was coming back. This had no effect on Burton, who said he had made up his mind "a decade ago." The recently logged areas looked "like a moonscape," he said. At a press conference, Burton said, "God knows, the lumber companies did very well in 1968, and God knows, they will do very well this time." Because working people would bear the brunt of the "decision we make," he again promised to guarantee federal help. "I do want to pinpoint some income protection."

Thousands of people jammed the front of the Humboldt County courthouse the next morning—before the hearing—to hear from Clausen, the mayor, and other local officials who opposed expansion. After the rally, they marched ten blocks to the hearing at the Eureka Municipal Auditorium chanting, "We Hate Burton" and carrying placards saying, "Keep Burton in San Francisco" and "Ship Burton and [Jerry] Brown to Japan with the Next Load of Chips." Park opponents with bullhorns exhorted the crowd to be rowdy and "let the SOBs know" they would not accept expansion. One labor leader shouted, "It's time these environmental radicals are stopped, and here is where we begin." Some 300 logging trucks followed the marchers blowing their horns.

The hearing was so tumultuous that at times it bordered on an open riot. Jammed to twice its capacity of 2,300 people, the auditorium was an old movie palace with large balconies. The three congressmen were to sit on stage. Burton, suffering from painful hemorrhoids, carried a pillow. When he walked on stage, a loud chorus of boos greeted him and lasted for several minutes.

"You're not so tough," he told a group of loggers lining the sides of the auditorium. "I've got longshoremen in my district who are much tougher than you are." Cleve Pinnix, however, was so worried about what might happen that he had already spent hours with Eureka police discussing escape routes and exits and what to do if the crowd stormed the stage.

Burton advised Clausen to oppose expansion, "because that's where your people are," but then added a dose of reality. "I'm going to beat you on this," he said, "but you and I will work to make the best possible arrangement for them." Pinnix interpreted Burton's remarks to mean, "Let me be the son of a bitch, and let them get it out of their system." But it angered Pinnix that Clausen continued to play to the mob. "We kept waiting for his speech asking for courtesy even if they disagreed with us," Pinnix recalled, "but it never came. Instead, he whipped them up and played cheerleader."

When it was Clausen's turn to speak, he said, "Take a look at this audience. They are concerned what will happen if this expansion goes through. The timber people will get their money, but these people will lose their jobs and their livelihood. If you had an ounce of decency, you would commit yourself to taking care of them." Burton pledged a third time to "take care of the workers."

For hours, Burton let every opponent testify. Amodio thought no other congressman would have even permitted the hearing in an atmosphere of such intense hostility. At one point, he left the stage to answer a call of nature, and a man at the microphone complained, "He doesn't even have the decency to listen to what I'm saying."

From the men's room at the rear of the auditorium Burton's voice boomed out: "I'm back here taking a leak, but I can hear you."

The environmentalists needed a police escort to the stage to testify. Amodio said he felt like he was in a B-grade gangster movie. Four or five heavy-set loggers positioned themselves in his line of vision. Every time they caught his eye, they whispered, "You motherfuckers. We're going to get you before this is over." Boos and hisses drowned out most of the environmentalists' statements. They required a police escort out of the building. Amodio thought he knew these people. He lived in the community, but their anger terrified him.

The next day, the hearings moved south to the Federal Building (later renamed the Phillip Burton Federal Building) in San Francisco, where several hundred truckers circled the building blasting their air horns. But after the passion of the previous day, this hearing was calm. Only 200 people were allowed into a tightly packed courtroom where economists argued over the impact of Burton's bill. The most emotional testimony came from John Henning, head of the state AFL-CIO, who was careful not to blame Burton specifically for antiworker sentiment. Nevertheless, Henning bellowed, "Where the hell are the liberals to stand up for our people? What the hell are the jobs they'll get? Where are they? There are none." Reacting to what Burton called a climate of fear that engulfed the timber workers, Henning said, "It is more than fear, it is a sense of rage and hatred for those who will displace workers. Believe me, Mr. Chairman, I know you are a friend of labor. . . . Don't underestimate the passions of the rank and file on this. The people come first, the trees come next."[10]

Burton returned to Washington more determined than ever to protect the workers. Borrowing from what he knew about income transfer programs and from what Nat Weinberg, chief economist for the United Auto Workers, did for displaced workers after a railway reorganization act, Burton added a new title to the bill. It ensured that no forestry worker would suffer economically from expansion. While the 1,200-member Lumber and Sawmill Workers, Local 2592, vowed to defeat Burton at the next election, Burton readied HR 3813.

The $40 million Title II that Burton added, later known as REPP (Redwood Employee Protection Plan), was not just some afterthought to cool the anger of the timber workers who had cursed him. It was more than even they could have imagined in their wildest dreams. Burton's Title II became the most generous bailout of workers ever enacted. It was the first time that legislation to acquire land for a national park would compensate affected workers as well as landowners. As with his welfare reform bill in California and his black lung program for coal miners, the costs of the redwood park expansion rapidly soared beyond anyone's imagination.

The cost for acquiring the extra land plus the worker protection element eventually came to nearly half a billion dollars. Those with more than five years of work got their average weekly take-home pay, tax-free, for up to six years, depending on how long they had worked. Older workers who turned sixty before 1984 got their weekly pay for up to eleven years, or until they turned sixty-five. Burton chose to "overcompensate" them. "I made the judgment," Burton said later, "to, in effect, induce the old-timers who worked all their lives . . . to leave the work force so the younger ones with families could stay." Workers with less than five years' work got one week's severance pay for every month worked. There was no lid or maximum amount. A highly skilled timber faller who earned $35 an hour, was guaranteed that weekly wage until 1984.

Just as he taught Dolores Huerta to lobby decades earlier, Burton now taught John Amodio and Sierra Club lobbyist Linda Billings how to do their jobs better. They arrived at his office about 7 P.M. most evenings for a full debriefing after others went home. He armed them with information and then pointed them at members of his subcommittee, such as Goodloe Byron of Maryland, a conservative Democrat with labor unions and timber interests in his district. Burton was not sure how Byron would vote, so he told them to lay out the facts but also let Byron know that if he did not support this bill, the Sierra Club would defeat him in the next election. When they began their talk, Byron was noncommittal, but Burton had sized him up well. He came around quickly when they threatened him. With other members, the advice changed. "Show him the pictures," Burton advised for Lamar Gudger of North Carolina. "No hardball." He, too, came around. Burton told them to get their local chapters to work editorial boards to produce editorials he could use to pressure members. The tactic worked, and they delivered them from large papers across the country and from small papers in key districts.

"We could not have had better intelligence or direction," Amodio recalled. "It made us very effective." Yet sitting in Burton's office, Amodio often wished he could disappear as he watched Burton intimidate one member after another. "Listen, you motherfucker," Burton would scream into the phone. "Do it this way or your asshole will be turned inside out." Then Burton staffer Judy Lemons would peer in to say Sala was on the phone, and Burton instantly transformed himself: "How's my little bride?"

Burton continued to work with Pinnix on the details of the legislation, pressing his labor contacts for information about the timber companies. That knowledge gave him extra leverage. Then he met with timber executives and threatened to annex more of their land if they did not go along with him. Meanwhile, he lobbied committee members individually. Because Burton worked everything out in advance, there was no need for substantive debate once the subcommittee met. Supportive members got what they needed. Opponents stated their opposition for the record so that their constituents would know that at least they had tried. But Burton had poor Clausen turned inside out. Clausen did not know when to be hard-nosed or when to compromise. Some observers said Clausen was so unnerved by what Burton might do next to "rape" his district that he sometimes shook at the markup sessions.

On July 26, 1977, sixteen minutes after his subcommittee convened, Burton reported the bill out by voice vote. Clausen and other Republicans filed a minority report stating their opposition. Five days later, the bill cleared the full committee. Senate Majority Whip Alan Cranston introduced President Carter's version in the Senate, which did not include the income protection plan. The House Appropriations Committee reluctantly appropriated the money for Title II, even though Subcommittee Chairman Sidney Yates of Illinois said, "This is unprecedented. There hasn't been a new entitlement program in years."

As the bill progressed, Charles Nichols, an old labor friend of Burton who headed the Carpenters' union, and Carpenters lobbyist Jay Power readied themselves to oppose the bill. They might not have been fully conversant with Burton's economic protection plan. Or they might have known but wanted to show their 900,000 members, including nearly 100,000 workers in the lumber industry, that they had the clout to stop the bill.

"Once Phil Burton put his bill in, we knew he'd win," Power recalled. "It didn't occur to us to ask for a Great Society program. We just hoped to slow Burton down and get his attention on a bill that would put 2,000 people out of work." The opportunity soon came. A top staffer to Majority Leader Jim Wright tipped Power that within a week Burton would ask the Rules Committee for a rule to bring his bill to the House floor. Wright's interest in not wanting his chief rival to succeed was understandable. Power and Nichols plotted a shrewd strategy. They got George Meany to ask Tip O'Neill for a favor: block the bill in Rules. Less than a year after the bitter race for majority leader, they figured Tip O'Neill would be happy to throw a monkey wrench into Burton's legislation.

"Our hope was," Power said, "that even though Burton would be hugely angry, maybe he would expand timber cutting on adjacent federal land or reduce the size of the expansion."

They guessed right. On October 18, O'Neill blocked the bill in the Rules Committee, saying he was only delaying it, not killing it outright. O'Neill said it was the first time George Meany had ever asked him for a favor. "Meany came to see me," O'Neill told reporters. "He talked about redwoods. . . . He wanted some time to try and work something out—you know, he hasn't had many victories around here—and I didn't see any harm in delaying the bill for a little while." O'Neill said he expected the bill to reach the floor as early as January. It also must have given ranking Rules Committee members Dick Bolling and Bernie Sisk special satisfaction to torpedo Burton's legislation. As a park proponent told *Congressional Quarterly,* "Nobody went out of their way to shoot us down, but nobody lifted a finger to help us, either."[11]

Unhappy with his low salary, Power wanted a better job lobbying for the AFL-CIO. Burton cornered him that week, so enraged that Power and Nichols had been smart enough to get to O'Neill, that he "got in my face and said I was dead meat in Washington. I'd never get hired at the AFL. I was finished. He was raving and spitting and waving his arms." For several weeks, said Power, "it was the talk of Capitol Hill that Burton had been blocked on something he wanted." Republican S. I. Hayakawa, who defeated John Tunney in 1976 to become California's junior senator, meanwhile worked with Alaska Republican Ted Stevens to block the bill in the Senate. Stevens was worried about creating an undesirable precedent for federal lands in his state.

With Congress in recess, Amodio went home to California. Soon Burton called and said he wanted to see Amodio in his district office the next morning. Amodio took a Greyhound bus and went directly to Burton's San Francisco office, nervous about Burton's reaction to the delay of his bill. Burton explained that in return for park expansion, the timber industry wanted a larger area of national forest available for dramatically accelerated clear-cutting, including important and environmentally sensitive tracts in the Siskiyou Wilderness. This would include road building in an area with no roads. How important was park expansion? Would the environmentalists trade it for loosening restrictions on logging in the national forests? Still intimidated by Burton, Amodio gathered his courage and said no. If what the timber industry wanted went into the bill, the Sierra Club would oppose it. Having nearly destroyed the areas adjacent to the park, why should the timber industry be rewarded with a whole new area to cut? Burton was only exploring the possibility, but Amodio left feeling queasy. To his immense relief, the subject never came up again.

When the House returned in January, Burton submitted a substitute amendment with a refined Title II, explained it to the AFL-CIO, and got labor's support. Once O'Neill learned that labor was on board, he cooperated with Burton in moving the bill quickly. On January 31, the Senate passed its version 74-20. Cranston and Jim Abourezk of South Dakota, who had moved up to the Senate and now chaired the Senate Energy Subcommittee on Parks and Recreation, led the fight. Supporters included the Department of Interior, the Carpenters' union, the AFL-CIO, the UAW, the Sierra Club, the Environmental Policy Center, the National Recreation and Park Association, the Conservation Foundation, the Friends of the Earth, and the Wilderness Society. Rules was scheduled to hear the bill on February 7. The vote was the next day.

"The very serious concerns we had about this bill," AFL-CIO Director of Legislation Biemiller wrote Burton, "have been addressed by the Burton substitute, and we urge its adoption without weakening amendments by the House." Burton was so happy the AFL-CIO was finally in his corner that when he spotted Jay Power, he threw an arm around him and said, "Once again, Jay, you're in your mother's arms. And don't worry about the future, kid, I'm going to let you go." Power knew in his rational moments that Burton's threat to kill his job prospects had been empty. But he had been terrified nonetheless.

More important, Burton's new coalition provided indisputable evidence that he now occupied a unique position in Washington. More than any other politician, more than Udall or Scoop Jackson, chairman of Senate Energy and Natural Resources, Burton had the complete confidence of labor and environmentalists. He bridged a gap between two warring interest groups that no one else had ever been able to reconcile. To take a New Deal labor base, whose interests Burton grew up representing, and wed it to a burgeoning upper-middle-class environmental movement was truly breakthrough politics.

As Burton rode up the elevator with Charlie Rose the day of the vote, it was crowded with lobbyists from a chainsaw manufacturers association, wearing buttons that said, "Defeat the Burton Bill." As they got out, Burton doubled over with laughter. He was delighted that his activities prompted chainsaw manufacturers to form a lobby and send representatives to Washington to defeat him. Even better, he could not have invented a more odious opposition. This group symbolized the worst excesses of the other side. "To him, it was manna from heaven," said Rose.

It was an easy win. The House approved Burton's bill 328-60. In the House version, Redwood National Park would nearly double, from 55,000 to 103,000 acres. Another 30,000 acres was designated as a "park protection zone," subject to acquisition by the Secretary of Interior if the park was endangered. Veteran workers would be compensated their full wages for years. And another $33 million would be authorized to rehabilitate the park and repair the damage that logging and erosion had created. But trouble was brewing. The Senate killed the economic protection plan. Burton had to get it back in conference.[12]

Conference committee was where Burton was at his best, where opponents gave in just to get this ferocious, saliva-spitting maniac off their backs. House conferees were Udall, Paul Tsongas, Bob Kastenmeier, John Krebs, and Republicans Keith Sebelius and Clausen. Burton had all the Democratic proxies, so no one else needed to show up. Everything was worked out in advance, anyway. Having lost on the expansion, Clausen became a Burton ally in getting as much economic aid for his constituents as possible. Senate conferees were Abourezk, who loved Title II, Jackson, Spark Matsunaga of Hawaii, and Republican Robert Packwood of Oregon.

In other words, Burton had reduced the conference to himself and a couple of senators sitting down in a back room to cut the deal. In return for a few compromises Burton could easily live with, Title II went back into the bill. On March 14, with little debate, the House passed it 317-60. As the members filed onto the floor to vote, they were startled to see Phil Burton standing by the door where the lobbyists traditionally stood, with Jay Power of the Carpenters' union and John Amodio and Linda Billings of the Sierra Club. All were giving the "thumbs up" signal to vote yes. It went to the Senate a week later.

As Jim Abourezk got up to give his speech, Senate aide Jim Bierne, who worked for Jackson, knew they already had the votes. "Let's put it in the record and get out," Bierne suggested, trying to discourage him. Why needlessly endanger what had taken so long to put together?

"No," said Abourezk. "I want to read my speech."

"Sir," Bierne suggested, as respectfully as he knew how, "it's an old rule that when you've won, you get out quickly." But Abourezk plowed ahead. As he spoke, Strom Thurmond of South Carolina waited on the Senate floor for a bill of his own to come up and flipped through the park bill. When he got to Title II, Thurmond became enraged. He had never seen anything quite like it. Bierne saw what was happening and muttered, "Oh, shit," under his breath, knowing Thurmond could derail everything. Thurmond asked Abourezk if he would yield.

"Can you explain Title II?" he demanded. Abourezk said it was compensation for workers. "Why are we doing this?" Thurmond insisted. Abourezk replied that this was a "legislative taking."

"I understand that," Thurmond said. "But this seems to be about jobs."

Thinking quickly, Abourezk said, "The federal government has the power of eminent domain. If you take a man's property, you have to compensate him. What's more important to a man than his job?"

"Yes," said Thurmond, "I guess that's okay," and sat down.

Coming off the floor, Abourezk turned to Bierne. "I did good, didn't I," he grinned, obviously pleased with himself.[13]

The long battle was over. The Senate approved the final version 63-26 on March 21, 1978. Interior Secretary Andrus supported the legislation. But Carter's Office of Management and the Budget hated the economic protection plan. The last thing OMB wanted was another entitlement built into the budget, but Carter was caught. Six days later, honoring a campaign pledge he made seventeen months before and expressing reservations about Title II, President Carter signed the bill.

As a teary-eyed Phil Burton celebrated his great victory in his subcommittee office, John Amodio was curious why Burton had invested so much time and effort in this fight. He wanted to know why.

"Once when I was a kid, my parents took me to see the redwoods," Burton said. "I've never forgotten that. This was easy."

Amodio was given a rare insight. Nobody ever heard Phil Burton talk about his personal motivation, let alone his family. But that family trip from Milwaukee to California some thirty-five years before, including the detour through the giant Sequoias, had special meaning. The trees were impressive, but perhaps they also evoked some rare moments of special family togetherness that Phil Burton treasured.[14]

Despite his almost total absorption in the redwoods fight, Burton managed to find the time and energy to take over acting chairmanship of the Education and Labor Subcommittee on Labor Standards in July 1977 when John Dent underwent eye surgery. In that capacity, Burton wasted little time in using the power of the federal government to improve conditions for working people and played a key role in guiding a new minimum wage bill into law. The minimum wage stood at $2.30 an hour. With the close collaboration of organized labor and the Carter administration, Burton produced the largest increase in history, a four-step series of hikes that took the minimum wage to $3.35 an hour in January 1981, a jump of $1.05. Even so, labor's weakness on the Hill surfaced when the House defeated an effort to index the rate and make increases automatic. It took Speaker O'Neill to break a tie and defeat a Republican plan to create a subminimum wage of 85 percent to workers under eighteen. Burton's bill gave three million workers pay boosts and extended minimum wage protections to another two million workers.

By mid-1977, Burton had little use for Carter or what he saw as incompetent White House aides, especially those on the congressional side. But his efforts on the redwoods bill and minimum wage prompted a mash note from the president. "In your years in the House," Carter wrote on February 9, 1978, "you have compiled an impressive record of leadership and achievement. Your efforts as Chairman of the Subcommittee on National Parks contributed to today's passage of the important bill expanding Redwood Park. Your work with the Speaker helped to shape the most significant minimum wage bill since 1935. Throughout your career, you have been responsible for changes which have helped make the House more open, vibrant and Democratic."[15]

Still ambitious for leadership and stung by Tip O'Neill's temporary intervention to halt his redwoods bill, Burton prepared to challenge Jim Wright when the new Congress convened again in December 1978. He made Mark Gersh his chief aide to help launch another run. Gersh, who worked for the National Committee for an Effective Congress, thought there was dissatisfaction with Wright among liberals who believed that he was an accidental majority leader, one who benefited from the Burton-Bolling schism. Gersh began studying the next election cycle to see which progressive Democratic challengers Burton could support and finance. Burton also hired his first press secretary, a young *Roll Call* reporter named Myron Struck, who began putting out the sorts of press releases crediting his boss that Burton never previously cared about. Since his defeat, he may have appreciated, at least in principle, the need for good public relations.

In January 1978, Struck had breakfast with Craig Raupe, Wright's top aide, in the majority leader's office. Raupe's message was unambiguous: if Burton thought he could challenge Wright, forget it. He would get crushed. Struck sent Burton a two-page memo summarizing what Raupe said, including his analysis of vulnerable Democrats in the Texas and California delegations.

"I don't think Phil is seriously thinking of challenging an incumbent who has done nothing seriously wrong," Raupe told Struck. "I don't think anybody will. We've been able to build up support continuously among our colleagues." Raupe predicted that if any challenge came, it would be from a "dissatisfied" faction leader. "Jim's voting record is not that different from Phil's," Raupe said. "We know that Burton could challenge us. We're not naive. But that would be a mistake, I think. That race wouldn't be close. One just doesn't challenge an incumbent member of the leadership without good cause," Raupe said. Wright expected to wait three to five years before O'Neill stepped down. "That's when the real dog fight will occur."

Raupe also said that after "months and months" of giving President Carter credit for being new and waiting for his staff to learn their way around, "now I think they're just fuck-ups. Plain and simple." Raupe, not Struck, brought up the redwoods bill, which was not resolved at the time of their breakfast. "We knew he [Burton] is pushing hard for it, and we're not trying to screw him. But we know labor's position, and we know that we can't schedule it or push O'Neill to schedule it as long as labor is opposed," Raupe said, a twinkle in his eye. When Struck asked whether O'Neill promised to pull the bill out of committee by March, Raupe replied, "Maybe he has, but that bridge hasn't been crossed totally yet. You know, every time Burton has something up for suspension [of the rules], it goes right to the top of the calendar—and we make up the calendar—there is no question that we're not trying to foul him up."

The Raupe-Struck breakfast had not happened by chance. Word had spread that Burton was on the march again. "Now Burton seems prepared to resume playing a larger role in House politics, including issues outside his committee jurisdictions," Richard Cohen wrote in the February 4, 1978 *National Journal.* "But while he won't say so publicly . . . it is clear from interviews with him and some of his friends that Burton is itching to take on Jim Wright again. And despite the obstacles facing a once-defeated candidate for a top leadership post, he could win—given some breaks." Cohen reported the House leadership so worried about Burton that "whenever anything is amiss in the Democratic ranks, O'Neill and Wright look to see if Burton is around. A Burton associate called the leadership 'paranoid about him.'" So paranoid that the once-active Democratic Caucus did not even meet in 1977—which prevented Burton from using it as a forum. When Cohen asked Burton whether Wright's performance during his first year in office was what he expected, Burton said, "In all candor—no."[16]

The prospective Burton challenge gained wider currency a few weeks later, when, during an AFL-CIO meeting in Bal Harbor, Florida, Burton sharply rebuked the House leadership for failing to pass key labor legislation, including a common situs picketing bill that was at the top of organized labor's agenda for the year. That criticism produced a *New York Times* headline: "Rep. Burton Held Likely to Seek House Leader's Post." The article said Burton "apparently intends" to challenge Wright after the fall elections. Labor leaders said Burton left no doubt "that he intended to run." Asked directly, Burton said, "I am certainly headed in that direction." Asked if it would be in 1978, he replied, "I certainly don't expect to wait until the next century."

Tip O'Neill also spoke at the labor meeting. He blamed the common situs picketing defeat on labor itself. He warned labor leaders in advance that the bill was "doomed" and that labor had to learn how to deal with a new generation of independent and better educated House Democrats who did not unquestioningly follow labor's cue. Burton spoke next and praised O'Neill, but then spoke of "doing something" about the leadership problem, which participants interpreted to mean he would challenge Wright. At a press briefing, George Meany indicated that he was especially unhappy with Wright. Wright originally opposed the common situs bill, then changed his vote at the last minute. Meany believed his first vote liberated other Democrats to oppose the measure, thus costing "valuable" support.[17]

As these reports reached Wright, he moved quickly to shore up his base. Supporters told him what happened at Bal Harbor. If Phil Burton were to become number two, they said, Tip O'Neill would be like a Roman emperor who needed a professional food taster at all times. Wright called twenty key supporters from various states and committees, people whom he trusted completely, and said he would be a candidate for majority leader again. Each one took twelve to fifteen names—enough to cover all the Democrats—and fanned out. By the next morning, Wright said he had pledges of support from four-fifths of the members. "Word got back to him [Burton]—and that killed it," Wright recalled. "That's all it took."[18]

As was true with so much of Phil Burton's legislation, the true costs of the redwoods expansion bill came in after the fact. Barely a year after President Carter signed the legislation expanding Redwood National Park, revelations in the *Sacramento Bee*, versions of which were later published in the *Washington Post*, documented excesses in the most lavish program to aid dislocated workers in American history. The reports focused on a few of the highest paid workers—highly skilled timber fallers who had earned $50,000 to

$60,000 a year—who were now earning $35,000 a year tax free, plus benefits, for doing no work. Attention also focused on former union business agent Alfred Lasley, who was given a $43,000-a-year GS-15 government job to coordinate the Redwood Employee Protection Plan. These revelations produced sensational headlines—and indeed there were some real abuses. But the average weekly benefits, including REPP payments and unemployment insurance for some 1,500 workers, added up to $270 a week, still a nice sum, but far less shocking than $35,000 a year.[19]

The real problem was not the extra costs—by October 1981, $45 million was spent on more than 3,100 workers, only $5 million beyond what was originally authorized—but the fact that union workers were colluding with the timber companies to get laid off so they could qualify for government benefits. The FBI promised to investigate whether fraud had been committed. Burton had written into the law a presumption that virtually any worker layoffs between a "window period" of May 31, 1977 and September 30, 1980 were caused by park expansion. As a result, nearly twice as many employees as originally estimated qualified for benefits in the first eighteen months, according to a harshly critical report by the General Accounting Office. The report said 36 percent of the 1,735 workers who got benefits through September 1979 were victims of temporary work curtailments unrelated to the park. "Because no determination is required that a layoff is related to park expansion," the report found, "any employee laid off by an affected employer due to such things as routine maintenance, equipment repairs, inclement weather, road closures or for any other reasons can qualify for benefits."[20]

When the Reagan administration realized in January 1981 what Burton had created, AFL-CIO lobbyist Jay Power recalled, OMB Director David Stockman "went ballistic and tried to kill it. But he couldn't. We had enough friends on the Appropriations Committees of the House and Senate, plus Phil Burton, that the program stayed funded." A January 24, 1981 article in the *Eureka Times Standard* reported that Lasley was told to close shop by the next Monday. Workers were told their benefits were being cut off, pending new Department of Labor guidelines. Burton scrawled on his copy of the story, "Within 3 days of Reagan's swearing-in." But the woodworkers union sued the Labor Department to block the new guidelines.

"In order to prevent precisely the kind of tinkering with the clear intent of the legislation that the Secretary of Labor is now attempting," Burton wrote in an affidavit supporting the suit, "we included in the last section of the Act a requirement that the Secretary construe the Act's language in the manner most favorable to employees. I don't know what else we could have said or done to make this any plainer."

Beyond any problems with fraud and abuse, the $33 million that Congress appropriated to clean up the landscape and repair damage at Redwood National Park financed the most successful restoration program ever attempted in any unit of the national park system. "The rehabilitation of the watershed is in itself a wonderful story," said Dick Curry.

> The work done up there was extraordinary, both in scope and in technical application. Phil Burton was the only individual who could have shepherded [the bill] through because he was so effective, feared and respected. He was a champion of the environmentalists and of labor, and he applied a fundamental principle that sometimes we forget about in conservation matters: you may be doing a lot for the spotted owl, but what about the endangered timber worker? Phil Burton insisted on that and fought for it when there was not much support in the administration. Yet without that Title II element, there would have been no redwoods bill.[21]

When it was all over, Curry gave Phil Burton a plaque quoting Interior Chairman Mo Udall's words to Burton on the redwoods bill: "You unscrewed the inscrutable."

16

PARK BARREL

He turned parks into patronage, and believe me, it worked. He made
preservation issues sound like the most pristine, high-minded cause.
But they were a Thanksgiving turkey, baby.

MARTIN F. NOLAN
Boston Globe *associate editor*

Phil really believed in a package deal for Congress. He thought we really
ought to pass one or two bills a year around here with everything in it for
everybody. . . . What he did was get things past the House without serious
objections. They don't express themselves with great grandeur on the floor.
Their magnificence is that nothing happened to stop them.

CHARLIE ROSE
former House Administration Committee chairman

Instead of trying to confront by main force and overwhelm the opposition,
Phil tried to disarm it, demobilize it, and send it home, and then plow
the fields, so that literally the army was gone when the attack came.
It wasn't a military operation. It was a parade.

FORMER HOUSE SPEAKER TOM FOLEY

SOON AFTER PHILLIP BURTON became chairman of the subcommittee on
national parks, the Sierra Club's Dr. Edgar Wayburn dropped by to visit
with staff director Cleve Pinnix. "You have to think of Phil Burton as a big
engine," Wayburn advised him. "The job for the rest of us is to lay track."
Four years later, when Pinnix and staffers Dale Crane and Judy Lemons
finished laying track, Burton, in an extraordinary burst of legislative pro-
ductivity, had preserved more national park and wilderness land than all

presidents and congresses before him combined. His legislation preserved nearly 5 percent of California's landmass and, if the Alaska Lands bill is included—in which he played a significant, though not decisive, role—nearly 10 percent of the entire landmass of the United States.

Between 1977 and 1980, Burton created thirty new units of the national parks system (not including Alaska) and set aside almost two million acres of wilderness in nine existing national parks. He designated eight trails as new "national trails" and eight rivers as "wild and scenic." His omnibus parks bill of 1978, the largest single park bill in history, tripled the acreage of park wilderness, tripled the miles of national trails and doubled the miles of wild and scenic rivers. Besides expanding Redwood National Park, Burton added the pristine High Sierra wilderness area of Mineral King to Sequoia National Park, which the Sierra Club had been trying to do for sixty-five years; protected the largest outdoors area east of the Rockies—the Boundary Waters Canoe Area, nearly one million acres of lakes and wilderness in Minnesota; created the one million-acre Pine Barrens National Reserve in New Jersey; nearly doubled the acreage of the Golden Gate National Recreation Area; created the Santa Monica National Recreation Area; and added dozens of new historic and cultural sites. These sites honored Eleanor Roosevelt, Martin Luther King, Jr., and Georgia O'Keeffe and included a Women's Rights National Historic Park, a Holocaust Memorial Council, and an archeological preserve for prehistoric Chacoan culture in New Mexico. Many members claimed credit for portions of his bills, and indeed earned that credit. But without Burton to wrap all the myriad pieces together and steer them through Congress, these landmark bills would never by themselves have become law.[1]

How was it that a man less at home in Muir Woods than in a darkened cocktail lounge with an unfiltered Chesterfield in one hand and a tumbler full of Stoli in the other could amass such an astonishing conservation record? When Joe Beeman drove Burton to the GGNRA one day, Beeman suggested they get out of the car and look around. "Why the fuck would I want to do that?" Burton asked, stamping his cigarette out in the gravel. On another occasion, he turned to George Miller and said, "Isn't the GGNRA beautiful?"

"Yeah, Phil," Miller replied, "it's a nice place."

"Not the place," Burton said. "The bill."

Burton had neither the need nor the interest to experience nature firsthand. He told Pinnix the closest he got to being outdoors was heading fifty yards into the forest to relieve himself. But he understood the benefits of wilderness and solitude. It mattered to people who mattered to him.

For a man obsessed with coming back from a devastating defeat, Burton also recognized the political advantages associated with parks and wilderness: he could turn environmentalism into an elaborate system of chits. Moving beyond California and the redwoods, he gave legislators parks they always wanted but were unable to obtain. Conversely, his threats to preserve land made some apoplectic. Designating a stretch of river "wild and scenic," for example, often enraged the local Cattlemen's Association, which in turn created major problems for the representative. Either way, Burton had leverage: as with reapportionment, this was the raw power to profoundly affect someone else's district. It was a strategy by which a man whose institutional power had been destroyed could reassemble his power base for another shot at the leadership. If he criticized O'Neill or Wright for their inability to "package issues," well, he would show them a package or two of his own.

With the environment, even more than with welfare and black lung, Burton could dominate the field, dazzle his colleagues, reward friends, and punish enemies while "doing good." Recalled George Miller,

> His field of vision was so great that he could look at fifteen political equations and see the one missing name. He traded tobacco for minimum wage. Everyone tries to duplicate that but nobody can. Some people voted for his parks bill because there was *not* a park in their district. He looked at parks not as adding acres here or there but as a political statement. Some people want environmental impact reports. He'd say, "Get me a member impact report. How many members are hurt and how many are helped by this?"[2]

Moreover, Burton firmly believed that if you have a lemon, make lemonade. He moved faster on Interior than on Education and Labor, and no one let him join Ways and Means, although that hardly kept him away. With House leadership gone for now and possibly forever, the environment was his best hand. Had he instead chaired a Post Office and Civil Service subcommittee, Burton might have written equally ingenious laws dealing with federal pay or traded the congressional frank for who knows what. In accepting his assignment on Interior, he made lemonade: his subcommittee chairmanship coincided with a period when people were changing what they wanted the government to do about the environment. Beginning on college campuses with Earth Day in 1970 and spreading into the larger culture, many Americans increasingly said they no longer wanted more highways or bigger dams. They wanted parks, wilderness, recreation areas. Government should preserve, not just build mindlessly.

That sentiment was especially strong in San Francisco—home of the Sierra Club, one of the most influential of all the environmental groups—and just thirty miles north of the Stanford campus, where Earth Day was born. John Muir's love of Yosemite and the Sierras created the modern conservation movement and the Sierra Club. A four-hour drive by car from San Francisco could take outdoors enthusiasts east to Lake Tahoe or Yosemite, to Squaw Valley, or Kings Canyon and Sequoia National Parks. A three-hour drive south took them down the spectacular Highway 1 to Monterey, Carmel, and Big Sur. A five-hour drive north led to Mt. Shasta, the redwoods, or the Trinity Alps.

Sensitive to changing constituencies at home and the need to replenish them, Burton recognized that as his labor base aged and moved to the suburbs, it was being replaced by younger professionals moving back to the city. Many were environmentalists and many were gay—although it took a few more years before he understood what these constituents were about.

"You know, Bill," Burton told Wilderness Society director Bill Turnidge, articulating another reason for his interest in the environment, "all the guys here, myself included, run around like crazy passing legislation and taking great pride in it. But if you stay here long enough, you find everything you sponsor is either wrongheaded, because you didn't understand the problem or the solution, is emasculated by the bureaucracy, or is replaced by other legislation or a new program. I figured out the only thing that really lasts forever is parks. That's my accomplishment."[3]

For Burton to pass these enormously complicated packages that he alone understood was also the ultimate act of domination: as with his previous legislation, he could show he was smarter than anyone else. His technical expertise, intimidating style, and hard work wore down his enemies. If greedy developers or voracious timber companies were the losers, so much the better. "The ego satisfaction was knowing he could win, he could beat everybody, with all their computers," recalled longtime Burton associate Tom Joe.

Burton gave a three-hour interview in early 1979 to a scared young reporter named Joan Moody from *National Parks and Conservation* magazine. He said he did not "do interviews," but Moody persisted and knew Dick Conlon, which helped. In that rare interview, Burton revealed his operating principles:

I've got to put the squeeze on the cojónes of the exploitive industries in my state. You'd be shocked how well they'll behave. . . . You have to learn how to terrorize the bastards. . . . If you start *giving* these special interests what they should *end up with*, they don't lose a dime, because they have no limits on their greed or their view of their own self-worth and power. So you have to arm their lobbyists back here with ammunition to tell [their] local people that "we've got a messianic zealot [Burton] who is going to kill us unless we work out a solution." . . . I'll save them from me. Truly, they'll be heroes with their bosses. Do not make them figure out how much more they're going to get, but how much they've got that they're going to lose. Most of my colleagues work it the other end: they kiss the asses of everyone.[4]

For years, the Public Works Committee assembled "omnibus" bills to package public works projects. Including dozens of items in one bill that provided benefits to many members made House passage much easier. That was also one way in which Jim Wright, who managed these bills, accumulated his many chits. On a much smaller scale, the Interior Committee in the early 1970s began combining routine items into one bill. These items usually involved raising the funding in some national park by a million dollars or so or expanding a park boundary by a few dozen acres. Soon after Burton became chairman, ranking Republican Joe Skubitz approached him to increase an appropriation for Fort Scott in Kansas by $325,000. Burton later said Skubitz's "one interest in life was Fort Scott." This was the first stirring of Burton's omnibus parks bill strategy.

At the same time, Burton asked Pinnix and Crane, who came over from the Army Corps of Engineers, to compile lists of areas that merited protection. In many cases, these were areas where National Park Service staff work had already been done but where Congress had not taken action. In Wayburn's words, Burton was asking them to lay track. While Pinnix and Crane were assembling lists, Burton found that his enemies were stalling his redwoods bill in the Rules Committee. Meanwhile, President Carter sent over a bill to designate a forty-eight mile stretch of the Chattahoochee River near Atlanta a National Recreation Area and to appropriate $73 million to buy 6,300 acres of riverfront property. Carter had failed to make that happen while governor of Georgia. He was determined to succeed as president.

In a speech he gave to environmentalists in San Francisco at the end of

1978, Burton recalled that when Carter sent his bill over, Burton was worried about getting his redwoods bill out of Rules. "So I toyed with the idea of attaching redwoods to President Carter's Chattahoochee River bill but didn't." He could have held Carter's bill hostage in his subcommittee, in other words, until Rules freed his redwoods bill. In fact, Burton did eventually hold Carter's bill hostage, but for another purpose. He wanted to raise the $600 million Land and Water Conservation Fund by 50 percent. This was a fund to which oil and gas companies contributed from profits on lands leased from the federal government. A larger fund gave him more money with which to acquire land. But when Carter opposed the increase, Burton hinted he would approve the Chattahoochee bill only if Carter supported the fund increase. "He's not holding anything hostage," said Georgian Dawson Mathis, a Burton ally on the subcommittee. "He just bought a little insurance."

When Skubitz approached Burton with an omnibus package that had grown to thirty routine items, Burton said in his speech, "I thought, 'My God, maybe I can use *that* to bust redwoods out of the Rules Committee.'" Burton got his redwoods rule before that tactic became necessary, but the idea was born: if he could use Chattahoochee or the omnibus package as leverage, why not clear the decks of every worthy conservation project in the country, no matter how controversial? He could wrap them all into one huge bill, just the way Public Works did. "Give me all the park wilderness ever discussed or recommended," Burton told his staff. He was more explicit with Pope Barrow, a lawyer in the House Legislative Counsel's Office, with whom Burton worked closely in drafting the bill.

"Why not put the whole agenda in here?" he said. "Why not get something for everyone? Christ, we'll pork out." He would load up the bill until he had enough votes to guarantee passage. Burton thus became the first legislator with the imagination, patience, and skill to turn environmental issues into the political equivalent of a water project or a defense contract. Senator Alan Bible had used parks as leverage, but certainly not on this scale. Bob Neuman, an aide to Udall, was the first to call it what it was: park barrel.[5]

Armed with new lists from Pinnix and Crane, calling on his own vast knowledge of his colleagues' districts and assembling "member impact statements," Burton figured out what they needed before they knew they needed it. He also wanted national historic sites that celebrated a more diverse group of people than dead white men. Maggie Walker, for example, rose from poverty in Richmond, Virginia, to become the first black woman to head a bank. At a cost of $1.3 million, Burton honored her with a national historic site at her place of birth. And by targeting large urban recreation areas for improvements, he could create a bigger political constituency for the national parks.

As Burton scoped out the politics of getting a bill this huge through Congress, he also had to consider his relationship with Udall, the new chairman of Interior. Udall's thinking on environmental matters was often similar to Burton's, but his style was far different. "We both have minor ego problems," Burton quipped. "He thinks he should have been president of the United States. My ambitions are not that limited." Udall knew about bitter defeats, too. He incurred the wrath of the old bulls when he challenged John Mc-Cormack for Speaker in 1968. He spent months thinking he would become majority leader in 1971, only to lose to Hale Boggs. He spent half of 1976 running for president. He frequently placed second, but never won a primary. But like Burton, Udall was determined not to let defeat crush his spirit or hunger for accomplishment. Many of his colleagues loved Udall for his warmth, fairness, and dry and self-deprecating wit. He believed in consensus and often hoped that by making the first concession, the other side would soon follow. This drove Burton crazy.

"Mo's idea of a bargain is to give everything away in the first thirty seconds," he told one friend. When Udall was a presidential candidate, Burton quipped to another, "If he's elected, the Russians will be on the Mall before his ass hits the chair, because he can't say no." But the pair respected one another nonetheless. Unlike Burton, Udall was an outdoors man, a westerner used to open spaces. Nor was he a rebel. Udall's family was prominent in Arizona political and legal circles; he succeeded older brother Stewart in the House when Stewart became John Kennedy's secretary of interior. Udall used humor and goodwill to achieve his ends. Burton tended to run over people and only occasionally and unapologetically return to pick them off the floor.

But the two often worked together. In one notable example, Arizona miners were so angry at Udall's support for reform of an archaic mining law that they hanged him in effigy and threatened to circulate petitions to recall him. Faced with the prospect of an uncomfortably close re-election effort in 1978, Udall used the specter of Burton taking over Interior to scare the miners (and other voters) to death. Writing in *Pay Dirt,* an industry newsletter for New Mexico mine operators, Udall was neither bashful nor subtle about playing the Burton card: "Phil is one of the best legislative operators in the House, and as ranking majority member of the Interior committee (that means he would be chairman if I'm gone) he has considerable clout with the committee."

Udall enclosed a copy of *Pay Dirt* to Burton with a note that said, "Dear Bro Burton—You continue to be my shield. God bless you!" In another note, Udall wrote, "Dear Mr. Burton (you dangerous liberal), Please take good care of your health and avoid danger. You are critically important to my re-election. Your anxious friend, Mo." They cooked up a plan whereby Burton accompanied Udall to a press conference. Udall had planted a question with a reporter, who asked how important Udall was to the future of the Central Arizona Project. This was a $2 billion project that took water 300 miles across the desert to Phoenix and Tucson. Udall spent much of his early career working on the water project, which was an enormous boon to his state's growth.

"Arizona is dead if you lose Mo Udall," Burton said, playing his Darth Vader role to the hilt. "If he dies or is defeated, I'm chairman of this committee. You know what I think of the Central Arizona Project? It stinks."[6]

Udall said there were two kinds of bills: regular bills and Burton bills. He often teased Burton that Wayne Aspinall "would turn over in his grave," because Burton's legislative tactics "upset the regular order." Burton replied, "Mo, judge me by results." Even though Udall was chairman, Burton had a majority of votes on virtually any issue he wanted to push. Between seeding the committee with liberals, which Burton did over the years, adding delegates beholden to him from the offshore islands, and cultivating the Republican minority, the committee was essentially Burton's instrument. But there was often tension.

"Phil would get the train running," recalled George Miller, who closely observed their relationship. "But sometimes Mo would hit the switch, and the train would head off in another direction because Mo didn't go along with the package, maybe for legitimate reasons, and you'd say, 'Turn on the air conditioner. This room is getting real hot.' Brother Burton, as Mo used to call him, was a major pain in the ass in the orderly running of the operation."

If somebody voted "wrong" on a committee roll call, Miller recalled, "Burton would look up and the whole place would come to a stop. The poor clerk did not know whether to keep calling the roll or not, and the vote would either change or there would be a volcanic eruption later. He'd give you such a glare that the choice was to change your vote or die. He believed you had said you would vote for that bill, and this meant you either misled him or lied to him." Afterwards, Burton typically stormed down the hall searching for the miscreant.

"You dumb son of a bitch! You don't know what a serious fucking mistake you just made," Burton would scream. "But you are going to find out." This went beyond taking someone aside and expressing disappointment. "He told you you may never fly again," said Miller.[7]

But Udall and Burton agreed on fundamentals. Sierra Club, Wilderness Society, and National Wildlife Federation lobbyists knew they were extremely lucky to have Udall, Burton, and Seiberling heading key subcommittees. If Udall sometimes seemed too eager to make concessions, they went to Burton to get them back. When Udall wanted a smaller committee, which meant pro-development westerners would have more votes, the lobbyists urged Burton to persuade Steering and Policy to keep the committee from shrinking.

More than any other Democrat, Burton also worked the Republican side. The man who had few personal assets of his own badgered Udall into approving pay raises for Republican staff consultants, which earned him chits. He paid at least as much attention to Republican needs as he did to those of Democratic colleagues. He conducted intensive, one-on-one negotiations, at which he had become expert through his redistricting consultations. Some Republicans were hard-core conservatives, placed on Interior to "limit the damage." But Burton often explored what parks they wanted—and sometimes those they did not want—and worked with them until they were satisfied.

Joe Skubitz wanted Fort Scott expanded. Keith Sebelius wanted a dam. Robert Lagomarsino, his friend from Sacramento with whose wife he had once danced atop the El Mirador Hotel, wanted the Channel Islands off Santa Barbara and the Santa Monica National Recreation Area. And Robert Bauman of Maryland wanted $1 million to acquire the 1771 home of Dr. Thomas Stone, one of four signers of the Declaration of Independence from Maryland, as a national historic site. Burton kept his word, and they learned to trust him, even as they reported on him to the Republican leadership.

"He'd spend all night with the Republicans explaining the concept," said Miller. "The next morning, he'd spend twenty seconds with them, saying, 'This is what you agreed to, don't worry.' Then he was like a bull coming out of the chute, twisting and turning and belching and snorting and yelling for coffee."

Burton believed the best way to get his "packages" approved on the floor was by unanimous consent. If all the key legislators had already signed off, why risk muddying the waters with debate, or worse, with amendments? That made Bauman especially important, because he could object to unanimous consent items. Burton could bypass the Rules Committee, where enemies like Bolling, Sisk, and Gillis Long lurked, and pass his bills on either a unanimous consent voice vote—which permitted no amendments—or a suspension of the rules, which also bypassed Rules, but which required a two-thirds vote. A voice vote denied members the chance to record their vote, but his way was quicker and more efficient, and Burton always made sure their remarks were inserted into the *Congressional Record*, which they could mail home.

Seiberling was awed one day when Burton amended a unanimous consent bill by unanimous consent. He had never seen *that* done before or since. Foley saw him win a unanimous voice vote and ask to vacate it for a roll call, so he could win 402-0 and establish a better record.

Bauman, a former aide and protégé of ex-Congressman and Interior Secretary Rogers Morton of Maryland, was especially adept at parliamentary procedure. He succeeded H. R. Gross of Iowa as the Republicans' chief "objector." The objector stations himself on the floor to object to any bill on the consent or private calendar that he does not understand or believes violates his party's principles. Bauman never left the floor unless the Democratic leadership assured him there would be no more votes. If they ever played games with him, Bauman could tie the House in knots. Republicans looked to Bauman to protect them and kill embarrassing legislation. Democrats detested him. "Many times," Bauman recalled, "Burton would come to me with no deal and explain what was in his bill. More senior members saw me as an annoyance and tried to bull their way past me, and more than one lost a bill as a result. They soon learned I could stop it. Burton was one who liked to clear the path early."

Burton and Bauman became close—if unlikely—friends. They dined at the Monocle, true believers of opposite stripes. Bauman entered politics through conservative intellectual William F. Buckley and became national president of Young Americans for Freedom while in his early twenties. Like Burton, he believed most of his colleagues were motivated only by what would get them re-elected. They had few hard beliefs or agendas and were usually propelled by events or circumstances beyond their control.

"He would come eat with me," Bauman recalled. "We'd get roaring drunk and commiserate about how all these jerks in Congress didn't know what they were doing, and we did. Sala was there occasionally, but she did not have much use for me. Phil was for the little guy and talked in terms that were mildly Marxist. It didn't seem to matter that I was totally the opposite. It was just that we stood *for* something and fought for it, and that was the bond—plus the booze."

A few years later, Bauman, a married father of four and closet alcoholic and homosexual, was arrested for having sex with a teenage boy. As the scandal broke, Bauman hid in his office, protected by staff. Bauman's secretary knew they were friends and put Burton through. It was the only call he took. "My dear, dear friend," Burton said. "I feel so sorry. I'm praying for you."[8]

During the summer of 1977, former park ranger Cleve Pinnix and staffer Clay Peters suggested that Burton visit the "crown jewels" of the park system, Yellowstone and Grand Tetons National Parks. Pinnix had once worked for Yellowstone Park Superintendent John Townsley, who was sent there to clean it up and wrest control from the private concessionaires. Townsley, like Burton, was a big man with a large ego. He asked Pinnix to direct Burton's attention to the deplorable conditions at Yellowstone, including dilapidated hotels. For their arrival, Townsley arranged a sitting room with a perfect view of Old Faithful and a large comfortable chair for Burton to sit in next to the huge picture window. All Burton had to do was turn his head. But Burton was in no mood to play tourist. Drinking heavily, he interrogated Townsley on any and all subjects. When Old Faithful blew, everyone yelled at Burton to look at it, but in what seemed like a perverse point of pride, he never did. He questioned Townsley so long—in what staffers thought was a crude attempt to establish his own dominance—that the dining room closed and they had to thaw fish sticks for dinner. The next morning, Townsley did manage to get him up the six steps to the overlook at Yellowstone Falls.

From Yellowstone, they moved on to the Grand Tetons. They stayed at Brinker House, a rustic old lodge on Jenny Lake that the park service reserved for dignitaries. While Pinnix and much of the traveling party took a white-water raft trip down the Snake River, Burton stayed behind. They left early and returned in the late afternoon to find Burton more subdued than Pinnix had ever seen him. Was anything wrong? No, Burton said, it was just the longest he ever recalled being alone. He sat on the porch, looking out at the majestic Tetons, solitary and reflective. It was a unique experience for a man who constantly needed to be surrounded by other people, who often insisted that aides sit with him while he worked late, even if they had nothing to do.

They traveled next to Minnesota for field hearings on the Boundary Waters Canoe Area (BWCA), a divisive and emotional subject similar to the battle over the redwoods. The area contained some 1,000 lakes and hundreds of miles of streams and short portages for canoeists. North of Duluth along the Minnesota-Ontario border, it had been a hunting ground for the Chippewa and Sioux and a vital link in the early nineteenth-century fur trade, a water-way for French Canadians bringing furs east. In 1909, President Theodore Roosevelt proclaimed the land part of the national forest system. It was made a federal wilderness in 1964, with a waiver for logging, mining, and limited use of motorboats. BWCA was the most heavily used wilderness in the entire national forest system, besides Yellowstone or Yosemite. Its one million acres was half Yellowstone's size, and it was the largest remaining tract of virgin forest in the eastern U.S. Half its acreage had never seen logging, and it attracted hundreds of thousands of people a year. A large constituency from all over the country, but especially from Minnesota, Iowa, Wisconsin, and other Midwest states strongly supported preservation.

The local congressman, James Oberstar, opposed total preservation. Representing nearly fifty angry resort owners, half of whom would lose substantial business if snowmobiles and motorboats were banned, Oberstar wrote a bill to convert 300,000 acres from wilderness designation to a national recreation area, which would permit logging and motorboats. Minnesotan Don Fraser introduced a rival bill to preserve the entire tract and keep it free of commerce, development, or vehicles. On a still night, canoeists said, an outboard motor could be heard for two miles.[9]

Both bills came before Burton's subcommittee. Hence the field hearings, where passions ran so high that tires were slashed and proponents were burned in effigy. With both bills in contention, wrote *Sports Illustrated,* "Preservationists were pitted against developers, motor men against pure canoeists, little government advocates against big government advocates, economics against aesthetics. There was even a basic class conflict that matched blue-collar motorboat men and snowmobilers with a white-collar elite which seeks an abstraction called 'the wilderness experience.'"[10]

Outdoorsman and BWCA advocate Bud Heinselman was amazed at how much work Burton devoted to this issue. He met with resort owners personally, going over topographical maps of the proposed wilderness, listening to why each section was necessary. Heinselman, whose father had been an al-coholic, thought Burton was hitting the vodka "a little too hard." He spent several evenings with Burton going over the two bills, and then a third bill, sponsored by freshman Bruce Vento of Minnesota, which closely resembled Fraser's. More hearings were held in Washington that September, as angry Minnesotans descended on the Capitol. But it took months of contention to resolve the issue. When Oberstar came before Burton's subcommittee the following spring, Burton asked how many amendments he had.

"How many proxy votes do you have?" asked Oberstar, knowing there were forty-three members of the full committee.

"Twenty-two, plus my own," said Burton.

"Then I haven't got any amendments," replied Oberstar.[11]

Eventually, a House-Senate conference completed work on the BWCA bill. Burton worked with Bruce Vento to forge a compromise between Oberstar and Fraser. The bill, approved on the last day of session, banned all timber and mining, banned snowmobiles except for two portage routes to Canada, and permitted motorboats on 23 of 124 major lakes. In his interview with Moody, Burton talked about his philosophy of incrementalism:

> In the BWCA, I learned in part from going through the give and take
> with the redwoods. . . . We wound up with more [motorboat] use than we
> had originally planned—but much less than we already had under the ex-
> isting management—plus, we banned logging and restricted mining. So
> it's one thing to say, "Here's perfection, and I stand for it," and that's what
> we should do. But it's another thing to realize at some point that if you
> keep standing for perfection, you won't get anything, [while] the resources
> are becoming more endangered every day.

Joe Skubitz introduced the first version of what Burton eventually made the largest parks bill in American history on October 17, 1977. Udall and Sebelius were co-sponsors. HR 9601 contained thirty-seven routine items. "I viewed putting those items together into a bill as a bookkeeping kind of operation," Burton said later. In the first few months of 1978, while the redwoods bill was getting resolved, Burton held markup sessions on what *he* wanted in *his* omnibus bill: Mineral King, Santa Monica, Pine Barrens, and all the rest. "These were fake markups, the whole laundry list," Burton said. "But there was no [Burton] bill yet introduced. I wanted some sense of where the opposition would be, of who lines up against rivers or trails. I got a vague feel of the lineup, so I got a sense of how to put it together." Burton said his subcommittee happily tolerated this charade. "My colleagues aren't easily fooled. Incumbents would love to go through the entire two years without ever having to vote on anything. They don't mind this technique, because it protects them politically. I have a reputation for being able to tell them if something 'hurts' you in your district."[12]

The package grew quickly. "All of this was being done informally," Burton told Moody, "so that my colleagues weren't nailed to the wall on being for or against a proposal. . . . To these policy and bookkeeping items we added what I felt were all the outstanding national environmental issues that nobody had been able to resolve."[13]

Burton knew he had to move fast. By early 1978, he had come to view President Carter and his inept congressional operations with contempt. His administration was such a disaster, Burton told aides, that Carter would almost certainly lose to the likely 1980 GOP nominee, former California Governor Ronald Reagan. In that event, the window that had opened briefly for environmental issues would slam shut.

On February 24, 1978, a week *after* the House passed his redwoods bill, Burton moved Carter's Chattahoochee River bill out of his subcommittee. In other words, Burton did hold Carter's bill hostage a second time. The price: Carter's signature on Redwood National Park expansion, with its controversial Title II economic package for timber workers. Carter was not the only hostage, however. By now, it was common knowledge that Burton was assembling a huge parks bill with projects in 150 or more districts. "Phil had 150 members by the ears," said one lawmaker who closely watched the redwoods fight, and who spoke on condition he not be mentioned by name. "All he had to do was smile and remind them their park was going into the omnibus bill. The message was clear: on the Burton team, you give something to get something." Another member told the same reporter, "He didn't threaten anybody. He didn't have to. Phil just slaps you on the back and asks if you're still with him."

Burton denied using any of the parks as levers to prod members. "I never told anybody their park was in trouble if they didn't support redwoods," Burton told the *Chronicle*. "It doesn't work that way—you'd demean their intelligence." Nevertheless, he conceded, the pending omnibus package "helped create a calm and cooperative atmosphere for decision-making." Burton applied another principle: "Always tell them the truth," he advised Dale Crane. "They'll never believe you. Then you can do it to them, and they can't say a thing."

Before the House approved Senate amendments to the Chattahoochee bill in August, Burton also obtained administration approval for Santa Monica. "I held up Chattahoochee until Santa Monica cleared as an NRA," Burton said in his October 1978 speech to San Francisco environmentalists. "I was rougher than that. I said Chattahoochee was dead. I said, 'I'm going to win Santa Monica, but Chattahoochee is dead. Now go back and tell those Georgia crackers, will you?' . . . In five days Santa Monica was okayed. In six I cleared Chattahoochee."[14]

Burton introduced his magnum opus, HR 12536, on May 5. He drafted it with Pope Barrow, whose Legislative Counsel's Office was the very model of Richard Bolling's sense of order, rules, logic, and decorum. Consistent with that, Barrow put headings on all the titles and sections of the bill as guides. "Cut them out," Burton screamed. "You want them to find everything? You're making it too easy!" He wanted this bill approved before people figured out what was in it. Visibility in general was bad. Low visibility was better than high.

The scope, size, and cost of Burton's bill was unprecedented. The previous Interior omnibus bill in 1974 was 4 pages. This had 157 pages and seven titles. Its price tag was $1.8 billion, and its 150 projects affected more than 200 congressional districts in forty-four states. It authorized development funds for thirty-four parks, historic sites, and national seashores. It expanded twelve wilderness areas, created eleven new national parks, historic sites, and seashores, and added segments to eight wild and scenic rivers and four new national trails. It also incorporated 90 percent of Carter's preservation program, including $750 million for restoring inner-city urban parks.

Title I was Skubitz's original bill, the "bookkeeping" measures. Title II, which added money to individual park units, was where the eye-opening changes began. Burton had his mitts on the public treasury again and was spending like a drunken sailor. The acquisition cost for Big Cypress National Preserve in Florida, for example, shot up from $116 million to $156 million. Funds for the Cumberland Island National Seashore in Georgia nearly tripled, from $10.5 million to $28.5 million. Money for Sawtooth National Recreation Area in Wyoming went from $19.8 million to $47.8 million.

Staffers were floored. These increases were so huge that each ordinarily would have merited a separate bill, complete with public hearings. Here, each earned only a few sentences. "What Phil Burton was suddenly doing," recalled Pinnix, "was changing the definition of what is acceptable in an omnibus bill. If you are a good Republican, you might ask a whole lot of questions about why we are suddenly spending $40 million."

Title III consisted of boundary changes, which in previous bills added or subtracted a few acres. Some were innocuous. Others showed Burton at his most ingenious. Section 314, for example, added Mineral King to Sequoia National Park. With its 16,200 acres, Mineral King, however, was more than a minor boundary adjustment. One of the loveliest High Sierra backpacking areas, Mineral King was also one of the environmental movement's most important fights. Because it was also a natural downhill ski area, it was always threatened by major development. No project outside Alaska ranked higher on the Sierra Club's preservation list; it had been fighting since 1911 to place Mineral King in the national park, which surrounded it on three sides. Burton introduced a bill to accomplish that in 1969, but it went nowhere.

Mineral King was U.S. Forest Service land. Because the Forest Service strongly believed the area should be used for recreation, it granted Walt Disney Enterprises a three-year permit in 1965 to develop a master plan for a gigantic ski resort. Disney proposed a $35.3 million year-round resort for skiers and hikers, with an Alpine Village of five-story hotels, twenty-two ski lifts and gondolas, restaurants at 11,000 feet, skating rinks, swimming pools, a theater, and a five-acre parking lot. The five ski areas would be the largest in Central or Southern California. The plan envisioned up to 33,000 people a night, 8,000 skiers a day, and a million visitors a year in a valley two miles long by 1.25 miles wide. Disney also wanted a chapel and a twenty-mile access road to carry 1,000 cars an hour at an average speed of fifty miles an hour.

The area was just five hours from Los Angeles. Disney spent $500,000 on planning, visited twenty-two European ski resorts, and kept snow survey teams in Mineral King for four years. "We're happier with Disney than a frog in a mud puddle," Forest Service Supervisor Jim James told Arnold Hano, who described the battle for Mineral King in 1969 in the *New York Times Magazine*. Hano assumed Disney would win. "It is easy to be offended by the Disney project," he concluded, "and its threat to the ecology of Mineral King. Something is going to be taken forever from Mineral King: nature with the bloom of creation on it. In its place, Disney will leave another pleasure palace for Southern Californians, who have more pleasure palaces per capita than any other people in the world."[15]

But the threat from Disney galvanized environmentalists, who turned saving Mineral King into a crusade and spent years tying up the project in court. When John Krebs of Fresno introduced a bill to add Mineral King to the park, Burton pushed it through his subcommittee in fifteen minutes and then added it to his omnibus bill. Once the Carter administration signed off, Disney wanted reimbursement for $1.2 million, but Burton refused. "A company of that size and influence," he said, had to assume that "sometimes you win and sometimes you don't."[16] If Burton and Krebs had preserved Mineral King and nothing else, environmentalists would have celebrated a huge victory.

The next section in the omnibus bill was less controversial but more devious: "Section 2 (a) of the Act of Dec. 27, 1974 entitled 'An Act to provide for the establishment of the Cuyahoga Valley National Recreation Area' is amended by striking out 'Boundary Map, Cuyahoga Valley National Recreation Area, Ohio, numbered 90,0000-A, and dated September 1976,' and inserted in lieu thereof 'Boundary Map, Cuyahoga Valley National Recreation Area, Ohio, numbered 644-90,003, and dated May 1978.''

This seeming gibberish in fact added $29 million to buy land in the Cuyahoga NRA, a favorite of Seiberling's. "This was a blur, even to staff," said Pinnix. "If you weren't at it full time, you were lost and you would have to depend on me, or worse, on Phil, God forbid, to tell you what it does. You can't tell the acreage or if any widows are foreclosed. All you know is that Congress will spend $29 million. Until the Burton era, that $29 million alone is a big deal. And in the next subsection, he throws in an extra $26 million for development."

But if what he did with Cuyahoga echoed the technical games Burton played in Sacramento with AB 59, his costly and comprehensive California welfare bill, the next section involving Golden Gate National Recreation Area was even more stunning. In revising the boundary, he left blank both the map numbers and the dates. In other words, the co-sponsors—a who's who of the Interior Committee, including its most conservative Republicans—handed Burton a blank check to fill in as he saw fit.

Section 317 thus read: "New construction and development within the boundaries described in Section 2a [still blank because Burton had not yet cut the deal] on lands under administrative jurisdiction of a department other than that of the Secretary [of Interior] is prohibited." This section, indecipherable to anyone but Burton, was nevertheless unambiguous. The military could not build anything new on its base in the San Francisco Presidio or on any other military lands he had yet to define that were part of the GGNRA. Period. The army could renovate or demolish an existing structure and replace it with a building of the same size *but only* with the permission of the secretary of interior, who must first conduct a public hearing. All the concessions the army won during the 1972 GGNRA legislation thus disappeared. And no one realized what was happening. Burton was making doubly sure that when the Presidio ceased being a military base, as it would more than a decade later, it would remain open space, free of commercial development or new military construction. Another provision waived all admission fees to ensure that the public could always get in free.

Title IV established new wilderness areas in existing national parks, such as Big Bend in Texas, the Everglades in Florida, and Hawaiian Volcanoes National Park. Title V established new units, from a Guam National Seashore and a $16.5 million War in the Pacific National Historical Park, also in Guam, to the San Antonio Missions in Texas (later dropped because of Carter's objections), Edgar Allen Poe's home in Philadelphia (Joshua Eilberg wanted it; Burton wanted his vote), and the new trails.

This title also preserved the Pine Barrens in New Jersey, which came to national attention with the 1968 publication of *New Yorker* writer John McPhee's book about them. The Pine Barrens were too large, too developed, and too expensive to be made a national park. But working with Jim Florio of New Jersey, Burton wrote provisions to acquire the most ecologically sensitive areas and restrict development elsewhere. Title V also established, among others, another national park celebrating ancient Hawaiian culture in Hawaii and the Palo Alto Battlefield National Historic Site in Texas, which commemorated a major battle of the Mexican-American War.

Also buried inside Title V was Section 510, the Santa Monica NRA, "with an appropriation of not more than $50 million a year for 1979–81 FY inclusive." These words added $150 million to Santa Monica, where Phil and Sala spent their honeymoon. Any time it came up, Burton clutched his heart and said, "No one touches that. That's right here." The mountains, up to 3,000 feet, are the only range within a major U.S. city. They begin in downtown Los Angeles at Griffith Park and run west for some fifty miles, reappearing offshore as the Channel Islands. Thirteen million people lived within an hour of them.

Title VI was a miscellaneous grab bag that included $1.5 million to fix up the lodge at Old Faithful in Yellowstone. Burton also sought to re-purchase the presidential yacht Sequoia, which Carter sold as a cost-cutting measure in 1977 for $286,000. Preservationists argued that it was a unique part of American history, a place where Roosevelt and Churchill discussed World War II plans. But Burton withdrew the measure when gay activists reportedly talked him out of it. During the Nixon years, gay Republicans used the Sequoia for occasional floating sex orgies on the Potomac, protected by gay Secret Service men who kept a watchful eye out. Activists feared that if the yacht became a floating tourist attraction, its unsavory history would surface.

"The Sequoia could be rented privately," recalled a gay ex-Republican minor official who attended several such parties. "The masquerade was a fundraising 'trip' down the river. People did not use last names. It was taken for granted that it was 'impolite' to recognize anyone you knew, and it was definitely bipartisan. There would be an early evening cruise with readily available young men who got things started. It began about 1970 and lasted into the mid-70s."[17]

The seventh and last title of the omnibus bill added wild and scenic rivers—

and revenge. One such designation preserved a thirty-seven-mile stretch of the Delaware River where a $1 billion dam had been authorized at Tocks Island, a site environmentalists fought hard to protect. The major proponent for the dam was Frank Thompson of New Jersey, whose floor activities had kept Burton from becoming majority leader. A week after Burton's loss to Jim Wright, John Dent called Thompson and asked him to drop by. Burton was already there. Burton stood up, stuck out his hand and said, "Well, Thompy, I did it to you, and you did it to me. I guess I had it coming. We're even. Let's be pals." Thompson, who had a nickname for everyone, stuck out his hand and said, "Right, Philco." He had a drink, stayed twenty minutes and left, delighted that he had patched things up. Or so he thought.[18]

Burton talked freshman Peter Kostmayer of suburban Philadelphia's affluent Bucks County into sponsoring legislation that would kill Thompson's mega-dam and save Tocks Island. Burton then wrapped it into the bigger bill, which preserved pet projects in the districts of so many of his allies. A 1976 Burton supporter and former McGovern activist, Kostmayer had won his seat by only 1,300 votes. Saving Tocks Island would improve his re-election chances.

The dam, authorized in 1962 to provide drinking water, flood control, power, and recreation, would flood the Delaware Valley. This flooding, the *New York Times* editorialized, would destroy "fisheries, agricultural land and historic sites to create a shallow, algae-infested lake that would be clogged with silt within a generation." But construction would provide hundreds of union jobs. Building the dam, added the *Philadelphia Inquirer*, "would, in our estimation, make no more—or less—sense than filling the Grand Canyon with concrete, which also would employ a lot of people and spend a lot of money."[19]

On May 15, 1978, the Interior Committee approved HR 12536. It passed out of Rules on June 20 in five minutes. "Notice how quiet we all are," said Trent Lott, a Mississippi Republican. "We've all got something in there."[20] Six days later, Interior Secretary Andrus expressed "serious reservations" to Burton about the scope of the enormous bill "and real concern that the fiscal impact is more than we can ask the American taxpayer to accept." Even without Carter's $750 million urban parks program, this bill would still cost ten times more than the typical omnibus bill. Andrus asked Burton to scale it back from $1.8 billion to $1.2 billion. Burton trimmed about $200 million. As the bill headed to the floor, Burton called it "the environmental vote of the decade." He added, "It's broader in sweep than anything I've ever done. It was really easy. There was a lot of detail and hard work. But there wasn't the Gordian knot of the redwoods bill or the philosophical hang-ups of the black lung bill."[21]

The first of three days of debate began July 10 under an open rule, which permitted amendments. Burton asked for unanimous consent to add seventy technical amendments. He cleared all of it in advance with Sebelius and Skubitz. Skubitz, who was retiring at the end of the session, happily discovered a new item that ensured his continued cooperation: Section 611. It renamed Big Hill Lake in Kansas the Pearson-Skubitz Big Hill Lake.

Seiberling called it "the national parks and recreation bill of the century," but Republican William Goodling of Pennsylvania, with whom Burton apparently felt he did not need leverage, complained bitterly. To no avail, Goodling opposed expanding the Eisenhower Memorial Historical Site in his district, near Gettysburg National Battlefield.

"When one is considering purchasing land or transferring land in a district where the congressman has not asked for that favor," Goodling said, "it would be a good idea to check with him to see whether the barrel can take any more pork. . . . It is not a favor to me when people purchase one additional drop of land for Gettysburg Battlefield or Eisenhower Park. There is not much land left for the farmers to farm or for anyone to build on or anything else."[22]

Thompson stood up next to kill the "wild and scenic" designation for the middle Delaware River, thus restoring the dam project on Tocks Island. Thompson was raised on the banks of the Delaware, learned to fish and swim in the river and even now lived just one block from its shores, he said. He witnessed the devastating floods in 1955 that destroyed hundreds of homes in New Jersey, New York, Delaware, and Pennsylvania. Now, he said, fifteen million people depended on construction of this dam for flood control.

Thompson wanted to know why Burton was being so sneaky. If the dam was going to be "de-authorized," why did it go to Interior, rather than to Public Works, which originally authorized it? He knew the answer, of course. If it went to Public Works, the dam would not have been de-authorized. Thompson's amendment was defeated overwhelmingly, 110-275.

"He did a gorgeous job on me," Thompson said of Burton. "We wanted that dam. The bunny rabbit lovers opposed it. We were going to win. There were a colossal number of jobs and we had the unions. . . . They sneaked the Delaware River in as wild and scenic. They sandbagged me. It was brilliant. I couldn't even get mad, I admired their legislative skill so much."[23] He did not know the half of it. Buried elsewhere in the bill was a provision making Tocks Island a national recreation area. Even if Thompson's amendment had passed, the dam still could not have been built. It would have been illegal to flood it.

Over the next few days, Burton lost votes on amendments that reduced various wilderness areas. Max Baucus of Montana deleted nearly a million acres in Glacier National Park. Jim Oberstar delayed designating portions of the upper Mississippi River in Minnesota wild and scenic. Other legislators reduced wilderness in Cumberland Gap and Guadaloupe Mountains National Park in Texas. "The Texas delegation wanted to delete 19,000 acres [to] build a tramway," Burton said. "They got their acreage, but there was no development money in there at all if they tried to build their tramway. They didn't catch that."

Burton also restored an item that the House twice passed—only to lose in the Senate—to expand Manassas Battleground in Virginia, the Civil War sites of the first and second Battles of Bull Run. Just thirty minutes from Washington, Manassas attracted a million visitors a year, but Virginia Senators Harry Byrd, Jr., and William Scott opposed expansion. Burton also introduced an amendment to honor the late William Ketchum of California, a conservative Republican who worked closely with Burton on negotiating the Northern Mariana Islands Covenant. This amendment authorized "appropriate recognition" of Ketchum in the War in the Pacific National Historic Park in Guam. Members quickly agreed after Burton asked "that we stand and bow our heads for a few moments of meditation." It was not entirely a cynical ploy for Republican votes, however. Burton really liked and admired Ketchum.

On July 12, the final day of floor argument, the House spent most of its time wrangling over whether to rename the Indiana Dunes National Recreation Area for the late Senator Paul Douglas of Illinois, who spent the last years of his life fighting to preserve them. Douglas once said: "As a young man, I was somewhat of a revolutionary and wanted to save the world. Later on . . . as a Senator, I wanted to save the United States. But now, in the twilight of my career, I want only to save the Indiana Dunes."

The dispute arose because of an amendment to authorize $1.5 million for a Jean Lafitte National Historical Park in New Orleans, which the Senate had already passed. It was an urgent priority for Bennett Johnston of Louisiana, chairman of a key subcommittee of Senate Energy and Natural Resources. Because Congress was reluctant to name national parks or monuments after people—the temptation for abuse was obvious—Sid Yates of Illinois wanted to know why it was all right to name one park after a pirate, even if he did help General Andrew Jackson win the Battle of New Orleans, but not all right to name another one after a great U.S. Senator. Burton could not resist a dig.

BURTON: I have not yet constructed a rationale to distinguish the difference between the Jean Lafitte situation and the Paul H. Douglas situation, except for the fact that one was dead longer than the other and that one was a pirate and the other served in the U.S. Senate.

YATES: That is not sufficient. I do not see why [Burton] prefers to honor a pirate over a distinguished U.S. Senator by naming a park after him.[24]

Burton voted for Yates's amendment, which carried. Pinnix watched in amazement as the argument unfolded. Huge, expensive, controversial items were sailing through: Mineral King, Pine Barrens, Santa Monica Mountains, a 1.3 million-acre expansion of the Everglades, and those guys were arguing over something as trivial as why Indiana Dunes was not being named for a senator. "I cannot say that he orchestrated this part of it, too," Pinnix said. "But it fit Burton's purposes perfectly." Added Dale Crane, "The fight on Indiana Dunes had nothing to do with the merits. It was pure emotion. He could have thrown it in just to give them something noncontroversial to fight about."

The House approved the bill 341-60. The margin was no accident, given the states and congressional districts the bill affected. Burton was particularly generous to his subcommittee, whose bills he incorporated, and to other key members of Congress. In Arizona, for example, Mo Udall got one national historic site, three national historic monuments, two rivers designated wild and scenic, and two more rivers placed under study as potentially wild and scenic. Goodloe Byron got a national historical park at Harpers Ferry and the Chesapeake and Ohio Canal and national battlefield designations for Civil War battles at Monocacy and Antietam. Joe Moakley of Boston, chairman of a subcommittee on Rules, got Dorchester Heights added to the Boston National Historical Park. Trent Lott, also on Rules, got the Gulf Islands National Seashore and study of two rivers. Even Dick Bolling's Missouri district included the Oregon National Historic Trail. Lamar Gudger of his subcommittee—"Lamar Gudger, the man's a poet," Burton said of him—got a national historic site for Carl Sandburg's home, the Overmountain Victory Trail and study of the Chattooga River. Al Ullman of Oregon, chairman of Ways and Means, got five items: a national monument, Crater Lake National Park, the Oregon National Historic Trail, the Hells Canyon

NRA, and study of the Rogue River. At a key moment, Tip O'Neill got an extra $5 million for the Cape Cod National Seashore. Jim Wright got nothing, Dan Rostenkowski got nothing, and Frank Thompson got the "wild and scenic" Delaware River shoved down his throat.

The *New York Times* carried a short account of the bill's passage, much of it devoted to an account of the controversy over Jean Lafitte. But in an interview with the *Los Angeles Times* the day the bill passed the House, Burton denied charges "made privately to a reporter by four House members," that he used the bill to retaliate against people who had voted for Jim Wright.

"The charge that Burton was using the bill to punish political enemies," the *Times* wrote, "was a lively topic in the House cloakroom, but apparently was considered too risky to mention in floor debate. However, sources said it was the driving force behind several floor fights in which members from New Jersey, Pennsylvania, Montana, Minnesota and Texas sought to amend provisions they believed adversely affected their districts." The story said Oberstar and Richard White of Texas, whose amendment reduced acreage in the Guadaloupe Mountains, believed Burton's original bill retaliated against them for their support of Wright. Burton denied it. "To use something like this bill as an instrument of pique is absurd," he said. "It would be very counter-productive."

Even so, Burton was reported to have approached Oberstar and said, "Jim, I'm going to get even with you one of these days. I'm going to make the whole fucking Eighth District a national park." To which Oberstar replied, "I thought you already had." In his review of the bill, Burton said: "Oberstar will never talk to me again, but that's his problem, not mine, because next year, I'm going to do the Upper Mississippi." Asked about suggestions that he was using the bill to earn chits for another race against Wright, Burton replied, "I hope to God I don't have to apologize for passing a bill that gives the administration nearly everything they asked for and is being praised as one of the most significant pieces of parks legislation ever put together."

The bill faced big problems in the Senate, however, because Henry Jackson, chairman of Senate Energy and Natural Resources, "is not the legislative wheeler-dealer that Burton is," a source told the *Los Angeles Times.* "It is not as easy institutionally for the Senate to pass a huge omnibus bill."[25]

Burton already knew that and prepared himself. "At first," Burton said, "the administration was hostile . . . and the Senate was even more hostile. I was assured more times than I care to think that it was never going anywhere." Jackson's committee, bogged down with other legislation, was just getting to the bill as adjournment loomed.

While Burton was awaiting Senate action, the Wilderness Society honored him at a dinner. Just as Interior Secretary Andrus praised Burton for preserving wilderness for "our grandchildren," Sala Burton walked in leading her two grandchildren, five and six, by the hand. They had just stepped off a plane from Spain, where their parents—Sala's daughter Joy and son-in-law—lived. Surprised and overcome by emotion, Burton kneeled down to hug them, tears streaming down his face. "They are what it's all about," Burton said.[26]

As Congress neared adjournment, Burton knew his bill could die. There was no time for a conference to resolve differences between the two chambers. So in an unprecedented series of legislative maneuvers, he became a one-man conference, shuttling between House and Senate negotiating different versions. He passed the bill, sent it to the Senate, found out what key senators wanted, negotiated individually with them, returned the latest version to the House and passed it again. He likened himself to a "postal worker," collecting amendments by day. "Then I call later, at night, and get changes in their position, and then I call in the morning and I get still further changes, and I try to accommodate them." All told, he passed the same bill four separate times.[27]

Worried the Senate still would not pass his bill, Burton on October 4 hijacked S 791, which authorized money for the Sawtooth National Recreation Area—a priority for Idaho Senator Frank Church, ranking Democrat on Energy and Natural Resources, and House Republican subcommittee member Steve Symms—and dumped the entire omnibus bill into it, complete with twenty-seven amendments. He dropped expansion of Manassas National Battlefield to avoid objections from the Virginia senators and dropped Crater Lake National Park expansion to avoid protests from Mark Hatfield of Oregon. He got the bill through the House on unanimous consent and sent it back to the Senate. But just to make doubly sure, Burton also grabbed S 491, a minor Senate bill to establish the Fort Union Trading Post National Historic Site in North Dakota and Montana. Then he attached most of the important provisions of the omnibus bill to S 491, as well, trimmed another $150 million to avert a threatened Carter veto, but added $5 million more for Redwood National Park.

Floor debate made it clear that no one but Burton had the foggiest idea what he was doing, but ultraconservative John Rousselot of California got suspicious. He asked Sebelius to explain the latest version. Rousselot's intrusion infuriated Burton, who cut his deals with relevant Republicans on the committee and thought outsider Rousselot should butt out.

SEBELIUS:	This actually includes provisions that were contained in the omnibus bill.
ROUSSELOT:	So what we have done now is to split it three ways?
SEBELIUS:	Perhaps the gentleman from California could explain it. . . .
ROUSSELOT:	Mr. Speaker, further reserving the right to object, will the gentleman from California explain what we have done here? Is this divided or split among three bills?
BURTON:	It is divided. We did not include this in our earlier unanimous consent request.
ROUSSELOT:	Which piece does this include?
BURTON:	This includes Redwood National Park and a number of other very important pieces of legislation that have been authored by and approved.
ROUSSELOT:	The Redwood National Park, among others?
BURTON:	Yes.
ROUSSELOT:	Is that in this third bill?
BURTON:	Yes.
ROUSSELOT:	What does it include besides the Redwood National Park?
BURTON:	Mr. Speaker, I am again delighted to welcome for the second time our distinguished colleague, the gentleman from Southern California, to the Committee on Interior and Insular Affairs.
ROUSSELOT:	I am glad to find out what is going on. California is my state, too. I just wondered what is in the bill besides the Redwood National Park.
BURTON:	This permits consideration, as optional and additional, the Redwood National Park, the San Antonio Missions, the Golden Gate National Recreation Area and a number of other very important national considerations.
ROUSSELOT:	So it is now in three bills, or what?
BURTON:	Four.
ROUSSELOT:	Four?[28]

The dialogue continued until the still-perplexed Rousselot dropped his objection, and the bill sailed through on unanimous consent.

During the following week, Burton kept talking with appropriate senators and their staff. To please Bennett Johnston, he kept the Jean Lafitte site in the bill. To please Church, the Sawtooths were in. He already included Ebey's Landing in Washington to pacify Scoop Jackson. He added New River Gorge in West Virginia. "Robert Byrd is the majority leader in the Senate," Burton said later, "and I didn't think it hurt if we got something from West Virginia in this bill. They had Senate hearings at noon, and I swear to God, by ten that night, I had another omnibus bill to the Senate with New River Gorge in the bill." Burton admitted he held the Sawtooths "ransom for fourteen months." If Burton signed off on the Sawtooths, he lost his leverage with Church. So he refused to sign off until the omnibus parks bill was part of the Sawtooths final version.

The provision commemorating native Hawaiian culture, including the burial grounds of King Kamehameha, faced opposition from Hawaii Senator Spark Matsunaga. "Matsunaga wanted it like he wanted to swallow arsenic," and deleted it at the last minute, Burton said afterwards. He alerted Abourezk, who was half Lebanese and half Sioux Indian. Abourezk was deeply committed to Native American issues and had hosted native Hawaiian leaders at his house the night before the vote. Abourezk put Matsunaga on the spot, saying Matsunaga had been fighting *for* this provision for years. "Sparky gulped, and we won," Burton said.

"It will take an unbelievable series of pratfalls" for the bill to fail, Burton told a reporter. "There isn't a senator who won't like this bill," he added, noting that nearly ninety senators now had projects located in their states covered by the bill. Dick Curry of the Park Service said he felt like "Captain Ahab on a Nantucket sleigh ride. I had hold of a whale, and I was in this little boat, and I was being dragged all over the sea by this behemoth."[29] But there were still perils.

With just days before adjournment, Burton ran into what seemed like an insurmountable roadblock involving Mineral King. Any senator could block the bill in the closing two weeks of the session. Hayakawa of California opposed Mineral King becoming part of Sequoia National Park. But if it was going to happen, he wanted Disney compensated. Abourezk said he would oppose everything if Disney was paid off.

"I had to screw somebody, so I thought I'd screw Abourezk," Burton said afterwards.

> He's a liberal. I could communicate with him in the last four days. There's no way I could touch Hayakawa. So I put in the payoff to Disney in the third omnibus [version]. Abourezk picked up not the third version, but

the second version and tucked in the ban on skiing and no money for Disney and Hayakawa didn't pick up on it. I was worried. This was insoluble. One senator [was] saying no bill if the payoff isn't in there. And the other senator [was] saying no bill if the payoff is in there, and it's very late in the game.

Fortunately for Burton, Hayakawa couldn't keep up with him.[30] On October 11, the House approved Burton's fourth version, HR 6900, originally designed to amend the National Trails System Act. He threw in key elements of the omnibus bill again, plus the twenty-seven amendments. Cranston pressed to get the bill on the Senate's priority list and secured the necessary debate time. On October 12, the Senate took up S 791 instead, and HR 6900 died. In passing the bill, the Senate defeated amendments to save the dam at Tocks Island and to delete Mineral King.

"Is there any state other than Kansas that did not end up with a park?" Senator Robert Dole of Kansas asked.

"Did we leave you out, Bob?" asked Abourezk.

"I have two more years in my term," Dole replied.[31]

The bill returned to the House for final approval on October 13, where Burton offered it a fifth time on unanimous consent. But Republican Bob Livingston of Louisiana stood to object. Spotting him rise, Burton ran full throttle across the House chamber screaming, "There will never be another fucking nickel for sugar. I'll get you!" Livingston blanched, sat down, and the bill went through without a hitch. It took less than five minutes. "You're the only one who could have done it," Lagomarsino told Burton, whose thank you list took up two entire pages in the *Congressional Record* of October 13.

Pope Barrow recalled the night before, however, when Burton was anything but calm.

> My closest experience with him was on the final passage of the omnibus bill. He's ripping it up and taking things out and yellow paper is flying all over, and he's screaming, "Get this in. Get this in." It was some deal he'd cooked up or something flying into place at the last minute. He was sitting there chain-smoking, looking like he was going to have a heart attack at any moment, blood vessels popping out, talking on the phone constantly, and writing—all at the same time. People had never seen anything like it. Udall was appalled, probably because there were so many moving pieces. Interior had never worked that way before and probably never will again.[32]

Burton had one more trick to play on the Senate. Three times Scott and Harry Byrd of Virginia had scotched a House bill or amendment to expand the 8,000-acre Manassas National Battlefield. The land was valuable and developers were clamoring for it. Finally, Burton pulled aside Senate staffer Peter Bevinetti and said, "I'm tired of this shit. I'm going to slip it into some bill, but I'm not going to tell you where."

When Byrd heard this the last night of the session, he had what Abourezk described as a "klong—a medical term that denotes a sudden rush of shit to the heart"—and demanded that every bill relating to parks be brought to him so he could examine every word. All he knew was that somewhere in some bill was a map change and some numbers.

At 3 A.M. Sunday morning, October 15, a sharp-eyed Senate staffer spotted one sentence in another Jean Lafitte bill: "Notwithstanding any other provision of the law, the Secretary is authorized to acquire the lands and interest generally limited and depicted in the map numbered 379–80, 005-G and dated July 1978." This was the crucial sentence they were looking for. Byrd confronted Burton, "who told me . . . it would [also] be in three or four other House-passed bills. When I asked him which, he refused to say."

Burton did not put Manassas in any other bill. He just wanted to torture Byrd, who searched in vain for the other battlefield references for the next seven hours. Things slowed to a crawl in the Senate in the early morning hours before adjournment. Byrd stood with his back to the clerk's desk, trying to read every bill and occasionally nodding off. Whenever a Burton item came up, Burton, one of the rare House members who barged onto the Senate floor whenever he felt like it, walked over to Abourezk's desk and said, "Look at Harry. He can't keep his fucking eyes open."

The Senate moved at a snail's pace, waiting for Byrd to read everything before voting. Finally, it passed a unanimous consent item to direct the enrolling clerk to re-read every bill and delete any reference to Manassas, direct or indirect. Once Byrd was assured this would happen, he released the rest of the bills so the Senate could adjourn.

"This was the biggest joke he ever pulled on the Senate," recalled Senate aide Jim Bierne. "He never put that bill anywhere, and he just had a wonderful time thinking about Harry Byrd sitting there reading every single line of every bill and never finding it."

Furious, Byrd released a statement the next day calling Burton's actions "reprehensible." A *Washington Post* reporter asked Burton if he tried to sneak Manassas past the Senate. "Yup," Burton said. He was not going to "lay down and die," just because the Senate "wasn't going to give it the time of day."[33]

On November 10, President Carter signed the $1.4 billion National Parks and Recreation Act of 1978. When the legislative histories of his bills were bound and published, Burton liked to sign them and inscribe them to favored allies, as if he were the artist and these were numbered prints of an exclusive edition. On Wayburn's copy Burton wrote, "To Ed Wayburn—Thanks for your guidance and assistance. Another fruit of your efforts. Your protégé, Congressman Phil Burton." On Pinnix's he wrote, "To Cleve Pinnix—Thanks to your skills and untiring efforts we did in the bastards. Phil Burton, MC."

One week later, on November 17, Burton received a letter from Tom Winnett, his old friend from Young Democrats days and co-editor of the now-defunct *liberal democrat.* He still lived in Berkeley, where he founded a small publishing business, Wilderness Press, which publishes books and maps for hikers and backpackers.

"Whatever you do in the future," Winnett wrote, "I think you will be remembered for this bill."

> Thousands of people who over a decade and more sought to preserve Mineral King Valley won't forget you. The Santa Monica Mountains partisans won't forget you. These places I know about because I am a Californian. There must be hundreds of similar places around the country.
>
> I have often wondered whether my political efforts were really worth it. Now I can feel that if I did nothing else, I did in some small way contribute to your election to the House, and if that hadn't happened, this bill wouldn't have happened.[34]

17

PROXY FIGHTS AND MORE PARKS

*Phil Burton was still thinking he could put together a coalition for Speaker.
He never gave up that ambition. He was working on the younger guys in
our delegation, expanding his base, finding the weight of gravity.
But there was still some bitterness.*

CONGRESSMAN ROBERT MATSUI

*Others didn't carry the baggage Phil Burton carried. His personality was so
overpowering and his views were so controversial that they were restraints
on his success. Others went further because they had more moderate
personalities, more moderate views. He had more ability,
but others didn't have to overcome as much.*

FORMER HOUSE DEMOCRATIC WHIP TONY COELHO

*The only thing Phil Burton did not like about winning
was it meant the game was over.*

JIM BIERNE
Senate Energy and Natural Resources staff aide

EVEN DURING THE MOST critical stages of Phillip Burton's fight to pass his
enormous parks bill, he never lost sight of his larger objective: to challenge
Jim Wright again, sooner or later. Chits piled up, and as George Miller
observed, "they were never accidental." Between his original support, some
of which dissolved with his 1976 loss, his moral authority to force colleagues
into making the "right" vote whenever possible, his park barrel legislation,
his appointments to the North Atlantic Alliance delegation, and junkets he
awarded colleagues to Guam, American Samoa, or the Virgin Islands, Burton

dominated congressional affairs far more than any recently defeated leader had reason to expect.

Burton's management of the minimum wage bill and his new entitlement for displaced timber workers in Northern California kept his labor credentials burnished. While his crudeness offended some high-brow environmentalists, the shrewder ones knew how valuable it was to have the Mayor Daley of the movement on their side. Maybe he never did go outdoors, but they never saw a politician quite like him before, one who would not hesitate to crush people to preserve wilderness. Robert Lagomarsino called him a "benevolent steamroller." Others were less charitable. But all knew only he could have brokered the redwoods expansion deal between labor and environmentalists and guided that bill to a presidential signature against all but impossible odds.

Signs of Burton's interest in moving back into the leadership were evident everywhere. In July 1978, congressional challenger Vic Fazio of Sacramento came to Washington for a fund-raiser. He hoped to succeed Robert Leggett, who, it turned out, maintained separate wives and families in his district and in Washington. When the story became public, Leggett prudently decided to retire. Wright and Burton showed up at Fazio's reception but at different times. A month later, Robert Matsui, another challenger from Sacramento, arrived in Washington to raise money. Again, Wright and Burton were on hand separately to court him. Burton supported Matsui's primary opponent, Phil Isenberg, an old ally from Young Democrats days, but the night Matsui won the primary Burton was on the phone congratulating him.

"I have $2,000 for you for the general," Burton said. Matsui's campaign manager, Clint Reilly, had also managed Father Eugene Boyle's 1974 assembly race against John Foran, whom Burton supported. Burton invited Matsui to dinner. "Clint's not invited," he said. "Get rid of him." Matsui was floored by Burton's presumption but obeyed.

Later, Matsui dropped in on Burton at his office. As Matsui arrived, Burton was meeting with another challenger, Tony Hall, of Dayton, Ohio. Burton, who knew Hall's district better than Hall did, was telling Hall how important it was to hold the black vote. "I'll talk to the labor guys and make sure they help you," Burton said, handing Hall an NAACP brochure of Ohio leaders. Matsui wondered why Burton was so interested in an obscure politician in a district far from California. But to those who knew Burton, his interest was obvious. He was working the prospective freshman class just as he had in earlier years.

Burton raised $67,000 at a February 1978 fund-raiser in San Francisco.

Perhaps to buy some peace, Speaker Tip O'Neill attended as the featured guest. Dinner receipts provided the $2,000 Burton had promised to Matsui and to other fall challengers. Using his extensive contacts in the labor, environmental, and consumer movements, he directed additional money to Democrats likely to win. Wright was not idle, either. By May, he had raised $300,000 for the same purpose. Wright kept a map of the U.S. in his office showing every congressional district. The eighty-three red pins indicated those he visited in the seventeen months since becoming majority leader. But Burton was skeptical of the 193 pledges of "firm support" that Wright hurriedly rounded up after reports surfaced from the AFL-CIO convention that Burton was looking to challenge him again. "One view is that it is easy to get 193 votes when a candidate is running unopposed," the *National Journal* wrote. "Another is that [Wright's] survey itself bears out Burton's view that Wright is scared."[1]

Burton's performance at the end of the Ninety-fifth Congress intensified the talk, and Burton, who never cared about good press, saw that his environmental success helped erode his image as a power-mad inside broker. By late fall, however, Burton and Mark Gersh reluctantly concluded they could not unseat an incumbent majority leader who had not slipped up. That did not stop Burton from doing everything possible to maximize opportunities should they come or stick it to rivals. Nor did it stop O'Neill and Wright from seeing Burton's scheming mind behind every plot, real or imagined. Thus ensued a series of proxy fights between Burton allies and O'Neill-Wright-Bolling supporters that determined the composition of key committees, the chairmanship of a critically important health subcommittee, and the tenor and tone of the House for the next several years.

After the 1978 midterm election, *National Journal* returned to the prospective battle, noting that thirty-nine House Democrats had died, retired, or been defeated since 1976, two-thirds of them Wright supporters. "Anyone who has any doubts of Burton's continuing interest in House leadership need only have observed his activity in the last few weeks of the 95th Congress," wrote correspondent Richard Cohen. "Working at an often frenetic pace, Burton seemed to be everywhere." Besides his parks bill, Burton "appeared to be stage managing the tactics" for several major issues on which he opposed Wright. Unlike Wright, Burton supported President Carter's vetoes of public works and defense authorization bills and opposed Wright on energy legislation and school busing. But Cohen also noted that the House leadership, including Foley, opposed a new Burton challenge, and Bolling was in line to chair the Rules Committee.[2]

Equally discouraging to Burton were the soundings he took from new members, especially in California, where voters in June 1978 approved a huge property tax–cutting measure called Proposition 13. The measure indicated a swing to conservatism, indeed, helped set the stage for Ronald Reagan's national success in 1980. "I like and admire Phil, but we all had to campaign as fiscal conservatives this year," one new member told the *Sacramento Bee*. "How would it look in my district if the new House immediately got tagged with big-spending liberal Burton as Majority Leader?"

Sometimes Burton backed the wrong person. In Massachusetts, for example, he supported street-tough Brian Donnelly's opponent in the Democratic primary. "Let me tell you something I don't think you know," Donnelly told Burton. "While you were trying to keep me from getting elected, Jim Wright was raising money for me. I told him that however long it takes, he had my vote for Speaker. Do you think I'll screw him for Majority Leader?"

Forty-one new Democrats were elected, but many were more ideologically attuned to Wright than to Burton. "There is speculation on Capitol Hill," *Bee* reporter Leo Rennert wrote, "that Burton may postpone a direct confrontation with Wright until O'Neill eventually retires and then make a direct bid for Speaker."[3] That is precisely what Burton prepared to do. He would sit tight, broaden his base, pass bills, and wait for Wright to err or O'Neill to retire.

But a few days later, Burton's feud with Jim Oberstar burst into the open, raising anew his leadership ambitions. Oberstar told a St. Paul newspaper that Burton offered to delay the Boundary Waters legislation in Minnesota that Oberstar opposed in return for Oberstar's vote for majority leader. Burton exploded, calling Oberstar's accusation "obscene, absurd. . . . A total flat lie without a scintilla of fact to support it. . . . How was I supposed to pull that off with Fraser and Vento and Bud Heinselman looking?" Oberstar stuck by his story that Burton "indirectly indicated" such a deal, but conceded that no third party heard it and that he told no one else about it. Burton aides Pinnix and Crane said years later they did not believe Burton would squander his reputation by swapping wilderness for personal gain. His vehement denial also contrasted with other times when he readily confessed to various shenanigans, such as trying to sneak Manassas expansion past Senators Byrd and Scott.[4]

Burton's immediate plans became explicit in the December 3 *Dallas Morning News*, which Wright was sure to see. It quoted a Burton "source" saying Burton "absolutely" intended to run for Speaker when O'Neill retired but would "never run against O'Neill." A Wright aide said, "We have 220 pledges right now. Give us two more years."[5]

Even so, Burton kept up the pressure. A few days later, Foley appointed him to chair the former Hansen Committee to review the size, structure, and authority of all House committees. Wright became "visibly agitated" when Foley informed him, Foley recalled. The steam had gone out of House reform, but they did not underestimate how Burton could turn up the heat again. O'Neill insisted that Foley "pack" the committee with anti-Burton people, including Bolling, Gillis Long, Thompson, and Rostenkowski as vice chairman.

Earlier that day, the California delegation chose Burton to represent it on the DCCC, replacing Yvonne Brathwaite Burke, who left Congress to run for state office. Jim Corman tried to block Burton's selection, suggesting that another black should get the job. But Ron Dellums of Berkeley ended that ploy, saying, "No. Phil is a soul brother. I'm all for him."[6]

The delegation also voted 18-7 to endorse Jerry Patterson of Orange County to succeed Sisk on Rules. When Bizz Johnson told O'Neill about the vote, O'Neill said, "I wish you hadn't done that." Having finally won the right to name who he wanted to Rules—the only committee to which he could appoint every member—the Speaker was not about to let state delegations dictate his choices. Johnson and Burton then compounded their error. If O'Neill appointed someone else, they warned, the Californians would be offended.

O'Neill ignored their concerns and picked Tony Beilenson, who forged his own relationship with Bolling, over Patterson. "I'll bet Burton has really got steam coming out of his ears now," a leadership aide said.[7]

These skirmishes were just the most visible signs of the intense proxy war between Burton and the House leadership, which used the Steering and Policy Committee to deny Californians one seat each on Appropriations, Budget, Interstate and Foreign Commerce, and two seats on International Relations. California newspapers attributed the delegation's weakness to rivalries, clashing ambitions, and leadership efforts to keep punishing Burton allies. Beilenson deliberately avoided seeking the delegation's help and cut his own deal, said Burton pal George Brown of Riverside, "because the delegation is not all that important."

But the retirement of powerful health care baron Paul Rogers of Florida gave Henry Waxman, a Burton liberal just beginning his third term, the chance to score a major coup. Rogers chaired one of the most important panels in Congress, the Health and Environment Subcommittee of the Committee on Interstate and Foreign Commerce. The subcommittee had enormously broad jurisdiction, including public health, hospital cost containment, mental health, biomedical research, Medicare and Medicaid, national health insurance, food, drugs and drug abuse, the Clean Air Act, and environmental protection. Aided by political advisor Michael Berman, Waxman set out to win the chairmanship.

Under rules pushed by Burton and the DSG in the mid-1970s, members of full committees could vote on subcommittee chairs. Waxman was in a position to go for it only because he was lucky following his 1974 election. Of all freshmen on that committee, he won the senior draw, giving him the most seniority. Even so, after four years Waxman ranked only fourth, thirteenth on the full committee. His opponent was L. Richardson Preyer of North Carolina. At fifty-nine, Preyer was twenty years older. He had six more years of seniority and was two slots ahead of Waxman on the subcommittee. But for Waxman, the power to be derived from such a huge and important jurisdiction made the risk of defeat worth it. Mortified when they discovered Waxman's intentions, House leaders became determined to defeat this upstart.

The Waxman-Preyer contest thus turned into the biggest power struggle of the new Congress and the first serious test of the seniority system since the class of '74 deposed the committee dinosaurs. This was not some effort to put a feeble, reactionary, or autocratic chairman out to pasture. A highly respected progressive southerner and former federal judge who supported civil rights, Preyer was once a serious candidate to head the CIA and had introduced bills to provide guidelines for federal busing orders. But he was vulnerable to Waxman's argument that the heir to the Richardson-Merrell drug fortune, which included Vicks Vapo-Rub and prescription drugs, should not direct the nation's health care legislation. Even though Preyer likely would have done everything possible to avoid any conflict of interest, the appearance was there. And his votes to continue tobacco subsidies—necessary in his tobacco-growing district—were a mark against him with the powerful medical establishment.

Preyer had backed Richard Bolling for majority leader, while Waxman was one of Burton's most vigorous supporters. The leadership therefore interpreted this contest as a replay of Burton-Wright-Bolling, which gave it a dimension beyond its importance. Taking advantage of recent federal election laws, Waxman created a political action committee and distributed $40,000 in campaign contributions to colleagues, many on his committee. Bolling was appalled. He felt Waxman was trying to buy the subcommittee chairmanship. O'Neill, Wright, and Burton all had PACs. But some members were offended that a *junior* member should so presume. Committee Chairman Harley Staggers of West Virginia, a Wright supporter, returned Waxman's $1,000.

Despite the heavy overtones of 1976, Waxman never consulted Phil Burton before making his move, which angered and embittered Burton. He thought the ploy too risky and treated Waxman badly for a month. Moreover, it upset his southern coalition. O'Neill, Wright, and Bolling, however, saw Burton's hand everywhere and mobilized to defeat Waxman, who was rounding up support from Nader, environmental groups, and organized labor, which saw Waxman as its vehicle for national health insurance. A month before the vote, O'Neill aide Ari Weiss approached freshman Bob Matsui, who had bid to get on Interstate and Foreign Commerce, a premier assignment that would also give him a vote in the Waxman-Preyer contest.

"Are you a Burton guy?" Weiss asked.

"Gee, I like Phil, but I only met him in August," said Matsui, naive and oblivious.

"Oh come on, you're a Burton guy," Weiss said.

Soon after, Preyer asked Matsui for his support. Less naive and no longer oblivious, Matsui said he was a friend of Waxman, and Waxman, a member of Steering and Policy, was going to nominate him for the full committee.

The crunch came at the January 1979 Steering and Policy meeting to determine Democratic committee assignments. There were five openings on Interstate and Foreign Commerce. Determined to block Waxman's ascent, the leadership made sure none of the five went to a Waxman supporter, who could then vote for him. Wright used his influence to get freshmen Phil Gramm and Mickey Leland of Texas on the committee and to keep Matsui off. Second-termers and Burton allies Peter Kostmayer and Bruce Vento also lost out. Bolling at one point began shouting at Waxman about challenging a more senior member and threatened to boot Waxman himself off the committee.

After the tense session, Staggers went up to Matsui on the House floor and said, "I voted for you, young man." This infuriated Burton, who grabbed Staggers by his lapels and snarled, "Don't lie to him."

"I didn't," Staggers said.

"You did," Burton replied. Other freshmen were stunned by Burton's assault on the integrity—and the lapels—of a senior committee chairman. "Phil had a way of holding people accountable," Matsui recalled. "He knew everything. He had ears everywhere."

But Wright and Bolling made a mistake Burton would not have made. They neglected to tell the five new members they put on this highly desirable committee how to vote in the Waxman-Preyer contest. The newcomers did not realize the price of their selection was to support Preyer. Burton told Waxman he should call all five and ask for their vote. Waxman said that was ridiculous. But he took Burton's advice and got commitments from Leland and Al Swift of Washington, whose votes proved crucial to the outcome. Second-term liberal Barbara Mikulski, whose vote Burton mistakenly counted on in 1976, also voted for Waxman, as did Tim Wirth, one of the 1974 freshmen who led the charge against Burton two years later.

The full committee rejected Preyer 15-12. Members then voted for Waxman, 21-6. Afterwards, Waxman said he believed seniority alone should not decide such votes. In a comment that echoed Burton's philosophy, Waxman said, "Dick Bolling worries about the instability of the institution. My commitment is not to the institution, but to the issues it deals with."

Burton was so thrilled that when he spotted Michael Berman, he hugged him, squeezed him, and kissed him on the cheek. "I don't believe you guys did it. I didn't think you could. Terrific," he yelled jubilantly. After his initial anger, Burton had rounded up several other votes Waxman could not have gotten on his own. Waxman and Burton won. Wright and Bolling lost. As with Frank Thompson and the Tocks Island dam, it was a small measure of revenge.[8]

It took until the end of February 1979 for anyone to say out loud and in print what House insiders had been watching for more than two years: Democrats were badly split between the O'Neill-Wright-Bolling faction and Burton. Virtually every contest, no matter how trivial or how much a sideshow, was viewed through that filter. When Abner Mikva stepped down as chairman of the Democratic Study Group, battle lines hardened again. The leadership's candidate was David Obey of Wisconsin, a Bolling protégé. His opponent was fellow liberal Richard Ottinger of New York, whom Burton endorsed.

"Rightly or wrongly," wrote the *Washington Post*, "DSG is perceived as under the influence of the Burton faction. DSG Chairman Abner Mikva spent the last two years reassuring the leaders that DSG was not out to get them. 'There's still a little bit of paranoia that we're being masterminded by Phil,'" Mikva said. Just as Obey denied he would be a "tool of the leadership," Ottinger declared, "I'm not an instrument of Phil." Summing up what many Democrats may have felt, Obey said, "I'm sick and tired of everything that comes up around here being a replay of the last Majority Leader race. We ought to quit fighting old personality battles and grow up. We ought to quit niggling over a one percent difference in philosophy and get together and agree to be a real force." Brave words, but Norm Mineta said the antipathy between Burton and the leadership "is a cloud that is going to be with us forever, influencing everything that goes on." Waxman's victory over Preyer, he said, "was like salt in the wound."[9]

Obey was elected, ending for a while talk of Wright versus Burton. A "Capitol Comment" page in the October 1979 *Washingtonian* said O'Neill might retire in 1982 and Wright had to be the "early favorite." Liberals could turn to Burton, except those who found him "too devious," the magazine said.

Despite his inability to get Patterson on the Rules Committee over Beilenson, Burton still dominated the California delegation, and new members, in particular, were terrified to cross him. Leon Panetta, a second-termer from Monterey who was close to Burton, nevertheless took the full brunt of Burton's fury over an item that, given Panetta's obvious anguish, wasn't all that earthshaking. Panetta had started out in politics as a Republican and had worked for Senator Tom Kuchel of California in the late 1960s. After Kuchel lost his primary, Panetta went to work in the Nixon administration as head of HEW's Office of Civil Rights but got fed up, resigned, and changed parties. He went home, practiced law, and in 1976 was elected to Congress as a Democrat.

The trouble began over Burton's desire to get more money in President Carter's budget for a conservation fund, which he could use to acquire more public lands. As a new member of the Budget Committee, Panetta was in a position to ask for it. Burton had already gone to Panetta's chairman, Robert Giaimo, to ask for an amendment. Giaimo, who represented a heavily Italian-American constituency in New Haven, Connecticut, and who was on Burton's handwritten list as having voted for Wright in 1976, told Burton not to waste his time because he had the votes to kill it.

Panetta found himself in an impossible situation. On one side, his chairman, no friend of Burton, told him not to offer an amendment because it would lose, but Giaimo also said he would see what he could do in conference. On the other side, Burton was breathing fire as only he could. Panetta reluctantly sided with his chairman. When Burton found out that Panetta never even offered the amendment, Panetta recalled, "he went through the ceiling," telling Panetta, "I don't give a good goddam what your chairman says. When I tell you to do it, do it." Burton was so angry, Panetta couldn't even talk to him. So he wrote a note.

"Dear Phil," Panetta's letter began.

I am upset enough by your anger and remarks that I felt I had to sit down and try to convey to you some personal thoughts before I left for California. I love and respect you too much to allow this or any misunderstanding to in any way impact on our relationship. What happened was in part the result of mistake and partly the result of misjudgment on my part. This is not the first mistake or misjudgment I have made nor do I expect it will be my last. But my Catholic faith tells me that since "infallibility" belongs only to the Pope, members of Congress must simply get up and try again. And that's what I pledge to you.

Whatever your anger and outrage, please know that my love and my loyalty will always be to you and what you stand for—not because of . . . a bill or an amendment in exchange—but because your causes are right. My Italian ancestors tell me even Garibaldi failed a few times before he finally delivered a unified Italy to his people. I hope you'll give me the same chance.

From the intensity of Panetta's language, one might have thought he had changed parties again and endorsed Ronald Reagan for president or committed some other unpardonable sin. That he hadn't and yet still felt compelled to apologize in such a personal way was a reflection of the respect—and fear—that Burton's junior colleagues held for him.[10]

Panetta soon got his chance to make it up to Burton, who was now refocusing on parks: specifically, Big Sur in Panetta's district, Lake Tahoe, and all the others that had been compromised out of the last big bill. First, however, Burton turned to the matter of Chief Turkey Tayac and Goodloe Byron.

Byron, a conservative Democrat from Maryland, died while jogging on his beloved Appalachian Trail in Maryland in 1978. A month later, prominent Native American Turkey Tayac died of pneumonia at eighty-three. Neither had a clue that fate and Phil Burton's fertile imagination would enshrine them forever in federal law. Turkey Tayac claimed to be the last full-blooded Piscataway Indian. A knowledgeable herbalist and an important Indian leader for decades, he was the last of his tribe to speak its language. He wanted to be buried with his ancestors in his tribe's historic burial grounds along the Potomac in Prince George's County. In the 1960s, the chief donated much of this land, including the burial ground, to the government for a national park. He believed he had an oral agreement that would allow him to be buried in the park. But park regulations prohibited burials. He needed an act of Congress.

Soon after Turkey Tayac died, Burton sent a bill to the Senate, written by

Gladys Spellman and the rest of the Maryland delegation, to permit his burial. But cynics there said John Smith eliminated the last of the Piscataways 300 years earlier and killed the bill. During this bickering, Turkey Tayac spent a year on a marble slab in the deep freeze of a coroner's office. Then Burton got a brainstorm. In a bill to commemorate Byron's efforts to preserve the Appalachian Trail—Byron's widow Beverly succeeded him and was lobbying the Senate hard for passage—Burton tossed Turkey Tayac's burial in as Title III. The House passed it on October 9, 1979, and the Senate quickly followed.

Burton was so proud of his handiwork that he called Senate staffer Jim Bierne to say "gotcha." But in one of the few times anyone ever got him back, Bierne said, "Congressman Burton, there is a reason why we have rules here in the Senate and why we have a deliberative process."

"I don't need that crap," Burton said. "This bill is going to the White House."

"That may be," said Bierne, "but you got the pages mixed up. You dedicated Piscataway to the congressman and buried the Indian on the Appalachian Trail." Bierne did not tell Burton he was kidding, and it was just plausible. There was dead silence on the other end.

"Shit!" Burton said, slamming down the phone and ordering the bill back from the White House. When he realized what Bierne did, Burton called back.

"That was good," he said. "I'm going to get you."

Others were more grateful. "Dear Phil," Spellman wrote. "You were magnificent! Thanks to you, Turkey Tayac's dream of burial in Piscataway Park is about to become a reality. We couldn't have done it without you."[11]

On November 11, Turkey Tayac was laid in the rich Maryland earth amid his ancestors. Wild turkey feathers were distributed among 300 relatives, tribe members, and friends. It was the first "full Indian burial service" in sixty years, his son, Billy Tayac, said. Some mourners permitted Bill Eagle Feather, a Dakota Indian chief and close friend, to cut tiny pieces of flesh from their arms to place on the grave as a sign of respect.

The Indian and the congressman behind him, Burton began work on a new bill to fix technical errors in his omnibus parks bill. When the new bill passed in February 1980, it had evolved into a $70 million piece of distinctively Burtonesque park barrel. In his hands, what had started out as "routine" ended up creating the $30 million Channel Islands National Park—Lagomarsino's bill—adding $5 million to buy 2,400 acres at Point Reyes, $15.5 million for up to 5,400 acres at Golden Gate National Recreation Area, and

$10 million for Olympic National Park in Washington. Burton said the new land at Point Reyes completed the National Seashore, but he had still more plans for GGNRA. "I'm moving south," he said, meaning San Mateo County. The bill changed appropriations and boundaries for twenty-one other national parks, battlefields, and monuments.[12]

Burton pushed to preserve as much land as he could, especially in California, before the Republicans returned to power. He drafted legislation for Big Sur and Lake Tahoe, where for years encroaching development and pollution bedeviled environmentalists, planners, builders, landowners, and bureaucrats from California and Nevada.

Burton and Jim Santini were already friends. A former county district judge who was his state's sole congressman—he represented conservative, rural Nevada and libertarian Las Vegas—Santini voted for Burton for majority leader and relied on Burton for political advice. His state gave birth to the Sagebrush Rebellion in 1979, a movement by many of the thirteen western states to reclaim some 544 million acres of land the federal government owned. Supporters called it the "Second American Revolution" and said they wanted to equalize western states with eastern states, where federal ownership of land was minimal. But opponents, including most Democrats and virtually all environmentalists, saw the Sagebrush Rebellion as an ill-disguised land grab to permit oil and gas, development, timber, and mining companies to cash in and exploit the natural resources on federal lands. One of their champions was a lawyer for the Mountain States Legal Foundation named James Watt.[13]

Santini, like Burton, was frustrated by the failure to preserve the once-glorious Tahoe region on the California-Nevada border. The largest alpine lake in the Western Hemisphere, twelve miles wide by twenty-two miles long, and once crystal clear all the way to the bottom, Tahoe was now covered with green algae from pollution. A massive building boom had gone unabated for years. The combination of vacation-home builders on the California side, summer and ski resort operators, and casino-hotel developers in Nevada degraded the region. Until recently an area of unsurpassed high-country beauty—once the summer home of the Washoe Indians—Tahoe now endured strip development, traffic congestion, and smog equal to San Francisco levels. Some 47,000 people inhabited the Tahoe Basin year-round, with another 300,000 visitors on a busy day, compared to 2,500 year-round residents in 1950 and 30,000 daily visitors. A drive around the lake took a visitor past 107 restaurants, 56 gas stations, and 218 hotels. Efforts to control growth foundered as competing jurisdictions, powerful landholders, and environmentalists tangled bitterly.

Santini was also frustrated by what he saw as "ridiculous" Bureau of Land Management checkerboard landholdings just off the extremely valuable Las Vegas strip. One block from some of the world's most garish—and profitable—hotel-casinos, BLM owned 150 undeveloped acres. From the juxtaposition of those two unresolved situations—Tahoe and Las Vegas—Santini evolved an audacious idea: sell the BLM holdings near the Vegas strip for big money and permit the federal government to use that money to buy undeveloped, environmentally sensitive lots in Tahoe to stop expansion. This was a kind of Sagebrush Rebellion in reverse, but the political obstacles were overwhelming and took more than a year of intense, late-night Burton-Santini negotiations to resolve.

Burton had to convince environmentalists that it was suddenly okay to sell federal lands in the West to private developers in exchange for preserving something as valuable as Lake Tahoe. Eternally wary, environmentalists initially believed this could establish precedent that Sagebrush Rebellion activists would use less benevolently elsewhere. As Santini recalled, all Burton could say was, "Trust me. I've never screwed you before. I won't screw you now. Look at my track record." Burton's assurance carried great weight. But Burton also had to deal with Bizz Johnson. He represented enraged landholders who wanted to build. Burton realized early that while California interests came to him to resolve the problems of the Tahoe Basin, they, far more than Nevadans, were responsible for having ruined the once pristine area.

Santini's political problems were even thornier. Most of his constituents lived in Clark County around Las Vegas. Not only did they not care about preserving Lake Tahoe, they would want to know why money from the sale of valuable land in their backyard should be used to save a lake hundreds of miles away. Moreover, some of the biggest property interests in Las Vegas, including the Howard Hughes estate, did not want land near the strip to suddenly come on the market and depress the value of their holdings.

The Carter administration was also opposed. OMB hated earmarking funds for anything. Money from the sale of federal land should go to the general fund, not some private pot to save Tahoe. There seemed little in it for Santini, other than the knowledge that he helped preserve a beautiful area. His leverage was a Vic Fazio bill to make the entire area a national recreation area. There was no chance of that happening, but Santini could position his bill as the lesser of two evils and use the Fazio bill as a club.

Burton and Santini typically got started about 7 P.M. in Burton's office and argued for three hours each night for months. As their aides recalled, both men loved the combat. Each night, Dale Crane readied a new draft of some portion of the bill for the next morning. All told, he did thirty-six. Santini's staffer, Mary Lou Cooper, was handed the issue her first day on the job in August 1979. At an early negotiating session Santini asked Cooper for her political assessment. When she finished, Burton exploded, spittle flying: "How dare you tell me about political reality! No one knows more about political reality than I do." Cooper, who felt like she had just been thrown into a cage with the toughest lion in the zoo, was determined not to cry until she got home. But she, like her boss, ended up enjoying Burton.

"Russian vodka was way down on my list," Santini recalled, "but this was my baptism of fire. His mind worked so fast that it was a challenge to keep up with him. . . . It took a lot of political spadework on my part and masterful engineering on his." Santini impressed Burton. "Goddam it, Jim," Burton told him, "one thing I like about you is that you're operational. I hate these fucking ideologues." This was Burton's ultimate compliment.

On May 8, 1980, Burton and Santini introduced their bill. "That day the fighting stopped and the celebrating began," Cooper recalled. "For them, the hard times were over. This is the opposite of how most legislation is done. The environmentalists felt left out, and Santini's constituents felt left out, but it might not have been done any other way." For Mary Lou Cooper, however, the hard times were just starting. That day, the National Inholders Association in Tahoe besieged Santini's office with a thousand telegrams protesting the bill.

Their arrival was "the most vivid thing that ever happened to me in my sixteen years of politics," Cooper said. "Those yellow telegrams just kept coming. Santini was worried, but he didn't say anything." Most homeowners mistakenly believed that the government was planning to buy *their* land, whether or not they wanted to sell it, rather than buy undeveloped lots. But speculators who bought lots hoping to sell them at a huge profit were correct in interpreting the legislation as an effort to shut down growth.[14]

HR 7306 directed the Interior Department, acting through BLM, to sell no more than 700 acres a year near the Las Vegas strip and deposit the money in the U.S. Treasury. All told, the government could sell up to 9,000 acres, 7,000 in Clark County and 2,000 in Washoe County. Seventy-five percent of the proceeds would be used to buy up to 16,000 undeveloped lots at Tahoe, especially land with steep slopes and high erosion potential where runoff was great. Another 20 percent of the money from the sales would return to the county of sale for recreation—Santini's compromise with Clark County officials who wanted something out of the deal—and 5 percent would be used for state education. The bill provided up to $150 million over ten years. In the most controversial section, the bill authorized $30 million to acquire homes on the California side "if the owner consents or if the Department of Agriculture determines that use of these lands jeopardizes the air, water or visual qualities of the basin." This meant the federal government could condemn and purchase improved property.

Four days after the bill was introduced, Burton held hearings. Two days later, on May 14, the Interior Committee approved the bill on a voice vote. "It was a classic Burton coup de grace," recalled Santini. "Not a single dissenting vote." On May 30, the week before the 1980 California primary, President Carter endorsed the bill. Burton, campaigning in San Francisco with Carter rival Ted Kennedy, said he was delighted. Nevada Republican Paul Laxalt and Alan Cranston said they would introduce it in the Senate.

The bill went to the House floor on September 8. The only dissenting voice was Bizz Johnson's. But it faced an uncertain fate in the Senate, where Laxalt and Howard Cannon, a conservative Nevada Democrat, opposed the federal condemnation powers. With the likely election of Laxalt's close friend Ronald Reagan just two months away, Burton felt he had no choice but to negotiate. He reluctantly agreed to Senate amendments that gave the Tahoe Regional Planning Agency veto power over any federal condemnation action. It was that, Burton said, or risk losing everything. Burton told Santini that if Laxalt let the Tahoe bill go this year, Laxalt could say no to any other environmental legislation affecting his state the following year. When Santini relayed that message, Laxalt's "eyes lit up."

Carter signed the bill on December 23, barely a month before leaving office. It was another master stroke for Burton, stepping in with a solution to a problem no one else had been able to solve. With Santini, he passed the first legislation in which public land was sold at auction, the proceeds designated for environmental protection. But the cost was great. The weakening amendments returned power to the pro-development forces on the local agency, subject to pressure from Tahoe-area landowners. "It was an ingenious trade-off—a concession to the Sagebrush Rebellion," Leo Rennert wrote in the *California Journal.* But "what began as a land-planning and protection bill emerged as a revenue-sharing measure. Nevada lawmakers grabbed the money and ran. An unhappy Burton, left with no maneuvering room, went along. . . . Almost everybody found something to cheer about. In coping with man-made threats, the lake gained some time. But not much."[15]

The fight to give federal protection to Big Sur and the rugged and spectacular coastline of Central California did not succeed, even a little bit. Had Burton won this battle, the sum total of his legislation would have created hundreds of miles of federally protected coastline from Point Reyes north of San Francisco virtually all the way to San Luis Obispo County, where William Randolph Hearst's San Simeon castle stood. The Big Sur loss was one of Burton's few setbacks. The good news was that he met Ansel Adams, the famous nature photographer and conservationist. Late in their lives, these two passionate, brilliant, and wildly idiosyncratic men from San Francisco developed an intense, albeit brief, friendship.

"There are only two people in the world of whom I stand in awe," Burton told Wilderness Society director Bill Turnidge, a close friend of Adams. "One is Cesar Chavez and the other is Ansel Adams. I'd like to think I have dedicated my life to the betterment of my fellow citizens. That, unquestionably, is what Cesar Chavez and Ansel Adams have done. But they did it without being mean, nasty sons of bitches like me. They did it entirely through spirituality. And that is something I admire more than I can tell you."

Adams told Turnidge that Burton was one of the most authentic politicians he ever met. He was uneasy about most, respectful, but not convinced they were sincere. With Burton he developed an immediate and intuitive emotional rapport, which grew out of his interest in preserving Big Sur, his home. Adams invited Phil and Sala to visit. Burton considered it one of the great privileges of his life. As Adams, who detested cigarettes, drove him up and down the coast, he suggested they stop so that Burton could smoke. That way at least he could get Burton out of the car and maybe also look at the view. "I'll tell you how much I respect Ansel Adams," Burton told Turnidge. "It's the only time in my life I spent two days without smoking cigarettes. I snuck out a few times. But thank God he likes to drink. That's what saved me."[16]

Action on Big Sur began in the Senate with a $150 million Cranston bill to preserve 160,000 acres—75 miles—of coast between southern Monterey County and San Simeon. But some homeowners adamantly opposed any federal intervention, arguing that the California Coastal Act of 1976 already ensured protection. They did not need the government to tell people how to run their lives. They said they were as determined as anyone to preserve Big Sur's physical beauty and cultural ambiance, despite the nearly three million visitors a year who drove through on scenic Highway 1, and pointed out that 90,000 of the 160,000 acres in question were already publicly owned.

Leon Panetta tried another approach with Burton and the Wilderness Society: a preservation plan and local-state-federal commission, comprising mostly local residents, to manage the Big Sur area. It included $30 million for land, one-fifth of what was in the Cranston version. Even despite these concessions, some landowners flew to Washington to tell Congress there was no need for federal action. "I don't believe that. Not for a second," said Burton, who called Big Sur "so gorgeous it beggars description."[17]

When Burton called HR 7380 up on a suspension of the rules, it barely passed. A shift of eight votes would have killed it. Cranston agreed to move the Burton-Panetta version, but Senate colleague S. I. Hayakawa prevented the bill from coming to a vote, ending preservation efforts on Big Sur. Burton was angry at Panetta for years afterwards for not continuing to press the issue. In defense, Panetta said that with Reagan and his Interior Secretary James Watt in place, even Burton gave up.[18]

"I have neglected writing you only because I have had little thought of consequence in my head in relation to the debacle in Washington," Adams wrote Burton a month after Reagan's inauguration. "I told Bill [Turnidge] that when you put on your armor, take your spear in hand and start on the Great Crusade, I would like to ride behind you, catching arrows and making direful faces at the Administration." Adams said he hoped there were ways to reach the new president, but he was not encouraged.

> I become impatient and disturbed over the leisurely tempo my friends display; where is the fire and the immediacy of action? We can lose the fruits of at least thirty years effort for the protection of the Environment within a year or so—and then it would require thirty years or more to reconstitute the loss (if such were possible). . . . With a few leaders such as you in various fields we have been able to move ahead with a minimum of "glorious battles." But perhaps we were too complacent, too assured? We now face a kind of Pearl Harbor. We cannot be complacent. . . . I think we have to fight like Hell—starting Monday Morning![19]

As part of a work schedule that would break men half his age, Burton also continued to press hard on insular affairs and trust territories. His work in this area prompted the only Burton profile the *Washington Post* ever published. Congressional reporter Ward Sinclair said Burton had created "an empire" on which the sun never set and over which Burton reigned as lord and master. "If Guam wants a debt excused, the man to see is Burton," he wrote. "If the Virgin Islands need tax-law changes, Burton is where they begin. When American Samoa wants a seat in the House, Burton can arrange it." Sinclair said Burton created a nonvoting House seat for American Samoa for his staff assistant, Eni Hunken, who ran and lost. He ran again, was elected and took his full Samoan name, Eni Faleomavenga.

But even here, Burton could not escape talk of an eventual rematch with Wright. Critics said he created the seat for Samoa to gain one more vote in the Democratic Caucus. Burton denied that, saying he delayed the final vote on the new seat as long as he could "to cut the crap about me running against Jim Wright." The article also noted Burton's generosity toward the islanders: "The rap, if any," Sinclair wrote, "is that he will give them anything not nailed down." Burton and Antonio Wan Pat of Guam—"who may have no equal on Capitol Hill in sending federal bacon home"—got $99.7 million in federal grants in 1980 for a population of 85,000 people 9,000 miles from Washington.[20]

Burton also loved his junketing trips to these exotic locales, although he tended to so dominate everyone else's agendas and schedules that it was hardly a tropical holiday. On one Virgin Islands trip, for example, Burton stood waist-deep in the ocean, forcing NPS staff to stand next to him while he barked orders. He was on the beach in Puerto Rico one day when he noticed a Puerto Rican family nearby get up to swim. While they were in the water, Burton rearranged their towels and beach chairs. "Things had to make sense, or they would distract him," explained Judy Lemons. "He needed to organize their things." Back in the office, "certain things were underlined once, and other things were underlined twice, and that made his world clear at a glance."

Another time, Utah Mormon Larry Burton got so drunk at a Puerto Rican reception that he had to be carried off the plane. When a member of the delegation saw him a few days later, the congressman still looked hung over.

"Larry, do you know how dangerous that was?" his colleague asked.

"I have a deal with Phil Burton," Larry Burton replied. "Phil told me it's okay if anyone ever has a question about my personal behavior to say that one of the terrible plagues of my life is to have the same name as that outrageous rapscallion libertine from San Francisco who drinks and swears and carries on. Undoubtedly, this terrible report about my lurid behavior comes from my association with the other Burton."

On trips to the South Pacific, Burton often got off the plane in Hawaii and stayed put. Even there, he held court in the hotel swimming pool or bar, where local pols eagerly came by to report on the latest gossip. Tom Foley accompanied Burton on a trip to Samoa for a congressional hearing. Like most visiting dignitaries, they were treated like potentates. "We had this great meeting with three paramount chiefs and high talking chiefs and orators," Foley recounted. "One paramount chief gave an invocation . . . thanking the great God for bringing us safely over the seas. It was poetic and heartfelt. After he finished, there was a great outburst of antiphonal singing, and the whole public school auditorium broke into singing a hymn of welcome. It was marvelous. As the testimony proceeded from all the members of the Samoan political and cultural hierarchy, Phil, in due American course, asked for the opposition. There were blank stares and murmuring in the audience. Phil insisted that those who disagreed with the previous testimony come forward. Finally, someone got up and said, "Our paramount chief has spoken. The dignitaries and orators have spoken. There will be no opposition."[21]

House rules limited any bills that came up on suspension of the rules to $100 million. To stay under that limit, Burton divided what would have been one omnibus bill into several. The first was the $70 million measure that established Channel Islands National Park. The second was HR 3, the National Parks and Recreation Act of 1980, an omnibus bill that nearly completed the list Pinnix and Crane had drawn up for Burton. They did their job well. They laid the track. And the "big engine" that Ed Wayburn described was barreling along at full throttle.

Burton began hearings in December 1979 on potential new parks submitted by NPS. HR 3 grew out of these hearings. It established seven new park units, adjusted the boundaries of thirteen, and increased acquisition funds at four more. Burton was up to his old tricks. "The administration has not had an opportunity to review this omnibus legislation," Bob Herbst, assistant secretary for fish and wildlife and parks wrote Udall on May 14, the day the full committee was scheduled to vote. "In fact, it would have been impossible to prepare a complete legislative report because new provisions have been added that have not even been printed at this time." Indeed, the report explaining the bill had not yet been printed, either, and was not available even to members. Nevertheless, Interior approved the bill that day. As Burton rushed the bill to the floor on suspension of the rules—again to bypass the hostile Rules Committee—the Carter administration asked the House to delay voting until the bill could be analyzed. Not only was HR 3 not yet printed, Interior said, it was "undergoing amendments even after the Committee ordered it reported." But Tip O'Neill ignored the request and it went to the floor on May 19.[22]

Burton greased the bill as only he could. Republican Keith Sebelius of Kansas was serving his last term. Before his career in the House, Sebelius was the city attorney for Norton, Kansas. In 1958, the city built an irrigation and recreation dam on the Missouri River, which created a lake. Under Section 508 of HR 3, the water impounded by the dam would now be known as "Keith Sebelius Lake" (not to be confused with the Pearson-Skubitz Big Hill Lake Burton put in an earlier bill to buy off Republican Joe Skubitz). Any time Burton wanted to move this bill out of committee by unanimous consent, he needed Sebelius's permission. "Is my lake still in it?" Sebelius asked. Assured that it was, Republicans on the committee let it go. To reward Republican House floor objector Robert Bauman, Burton commemorated the late Rogers B. Morton, Bauman's mentor, a former Interior Committee member and secretary of interior. The bill established a monument honoring Morton at Assateague Island National Seashore in Maryland, whose preservation Morton had championed.

In one of the supreme acts of chutzpah that Udall ever witnessed in the House of Representatives, Burton presented HR 3 as a two-line bill to add a few acres to the GGNRA. Then he asked unanimous consent to add "technical and conforming amendments," which turned out to be the entire seventy-five-page bill. Even so, many of his colleagues knew what he was up to. HR 3 created a Women's Rights National Historic Park in Seneca Park, New York, the birthplace of women's rights in the nineteenth century; the Georgia O'Keeffe National Historic Site honoring the great American artist at her home and studio in Abiquiu, New Mexico; the Chaco Culture National Historic Park in the San Juan Basin of New Mexico to protect and interpret valuable archeological sites from the prehistoric era; a Mary McLeod Bethune National Historic Site in Daytona Beach, Florida, and the Martin Luther King, Jr., National Historic Site and Preservation District in Atlanta. It eventually included the home where the civil rights leader grew up, the church in which his father and he preached, and a museum honoring King and the civil rights movement.[23]

These additions typified how Burton expanded Park Service definitions of people worth honoring. Bethune, for example, left her South Carolina home for Daytona Beach to help educate a community of black construction workers, then founded the Bethune-Cookman College. She served in the Roosevelt administration and later at the United Nations. She founded the United Negro Women of America and was an early civil rights activist.

HR 3 also added 89,000 acres to Big Bend National Park in Panther Junction, Texas, and expanded the Lyndon B. Johnson National Historic Site by 1,200 acres. Burton even visited the Johnson ranch and met Lady Bird, who was so taken with him—"he reminds me of my Lyndon," she said—that she loaned him "Lyndon's" bathrobe to wear, which fit.[24]

Burton added yet more acres to his beloved GGNRA. As promised, Burton "moved south," adding hundreds of mountainside acres known as Sweeney Ridge. In researching valuable city-owned land near a large reservoir on the Peninsula, Dale Crane discovered an agreement between the city of San Francisco, San Mateo County, the state Department of Fish and Game, and the Department of Interior to manage that land for fish, wildlife, and limited recreation, such as hiking trails. Worried that San Francisco might sell the land to private developers for huge amounts of money some day, Crane and Burton put the language from that agreement into HR 3, making it federal law. Burton also reduced or abolished entrance fees to the national parks for the blind and disabled and directed studies for future sites for former President Gerald Ford and AFL-CIO President George Meany.

As the bill was debated—actually, more like celebrated—John Myers of Indiana questioned its necessity. Myers, a former banker, was the ranking Republican on Appropriations's public works subcommittee. Burton's sudden solicitude for the public treasury, if not the English language, as his response to Myers indicated, would have been touching were it not so laughable.

MYERS: Why [did] this very complicated, very large, very expansive bill, one covering a lot of districts in the country, come up under suspension, where we do not have the opportunity to discuss it or to even offer amendments?

BURTON: I will be very frank in this respect. It is because we did not want this bill Christmas treed. We turned down innumerable members who wanted to add expensive items. We rejected them. . . . It is very difficult to say no to a member. The easiest way to say no is to preclude sweeteners and add-ons and Christmas treeing by putting the item on suspension.

MYERS: I think every one of us would like to avoid Christmas treeing our bills. . . . The members would like to know more about what is in here. The report is not out. The impact on the budget should be included. . . . This is not the proper way to legislate. About two weeks ago the *New York Times* editorialized against our appropriations bill on energy and water . . . calling them pork barrel.

BURTON: Mr. Speaker, I have a distinct feeling that the several billion dollar item perhaps generated some of the gentleman's concern about this less than $100 million item. [At this, Burton waxed nostalgic about his father's semi-pro baseball league and sounded wistful as he expressed how much he would love to have Myers's budget to play with, rather than Interior's piddling sums.] . . . If in my wildest dreams I could have a bill that authorized or appropriated the magnificent sums . . . in the public works bill, I would be willing to take to the floor and even to suffer the slings and arrows that might be inflicted upon me for rejecting further sweetening amendments. Incredibly, this bill amounts to about two percent or thereabouts of the efforts that the gentleman has been concerned with over his great number of very effective years in the House, so we are not quite in the same ballpark. I wish we were in the same league, but I suspect we are in the 3-I league, whereas the gentleman is talking about the World Series. I wish we were in the World Series.[25]

Myers alone objected. Other Republicans looked to Bauman, who, confident that Morton's seashore was in the bill, proclaimed, "I love national parks. If it were foreign aid, I'd be out there raising all the procedural objections in the world." HR 3 passed 300-102. The margin attested to Burton's strategy of honoring Martin Luther King, Jr., women's rights, George Meany, Lyndon Johnson, and Republicans Jerry Ford, Keith Sebelius, and Rogers Morton.

With the Republican administration on the way in, Burton's work on the environment was virtually done. Now it was time to play defense, help his friends in California, create new Burton votes for the rematch to come and return to his first love: reapportionment. When he was finished, critics and admirers alike called it the most brazen redistricting since 1812, when Massachusetts Governor Elbridge Gerry's Jeffersonian minions put every Federalist they could find into one grotesquely-shaped, salamander-like district and created a new transitive verb: to gerrymander.

18

YOUR MOTHER'S ARMS

Everyone north of the Tehachapis is in their mother's arms.
Los Angeles is dog meat. And San Diego takes care of itself.

PHILLIP BURTON

My mother is in Forest Lawn.

REPUBLICAN CONGRESSMAN ROBERT BADHAM

While all states struggle with reapportionment,
the situation in California seems to have gotten out of hand.

PRESIDENT RONALD REAGAN

LEO MCCARTHY'S SPEAKERSHIP, which began on a promising note in 1974 and continued the following year with the peace accord between the Mc-Carthy and Burton factions in San Francisco, was starting to unravel by 1978. This had enormous implications for reapportionment in California, which Phillip Burton dominated as even he never had before. A Democratic gerrymander could help guarantee continued Democratic control of the House of Representatives, further Burton's own leadership ambitions, and help combat the dramatic rise of fiscal conservatism, which took off and moved east like a tidal wave. The next two years of political war pushed nearly everything else off the table and determined politics in the nation's largest state for the next decade and beyond.

McCarthy erred badly; he said aloud that he was using his speakership as a springboard for higher office. That meant he was paying less attention to his true constituency—the assembly Democrats who elected him—than was wise for any leader. Not that he had immediate worries. The Democrats owned fifty-seven of the eighty seats—three more than needed for a veto-proof house. Even conservative Orange County sent five Democrats to the assembly.

But at the worst possible moment, Democrats dithered over property tax relief. California home values were soaring, and with them, property taxes. Elderly couples, and younger middle-class families, were being priced out of their homes, and politicians could not agree on how to help them. Governor Jerry Brown, still itching for the White House, sat on billions of dollars in state surpluses rather than refund them to taxpayers. Into this leadership and policy vacuum stepped Howard Jarvis, a crusty right-wing crusader for property tax relief and a lobbyist for apartment owners. Along with another cantankerous conservative named Paul Gann, he sponsored a ballot initiative called Proposition 13, opposed by virtually the entire state political establishment. It was designed to reduce property taxes by a whopping 60 percent, change the formula by which they were calculated, and thus slash the amount of money available to cities and counties to finance local government.

In June 1978, Proposition 13 passed easily. The victory made Jarvis a folk hero and put him on the cover of *Time*. UC Berkeley political scientist Jack Citrin described him as a "neglected, though shrill voice in the political wilderness" until 1978. With Proposition 13 and Reagan's 1980 election, Citrin wrote, his tax goals "became enshrined as national policy."[1] The Democrats also lost seven assembly seats in California that November—a worry to any Speaker—even though they still had fifty. The new Republicans, "Proposition 13 Babies," were so conservative they preferred their own name, the "Cavemen."

But bigger shocks quickly followed in the Bay Area. In 1977, revelations in *New West* magazine and in the *San Francisco Examiner* about a bizarre religious group called Peoples Temple and Jim Jones, its charismatic leader, drove the group to a remote jungle outpost in the tiny Caribbean nation of Guyana, formerly British Guiana, on the northeastern slope of South America. The stories by Marshall Kilduff and *Examiner* investigative reporter Tim Reiterman described a racially mixed, liberal-radical group of several thousand members that grew powerful in Ukiah, a few hours north of San Francisco, and then established an even bigger congregation in the city itself. Mayor George Moscone appointed Jones to chair the Housing Authority in 1976, and it was widely—if inaccurately—believed that Peoples Temple provided the margin of victory that elected Moscone in 1975. With the perception of power came power, even if dishonestly arrived at.[2]

The advent of district elections in San Francisco in 1977 transferred power from downtown-financed candidates who ran citywide to neighborhoods that now elected supervisors from each of eleven districts. This gave newly emerging groups the political clout to influence events far beyond their numbers. The first district elections saw the rise of a new generation of neighborhood-oriented leaders. They included gay activist Harvey Milk and a conservative ex-firefighter and cop named Dan White, who represented a constituency threatened by Moscone's liberalism and Milk's gay followers. Jones and his Temple cultivated powerful politicians, such as Willie Brown, Sheriff Richard Hongisto, District Attorney Joseph Freitas, newspaper publisher Carlton Goodlett, black minister Cecil Williams, Republican state Senator Milton Marks, and other beacons of the city's liberal establishment.

Ominously, the Peoples Temple exposés documented beatings, cult-like mind control, theft of the life savings of people who wanted to leave the group and a bizarre paternity suit involving Jones that led to legal action on two continents. As the stories broke, Jones hurriedly moved hundreds to his jungle hideout in "Jonestown," eventually cramming nearly a thousand people into a small, inaccessible compound, far from civilization, where conditions were crowded and miserable, mind-control techniques primitive but effective, punishment severe, and escape extremely difficult.

In October 1978, just as Phil Burton was getting his park barrel bill through Congress, Leo Ryan announced that after the November elections he would lead a congressional delegation of "concerned relatives" and former members to Jonestown to investigate conditions firsthand and to bring home relatives they believed were being held against their will. In part because he was a loner and had a reputation for headline-grabbing stunts, Ryan could not persuade House colleagues to join him. But he did lure journalists from NBC, the *Examiner, Chronicle,* and *Washington Post.* Their trip began on November 13. Five days later, the world woke up to shocking headlines. As he attempted to board a small-engine plane on a tiny jungle airstrip to take home "defectors" whose stories Jones knew would blow his Peoples Temple apart forever, Temple gunmen shot Ryan from afar and again at point blank range. Four others were also killed, a mother leading her family out, and three journalists.

As the wounded survivors huddled for cover in the jungle, seven miles away the paranoid, drug-addicted Indiana preacher led 913 of his followers, including more than 200 children, to their deaths. It was a ghastly, well-rehearsed ritual of murder and suicide. Nowhere were people more horrified than in San Francisco, where this world tragedy was also a local story, where the victims were not nameless faces or crazed cultists but friends and neighbors. "When I heard the news, I proceeded to vomit and cry," Moscone said. Majority Leader Jim Wright flew west to deliver a eulogy at Ryan's funeral. Phil Burton, who had kept his distance from Jones, was in Portugal for a North Atlantic Alliance meeting and did not return.

Nine days later, it got worse. On November 27, 1978, George Moscone and Harvey Milk were assassinated in their City Hall offices. The killer was Dan White, who, under intense pressure, had resigned from the board of supervisors two weeks before. White had quit his $9,600-a-year job to earn more money for his young family. When friends and family offered financial help, White asked Moscone if he could change his mind. Moscone agreed. But over the next few weeks, other supervisors, including Milk, persuaded Moscone that the six-to-five conservative board majority would continue if White got his job back. With White gone, Moscone's new appointee could tip the balance to the liberals. Moscone, who could finally begin to implement his programs, sided with them. It was not personal.

Milk had also "betrayed" White, who was narrowly elected the year before, in part by opposing a campus for disturbed teens in his district. Milk had initially agreed to support the campus but had changed his mind without telling White.

Moscone scheduled a press conference for November 27 to announce White's successor. Except for White, Willie Brown was the last person to see his friend alive. Brown and Moscone talked about Jim Jones and the deaths at Jonestown, about Moscone's birthday, and about his decision to hang tough on White. Moscone said he had to give White the "bad news."

As they spoke, White snuck through a basement window of City Hall to avoid setting off the metal detector his .38 caliber revolver would activate. When he arrived, Moscone led him into his inner office. As he turned to fix White a drink, Moscone began to explain why he could not reappoint him. In his taped confession, White said he heard "a ringing in my ears." He pulled out his revolver and shot Moscone twice. As Moscone fell, White fired twice more into his brain. White reloaded and let himself out a side door. That put him in the marble corridor on the second floor, where he spotted an aide to Milk. As White walked into his former office, he asked to see Milk for a moment. "Sure, Dan," Milk replied. They stepped inside Milk's tiny office. White shot him five times at close range.[3]

Board President Dianne Feinstein heard the shots and was the first to discover Milk's body. Moments later, standing on the steps of City Hall and in a trembling voice, she announced the two men's deaths to a city already in deep shock. Feinstein had just returned from a vacation in Nepal. Two hours before the killings, she dropped by the press room. After losing two mayoral races, she told several reporters, she had decided to finish her term and retire from politics. But after some quick maneuvering to nail down six votes of her colleagues', a majority, the board elected her to serve the last year of Moscone's term.

Feinstein, like the city she led, was traumatized by the killings. A moderate to begin with, these horrendous events convinced her it was more important than ever to "govern from the center." Anything else could—and did—unleash murderous rage. She kept on most of Moscone's appointees and a year later won a full term. San Franciscans searched themselves to explain the dark events that cast such a pall over the city that had always been considered a tolerant, fun-loving place. Moscone's death also devastated his best friend, John Burton, who had developed a serious cocaine dependency and whose second marriage was foundering. He began sinking further.

Compared to the Peoples Temple horrors and the killings of Moscone and Milk, the political wars in Sacramento seemed petty indeed. But real power was at stake. With the loss of seven seats in 1978, Burton protégé Howard Berman, McCarthy's majority leader, worried whether his party could retain even a bare majority to control the 1980 reapportionment. Annoyed with what he saw as the speaker's neglect of the property tax crisis that led to Proposition 13, Berman thought McCarthy's plan to run for higher office—as former speakers Unruh and Moretti did—would make matters worse. Assembly Democrats needed a speaker to work full time for them and raise money to protect them in the 1980 elections, not to stockpile it for himself.

In November 1979, the *California Journal* headlined an article, "The Next Speaker? Probably Howard Berman." But the article gave no hint of trouble. It was "taken for granted" in Sacramento, the piece said, that McCarthy would run statewide in 1982, and there was "near-unanimous agreement" that Berman would succeed him. Willie Brown could be a factor, but he rated only two paragraphs. His thriving law practice was "an indication of waning interest in the Speakership." That it took nearly three years for the *Journal* to even discuss McCarthy's speakership was a sign of his low profile.[4]

Berman saw it differently. What already happened was scary enough: the loss of seats, Proposition 13, Governor Brown's absence—he was plotting a second White House run—President Carter's obvious vulnerabilities, McCarthy's failure to tend to business with reapportionment coming up. The Democrats could lose it all. As heir apparent, Berman asked McCarthy for a personal favor. He wanted assembly rules changed to permit only the majority caucus, not the entire body, to elect the speaker. Why should the Republicans have any say? McCarthy agreed but did nothing. Berman took McCarthy's failure to change the rule as a personal affront.

Confident of his power, oblivious to the seething Berman, his future seemingly unlimited, McCarthy blundered again. He hosted a $500,000 dinner at the Los Angeles Convention Center with Ted Kennedy and a thousand guests. He wanted all the assembly Democrats there, part of his entourage, part of a command performance for him. But the money would go to a separate McCarthy account, not to them. Worse, McCarthy introduced the members en masse and asked them to stand as a group, rather than identify each one by name to the biggest Democratic donors in the state. Outraged by what they considered a double insult, some met immediately after the dinner and complained bitterly that McCarthy was using them to further his own ambition.

The dinner crystalized growing antipathy to McCarthy. Money raising aside, to be an effective speaker one should be loved or feared. To many members, McCarthy was neither. He was remote, often too busy to meet with individual members, who had to settle for staff. He rarely convened caucus meetings, and some felt he delegated authority to a cadre of rigid associates, including caucus chair and protégé Art Agnos.[5] McCarthy drove ninety miles home to San Francisco every night for dinner. While that was admirable for a man trying to preserve a semblance of family life, it also meant McCarthy was not in the capitol to schmooze with colleagues, find out what they wanted, get a feel for what was happening on the floor. A member who voted wrong would sometimes be yanked out of committee, told how to vote, and sent back. If McCarthy had spent more time with his colleagues, they complained, this demeaning exercise would not have been necessary.

"People told me a challenge was coming," recalled John Foran, McCarthy's law partner and close friend. "They said Leo was not responding to requests of his own members. I told Leo, but he didn't put any credence in it."

It thus came as a complete shock to McCarthy when Howard Berman walked into McCarthy's office on December 10, 1979. Fueled by ambition, personal grievances, and a sinking feeling that unless he acted he might be minority leader instead of speaker, Berman asked McCarthy to step down to become speaker pro tem and let him take over. Berman had been loyal for five years. It was his turn. This was not a fight over ideology. Both men were liberals. The meeting lasted all day. Feeling betrayed by the man he made his majority leader, McCarthy said he wanted to think about the proposition overnight. He felt Berman had used his position to round up votes against him. The next day, McCarthy turned him down. Berman said he would challenge McCarthy when the caucus met in January.

"It was a very tough decision to challenge Leo for speaker directly," Berman recalled. "I thought it would be a one-month war. I was an idiot in that sense. I never fully contemplated what might happen." Said McCarthy: "I had no knowledge of the war brewing. Howard comes to my office and says they want me to move over to speaker pro tem and they will put up the money to fund a statewide organization. I had made a serious mistake by saying I wanted to run statewide in '82. . . . Berman capitalized, saying, here was a speaker who was not watching out for his own members."

The bloody speakership war that followed lasted an entire year, drained and embittered the Democrats, cost millions of dollars, strained friendships to the breaking point, and brought policy impasse to the state for all of 1980. But the protracted dispute also had one positive—if wholly unexpected—result. Once the smoke cleared, the surviving Democrats emerged as a stronger organization, in time for reapportionment.

Phil Burton did not participate. He was not consulted in advance and thought Berman's play was foolish and risky, just as he thought Waxman's subcommittee challenge to Richardson Preyer was also foolish and risky the year before. His protégé, moreover, was mucking around in his backyard, disrupting the peace that had taken so many years to establish. There was no way he could support a Los Angeles power grab, whatever the rationale, if it meant costing San Francisco the speakership.

It was a go-for-broke gambit. But the stakes were huge. Unlike traditional speakers beholden to special interest campaign cash, which allowed them to retain power, Howard Berman had a different financial base: fabulously wealthy, ideologically driven, pro-Israel Jews on the west side of Los Angeles. If he won, Berman could run the speakership from Beverly Hills. He could be as liberal and as partisan as he wished, while brother Michael ran the computer-targeted direct mail for Democrats. Michael could knock Republicans off one by one, and help Burton do the 1981 reapportionment. With forty rich liberals in West Los Angeles bankrolling the operation, the Bermans would not have to cut deals with the trial lawyers, the beer wholesalers, or anyone else in return for campaign cash. The Republicans were terrified. Even Unruh had to carry somebody's water much of the time.

The day after Christmas, Berman turned two key votes: Hispanics Art Torres and Richard Alatorre. Both were pressured by Cesar Chavez to back Berman, who wrote historic farm labor legislation that enhanced Chavez's union. Torres and Alatorre were reportedly threatened with retaliation if they stayed with McCarthy. These votes gave Berman a majority in the caucus. When it convened in January, Berman resigned as majority leader and challenged McCarthy, winning twenty-six votes to McCarthy's twenty-four. But neither had the assembly majority of forty-one needed to be elected. McCarthy refused to step down, insisting that he had been elected speaker for the full term and that Berman's majority was tainted by the last-minute Torres-Alatorre conversions. Berman's allies elected him caucus chairman, which came with a suite of offices and five-person staff. Neither man could form a majority, and they remained at impasse, McCarthy fatally weakened and Berman chairman of a badly split caucus. There it remained for the next ten months.

The Republicans wisely stayed out and let the Democrats beat each other up. As friendships frayed and then snapped, Speaker Pro Tem Jack Knox, a twenty-year veteran, called the war the "bloodiest fight this town has ever seen." Former allies were actually trying to defeat each other's candidates, including incumbents, in the Democratic primary. "It was awful," recalled Phil Isenberg, a former consultant to Willie Brown who was mayor of Sacramento and trying to be friendly to both sides. "Howard and Leo were flying all over the state to talk to members and hold secret meetings. Former friends now hated each other." McCarthy installed Willie Brown, no stranger to leadership fights, as majority leader. His political rehabilitation thus came full circle from 1975, when McCarthy exiled him to an office so small that visitors waited in the hall and his staff consisted of two secretaries. It was a "terrible bloodbath," Brown recalled. "Every day the entire program was geared to attack Leo McCarthy. They [the Bermanites] were very good at it, and if they ever ran out of gasoline, the Republicans always delivered an extra can to keep the fire going."[6]

As both sides geared up for the June primaries, they supported candidates who would pledge their loyalties accordingly. In one particularly nasty campaign, the Berman forces backed Hispanic newcomer Matthew Martinez, against popular eight-term assemblyman Jack Fenton, a McCarthy supporter. Martinez defeated the veteran legislator. Fenton's colleagues were shocked that Berman would target an incumbent Democrat and then mail hit pieces to voters in his district.

A perceptive member looked beyond the immediate battle. "Willie has one clear agenda," he said. "He's propping Leo up for now only because he needs him. But when Leo's dead, Willie will carry the casket. I overheard him say the next fight won't be between Leo McCarthy and Howard Berman. It will be between Howard Berman and Willie Brown."[7]

As the battle wore on, McCarthy tried to punish committee chairmen who supported Berman. But lacking the clout to dump them, he had to pull back and tolerate them—a profound admission of weakness. The *Los Angeles Times* described a $5 million war in which "longtime friends and associates don't trust each other or even talk anymore." But the war also hurt the other side. "Most Republicans now realize," *California Journal* editor Ed Salzman wrote in August, "that the Democratic internecine feud is not healthy for the GOP. Democrats are now running with increased intensity, more money and with more professional management than would have been the case without the leadership struggle."[8]

That became clear on election day. Despite the Reagan landslide on November 4, assembly Democrats lost only three seats and finished the year with a 47-33 majority. They also retained their 23-17 margin in the senate. With Jerry Brown still governor, they could remap the state for the next decade. On the down side, four congressional Democrats lost in California, including longtime Burton enemy Jim Corman.

The next day, Berman announced he had twenty-six votes, to McCarthy's eighteen. McCarthy, who said he would not serve without a majority of Democrats, withdrew and told supporters to look out for themselves. Feeling vulnerable, many, including committee chairmen about to be dumped, turned to Willie Brown to feel out how fair Berman would be and to negotiate how many chairmanships they would retain. Brown did not report back positive news. "The meeting was held in my office in San Francisco," Brown recalled. "He [Berman] flunked all the answers. The members became enraged and suggested another speaker. That's when I emerged." The wily veteran of sixteen years and one intense leadership fight six years earlier was now perfectly positioned to take over.[9]

Two days after the election, Elihu Harris of Oakland and Maxine Waters and Mike Roos of Los Angeles—all rookie legislators—told Brown what he already knew: Berman was unacceptable to most McCarthy supporters. Moreover, the Republicans liked Willie Brown and considered him fair. In other words, when combined with his Democratic support, GOP votes could make him speaker. (This was why Berman had never wanted GOP members to vote.)

Brown sent the three freshmen to McCarthy to see how he would feel about such a coalition. "They backed Leo into a corner," Brown said. "He was reluctant, but they pointed out how they had stood with him and saved his Speakership and he owed it to the membership." McCarthy said he needed first to talk to Agnos. Fortunately for them, Agnos, who opposed any deal with the Republicans, was leaving town the next day.

"We had about seven days [until Agnos returned] to put it together," Brown said. "We got on the phone to about four or five Berman supporters and said we needed their help. They said, 'If you announce, we'll support you.' Leo and Art didn't like the [GOP] deal. We paid no attention. We gave Howard a second meeting, and he failed even more miserably. Then we started talking with the Republicans."[10]

While this was going on, GOP strategist Ed Rollins, chief of staff to Minority Leader Carol Hallett, chatted about the speakership over lunch with Martin Smith, political editor and columnist for McClatchy Newspapers, which publishes the *Sacramento Bee*. Rollins told Smith his caucus could play a role.

> Our main objective was to keep it [the speakership] from Berman. Leo was partisan and damaged goods. Berman was close to Phil Burton and not flamboyant. We could never make him a target. He had the only significant political machine in the state and he could be a long-term speaker. Smith asked me if I had an alternative. I said Willie Brown tried to make a deal with the Republicans once before, and that was a possibility. He ran the story that Sunday. I circled it and sent it to Willie. He called me an hour after he got it and said, "When do we meet?" We met an hour and fifteen minutes later.
>
> Brown said, "How many chairmanships do you want?" I said, "I don't want any. It's a sterile gavel." I wanted vice chairmanships. I wanted a staff person for each vice chairman to build up a political staff. I wanted half the money that would be spent on reapportionment. I wanted Hallett to have the same authority as Minority Leader that Willie would have to appoint and remove Republicans from committees. He agreed to all but the last. He could not give up that power but said he would do what she wanted, and he lived up to his word.

Berman, meanwhile, was wooing the wrong guy, Republican Caucus Chairman Charles Imbrecht, in hopes of clinching his own deal. "But he didn't realize Imbrecht didn't have influence in the caucus," said Rollins. The Republicans also figured an ultraliberal black speaker from San Francisco would be a wonderful foil as well as a hostage. They could run against him in every district in the state. If he did not do what they wanted, the Republicans could threaten to withdraw their votes.

Brown had one more secret weapon: State Treasurer Jesse Unruh. Unruh lost to Reagan for governor in 1970 and lost again for mayor of Los Angeles a year later. But he was elected state treasurer in 1974 and turned the sleepy office into a powerful financial center. With billions of dollars of state employee pension funds to invest and bonds and notes to sell, Unruh soon had Wall Street bankers wooing him as they would an Arab oil sheik. Unruh never liked Leo McCarthy, never felt Leo paid him proper deference. As long as McCarthy was speaker, he had never set foot in the house he dominated for more than a decade. He also disliked Berman. But Unruh had great affection for Willie Brown, even though Brown's first vote in the assembly sixteen years earlier had been against Unruh's continuing speakership, and said he would help. (Brown and Unruh eventually patched things up, as Burton and Unruh had, in Robert Kennedy's ill-fated 1968 presidential campaign in California.)

Unruh's help took the form of legitimizing Brown to a band of conservative Republicans, including "Cavemen" Ross Johnson and Pat Nolan and others who were Unruh's drinking companions several nights a week at Sacramento watering holes. He told them Brown could be trusted to keep his word and would be a good speaker. Unruh also worked on Republican Lieutenant Governor Mike Curb, a former Hollywood record company executive and young conservative who was planning to run for governor in 1982. Curb could also validate Willie Brown to the Cavemen and provide enough political cover that assembly Republicans could safely vote for him.[11]

Over the next few weeks, the jockeying for power intensified as the legislature approached its December 1 opening session. The upper house had its own leadership fight. Senate Democrats, scared of the Reagan landslide and of a new partisanship among senate Republicans, worried that senate President Pro Tem Jim Mills of San Diego was too much the old school gentleman and member of the club to return the fire. He was toppled by the more partisan David Roberti of Los Angeles. But next door, the forty-seven-member Democratic Caucus was tied: twenty-three for Berman, twenty-three for Brown and one who wanted nothing to do with either.

On November 20, Brown announced his deal with the Republicans but did not say he had the votes. In Washington, meanwhile, Berman ally Henry Waxman produced a letter from eighteen anxious Californians in Congress. They said a Democrat-Republican coalition would be a "disaster," that would "seriously endanger the critical reapportionment you [assembly members] are about to undertake." Burton did not sign it. To avoid having to choose between two competing protégés—Berman and Brown—he fled to Hawaii.[12]

On November 24, Brown said he had fifty-one votes, ten more than he needed: twenty-three Democrats and twenty-eight of thirty-three Republicans, whose proxies Minority Leader Carol Hallett held. Berman refused to concede. Four of Brown's new votes were former Berman supporters, including Torres and Alatorre, who began with McCarthy, switched to Berman and now switched again. Cesar Chavez, who contributed more than $100,000 to Berman's assembly fund, angrily but unsuccessfully urged them to go back to Berman. Just as their first switch doomed McCarthy, this one doomed Berman.

On December 1, Willie Brown defeated Howard Berman to become California's first black speaker. McCarthy was elected speaker pro tem 75-0. "Now the little black kid can count," Brown said, referring to his 1974 loss to McCarthy. Moments after his victory, the assembly voted on a routine matter. Brown asked his seatmate—Howard Berman—to push his electronic button for him. "That's not considered ghost voting," Brown quipped, "even though it's done for a spook." Even Berman, who just witnessed a hellish year of work go up in smoke, had to laugh. Most postmortems said Berman's "slashing" attacks against fellow Democrat Fenton in June angered and scared non-Bermanites, and he could not reassure them afterwards that he would not punish them.

"Most people feared that a cold, ruthless machine would suddenly grip the state with Howard at the head of it, [with] everyone else impotent in the face of it," said Brown supporter Doug Bosco. Even so, others said, if Berman had been just a little more reassuring in his postelection meetings with the McCarthy forces, the job could have been his.[13]

Only forty-six, Brown was starting his ninth term. Flamboyant in his expensive Italian suits and black Porsche ("my body would reject a Plymouth"), he was known for his liberal politics, including a 1975 law legalizing private homosexual acts between consenting adults. Mike Roos, his new majority leader, would carry the fundraising load. The new chairman of Elections and Reapportionment was Alatorre, a Hispanic in a year when MALDEF, the Mexican-American Legal Defense and Education Fund, was determined to gain more Hispanic seats. Alatorre wanted a congressional district in East Los Angeles, one of two new seats to which California was entitled.

Brown pledged to be a speaker for everyone and said he would not use his office to promote Democratic political objectives. He could hardly say less, given where the majority of his votes came from. Even so, he told the *Los Angeles Herald Examiner* in a front-page interview, "I think the party has gained the most liberal Speaker in the history of the state" and also called his victory a benefit for race relations. Brown said he would "share the powers of the Speakership like no other Speaker has ever shared them." As to Berman's future, Brown said, "Howard is a young man. There is plenty of time and plenty of room for him to ultimately be Speaker or any other kind of thing that his enormous talent may offer him." Brown had lost once and been able to rebuild. "Howard Berman needs to go back and do essentially the same thing."[14]

Brown moved quickly to heal the wounds. He appointed Berman to the Ways and Means Committee and to Elections and Reapportionment, where Bermanites got four of the eight Democratic seats. Then Brown met with congressional Democrats in Washington. He assured them that he made no deals with the Republicans on reapportionment and that any plan "would be fair and equitable" and would yield "as many Democratic seats as possible." The delegation had already named Burton to "head" its redistricting committee. Brown said he would pass any plan Burton sent him. Back home, Brown made Jesse Unruh the honorary eighty-first assemblyman with full floor privileges.

In a story about why the Republicans turned to Brown over Berman, Gannett reporter Eric Brazil said Carol Hallett believed Waxman would have been the congressional point man on reapportionment, not Burton, and would have been more partisan. By instructing her caucus to vote almost en masse for Brown, she argued that a more flexible Burton would not punish congressional Republicans. This was not implausible, given Burton's history in preserving seats for incumbent Republicans. But that was when he had to. This time around, he didn't have to.

The mistake Hallett and Rollins thus made was in ever thinking Waxman would have supplanted Burton as the lead Democrat on reapportionment, even if Waxman's close friend Howard Berman became speaker. They also wrongly assumed Hallett's deal with Brown would temper Burton. The key was not who would be speaker, but which party the governor belonged to. As long as the Democrats controlled the state house, Burton would do everything in his power to maximize Democratic gains.

"He'll be tough," Hallett said of Burton. "No question about it. But . . . we're convinced that Willie Brown will have certain things he has to do as Speaker," one of which was to be "fair to minorities in reapportionment— and we're a minority." On his copy of Brazil's story, Burton put an asterisk by Hallett's comments and sent it to Waxman. On the bottom he scrawled, "Henry—I never thought I'd see the day when I'm less threatening than you! Phil."[15]

Michael Berman was in his office exhausted and in a self-described "deep psychological snit" when the phone rang. After a nightmarish year and what looked like victory at last, the Bermans came up short. Phil Burton was calling from Washington.

"I want you to work on reapportionment," Burton said.

"Fuck you, Phillip."

But Burton had a plan. Throughout their war, the Bermans told supporters that even if they lost, they would be better off losing with Howard than winning with Leo. Burton's plan would guarantee it. Here was the pitch: move the entire Berman operation to Washington. Burton would draw the districts. California was getting only two new seats, but Burton wasn't a wizard for nothing. One seat for Howard, one for Mel Levine, one for Rick Lehman, one for Marty Martinez, the latter to comply with the Voting Rights Act and pressure from Hispanics. Next, "marry" Alatorre—the double-crosser who switched from McCarthy to Berman to Willie Brown and who now headed the redistricting committee—by telling Alatorre they would create more Hispanic congressional districts. He could run for one of the new ones or stay where he was and position himself to succeed veteran Ed Roybal when Roybal retired.

They could sell the plan easily to Willie Brown by arguing that it "promoted" most of his enemies out of the assembly. Berman and his friends would not challenge Brown for speaker again if they were in Washington. David Roberti's new partisan senate districts also allowed more Berman supporters to move up to the senate. With a united Democratic Party, Willie Brown no longer would need the Republicans who made him speaker. He could be, as Burton put it, "the Democratic Speaker you always wanted to be" *and* keep his bargain with the Republicans. "I gave them what we agreed," Brown recalled, still speaker, ten years later. "I handed them the money [for reapportionment] . . . and I let Phil Burton rip their hearts out in Congress. We didn't have a deal on that."[16]

What was Phil Burton getting from the deal? At the very least, by taking charge of reapportionment, Burton could design a district to protect brother John, who almost lost in 1980 and who was likely to face the same, better-financed opponent in 1982. In other words, if Burton wanted to draw his own and his brother's district, he would have to draw them all. Otherwise, someone else would. He could also eliminate several Republicans and put others in fewer congressional districts where they would have to run against each other. With clever line-drawing, he could put a dozen votes just from California in his pocket for when the time came to challenge Wright, either for majority leader or directly for speaker. Not least, he could deliver some good news nationally for the Democrats in what was otherwise a bleak period.

"Phillip used reapportionment to get over the 1976 race," Michael Berman said. The environmental legislation had been important, restorative, satisfying, and lasting. But reapportionment involved hard-core power politics, and that was where he thrived. Burton could deliver more House Democrats with his pen than any of their "leaders" could by campaigning for them.

With Reagan's 1980 landslide, Republicans regained control of the U.S. Senate for the first time in decades and were within twenty-six votes of controlling the House. GOP strategists estimated they could get fifteen of those twenty-six seats back—just through reapportionment—after 1980. If they waged a strong 1982 campaign, they could take over the House for the first time since 1954. With Reagan in the White House and the Senate already in GOP hands, there would be no stopping what some political scientists were calling a fundamental realignment in American politics.

In 1980, Republicans targeted—and defeated—Ways and Means Chairman Al Ullman in Oregon, Democratic Whip John Brademas in Indiana, and DCCC Chairman Corman, the ranking Democrat on Ways and Means. Burton deplored the loss of seats but did not regret saying good-bye to Corman or Bizz Johnson, who was also defeated. Both had voted against him for majority leader and were longtime adversaries.

Burton was determined to frustrate the GOP plans and prove there had been no realignment. With this much at stake nationally, the intramural battles in California looked less consequential. Burton also prepared to lead the charge against Reaganomics, one of the few Democrats who even wanted to try. Even after his 1976 loss, he remained one of a select group in the House who made things happen, along with O'Neill, Wright, Bolling, Rostenkowski, Jack Brooks of Texas, and John Dingell of Michigan.

Despite his strategic value, however, the House leadership took new steps to prevent a Burton comeback. In a direct repudiation, O'Neill and Wright elevated Tony Coelho to succeed Corman as chairman of the DCCC, even though Coelho had just finished his first term. But Coelho had worked on the Hill since 1967 as B. F. Sisk's top aide, was obviously talented, and had hosted fundraising events for Wright, Brademas, and other important Democrats. Coelho thus became the new California rival to Burton. Like McFall before him, Coelho in theory could keep Burton's home base divided. Soon after his appointment, he and Burton talked.

"You've got a future. Let's make a pact," Coelho recalled Burton telling him. "I don't know if I can get anywhere now," Burton went on. "But if I do run, I want you to support me. If you are in a position to run, I will support you." Coelho said yes. "That was our agreement," Coelho recalled.

> Just the two of us were in the room. It was quick and easy because we both felt strongly that the delegation got hurt by not having anyone in the leadership. Everyone ran for different things, and they all got defeated. Phil wanted to run again. There was no doubt about it. I was more interested in the future. I didn't think in 1981 that I would be elected Whip [in 1986]. I knew I had a future. . . . I thought he would move before I would. I realized that if you get a Californian in the leadership, it helps everyone.

Other Californians challenged Coelho's version of events. Sure, the delegation was fragmented and unity would help, but they doubted whether either man would have agreed to support the other's bid. Each wanted it too much for himself, and there was not enough room at the top for both.[17]

As organized labor surveyed the wreckage of 1980, which also included the arrest, conviction, and defeat of Frank Thompson after involvement in the FBI's Abscam political corruption probe, labor lobbyists pressed Phil Burton to give up his national parks subcommittee and take over Thompson's Labor-Management subcommittee. Burton was needed not so much for new labor programs but to block Reagan administration efforts to gut programs that already existed. Burton persuaded John Seiberling to take over his parks committee and maintain a strong commitment to the trust territories and offshore islands. Then he hired environmental writer Joan Moody as his press secretary, mostly to keep him up-to-date on the environmental movement.

"I reached the decision to switch to a different subcommittee with great reluctance," he said in a prepared statement announcing the move. "I remain deeply committed to protection of the natural and historic resources exemplified in our National Park System. However, the new political climate in Washington makes it imperative for me to focus my primary efforts on the rights of the American worker . . . I intend to uphold the minimum wage and the right of American citizens to expect a decent wage, collective bargaining, adequate pension benefits and a safe and healthy workplace."[18]

In a *Washington Post* article about how key House Democrats were regrouping to protect liberal programs from Republican budget cutters, Burton elaborated: "I'd rather spend my time passing laws. But people like me can hardly expect much progress in the next few years, so I guess the effort is to hold the fort." The Reagan administration was keying on education and labor programs. It proposed cutting $2.8 billion, or 28 percent, from elementary and secondary school assistance (the main source of federal money for teaching poor children); $6.1 billion, or 58 percent, from employment programs, including public service jobs; and $1.9 billion, or 38 percent, from child nutrition funds. All told, Reagan proposed cutting $11 billion of the $33 billion authorized by the House Education and Labor Committee and the Senate Labor and Human Resources Committee, where Senator Kennedy was doing what he could to block the cuts.[19]

The most important thing about his new chairmanship, however, was that it freed Burton for reapportionment, which took three-quarters of his time in 1981, much of it on the phone to Michael Berman or on his office floor digesting maps and census tract data. It became an obsession, Burton's chance to protect as many as ten progressive votes in the House. He told aides this was the most significant thing to which he could devote himself. Ed Davis, his new administrative assistant, could barely get Burton's attention for anything else.

His constant work schedule and near-total focus on reapportionment notwithstanding, Davis, Mark Gersh, Judy Lemons, and Fred Feinstein, the staff director and general counsel to the labor subcommittee, believed Burton knew his moment had passed. He might never be speaker. At best, he might become chairman of Interior, where he was the ranking Democrat after Udall. He still had his alliances and still kept everything going, but these staffers thought that deep down he was going through the motions, in part to keep alive the perception of power.

The liberalism of the 1970s was no longer ascendant, and his health was deteriorating. He was grossly overweight, suffered from terrible piles and bad teeth, and never took care of himself. Hospitalized twice for heart problems, he still smoked heavily. His drinking got more excessive at night. He watched the clock until 6 P.M. and then brought out the vodka. When *Boston Globe* reporter Marty Nolan visited him in San Francisco, Burton said, "Hell, you're the first straight white male to walk into this office in months. Let's have a drink." It was only 2 P.M., but Burton justified it because it was 5 in Washington.

But others weren't convinced that Burton had taken himself out of contention. Charlie Rose thought he was pacing himself, getting ready if the opportune moment came. Burton began holding quiet meetings at his home to discuss comeback plans. Labor reps, including Ken Young of the AFL-CIO, Bill Holayter of the Machinists, California Teamster leader Chuck Mack, George Gould of the Letter Carriers, Dick Murphy of SEIU, and other "guests" and members, such as Bob Kastenmeier, Rose, and George Miller and his wife Cynthia were invited to dinner every month or so. The plan was to build his reputation and show he could be more effective than O'Neill and Wright. "I will give you something the leadership isn't giving," he told them. "I'll make the place work."

> Half the people in the room were background noise [Miller recalled]. This was not a dinner party where you talked about the latest movie or a trip or even the current political situation, with everyone chiming in. Cynthia and I were there to keep people entertained while others were pulled off to the side, so it would stay polite. You never sat at a table. Phil worked the room while Sala and Cynthia and I kept it social, and others could see in a relaxed setting that Phil had the political smarts to diagnose, analyze, and prescribe how the House should act. Sometimes these dinners ended quickly if Phil exploded.

Not even Miller was sure whether Burton felt he could mount the comeback. "On the one hand, he was on track," Miller said. "The chits and obligations kept accruing. But he had to confront the fact that other people had slipped into the chain of leadership. There was a new tier. But I also think he never believed that new cast of characters had the fundamentals to make themselves successful. He just didn't believe this was a group of individuals to lead us to the greater public good. Other times, he'd have a lapse of energy. And then you'd have to ask, what was the timetable?"

Often at night, Burton summoned Miller, whom he still called, "the kid," to his office. Miller would sit on a couch in the labor subcommittee office and say to Feinstein, "What have I done now? What does he have on me, Fred?" Usually, Burton just needed a warm body around. Once Burton summoned Miller and motioned him to sit down while he talked to Sala on the phone. Miller waited and waited and finally got up to leave. Burton motioned him to stay put. After a few more minutes, Miller got up again, and again Burton motioned him down. Finally he heard Burton say, "The kid's here. I'll be home soon."

"What was that all about?" said Miller after Burton finally hung up.

"I've used that line so many times with Sala," Burton replied, "that I wanted you to be here at least once when it was true."

Sometimes Sala got so angry about his impossible work hours that she locked him out of the house. He kept a pillow and pajamas in his office. Judy Lemons once heard them argue for hours over where to get a hamburger. When they found a place, Sala was uncharacteristically quiet. "Want a french fry, Poopsie?" he said, trying to make peace. It was an image of sweet solicitude no business lobbyist would have found believable. When Sala came into the office, the vodka immediately went into the desk drawer. If she ever found a bottle, she poured it down the sink. Even so, she never really wanted to admit to herself or anyone else that her husband had a drinking problem and often made excuses for him to others.

Fred Feinstein arrived on the labor subcommittee staff in 1977, shortly after Burton's loss to Wright, when chairman Thompson was, in Feinstein's words, "still basking in the glow of revenge." But Thompson often talked to Feinstein of the mixed feelings he had about opposing a man with whom he so often agreed and questioned his role in that race. Labor lobbyist Bartley O'Hara, who knew both men well, described their relationship—and what might have been—as the stuff of grand opera. After Thompson's defeat, Feinstein and the rest of the staff awaited the new boss with trepidation.

"We were all here one morning about eleven," Feinstein recalled, "when this huge figure comes bursting through the door. 'Hi. I'm Phil Burton. All of you come around. I want all your résumés. You—what do you do?' We all trembled while he interrogated us, and then he left. . . . A few days later he said, 'I'll try it with all of you for a few months.'" Feinstein, who thought it was Burton's way of making up to Thompson, asked Bill Ford of Michigan whether he should stay. Allied with liberals often hostile to Burton, Ford said, "Do it. Phil's a genius." Feinstein proved "operational" and Burton came to rely on him. Thompson, meanwhile, was facing jail, and Feinstein often felt Burton was talking to Thompson through him.

The subcommittee had jurisdiction over labor law and the National Labor Relations Board. Its reach defined much of the relationship between management and labor, including the right of unions to exist. Labor feared Reagan would help management win take-backs. "No one felt we could move forward," recalled Feinstein. "We had to fight to protect what was there. Burton never saw the subcommittee as a vehicle to do anything but guard the safe."

One typical Burton tactic came during a conference committee on the Gramm-Latta budget reconciliation bill. This was the 800-page Reaganomics package of deep domestic spending and tax cuts Congress approved in 1981 with the help of "boll weevil" southern Democrats like Phil Gramm of Texas. Education and Labor Chairman Carl Perkins was absent, so Burton led the House negotiations with conservative Republican Orrin Hatch of Utah, the new chairman of Senate Labor and Human Resources. Over Burton's objections, the House had slipped into the bill a provision cutting FECA, the Federal Employee Compensation Act, which provided worker compensation for federal workers. Hatch was no doubt counting on putting the FECA cut in the final version, figuring that if the more liberal House had already passed it, the Senate would follow. Hatch did not count on Burton turning the entire process upside down. Instead of hanging tough for the House version—typical of conference negotiations—Burton made a concession neither the House nor Hatch wanted him to make.

"The House will recede to the Senate position," he said, meaning there would be no FECA cuts, Burton's position all along. "You can't do that," Hatch said, incredulous. "No, we're receding," Burton replied. "This meeting is adjourned." With that, he and Miller walked out, leaving Hatch sputtering.

The budget bill presented challenges to everyone. The House Budget Committee said every nonmilitary committee should cut a percentage of the funds it authorized. But the question was, cut from what? It was not clear whether the reductions should come from Reagan's budget or from the previous year's authorization. The Congressional Budget Office then produced a number, which every committee was told to use as a baseline from which to reduce spending. This baseline number became pivotal. A staff member on the Interior Committee described an informal meeting in Burton's office to figure out how much to cut the programs in its jurisdiction.

> We went over to Phil's office. He was in front, with his chair to the side of his desk, and a small table for a phone, a drink, and an ashtray. The rest of the chairs were set up auditorium-style, facing him, for members and staff. The meeting started about 5:30. A secretary took drink orders, and Phil sat there, drinking and smoking and kicking it all around like a talk show host. He said, "I don't know where the junior accountant in CBO is getting these baselines, but I'm going to find him, and next time we're going to have a say in establishing these numbers." It was remarkably perceptive

to figure out that a particular person at CBO had established the numbers, that Burton would find out who and then get to him. He assessed the power situation immediately.

Where other legislators would have accepted the numbers and worked with them as best they could, he realized that creating them was itself a political act, which he could influence, once he discovered who did it.[20]

Burton was so angry at the House leadership for its complicity with Reagan's budget cuts and fiscal program that he blasted O'Neill and Wright in a remarkably candid interview with Leo Rennert of the *Sacramento Bee*. What he said was the public version of what took place at his "dinner" parties. The leadership's first problem, Burton said, was making undue early concessions to conservative southerners who then bolted to Reagan. Instead of "rewarding the Phil Gramms and other boll weevils," he said, O'Neill and Wright should have rewarded other southern conservatives who showed party loyalty. Burton said he fought with O'Neill and Wright in closed-door meetings of Steering and Policy. They put Gramm on the Budget Committee over Burton's objections, for example. Gramm, a former Texas A & M economics professor, later resigned, switched parties, ran for his old seat, and was elected as a Republican.[21]

The leadership also missed key opportunities to set legislative traps for the GOP, Burton told Rennert. O'Neill and Wright should have forced the Republicans to cast recorded votes that pitted their own region's economic interests, especially in farm areas, against Reagan's budget cuts. For example, Burton said the leadership should have forced a roll-call vote when the House passed a Reagan bill to reduce dairy price supports. Even if a recorded vote would not have changed the outcome, he said, dairy farmers at least would have known who voted against them. "We must put Republicans on the spot," he said. "It's time for them to show their true colors—whether they're Reagan zealots or whether they're more sensitive to their own constituents."

"In politics," Burton said, "you have to nurture your own basic strength while you erode the basic strength of the enemy. We've managed to reverse that. The malaise speaks for itself. Reagan is trampling our leadership." But when Rennert asked if he was preparing to challenge the leadership, Burton said, "I'm too smart to answer that question in an odd-numbered year. You replace them in an even-numbered year—at the end of the year."

The Republicans were careful not to let House Democrats see their final budget reconciliation bill, Gramm-Latta, also known as the Latta substitute, which incorporated all the Reagan spending cuts and tax breaks. Written in OMB Director David Stockman's office and in the Senate, it was assembled so quickly that it was nearly impossible to follow, a jumble of cut and paste and pages out of order. "We've got to plug the bill into the computer," Burton told Feinstein.

Because Vic Fazio chaired a subcommittee of the Appropriations Committee with jurisdiction over the House clerk, Burton summoned Fazio and headed to the Clerk's Office to intercept the bill, the only copy of which was about to go to the printing office. Knowing who controlled his budget— Fazio's subcommittee—the clerk reluctantly parted with the huge bill and accompanied them to H324, a small room in the Capitol where Burton began reading it and jotting down a few notes and code numbers. He had the bill at most for ten minutes. "We were frantic to determine what the bill would do," Fazio recalled. "But as we reviewed it, we didn't get much out of it." The legend quickly grew that Burton threw the entire 800-page bill into the air, deliberately creating chaos.[22]

The next day, Republican Minority Leader Robert Michel of Illinois took to the floor in a fury to blame Fazio and Burton for the poor order the bill was in and for violating House rules by intercepting it. "It is outrageous. It is wrong, and you might as well face up to it now," Michel fumed.

Burton replied that he had the bill for a few moments only to ascertain whether he could photocopy it. He most certainly did not "throw it out on the table and spread it all around," as Michel alleged. But in equally firm, if tortured, language, Burton said, "If this be a culpable act, I will admit it. I affirm it was an act in an effort to ascertain . . . to what extent the sweeping scope of this amendment was, because obviously, when the people voted for the [Gramm-]Latta substitute, they had no idea in the world what was in it, and we do not have today any idea of some of the barnacles on this 'ship of state.'" Second-termer Newt Gingrich of Georgia, the ranking Republican on the Joint Printing Committee, said disciplinary action was "clearly warranted." Fazio later said Burton went to the floor "to take the arrow so it wouldn't land on me."[23]

Burton condemned the Reagan package unequivocally in language other Democrats wouldn't use for another decade, when it helped them win back the presidency. "I rise in opposition to the Latta-Reagan substitute," he said. "I predict that this is going to prove the economic equivalent of the Tonkin Bay resolution to declare war in Indo-China. This substitute is a declaration of war against America's poor and powerless, against the working people of this country, and against the environment. This proposal will make the rich richer and the poor poorer. It is, in short, a blueprint for economic disaster. I urge its rejection."[24]

Most members of Congress relied on staff to make them look good, brief them on the substance of legislation, fill them in on details the members were far too busy or preoccupied to keep track of themselves. Not Burton. Staff director Feinstein had always prepared an opening statement for his former boss, Frank Thompson, to read when he conducted hearings. Feinstein stopped when he realized his new chairman never read them. And the first time he handed Burton a list of questions to ask witnesses, Burton said, "These are interesting. Why don't *you* ask them? I'll ask my own." Staff had a word for what happened if Burton found them late in the day. They would get "captured," and plans for the evening went out the window.

Feinstein grew to admire and respect Burton tremendously. But he had to endure a painful and traumatic episode first. One night, Burton began drinking heavily while talking to a new employee. She wanted more status on the subcommittee. She complained about others, including Feinstein, who she thought were pawning off less important jobs on her. Soon Burton was roaring drunk and in the grip of a blind and irrational rage. He spotted Feinstein and began screaming at him, mostly about the "Princeton elite," Frank Thompson, and "effete fucking liberals." Five years later, his bitterness, despair, and anger over losing his 1976 race came boiling to the surface. Feinstein, who was totally blameless, and Judy Lemons, who was also in the office, became convenient targets of his fury. Even though Thompson had gone to Wake Forest, Princeton was in his district, and it symbolized all that Burton hated about the liberals who had chosen Bolling and Wright over him.

"I'm the Maoist. I'm the street-fighter. I'm the bomb-thrower, and people who work for me have to be guerrillas," he screamed, insisting that no job should be beneath them. "People who work for me have to be willing to clean the toilets." At first, Feinstein tried to respond, but nothing would satisfy Burton. This was a savage rage at the world. Feinstein and Lemons tried to leave, but he screamed, "Stay right there!" and vented his fury for another hour. He made constant reference to the 1976 race, but he was incoherent much of the time. Feinstein was so devastated that he agonized over whether to come to work the next day. Was he fired, and if not, how could he continue working for a man like that? But he showed up and Burton came up to him immediately.

"Don't say a word. I completely apologize," he said. "I lost it. It happens to me now and then. It's like howling at the moon. It's better than shooting my wife." Burton never let Feinstein say a word and never abused him again.[25]

Burton began preparing for the 1981 reapportionment as soon as Jerry Brown's 1978 re-election guaranteed his signature on a redistricting plan. But the man who began the hostilities was not Burton, but nemesis John Rousselot, a one-time chairman of the John Birch Society from San Marino, a wealthy Los Angeles suburb. Burton helped redistrict Rousselot out of the House after one term in 1960. He was elected from a different district a few years later, rising to become vice chairman of the Republican National Campaign Committee. From that spot, he shipped money to GOP challengers in California in 1980. He persuaded Bobbi Fiedler, a popular Jewish Republican on the Los Angeles school board, who led an anti-busing crusade in the San Fernando Valley, to run against ten-term incumbent Jim Corman, the ranking Democrat on Ways and Means, in an increasingly conservative district. Her victory would have enormous implications for the House. When Fiedler defeated Corman in 1980 and Chairman Ullman also lost, Tip O'Neill gave Dan Rostenkowski a choice: he could become whip, succeeding Brademas, or take over Ways and Means. Rostenkowski chose the latter. Tom Foley became Whip and eventually Speaker.[26]

Rousselot also recruited a moderate Republican named Dennis McQuaid in 1980 to run against John Burton, much of whose district was in Marin County. John hated Washington and wanted to leave but would not walk away from a fight, even if his as-yet unpublicized drug problems made it hard for him to concentrate on his job. McQuaid attacked him as unconventional and "off the wall" and beat him in Marin. But Burton's strong San Francisco base delivered a six-point victory. Phillip was furious, however. In an angry encounter at a California Bankers Association–sponsored dinner on a boat cruising the Potomac, a well-lubricated Burton cornered Rousselot and threatened him with political oblivion.

"You're just a no-good jerk," Burton said, putting his beefy arm between Rousselot and the boat rail, making escape difficult. "You tried to beat my brother. Now you'll pay the price. . . . Nobody pisses in my family's sandbox." Burton denied calling Rousselot a "no-good jerk" but threatened to draw a line from Rousselot's district up Interstate 5 "and put you in the gayest part of San Francisco." John Burton was less upset. "You really ticked my brother off," he told Rousselot. "I'm not sure I want to stay here, anyway."[27]

As 1981 dawned, conventional thinking held that Burton would behave responsibly and protect incumbents of both parties. Everyone knew he would take care of his brother, but the GOP thought he would evenly apportion California's two new seats, which would make the 22-21 Democrat-Republican split in the delegation 23-22. That at least was what Robert Naylor, the California Assembly Republican Caucus chairman, believed when he visited Washington for the Reagan inaugural and paid a courtesy call on Burton. Naylor, in his third year from San Mateo on the San Francisco Peninsula, was the GOP's designated point man on reapportionment.

Burton made Naylor wait twenty minutes while he carefully organized his national park files. Then he handed Naylor a glass, some ice, and a bottle of Stolichnaya. Over the next two hours, as Naylor slowly nursed his vodka, Burton "dazzled" him with his knowledge of California, his grasp of new census data, and of where population growth pressures might appear over the next decade. For the first time, Naylor heard the phrase, "He's in his mother's arms" to signify someone Burton would protect. But at the end of the conversation, Naylor realized he told Burton more about what Burton wanted to know—who hoped to move up to Congress from the state legislature—than Burton told him.

GOP reapportionment consultant Tony Quinn, who accompanied Naylor to the meeting, recalled Burton wanting very much to protect California's interests by protecting the senior members of both parties, as he tried to do in 1971. With safe districts, Burton said, they would not have to fly home every weekend. They could remain in Washington to fight the other big delegations in Texas and Illinois and New York for their share of federal pork.[28]

Naylor's and Quinn's experiences were typical. Only Michael Berman really knew what Burton was doing. But even he never saw John's district. As in previous years, members did not want to devote the time, were precluded, or were too scared to challenge Burton. "He's the one who wants to do it," Glenn Anderson told the *San Diego Union*. "I don't have time. He loves this stuff. I'm not really concerned where the lines are drawn in San Francisco." Anderson should have known better. He discovered to his chagrin what Burton did to his district.

"I'm sure he will be cold and surgical," right-winger Robert "B-1 Bob" Dornan of Orange County said. In fact, after hearing rumors that Burton would eliminate his district, Dornan went up to him and said, "Phil, I hear I'm number one on your hit list. If so, I take that as quite a compliment." Burton patted him on the arm. "Just doing the Lord's work, Bobby," he said.

Just as assembly Republicans designated Naylor, House Republicans designated Bill Thomas to keep track of Burton. In a hopelessly misguided analysis, Thomas said that if Burton was "really creative, of the two new seats, he can keep one." Democrat Tony Beilenson was more realistic: "He's a good friend of mine, but I want to keep an eye on him, too."

Assemblyman Terry Goggin, who wanted to go to Congress, learned manners the hard way. In mid-February, Burton spent ten minutes in Goggin's office waiting to see him. That was ten minutes too long. "If Mr. Goggin wants a congressional seat," Burton yelled to a secretary as he stormed out, "tell him to visit me in Washington." There went Goggin's dream of a House career.[29]

In mid-March, state legislators gathered at the Madison Hotel in Washington for their annual dinner with the California congressional delegation. Burton spotted Naylor, sat him down at a side table, and offered him a new House seat on the peninsula. Pete McCloskey was giving up his seat to run for governor in 1982. If Naylor cooperated and helped round up Republican assembly votes for the congressional plan, Burton implied he would design the new district for him. Burton drew the district he envisioned for Naylor on the tablecloth, complete with boundaries, arrows and census data.

Naylor listened politely to Burton but refused. He could not sell out House Republicans in exchange for his own ticket to Washington. He was also on the leadership ladder in Sacramento and did not want to disrupt his young family. (The hotel manager was furious about his ruined tablecloth. Former Burton secretary Martha Gorman, who had become a lobbyist for the California Medical Association, went back the next morning and bought it for $17.)[30]

Burton had already begun intensive one-on-one negotiations with House members on the shapes of their districts. Nobody saw what other districts looked like or the complete map of the state. Members fell into three distinct categories, Burton told them: "You're in your mother's arms," or "You're going to have to work a little harder," or "You're totally fucked." Few were completely happy, even safe Democrats. Burton was trying to maximize Democratic seats. To do that meant he had to spread Democratic voters into as many districts as possible. That lowered Democratic registration in each— and thus made re-election a little harder.[31]

The Republicans, for their part, tried to force the Democrats to create more Hispanic seats. Their goal: bunch so many Democrats into safe Hispanic districts that there would be fewer Democrats in the surrounding non-Hispanic districts. That would permit Republicans to carry the outlying, now Republican, suburbs. Burton saw their move and had a surprise waiting.

Burton knew he would have to steal Democratic voters from Fazio, whose

Sacramento district stretched south to Vallejo, and from freshman Tom Lantos, who now represented Leo Ryan's district immediately south of San Francisco, his brother's district. When a letter came to Burton from the Solano County Central Labor Council expressing worry they would "lose" Fazio, Burton called him in. "I've told you you're in your mother's arms," Burton said. "This is unnecessary." Then came a chamber of commerce letter saying the same thing. Burton told Fazio to knock it off or he would be the only Californian with a district in Oregon.

Fazio knew reapportionment cold from his days as an assembly staffer. He had no alternative but to sign off on the loss of Vallejo, however painful. He agreed to divide Sacramento with Bob Matsui, even though he knew his new district would get weaker, not stronger, as the decade progressed. Fazio was a team player, and Burton considered him "operational." But it was more complicated than that. Burton also regarded Fazio as one of his "upwardly mobiles," young, ambitious career pols who did not want to spend their entire careers getting their marching orders from Burton.

Tom Lantos, on the other hand, considered the loss of Daly City a "disaster" because his votes declined as he moved south. "He did not ask," a Burton staffer wrote of a phone conversation with a Lantos staffer, "but the thought was there: why not more of Solano [for John Burton], not Daly City?" And: "Why doesn't Phil take part of Marin and give John more of SF?" The unspoken answer, of course, was that "Phil" was "taking" from everywhere. He was giving John plenty of Solano and San Francisco and Daly City. Lantos lost 60,000 Democrats in Daly City, which forced him to move out of his Hillsborough home and into a San Mateo condo. But to keep the district safe, Burton pushed Lantos into McCloskey's district, where he picked up Democratic voters in Palo Alto and Stanford.[32]

That, in turn, required pushing McCloskey's district further south as well. It was later described as being an "urban cowboy" district, beginning at San Gregorio Beach, jumping over the Santa Cruz Mountains to affluent Atherton and the Silicon Valley suburbs in the Los Altos Hills, Sunnyvale, Cupertino, and Saratoga. Then it then headed south into lower-middle-class Morgan Hill, Gilroy, and rural San Joaquin Valley. This became Republican computer executive Ed Zschau's seat. After Zschau was elected, a constituent walked into his office, noticed an interesting piece of art on the wall, and asked what it was.

"That's my district," Zschau said. An analysis by the Republican-backed Rose Institute at Claremont Men's College called Zschau's district "the most serious violation of the principal of regional integrity."[33]

There was little doubt Burton was using redistricting to punish Democrats who voted against him in 1976. To create a new district for Howard Berman on the west side of Los Angeles, he shoved Tony Beilenson of Beverly Hills into portions of the more blue-collar San Fernando Valley. At the same time, he removed other Democrats from Beilenson's southern border and added them to Dornan's district, which he tailored for Berman ally Mel Levine. "I wanted you to know that I am angry and hurt about the proposed new district in my area," Beilenson wrote in a May 14, 1981 letter to Burton. "When we transferred the description that you had given me to a map, we discovered that it reaches all the way to the Ventura County border and looks about as gerrymandered as a district could look."

Conceding that there had been "shouting matches," Beilenson said years later that Burton "wasn't trying to get even with me. He was trying to create as many districts as possible. That worried some of us who thought we knew more about our locales than he did. He left much of Southern California to Michael Berman. They didn't do it nicely or well, and we didn't see the maps."

Norm Mineta, the former San Jose mayor whose loyalty on the critical third ballot Burton allies still questioned, was given a safe district but gained less than ideal territory. "I was the dean of the [California] delegation," recalled Don Edwards, whose district bordered Mineta's and whose office was next to Burton's in the Rayburn building. "Phil summoned me from twenty feet away. He was sitting in his office in the dark, and I couldn't see him, and in a big voice, he said, 'Why in the hell do you want to accept Santa Clara? That's a rotten place. You'll be un-elected. Don't be a good guy. Don't do it.'" Mineta got Santa Clara.

Burton was so delighted Fiedler beat Corman that he gave her what she wanted. Because Barry Goldwater, Jr., was planning to run for the U.S. Senate in 1982, Burton could slide Fiedler into Goldwater's solidly Republican district in Woodland Hills, which left more Democratic terrain for Howard Berman.

"I had been elected to the school board at large from the city of Los Angeles," Fiedler recalled. "I had a strong, large base and I knew there wasn't anywhere he could put me I couldn't win. I had won a 60 percent Democratic district, but he wanted that for Howard Berman. He wanted both of us to be happy, and he had a big grudge against Glenn Anderson, so he gave me the jewel of Anderson's district, Santa Catalina Island. Emotionally, Anderson was very attached to that, but he voted for Wright." Worse for Anderson, Burton also took the predominantly black city of Carson out of his district to strengthen Mervyn Dymally's district. "I told him the one city I really wanted to keep was Carson," Anderson complained. "He told me I couldn't have Carson."

Alarmed by rumors of devastation to Republican districts, Bill Thomas kept talking with Burton, Willie Brown, and Roberti, the California legislative leaders whose houses would vote on the plan. The Republicans agreed not to cut individual deals with Burton. But by the time Burton called Fiedler into his office, he told her every other Republican had already come in to bargain. Virtually all of them had.

The Democrats could not get information from Burton, either. If they asked, he'd say, "You're in your mother's arms." If they saw him across a room and shouted, "Phil, how'm I doing?" he cradled his arms in front of his chest and made a rocking motion. Once the Democrats realized Thomas was piecing together data on Burton's plan from discussions he had with other Republicans, they came to Thomas for scraps of information.

Thomas developed an odd friendship with Burton. He visited Burton in his darkened office, and like so many before him, drank vodka in tumblers. Thomas asked questions, and Burton would decide whether he thought they were naive or perceptive and answer accordingly. Thomas was trying to provide information to fellow Republicans and build a file for potential court action.

"Over time, even the prison guard and the prisoner develop some kind of relationship," Thomas recalled. "It got to the point where he would ask if I could take him home, and I would. He pulled on one mask and took off another, and he'd talk about how no one had ever done with him what I was doing, that is, come back for more. I assumed he enjoyed dangling me around, but over time I picked up information."[34]

Computer technology for redistricting was available, but Burton never used it. The technical challenges Burton thus faced were awesome. "One man, one vote" court rulings dictated that each of the forty-five districts possess near equal population. The Voting Rights Act called for minority districts where possible. Proposition 6, a Republican-backed measure approved on the June 1980 state ballot to establish reapportionment guidelines, required Burton to make the districts contiguous, which meant they should be in contact on all or most of one side. Each district, moreover, was supposed to reflect a "community of interests." When Burton's district for Thomas appeared, however—it stretched from Pismo Beach to the Mohave Desert— Republicans said its only community of interest was sand. Districts were also supposed to be compact, and cities and counties not split into more than one district.

In conforming to these guidelines, Burton accumulated hundreds of pages of yellow work sheets. On these sheets he moved blocks of voters census tract by census tract to achieve population equality. Stapled to the work sheets were hundreds of adding machine tabulations of population figures by census tract, each broken down by number of Democrats, Republicans, independents, blacks, Indians, Asians, and Hispanics. His demand for precise information that went beyond census data was insatiable. Dr. Leroy Hardy of Long Beach State, who still consulted for him on reapportionment, cruised neighborhoods on the lookout for makes of car. When the cars changed from Chevy to Buick, he knew the neighborhood had changed from Democrat to Republican. When the cars became Volvos and Saabs, he figured he was in upper-middle-class Democratic territory.

Burton sometimes did his own growth projections. In Contra Costa, for example, the fast-growing suburban county east of San Francisco, county planners projected growth at "perhaps 1,000 additional units" for Census Tract 3452.04. Next to that was Burton's scrawl: "No more than 500 will be okayed." Burton had not even taken the Planning Department's projections at face value. He went the extra step to see how many new housing units the county would likely *approve* over the next decade, which told him how to exploit that growth for Democratic advantage in devising the congressional district.

Robert Brauer, a staff consultant to Ron Dellums, sent Burton a list of Richmond's black population census tract by census tract. "Bob—you've made my whole week!" Burton replied. "Can you give me equivalent data for Hunters Point, Compton and San Diego Inner City?" Burton even asked the Census Department how many people were on ships in California by census tract.[35]

While Burton and Michael Berman worked on adding machines and a $300 hand-held calculator, Republican-oriented corporations and business groups gave nearly $1 million to the Rose Institute for sophisticated computer work and maps. GOP analysts wanted to be able to instantly compare plans once the Democrats produced them. The California Roundtable, a business organization, gave Rose $688,000 to get started. The American Medical Association PAC gave another $40,000; Fluor Corporation gave $25,000; and Hewlett-Packard donated a $90,000 computer.[36] Other PACs saw control of the House at stake and kicked in more money to help the Republicans.

But for Burton, this was AB 59, black lung, and Redwood National Park packed into one. Through manipulation of technical data, hard work, prodigious feats of memory, and intense determination, he "terrorized the bastards" yet again. Phillip and Michael versus a million dollars and Republican computers. But he held the trump cards and carried his computer in his brain.

On April 30, 1981, Indiana Republicans approved a reapportionment so blatant that it changed a six-to-five Democratic advantage in the Indiana House delegation to a seven-to-three Republican edge. This gave Burton the pretext, although he hardly needed it, for doing the same thing in California. "The [Indiana] plan is a textbook case of partisan redistricting," *Congressional Quarterly* wrote. "Its lines weave freely in and out of counties, concentrating Democratic voting strength into the districts of just three of the state's six Democratic incumbents and damaging the re-election prospects of the other three." In Washington State, meanwhile, Republicans gained control of the legislature in February, immediately dispatched $175,000 to the Rose Institute for consulting work on that state's remap and came up with a plan almost as partisan as Indiana's.[37]

In return for its approval of the congressional plan, the California legislature exacted a heavy price from the delegation. The IRS had ruled that state legislators' untaxed per diem allowance of $75 a day for 200 days in session was taxable income, retroactive for up to ten years. State legislators could be liable for thousands of dollars in back taxes. The solution: get Ways and Means to fix it. When Californian Pete Stark would not touch it, Burton hit up Bob Matsui. Burton had cooked a deal with the Texans, who wanted one of theirs to get the next Energy and Commerce opening. In return, Burton got Matsui on Ways and Means, assuming the California slot Corman left.

After just one term and with Burton's help, Matsui shepherded an amendment through Ways and Means to allow state legislators to treat their district home as their residential home for tax purposes and thus deduct without verification "an amount equal to the number of legislative days times the per diem." Without this change, state legislative leaders told the delegation privately, there would be no approval for Burton's redistricting plan. But California had to wait its turn, because Rostenkowski had to take care of the same problem with Illinois legislators first. Greasing passage of the amendment required several large meetings in Tip O'Neill's office.

Burton put the deal together behind the scenes, and Matsui wrote the amendment into the 1981 tax bill. On June 17, it was approved unanimously and became part of Reagan's tax package. The public never knew a thing about these maneuvers. Rousselot, a member of Ways and Means, could have held up the deal by insisting that he see Burton's congressional lines before agreeing to anything. "He was dumb," said one California Republican, still angry at him a dozen years later. "He was the only man in U.S. history ever to get redistricted out of office twice."

By July, word was leaking about some elements of Burton's plan. Beilenson and Anderson complained publicly about what they thought Burton was doing to their districts. Bill Thomas went further: "Phil wants me to get on my knees," he told the *Los Angeles Times* in one version of his comments that was printable. "That's not a wholesome relationship." Thomas said Burton told him every seat was fixed but his. "He asked me for a map of Bakersfield with a dot where my house is." In the Central Valley, the *Fresno Bee* heard Burton was handcrafting a district for another Berman ally, assemblyman Rick Lehman. The plan divided Fresno into three congressional districts, one of which looked like a telephone receiver, with Stockton at one end and the city of Fresno at the other and no direct access in between. This was more Coelho's idea than Lehman's, who said he would accept it as long as it was clear he was not responsible for it.

"He drew a district I couldn't run in," Coelho recalled of Burton's first plan. "I said, 'Phil, that's well and good, but I'm going to run in the other district you created for Rick Lehman. It has my home town of Merced in it, and I can win that district against anyone, and you know it. In the other seat I'll run my own candidate against anyone you put up, and after all, you're only concerned about electing two Democrats, right?' He wasn't too happy with me. He came back later and said, 'You'd win that seat, so let's redraw the lines. I'm told he didn't do this with anyone else." Michael Berman confirmed Coelho's story. Coelho was an "upward mobile" on whom Burton had no claim. "Tony doesn't want that district. I don't want to have that war," Burton told Berman.[38]

By late August, Beilenson was so angry about his proposed district that he canceled a trip to the Soviet Union and Israel and headed to Sacramento, where he plotted with David Roberti to stop Burton's plan. A former state senator, Beilenson still had friends there, and Roberti, also angry, announced he would do his own remap. After a two-hour meeting with Burton, Roberti said, "He didn't show me any lines, and it was not a very interesting conversation." Other senators agreed that Burton's style was "bullying and manipulative." Roberti said of the three liberal Jewish Democrats—Waxman, Beilenson, and Howard Berman—competing for turf in West Los Angeles,

"I view it as a blood feud between children in the same family fighting over the family inheritance."

Some Democrats thought Beilenson had no case. He still had a safe, 59 percent Democratic district. But to make room for Berman and Levine, he would have to trade his silk-stocking district of rich liberals in Beverly Hills for loyal blue-collar Democrats in the San Fernando Valley. One Democrat quoted Beilenson as saying, "Give me Gucci or give me death," but Beilenson said, "I don't say crazy things like that." Willie Brown, not surprisingly, sided with Burton. "I want to make sure Howard Berman has a seat," he said of his rival. "I think Mr. Berman would make an excellent congressman."[39] Eventually, they worked out a compromise.

On September 9, 1981, Burton finally went public with his redistricting plan. During a two-hour bravura performance before the Sacramento press corps, Democratic legislators chortled at Burton's deadpan delivery, while Republicans lined the back walls of the briefing room fuming. Asked how many seats his plan would cost the Republicans, Burton said with a straight face, "I would have no way of making that estimate." The "loudest guffaw," the *San Jose Mercury News* reported, "came from Richard Alatorre."[40]

There were no maps to show Burton's extensive handiwork in Los Angeles or the San Fernando Valley. Rough maps of other areas were tacked up. Even so, Republicans knew immediately that Burton's new lines would change the ratio in the delegation from 22-21 to 28-17. Burton was single-handedly delivering six Democrats to Tip O'Neill for a net change of ten House votes, which not only strengthened O'Neill's hand enormously in dealing with the Reagan administration, but represented nearly one-fourth of the twenty-six House seats the Democrats picked up nationally that year. The severe 1982 recession convinced GOP strategists they could not take over the House. But no one expected this.

One columnist compared Burton at the press conference to "Reggie Jackson taking batting practice with the Toledo farm team." *Sacramento Union* columnist Dan Walters said the plan "resembles nothing so much as a jigsaw puzzle designed by an inmate of a mental institution." Speaking without notes, Burton recited the precise number of people in each district, where the splits in cities and counties occurred, down to the street names. Despite the twisted lines, his plan conformed almost perfectly to court requirements: minority seats and near equal population per district. He split fewer cities and counties than the special masters did in 1973. No district deviated by more than 223 people from any other. The average deviation was 67 people. But despite the technical genius, Burton's contempt for public input and his raw partisanship came through so strongly that virtually every editorial page in the state lambasted him for weeks. Even Willie Brown was forced to concede that Burton "gives arrogance a bad name."

The pièce de résistance was John Burton's district, the district he would let no one else see, not even Michael Berman. It included parts of four counties, San Francisco, Marin, Solano, and San Mateo. Critics said one needed a boat to get around and that it was contiguous only at low tide. Burton himself called it "my contribution to modern art," and added, "It's gorgeous. It curls in and out like a snake." So much for compact and contiguous. Two of the four portions were connected only by water, and two by railroad yards. "We discovered that Sacramento, Yolo and Solano [had] 80,000 people too many," Burton explained. "So we wondered, 'Is there a whole city in Solano [County] we can attach to [John's] district?'" After a long pause for effect, he added, "Would you believe we discovered Vallejo?" The room erupted in laughter, because everyone knew it was the other way around. Burton grabbed Vallejo for John, whose new district jumped from 52-28 percent Democratic to 57-25. It was 26 short of possessing the numerically perfect 525,968 people.

But to achieve this, Burton weakened himself. He took from John the more conservative Richmond and Pacific Heights districts of San Francisco and gave him the predominantly black Bayview and Hunters Point sections, along with portions of Chinatown, North Beach, and Telegraph Hill. Forty percent of John's new district was still in Marin County, which, despite its trendy reputation, voted for Reagan in 1980. Another 33 percent came from San Francisco. The rest came from Democratic pockets in Vallejo, which was closer geographically and culturally to Sacramento than to the Haight Ashbury, and from Lantos precincts in Daly City. John Burton's 1980 opponent Dennis McQuaid said Vallejo did not bother him. What killed him was the addition of Daly City and the removal of the Richmond District and Pacific Heights from San Francisco, where McQuaid invested enormous effort in 1980—now wasted.

Burton also put more blacks and Democrats in all four black districts, those of Augustus Hawkins, Mervyn Dymally, Julian Dixon, and Ron Dellums. Describing Dellums's new district, Burton said: "It decreases his vulnerability from a blatant, non-black primary challenge." Asked to translate, Burton replied, "He can't be beaten by a honky in the primary. He's in his brothers' arms."

But the biggest howls of protest came from the six GOP incumbents he collapsed into three districts in the south. To no one's surprise, he combined

Fiedler's and Goldwater's district. He forced Rousselot to run in a Democratic Hispanic district against Marty Martinez or face GOP incumbent Carlos Moorhead (Rousselot chose the former and lost). And he put incumbents Wayne Grisham and David Dreier in the same Pomona-Whittier district, forcing them to run against each other. (Dreier, a product of Claremont and the Rose Institute, defeated Grisham in the 1982 primary.) As advertised, he eliminated Dornan's district (Dornan and Goldwater ran for the U.S. Senate and lost in the primary to Pete Wilson). He also weakened Don Clausen's district in the far north. With these maneuvers, plus the two new seats, Burton drew districts for Berman, Levine, Lehman, San Diego Supervisor Jim Bates, and Marty Martinez.

But Burton had one more shocker: a third Hispanic seat, which not only brought Alatorre and the Hispanics on board, but undercut Republican criticism that Burton would not do enough for minorities. The first Hispanic seat belonged to veteran incumbent Ed Roybal. The second was the new seat that Martinez picked up. For years, Congressman George Danielson barely survived Democratic primary challenges in an increasingly Hispanic district. Recognizing that it was only a matter of time before he would lose, Burton convinced him to accept an appointment to the California Court of Appeal. Burton then created a 54 percent Hispanic seat in what had been Danielson's district. In testimony to an assembly committee, Burton said: "Congressman Danielson is a person of great judicial temperament and may well find other areas to continue his superb service to the people."[41]

Meanwhile, Burton harassed Governor Brown until he appointed Danielson. This permitted Martinez, who had served less than one assembly term, to run in the special July election, which he won with only 51 percent of the vote. (He took just 54 percent in November against Rousselot.)

Nobody expected a third Hispanic seat. Burton created it from the results of the 1980 census. The district was 48 percent Hispanic. Esteban Torres, another Waxman-Berman friend, was the candidate. Torres, a former UAW representative and auto worker, worked his way up to head a federal antipoverty program in East Los Angeles. He ran for Congress in 1974, eight years earlier, lost to Danielson, and then went to Washington. After serving in the Carter White House, he became ambassador to UNESCO. Torres had been away so long he did not even have a California driver's license. MALDEF, set to protest the plan, was so excited about the Torres seat that MALDEF director John Huerta called the remap "historic and unprecedented for Hispanics."

Burton regretted weakening Clausen's district. They served together nearly twenty years, all on the Interior Committee. But Burton was so successful moving the Berman operation to Washington that Bermanites were getting all the plums. Willie Brown supporters, the winners in the speakership fight, got almost nothing. This posed a problem for assembly members who still had to approve the plan. Brown supporters weren't stupid. They would notice such things. Berman, Levine, Lehman, and Martinez were moving to Washington. Four more Berman supporters were likely to move up to the Senate, compared to only one Brown supporter. Fearing a revolt and feeling the need to give Brown's people something, Burton removed Napa and Lake Counties, Clausen's GOP strongholds, from his district. Brown supporter Doug Bosco saw the opening, challenged Clausen, and won the seat.[42]

As the full audacity of the plan emerged, Republicans in Sacramento and Washington were enraged but helpless. According to a declaration filed with the California Supreme Court by GOP Caucus Chairman Robert Naylor, the entire public hearing took thirty minutes, and less than twelve hours elapsed between that hearing and passage of the bill. Even then, there were few maps available. The only descriptions consisted of lists of census tract numbers in each district, which made them unreadable to all but the most sophisticated insiders, who still had to plug the data into their computers to see what things looked like. When Naylor, the only Republican on the conference committee, offered his 206-page counterplan, Burton dryly noted on his file copy, "Died for lack of a second." The Republicans had the money and the fancy computers, but lacking the power to schedule or assign, could only stand by frustrated.

"First of all, I must congratulate Congressman Burton on what certainly is a masterpiece, a diabolical masterpiece," Naylor testified. "It represents almost a total disregard for every standard of fair representation." In response, Burton said he had to bunch the GOP incumbents together to gain Hispanic seats. "The Republican Party has stated they have a deep and abiding interest in improving the Latino representation. Of course, in their congressional plan," he said, "they don't have any. None at all. . . . You couldn't open up a whole new seat without putting some incumbents in another incumbent's district."[43]

The Republicans announced they would gather signatures for a ballot initiative to change the lines. It would cost upwards of a million dollars, but "money is no object." In a typical editorial, the *San Francisco Examiner* said Burton "is rightly known as a politician of consummate skills, a master of manipulation, but this time he has gone too far." Burton's lines, the newspaper said, provided "such wild shapes as would give Salvador Dali night-mares." The *San Jose Mercury News* called it a "pious fraud," and the *Sacra-mento Union* called it a "travesty of greed." But a Washington Democrat quoted in the *Examiner* said, "They mugged us in Indiana. They mugged us in Washington. Phil is one of our strongest guys. All's fair in reapportion-ment." Another Democrat added, "We're talking about more than the makeup of the California delegation. We're also talking about control of the House and saving essential programs from Reagan's ax. Phil's looking at the bigger picture." Burton said the Republican/Rose remap would have turned seven Democratic seats over to the Republicans. While each of his districts deviated from the norm by an average of 67 voters, the Rose plan deviated by 453 voters, and his plan kept more cities and counties intact. He beat them at their own game.[44]

In his declaration to the state supreme court, GOP consultant Tony Quinn said it was impossible to analyze Burton's plan prior to passage because Burton refused to provide maps. Quinn said, "I can say with confidence that no staff person working on reapportionment for the California legislature either drew up this plan or undertook a thorough analysis of its provisions. AB 301 was entirely the product of Congressman Burton and his privately employed staff and was presented to the legislature as a finished product." Quinn said one congressional district crossed five mountain ranges. John Burton's district was contiguous only at some "geometric point over the Bay." Census tract 107 was split between the Sixteenth and Seventeenth Districts, with one portion assigned to the Sixteenth described as the "trailer park in the north-east corner."[45]

In a highly orchestrated media event, President Reagan became the first Californian to sign the ballot petition. After a *Washington Post* article described how the GOP could lose five House seats, Phil Jourdan, aide to William Broadhead of Michigan, wrote Burton: "There has been precious little of late for which Democrats can cheer. We Democrats would like to thank you very much for this piece of news. We love it."

Having ignited the controversy, Burton could not stay away from Sacra-mento, where even some Democrats, including Beilenson, were blasting his plan. When someone asked what Burton was doing in town, Howard Berman quipped, "He's like a pyromaniac at a fire." Burton made the rounds at Frank Fats, the popular political dining spot, accompanied by a magazine reporter, who recorded his anti-Beilenson diatribes. "Every Democrat in California would exchange his seat for Tony's," Burton roared at one point, reaching for his fountain pen and rapidly scribbling registration figures on yet another tablecloth. "Beilenson, 59 percent," he shouted. "Beilenson's a shit. That's on the record. 'Beilenson's a shit.'"

After another cascade of shouted obscenities, a man appeared at Burton's table. "Phil," the man said in a quiet voice, "I don't mind 'shit' and 'damn,' but I'm with my wife, and she doesn't like the f-word. Please keep it down." Burton followed the man to his table, bowed, and apologized.[46]

During all the fuss over Burton's plan, assembly Democrats and Republicans complained about their new districts, too. Michael Berman's appearance on behalf of assembly Democrats cemented Willie Brown's break with the Republicans. They had voted for him for speaker to keep Berman out. On September 15, on a strictly partisan vote, Democrats rammed through the new boundaries for the 1980s and then adjourned. Howard Berman was so impressed by Brown's role in protecting Democrats during the contentious redistricting squabbles that he called Brown's leadership "fabulous."

"You're the best Speaker I never voted for," Berman said. Another Democrat said Brown "had to divorce" the Republicans "sooner or later. The perfect divorce vehicle was reapportionment." Added a third, "Willie Brown is a unified Democratic Speaker now and will only lose the Speakership if he really screws up. There is no one on the horizon who is even close to challenging him, not in the remotest way."[47]

Republicans had just ninety days to collect nearly half a million petition signatures. Fueled by wads of money and continued editorial blistering of Burton, they turned in more than a million. Democrats sued to stop the measure. They argued it was not permissible. Staying the plan—as the Republicans requested—would muddle the 1982 elections and would violate one man, one vote requirements, given population changes since 1973. The case quickly went to the state supreme court. The secretary of state needed to know whether to use new or old lines for the 1982 elections. The GOP proposed electing 43 members from the old districts and two new ones "at large."[48]

On January 28, 1982, the court ruled for the Democrats. The vote was four to three on the state legislative plans and unanimous on Burton's congressional plan. Republican activists believed Chief Justice Rose Bird, a controversial appointee of Jerry Brown, was so clearly partisan in her decision that they met almost immediately to begin a recall campaign against Bird and three of her liberal court allies. They dropped the effort soon thereafter, but other Republican activists later picked it up—after Jerry Brown was gone. That June, voters rejected all three plans. But as Republican reapportionment expert Tony Quinn later wrote, "By then, the referendum was meaningless: the now-rejected districts were the law of California for the 1982 election."[49]

On February 4, 1982, Governor Brown appointed George Danielson to the California Court of Appeal. His resignation from Congress paved the way for the third Hispanic seat in Los Angeles, which Marty Martinez won. At a Howard Berman fund-raiser in Los Angeles soon after, Burton spotted his friend Dolores Huerta of the United Farm Workers. Huerta nearly fell off her chair when Burton asked her to dance, but she knew why. Her union had targeted Richard Alatorre for defeat, because he "betrayed" Berman in the speakership war. Hoping to maintain peace, Burton tried to talk her out of it. While he led her around the dance floor during a slow tune, Burton said, "You've really got to think about what you are doing. This is important to me." To which Huerta replied, "Yeah, Phil, but I really don't trust this guy at all. He's a rat."[50]

A few years later Burton ran into his friend Robert Bauman, the former House "objector" who was persona non grata in the Republican Party after his homosexual sex scandal. "I heard you were thinking of running again for Congress," Burton told him. "Why didn't you tell me? I would have drawn you a gay Republican district in California."[51]

Editorial abuse notwithstanding, Phillip Burton's reapportionment plan was a personal triumph. It would cost him dearly in his own district in 1982, but he did not yet know that. What he did know was that between 1976 and the aftermath of the 1982 elections, he picked up at least a dozen and possibly as many as seventeen votes against Jim Wright in the California delegation alone. Coupled with his other allies in the House, this was no small base. Seven of those votes were directly attributable to his 1981 labors: Bosco, Berman, Lehman, Levine, Martinez, Torres, and Bates. Seven anti-Burton Democrats lost or retired, and an eighth, Leo Ryan, was murdered in Jonestown. Many were succeeded by men certain to vote for Burton, including Robert Matsui, Vic Fazio, Tom Lantos, and Leon Panetta.[52]

If Burton was preparing himself—should the opportunity to challenge Wright present itself—this was not a bad start.

19

AIN'T THAT A BITCH!

Phil Burton was absolutely convinced his record, his performance in office, entitled him to never be challenged by mere mortals. To this day, he has not forgiven Milton Marks.

CALIFORNIA ASSEMBLY SPEAKER WILLIE BROWN

The 1982 campaign was good for Phillip, even though Sala thought it killed him, because he saw that people really cared and responded. They came out of the woodwork to help him. If he had to die, we were all glad this campaign happened before he did.

JOHN BURTON

JOHN BURTON WAS GOING downhill fast. As his cocaine dependency increased, his behavior became erratic. Friends saw him walking around Capitol Hill looking disheveled. Rumors surfaced that a dry cleaner found packets of cocaine in his coat pockets. His brief but wild speeches on the House floor on any and all subjects provided amusement to some, but concern to those who knew him. He was not showing up for meetings of the Subcommittee on Governmental Activities and Transportation, which he chaired. When he presided over explosive and widely covered hearings into the safety of DC-10 aircraft, a number of which had recently crashed, he pulled himself together. But it took constant staff work to keep him on track. Sometimes he disappeared for days and staff worked frantically to locate him. As rumors of federal drug probes of Capitol Hill surfaced, one aide got a phone call from another staffer saying, "If subpoenaed, I will go to the grand jury and tell the truth." Others said John was at rock bottom. Friends feared they would find him dead somewhere.

Phillip, who labored so long to protect John's district, was not prepared for news of this sort. Just when he pulled off one of the political coups of his life and laid the foundation for a comeback, another crisis erupted. What coalesced was a combination of factors so dangerous that it threatened to end his career. These factors included his brother's ongoing problems, a lingering and bitter aftertaste from his reapportionment plan, his own weakened district, an arrogance born of neglect of his home base, and an emboldened Republican Party suddenly energized at the prospect of ending two Burton careers in the same year. Slow to react, Burton eventually realized he could lose everything.

He knew his brother was in trouble. But although he loved John, Phillip Burton did not understand how to approach him. "His only problem with me," John recalled years later, "was he didn't know how to deal with it. He wanted to do things for me, but he didn't know what to do. And he had his own problems with alcohol." Part of the difficulty was generational. Phillip was from the hard-drinking old school. John, always a free spirit, was only six years younger. But it was an important six years. John had been touched by the drug-tolerant 1960s counterculture. Phillip's habit was legal. He knew nothing about smoking dope, doing lines, or buying drugs on the street at midnight from disreputable people.

Phillip used George Miller, one of John's closest friends, as a go-between, putting Miller in an impossibly awkward position. The way Miller saw it, John seemed "like a shotgun victim, standing on the sidewalk with blood pouring out of his chest," while his older brother refused to acknowledge the wound. The go-between role Miller performed in Washington, Willie Brown performed at home. "Those two brothers were very different and equally smart," Brown recalled. "But they had mammoth arguments. John would ask me, 'Did you talk to Phil? What did he say?' And Phil would ask, 'Did you talk to Johnny? Did you tell him?'"

The relationship had long been awkward. John Burton loved and respected his older brother and usually did what Phillip wanted. But he was angry at Phillip's inability to understand him. They were never closer than when John was first elected to the assembly. Phillip called often from Washington with advice and direction on strategy and legislation. John accomplished things in California on his own that Phillip never could. He was elected president of the California Democratic Council and later the state Democratic Party. He chaired the important Assembly Rules Committee. But in Phillip's mind, John was always the kid brother who needed Phillip to plan and make decisions. When he ran for chairman of a subcommittee of the House Select Committee on Aging, Phillip gave him hell for even trying.

"Fuck you, I've got the votes," John said.

"You got the votes?" Phillip said.

"Yeah," John replied. "I got the votes. Me, not you."

"You hear what the kid did?" Phillip later bragged to Charlie Rose, after his brother was proved right. "He knocked off Ike Skelton."

Phillip also made light of John's major committee assignment on Government Operations, which primarily involved oversight of federal agencies. "You ought to try legislating some time," the elder Burton said. "That's what it's all about." But Phillip bragged some more about the publicity John generated with his DC-10 hearings.[1]

Phillip was the consummate strategist and power broker, John the idealist and cut-up. In a February 1979 letter to constituents, John wrote: "The horrendous news [from] Guyana and the death of Leo Ryan . . . had hardly hit home when my closest friend, George Moscone, and Supervisor Harvey Milk were slain." In what could have been a subconscious plea to his brother, John added, "Those senseless events brought me face to face with grief, making me realize that friends are precious and life is all too short. We should remember to take time from our own activities to spend more time with those we care about, rather than so totally immerse ourselves in our jobs and businesses that we are always too busy to relate to people." Phillip Burton, who buried himself in his work to submerge his demons, could never have written such a letter.

John Burton had always hated Washington. To make matters worse, his second marriage collapsed. In 1980, he told his brother he was thinking about retiring at the end of the term, but the Republicans were challenging him, and he was not one to turn his back on a fight. That was a "lousy" reason to stay if he was not happy, Phillip said, but John decided to stay, anyway.

Meanwhile, John Burton began behaving strangely in his district, too. In 1981, his staff invited forty Marin County business leaders to an 8 A.M. breakfast with John to improve relations. Most were gone by 9:30 when word came that John had overslept. He said the motel desk clerk failed to wake him. *Examiner* columnist Bill Barnes wondered why Burton, who had so narrowly dodged defeat in 1980, was not in the district every weekend to mend fences and fortify his base. When a storm battered the Northern and Central California coast, especially Marin, coastal representatives like Leon Panetta immediately flew home. Where was John Burton, Barnes asked. Had he "blown a fuse, flipped out, gone bonkers, had a nervous breakdown?" At a recent fund-raiser, Barnes wrote, Burton had "flipped off" a guest and referred to close friend Willie Brown as "the little bastard." After days of not getting his calls returned, Barnes met John Burton's plane. John disembarked wearing a tan and a smile. He said his only health problem was "piles," which seemed to be the generic Burton family reply to all health inquiries. They knew it stopped follow-up questions.[2]

But it was not piles and few were fooled. Gary Sellers, who worked with Phillip Burton years earlier on the black lung legislation, had become general counsel to John Burton's subcommittee. Driven to near distraction by John's erratic behavior, he finally approached Phillip. "We've got a problem with John," Sellers began, awkward and uncomfortable for going around his boss and never mentioning the exact nature of the "problem."

"What do you mean John's got a problem?" Phillip said.

"We've got a problem we've got to deal with."

"Gary," Phillip said, "I've known you a long time. You're a worrier. You're a hand wringer."

"Goddam it," Sellers said. "I've kept my mouth shut for two years. The problem isn't getting any better. It's getting worse. I can't deal with it anymore." As he started to walk out, Burton called him back. It couldn't be true, Burton said. He had someone "watching" John. But that person was pulling his punches.

Sellers went to see George Miller. "If this were alcohol, you'd wrap him in a fucking blanket and get him out of here," Sellers said. John was furious when he learned that Sellers had confronted Phillip.[3] But the long ordeal was nearly over. Not long after, friends took John Burton to Bethesda Naval Hospital. The man was barely able to function, let alone stand for re-election. On March 6, 1982, two days before the filing deadline, John announced that he was retiring from Congress. Miller broke the news to Phillip, who had endured so much editorial abuse for designing John's district. But Phillip did not try to talk John out of his decision. He knew Sellers was right. Now John could get some help. More than anything, Miller said later, Phillip was relieved. Problem solved.[4]

The decision to seek treatment saved John Burton's life. Somewhere in his mind, he seized on the image of his teenage daughter Kim, and the thought of her gave him strength to begin his long painful recovery. Kim gave him back his life. He gave Kim back her father. When San Francisco reporters called to confirm reports of his departure from politics, he said, "I just want to go home. I'm happy I did what I did. It's a load off my back." He said he was at Bethesda for treatment of a "back injury" he received slipping on some ice. When pressed, Burton told *Examiner* reporters Dennis Opatrny and Carol Pogash that the Moscone assassination "just took the stuffing out of me." The breakup of his second marriage, he said, plunged him into despair and loneliness. "I'm basically back here alone. I don't like it. I want to get out. It isn't my town. . . . I've done 18 years of public service. It isn't fun anymore."[5] At a press conference in San Francisco a few days later, a reporter asked him about rumors of cocaine use. "One of the good things about not running for re-election," John said, "is you don't have to answer stupid questions." Shortly thereafter, he flew to Arizona, where he spent three weeks in a drug rehabilitation center.

Phil Burton wasted little time trying to find another candidate. The obvious choice was Art Agnos, who represented his brother's former assembly district on the eastern side of San Francisco. Burton called Agnos before the official announcement. John was okay, he explained, in the hospital. But Agnos wasn't interested in the job. He had two young sons and didn't want to move.

"You don't understand," Burton said. "It's a free ride. You'll get labor, the environmentalists, everyone."

"I don't want to go to Congress," Agnos explained. "I don't want to commute back and forth."

This exchange went on a few more times. But it was Burton who did not understand. How could someone pass up a free ticket to Congress? He was handing Agnos a gift of almost unimaginable value. No one had ever handed Burton anything. He had to fight and claw every step of the way. Agnos took his sons' photos out of his wallet and slapped them on the table. "Here's reason number one," he said. "Here's reason number two." Burton stared at the photos for the longest time. "What am I going to do for a candidate?" he sighed.

Burton also sounded out Nancy Pelosi, who was chairing the state Democratic Party. Pelosi grew up in a political family. Her father, Thomas D'Alesandro, had served four terms in the House and three terms as mayor of Baltimore. A brother also served in the House and as mayor. Her work in the 1976 presidential primaries helped Jerry Brown win Maryland and California. But not all of Pelosi's five children were grown, and she was not yet ready to start a congressional career.

Burton turned next to San Francisco Supervisor Jack Molinari, who was in Mount Zion Hospital with pneumonia when Burton called. A liberal Republican, Molinari considered switching parties, particularly after what passed for the GOP in San Francisco tried to kick him out of the party in 1980 for supporting John Anderson for president over Ronald Reagan.

"I told you you should have changed parties," Burton said, explaining that his brother had just pulled out. "I've been checking the law. We could run you as a write-in Democrat."

Sick as he was, Molinari was intrigued. But after checking with his political advisor the next day, he concluded he could not get enough write-in votes to win the Democratic nomination. By now, Marin County Supervisor Barbara Boxer, who also ran John Burton's Marin County office, had talked John into supporting her. She easily defeated San Francisco Supervisor Louise Renne, Mayor Feinstein's candidate, in the June primary. Reagan political director Ed Rollins, who fifteen months earlier brokered the deal that made Willie Brown assembly speaker, had a characteristically acerbic reaction to the succession battle: "Let's not let John Burton be replaced by someone who's every bit as liberal but willing to work. At least Burton stood back in his stupor and didn't do much but vote wrong."[6]

The Republicans, meanwhile, still steaming over Burton's humiliating reapportionment, discovered that Burton, in giving much of his old district to his brother, had let Democratic registration in his new district fall below 60 percent. Harvey Hukari, the Republicans' regional political director in San Francisco, suddenly got interested. Rousselot, a bitter enemy still on the Republican campaign committee, did not need convincing. Burton became number one on the GOP's 1982 hit list.

There were two obvious challengers, Democratic curmudgeon Quentin Kopp for the primary, or liberal GOP state Senator Milton Marks for November. Burton was worried about Kopp, who had a large following in conservative western city precincts, and relieved when Kopp chose not to run. Marks was another matter. He defeated John Burton in the 1967 special election and kept his seat by satisfying his predominantly Democratic district. Burton made sure Marks never faced a serious opponent, because he considered Marks a more reliable liberal vote than many Democrats.[7] Even though Burton viewed him as a lightweight, Marks could prove formidable; his senate district encompassed nearly all of Burton's new district, whereas Burton was new to 35 percent of it. To help John, he gave up many of his most loyal liberal voters, those who launched him in 1956 and whom he represented for twenty-six years in Sacramento and Washington. All the affluent areas he had never represented—Sea Cliff, Pacific Heights, the Marina, the Inner Richmond—were in the new district. Asians and blacks constituted only about 8 percent of the new district, Hispanics 6 percent.

Rousselot, Hukari, and Ed Rollins, who had moved to the White House as Reagan's political director, commissioned a poll. The results were shocking. Taken in late February by Reagan's own firm, Richard Wirthlin's Decision/Making/Information, Inc., the poll found Marks leading Burton by nearly 10 points. Eighty-nine percent of the respondents had heard of Marks, and 58 percent had a favorable impression, compared to only 14 percent who did not. Just 40 percent had a favorable impression of Burton, and 31 percent did not. Only 30 percent said Burton was doing a good job; 45 percent said he was doing a poor job. Worse, only 34 percent said he deserved re-election, 81 percent said they did not believe he was "conversant" with their concerns, and 63 percent of the Democrats polled had voted for Marks at some time in the past.

Between the poll and the promise of $70,000 from the Republican National Committee and help raising another $500,000, it was not hard convincing Marks to run. Getting rid of both Burtons, a Republican in Washington said, "has everyone here fired up, believe me." Burton got endorsements from every political and labor group he could and instructed aide Kevin Shelley to slip them under the door of Marks's office to scare him off.[8] But it did not work.

Marks announced his candidacy on March 12, less than a week after John Burton said he was leaving office. As the 1982 national recession deepened, Marks said San Francisco voters were saddled with a "missing" congressman whose failures had cost the city jobs. For his part, Burton said the campaign would be a "welcome referendum on Reaganomics and its devastating impact on urban America."[9]

In Milton Marks, or "Uncle Miltie," as he was sometimes called, Republicans had found the perfect challenger. A master of "retail politics," he hit every bar mitzvah, wedding, confirmation, baptism, and birthday party in town. While Burton expressed opinions on virtually everything, no matter how controversial, and rarely set foot in his district, Marks almost never took a public position on anything, but was everywhere. People who never heard of him got letters congratulating them on graduating from high school, winning the Rotary Club speech contest, or becoming parents. A Stanford undergraduate, Marks went to San Francisco Law School and finished World War II as an army major. He was elected to the assembly in 1958 and served eight years until redistricted out of his seat. Pat Brown appointed him to the bench, but he lasted only seven months, before running for the late Eugene McAteer's senate seat.

Marks chaired the Committee on Local Government and subcommittees on the disabled and on the maritime industry. He was known as a blow-with-the-wind moderate who avoided controversy and never got out front on an issue. Something of a loner, he set the senate record for sending out honorary scrolls. But he was not completely vacuous. His bills improved worker compensation benefits, set flammable standards for children's clothing, reformed small claims court, and provided tax relief for elderly and disabled renters. A *California Journal* article that rated state senators, however, saved Marks for the "once over lightly" category, saying he "wears down his opponents with whines and complaints."

Marks once told Reagan aide Lyn Nofziger he was the only Republican who could win a district that was 19 percent Republican. "That's because you're only 19 percent Republican yourself," Nofziger replied. When uncertain how to vote, Marks watched how San Francisco colleague George Moscone was voting. But Marks came before Moscone in the roll call, and so he would pass until after Moscone voted. On occasion, the mischievous Moscone voted, waited until Marks voted the same way, then switched at the last minute, catching Marks flat-footed.

Burton reacted to Marks's entry with cold fury. He believed his legislative record was so outstanding he should never have to face any threat more real than Tom Spinosa, a fringe Republican perennial challenger, who in one campaign year sent out a record featuring "Tom, the Singing Candidate." Spinosa doctored photos of Presidents Nixon and Ford, pasted them next to photos of himself in his homburg, and then photocopied them.

The Marks challenge also angered Burton because he had important business in Washington and this would divert his attention. He did not even live in the district, had spent only nine days there the year before—at that, in a suite at the Sir Francis Drake Hotel. He believed his value to the district was his record. Period. His district office, which pioneered the concept of constituent services, had grown lazy and fat. Earlier in his career, he had sent press releases to the ethnic media, to "big families," to every black, Asian, and Hispanic lawyer, dentist, and physician in San Francisco. But he had not sent a piece of mail to anyone in years. It was little wonder that voters had forgotten him. In Washington, Ed Davis grew so concerned he ordered the 1980 San Francisco office mail counted. Burton had received only 5,000 letters from his district, a pathetic figure for a modern congressional office. His aides rarely got out of the office, did not sink roots into emerging communities or constituencies, did not even know how out of touch they were, the Washington office learned.

On his occasional trips home, Burton summoned a few old friends, pols and labor leaders to brief him. He held court at his office or in Agar Jaicks's living room, then headed to the House of Prime Rib for dinner. This time-honored technique for gathering political intelligence did little to help him comprehend the crosscurrents of city politics in 1982. But such was his brand of political egotism that he could not understand why voters needed to be reminded who he was or why he mattered.

He had given his life for these people, rising to a position of leadership in the House, which enabled him to wield real power on their behalf. Why should he send out puff pieces advertising his accomplishments? When campaign fund-raiser Duane Garrett, a rising young political lawyer, brainstormed with him over how to distill his Washington clout into a campaign message for voters, Burton said, "I can round up 110 votes to have dog shit declared the national food." That was not exactly what Garrett had in mind.[10]

A few weeks after Marks's poll, Burton was shaken to his core. He never took Marks's poll or lead seriously. But when he took his own, it confirmed the DMI poll. Marks led by seven points. Aside from people identified as pro-environment, he was losing among those who cared about labor, consumer, and civil rights and women's issues—everything he had championed. The night he got those results, Shelley recalled, Burton became deeply depressed.

Burton's entire identity and sense of self-worth hinged on his conception of being a powerful and effective legislator who got things done for people and improved their lives. It was a jolt to find that the people for whom he toiled with such consuming passion did not appreciate him—or worse—that many did not even like or approve of him. Yet the numbers did not lie. Labor leaders in Washington knew his value. So did environmental lobbyists. But many voters did not follow the nuances of Washington or even of San Francisco politics. If all they knew was what they read in the newspapers of late—that Burton was an arrogant, out-of-touch pol who abused the system to benefit himself and his brother—then he was in for the fight of his life.

This was no longer merely a nuisance, a distraction that would force him to spend money and time back home fighting Marks off. Burton might lose. His political career—the only thing that drove him for more than thirty years—might end. That would be like death itself. Just to imagine Burton with time on his hands, let alone booted out of office, was inconceivable. For Burton, who filled his life with agendas, accomplishments, and forward movement, as if to forever banish doubt, anxiety, or even a quiet moment to reflect on something other than politics, the notion must have been terrifying. For nearly a month, he fell into a tailspin, not emerging until April. And then finally, gradually, he pulled himself together. It was time to get operational.

At the county central committee, Rich Hays was looking at the same data

Hukari had studied. Hays, a former activist from the Saul Alinsky school of organizing poor people at the grass-roots level, was hired in January, after Jaicks convinced Burton he could have a problem if his Democratic registration dipped under 60 percent. Hays's job was to mount a voter registration drive, but as the Marks challenge took shape, he saw that a field operation was also necessary. In Washington, Mark Gersh analyzed the district precinct by precinct. Hays began with that.

Once Burton came out of his funk, he hit the phones. First he called his labor friends in Washington and screamed for money. "They are coming at me for real," he said. "This is a serious threat with national implications, and Milton Marks has nothing to do with it." Michael Berman called from Los Angeles, offering to do the mail and television campaign and provide strategic advice.

Burton made two other phone calls that proved pivotal. One was to Bill Kraus, president of the Harvey Milk Gay Democratic Club. Kraus was an aide to Harry Britt, Milk's successor on the board of supervisors, and a leader in the gay and lesbian community.

The second call went to the San Francisco Police Officers Association. The POA was a potent political force. Liberal, pro-labor Democrats took over the leadership in the late 1970s, among them Paul Chignell, who was also running for a Marin assembly seat. Burton phoned Mike Nevin, a POA board member whom he knew years earlier as Mayor Alioto's driver, and asked him to come over. A POA endorsement carried great weight in the conservative areas where Burton was weakest. A POA mailer on his behalf would be even better. He knew this was not an easy sell. One of the few national politicians to advocate decriminalization of marijuana, Burton was not exactly Mr. Law and Order. But he was determined to crush Marks, he told Nevin, "and besides, I have his rabbi." That was true. Rabbi Joseph Asher of San Francisco's famous Temple Emanu-El, just a few blocks from Marks's home, had already endorsed Burton.[11] But POA President Bob Barry was close to Marks, who was helpful on labor issues in Sacramento. Barry was also facing reelection. A POA leadership-rigged endorsement of Burton could cost him the union presidency.

The chance to win over Barry came on April 24, when Tip O'Neill, who had gotten over his problems with Burton, arrived in town to campaign for him. It happened on the back deck of Mayor Feinstein's Pacific Heights home, where Chignell told O'Neill that Bob Barry's mother in Waltham, Massachusetts, was O'Neill's constituent. Understanding at once what he needed to do, the Speaker introduced himself to Barry as "a member of Phil

Burton's Congress." Draping his giant arm around Barry's shoulder, O'Neill said, "You have a large family. They are loyal Democrats. Phil Burton is needed in the Congress. He is important for labor. You should endorse him." Barry was overwhelmed.[12]

Later that day, O'Neill told reporters that Burton's defeat would be "just about the worst thing that could happen. . . . I can't imagine the people of San Francisco being that foolish."[13] Then they headed to the Irish Cultural Center for dinner. Burton had never been close to the San Francisco Irish community, but he visibly warmed to O'Neill as Nevin and the Speaker sang Irish songs together, Tip holding a twin baby in each arm.

Around the time of O'Neill's visit, Burton flew home from Washington with his brother. After a few drinks, he started picking at him. Nervous and tense, he knew he had neglected his district, and the strain of Marks's challenge was showing. John had just sent out a fundraising letter for Barbara Boxer, running to succeed him. "Why don't you send out a letter for me?" Phillip asked angrily.

"Her problems are in the primary," John said. "Yours are in the general."

"How much money do you think I have to raise?" Phillip asked.

"As much as you need," John replied. He said he would talk to Eddie DeBartolo, the fabulously wealthy owner of the Super Bowl champion San Francisco Forty-niners. DeBartolo might be willing to host a fundraising party.

"Why?" said Phillip. "They're your friends."

"That's right. They are my friends. You are my brother. They'd help my brother. They understand family." John was insulted his brother would think so little of him or of their relationship that he would question DeBartolo's willingness to help.

Phillip kept it up, eventually getting to what was really bothering him. Two of John's aides never showed up to vote for Phillip at a local endorsement session of the National Women's Political Caucus. He was furious that John would tolerate such sloppiness. In passing, however, he let slip that his *own* district aides had not bothered to show up, either. Worried that the no-shows might have cost Phillip a key endorsement, John asked what the vote was. Phillip had won 23 to 4. The extra votes were not even needed. He was just venting his anger. He screamed at John when he should have been screaming at his own staff, if not at himself. Free of drugs for several months but still in a recovery program, John shook with anger as the plane landed. He wanted cocaine. But he pulled himself together and resisted the urge.[14]

Despite his anxiety, Burton was not taking the race as seriously as his aides felt he should. He had not even hired a campaign manager. The very idea of anybody "managing" Burton was ridiculous. A good field operation was all he needed. He might not even be home for the primary. "I've spent most of my time in Washington, I agree," he told *Examiner* reporter Bill Boldenweck. "But that's what I'm being paid to do and that's what my constituents expect me to do."[15] Meanwhile, newspapers outside San Francisco discovered the race. "Godfather of California Politics May Be Mortal," the *Los Angeles Times* headlined. One Democrat told reporter Ellen Hume that Burton was "the most unpleasant man in American government . . . but the most competent congressman in the country."

Marks damned himself with his own words. Noting Burton's strategy to tie Marks directly to the Reagan administration, Hume asked whether Marks felt Reagan was doing a good job. "I can't answer a question like that," Marks stammered. "It's mixed." Asked whether he would press Reagan to delay tax cuts to ease the budget deficit, Marks bobbed and weaved: "It's too early to tell whether tax cuts would work or should be modified." Hume asked whether he favored cutting the defense budget, as Burton advocated, or cutting the increase in the defense budget, as many Republicans urged. "I think they both could be looked at," he said.[16]

The first dinner with gay political activist Bill Kraus was critical. Kraus, raised in Catholic schools in Cincinnati, went through the antiwar years at Ohio State but never really found himself until he moved to San Francisco's Castro District in 1972. The Castro was where gay liberation first bloomed, three years after the famous Stonewall Bar riots in New York that began the movement. As young gay men from all over America arrived to celebrate its open sexuality and revel in their out-of-the-closet freedom, the Castro took off, led by a quirky but charismatic camera-shop owner named Harvey Milk.

Kraus grew up politically with Milk, learning the importance of good precinct maps, voter turnout, and reaching out to other communities. Over time, he became the Castro's top political strategist. Kraus knew who to bring to the table to cut the deal or expand the coalition. He followed Milk to city hall and stayed to help Harry Britt, Milk's successor. Twice elected president of the Harvey Milk Gay Democratic Club, Kraus was a Kennedy delegate in 1980 and the first openly gay man to address a major presidential convention. Once approached, a choice between Burton and Marks was for Kraus an easy call.

Kraus's personal transformation mirrored the Castro's evolution from Irish working-class neighborhood to gay Mecca. A self-contained community, the Castro included more than 100 gay bars and restaurants, plus bathhouses, health clubs, book stores, medical services, clothes shops, and even a movie palace. It was estimated that more than 100,000 of San Francisco's 700,000 people were gay, half or more of whom had arrived in the previous ten years. This was a higher proportion than any other city in the nation, if not the world. Nearly a dozen gay newspapers flourished. Gay people voted, and Milk's 1977 election catalyzed the community and made it a potent political force.[17]

Burton did not speak with Harvey Milk until October 1978, when Milk brought him to the headquarters of the "No on Six" campaign, which was devoted to defeating an anti-gay state ballot measure. Agar Jaicks, Burton's eyes and ears on the county central committee, tried for years to tell Burton about the emergence of sophisticated gay political activists. Burton could see that the campaign's 700 volunteers canvassed 98 percent of the city's districts. Gays were active in Moscone's 1975 election. But the "No on Six" campaign marked the beginning of gay participation in mainstream politics.

Now, with the same intensity and hunger for detail he showed in 1956 in creating a constituency in Chinatown, Burton looked for entrée to a foreign community. Bill Kraus was tapped to be Phil Burton's Lim P. Lee of 1982 and open up the Castro as Lee had opened up Grant Avenue twenty-six years before. This time, however, Milton Marks was no Tommy Maloney. He was widely known and liked among gay voters and always supported their issues. If the vote had been held then and there, Marks would have beaten Burton handily in gay precincts.

Burton had other problems with the gay community. It was his machine that endorsed Agnos over Milk for the assembly in 1976, and Burton supported another candidate over Milk for the board of supervisors a year later. To repair the damage, Burton began a systematic study of the gay community, combing through gay newspapers as he once had Chinese newspapers, underlining the names of key leaders. He studied the gay political clubs and noted gay appointments to various boards and city commissions.

"What's the most important issue today?" Burton asked Kraus over dinner with Britt and Jaicks.

"Gay cancer," Kraus said quickly, surprising himself.

It was less than a year since the first Kaposi's Sarcoma case had been diagnosed in San Francisco. They did not even have an official name for this baffling constellation of deadly infections, but what four months later became known as Acquired Immune Deficiency Syndrome was poised to explode in the gay centers of America, even though less than a thousand people had been diagnosed and no one knew what it was or how it spread. It would take another year until scientists identified the AIDS virus. If Kraus was going to be Burton's liaison, this was the time to explain that gay men were beginning to die and that the federal government did not seem to care.[18]

News of Kraus's hiring hit the *Bay Area Reporter*, San Francisco's most influential gay paper, on April 22, complete with photo and biography. In his regularly featured column, Britt called Kraus "the finest gay political leader I know." A few days later, Kraus sent his first memo to Burton: "I think you made a hit at Harry's party, and it gave me some ideas for appearances in the gay community."[19] Kraus made gay freedom real to Burton. It was one thing for Jaicks or Kevin Shelley to tell him why gay rights mattered. It was quite another for his own staffer to say, "This is my life story." Kraus made Burton see that equal rights for gays was no different than equal rights for other minorities. Burton began rounding up co-sponsors for a national gay rights bill.

In June, Kraus told Burton he should appear in the annual Gay Freedom Day parade, an international event that drew hundreds of thousands of raucous and colorfully garbed and ungarbed activists. "They know who comes and who doesn't," Kraus said. In fact, it was still a point of major irritation that after three years as mayor, Dianne Feinstein refused to appear. She said she did not want to glorify homosexuality or the gay lifestyle. Going into its fifth year, the parade had become world famous and boasted its own ceremonial start—the gunning of motorcycles by a contingent of "Dykes on Bikes." It included every conceivable interest group from Gay Lutherans to Lesbian Taxi Drivers of San Francisco. There were cowboys and drag queens, superheroes with sequined jockstraps, Marilyn Monroe look-alikes, and oceans of flesh.

Burton happily rode on the back of a convertible with Harry Britt. It was his first appearance, and the crowd responded well. Later, he insisted that Kraus take him to the Castro. He even ducked into a notorious leather bar, where men wore chaps that covered their thighs and little else. Unfazed, he plunged into the dimly lit bar, held out his hand to the bartender and said, "How do you do. I'm your congressman, Phil Burton." He worked the room like it was a union hall, looking each man directly in the eye—possibly the only safe place to look—and chatting briefly. They respected him for visiting, Kraus told friends later, and this was a crowd that did not show much respect to anybody.

Burton made his biggest hit at the first annual Gay Games in Kezar Stadium that summer. The International Olympic Committee went to court to prevent the group from using the word "Olympic" in its title. Burton showed up with Kraus, Shelley, and Pat Jackson, an SEIU friend from the 1950s, who was coordinating gay and labor groups for the campaign. Kraus wrote the speech and as Burton walked to the stage, he clung to Jackson for security, glanced over the speech and thrust it in his coat pocket. "I welcome you all," he began to loud cheers, his voice booming over the public address system, "TO THE GAY OLYMPIC GAMES!" Without taking the speech out of his pocket, he delivered Kraus's lines: "In every generation, there is a community that struggles to be free and which, in that struggle, becomes stronger and teaches something about freedom to all of us. In this generation, you are that people." The crowd roared its approval.[20]

Despite the good news, the next poll taken for Burton was almost as devastating as the first. It was conducted in June by Jim Lauer and Brad Bannon of DSG Survey Research in Washington. Although Burton had improved slightly in the head-to-head race against Marks, now trailing by 4 points, only 34 percent rated him favorably, compared to 47 percent who rated him negatively. He did well only among self-identified "strong Democrats," winning 45 percent favorable and 41 percent unfavorable. Among the young, it was 23-47, a sign of his low profile in the district. Among union families, it was 39-49. Among minorities, it was a horrible 27-61, and among those earning less than $20,000 a year, those whose lot he had devoted his life to improving, his favorable to unfavorable rating was 34-46. Marks, by contrast, had favorable ratings of 58 percent and unfavorable ratings of only 10 percent. He scored well with all demographic groups. Even "strong Democrats" rated him 58-12 favorable to unfavorable.

The DSG poll did show some encouraging signs, however. Among those surveyed, 58 percent they would be more likely to vote for a candidate endorsed by environmental organizations. President Reagan was more unpopular in this district than in almost any district the pollsters had surveyed. Only 31 percent gave Reagan a positive rating, 69 percent a negative one. The poll found that the reapportionment issue had caused damage to Burton only among older, Republican voters who would tend to vote for Marks in any case. Meanwhile, 62 percent said they would vote against a candidate who wanted to increase the defense budget, and 51 percent said they opposed Reagan's budget cuts, "the highest level of opposition to the budget cuts I have seen this year," Lauer concluded.

Lauer identified what would turn out to be a major theme:

One of the most striking findings of this poll is that so may voters *respect* Phil Burton for his effectiveness and ability. In fact, there is a 12-point difference between the number of voters who believe Burton is effective and the number of voters who give him a positive job rating. . . . What Burton must guard against is the notion that he is out of touch, disinterested in the problems of San Francisco and doesn't care about the average voter. Therefore, he must demonstrate that his effectiveness benefits the voters of the 5th district.[21]

An April fundraising appeal enclosed portions of the DMI poll showing Marks beating Burton. "The results of that survey were so encouraging, they convinced me to run against Burton," Marks wrote. "When I filed for this race, the Congressional Committee picked Phil Burton as one of the top incumbents in the country to defeat." Marks carefully refrained from saying it was the "Republican" committee.

Marks's next fundraising letter proved disastrous. While campaigning as a liberal, he solicited money from some 650 PACs across the country by portraying himself as a pro-business conservative. Marks said it was important to get rid of Burton because Burton voted against the MX missile and the B-1 bomber and for a moratorium on nuclear plant construction. He voted against capping food stamp programs, against capping funds for occupational health and safety programs. He opposed lowering the minimum wage for youths and banning aid to Nicaragua. Marks likely would have voted the same way on virtually every issue. But he said he supported pro-business state legislation.

The letter was dynamite. While seeking votes in liberal San Francisco, he was also seeking money from the most conservative business interests in the country, strongly suggesting he would vote their way. Moreover, the letter confirmed the campaign message Burton had wanted to use all along: that Marks was a tool of Ronald Reagan and corporate America, programmed and aimed like a heat-seeking missile at one of their toughest adversaries. The Burton campaign got a copy of the letter, waited for a propitious moment and then leaked it. "I think this will be VERY useful, especially after it appears in the *Chronicle*," Kraus wrote.

The story appeared July 9. Marks campaign manager Ed Slevin, a former state Republican Party executive director, defended the letter, saying, "We're after money. We point out certain aspects." Even though the letter implied that Marks's positions were diametrically opposed to those of Burton's, Slevin said he would urge Marks—who was on a cruise ship heading to Latin America—to avoid revealing any specific positions on national issues until September or October.[22]

In late July, Marks got some good news. A new DMI poll showed him still leading by six points. But soon the Marks campaign was hit by another political bomb. At a Washington fund-raiser a few days later, Marks was shocked to see Jim Watt, the notorious anti-environment interior secretary, drop in uninvited and offer to do all he could to help defeat Burton. "I'll come to San Francisco as often as you want or I'll stay as far away if you want," Watt told Marks. As reporter John Fogarty recorded the conversation, "A somewhat flustered Marks demonstrated the political touchiness of the situation after Watt's departure, when asked if he was surprised the secretary came to the fund-raiser."

"'No. I mean yes. I mean, he wasn't invited, and it was a surprise to see him,'" Marks said. "'I recognized him right away, and I thanked him for coming. . . . I don't know what I'm going to do.'" In another show of mushiness, Marks refused even to comment on Watt's policies.

Among environmentalists, however, Watt was not just a conservative buffoon who wanted to pave national parks and drill for oil off every coast. He was Reagan's thumb in the eye of the environmental movement, Reagan's announcement that the gains of the 1970s were over. Watt had also become the single biggest reason for a national surge in Sierra Club memberships, and Burton was his toughest congressional adversary. Having Watt in his opponent's corner was like fighting the chainsaw manufacturers over the redwoods. He could hardly have invented a better "bad guy" to run against.

Soon after his appointment, for example, Watt took out after Burton's precious Land and Water Conservation Fund, the $900 million a year used to purchase wilderness areas, the same fund Burton had given Leon Panetta such a hard time about. Watt also said he would end the $750 million urban parks program Burton's 1978 parks bill established and said he would acquire new parks only under court order. He reduced money for new parks from $282 million in 1980 to $45 million in 1982. Hitting even closer to home, Watt said some parks were "not worthy" of federal protection. Referring to land Burton included in his original GGNRA legislation, Watt said, "The City of San Francisco has dumped a playground on us. . . . How we got conned into it, I'll never know. Here's a playground that all of a sudden the taxpayers from all over the nation are supporting."

The park, Julius Kahn Playground, had a sweeping view of the Golden Gate Bridge and of San Francisco Bay. Adjacent to the Presidio, it was among the city's most scenic and valuable land. The park was deeded by the army, managed by GGNRA park administration, and named for a prominent Republican congressman from the 1920s. "The environmentalist nightmare is taking the form of cold reality," Burton responded. "The secretary of the Interior is either uninformed, ill-advised or both." Burton called Watt's many pronouncements "a declaration of war on the nation's great outdoor areas."[23]

After Burton introduced the Wilderness Protection Act of 1982 to protect such areas from Reagan-Watt leasing and mining threats, Watt released an administration bill with the same title that would do exactly the opposite—eliminate much of the protection that Congress already provided wilderness areas. Burton called Watt a "rotten apple," urged him to resign immediately, and said his bill was a "complete fraud and deception . . . a devastating anti-wilderness measure masquerading as a wilderness protection bill."[24]

Environmentalists were San Francisco's other large, untapped constituency, mostly white, middle-class professionals. If they needed any jacking up, the Watt offer of help to Marks did it. The story hit just as Rich Hays began organizing a field operation. Carl Pope, the Sierra Club's political director, and John Amodio, Burton's former junior partner in the redwoods fight, convened a meeting of fifteen environmental groups, among them the Sierra Club, the League of Conservation Voters, and Friends of the River, to protect the movement's most powerful congressional champion. These environmental foot soldiers became the largest component of the precinct worker army, supplying nearly a thousand volunteers. It was the most intense effort environmentalists ever made for a politician. Just as Burton belatedly brought gays into the center of political power, he was doing the same for environmental politicos.

Ansel Adams hosted a fund-raiser for Burton at his Big Sur home, where he auctioned off one of his famous Sierra photographs. When Burton wanted to smoke, however, Adams banished him outside to the front deck, Chesterfield in one hand, Stoli in the other. A solitary figure, he stood huddled against the wind whipping in off the ocean, his back to some of the most gorgeous coastal scenery in the world—a landscape Adams and he had worked so hard to preserve. Apparently, it never occurred to Burton to turn around and look at it.

"I'm good, too," Marks pleaded to Carl Pope.

"It doesn't matter," Pope said. "You're a Republican. You will never be chairman of Interior."

Burton insisted that the Sierra Club feature him on the cover of its October *Bulletin*, the glossy magazine sent to its 300,000 members worldwide. Pope tried to explain that this was not customary.

"Listen, you little shit!" Burton exploded. "If I'm not on the cover of that next issue, you'll never get another piece of legislation, and if you don't believe me, don't put me on. Who's the greatest friend you ever had? Who's better than Udall? Who's better than Scoop Jackson?"

"You are, Phil."

"Then put me on that fucking cover." Some of its more conservative members protested, but Pope kept his word. "Boy," labor lobbyist Jay Power told Pope after the photo appeared, "You guys really stick by your friends."[25]

Despite some progress, Burton still had not hired a full-time campaign professional, someone to talk to the press, help with fund-raising, pull things together, and keep them on track. Mike Novelli, a consultant who left California for Washington in 1976, was at the beach in Rehoboth when Burton called and summoned him to his D.C. office. Padding around in his bare feet and obviously worried, Burton asked Novelli if he would return to San Francisco to run the campaign. They talked for nearly five hours. At one point Burton said, "Keep talking. I'm going to the bathroom. But unlike Lyndon Johnson, you don't have to watch." Novelli accepted the job that day. The awkward moment hinged on Novelli's job title. Burton never needed a "manager," he explained, and the title bothered him. He always did it out of his back pocket. Novelli knew no one could ever manage Burton anyway.

"Phil," he said, "call me the campaign coordinator." Burton sighed with relief and said he thought that was "wonderful."[26]

Coming from the Bay Area, Novelli also provided the political cover that allowed Burton to use Michael Berman and his new partner, Carl D'Agostino, both of Los Angeles, to do his direct mail, television, and overall campaign plan.

Burton *was* impossible to manage and it drove people crazy, including Berman and D'Agostino. In Burton's mind, he wrote the book on modern campaigning. No one could tell him anything new. In truth, however, he had not run for office seriously since 1956. Everything had changed. Berman wanted to send out thousands of pot holders with Burton's name on them, a wildly successful stunt in other campaigns. Burton thought it demeaning, a cheap gimmick. But he relented and 50,000 pot holders were distributed. Novelli walked into the headquarters on Van Ness Avenue one day and saw Burton examining a pot holder as if it were Yorick's skull. "My career has come down to this," he said. "A goddam pot holder. Eighteen years in Congress."

At a seafood restaurant he got into a screaming match with Berman and D'Agostino. Although the pair developed into one of the most respected and feared teams in California, this was one of their first campaigns. Burton thought they should do it for nothing. As he ate his crab entrée and gestured wildly with his fork to punctuate his points, pieces of crab and cocktail sauce flew across the table, landing on D'Agostino's shirt. When D'Agostino, who could not stop laughing, looked in the mirror that night, his entire shirt front was spattered.

Berman's sixty-two-page strategy memo reflected the challenges of trying to tell Burton what to do. "Our goal is to help save Phillip—whether he likes it or not," Berman began. "We figure that if he loses, he'll blame us, and that if he wins, it's because of his genius, his reputation, his talent, his (we don't believe this) reapportionment plan, his incisive strategic analysis, his sense of San Francisco, his knowledge of modern campaign techniques and his sense of honor—and he will be right. But in the meantime, we know Phillip will be swayed by our views and play this hand the way we deal it. After he wins, he'll take his revenge. The point of this is the following: the last time he didn't listen to Michael, he lost by one vote. The last time Michael didn't listen to him, Howard lost by one vote. The ball is back in Carl and Michael's court."

The Berman memo coldly analyzed Burton's political problems, including arrogance, "bossism," and Marks's theme that Burton was a "power hungry backroom politician who should be retired from office." Moreover, Berman summarized the delicate problem that voters were confusing Phillip with brother John, who still represented the district, and who had just resigned amid rumors of cocaine abuse. "You can communicate that Phillip is effective," he wrote. "But so were Boss Tweed and Dick Daley." The correct response, he argued, was to devote everything to "exposing Marks as the pawn of disreputable interests that he is." They settled on one strategic theme: "Why is Milton Marks running against Phillip Burton? Because big money special interests offered him the money to run against San Francisco's great congressman. It's the money!"[27]

Burton had much to re-learn about connecting with people. One day Shelley drove him to a junior high school to meet several hundred members of the local chapter of the American Association of Retired Persons. One of the foremost champions of the elderly, Burton launched into Washington Speak, a detailed, jargon-laden description of entitlement programs, federal matches, and mysterious agencies known only by their initials. He was so out of touch he did not know most of his listeners had no idea what he was talking about. A few even came up to him afterwards and urged him to please keep it simple. He needed Berman to tell him, "Don't use jargon. Don't use code words or phrases. Assume that no listener, especially the swing voters you most need to impress, have any understanding of politics or the vocabulary we commonly use. They don't know what a PAC is. Famous legislation to us is obscure or totally meaningless to them. Big oil companies are bad only if you say they support oil drilling on San Francisco Bay."[28]

The strain wore on Burton throughout the summer, and he drank heavily. Although never drunk in public, he missed several appearances. When he visited Dave Jenkins, the longtime ILWU organizer who knew Burton's father, he introduced himself as though for the first time to Jenkins's wife, Edith. "Phil," she snapped, "I've known you for 25 years and I've always voted for you, because I've always admired your politics. But that doesn't mean I have to like you." Embarrassed, Burton stumbled down the front steps of the Jenkins home. A large bouquet of flowers and an apology arrived the next day. Dick Murphy, SEIU's Washington lobbyist, hearing the stories of Burton's drinking, flew out to San Francisco and quietly confronted Burton in the only way that might get his attention. Marks was already making references to the drinking, Murphy told him. They would use it against him. Burton listened in silence. But the message sank in. A week later, back in Washington, Murphy got word that Burton was drinking Calistoga until November. Burton did not eliminate the Stoli entirely, but he drastically cut back.

Because of its political sophistication, ethnic diversity, and compact size, San Francisco had become a direct-mail targeter's dream, a social laboratory where a campaign consultant could use a computer to isolate, for example, same sex, Hispanic-surnamed couples interested in housing issues. Berman was a pioneer in the field. But Marks campaign manager Slevin was also capable of producing first-rate political mail. Mail was much cheaper and more efficient than television, where candidates were required to invest huge sums for the entire Bay Area media market, even though they were aiming at only the San Francisco slice of it.

The "hit pieces," or distorted attacks that landed in mailboxes, started with Marks. One mailer, with two inside pages, showed drawings of nineteenth-century workers tossing papers marked "debts" into a large safe marked "social security." On the other side, fat cats drank champagne around a table identified as the Sir Francis Drake Hotel. The wording on the front: "Power Corrupts," and inside, "Absolute Power Corrupts Absolutely." Copy on the back accused Burton of not having a home in San Francisco, of spending

$1,000 a week on a suite at a "luxury hotel," paid for with campaign contributions, of spending thousands of dollars of "taxpayer money" on thirty-two junkets to foreign countries, of missing "key committee and House votes while lounging on the beaches of the Virgin Islands and dining in fancy restaurants in Italy."

To anyone who really knew Burton's career, these charges were absurd. But they represented the latest in the technology of negative campaigning, of selectively stringing isolated facts together in a completely distorted fashion to smear an opponent. If they worked, it was only because Burton had so lost touch with his district, had taken so much for granted. Voters did not have the knowledge or information to counter these claims.

One particularly effective mailer targeted to gay precincts called Burton's behavior towards gays a "stab in the back." It described his "sellout" of Harvey Milk and said that he had not appointed a gay aide "until this year." Another Marks mailer said Burton had authored only five minor bills in two years that had become law, while voting for four pay raises. Other "positive" mailers showed Marks in his World War II army uniform, as a young lawyer "with his radiant bride Carolene," and being sworn into the assembly in 1959.

Burton's mail featured quotes lavishing praise on him from Ansel Adams, Cesar Chavez, Ted Kennedy, Martin Luther King, Jr., Elie Wiesel, Ralph Nader, Benjamin Spock, and Tip O'Neill. "Any politician can make promises," one said. "Phil Burton makes things happen." It listed some of his best-known legislation, including his GGNRA and redwoods bills. Two pieces to gays countered Marks's mail. A lavender-colored mailer from the Milk Club said, "The best judge of a person is the company he keeps. . . . Milton Marks and Phil Burton are keeping very different company these days." It showed Marks with Ronald Reagan, George Bush, James Watt, Gerald Ford, and Alexander Haig and listed his contributors as all seven major oil companies, mining and chemical companies like Dow, Alcoa, and Fluor, timber companies like Boise Cascade, Louisiana Pacific, Weyerhaeuser, and defense contractors like Bechtel, Boeing, and Honeywell. Burton's "company," meanwhile, included the Milk, Toklas, and Stonewall clubs, the Sierra Club, League of Conservation Voters, the National Women's Political Caucus, and a huge list of elected officials.

Another mailer highlighted Burton's speech at the Gay Games and quoted prominent lesbian Del Martin saying, "I'll never forget Phil Burton being at gay organizations 20 years ago—when no other public official could have dreamed of coming around. It makes me angry when some people say he's just now 'discovering' the gay community. I know better. I was there—and so was Phil." Burton was there, but most gays arrived later, while Burton was making his mark in Washington, and never saw him.

On August 23, Marks held a press conference to publicize his new media campaign: billboards featuring large photos of Burton wearing a button that said, "I'm for me." Big red letters spelled out the words, "The Arrogance of Power." Marks announced a two-week, $30,000 TV and radio campaign of man-in-the-street interviews, and repeated charges about the $11,000 Burton spent in hotel bills, his thirty-two "globe-trotting junkets," and the way he "carved up California like a Christmas goose and gave the choicest portion to his brother."

"If I'm so arrogant and selfish, why did I weaken myself?" Burton told the *Wall Street Journal.* "What does that make me, an idiot?"[29] Burton held a press conference the same day with Public Works Committee Chairman Jim Howard of New Jersey to announce that a long-sought $16 million breakwater to protect the fishing boats at Fisherman's Wharf would soon pass Congress.

As Labor Day approached, Burton called a meeting of labor supporters to plan the march. One group of gay activists was set to march up one block, while labor was marching on a nearby block. They planned to converge at City Hall for a massive rally. Turning to the Teamster representative, Burton said, "Just one thing. Don't let your Teamsters go near my cocksuckers."

With Labor Day also came new endorsements, including that of the pivotal Police Officers Association. POA President Bob Barry wondered what he was turning his law and order organization into as Burton lumbered up the stairs to the POA's headquarters near the Hall of Justice to meet with the POA executive board, Sala trailing behind. On the merits, the only thing going for Burton was his support for a $50,000 death benefit for cops slain in the line of duty, and he pushed it for all it was worth. Marks was also counting on the POA endorsement. But after the April session with Tip O'Neill, Barry and Chignell quietly lobbied the membership. The room was wired for Burton, who lost no points when he asked, "Who do you want, the third most powerful Democrat in Congress or some freshman Republican who won't do shit for you?"

For added insurance, Burton was readying a plan so audacious that it stunned San Franciscans. The coalition-building, eye-opening ramifications of the deal were a metaphor for his entire political career. He brought southern farmers and black lung victims together. He brokered a deal between timber workers and environmentalists. Now he was going to unite homosexuals and the police.

The gay community despised the SFPD, which beat and harassed them with seeming impunity. Gay rage erupted in the 1979 "White Night" riots that broke out after Dan White was convicted of manslaughter, rather than murder, for the point-blank shootings of Moscone and Milk. Despite killing two revered public officials, he was eligible for parole after five years. Convinced that old-boy networks in the Police Department had gone easy on White, a former cop himself, young gay men trashed City Hall and set police cars afire. Now the gay community was aiming a new weapon, a ballot proposition called Measure A, to establish an Office of Civilian Complaints that would investigate claims of police brutality. The POA had qualified two ballot propositions of its own, Measures I and J. The first would pay officers time and a half for overtime. The second would increase police pensions. Under the city charter, both required a vote of the people. POA leaders knew they could easily defeat Measure A. No self-respecting fraternal organization of police could permit such a thing to pass.

Enter Phil Burton with the deal. Gays, specifically the Harvey Milk Gay Democratic Club and other gay groups, would support the POA's pocketbook issues. They would campaign for and distribute slate cards that would be mailed to their memberships for Measures I and J. This alone was so mind-boggling that Milk Club President Gwen Craig spent hours reassuring her executive board, many of whom felt that even to sit down with the cops, let alone agree on anything, was a total sellout. In return, the POA would stay neutral on Measure A, the citizens commission to investigate complaints against the police. Supporting it was completely out of the question, but even staying neutral would arouse howls of protest. The *Chronicle* broke the story in early September, calling it an "unprecedented political alliance." The deal was "dynamite," one police leader told the newspaper.[30]

How had Burton pulled it off? On one side, Chignell and Barry ran the POA, and they saw firsthand what Burton earlier accomplished for them. Barry and Reno Rapagnani, another POA board member, went to Burton to ask for help with Chignell's assembly race. They wanted a Sierra Club endorsement and money from Speaker Willie Brown.

"Did you get a commitment from Willie?" Burton asked, sitting in his darkened office, a nervous aide walking in with tumblers of vodka. They had not. Burton called Brown on the spot and made their pitch for them.

"Has the Sierra Club committed yet?" he asked. Rapagnani equivocated. Chignell had been lobbying the club for two months, getting nowhere. Burton picked up the phone again and reached Carl Pope. "Chignell needs your endorsement, Carl," Burton said. "Deliver it."

Within 48 hours, a check and endorsement arrived at Chignell's house from the Sierra Club. Money from Willie Brown's assembly account soon followed. It had taken all of ten minutes. They would follow Burton anywhere after a performance like that.

With the gay community, it was much the same. In a few short months, Burton became like a father to Kraus, who soaked up Burton's knowledge and wisdom. Through him, other smart young gay activists like direct-mail specialist Dick Pabich, another Harvey Milk acolyte, got a chance to study with the master over dinners at the House of Prime Rib or in his office. Kraus and Pabich had credibility and were trusted. The alliance with the POA made sense.

A week after the story ran, the POA endorsed Burton. The Milk Club soon followed. Burton took Rapagnani to a fund-raiser at the huge Pacific Heights mansion of famed trial attorney Melvin Belli and his politically ambitious wife Lia. When it came to radical chic, Leonard Bernstein's 1960s Manhattan soirees for the Black Panthers had nothing on this crowd. "This is Reno Rapagnani of the Police Officers Association," Burton said. "He's helping us out, and we've got to help the POA with their benefits." There was not a murmur of disapproval. It was a bizarre alliance for Rapagnani, who had broken up his share of radical demonstrations over the years. "I haven't seen this many leftists in one place since I was on the Tac Squad," he thought.[31]

The Burton for Congress headquarters officially opened in September, although it had been operating for weeks, as dozens of gay and environmental activists came in nightly and on weekends to walk precincts and work phone banks. Britt's mission that night was to get the POA to lobby Wendy Nelder, a pro-police supervisor running for re-election and the daughter of a popular former police chief, to stay neutral on Measure A. Hundreds of people packed in as Burton slowly made his way through the crowd and onto the stage. Sensing the excitement in the room, Burton tossed out his speech, substituting an impromptu mishmash of such raw emotion that Shelley thought Burton would have a heart attack on the spot. Burton looked out over the crowd, packed like sardines in the one-time auto showroom, grinned broadly and said, "I got the cops, and I got the gays. Ain't that a bitch!" As the crowd erupted, Britt saw Rapagnani and said, "Ask her now." But before he could even get the words out, Nelder said, "Do you think I should support Measure A?"

After months of hard work and no little panic, it was all beginning to click. Berman's TV ads featured Jack Klugman, star of the TV series "Quincy," linking Marks to Reagan and big business. The targeted mail was eroding Marks's credibility. The Milk Club and the POA sent their own mailers on Burton's behalf. The Saturday crowds swelled at Burton headquarters as people came in for precinct kits and walking instructions. Besides environmentalists, gays, and union activists, old CDC activists and Young Democrats from Burton's past, such as Mary Louise Allen and Jane and Jack Morrison, also plunged in, putting aside long-held grievances with Burton for the sake of keeping him in Congress. Burton called Morrison and others from Washington nearly every night asking how the canvassing had gone and what people said.

All the various elements of his life were emerging to help him in his time of need. All the coalitions he once assembled and the new ones he just created were united by one goal: their overwhelming desire to re-elect Phil Burton. "There may come a time," *Sun Reporter* publisher Carlton Goodlett wrote, "when some of us again can support Marks for public office. But not this time, not this race. Too much is at stake."

Though he would never admit that he was enjoying a minute of it or that he was glad Marks forced him to re-acquaint himself with San Franciscans, Burton seemed energized by the human contact. At a seniors home, he danced with an elderly woman and was moved by her enthusiasm. Walking through Washington Square after a dinner in North Beach, he turned to campaign consultant Novelli and said, "This is the most wonderful, cosmopolitan city."

After a late dinner at the House of Prime Rib on a cold, foggy night, Burton walked outside with Rich Hays and Rich Schlackman, another young political consultant. "They hate me out there," Burton began, pointing to the downtown high rises. "They are out to get me. They are doing everything they can to make me lose this election. You don't understand. This goes way back. They didn't like me from the beginning. In 1956, we walked every precinct in the district. They didn't like me then. They still don't. They talk about the Burton Machine. Do you want to see the real Burton machine?"

With that, Burton grabbed Hays and Schlackman by the shoulders and marched them down the street and into a dark alley. Reaching against the side of a building, he pulled open a large steel sliding door. Inside, fourteen bakers were making doughnuts. It was 11 P.M. "Hey, Phil," they said when they spotted him. "How ya' doin'? Long time no see." Burton greeted them, explaining to Hays and Schlackman that these guys made the best doughnuts in the city. He stopped to chat with each one, asking about the wife and kids.

As they shook hands and said goodnight, they handed him a bag of doughnuts.

Back on the street Burton turned to the two young men with him. "That's the real Burton machine," he said, jabbing his finger in Hays's chest. "That's what's missing now. The passion factor. All the money. All the newspapers. They miss it. They don't get the passion factor. That's what this campaign is all about." With that, Burton got into his waiting car and was driven home.[32]

Burton was never what anyone would call a "cool" television presence. In part, that may have contributed to his defeat as majority leader. As House leaders became TV spokespersons for their parties, the idea of Phil Burton offering "sound bites" on the evening news was ludicrous. He could no more frame a pithy ten-second response for TV cameras than scale Yosemite's Half Dome. But he had accepted a debate challenge from Marks—fortunately on a small cable channel—and they had to get him ready. Ed Davis took Burton to a House TV studio to rehearse. But with tie askew and Burton looking down, rather than directly at the camera, Davis thought he looked like evil incarnate.

Kraus prepped Burton on questions to expect and on how to respond to gays. "There will be a question about Kaposi's Sarcoma and related diseases," he wrote. "Focus on long-term commitment through me." Kraus suggested Burton explain that he ate lunch regularly with the chairman of the health appropriations subcommittee and that health subcommittee chairman Henry Waxman was a friend. On the always delicate subject of why he had never supported Harvey Milk, Kraus wrote, "Careful on this one. You didn't know him, but he brought you to No on Six Headquarters before he died and you are pleased most of his subordinates are with you, not Marks."

The first debate was September 25 and went as predicted. Marks called Burton "a ghost who occasionally haunts our city" and attacked his reapportionment plan. Burton said he was proud that Reagan and Watt had placed him "at the top of their hit list." Few people watched.

Michael Berman blamed himself for what he called a "disappointing" debate performance and for filling Burton's head with contradictory advice. Summing up the debate, Berman wrote:

> Phillip, you are one enormously imposing figure. You do not look like the
> normal ad agency ideal of a politician. And there is nothing you can do
> about it. Of course, all things being equal, it is better for no bead of sweat

to show on your brow and better for you to smile rather than grimace (and of course it's essential that you don't cuss). But the preoccupation with mildness of style inhibits you from maximizing the political advantages that are the reason you are debating in the first place—to use your wits and your intelligence to force Marks to make the mistake that loses the election, or to at least prove, by virtue of your performance, that you are indeed the best congressman in America. We believe it is impossible for you to persuade an effete Marina area person that you are the ideal politician whom he would like to have over for dinner. We do believe that it is within your power to convince a Marina resident that you are an extremely knowledgeable and powerful man who has done tremendous good for San Francisco and who is being unfairly challenged by a nice but lightweight politician tempted into the race by evil forces that fear you for your effectiveness.[33]

A few nights before the final debate, everything changed. According to a KGO-TV poll conducted October 7 and 8, Burton suddenly led Marks by ten points, 38-28 with the rest still undecided, a seventeen-point turnaround. Burton let out a whoop. Moreover, by October 13, Burton had raised nearly $500,000, with some $230,000 left to spend in the campaign's final weeks. Marks, records showed, had raised only $410,000, including a $125,000 loan to himself, with only $71,000 left to spend. Before it was over, Marks and his wife loaned the campaign $300,000. Marks found himself in the worst of all possible worlds. He was getting blasted for taking money from every special interest in America. Worse, they were not giving him enough to compensate for the bad press. Not surprisingly, both major papers endorsed Marks. The *Examiner*'s endorsement ran two columns and included a map of the district Burton drew for his brother. Titled "Burton: The Arrogance of Power," it said Burton acted as though he were invincible and said District 6 "perform[s] gyrations that leave us dizzy—and sick." But the newspaper, which endorsed Reagan in 1980 and 1984, was increasingly out of touch with its readers.

Burton's renewed confidence did not stop him from blowing the answer when Marks accused him of living in hotel suites. Burton admitted that he and Sala had spent only nine days in the district the previous year. He kept the hotel suite because he did not want to intrude on his elderly mother's Sloat Boulevard home, where the phone calls would disturb her. And why not use a hotel if you don't get back that often, he said.[34]

But the Marks theme was no longer working. His summer gaffes allowed

Burton's charge that he was a tool of Reagan, Watt, and the "special interests" to resonate. Meanwhile, even with a U.S. Senate and governor's race on the California ballot, people finally woke up to the importance of this election. Ed Davis arrived from Burton's Washington staff to handle press, and Chuck Hurley, his press secretary from the 1960s, also helped out. Judy Lemons coordinated precinct work with Hays. Labor lobbyists and old friends showed up to pitch in. Volunteers returned from canvassing with favorable responses about Burton's effectiveness in Congress. This was, after all, still a liberal district. Toward the end of October, Burton and Kevin Shelley drove to one of the final candidate's nights. Shelley dropped him off and went to park. By the time he arrived at the hall ten minutes later, Burton said, "This thing's over."

"What do you mean?" asked Shelley.

Burton said he greeted every person as he or she walked in. Virtually all said they were going to vote for Burton. "If they weren't going to vote for me, they wouldn't have said anything," Burton concluded.

On October 28, political scientist Marshall Windmiller, Burton's friend from CDC and Young Democrats thirty years earlier, was walking out of a class at San Francisco State University when he heard a familiar voice booming out over the loudspeaker. He arrived at the rally just as Burton concluded, and Burton, who was with Daniel Ellsberg that day, asked him to join them for coffee.

"He looked old and tired and his hands trembled," Windmiller wrote in his diary. "He was grossly overweight but still intense, hard driving. . . . He doesn't seem to have mellowed. He was touching base but without real contact. The conversation was inconsequential. He has plenty of money for the campaign but needs workers to get out the vote. He asked me to help on that—the bottom line of the conversation."[35]

As the campaign headed into its final week, environmental activists got creative. Wearing James Watt masks, they gathered every morning at Marks's home and followed him to campaign events, where they passed out what they called "Watt bucks." Marks had to shelve half his daily schedule. Everywhere he went, the message became, "Why are you taking money from Jim Watt?"

The night before the election, Hays assembled his coordinators to go over the city one final time, precinct by precinct, and make the final call on where to send nearly 1,200 volunteers, the largest grass-roots army in the city's history. When they finished, Burton looked at his nervous assistants. "We've got 52 percent," he said, "54–56 percent if we're lucky."[36]

Burton's campaign headquarters was packed when the first returns trickled in. Marks led among absentees, who tended to be affluent, Republican voters. When the first returns were announced at 8:46, Marks jumped out to a 63 to 36 percent lead. But the numbers changed quickly, and the excitement grew steadily. Within an hour, Marks slipped to 53 percent. Ten minutes later he was under 50 for the first time. At 10:06 Burton took the lead, never to relinquish it. His victory was convincing, nearly 58 percent to Marks's 40.5 percent, for a 31,000 vote margin. Marks won only one precinct. In a public housing precinct, Burton beat him 458 to 16. The hard work, fund-raising, calling in of chits, brokering of new deals, and unprecedented alliances all paid off.

"They [Marks] made a bad mistake with the PAC letter," Novelli wrote in an exit memo. "We made none. Campaigns are won on such differences."[37] Burton could return to Washington stronger than he had been in years and again nurture his dreams of returning to the House leadership.

"I am very grateful to the people of San Francisco," Burton told the *Examiner* that night. "We made an effort to run a clean campaign on the issues, and the Republican candidate took a different road." Burton conceded that he was "initially surprised" that voters weren't familiar with his record. "I made some assumptions about people knowing what I had done," he said. "I was taken aback by the fact that [the record] was not known by many people."[38]

It was not just a triumph for Phil Burton. The coalition he created also triumphed. All three ballot measures, Propositions A, I, and J won, taking more than 60 percent of the vote in the gay precincts. Wendy Nelder, who decided that night in September to support the police review office, got more votes than any other candidate and became president of the board of supervisors.

At the election night party, AFL-CIO lobbyist Jay Power, who spent a month working on the campaign, congratulated Burton. "So what are your plans?" Power asked, expecting Burton to talk about a vacation or at least a few days off to recover from the rigors of the campaign.

"Jay," Burton said, "my plan for the immediate future is to wipe Milton Marks off the face of the planet."[39]

20

THE MAN WHO WOULD BE SPEAKER

I get my exercise acting as pallbearer at the funerals of my athletic friends.

PHILLIP BURTON

He was always afraid of being sick or disabled. He didn't want to be laid up or an invalid. He died the way he wanted, though a little early.

JOHN BURTON

AS PHILLIP BURTON LOOKED back over the past two years, he had reason to feel triumphant. He performed the seemingly impossible: he exploded the Willie Brown–GOP coalition, united the Democrats in California, and saved the guts of his masterful—if infuriating—reapportionment plan. He almost single-handedly brought six new progressive votes to Congress with him, one-fourth of his party's national gains, amazing his colleagues and delighting Tip O'Neill. He convincingly defeated the toughest, best-financed Republican candidate he likely would ever face and created new and promising political alliances back home. All of his candidates won, although over dinner at the House of Prime Rib one night when somebody questioned whether Marin Democrat Barbara Boxer could hold John Burton's seat, Burton directed his withering stare at the presumptuous questioner. "Give me a break," he snapped. "I designed that seat so Attila the Hun or Winnie the Pooh could win it."[1]

All of this increased his stature at home and in Washington, where longtime adversary Richard Bolling was leaving Congress. This meant Burton was beginning a new Congress, the Ninety-eighth, without having to worry about one of his most implacable enemies. With Reagan's election two years earlier, these two giants of Capitol Hill had put aside their personal feelings about each other. Bolling's powerful perch as chairman of the Rules Committee and Burton's ability to put votes together occasionally allowed them to join forces to block Reagan raids on New Deal and Great Society programs. Neither, of course, forgot what happened in 1976, and Burton was not yet ready to challenge Jim Wright. But knowing how Bolling had blocked his leadership ambitions once before, it was better for Burton that Bolling was gone.

All things considered, he was making progress. Burton's ebullience was obvious at a January 26, 1983 Interior Committee meeting, at which Interior Secretary James Watt testified on his department's plans for the coming year.

"I would be remiss," Burton said, "if I didn't on behalf of my brothers and my mother, my wife and myself, thank you very much for the extraordinary contribution you made to my successful re-election effort."

Watt, who enjoyed bantering with Burton, replied, "I hope America benefits by the contribution." But Burton, who despised Watt, did not leave it there. "I think your stewardship has been essentially an abomination," he said. "In the view of many of us, we think you have defaulted on [your] responsibilities."[2]

These upbeat signs, however, clashed with disturbing indications that Burton's mental and physical health were deteriorating. The campaign had exacted a dreadful toll on his body, but he refused to see a doctor. After months of near-abstinence to beat back the Milton Marks challenge, Burton was drinking heavily again. There were several alcohol-induced public lapses.

Before he could think about his next crusade, Burton had important unfinished business involving reapportionment, which beckoned again after the November 1982 election. Because of the January 1982 state supreme court ruling for the Democrats, Burton's 1981 plan was valid for all of 1982. But in June, voters approved the initiative that angry Republicans had qualified for the ballot. It invalidated the Democratic plan, including Burton's congressional lines, beginning with 1984. It meant that after November, the legislature had to approve a new plan that incorporated these changes for the rest of the decade.

To prevent the Democrats from ramming through another Burton-style gerrymander, the Republicans went beyond their June initiative and teamed up with California Common Cause and qualified Proposition 14 for the November 1982 ballot; its purpose was to remove redistricting from the politicians entirely and give it to a bipartisan commission. The Republicans, however, gave the issue scant attention and little money, and it lost. That liberated the Democrats to do what the GOP most feared—a plan that tinkered around the edges of Burton's remap and left his overwhelmingly Democratic margins intact.

With Republican George Deukmejian's election as governor over Los Angeles Mayor Tom Bradley (by sixth-tenths of one percent), the Democrats had to act quickly to get Jerry Brown's signature on the new plan before he left office. They needed to change the congressional map enough to satisfy a judge (in the likely event the Republicans would sue again) that it was substantially different, but still retain their 28-17 majority and keep in office all the new Democrats who had just been elected. Burton and Michael Berman went back to work, but Burton was told to stay away from Sacramento. His mere presence inflamed the media and the Republicans.

"Phil Burton is not going to be involved in reapportionment," Richard Alatorre told an assembly hearing. But even as Alatorre spoke, Burton was contradicting him. "Before I submit a new reapportionment plan to the legislature," Burton told reporters, "I will meet with all my colleagues, Democrats and Republicans, and review their individual needs."

Although he kept a lower profile, Burton was as much involved as he had been in the original plan. He worked on the new lines in Washington, while Howard Berman remained in Sacramento to secure votes for passage. But Burton did appear at Frank Fat's in Sacramento one night, telling Minority Leader Robert Naylor he did not appreciate the Republicans' June ballot measure, which was the cause of all this extra work.

If Burton had made a fair split of the new seats, Naylor replied, there would have been no need to go to the ballot. Furthermore, if the next remap was also unfair, Naylor warned, he would put another measure on. Agitated, Burton spilled his Stolichnaya all over Naylor's steak dinner. Refusing to acknowledge the spill, he continued his harangue even as small rivulets of vodka cascaded onto Naylor's lap.[3]

Some districts were easy to fix; Burton's own, for example, and his brother's, which now belonged to Boxer. To avoid a repeat of the Marks challenge, he restored to his district almost all of the strong San Francisco precincts he had given to John, and he divided gay precincts between his and Boxer's district to discourage a gay candidate from challenging him later.

"Phil," said Bill Cavala, one of Willie Brown's consultants, "you just won a career race. You don't need all this." But Brown said, "Give him what he wants. He earned it." Burton and Michael Berman also toned down Boxer's egregious four-county district, extending it north and removing Daly City. They took Lantos out of Palo Alto and Zschau out of the rural portions of his district. They redrew part of Lehman's Central Valley district and added

Democratic Cerritos to Jerry Patterson's Orange County district. Most of the other changes were cosmetic. Of the forty-five seats, said *Congressional Quarterly*, twenty-eight were virtually unchanged, fourteen slightly altered, and three dramatically re-arranged.

A more serious change since the election was Willie Brown's decision to substitute tough-minded Maxine Waters of Los Angeles for Alatorre as chairman of the Assembly Elections and Reapportionment Committee. Waters, one of thirteen children raised in St. Louis public housing projects, was a factory worker and telephone company employee in Los Angeles before joining a Head Start program. She got involved in community work and then politics and was elected to the assembly from Watts in 1976 when she was thirty-eight. Like Alatorre, she wanted to go to Congress and planned to inherit Gus Hawkins's seat. Unlike Alatorre, she was passionate and uncompromising. Although she shared Burton's ultraliberal politics, he did not scare her one bit. Alatorre had not interfered with any of Burton's boundaries. But Waters did not hesitate to play her own game of brinkmanship and caused Burton so much grief that he told Cavala, "I'm going into the hospital. Maxine has given me piles." In this instance, he really did have a painful anal lesion that required surgery.

To convert Republican Bob Dornan's district for liberal Democrat Mel Levine, Burton and Michael Berman extracted middle-class black voters in South Central Los Angeles from Julian Dixon's district and combined them with affluent white voters in Malibu. But that started a chain reaction. To balance population, they gave the city of Downey—nearly 80,000 white working-class "Reagan Democrat" voters—to Hawkins. Even though Hawkins still had a majority black district, Waters worried that when he retired, a white candidate from Downey could defeat three or four black candidates, including her, who might split the black vote in a primary.

Waters wanted Downey taken out and more blacks from Dixon's district put in. Berman thought Waters was making trouble just to assert herself—she was one of Brown's top lieutenants and Brown had defeated his brother, after all. But Waters made it clear she would kill any bill that kept Downey in Hawkins's district. The problem seemed insoluble. If Levine lost his black voters, he was at risk in 1984. Alatorre asked Bruce Cain, a Cal Tech political scientist who had worked on the assembly plan, to figure a way out of the mess. After intensive compromise, they moved Downey into Glenn Anderson's district, kept Levine's district safe and put a plan together all incumbents could live with.

"Maxine did to Burton what Burton had been doing to everyone else for years," Cain recalled. "She said, 'I will hold up the bill if I don't get what I want. Here's the grenade. I'll pull the pin.' Up until the last twenty-four hours, she had Burton sweating. She was willing to blow up the whole plan and let it go to the courts. Nobody wanted to test her. It was the first time Phil Burton's authority on reapportionment was challenged."

They rounded up assembly votes for the congressional plan, but as it headed to the senate, big trouble was brewing. They were one vote short of passage. It was December 29, and with Governor-Elect Deukmejian heading into office in days, and Willie Brown having trouble keeping his house, which needed to vote on any senate changes, from going home, they were down to their final hours. The chairman of the senate elections committee opposed the plan. Democratic Majority Leader John Garamendi also objected, as did Senator Henry Mello of Monterey. His congressman, Leon Panetta, was in the Senate chambers vociferously objecting. Panetta wanted 14,000 Republicans in Santa Cruz County, whom he once represented, restored to his district. This enraged Burton, who was keeping track of events by phone from Washington, and Michael Berman, who knew that the political and legal brilliance of the congressional plan was its mathematical near-perfection. Taking 14,000 votes out of one district and adding it to another would up-end everything.

Mello and Panetta would not budge, but the Democrats weren't worried, because they had the missing vote they needed. It belonged to Democratic Caucus Chairman Paul Carpenter. But Carpenter, never much of a team player, announced on the spot that he was leaving for a vacation in Hawaii. Desperate to keep him there, Democrats rounded up a private plane for Carpenter, but he disappeared anyway, without a word to anyone. (Twelve years later, after being convicted in federal court on serious political corruption charges, Carpenter again flew the coop, escaping to Costa Rica to beat prison. But after a few months, he was returned to the U.S.) It was now 9 P.M. Burton was screaming on the phone. Berman was screaming at Mello and Panetta, all to no avail. Finally, they accepted Mello's amendment and added the 14,000 Republican votes to Panetta's district. They passed the bill, sent it back to the assembly for concurrence, and everyone went home relieved to have the matter behind them. On January 2, in one of his last acts as governor, Jerry Brown signed the bill. Burton's districts were safe through 1992. It was only later, when Michael Berman convinced the Secretary of State's Office to accept a series of "technical submissions" to correct errors in the bill, that those 14,000 Panetta voters quietly disappeared from his district.[4]

Back in Washington, however, Burton quickly squandered much of the goodwill he had built up during his year of "good behavior." It came to an abrupt end at a late November social gathering of new members, including John Bryant of Texas, at The Dubliner, a Capitol Hill watering hole. Bryant was running for the freshman spot on the Steering and Policy Committee. He was backed by Wright, Dingell, Rostenkowski, and Coelho. His opponent was Howard Berman. Six years after the fact, House Democrats again divined a Wright-Burton replay. The vote was scheduled for December 6, a week later.

By the time Burton arrived at the bar with an aide, he was already drunk. When he saw Bryant and a half dozen other freshmen and their wives having a drink, he joined them. Burton collared Bryant almost immediately, calling him a "stalking horse" for Wright and threatening to "squash" him unless he withdrew.

"I'm going to pulverize you and make your life miserable," Burton shouted, as Bryant's wife looked on, no doubt horrified. "We'll redistrict you out of existence. When I'm through with you, you'll be no better than a used condom." Burton's aide was appalled. It was the first time he had ever seen his boss lose control in public. People tried to change the subject, and Bryant did his best to keep things light and divert attention from Burton's nonstop invectives. But Burton kept it up for another twenty minutes. "You'll be a fucking one-term congressman," he threatened again, in a voice heard throughout the bar. "Get him out of here," a Burton colleague whispered urgently to the aide. They finally left. "The demon got me," Burton said later.

By the next day, the incident was all over Capitol Hill. Berman defeated Bryant, 29-27 in a vote of the freshman, but it was closer than it should have been and raised questions about Burton's fitness and conduct. "After a year of behaving himself," a California Democrat told the *San Francisco Chronicle*, "the old arrogant Phil Burton is re-emerging. His enemies relish it, and his friends regret it." Bryant was said to have been shocked by the outburst, because he considered Burton a hero. Berman conceded that the incident cost him votes. But he thought it wrong to play up the contest as any kind of test of strength between Wright and Burton. "I'm in a fight with a guy I never met over something bigger than anyone thought, and Burton helped me win," Berman recalled. "He called up the other side and used his contacts with the freshmen. But it was a big fight over nothing."[5]

Shortly thereafter, Burton almost lost control on the floor. At nearly 1 A.M. on December 17, as the House was set to adjourn, Burton asked for unanimous consent on a bill. The request caught temporary chairman Roman

Mazzoli of Kentucky by surprise. House leaders had gone home without saying anything about any Burton item. Burton, who had already cut a deal with the Republicans, was trying to sneak through the $16 million breakwater for Fisherman's Wharf that he had promised during the campaign. It was buried at the end of a long bill to study "water resources development in the Central Platte Valley, Nebraska," and other such projects.

Mazzoli repeatedly asked Burton to withdraw his motion, but Burton refused. He had waited nearly four hours for just such a moment. In fact, hours earlier, when Burton first brought it up, Floyd Fithian of Indiana objected. Burton flew across the floor toward him screaming. "When Phil ran, his legs moved but the body from the waist up did not," Matsui recalled. "So it looked like he was just sailing across the room. He dropped his glasses and he grabbed Floyd around the collar."[6] Fithian, however, did not drop his objection. Burton waited until Fithian, too, went home, but Mazzoli still refused to recognize him.

Mazzoli asked Coelho and George Miller, who witnessed the scene from the back of the chamber, to get Burton off the floor. "We stood in the back like two scared chickens, saying, 'Whoa, I'm not touching this guy. I don't want to be electrocuted,'" Miller said. While Burton was screaming, "You're dog shit!" at Mazzoli, Coelho and Miller wisely decided not to tackle him. Finally, Robert Walker of Pennsylvania, who had assumed Robert Bauman's role as Republican "objector," calmed Burton and asked if he could withhold his motion until the next morning. Burton reluctantly agreed. The next morning, Udall handled the unanimous consent item, Fithian dropped his objection, Burton made his case, and the measure passed.[7]

He could still be civilized, indeed for him eloquent, when the situation required it, however. On December 21, John Burton's fiftieth birthday, Phillip paid tribute:

> Mr. Speaker, This will be the last day my brother John serves as a member of the House of Representatives. I am pleased John will be returning to the city he loves, but I also have a special sense of loss at John's departure. . . . Now that the Burton brothers act has split up here in Washington—we still have another brother in elective office in San Francisco [Robert was on the Community College Board]—I suppose I will have to redouble my efforts to champion those causes John and I have worked for in Congress. I, of course, wish him well and look forward to seeing him back in San Francisco.[8]

As the House convened in early January, most of the freshmen were angling for the big committees—Ways and Means, Appropriations, or Energy and Commerce. But few had any chance, and it fell to the senior members of each delegation to tell them what they could realistically expect. Wright made sure John Bryant was put on Energy and Commerce. But it took that kind of leadership intervention. Eager to consolidate his gains and get the best possible assignments for the new Californians, Burton insisted that the three other Californians on the 30-member Steering and Policy Committee—Coelho, Berman, and Norman Mineta—caucus at his home beforehand to plot strategy.

Their preparation paid off. Berman and Levine both landed on Foreign Affairs, a key committee for representatives of strongly pro-Israel West Los Angeles, and Berman, a strong civil libertarian, got Judiciary. Lehman got Interior—important for his Central Valley constituents. Bosco got Public Works and Merchant Marine and Fisheries, important for his coastal district, as did Boxer, who also took John Burton's slot on Government Operations. Waxman-Berman protégé Matthew Martinez was put on Education and Labor.

Burton did not stop there. He got Jim Bates of San Diego on Energy and Commerce and on House Administration. Both assignments were coups, but the latter reflected the House leadership's willingness to accommodate Burton at almost any cost. O'Neill and Wright wanted to make Administration a tool of the leadership and add Foley and Coelho. But Burton insisted that Bates be added. Burton also had to work harder to get his California freshmen on the Banking, Finance, and Urban Affairs Committee. Lehman made it, but Torres came in ninth for seven Democratic slots.

A few days later, at the California delegation's weekly breakfast, Berman showed Burton a quote in the *Washington Post* from second-termer Buddy Roemer of Louisiana, who got the seventh slot on Banking Torres had sought. If the Democrats had not given him the Banking post, Roemer said, the Republicans would have. This appeared the day after Steering and Policy stripped Texan Phil Gramm of his Budget Committee slot because he spent two years collaborating with the Republicans on the Reagan budget package.[9]

Enraged by Roemer's stated willingness to sell out his party for a better offer, Burton grabbed Berman and said, "Follow me." He led Berman over to the House Annex and into the office of Democratic Caucus Chairman Gillis Long. There, Burton threatened to take the issue of Roemer's committee selection to a vote of the caucus, which had the power to reject Steering and Policy recommendations.

"Please don't, Phil," Long said, aware that Burton could win a caucus fight to boot Roemer off the committee and thus embarrass the leadership. "Anything you want. I had to produce for Louisiana." Once again, Burton's bluster worked. To accommodate Torres and quiet Burton, O'Neill and Long expanded the committee by three slots, two Democratic and one Republican. "His willingness to be the most irritating and contentious guy possible made the leadership do things for him that would have been otherwise unthinkable for a guy who had lost," said Berman.[10]

But Burton's one committee failure was almost more impressive than his victories. The night before Steering and Policy met, Burton dropped into Billie Larsen's office about 10 P.M. Larsen was O'Neill's aide for Steering and Policy and the younger sister of Nancy, Burton's longtime aide on insular affairs. Burton had helped her get the job. He was after a loose-leaf binder that Larsen kept in her office. In it, she listed all the committee openings and what slots people bid for. After a cursory glance, Burton told Larsen her information was outdated. Nonetheless, he studied it for a long time, peering wordlessly through his half-moon reading glasses. In what seemed to Larsen like an offhand remark, he said, finally, "I'm putting Barbara Boxer on Appropriations."

This was news to Tip O'Neill. There was only one freshman slot on Appropriations and O'Neill was determined to give it to Robert Mrazek of Long Island. Mrazek had just defeated John LeBoutillier, a brash, 29-year-old first-term Reagan Republican, who had been quoted in *Time* magazine the year before saying that O'Neill was "fat, bloated and out of control, just like the federal government." The Speaker said little at the time. It was not his style to make personal attacks, especially against one so inconsequential. But if there was anyone he wanted to reward, it was the man who took out LeBoutillier. Boxer had not lobbied for the slot; indeed, she did not even know Burton was putting her up against the Speaker's personal choice. Mrazek won, but by a shockingly close one-vote margin. Boxer was floored. "My God. Did you hear? Phil almost got me on Appropriations," she told Larsen after the vote.[11]

True to his campaign commitments, Burton turned his legislative efforts to two key areas: gay rights and AIDS and again to the environment. One of the first members of Congress to grasp the national significance of AIDS, Burton hired Bill Kraus, his 1982 liaison to gays, as a district aide. Kraus was soon shuttling between San Francisco and Washington, where he lobbied for money to fight the disease, still in its infancy. Burton also talked with gay consultant Dick Pabich about producing newsletters to his constituents so that he never again would be as out of touch with his district as he had been in 1982.

In March, Burton introduced a bill to appropriate $10 million for "massive research" on AIDS to the Centers for Disease Control, then studying the epidemic under a $2 million federal grant. More than a thousand people had contracted the frightening virus, 38 percent of whom had already died. "That the federal research effort in this area has not expanded more rapidly and involved much larger sums of money is a tragedy," Burton said.[12]

Burton also plunged back into a frustrating and long-simmering environmental issue, which he characteristically converted into the second largest wilderness preservation bill in American history. In 1977, the Carter administration began compiling an inventory of undeveloped national forest land to determine which should be preserved as wilderness. Known as RARE II, an acronym for the Second Roadless Area Review and Evaluation, the inventory covered more than 46 million acres in the continental U.S. In May 1979, Carter recommended that Congress designate nearly 10 million acres as wilderness, 28 million acres as nonwilderness, and nearly 8 million acres as areas for further planning. The timber industry and the environmental movement had great interest in how this review got resolved. The largest portion of potential wilderness was in California. What happened there would help determine what happened in the rest of the country.

That same year, 1979, Burton and Bizz Johnson, dean of the delegation and powerful chairman of Public Works, assembled rival California wilderness bills. Johnson, a timber industry ally, called for nearly 1.3 million acres to be designated as wilderness. Burton's "California Wilderness Bill" called for preserving 5 million acres, virtually every remaining acre, for Forest Service land in the state. He then set out to negotiate with each member of the California delegation, much as he would over the following two years on reapportionment. The fact that many districts in California included Forest Service land meant he could play the two issues against each other, telling Don Clausen, for example, "Support me on wilderness or I'll fuck you on reapportionment." Or vice versa. Or both. These issues permitted him to do what he loved most: invading another member's district and somehow altering it, for better or worse. Either way, he established his dominance and encouraged continued "cooperation"—and resentment.

Working with Sierra Club lobbyist Tim Mahoney and Seiberling aide

Andy Weissner, Burton picked off California Republicans one by one, starting with Lagomarsino, his longtime colleague on Interior. "We gotta have Largo," he told Mahoney, mispronouncing his Lago nickname. "Whatever Largo wants, we put in this bill. Once I have Largo, we go after the others." When Mahoney showed him how Robert Badham's Orange County district was affected, Burton said, "Don't tell me about Badham's district. I don't understand that man. He doesn't care about government. He doesn't care about legislation. I can't work with that man. Just put the wilderness in his district. I can't talk to him." In the far north, Burton played Clausen against Johnson, whom he called "the Bizzer." Their districts included large portions of disputed wilderness.

When Clausen wavered over supporting a particular compromise, Burton tried to help: "Don, the fucking votes aren't here, Don. They're in L.A. and San Francisco." In other words, if Clausen fought, he would get rolled by the great urban masses who wanted wilderness and had the votes. It was sign off or die.[13]

But because he could not get "the Bizzer" to support 900,000 acres of wilderness, Burton presented his bill with asterisks and blank spaces in place of the deals not yet cut with Johnson, a technique known around Congress as "Burtonizing." On the day the bill sailed through his subcommittee, blank spaces and all, he used a wedding night metaphor uniquely his own: "Congressman Johnson has come in with one problem we know of that we will deal with in full committee. . . . It is not unlike the night when marriage must be consummated; everybody looks forward to this process with a great deal of anticipation and concern. I don't know how many people are going to go back to the washroom and rebrush their teeth, but with any luck at all, I suspect we will find that this matter will be unanimously supported by our delegation."[14]

From Johnson's perspective, the deal more closely resembled rape than lovemaking, and he was not about to rebrush his teeth and hop into the sack with Phil Burton. Johnson negotiated with Burton for a year but was not shown the bill until sixteen hours before the subcommittee meeting. When the House passed the Burton bill on August 18, 1980, it did so over Johnson's objections. The measure consisted of 3.5 million acres of wilderness, or 3.5 percent of the entire state of California. The land to be preserved was twice the amount contained in his 1978 omnibus parks bill. Of that total, 1.4 million acres—90 percent of Yosemite and Sequoia and Kings Canyon National Parks—was already preserved. But this designation provided extra protection by upgrading them to wilderness status, thus preventing new campgrounds, roads, and other development. The bill also created two new major wilderness areas, the 500,000-acre Trinity Alps and the 101,000-acre Siskiyou Wilderness, in the far north. Despite Cranston's strong support, Republican S. I. Hayakawa killed the measure in the Senate.

Burton passed a virtually identical bill again a year later, and again Hayakawa blocked it in the upper chamber. The second passage was trademark Burton. A weekly newsletter on Congress said the bill took fifty seconds in subcommittee, but "much longer—ten minutes"—to get through the full committee and four days to get through the House, eventually passing on unanimous consent. Eugene Chappie, who defeated Bizz Johnson in 1980 and who opposed the bill, was not notified it was coming to the floor. Burton rolled over Chappie, a freshman Republican with no clout. Chappie was in his office, watching the proceedings on closed circuit television and talking on the phone, he told the *Eureka Times Standard.* "I saw Burton rise to speak. By the time I turned the volume up, it was all over."

During the negotiations, longtime acquaintance William Newsom III, son of the trusted associate of former San Francisco boss William Malone, lobbied Burton to preserve the Granite Chief Wilderness on the eastern side of Squaw Valley. As Newsom's associates began taping topographical maps to the wall in his office, Burton asked "what the hell" they were doing.

"I want to lay this out carefully, so you know where it is," Newsom replied.

"Bill, get the goddamn stuff off the wall," Burton said. "You want to save it or you want to give me a fucking geography lesson?"

Later Burton called Newsom and said he was working on a new stealth strategy: all the Republicans who thought they were voting against the bill were actually voting to preserve the land but did not realize it. "This is a new formula," Burton crowed. "I'm going to take their pants down." When Newsom ran into him again during the Marks campaign, Burton said, "Billy, I've got some good news for you. What's the name of that place? Granite something? Well, all the Reagan guys voted for it."

Often, Sierra Club volunteers arrived in Washington to lobby for a pet bill. One of their psychic rewards was the chance to meet the legendary Phil Burton, who had no patience for such niceties and total disinterest in the environmental passion that motivated them. Mahoney tried unsuccessfully to dissuade one group but eventually got Burton's staff to request a precious half hour of the great man's time to meet with another group. Then Mahoney prepped the volunteers, underscoring the importance of not wasting Burton's time.

To Mahoney's surprise, Burton was uncharacteristically gracious, never once acting impatient or boorish. When one earnest young woman from Chico went on at great length about the Ishi Wilderness—an especially difficult and controversial area in Johnson's district—Burton picked up a yellow pad and scribbled furiously. Curious about what Burton had just heard from the woman that might trigger a new approach, Mahoney peeked over Burton's shoulder. "ISHI good!" Burton had written. It was all the information he needed.[15]

By 1983, Hayakawa was gone, replaced by more conservation-minded Republican Pete Wilson. Burton went back to work on the bill. On March 11, it passed out of subcommittee. The House was scheduled to take it up in April.

Burton continued to be obsessed with getting another shot at the leadership. He talked to his former caucus aide Ben Palumbo and to DSG Executive Director Dick Conlon about running for his old job of either DSG or caucus chairman. It would put him back on the ladder. Palumbo advised him to wait and run for the job he really wanted. If he were defeated in a "sideshow," he would be out of it for good.

Conlon was more blunt. "You are never going to be anything around here because people think you are a slob and a drunk," he said. Conlon's words must have penetrated, because Burton actually went on a diet. "Take a look," he said a few weeks later. He had lost a few pounds and had bought new clothes. Conlon interpreted that as renewed interest in challenging Wright.[16]

But Burton could not transform himself so easily. At lunch one day, *Chronicle* columnist Herb Caen watched as he slathered butter on his sourdough bread.

"You don't believe in the cholesterol theory?" Caen asked.

"I'm carrying a bill to outlaw it," Burton replied. He made jokes but his friends continued to worry. His health was bad and it showed. Friends tried to get him to see a doctor, but he refused, sometimes defensively. Shortly after he defeated Marks, Dolores Huerta paid him a visit, and Burton said, "Is there anything I can do for you?"

"Yeah, Phil," she said. "You can take care of your health."

"What do you want me to do, be like Jane Fonda?" he said.

"No," Huerta replied. "I'd like you to be like Cesar Chavez. He takes care of his health." Burton did not say anything. "Phil," she pleaded, "you are the only person we have that poor people can depend on."

AFL-CIO lobbyist Jay Power, worried about Burton's weight and heavy drinking, screwed up his courage late one night as he drove Burton home.

"Phil, I know you're going to get mad," he began. "I love you. We in labor really need you. Why don't you see a doctor and really start to take care of yourself?" Burton exploded. He told Power that it was "none of my fucking business and never to raise it again."

When his anal lesion got so painful that he needed surgery, Ed Davis drove him to Bethesda Naval Hospital. "Why don't you stay a couple days, get a physical and some rest," Davis suggested.

"No," said Burton. "I know what the bottom line will be."

"He didn't say what it was," recalled Davis, "but he knew what the doctors would say, 'Don't drink, don't smoke, eat better, exercise,' and he did not want to face that. He had the procedure done and was out in a couple of hours."

In April, Sala and Phil Burton flew home and then to Hawaii for a brief rest. Back in San Francisco, he took some friends, including Agar Jaicks and POA President Bob Barry, to dinner at his favorite restaurant, the House of Prime Rib, where he chain smoked and put down one vodka after another. After shaking Burton's hand, Barry noticed that it was dripping with sweat. Drinking and smoking too much himself, Barry began talking about his own health and pointed out Burton's sweaty hands. Burton was surprisingly receptive. "He said he wanted to cut down on the booze and lose weight," said Barry. "He seemed very genuine about it. The conversation lasted ten or fifteen minutes."[17]

That Tuesday, Burton, tanned, rested, and relaxed—at least by Burton standards—showed up for Opening Day at Candlestick Park. He sat in the VIP box, chatted with fellow politicians, and watched the San Francisco Giants play the San Diego Padres. To Supervisor Jack Molinari, Burton seemed "ebullient" and "rejuvenated" after defeating Marks. He told Molinari the election was a "watershed" and gave him increased stature for a future leadership race. After the sixth inning, Molinari drove Burton back to his office. Burton had a special reason for talking to Molinari. He wanted a candidate to run against Marks in 1984 and hoped Molinari would do it. Molinari, however, was running for re-election and then mayor in 1987. Burton said that would likely put him on a collision course with Art Agnos, who also wanted to be mayor.

Burton told Molinari he wanted to "get back into the game," meaning the leadership. O'Neill was planning to retire at the end of 1986. His dilemma: should he challenge Wright in 1984 for majority leader or wait two years until O'Neill stepped down and challenge Wright directly for Speaker?[18]

That Friday, Burton felt poorly and thought he had the flu. He took it easy over the weekend. Early Sunday morning as they were preparing for bed in their hotel, he turned to his wife, complained of chest pains and said, "Jesus, Sala, I don't feel good." It was 1:44 A.M. Thirty seconds later, he collapsed. Two thousand miles away, by some weird coincidence, Charlie Rose woke up with a jolt in his North Carolina home, thinking about Phil Burton. Burton was rushed by ambulance to the hospital, where he was pronounced dead of a spontaneous ruptured artery in his abdomen. He was fifty-six. The death certificate listed the cause of death as "abdominal aneurysm with retriperitoneal hemorrhage." A secondary cause was "severe arteriosclerotic heart disease."

Internist Edgar Wayburn, his longtime friend and counselor, and Dr. Seymour Farber, his father's colleague who had become chairman of UC San Francisco's Department of Medicine, both agreed that this was a preventable death. Farber had seen Burton a few months before and urged him to get a checkup. Wayburn had been urging this for years. "Any doctor," Farber said, when he heard the cause of death, "could put his hand on the area around the liver and the kidney and feel the pulsation from the aneurysm. You do an arteriogram to outline it and then repair it. You replace six to eight inches of aorta, and he could have lived indefinitely. This was a life lost needlessly."[19]

In a huge Monday banner, the *San Francisco Examiner* headlined its edition, "Death of a Titan" and devoted nearly its entire front and back pages to Phillip Burton's life and death. The next day, his beloved House of Representatives devoted three hours and twenty-seven minutes to extended eulogies from hundreds of members. His friend Don Edwards said the outpouring of affection and respect for a departed member was unmatched in his twenty years in the House. As a memorial earlier that day, the House passed for a third time his California Wilderness Act. Udall and Seiberling managed the bill, but it was difficult. Burton had cut so many deals, the totality of which only he was aware, that colleagues were at a loss to know who was going to get what. Even so, in an extraordinary tribute, the House approved HR 1439 on a vote of 297-96. "If he had known he was going to die," said Udall in his eulogy, "he really would have loaded up the bill. . . . Leave it to Phil Burton to make the most of his own demise."

EPILOGUE

Phillip's death made us all put on long pants.

CONGRESSMAN GEORGE MILLER

As PHILLIP BURTON'S BODY lay in state in the imposing beaux arts rotunda of San Francisco's City Hall, thousands of people lined up to view the casket and pay their final respects. Although a large number of public officials turned out, along with much of the city's liberal intelligentsia, many of the mourners were public employees, longshoremen, transit workers, welfare recipients, immigrants. They came from the housing projects of Hunters Point and Chinatown and other low-income enclaves. They took the bus or walked from the Tenderloin or from south of Market. These were the people whose daily struggles Burton had championed throughout his career; many had voted for Phillip—and brother John—all of their adult lives. Hundreds sent letters of condolence and personal reminiscence to Burton's office, recalling a kindness or help in dealing with the bureaucracy, telling stories of how Burton had touched their lives.

Sherrie Keith, a sixty-two-year-old retired seamstress, typified many of the mourners. She came to pay tribute an hour before the flag-draped oak coffin was brought into the rotunda. "He helped me get my SSI when I was hospitalized," she told a reporter. "They kept putting me off, so I went to see him personally, and he told me he would do all he could. Right after that, I got it."

One distraught mourner was Michael Berman. Mike Novelli, Burton's 1982 campaign consultant, found him "hiding" behind a pillar near the body, devastated by Burton's death.

"Why are you standing there?" Novelli asked.

"I'm afraid to go any closer," Berman replied. "I'm afraid he's going to get up and start yelling at me."[1]

House Speaker Tip O'Neill led a congressional delegation of 117 members plus additional friends to San Francisco for the memorial service. They flew out on two planes from Washington. Richard Conlon, his longtime colleague at the Democratic Study Group, caught the moment as well as the man when he said, "Half of you are here to pay your respects. The other half to make sure he's really dead."

Recalling the pledge he had made to Burton eight years earlier to look after Sala, Art Agnos drove directly to the Sir Francis Drake from Sacramento when he heard the news. He quickly went upstairs to Burton's suite, walking past a horde of people in the corridor who wanted to know if he was going to run for Burton's seat. Expressing his sympathy, Agnos told Sala Burton he was there to keep the promise he had made to Phillip in 1975 and would do whatever she asked.

"Thank you very much, Art," Sala replied. "I'm going to run to take Phillip's place."

"Put my name down as a supporter," Agnos said.[2]

Sala Burton's rapid declaration of intent quickly froze the field and showed again this extraordinary couple's commitment to politics. There would be time for mourning, but not at the expense of losing control of a congressional seat that had been their whole life. No other prominent Democrat dared enter the race. Sala was easily elected to fill out Phillip's term and was reelected in her own right in 1984 and 1986. She quickly gained assignment to both the Interior and Education and Labor committees, where her husband had been such a powerful presence. On January 29, 1985, Speaker O'Neill, reflecting the warm friendship that had developed between them in the two years since Phillip's death, named her to the House Rules Committee.

It would have been impossible for anyone to step in and fill the shoes of Phillip Burton, even the widow who stood at his side for thirty years. Sala Burton tried but faltered. She lacked his intimidating personality and lightning-quick mind. By early 1986 it became clear something else was wrong: in August, she had surgery for colon cancer. Forced to disclose the cancer before the November election, she promised to beat it and was reelected, but those closest to her knew she was terminally ill. The following January, too weak to take her oath of office, Sala summoned her closest friends and family to her hospital bed—her daughter Joy, John Burton, Don Edwards, Agar

Jaicks, Mary Rose Oakar of Ohio, several longtime aides and relatives, and former state Democratic Party Chair Nancy Pelosi.

Pelosi, who had turned down Phillip's offer to run for John's seat five years earlier, knew why she was there. Sala wanted Pelosi to carry on the Burton tradition. An independently wealthy resident of Pacific Heights who was at home in some circles where it was impolite to mention Phillip's name, Pelosi seemed an odd choice. But this daughter of one congressman from Baltimore and sister of another was a partisan, liberal Democrat to her core.

From her sickbed, Sala questioned Pelosi closely on whether she was truly interested in the job. She would be 2,500 miles from her husband and five children; the hours would be long and grueling. Was Nancy Pelosi fully committed to serve? She looked at the dying woman and said, "I expect you to get well. If you do not, I would be honored to succeed you."

Thus, in a dramatic deathbed gesture, Sala designated Pelosi as her successor, the person she believed best qualified to represent the people the Burtons had served for twenty-four years in Congress. Pelosi defeated all comers in April 1987 in a spirited special primary. She won votes from moderates and conservative Republicans on the city's west side, who preferred her to Supervisor Harry Britt, a gay socialist who was her most serious opponent, and easily defeated Republican Harriett Ross in June. Pelosi's campaign chairman and trusted advisor was John Burton.

Free of drugs and alcohol, back in politics for the first time in five years and having fun again, John Burton decided to run for his old seat, which Agnos was vacating to become mayor of San Francisco. Burton was elected over token gay opposition.[3] A few years later, after having lunch with Pelosi and several reporters, Burton laughed out loud as he recalled how Sala had so carefully and theatrically designated Pelosi to be her political heir, even as many were writing the obituary for the "Burton Machine."

"I can't believe we pulled it off," he said, still delighted by the image of the Burtons and friends rallying yet again for their candidate. In 1992, Assembly Speaker Willie Brown appointed John Burton, his friend of forty years and his closest ally, to chair the Rules Committee, a job he had held twenty years before. And whenever anyone in his house showed signs of a drinking problem or other substance abuse, Brown sent John Burton around for a little talk.

Between 1982 and 1988, there were 180 congressional elections in California. Thanks to Phil Burton's reapportionment lines, only one Democratic incumbent, Jerry Patterson, was defeated. Yet the plans that he and the assembly

Democrats created led to so much partisan rancor that it poisoned the relationship between the two parties for most of the decade and beyond. The great battle to turn liberal Supreme Court Chief Justice Rose Bird out of office in 1986, for example, succeeded because many people, especially Governor George Deukmejian, were angry that her court had overturned so many death penalty sentences. But the bitterness that drove some of the true partisans, said GOP consultant Tony Quinn, "came directly as a result of reapportionment" and her 1982 ruling to let the newly drawn Democratic districts stand.

Against all expectations, Willie Brown survived and prospered during the 1980s and early 1990s. He was helped in no small measure by the reapportionment skills of Phillip Burton, Michael Berman, and Richard Alatorre, which gave Democrats a decade of hegemony in the state even as it was growing more Republican. In 1988, Brown chaired the national presidential campaign of the Rev. Jesse Jackson. Required along with John Burton to leave office in 1996 by a 1990 term limits initiative that limits assembly careers to six years and senate careers to eight, Brown was elected speaker again in 1995. Easily the most gifted politician in Sacramento and certainly one of the two or three key black politicians in America, Brown was on his way to completing the most durable and important speakership in California history, doubling the eight-year reign of the late Jesse Unruh.

Critics of Brown said he had no bottom line, that in the end, he did business every day with the same corporate and business interests that Phil Burton spent his life fighting. He took their campaign money and did much of their bidding. There is truth in this assessment, although Brown might reply that for all but the first two years of his speakership he was forced to deal with Republican governors, first George Deukmejian and then Pete Wilson, who could veto his bills, as well as with the punishing fiscal consequences of Proposition 13. During these years, he protected public education from cuts proposed by Deukmejian and Wilson, fought repeated attempts to cut spending for most social programs, including welfare, and maintained his majority, which allowed him to name liberal Democrats to chair the assembly's most important policy committees.

But the partisan bickering took its toll as the 1980s ended, as did the inability to reach consensus, the noncompetitive districts that allowed very liberal and very conservative legislators to serve in the same body with few centrist peacemakers, and the explosion of ballot initiatives as citizens sought solutions the legislature seemed unable to enact itself. "The real progeny," said Quinn, "was term limits."

One of Brown's most remarkable feats came after the November 1994 elections, which saw his party lose eight seats and apparent control of the assembly for the first time since 1968. Even so, with just thirty-nine Democrats and one Republican-turned-Independent, Brown managed in late January 1995 to outmaneuver his Republican opposition and retain his speakership. It might only last for six months or so, but Brown was determined to choose the time and manner of his departure. At a Sacramento lunch several days afterward, Brown went on at length about how procedurally ignorant and inept his opponents were. When asked whether he knew all the rules and parliamentary tricks when he first got to Sacramento in December 1964, Brown said, "Oh, yes, I knew all that stuff before I ever got here." He added one word by way of confirmation: "Phil."

Brown's power play to keep the speakership—it involved converting a Republican to his cause and booting another Republican out of the assembly who had been elected to the senate but who wanted to stay put to vote against Brown—resembled Burton in his most clever and unapologetic power mode. The editorial abuse he took—similar to that which Burton earned for his 1981 reapportionment—Brown considered a small price to pay to preserve a Democratic majority and the tools to perpetuate it, as well as half the institution's committee chairmanships. He had learned from his mentor something far more important than mere parliamentary skills: he had learned that one never voluntarily relinquishes power when there is a fight to be made and possibly won.[4]

Another Burton protégé, veteran legislator Bill Lockyer, was elected president pro tem of the state senate in early 1994. "He's the last of us," said John Burton, as he looked on from the rear of the senate chamber. Amid the Republican sweep nationally and in California, Lockyer kept his narrow majority in November 1994. (Phil Burton had "discovered" him in the late 1950s, when, still in high school, Lockyer was organizing an East Bay Young Democrats chapter.)

John Burton reacted to the 1994 Republican landslide by introducing a bill to make poverty a felony and to create a statewide system of orphanages, with "direct gruel services" to be provided by the state Department of Social Services. "Republicans theorize that poor people are intentionally that way," Burton explained. "Republicans also feel that when something is a crime, it will change your behavior." His bill died in the Public Safety Committee.[5]

In Congress, Jim Wright succeeded Tip O'Neill in 1986 and proved to be a surprisingly strong and effective speaker. But three years into his job and after a year of negative stories generated primarily by Newt Gingrich over allegations of unethical conduct—that he converted honoraria to book royalties and accepted gifts from someone with a direct interest in legislation—Wright was forced to relinquish the speakership in 1989, profoundly embarrassing his party. That left Tom Foley, Burton's close friend, to succeed Wright. Some Burton loyalists criticized Foley for being passive and said no one had ever envisioned him in the top job. He was to have been the lieutenant to Burton, not the general. Burton had known better. He had told a few associates that Foley, who sometimes was passive, was the one Western legislator with the personality and political skills to win the job Burton wanted so desperately.

As Foley moved up, Democratic Whip Tony Coelho by rights should have followed him as majority leader. But amid the controversy over Wright came damaging revelations about Coelho's financial dealings with a highly paid savings and loan executive who, like Coelho, was a friend of convicted junk bond king Michael Milken. Questions were raised, as with Wright, about accepting a gift from someone who could benefit from legislation. With a Justice Department investigation likely and the Washington press corps cranking up to dig for more, Coelho quickly resigned.[6] Four years later, Coelho became an important but informal advisor to a new Democratic president.

The new majority leader was Richard Gephardt, whose mentor was Dick Bolling and who was first elected from St. Louis in 1976. Gephardt's election took just days, a sharp contrast to the fifteen months the 1976 majority leader contest had lasted. Bolling retired in 1982 and died a decade later, still angry that Burton had "thrown" votes to Wright to keep Bolling out of the final round of voting. Several commentators noted the curious parallel that Burton and Bolling protégés were now leading the House.

"The Bolling-Burton reform movement will be in charge of the House," David Obey told the *Wall Street Journal* in 1989. "It will mean very major institutional change." Obey read the two men wrong. It was the failure of Foley and Gephardt to enact any serious institutional change in the House, despite bank scandals, indictments, and arrogant committee chairmen who used their power to block needed reforms, that led in part to the stunning Republican House takeover in the 1994 elections and the elevation of Gingrich to speaker.[7]

Wright supporter Dan Rostenkowski dominated his Ways and Means

Committee throughout the 1980s and early 1990s. He won praise for guiding a massive 1986 tax reform bill through the House and for putting together difficult budget packages, including President Bill Clinton's important deficit-cutting legislation his first year in office. But by 1993, he too came under a cloud as the U.S. Attorney General's office in Washington began investigating him in connection with an alleged scheme to convert some $20,000 worth of postage stamps to cash over seven years. The investigation quickly snowballed, and he was indicted on seventeen felony counts in June 1994, alleged to have converted more than $500,000 of government funds to personal use over twenty years. As he prepared for trial, Rostenkowski was forced under caucus rules to relinquish his chairmanship. That November, the inconceivable happened: after thirty-four years in the House, the Chicago Democrat was defeated by a Republican.

Most of Burton's House loyalists and protégés fared well until the 1994 elections cost them their majority. He had often counseled patience to his younger California colleagues. With the safe districts he had drawn for them, they would keep winning elections and move up in seniority. One by one, they began to lead important committees. Longtime Burton ally George Brown ascended to the chairmanship of the Science, Space and Technology Committee. Henry Waxman kept the powerful health and environment subcommittee chairmanship he first won in 1978, which he used to press for tougher regulatory laws and to conduct explosive hearings into the addictive power of cigarettes. Pete Stark chaired a key health subcommittee on Ways and Means, and Bob Matsui, still in his early fifties, also rose to a senior Ways and Means spot and was planning someday to run for chairman, assuming the Democrats could retake the House.

Sacramento neighbor Vic Fazio, who gave up so much of his district in 1981 for John Burton, became the sole Californian in the House leadership after Coelho's fall. He chaired the Democratic Congressional Campaign Committee and was elected caucus chairman in December 1994. Fazio was one of the few Democratic incumbents in a competitive district to survive the 1994 GOP juggernaut.

In a startling development, given the history of the committee, ex-Berkeley radical Ron Dellums—who arrived in Washington in 1971 wearing bell-bottoms and talking about prosecuting American officials for "war crimes" in Southeast Asia—became chairman of the House Armed Services Committee in 1993 when Les Aspin resigned to become Clinton's first secretary of defense. He lost his chairmanship to a Republican after just two years.

Leon Panetta, who was elected chairman of the House Budget Committee by his peers, became Clinton's first director of the Office of Management and the Budget. In a June 1994 staff shake-up, he was named White House chief of staff. Burton's close friend Abner Mikva, meanwhile, embarked on a distinguished judicial career, becoming chief judge for the federal Court of Appeals for the District of Columbia. In August 1994, Clinton named Mikva his White House counsel.

After just a few years in the House, Nancy Pelosi was elected to the Appropriations Committee, thus following in her father's footsteps. In 1992, she was named co-chair of the Democratic Party's Platform Committee, which gave her an important role at the convention that nominated Clinton. Barbara Boxer, who succeeded John Burton in Congress, was elected to the U.S. Senate from California in 1992, joining Dianne Feinstein, also elected that year.

But the ascension that would have most pleased Burton was George Miller's. In May 1991, following Mo Udall's retirement for health reasons, Miller, only forty-five, became chairman of the House Interior Committee (later named the Committee on Natural Resources) and immediately vowed to end what he saw as the Department of the Interior's mismanagement of the nation's resources, including timber, oil, gas, minerals, and water.

After Burton's death, congressional aide Judy Lemons saved the office chair he had used throughout his career for Sala. When she died, Lemons kept the massive chair for Pelosi. But the diminutive Pelosi was never comfortable in it. Rather than return it to some government warehouse, Pelosi and Lemons cooked up a plan. The day Miller was formally installed as committee chairman, Pelosi threw a party for him, inviting members and staff of the Interior Committee and the California delegation. When all had arrived, she wheeled in the chair, wrapped in a big red bow. At first, Miller did not understand. Then Pelosi explained. "George," she said, pointing to the chair. "This was Phil Burton's. You're in your mother's armchair."[8](He would surrender the gavel to Alaska Republican Don Young in December 1994).

Following California's huge population growth in the 1980s, the congressional delegation grew by seven to fifty-two. Nearly one in eight House members was now from California. After a year of impasse over the 1990 reapportionment, Republican Governor Pete Wilson designated the state supreme court to come up with a plan, just as Ronald Reagan had twenty years earlier. The court appointed special masters who finally undid Burton's 1981 remap, creating competitive districts up and down the state. Republicans figured they could win thirty seats, but just as in 1974, when the Watergate scandal killed Republican congressional chances in California, the terrible economy and President George Bush's decision to write off California helped give Democrats thirty of the state's fifty-two seats. But even in 1994, the biggest Republican off-year victory in decades, California Republicans could pick up only three House districts, and Democrats still held twenty-seven of the fifty-two seats.

It is a remarkable tribute to Burton's legislative ingenuity that it took so long for his enemies to erode some of his most significant accomplishments. It was not until the early 1990s, when California went into the worst economic downturn since the Depression, that Republican officials were able to cut back the generous state welfare benefits Burton had created in the early 1960s. Congress eventually scaled back the black lung program for coal miners, and after a decade of neglect during the administrations of Ronald Reagan and George Bush, it became clear that many of the strict enforcement mechanisms Burton had built into the coal mine safety bill were being disregarded by a lax federal bureaucracy. Similarly, GOP administrations halted acquisition of new parks and open space and allowed many of the park facilities to deteriorate. Only in 1992 did Congress pass and the president sign a bill to increase the hourly minimum wage from the $3.35 that Burton had last set it at in 1978.

The 1994 elections also imperiled the future of the San Francisco Presidio and all of Burton's manipulations to ensure that, once the army base closed, no consideration would be given to letting private developers build on some of the city's most scenic and valuable land. Citizen commissions met for years to determine how best to use these 1,040 acres adjacent to San Francisco Bay for the greatest benefit to the public. But even Burton could not control the House appropriations process a dozen years after his death. By 1995, the House Republican majority was expressing grave concerns about how many millions of dollars the conversion from military base to national park would cost. Supporters envisioned the most unusual park in the entire system, with hiking trails, scenic vistas, historic architecture, a conference center, and surrounding buildings devoted to world peace and the study of science, the environment, and the Pacific Basin. It seemed doubtful, however, whether Congress would continue to support this costly a conversion. In Tahoe there was better news. Environmentalists cited the Burton-Santini act, which enabled land near Las Vegas to be sold and the proceeds used to purchase and thereby protect undeveloped land near the lake, as the land use decision that best improved the quality and clarity of Lake Tahoe.[9]

Phillip Burton's death was merciful in one important sense. History was unalterably moving away from him. The great liberal tide that began with the New Deal and crested with the Great Society had run its course by the late 1970s. Ronald Reagan's 1980 election confirmed the end of an era. Had he lived, Burton would have had to play defense constantly, as he did for the first few years of the 1980s, for another full decade, until Clinton was inaugurated in January 1993. Even then, he would not have felt at home with another southern Democrat who governed as a moderate and who sometimes seemed not to know what he really believed.

Moreover, Reagan's fiscal policies, which created enormous budget deficits, ruled out spending increases on most domestic programs, aside from entitlements, let alone creation of expensive new ones. The kinds of social programs Burton fought to create would have been inconceivable in the 1980s and early 1990s. By the mid-1990s, House Speaker Gingrich and his Republican majority were voting systematically to dismantle huge chunks of the welfare state. Even many liberals had already begun rethinking its fundamental premises, questioning whether some of its effects—welfare dependency spanning generations, rising illegitimacy, and a growing underclass that had all but abandoned hope of upward mobility—were worse than the ills it addressed.

Burton's SSI program, for example, had exploded, costing $25 billion a year by 1995 in payments to 6.3 million beneficiaries, 700,000 of whom were newly arrived immigrants and 250,000 of whom were addicted to either drugs or alcohol or both and using their $458 monthly stipend to feed their addictions. Journalists, meanwhile, were discovering people like Rosie Watson of Lake Providence, Louisiana, who spent years working the system until she was able to collect monthly SSI payments of $3,893—$46,716 a year—for herself, her husband and her seven children, ages thirteen to twenty-two, each of whom had failed to demonstrate "age-appropriate behavior" and thus qualified for SSI disability benefits.[10]

Clinton campaigned for the presidency in 1992 in part on a pledge to "end welfare as we know it." Once in office, his administration began working on a welfare reform plan that would begin to push people off the welfare rolls after two years. Republicans advanced harsher plans that included eliminating aid to teenage mothers, cutting back school lunches for needy children, and changing welfare from an entitlement guaranteed to those who met certain eligibility requirements into block grants for the states that would not automatically increase to meet rising caseloads. Burton would have found the entire discussion abhorrent.

Perhaps even more difficult than the rightist swing in the political climate was the likelihood that, had he lived, Burton would have faced an uphill battle to defeat Jim Wright for speaker in 1986, when Tip O'Neill retired. To the newer members, he was becoming something of an anachronism in the House, one who represented old politics. Members wanted to think they got a campaign contribution from a labor union or an environmental group because of their voting record, not because Burton put in the fix or somehow "owned" them. His success placing the 1982 California freshmen on desirable committees was more the exception than the rule. Fazio's assessment of Burton at the end of his life was brutal but accurate.

"Our delegation was in jail waiting for Phil Burton's fate to be determined," said Fazio, then one of Burton's "upwardly mobiles," the cohort of talented young California Democrats who were no longer rookies and who were becoming restive and increasingly difficult to control. "His peak had passed, and it was becoming counterproductive to always be seen with him. Phil couldn't always deliver. People wanted us to owe others, not him. . . . In the 1960s and 1970s, he was a master coalition-builder and tactician. But his style was fashioned in an era that was ending. His greatest attributes were now becoming liabilities. There was nothing else he could have done. It broke his heart that he didn't quite attain his goal."[11]

In important ways, Phillip Burton's death marked the end of an epoch, the exhaustion of a major strain of American liberalism. Yet it is worth reflecting for a moment on the power of one man to make a difference. His life underscores the critical role of powerful personalities in institutional settings. Many of his peers detested Burton, found him offensive at best and intolerable at worst. And yet many were drawn to him by his utter incorruptibility and by his passion for the causes to which he devoted himself.

Most who commit their professional lives to Congress choose one of two roles, insider or outsider. Leaders such as Tip O'Neill, Jim Wright, Robert Michel, and Bob Dole are the insiders. They forge consensus, fashion compromise, quietly build relationships, and move the body forward inch by inch. The outsiders—a Jesse Helms, an Adam Clayton Powell, a Robert Bauman—are also important. They are defined by their negative roles, their willingness to gum up the works, no matter how much it angers or inconveniences anybody else, to make their point. What made Burton almost unique, said congressional scholar Norman Ornstein, was his ability to play both roles so effectively. By temperament and style, he was the outsider. By virtue of his need for power to effect change, he willed himself to be an insider.

Burton's synthesis of these two modes of being took him further than anyone could have imagined. Had he achieved his dream, had he won his race against Jim Wright, American politics might have been different—but only at the margins. No one person, not even one as formidable as Burton, could have single-handedly extended the historical moment, could have prevented the rise of Reagan and a new generation of conservative political activists determined to roll back New Deal and Great Society programs. Yet Burton's life mattered because it was precisely at the margins where the power of what one man can do becomes so important, as millions of park enthusiasts and naturalists can attest, as well as millions more workers and disabled, elderly, and poor people.

There is one other American politician who recently was able to merge the insider-outsider skills of Phil Burton: Newt Gingrich, Burton's opposite number in the Republican Party, who began his House career as a bomb-throwing back-bencher and who consciously sought to discredit the House even as he reached for power in the hopes that more Democrats than Republicans would be destroyed in the fallout.

There are many differences between the two, not least that Burton believed far more viscerally in his causes than Gingrich ever had in his. Gingrich came to the speakership knowing little about crafting legislation or brokering deals among adversaries, whereas Burton could recite from memory every dot and comma of his complex legislation as well as the political crosscurrents in virtually all of his colleagues' districts. Burton, moreover, would never dream of passing out "reading lists" to his acolytes, of calling attention to himself by gabbing endlessly on television talk shows or in daily press briefings, or of seeking to capitalize financially on his newfound celebrity by writing political treatises and novels. He was far more interested in tangible results than in "ideas." But having come of age in an earlier political era, Burton also never would have understood how to exploit the media the way Gingrich did and make it complicit in setting his agendas.

Despite their large differences in style, outlook, and modus operandi, however, the two men resembled each other in important institutional ways. Al From, founder of the centrist Democratic Leadership Council and onetime aide to the late Gillis Long of Louisiana, said of Gingrich, "He's their Phil Burton. No question."[12] Like Burton, Gingrich had an agenda for governing the minute he seized power. His sweeping and highly ideological "Contract with America" was a right-wing version of what Burton might have done had he ever become House speaker (although Burton never would have tipped off his opposition by formalizing it or writing it down). Like Burton, Gingrich had a plan to consolidate power. His decision to reach down into the ranks of House Republicans and elevate junior members to committee chairmanships, thus bypassing the seniority system and a number of ranking Republicans on major committees, was a continuation of the House reforms that Burton and his DSG comrades began twenty years earlier.

Similarly, Gingrich's decision to limit committee chairs to serve no more than six years was something Burton would have endorsed. He also would have approved of subjecting Congress to the same laws to which it subjects everyone else. Foley and Gephardt could have implemented these sorts of internal reforms, but whether it was inertia or fear of challenging entrenched committee chairs, the Democratic leadership took no action until it was too late. "It is historically interesting that what the Democratic left began had to be finished by the Republican right," said journalist Lou Cannon.[13]

Both men sought to consolidate power so as to move an otherwise reactive institution: Burton from the left, Gingrich from the right. But there was, of course, a huge difference in the two men's agendas and bases of support. In his relentless quest to redistribute income, strengthen labor unions, and use government to help the poor, Burton challenged the most powerful corporate and business interests in America. His successes came in spite of these interests. For at least the critical first months of Gingrich's tenure, these same interests not only rooted him on and wrote key provisions of his party's legislation but also financed his rise to power and his efforts to maintain it.

After they defeated his leadership bid, Tip O'Neill and Jim Wright never let Burton continue the House reforms his caucus leadership had so successfully begun. They did not want to provide a vehicle through which Burton could reemerge as a threat. Years later, Wright might have achieved a historic speakership but for Gingrich's successful assault on him. In becoming the most powerful speaker of the modern era immediately on assuming the office, Gingrich thus became the first House leader since Burton to make the institution work.

Were Burton still alive and in a position to influence policy and politics in the House, there would be little of the hand-wringing and confusion that characterized Democratic responses to their loss of power in 1995. Though his policy views might have been repudiated by an angry and conservative electorate, that never would have stopped him from figuring out how to force Republicans in the grip of ideological fervor into choosing between that fervor and their own constituencies—and then paying for their choices in the next election. Nor would it have stopped him from devising ingenious ways of delivering votes to Republicans in return for benefits for his constituencies. As longtime Burton watcher Leo Rennert said soon after the 1994 elections, "Can you imagine how much fun Phil would be having now cutting deals with these guys?"[14]

On June 15, 1991, eight years after his death, the friends of Phillip Burton gathered at Fort Mason, near the headquarters of his beloved Golden Gate National Recreation Area. The occasion was the unveiling of a two-ton, ten-foot high statue of Burton in seeming mid-argument. Bethesda sculptor Wendy Ross brilliantly captured the man's energy and intensity. The bronze figure rises dramatically from its spot amid the gentle hills and two acres of lawns that surround it. The Golden Gate Bridge, San Francisco Bay, and the Marin Headlands sparkle in the distance. Tucked in the pocket of his suit, Ross stashed the replica of a note, the visible portion of which reads: "The only way to deal with exploiters is. . . ." Those familiar with the Burton aphorism can finish the sentence themselves: "to terrorize the bastards."

"In this generation," then-House Speaker Tom Foley said to the hundreds who had gathered, "I know of no more effective legislator than Phil was. . . . There are people who in generations will never know his name but who will have reason to bless him."

John Burton was characteristically more ambivalent—and more honest. "He had great love for people," John said of his brother. "It was just individuals he busted their chops." Turning to the giant statue towering behind him, John added, "Do you really think he is gesturing us to the gateway to the Golden Gate National Recreation Area? Or is he saying, 'Come on, Foley, let's go have a Stoli over ice.'"[15]

NOTES

I. BEGINNINGS

1. Most of these biographical details are from interviews with Robert and John Burton, who knew little of their family history. Robert was interviewed twice in November 1988 and on April 17, 1991, all in San Francisco. John was interviewed on May 5, 1989, and on August 1, 2, and 5, 1991, in San Francisco. Both were also called repeatedly to confirm details. Dr. Thomas Burton died in 1974. Mildred Burton suffered from Alzheimer's disease for years and could not be interviewed. She died in December 1992. The FBI, which opened a file on Phillip Burton because of his political activities in the early 1950s, corroborated some of these details. Indeed, the FBI files, obtained under a Freedom of Information Act request, contained precise dates and places of birth that neither surviving brother could supply. Most likely, this information came from military forms Phillip Burton filled out while in the navy's V-12 program and later in the air force. Several psychotherapists familiar with some details of their family life suggested that the lack of biographical knowledge was itself diagnostic of a dysfunctional family. The reference to FDR's speech is from Joyce Purnick, "Rep. Phillip Burton: Democratic Caucus Pick, Man in the News," *New York Post*, December 7, 1974.

2. For more on Milwaukee Mayor Dan Hoan, see Lloyd Gladfelter, "Dan Hoan after Thirty Years," *National Municipal Review* 39 (July 1940): 448–50, 487; Daniel W. Hoan, "A Mayor Counsels with Managers," *Public Management* 16 (November 1934): 346–53.

3. Two magazine articles describe the neighborhood that produced these politicians: Frank Aukofer, *Milwaukee Journal*, January 9, 1972, which recounted the incident with Burton and the "kikes," and Jim Anderson, "Growing Up Straight in Squaresville on the Lake," *Chicago Sunday Sun-Times*, December 2, 1973. Stark is still in Congress from California. Mikva was appointed to the District of Columbia Circuit

Court of Appeals by President Carter. In August 1994, President Bill Clinton named him White House Counsel.

4. The account of Burton's high school years is based on interviews with fellow Falcon Club members Jack Hanley, December 1, 1988, San Francisco; Matt Gately, December 19, 1988, San Francisco; Doug Brown, March 20, 1991, by telephone; Harlan Hoffman, November 29, 1990, San Francisco; Stan Perkins, February 13, 1991, by telephone; and Gerard Rhine, July 7, 1989, San Francisco.

5. The high school yearbooks are the June 1943 and 1944 *Surveyors*. All six members of the Falcon Club interviewed said Burton had no advance knowledge of the ballot-stuffing incident.

6. David Jenkins, interviews, July 9, 1988, January 8, 1991, San Francisco.

7. Dr. Seymour Farber, interview, December 13, 1988, July 21, 1991, San Francisco.

8. Siegfried Hesse, interview, April 29, 1991, Berkeley; Dr. Robert Peck, interview, August 7, 1991, by telephone.

9. John Burton, interview, May 5, 1989, August 1, 1991; Robert Burton, interview, April 17, 1991.

10. Walter "Buzz" Forward, interview, May 13, 1991, by telephone.

11. Gil Ferguson, interview, May 8, 1991, Sacramento.

12. Interviews with Forward; Ferguson; Hanley; Joseph Holt, April 24, 1991, by telephone; Patrick Hillings, April 8, 1991, by telephone; Chuck Brohammer, May 13, 1991, by telephone; Robert Tolstad, May 13, 1991, by telephone; Al Conti, March 8, 1991, by telephone.

13. Description of the political atmosphere on board ship in the late 1940s is from an interview with Patrick Tobin, March 9, 1991, in San Francisco, who worked on similar ships as a member of the National Maritime Union and Marine Cooks and Stewards Union, and confirmed by James Herman, December 12, 1993, by telephone, former president of the ILWU. Tobin later became the ILWU's Washington political director.

14. Many of the biographical details on Jesse Unruh are from Lou Cannon, *Ronnie and Jesse: A Political Odyssey* (New York: Doubleday, 1969). For more on Unruh's origins and years at USC, see pp. 9–13, 21–26.

15. Larry Margolis, interview, February 6, 1991, Sacramento.

16. Cannon, *Ronnie and Jesse*, p. 24.

2. BEATEN BY A DEAD MAN

1. See Frederick M. Wirt, *Power in the City: Decision Making in San Francisco* (Berkeley: Institute of Governmental Studies, University of California Press, 1974), pp. 20–42. Statistical data from Table 1, p. 33.

2. State Appeals Court Justice William Newsom III, interview, January 3, 1991, San Francisco. For discussion of the McDonough brothers, see Norman Elkington, "From Adversary to Appointee: Fifty Years of Friendship with Pat Brown," oral history, Bancroft Library, UC Berkeley, p. 19.

3. Newsom interview. Newsom is the grandson of William A. Newsom and heard about the political role of the church from his father, William Newsom, Jr.

4. See Bill Malone, oral history, Bancroft Library, UC Berkeley, 1978–79, pp. 3–4.

5. Ibid., pp. 39–40. For an excellent discussion of Irish political machines, see Steven

P. Erie, *Rainbow's End: Irish-Americans and the Dilemmas of Urban Machine Politics, 1840–1945* (Berkeley: University of California Press, 1988).

6. Malone, oral history, p. 58.

7. Joseph Holsinger, interview, May 8, 1991, Sacramento. As a young protégé of Malone, Holsinger heard Malone's stories of his role in picking Truman at the 1944 convention. See also Elinor Raas Heller, "A Volunteer Career in Politics, in Higher Education, and on Governing Boards," 2 vols., oral history, conducted between 1974 and 1980, Bancroft Library, UC Berkeley, pp. 250–59. Heller described how the California delegation was seated at the front and center of the convention hall, with the Missouri delegation immediately behind it. Truman was chairman and Heller sat in front of him and got to know him well. She said Malone urged the California delegation to play "practical politics" and "go with the winner" in the contest between Wallace and Truman.

8. Background on Malone and how he wielded power in San Francisco and in California is based on Malone oral history; Heller, "A Volunteer Career in Politics"; and on interviews with Cyr Copertini, formerly Cyr Mullins, Malone's secretary from 1942 to 1947, January 31, 1991, San Francisco; Holsinger; Judge Jack Ertola, January 3, 1991, San Francisco; Newsom; Justice Donald King, November 29, 1990, San Francisco; California Lt. Gov. Leo McCarthy, November 29, 1990, San Francisco; Jenkins; Morris Bernstein, January 16, 1991, San Francisco; Harvey Matthews, January 3, 1991, by telephone; Thomas Fleming (a longtime assistant to Dr. Carlton Goodlett), December 3, 1990, San Francisco; Joseph Williams, August 10, 1989, San Francisco; former San Francisco Assemblyman John A. O'Connell, August 11, 1989, San Francisco; former *San Francisco Examiner* political correspondent Jack McDowell, February 18, 1991, by telephone; former *San Francisco News* political editor Mary Ellen Leary, February 18, 1991, Berkeley. Aside from a few oral histories, there has been virtually nothing written on Malone or his powerful influence on the Democratic politics of California from the mid-thirties to the mid-fifties.

9. John Sheridan to San Francisco Teamster leader Jack Goldberger, n.d., "'54 Campaign," carton 1, Phillip Burton Papers, Bancroft Library, UC Berkeley (hereafter cited as PB Papers).

10. Bertram Coffey, "Reflections on George Miller, Jr., Governors Pat and Jerry Brown, and the Democratic Party," oral history, conducted by Gabrielle Morris, 1978, Bancroft Library, UC Berkeley, p. 37.

11. Accounts of the Young Democrat days come from interviews with Holsinger; Yori Wada, January 8, 1991, San Francisco; Jack Berman, January 21, 1991, San Francisco; Marshall Windmiller, December 30, 1990, Alameda; Fleming; Charles Warren, February 7, 1991, Sacramento.

12. Lionel Steinberg, interview, January 12, 1991, by telephone.

13. Malone's efforts to persuade Downey to stay in the race and keep Douglas out, as well as what Nixon told Downey are in Malone, oral history, pp. 70–75. The quotations from Downey and Boddy are from Stephen E. Ambrose, *Nixon: The Education of a Politician, 1913–1962* (New York: Simon and Schuster, 1987), p. 210. Malone's refusal to help Douglas is from Copertini interview.

14. Roz Wyman, formerly Roz Weiner, interview, March 8, 1991, by telephone; Toby Osos, interview, March 26, 1991, Pasadena. For account of Nixon-Douglas race, see Ambrose, *Nixon*, pp. 208–23.

15. Account of the courtship is from interviews with Osos; Joseph Williams; Tom Winnett, August 10, 1989, Berkeley.

16. Pierre Salinger, *San Francisco Chronicle*, August 25, 1952.

17. Matthews interview.

18. Steinberg interview; Warren interview.

19. The story of the bar exam incident is from Terrence Ryan, interview, August 12, 1989, San Francisco, who heard it from Sala Burton. The account of the Miller-Stevenson relationship is from Bert Coffey, interview, January 6, 1991, Richmond.

20. For Malone's reluctance to support Stevenson, see Elizabeth Gatov, "From Grass Roots Organizer to Treasurer of the United States," Bancroft Library, UC Berkeley, p. 138. Winnett quote is from Carlotta Herman Mellon, "The Rise and Fall of Grassroots Politics: The California Democratic Council, 1953–1966" (Ph.D. diss., Claremont McKenna College, 1972), p. 29. The Myers quote is from James Q. Wilson, *The Amateur Democrat: Club Politics in Three Cities* (Chicago: University of Chicago Press, 1962), p. 114.

21. Wilson, *The Amateur Democrat*, p. 110. See also Mary Ellen Leary, "The Two-Party System Comes to California," *The Reporter*, February 7, 1957, pp. 33–36.

22. Alan Cranston, "Report of the California Democratic Council: What the CDC Did in 1954," December 16, 1954. See also Wilson, *The Amateur Democrat*, pp. 114–21; Mellon, "The Rise and Fall of Grassroots Politics, pp. 32–42.

23. *People's World*, May 16, 1950.

24. Accounts of the Smyth scandal are from dozens of newspaper stories in San Francisco in 1951–52, including: Mary Ellen Leary, "What Gives with the Democrats? Bill Malone Says He's Not Mad at Anyone; Mrs. Heller Agrees," *San Francisco News*, March 11, 1952; Dick Pearce and Ed Montgomery, "House Probers Here; John Malone Linked by Agent to Backdating," *San Francisco Examiner*, February 6, 1952; and David Perlman, "Smyth Takes Stand, Denies Backdating," *San Francisco Chronicle*, June 4, 1952.

25. Mary Ellen Leary, "Malone Fighting for Party Post," *San Francisco News*, January 10, 1952, March 11, 1952; Holsinger interview.

26. Burton to Phillips, n.d., "'54 Campaign," carton 1, PB Papers.

27. Ibid. Accounts of the campaign are from interviews with O'Connell; Lou Cannon, March 25, 1991, Santa Barbara; the late George Hardy's daughter, Joan Tuomy, January 10, 1991, San Francisco; John Henning, February 7, 1991, Sacramento; Frank Mankiewicz, April 9, 1991, Washington, D.C.; Osos; Copertini; Holsinger.

28. "'54 Campaign," carton 1, PB Papers.

29. Phillip Burton file, Congressional Quarterly Library.

3. CHINATOWN AND THE BATTLE FOR POTRERO HILL

1. Sydney Kossen, "I'll Never Retire from Politics, Maloney vs. Burton, an Intense Local Fight," *San Francisco News*, October 31, 1956.

2. Leary, "The Two-Party System Comes to California," p. 35.

3. Hubert Bernard, "The Burton Machine," *San Francisco Examiner*, February 6–10, 1967; interviews with Cannon; Henning; and Joseph Williams.

4. Sala Burton's ability to speak six languages was now an asset. She went door-to-door in a district more polyglot than the Irish-dominated Twenty-third. Demo-

graphic data is from "20th AD Election Results," carton 17, and "San Francisco Census Data," carton 16, PB Papers; Rudy Nothenberg, interview, December 14, 1990. Burton continued his own demographic studies after his election. His files showed, for example, that while the white birth rate in 1959 was 15.2 per 1,000, the black birth rate was 44 per 1,000, the Chinese was 27.4 per 1,000, and the Japanese was 31.2 per 1,000. The white death rate was twice that of Chinese and 50 percent higher than that of blacks.

5. "20th AD Election Results," carton 17, PB Papers. See Nothenberg, "The Young Democrats and the Burton Victory," in "20th AD Election Results," carton 17, PB Papers.

6. For the Maloney-Samish connection, see Elmer Rusco, "Machine Politics, California Model: Arthur H. Samish and the Alcoholic Beverage Industry" (Ph.D. diss., University of California, n.d.), pp. 189–90. On his Republicanism, Pat Brown said in a July 5, 1989 interview in his Los Angeles law office that one day in 1933 he encountered fellow attorney Matthew Tobriner as Tobriner was on his way to City Hall to change his party registration from Republican to Democrat. "Changing your party is like changing your religion, isn't it, Matt?" Brown asked. "Well," Tobriner replied, "that's what you do when you don't believe in it anymore." Brown said, "By God, you're right," and decided to accompany Tobriner to change his registration, too. After he was elected California's second Democratic governor of the twentieth century, Brown appointed Tobriner to the California Supreme Court.

7. Background on George Hardy and on the Hardy-Burton relationship is from Tuomy interview; details on the "basement" of 240 Golden Gate Avenue are from interviews with Tuomy; Susan Kennedy, January 14, 1991, San Francisco; and retired SEIU organizer Pat Jackson, August 21, 1991, by telephone.

8. Details of Burton's 1956 labor support are from interviews with ILWU leaders David Jenkins and Patrick Tobin.

9. The statistics on Chinatown voting are from Bessie May Ferina, "The Politics of San Francisco's Chinatown" (master's thesis, UCLA, 1949), pp. 54–80.

10. Lim P. Lee, interview, March 8, 1991, San Francisco. Some biographical details are from Ken Wong, "Retired Postmaster Lee Still Going Strong at 70," San Francisco Examiner, September 17, 1980.

11. "AB 61: Chinese New Years," carton 15, PB Papers.

12. Lee's journal is quoted in his column in Asian Week, February 25, 1982.

13. State Appeals Court Justice Harry Low, interview, January 24, 1991, San Francisco. See also "AB 61: Chinese New Years," carton 15, PB Papers.

14. Mildred Burton to Phillip Burton, May 15, 1956; Winnett to Burton, n.d., in "1956 Campaign," carton 1, PB Papers.

15. O'Connell interview; Gene Marine, interview, February 20, 1991, Berkeley. See also Gene Marine, "How 'The Unbeatable' Was Beaten," Frontier, February 1957, 15–16.

16. Sydney Kossen, San Francisco News, October 5, 1956.

17. Maloney to Goodlett, "1956 Campaign," carton 1, PB Papers.

18. Steinberg interview.

19. These statistics come from Nothenberg, "The Young Democrats and the Burton Victory."

20. Cannon interview; Marine, "How 'The Unbeatable' Was Beaten."

21. Interview with the Burton friend, a Democratic Club activist who asked to remain

anonymous. Ann Eliaser, "From Grass Roots Politics to Top Dollar: Fundraising for Candidates and Nonprofit Agencies," oral history, Bancroft Library, UC Berkeley, pp. 53–54.

4. FIRECRACKERS AND FARM WORKERS

1. For a profile of Sacramento of that era, see Robert E. G. Harris, "The Busy Little Men in Sacramento," *Frontier*, July 1955, 7–10.
2. Quoted in David Farrelly and Ivan Hinderaker, *The Politics of California* (New York: Ronald Press, 1951), p. 177. See also Rusco, "Machine Politics, California Model," p. 169.
3. Cited in Rusco, "Machine Politics, California Model," p. 180.
4. California Assembly Committee on Governmental Efficiency and Economy, *Investigation of Arthur H. Samish*, p. 128, cited in Rusco, "Machine Politics, California Model," p. 187.
5. Rusco, "Machine Politics, California Model," pp. 405–41. See also Cannon, *Ronnie and Jesse*, p. 90.
6. This profile of Sacramento comes from interviews with former Assemblymen William Bagley, December 14, 1990, San Francisco; Jack Knox, January 5, 1991, Richmond, Calif.; Jerome Waldie, February 5, 1991, Sacramento; and from Harris, "The Busy Little Men in Sacramento"; Charles G. Bell and Charles M. Price, *California Government Today: Politics of Reform?* (Chicago: Dorsey Press, 1988), pp. 114–22.
7. Leary, "The Two-Party System Comes to California," p. 33.
8. Cannon, *Ronnie and Jesse*, pp. 98–99. For background on Unruh's early years running for office and in the assembly, Cannon's book is invaluable.
9. Tom Rees, interview, August 28, 1989, Scotts Valley, Calif.
10. "First Term Publicity," carton 16, PB Papers.
11. McDowell interview.
12. The more benign view is from an interview with Chuck Hurley, a former McClatchy reporter who later worked for Burton, March 4, 1991, Berkeley. The latter view is from Lee Nichols, interview, March 4, 1991, by telephone, a reporter for NBC News who later worked for Unruh as an assembly consultant.
13. Notes of this Burton-Lancione "understanding" are in "1959 YD Convention," carton 17, PB Papers.
14. Ibid. See in particular, Burton to Humphrey, October 24, 1959, and Humphrey aide Herbert Waters to Burton, November 2, 1959.
15. Joe Cerrell, interview, July 6, 1989, Los Angeles; Dick Nevin, interview, March 26, 1991, Pasadena.
16. Letters from Bamberger and friend to Burton are in "'58 Campaign," carton 17, PB Papers. The file also contains a brief unbylined article from *San Francisco Call Bulletin* about the controversy.
17. Tuomy interview.
18. For more on the Knowland-Knight switch, Pat Brown's electoral strategy, and Burton's discussions with Dutton, see Cannon, *Ronnie and Jesse*, pp. 56–57; Fred Dutton, "Democratic Campaigns and Controversies, 1954–1966," oral history, Bancroft Library, UC Berkeley; Don Bradley, "Managing Democratic Campaigns, 1954–1966," oral history, Bancroft Library, UC Berkeley.

19. Jack McDowell, "California Fact and Comment," *San Francisco Call Bulletin,* January 27, 1959. Dr. Thomas Burton to Phillip Burton, May 18, 1959, in "1959 Press," carton 17, PB Papers.
20. Dolores Huerta, interview, July 12, 1991, Berkeley; State Appeals Court Justice Coleman Blease, interview, February 7, 1991, Sacramento. See also Harry Farrell, Burton profile, *San Jose Mercury,* December 11, 1959, in "PB 1960 Primary," carton 17, PB Papers.
21. "Drug Hearings," carton 15, PB Papers; Hurley interview.
22. Huerta interview; "Civil Rights '60–61," carton 16, PB Papers.
23. John Seiberling, interview, June 28, 1991, by telephone.
24. Coleman Blease, "A Lobbyist Views the Knight-Brown Era," oral history, Bancroft Library, UC Berkeley, 1979, pp. 12–14.
25. Dymally eulogy, *Phillip Burton: Memorial Addresses Delivered in Congress* (Washington, D.C.: Government Printing Office, 1983), p. 32.
26. J. Edgar Hoover, "Communist Target—Youth" (House Un-American Activities Committee, 1960), cited in Department of Religious Liberty, "Operation Abolition: Some Facts and Some Comments" (New York: National Council of the Churches of Christ in the USA, February 1961).
27. Ralph Tyler, "Why It Happened in San Francisco: A Report on the Demonstrations against House Un-American Activities Committee by an American Generation Nobody Knew Was There,'" *Frontier,* June 1960, pp. 5–9. See also Dept. of Religious Liberty, *Operation Abolition;* Northern California Chapter of Americans for Democratic Action, "San Francisco and the Un-American Activities Committee," n.d.
28. Hadley Roff and Wes Willoughby, *San Francisco News–Call Bulletin,* January 26, 1961.
29. "Nixon Smear," carton 1, PB Papers. See also "Nixon Accuses Two Again of S.F. Riot Role," *San Francisco Chronicle,* October 4, 1962.
30. Blease, "A Lobbyist Views the Knight-Brown Era," pp. 22–24; interviews with O'Connell; Waldie; state Senator Nicholas Petris, February 22, 1991, Oakland.
31. Robert Lagomarsino, interview, April 11, 1991, Washington, D.C.

5. AB 59

1. Quoted in Cannon, *Ronnie and Jesse.* p. 105. See also James R. Mills, *A Disorderly House: The Brown-Unruh Years in Sacramento* (Berkeley: Heyday Books, 1987), pp. 13–16.
2. Lou Angelo, interview, February 8, 1991, Sacramento.
3. Ibid.
4. Interviews with reapportionment consultants Angelo; Leroy Hardy, June 29, 1989, Long Beach; former Assemblymen Knox; Rees; Waldie; Bagley; Unruh assistants Margolis; Jack Crose, February 7, 1991, Sacramento. See also Cannon, *Ronnie and Jesse,* pp. 106–12; Mills, *A Disorderly House,* pp. 31–46. Mills argues that the 1961 reapportionment plan resulted in a 28-28 standoff between Unruh and Bea and that what really gave Unruh the speakership was his breakfast club of nine uncommitted assemblymen deciding to vote for Unruh in a bloc. But Unruh insiders Rees and Waldie and political scientist Hardy dismiss that argument, saying Mills was not

inside enough to know what was really going on in 1961 and that Unruh had more votes than Mills knew about.

5. Angelo interview; Knox interview.
6. Carton 16, PB Papers.
7. Jack McDowell, *San Francisco Call-Bulletin*, April 26, 1961.
8. Margolis interview.
9. Jackson Doyle, *San Francisco Chronicle*, April 5, 1962, from "62 Items," carton 8, PB Papers.
10. See Eugene C. Lee, "The Stork and the Golden State," in *The California Governmental Process* (Boston: Little, Brown, 1966), pp. 6–7.
11. Margolis interview; Lee Nichols, "The California Experience: Recruitment, Training and Promotion of State Legislative Staff," unpublished monograph, Institute of Governmental Studies, UC Berkeley, July 1966.
12. Interviews with Martha Gorman, February 5, 1991, Sacramento; Tom Joe, April 1, 1989, Washington, D.C.; Knox; Nichols; Hurley.
13. Willie Brown, interview, August 21, 1991, Sacramento; John Burton interview, August 1, 1991. See also Robert Scheer, "The Flash, Power, Politics and Image—Willie Brown Style," *Los Angeles Times Magazine*, June 23, 1991.
14. "1960 PB Campaigns," carton 17, PB Papers.
15. See Richard J. Rapaport, "Those Bad, Bad Burton Boys and the Post-Modern Liberal Blues," *California*, April 1988, pp. 75–84. The story of the original arrest was first published in the *San Francisco Examiner* and *San Francisco Chronicle* of April 5, 1962.
16. O'Connell interview. Foran and McCarthy also survived a terrifying experience together. One night in 1953 as McCarthy was about to drop Foran off at home after a lecture, a man with a gun snuck up, tapped on the window, and ordered them to drive him to Los Angeles. He had just shot a police officer and left him for dead, had escaped a police dragnet, and was high on heroin. Training his gun on them for the next twelve hours, the man forced McCarthy and Foran to keep driving. They listened to radio broadcasts that confirmed the officer's death. Eventually the man was caught, and McCarthy and Foran returned home safely. But their close bond deepened. McCarthy interview.
17. Interviews with O'Connell; Willie Brown; Mary Louise Lovett, January 14, 1991, San Francisco; John Burton, August 1, 1991; Marine; McCarthy; King; Jane and Jack Morrison, January 12, 1991, San Francisco; Gorman.
18. "Big Daddy's Boo-boo," *liberal democrat*, October 1962, p. 2; Able Dart, "Politics Inside Out," ibid., p. 10; and "Unruh Loses at State Convention," a *liberal democrat* staff report, pp. 5–7.
19. *liberal democrat*, August 1963, p. 11.
20. For details of the ballot proposition, see Louis Garcia, "Yes on 23: A Reasonable and Moderate Proposal," *liberal democrat*, October 1962, pp. 7–8. Garcia was co-chairman of the Northern California Committee for Proposition 23.
21. Hale Champion, interview, March 21, 1991, Berkeley.
22. This section is based on multiple interviews with Tom Joe, April 1, 1989, February 1, 1991, March 8, 1991, and April 5, 1991, Washington, D.C., and by telephone; legislative advocate Tom Moore, January 24, 1991 and March 16, 1991, San Francisco; Legislative Counsel's Office attorneys Ed Percell, January 3, 1991, by telephone; and Tom Dooley, May 8, 1991, Sacramento; and readings of multiple and

sequential versions of AB 59, supplied by Dooley. The section on how Burton got the bill through the legislature is based on the above sources, as well as interviews with Dugald Gillies, February 7, 1991, by telephone; Champion; Gorman; Stephen Teale, February 13, 1991, by telephone; John Quimby, May 9, 1991, Sacramento; Joseph Rattigan, January 31, 1991, by telephone; James Cobey, January 31, 1991, by telephone; Winslow Christian, February 20, 1991, by telephone; Bob Williams, January 31, 1991, by telephone; Blease; Crose; Waldie; Huerta; and John Burton, August 1, 1991.

23. Tom Moore's appointment was itself an intriguing study of the intramural feuds between Governor Brown, Unruh, and Burton. Moore was hired by political pro Don Bradley as a reward for working in Brown's 1958 campaign. He was supposed to be the liaison between the governor's office and the legislature. Burton wanted to control the job himself, as did Unruh. At their first meeting, a final meeting of the Welfare Study Commission, Moore overheard Burton pounding the table and screaming, "No, goddam it! They're not jamming any political hack from Don Bradley down my throat." Burton later went over to Moore and said, "I don't know you, but you're not the right guy for the job. Nothing personal. I hope you have other plans." When Unruh aide Larry Margolis found out that Moore's father had been convicted for contempt of Congress for refusing to answer questions from the House Un-American Activities Committee, he spread the news all over Sacramento to torpedo Moore's appointment. But when Burton heard that, in Moore's words, he "flew into a rage, saying, 'I don't care if he committed sex with animals, they won't get him out of that job.'" Then he sought out Moore to say, "anyone being hounded for his politics is a friend of mine" and called off his own effort to get Moore fired. Tom Moore, interview, January 24, 1991, San Francisco.

24. Governor Brown press conference, May 21, 1963, transcript, State Archives Collection, Secretary of State's Office, Sacramento.

25. Jack McDowell, "Burton Smiles at Welfare Critics," *San Francisco News–Call Bulletin,* May 23, 1963.

26. California Taxpayers' Association, *CAL-TAX News* 4 (May–June 1963): 1–3.

27. Don Collin, "A Look at the New Welfare Program In Action," *California Farm Bureau Monthly* 45 (August 1964): 8–9.

28. Tom Joe, interview, September 27, 1991.

29. Quimby interview. *San Francisco Chronicle* editorial, May 6, 1963, from "Unruh-Bane Ploy," carton 15, PB Papers.

30. Gorman and Margolis interviews; *San Francisco Chronicle,* September 15, 1963; Waldie to Burton, September 21, 1963, from "Big Daddy Unruh," carton 7, PB Papers.

6. THE COCKATOO'S HEAD: LOOKING EAST

1. T. Anthony Quinn, "Carving Up California: A History of Redistricting, 1951–1984" (Ph.D. diss., Rose Institute of State and Local Government, Claremont McKenna College), pp. 14–17; Leroy Hardy, interview, June 29, 1989. Hardy did his doctoral dissertation on the 1951 reapportionment and was one of Burton's chief redistricting consultants for twenty-five years. Burton told the story of the effect of Havenner's

reapportionment on him during a talk to Hardy's students on the Long Beach campus in 1981.

2. California Assembly Interim Committee on Elections and Reapportionment, hearings, Los Angeles, December 15, 1960; John Burton interview, August 1, 1991.

3. California Assembly Interim Committee on Elections and Reapportionment, hearings, November 22, 1960, p. 59.

4. Mills, *A Disorderly House*, p. 56.

5. The story of San Francisco's fifth assembly seat is based on interviews with Angelo; Leroy Hardy, June 29, 1989 and March 26, 1991; Gorman; and Frank Kieliger, August 1988, Concord, Calif.; "1961 Reappo," cartons 16, 26, PB Papers. After three interviews with the author, Dr. Hardy wrote, "There was simply no way the loss of one seat [the eightieth] could have occurred. . . . It is inconceivable that two political giants such as Burton and Unruh would allow such a staff error to occur, regardless of the staff incompetence. When the decision was made, I cannot say. Who made it, I cannot say. I suspect some staff member (Lou or myself) brought the options to the attention of Crown, who in turn discussed it with Unruh and/ or ?, and a decision was made." Hardy added that it is always more convenient for politicians to blame things on staff, especially academics, "whom the average politician detests . . . than to say, 'You caught me. I was trying to screw you.'" Hardy to author, March 28, 1991. Assembly Speaker Willie Brown, who won the fifth seat in 1964 and who has retained it ever since, said: "It would not surprise me that Phil Burton would position himself to be dominant in a crisis situation to resolve the missing seat. Whether he did it deliberately, I highly doubt. He did give San Francisco an extra seat that San Francisco by population was not entitled to, and he did it by virtue of politics. It was not as colorful as legend reflects, but it is an accurate reflection of his skill and the superiority of his strategy." Willie Brown interview. After a helpful four-hour interview, former Burton staffer Kieliger said he was so outraged by the assertions of Angelo and Hardy vis-à-vis the eightieth seat that he refused to cooperate further.

6. California Assembly Elections and Reapportionment Committee, hearings, Sacramento, May 18, 1961, pp. 37–38.

7. "PB Items, Calif. State Assembly," carton 16; "1960 Burton Campaign," carton 17; and "1961 Reappo," carton 26, PB Papers.

8. Richard Reinhardt, "The Cockatoo Squawks," *San Francisco*, January 1964.

9. Morris Bernstein, interview, January 16, 1991, San Francisco; McCarthy interview.

10. The story of McAteer's withdrawal and Malone's role in it is based on interviews with McCarthy; Newsom; King; Joseph L. Alioto, November 30, 1990, San Francisco; Jack Ertola, January 3, 1991, San Francisco; Thelma Shelley, July 3, 1991, by telephone.

11. Sydney Kossen, "Shelley Aide Denies Deal," *San Francisco Examiner*, February 15, 1963.

12. Rhine interview. See also "They Hurl Their Last Charges," *San Francisco Examiner*, November 5, 1963.

13. Terrence Hallinan, interview by telephone, October 3, 1991; "Your Dobbs Vote Works 3 Ways," *San Francisco Examiner*, November 1, 1963; "Statements by Dobbs, Shelley," *San Francisco Examiner*, November 4, 1963.

14. Carton 2, PB Papers.

15. Transcript of Burton November 7, 1963 press conference in "PB Remembrance—1964," carton 2, PB Papers.

16. "Shelley Talks of the JFK He Knew," *San Francisco Examiner*, November 25, 1963.

17. Edmund "Pat" Brown, interview, July 5, 1989, Los Angeles.

18. Heavey to Burton in "1964 Special Election to Congress," carton 1, PB Papers; "Brown Says 'I'm for Burton,'" *San Francisco Chronicle*, December 12, 1963.

19. Ibid., cartons 1 and 10, PB Papers. Also Department of Justice, FBI, Burton file 89-184, which included "Burton's Embarrassing Fund Pitch" and Governor Brown's January 2, 1964 "letter" of invitation to the Burton dinner, *San Francisco Chronicle*, January 3, 1964; John Burton interview, August 1, 1991; Beeman, interview, January 9, 1991, San Francisco.

20. Margot Patterson Doss, *San Francisco Chronicle and Examiner*, May 26, 1991.

21. Thomas Winnett, "Phil Burton Runs for Congress," *liberal democrat*, December 1963, pp. 5–6.

22. "1964 Special Election," carton 10, PB Papers.

23. Wallace Turner, *New York Times*, February 20, 1964; Michael Harris, "Burton Restates Policies, the House's Newest Liberal," *San Francisco Chronicle*, February 20, 1964; Harry Johanesen, "Burton Plans to 'Earn Spurs,'" *San Francisco Examiner*, February 20, 1964; and Robert Strand, "Burton, Newest in House, Won Victory as Liberal," UPI, February 19, 1964.

24. Special Agent in Charge to Assistant FBI Directors DeLoach and Sullivan, February 19, 1964, San Francisco; M. A. Jones to DeLoach re Burton, February 20, 1964; A. Rosen to "Mr. Belmont re Anonymous political pamphlet Fifth District of California election laws," FBI Burton file 89-184.

7. CAPITOL HILL AT LAST

1. Richard Bolling, *House Out of Order* (New York: E. P. Dutton, 1966), pp. 37, 42, 108.

2. Ibid., p. 12.

3. Ibid., pp. 52, 54.

4. For a detailed discussion of the Rules Committee expansion, see Milton C. Cummings, Jr., and Robert L. Peabody, "The Decision to Enlarge the Committee on Rules: An Analysis of the 1961 Vote," in Robert L. Peabody and Nelson W. Polsby, eds., *New Perspectives on the House of Representatives* (Chicago: Rand McNally, 1963), pp. 167–94.

5. For an account of Albert's successful campaign for majority leader and Bolling's failure, see Nelson W. Polsby, "Two Strategies of Influence: Choosing a Majority Leader, 1962," in Peabody and Polsby, *New Perspectives*, pp. 237–70.

6. Christopher Madison, "The Heir Presumptive," *National Journal*, April 29, 1989, p. 1035.

7. Interviews with Irving Sprague, August 9, 1990, by telephone; Robert Kastenmeier, December 18, 1988, Washington, D.C., and May 4, 1994, by telephone; Beeman, January 9, 1991; Richard Bolling, April 11, 1989, Washington, D.C.

8. "Burton's Rap at Red Probers," *San Francisco Chronicle*, March 5, 1965.

9. I. F. Stone, *I. F. Stone's Weekly*, March 16, 1964; Gilbert Woo, *Chinese Pacific Weekly*,

April 9, 1964. Burton had Woo's article, written in Chinese, translated by the Orientalia Division of the Library of Congress.

10. Interviews with William Thomas, December 19, 1990, San Francisco; Peter Trimble, March 20, 1991, by telephone; Kevin Shelley, June 5, 1991, San Francisco; Thelma Shelley, July 3, 1991, by telephone. Thelma Shelley said she did not believe her husband would have made that call. Son Kevin, who later worked for Burton, said it was possible his father could have said to McCormack, "Look, old pol to old pol, don't do him any favors. Make him earn his stuff." The Dewey quote is from Gerald Rosen, "The Most Powerful Man in Congress?" *Dun's Review* (July 1975): 46.

11. Jack McDowell, "Politics Today," *San Francisco Examiner*, March 31, 1964.

12. Dr. Edgar Wayburn, interview, January 16, 1991.

13. Todd Gitlin, *The Sixties: Years of Hope, Days of Rage* (New York: Bantam Books, 1987), p. 147.

14. "Phil Burton in Mississippi," *San Francisco News–Call Bulletin*, July 4, 1964.

15. C. D. DeLoach to John Mohr, May 14, 1964, July 2, 1964; P. C. Morrell to C. D. DeLoach, July 6, 1964, August 14, 1964, FBI file 100-37609.

16. Gitlin, *The Sixties*, pp. 151–62; Don Edwards, interview, August 23, 1989, Washington, D.C.; then-ADA director David Cohen, interview, December 6, 1990, Washington, D.C.

17. Gitlin, *The Sixties*, p. 178.

18. Gilbert Woo, *Chinese Pacific Weekly*, August 13, 1964.

19. Lee interview. See also Sydney Kossen, "New Postmaster from Chinatown?" *San Francisco Examiner*, December 2, 1965, and FBI file 100-435576 on Burton, in particular, December 6, 1965 memo from SAC, San Francisco to J. Edgar Hoover re Lim Poon Lee, and December 12, 1965 memo from D. J. Brennan to W. C. Sullivan re Lee.

20. Nelson Polsby, interview, September 15, 1991, Berkeley.

21. Dick Murphy, interview, July 11, 1990, Washington, D.C.; Ken Young, interview, April 4, 1991, Washington, D.C.

22. Background on Frank Thompson is from William Dietz, Thompson's administrative aide for seventeen years, interview, April 4, 1991, Washington, D.C.

23. Chuck Stone, *Black Political Power in America* (New York: Dell, 1970), p. 196.

24. Ibid., p. 193.

25. For review of the Powell history, see "Controversies Surround Rep. Adam Clayton Powell," *Congressional Quarterly Almanac*, 1966, pp. 519–24.

26. Ibid., p. 523. See also Powell to Burton, September 26, 1967, from "1966 Material to Save, 2," carton 8, PB Papers.

27. Quoted in "Adam Clayton Powell Excluded from House; He Files Historic Lawsuit to Regain Seat," *Congressional Quarterly Almanac*, 1967, p. 543. See complete article (pp. 533–49) for fuller discussion of details of Powell case.

28. See C. Sumner Stone to Burton, March 11, 1967, Burton to the *Sun Reporter*, January 14, 1967, from "Adam Clayton Powell," carton 7, PB Papers.

29. Leroy Hardy interview, June 29, 1989.

30. George Gould, interview, April 9, 1991, Washington, D.C.

31. Hurley interview.

32. For a more detailed analysis of the 1967 congressional reapportionment, see Quinn, "Carving Up California," ch. 3, pp. 22–34, from which these statistics are taken.

33. Ibid.; Hurley interview. Burton's statement on Vietnam is from *Congressional Record*, March 1, 1966, vol. 112, no. 36. John Burton to Phillip Burton, March 2, 1966, PB Papers; Robert Peck to Phillip Burton, April 3, 1966, made available to the author by Dr. Peck.

34. Kastenmeier interview, December 18, 1988.

35. Will Sparks confidential memo to LBJ, September 27, 1967, from "National, Vietnam," carton 6, PB Papers. A copy of the memo was transmitted by Sparks to Burton on December 16, 1974. Sparks told Burton he "discovered" the memo while going through his files. "Since we had not quite invented the tape recorder in those days," he wrote to Burton, "this represents only my memory of your comments the following morning. What, if anything, the President did with them, I do not know. What I do know, re-reading it today, is that somebody should have listened."

36. Interviews with Kastenmeier, December 18, 1988; Edwards; Abner Mikva, April 10, 1991, Washington, D.C.; Bob Eckhardt, May 28, 1991, by telephone; Pat Kraus, December 12, 1990, Washington, D.C.

37. For discussion of the events leading up to the Chicago convention and the convention itself, see Nelson W. Polsby, *Consequences of Party Reform* (New York: Oxford University Press, 1983), pp. 16–35; Gitlin, *The Sixties*, pp. 319–36; Theodore H. White, *The Making of the President, 1968* (New York: Pocket Books, 1970), pp. 321–89; *Congressional Quarterly Almanac*, 1968, pp. 1015–24. Also, Larry Berg, interview, May 5, 1994. Berg was a Kennedy delegate in Chicago.

38. Polsby, *Consequences of Party Reform*, p. 24.

39. San Francisco attorney Duane Garrett, interview, July 9, 1988, San Francisco. Garrett heard the story directly from Ted Kennedy.

40. Gary Hymel, interview, July 13, 1990, Washington, D.C.

41. Text of Burton's statement to the Platform Committee is in "1968 Antiwar Plank," carton 7, PB Papers. His speech to the convention was published in the *New York Times*, August 29, 1968. A 16-millimeter film of his speech is included in carton 30, PB Papers.

42. Gitlin, *The Sixties*, p. 326; "Democrats Struggle over Plank on Vietnam War" and "Platform Approved after Landmark Debate on Vietnam," *Congressional Quarterly Almanac*, 1968, pp. 1020–21.

43. Hymel interview. See also Thomas P. O'Neill, Jr. (with William Novak), *Man of the House: The Life and Political Memoirs of Speaker Tip O'Neill* (New York: St. Martin's Press, 1987), p. 252; John Barry, *The Ambition and the Power: A True Story of Washington* (New York: Penguin, 1990), p. 21; Carl Albert (with Danny Goble), *Little Giant: The Life and Times of Speaker Carl Albert* (Norman: University of Oklahoma Press, 1990), pp. 326–27.

8. THE "BURTON MACHINE"

1. King interview.

2. Trimble interview.

3. Bagley interview; Bagley to Sala Burton, April 15, 1985, provided by Bagley to author; Charles Raudebaugh, "Ultra Right Plans Coup in State GOP," *San Francisco Chronicle*, April 27, 1964.

4. Hurley interview; Martin Eber, interview, March 2, 1991, San Francisco; Jim McClatchy, interview, April 30, 1994, Sacramento.

5. Joan Brann, interview, January 15, 1991, Oakland.

6. Coffey interview; *San Francisco Examiner*, September 30, 1966.

7. Hubert Bernhard, "The Burton Machine," *San Francisco Examiner*, February 6–10, 1967.

8. Thomas C. Fleming, Weekly Report, *Sun Reporter*, February 18, 1967.

9. Sydney Kossen, "McAteer's Death Has Big Impact," *San Francisco Examiner*, May 27, 1967.

10. Willie Brown interview, August 21, 1991; Jenkins interview, January 8, 1991.

11. Joseph Williams interview.

12. "Report Mayor Not Running for Election," *San Francisco Examiner*, September 7, 1967.

13. Jack Viets, "Burton's Remarks Serve to Obscure," *San Francisco Chronicle*, September 9, 1967. See also Michael Harris, "Mayor's Decision Medical," *San Francisco Chronicle*, September 8, 1967.

14. Alioto interview.

15. The meetings at the homes of Jaicks and Alioto are based on interviews with Agar Jaicks, July 2 and 3, 1988, San Francisco; Alioto; Jenkins; Morrison.

16. Alioto interview.

17. Tom Wicker, "In the Nation: Chicory Roots and Children," *New York Times*, July 1, 1969.

18. Ibid. See also *Congressional Record*, June 25, 1969, pp. H5211–524, and June 27, 1969, p. H5341.

9. "EATING ITALIAN" AND THE POLITICS OF BLACK LUNG

1. For both extensive coverage of the Farmington tragedy and a critical and invaluable discussion and history of the Coal Mine Health and Safety Act of 1969, see John R. Nelson, Jr., *Black Lung: A Study of Disability Compensation Policy Formation* (Washington, D.C.: School of Social Service Administration, University of Chicago and the Center for the Study of Social Policy, 1985).

2. Waldie interview. See also "Misc. 1956–1964," carton 7, PB Papers; *Service Union Reporter*, February 1967, for Burton letter explaining new provisions of the Fair Labor Standards Act of 1966, which increased and extended minimum wages.

3. Gary Sellers, interviews, August 9 and 10, 1990, December 7, 1990, April 6, 1991, Washington, D.C.; Charles McCarry, *Citizen Nader* (New York: Saturday Review Press, 1972), p. 228.

4. Ben A. Franklin, "The Scandal of Death and Injury in the Mines," *New York Times Magazine*, March 30, 1969; Sellers interviews; Thomas interview.

5. Robert G. Sherrill, "The Black Lung Rebellion," *The Nation*, April 28, 1969, p. 530.

6. Ibid., p. 532. See also Nelson, *Black Lung*, pp. 1–4; former West Virginia coal miners Tony Turyn, interview, May 28, 1991, by telephone; Harry Carter, interview, May 29, 1991, by telephone.

7. Sherrill, "The Black Lung Rebellion," p. 529.

8. Franklin, "The Scandal of Death," p. 27.

9. "Congress Clears Comprehensive Coal Mine Safety Bill," *Congressional Quarterly Almanac*, 1969, p. 736.

10. Nelson, *Black Lung*, p. 31.

11. The writing of the black lung provisions of the Coal Mine Health and Safety Act of 1969, in addition to Nelson, Franklin, Sherrill, and *Congressional Quarterly Almanac*, 1969, is based on Sellers interviews; Bob Vagley, interviews, April 1 and 23, 1991, Washington, D.C.

12. Sellers interviews. Burton aide Frank Kieliger also said he had heard something about a miscarriage by Sala Burton in the early 1950s, but knew of no details. Neither John nor Robert Burton, nor Sala's daughter Joy Temes, had ever heard about it.

13. Sellers interviews; Vagley interviews.

14. For an extensive and impressively reported account of "the deal," see Leo Rennert, "Strange Alliances in Lawmaking," *Sacramento Bee*, January 25, 1970.

15. Sellers interviews. Congressman David Obey refused repeated requests for an interview.

16. Nelson, *Black Lung*, pp. 32–33, 47–48; John Erlenborn, interview, April 4, 1991, Washington, D.C.

17. *Congressional Record, House*, December 17, 1969, pp. H12636–37.

18. Ibid., pp. H12636–53.

19. Ben A. Franklin, "President to Sign Mine Safety Bill Despite Doubts," *New York Times*, December 30, 1969.

20. Vagley interviews; Rennert, "Strange Alliances in Lawmaking."

21. Nelson, *Black Lung*, pp. 71–73, 78.

22. Ibid., p. 92.

23. Vagley interviews.

24. Nelson, *Black Lung*, pp. 97, 104, 135.

10. THE LEGISLATOR

1. Rosen, "The Most Powerful Man in Congress?" pp. 45–48; Marjorie Hunter, "A California Democrat Delivers the Vote in House," *New York Times*, May 23, 1975.

2. Ralph Nader, interview, December 12, 1992, by telephone; Sellers interviews; Dan Krivit, interview, July 11, 1991, by telephone; Young interview. See also U.S. Department of Labor, "Safety Standards"; "Job Health Safety Bill Passes, Goes to Nixon," *Washington Post*, December 18, 1970; Morton Mintz, "Dispute Mires Job Safety Bill," *Washington Post*, October 1, 1970; James M. Estep, "The Drafting of the Daniels Bill," unpublished paper, May 22, 1972, made available to the author by Dan Krivit.

3. Nader interview; Sellers interviews. See also "Passage of Job Safety Bill Ends Three-Year Dispute," *Congressional Quarterly Almanac*, 1970, pp. 675–82; McCarry, *Citizen Nader*, pp. 228–33.

4. Interview with labor lobbyist, who asked not be be identified, Washington, D.C., 1991.

5. Daniel Patrick Moynihan, *The Politics of a Guaranteed Annual Income: The Nixon Administration and the Family Assistance Plan* (New York: Random House, 1973), p. 4.

6. "Welfare Reform: Disappointment for the Administration," *Congressional Quarterly Almanac*, 1970, p. 1031.

7. It is interesting to speculate whether, had Finch chosen to become attorney general instead of former Nixon law partner John Mitchell, the Watergate scandal would have played out differently or even happened at all. For an extended discussion of the Nixon plan and of Burton's role, see Vincent J. Burke and Lee Burke, *Nixon's Good Deed: Welfare Reform* (New York: Columbia University Press, 1974), esp. pp. 195–98.

8. Pamela Duffy, interview, January 11, 1991, San Francisco; Joe interview, April 5, 1991.

9. Moynihan, *The Politics of a Guaranteed Annual Income*, p. 156.

10. Rick Merrill, interview, July 10, 1990, Washington, D.C.; Vincent J. Burke, "Key Democrats Back Nixon's Welfare Idea," *Los Angeles Times*, February 11, 1970.

11. Joe interview, April 5, 1991; Merrill interview.

12. Michael D. Green, "Life and Death of a Giant: Recollecting Phil Burton," unpublished ms., p. 13.

13. Jodie Allen, interview, August 8, 1990, Washington, D.C.

14. Burke and Burke, *Nixon's Good Deed*, p. 194.

15. Burton's remarks are taken from *Congressional Record*, July 15, 1968.

16. This section on the GGNRA is based on interviews with Ansel Adams's biographer William Turnidge, June 4, 1991; Amy Meyer, December 3, 1990; John Jacobs (no relation to the author), March 14, 1991, by telephone; Don Clausen, July 11, 1991, by telephone; Thomas; Edgar Wayburn, January 31, 1991, San Francisco; and carton 33 (GGNRA), PB Papers.

17. Thomas interview. Burton's foresight paid off. In the early 1990s, when a commission on military base closures ordered the Presidio closed, there was little question that anyone but the National Park Service would control lands worth hundreds of millions of dollars to private developers. Nearly a decade after his death in 1983, Burton reached out from the grave to help determine the fate of the Presidio and keep it accessible to the public as part of the GGNRA. In the late spring of 1994, Burton's successor, Rep. Nancy Pelosi, working with Burton's former staffer Judy Lemons, beat back Republican efforts to sell off the most valuable parts of the Presidio to keep down the price of conversion.

18. Cranston quote in file marked "SF-GGNRA Hearings 8-9-71 and 5-11-12-71" and "GGNRA Markup," carton 33, PB Papers; Meyer letter from Meyer and Wayburn interviews; Hebert to Albert, September 21, 1972, from "GGNRA 1971–72," PB Papers; Hebert "Dear Colleague" letter, October 9, 1972, and *San Francisco Chronicle* editorial, from "GGNRA Media 1970–72," carton 33, PB Papers; Burton to Mitchell, March 1, 1972, "S.F.-Fort Mason," carton 33, PB Papers. Burton did not stop with his letter to Mitchell. He sent a copy of his letter and an accompanying press release to the *Examiner* and to Alioto, prompting the *Examiner* to begin a news story by writing, "Mayor Alioto went through the roof today when he learned of the Justice Department's plans to build a new correctional institution for youthful law-breakers at Fort Mason." Within two weeks, Burton had a letter back from Mitchell saying such plans would not be "appropriate." An *Examiner* editorial said the proposal was met by "hoots, scoffs, sneers, snorts, expressions of disbelief and full gales of derisive laughter," and added, "Who in the name of Lucifer could dream up such a farce and sell it to a cabinet officer?" *San Francisco Examiner*,

March 2, 1971, Mitchell to Burton, February 24, 1971, and *Examiner* editorial, from "S.F.-Fort Mason," carton 33, PB Papers.

19. Thomas interview; Fort Mason Foundation Director Mark Kasky, interview, December 17, 1991, by telephone.

II. THE PATH TO POWER

1. Thomas Foley, interview, April 11, 1991, Washington, D.C.
2. Dennis Farney, "Ruler of the Land: U.S. Presidents Come and Go, but the Power of Rep. Aspinall Persists," *Wall Street Journal,* January 22, 1971.
3. Sala Burton recounted Doda story to Charlie Rose. Rose interview, April 10, 1991, Washington, D.C.; Lloyd Meeds, interview, December 5, 1990.
4. Report to Constituents, Congressman Sam Steiger of Arizona, February 19, 1971, from "Kudos, Awards," carton 9, PB Papers.
5. Congressional Quarterly, Inc., *Inside Congress: A Contemporary Affairs Report* (Washington, D.C.: Congressional Quarterly, January 1976), p. 104.
6. This account of DSG strategy meetings is based on interviews with former Common Cause President Cohen, December 6 and 10, 1990; Common Cause President Fred Wertheimer, December 12, 1990, Washington, D.C.; former DSG staffer Roy Dye, August 8, 1990, Washington, D.C.; Frank Thompson aide Dietz. See also Mary Russell, "Revolt on Capitol Hill: Seniority System's Downfall Began 6 Years Ago," *Washington Post,* February 4, 1975; Burton D. Sheppard, *Rethinking Congressional Reform* (Cambridge, Mass.: Schenkman Books, 1985), pp. 11–20, 38–45.
7. Russell, "Revolt on Capitol Hill."
8. Norman Ornstein, "The Democrats Reform Power in the House of Representatives, 1969–75," in Alan Sindler, ed., *America in the 1970s* (Boston: Little, Brown, 1977).
9. *Congressional Record,* House, March 18, 1969.
10. Transcript of Rivers's remarks to CBS News on October 30, 1969, was included in a November 7, 1969 memorandum from DSG Director Dick Conlon to all DSG members and staff assistants, and is from the congressional files of Walter Oleszek, photocopied with his permission. For a fuller discussion of the vote on ending teller voting, see Sheppard, *Rethinking Congressional Reform,* pp. 47–55; Ornstein, "The Democrats Reform Power"; also interviews with Cohen, December 6 and 10, 1990; Dye; Merrill; and Norman Ornstein, interview, July 11 and 12, 1991, by telephone.
11. Ornstein, "The Democrats Reform Power," p. 22.
12. See Norman Ornstein, "Causes and Consequences of Congressional Change: Subcommittee Reforms in the House of Representatives, 1970–1973," in *Congress in Change* (New York: Praeger, 1975), pp. 93–95. The conservatives on the committee were Phil Landrum of Georgia, with seventeen years in the House, Olin "Tiger" Teague of Texas, with twenty-four, and freshman Ed Jones of Tennessee. The moderates were led by Administration Chairman Wayne Hays and included Neal Smith of Iowa, Frank Annunzio of Illinois, and Hansen. The eleventh member was freshman Shirley Chisholm of Brooklyn.
13. Sheppard, *Rethinking Congressional Reform,* pp. 75–76.
14. Ornstein, "Causes and Consequences of Congressional Change," p. 97; Foley interview.

15. Hymel interview. See also Albert, *Little Giant*, pp. 326–27.
16. Jim Wright, interview, June 3, 1991, by telephone; Dan Rostenkowski, interview, April 5, 1989, Washington, D.C. See O'Neill, *Man of the House*, p. 260.
17. Hymel interview; Tip O'Neill, interview, December 17, 1988, Washington, D.C. See also O'Neill, *Man of the House*, pp. 259–60.
18. Democratic Study Group Special Report, "Age and Tenure of House Committee Chairmen," February 1, 1971, p. 1.
19. Lou Cannon, "Burton Will Spark Liberals," *St. Paul Pioneer Press*, March 15, 1971.
20. Marjorie Silverberg and Joan Claybrook, "Phillip Burton," Ralph Nader Congress Project, August 1972; Joan Claybrook, interview, July 11, 1990, Washington, D.C.; Sellers interview, August 9, 1990. The account of Burton's carousing in London is from the former staffer-turned-lobbyist who accompanied him and who asked not to be named. Burton's eating habits are from Rees interview; Beeman interview; conversation with Woodruff, October 1990, Los Angeles. The Conlon story of Burton eating corn is from Green, "Life and Death of a Giant," p. 14. Conlon concluded to Green: "When news of Phil's death was reported, all three of my kids called, and they all said the same thing: 'I'll never forget that day he was out at the house—eating.'"
21. Account of Sala Burton is drawn from interviews with Kraus; Judy Lemons, April 11, 1989, Washington, D.C.; George Miller, December 6, 1988; Nancy Larsen, February 28, 1991, San Francisco; and Eni Faleomavenga, December 11, 1990, Washington, D.C.
22. Rose interview; Pat Schroeder, interview, February 22, 1991, Berkeley.
23. DSG press release, March 13, 1972, from congressional files of Walter Oleszek.
24. DSG press release, April 20, 1972, Walter Oleszek files.
25. DSG memo from Conlon to Burton, "Impact and Implementation of the Democratic Caucus Resolution on Indochina," April 24, 1972, Walter Oleszek files.
26. In a fascinating retrospective essay on Congress, Nelson Polsby suggests one key development that allowed the DSG and the House Democratic Caucus to succeed: air conditioning. The spread of air conditioning in the South in the 1950s, he argues, drew northerners to what were formerly bedrocks of the Confederacy. Where once there had been Dixiecrats in Congress, over time they were replaced by Republicans. Where just 7 of some 100 congressional districts belonged to Republicans in 1960, he said, by the mid-1970s and 1980s, more than one-third were safely Republican (and 47 were by 1992). This trend, he said, aided the liberalization of the southern Democratic parties as well. "In Washington," Polsby writes, "the resulting drastic reductions in the number of Dixiecrats in the Democratic Caucus meant that for the first time in half a century, the mainstream of the Democratic Party could emerge in the House and insist that its leaders follow mainstream policies. This reduced the autonomy of committee chairmen by requiring them to pay far greater attention to rank-and-file Democratic committee members and to cut back on the cross-party alliances that many of them had forged with ranking Republicans." See Polsby, "Does Congress Work," *Bulletin of the American Academy of Arts and Sciences* 46 (May 1993): 30–45; Polsby interview, August 14, 1993, Berkeley.
27. O'Neill interview; Betty Stephens, interview, May 15, 1989, by telephone. Of the five people at the table, only they were alive to recount what happened, to the author. (O'Neill has since died.) Neither could precisely pin down the date, but O'Neill recalled that he was whip at the time and that as DCCC chairman he made

several fundraising appearances in Los Angeles in the fall of 1972. John Burton said that while he knew his brother frequently got into verbal scraps, he never knew him to challenge anyone to a fight. He said he found it difficult to believe that his brother would have threatened O'Neill in that manner. Interview, May 14, 1989, San Francisco. O'Neill said he did not include the incident in his memoirs because Sala Burton was still alive when the memoirs were published and he did not want to cause her pain.

28. Nancy Larsen interview; Hymel interview.

29. When Silvio Conte wrote another amendment to limit agricultural subsidies to $20,000, as he had before the black lung vote with cotton, Burton again defeated it and then infuriated Conte by teasing, "Keep up the good work, Silvio. We get real mileage out of your amendment." The first time Burton saved their subsidies, the southerners voted for the black lung bill. This time they gave Burton their votes for food stamps for striking farm workers.

30. "Burton Fails in Bid for House Post," *San Francisco Chronicle,* January 3, 1973.

31. "Contests: House, Senate Leadership Posts at Stake," *Congressional Quarterly,* December 23, 1972, p. 3207.

32. O'Neill, *Man of the House,* p. 270.

33. "Democratic Study Group: A Winner on House Reforms," *Congressional Quarterly,* June 2, 1973, pp. 1366–71.

34. Hymel interview. For discussion of the reforms, see Sheppard, *Rethinking Congressional Reform,* pp. 87–95; "House Reform: Easy to Advocate, Hard to Define," *Congressional Quarterly,* January 20, 1973, pp. 69–72; Marjorie Hunter, "House Democrats Given Power to Vote on Committee Chairmen," *New York Times,* January 23, 1973.

35. See Ornstein, "Causes and Consequences of Congressional Change," pp. 106–9; Sheppard, *Rethinking Congressional Reform,* pp. 98–101.

36. Marjorie Hunter, "Democrats Curb Secrecy in House," *New York Times,* February 22, 1973; Richard L. Lyons, "Democrats Vote to Open House Meetings and Rules," *Washington Post,* February 22, 1973.

37. David Broder, "The House: A New Era," *Washington Post,* February 18, 1973; Rowland Evans and Robert Novak, "Making the Caucus King of the House," *Washington Post,* February 28, 1973; Tom Geoghegan, "House Cleaning," *The New Republic,* February 24, 1973.

38. "Democratic Study Group," p. 1367. See also "Democratic Study Group: A Winner on House Reforms," *Congressional Quarterly,* June 2, 1973, pp. 1366–71.

39. Bolling interview.

40. Sheppard, *Rethinking Congressional Reform,* pp. 118–34, on setting up the Bolling Committee; Roger H. Davidson and Walter J. Oleszek, *Congress against Itself* (Bloomington: Indiana University Press, 1977).

41. Sheppard, *Rethinking Congressional Reform,* pp. 140–47.

42. Ibid., pp. 153, 179.

43. *Americans for Democratic Action Legislative Newsletter* 3 (June 1, 1974): 3.

44. Sheppard, *Rethinking Congressional Reform,* p. 186. See also Davidson and Oleszek, *Congress against Itself,* pp. 207–20; interviews with former Hansen Committee staffer William Cable, April 3, 1990, Washington, D.C.; former Bolling Committee staffer Linda Kamm, August 9, 1990, Washington, D.C.; political scientist Walter

Oleszek, December 6, 1990, Washington, D.C.; Dye; Merrill; Ornstein; Claybrook; Cohen, December 10, 1990; Wertheimer.

12. REVOLUTION IN THE HOUSE

1. Michael Barone, *Our Country: The Shaping of America from Roosevelt to Reagan* (New York: Free Press, 1990), p. 518.
2. "Rule on Oil Tax Bill," *Congressional Quarterly*, June 8, 1974, p. 1503; Wilbur Mills, interview, April 22, 1991, by telephone.
3. Milton Viorst, "Attacking the Baronies," *Washington Star-News*, June 10, 1974.
4. Mary Russell, "GOP Fears Return of 'King Caucus' in House Next Year," *Washington Post*, July 29, 1974; Wertheimer interview.
5. Interviews with Miller, April 19, 1991, Pleasant Hill, Calif.; Henry Waxman, July 6, 1989, Los Angeles; Murphy; Machinist Legislative and Political Director William Holayter, December 12, 1990, Washington, D.C.; former Hays aide Doug Frost, April 4, 1991, Washington, D.C.; AFL-CIO official Young.
6. Wertheimer interview; Cohen interview, December 10, 1990; *Congressional Quarterly Almanac*, 1974, pp. 630–31.
7. James R. Dickenson, "A Too Formidable Reformer?" *Washington Star-News*, November 20, 1974.
8. Paul Rosenberg, interview, February 1, 1990, San Francisco.
9. Mikva interview.
10. Joseph Crapa, interview, December 5, 1990, Washington, D.C.
11. William Schneider, "JFK's Children: The Class of '74," *The Atlantic*, March 1989, p. 39.
12. Ibid., pp. 35–37.
13. Wright interview; B. F. Sisk, interview, May 19, 1989, by telephone.
14. Mary Russell, "Jostling for Position Begins in House," *Washington Post*, December 1, 1974. See also Dickenson, "A Too Formidable Reformer?" *Washington Star-News*, November 20, 1974.
15. John Pierson, "A New Boss for House Democrats?" *Wall Street Journal*, November 29, 1974.
16. "GOP, Democrats, Pick Liberals as Caucus Heads," *Wall Street Journal*, December 3, 1974.
17. Mills interview; Mills aide Gene Goss, interview, April 22, 1991.
18. Waxman interview. The notable exception was Ron Dellums of Berkeley, elected in 1970 as an antiwar socialist. In winning his primary that year, Dellums defeated incumbent Jeffrey Cohelan, who was Burton's brother-in-law. Burton advised Dellums to seek an assignment on the Armed Services Committee, where he could make his case against the Vietnam War. Twenty-two years later, on January 27, 1993, the House Democratic Caucus approved Dellums as the new chairman of Armed Services, a startling development given the reactionary views of such predecessors as Mendel Rivers and Edward Hebert.
19. Stephen Green, "Mills under Fire for Weekend Visit to Stripper," *Washington Post*, December 3, 1974; Mary Russell, "Hill Unit Assignments Stir Dispute," *Washington Post*, December 5, 1974. See also David E. Rosenbaum, "House Democrats End Mills's Rule over Committees," *New York Times*, December 3, 1974; Albert R. Hunt,

"Mills May Lose His Ways and Means Post as Committee Democrats Look to Ullman," *Wall Street Journal*, December 3, 1974; Anthony Ripley, "Mills Goes into Hospital after Being Told of Plan to Oust Him as Chairman," *New York Times*, December 4, 1974; "Democrats in House Vote to Expand Size of Ways and Means," *Wall Street Journal*, December 4, 1974; Lyle Denniston, "Mills Out as Chairman," *Washington Star-News*, December 4, 1974; "New Congress Organizes; Duncan Spencer, "Old Grievances Pursue Wilbur Mills," *Washington Star-News*, December 5, 1974; No Role for Mills," *Congressional Quarterly*, December 7, 1974; "Wilbur in Nighttown," *Newsweek*, December 16, 1974, pp. 21–22.

20. *Wall Street Journal*, December 6, 1974; Leo Rennert, "Commander Phil Burton and the 'Children's Crusade,'" *California Journal*, February 1975, p. 49.

21. Mary Russell, "Democrats End Hill Era," *Washington Post*, December 8, 1974; Mary Russell, "Liberals Are Added to Ways and Means," *Washington Post*, December 12, 1974.

22. Rowland Evans and Robert Novak, "New Era? From Mills to Burton," *Sacramento Union*, December 14, 1974.

23. Mary Ellen Leary, "I Aim to Open Up the System," *The Nation*, January 18, 1975, pp. 38–40.

24. *Congressional Record*, October 28, 1971, p. E11451; Richard D. Lyons, "Searching for Subversives: Dwindling but Not Dead," *New York Times*, October 20, 1974.

25. Mary McGrory, "The Old Terror Is Gone," *Washington Star-News*, January 23, 1975; interviews with Edwards; Mikva; Kastenmeier, December 18, 1988; *Congressional Record*, April 5, 1967, p. H3540; "Internal Security Committee," *Congressional Quarterly*, April 6, 1974, p. 905; Mary Russell, "House Panel on Security Periled Anew," *Washington Post*, January 6, 1975; Haynes Johnson, "Subversives Were Its Targets," *Washington Post*, January 14, 1975. See also Paul Rundquist, "Abolition of the House Internal Security Committee," March 9, 1988, Congressional Research Service Report for Congress.

26. Norman Mineta, interview, April 11, 1991, Washington, D.C.

27. Common Cause, "Report on House Committee Chairmen," January 13, 1975.

28. Interviews with Joseph Williams; Frost; Dawson Mathis, May 10, 1989 and April 10, 1991, Washington, D.C.; Frank Thompson, May 22, 1989, by telephone; former Thompson aide Don Koniewski, April 2, 1991, Washington, D.C.; Dietz; Mikva; John Burton, April 10, 1991; and Meeds. See also Sheppard, *Rethinking Congressional Reform*, pp. 202–7; Richard D. Lyons, "2 More Chairmen Ousted; 4 House Panels Unsettled," *New York Times*, January 17, 1975; Walter Taylor, "Wayne Hays Quick Rebound," *Washington Star-News*, January 17, 1975; "Half Rebellion," *New York Times* editorial, January 19, 1975; Walter Taylor, "Thompson Eyes Renewing Fight for Hays' Post," *Washington Star-News*, January 21, 1975; "The Trouble with Mr. Hays," *Washington Post* editorial, January 22, 1975; Richard L. Lyons, "Hays Is Challenged for Committee Chair," *Washington Post*, January 22, 1975; Michael J. Malbin, "Congress Report: House Democrats Oust Senior Members from Power," *National Journal*, January 25, 1975; "House Democratic Revolt Claims 3 Chairmen," *Congressional Quarterly*, January 25, 1975.

29. Paul Houston, "'We Got Him'; Ouster of Hebert Signals Fall of Seniority, Power Shift in House," *Los Angeles Times*, January 20, 1975.

30. Interviews with Frost; Mathis, May 10, 1989 and April 10, 1991; Koniewski; Dietz;

Thompson. See also Mary Russell, "Freshmen-Led Drama Yet to Be Played Out," *Washington Post*, January 19, 1975.

31. Lyons, "Hays is Challenged for Committee Chair"; Taylor, "Thompson Eyes Renewing Fight." Interviews with Frost; Mathis, April 10, 1991.

32. Mary McGrory, "It's Like Having Your Own Hit Man," *Washington Star-News*, January 20, 1975. "Half Rebellion," *New York Times* editorial, January 19, 1975; "The Trouble with Mr. Hays," *Washington Post*, January 22, 1975; Joseph Williams interview.

33. Arthur Siddon, "The Congressman Who Pushed His Way into No. 3 Post," *Chicago Tribune*, February 9, 1975.

34. "Chairman Phillip Burton: A Maverick Takes Control of the Democratic Caucus," *Democratic Review* (February-March 1975): 12–15.

35. James M. Naughton, "Leadership in the House: No Longer Order-Giving," *New York Times*, March 2, 1975; Martin F. Nolan, "A Would-Be Speaker," *Washington Star-News*, March 4, 1975; Martin Nolan, interview, July 20, 1988, Boston. At one point during their tour of San Francisco, Burton pointed to a building and told Nolan, "There are four Finnish families in that apartment building. I usually get a good vote from them." And later in the tour, Nolan said, "We went to a meeting of Filipino-Americans for Burton, Chinese-Americans for Burton, and then the Alice B. Toklas Club, at which a young man grabbed my arm and said, 'Congressman Burton is good for gay people,' and Burton came over laughing and said, 'Congressman Burton is good for straight people, too.'"

36. Henry Bradsher, "House Democrats Reject Arms Aid," *Washington Star-News*, March 12, 1975; John W. Finney, "House Democrats Opposed, 189-49, to Cambodian Aid," *New York Times*, March 13, 1975; Walter Taylor, "Caucus Role Strains Party Unity," *Washington Star-News*, March 30, 1975.

37. Rowland Evans and Robert Novak, "A Warning About Vetoes," *Washington Post*, March 30, 1975; Robert Gruenberg, "Ford Team Told: Stop the Cheap Shots at Congress," *Chicago Daily News*, March 31, 1975.

38. William Safire, "Escape Hatch for the Democratic Chairman," *New York Times*, April 28, 1975.

39. "Phillip Burton on Influence of Caucus," interviewed by Norman Kempster, *Washington Star-News*, May 19, 1975.

40. Rosen, "The Most Powerful Man in Congress?" p. 45; Hunter, "A California Democrat Delivers the Vote."

41. "House Democrats: Dispute over Caucus Role," *Congressional Quarterly*, May 3, 1975, pp. 911–15.

42. Tom Wicker, "Democrats in Disarray," *New York Times*, June 15, 1975; David E. Rosenbaum, "Congress Once Again Shows It Is Not 'Veto-Proof,'" *New York Times*, June 5, 1975; Marjorie Hunter and David E. Rosenbaum, "House Democrats Bitterly Split by Defeats and Generation Gap," *New York Times*, July 2, 1975; The *Times* article of July 2 noted, "Rarely has a party in Congress promised so much and accomplished so little," and cited a "generational chasm between young and old, between newly elected Representatives and their leaders . . . [who] are bewildered by the freshmen, find them politically naive and accuse them of seeking instant solutions to complex problems." Speaker Albert recited changes that had enhanced his leadership. But Les Aspin countered, "He's absolutely balmy. He's got no carrots and no sticks. Albert's got no levers." See also William Greider and

Barry Sussman, "The House Today: A Badly Tattered People's Institution," *Washington Post*, June 29, 1975; "Overestimating the Capability of Congress?" *Congressional Quarterly*, June 28, 1975, pp. 1343–57; "Capitol Marshmallows," *Newsweek*, June 30, 1975, pp. 14–16.

43. Richard P. Conlon, "Putting the 94th In Perspective," *Harvard Political Review* (Winter 1976): 25–31.

44. Marianne Means, "House Speaker May Retire at End of Term," *Los Angeles Herald Examiner*, June 29, 1975; Paul Houston, "2 House Leaders Who Want Promotions Plan to Donate to Colleagues' Campaigns," *Los Angeles Times*, August 2, 1975. See also Polsby, "Two Strategies of Influence," p. 245.

45. Walter Taylor, "Burton's Tactics in Caucus Draw Fire," *Washington Star*, September 23, 1975.

46. Joseph Albright, "Phillip Burton in Hospital; Heart Ailment Suspected," *Washington Star*, November 8, 1975.

13. TRIUMPH AT HOME

1. R. W. Apple, "Population Shift Likely to Give California GOP New Power," *New York Times*, September 26, 1970.

2. Gould interview; Gately interview. See also Alan C. Miller, "Mr. Inside and Mr. Outside: The Audacious Berman Brothers Built a Powerful Progressive Machine in California. But Can They Survive a New Political Order?" *Los Angeles Times Magazine*, March 29, 1992.

3. Leroy Hardy interview, June 29, 1989. For an excellent history of the 1971–73 California reapportionment, see Quinn, "Carving Up California."

4. "Critique of Gordon Knapp of Temporary Congressional Districts," part 2, submitted to the Supreme Court, carton 20, PB Papers. See also Michael Barone, Grant Ujifusa, and Douglas Matthews, *Almanac of American Politics* (Boston: Gambit, 1974), p. 133; T. Anthony Quinn, interview, March 29, 1994, Sacramento.

5. Theodore H. White, *The Making of the President, 1972* (New York: Atheneum, 1973), pp. 161, 177; Willie Brown interview.

6. Mankiewicz interview.

7. "1973 Masters Plan," carton 20, PB Papers. See also Sydney Kossen, "Remap Ruling—Demos Cheer, GOP Grumbles," *San Francisco Examiner*, November 29, 1973; George Murphy, "State Court OKs Redistricting Plan," *San Francisco Chronicle*, November 29, 1973. Mailliard to Special Masters, September 21, 1973, from "1973 California Supreme Court Masters Plan," carton 20, PB Papers.

8. Welfare rights attorney Ralph Abascal, interview, January 30, 1991, Berkeley. See also Rapaport, "Those Bad, Bad Burton Boys," pp. 79–80.

9. Jack Welter, "Next Speaker, Is It Brown or McCarthy?" *San Francisco Examiner*, June 7, 1974; Ken Maddy, interview, May 16, 1994, Sacramento; Dennis J. Opatrny, "McCarthy Is Sure He's Got the Votes," *San Francisco Examiner*, June 14, 1974.

10. Opatrny, "McCarthy Is Sure He's Got the Votes"; Opatrny, "McCarthy Assembly Speaker," *San Francisco Examiner*, June 18, 1974; Opatrny, "How McCarthy Beat Brown for Speaker," *San Francisco Examiner*, June 23, 1974; Ed Salzman, "How McCarthy Won the Speakership," *California Journal*, July 1974, p. 245. See also Ed

Salzman, "The Constant Quest for the Speakership," *California Journal,* March 1974, pp. 95–96.

11. "Willie Brown Off Key Panel," *San Francisco Chronicle,* August 6, 1974; Jack Welter, "McCarthy Beats Back Brown Bid for Speakership," *San Francisco Examiner,* December 2, 1974.

12. Willie Brown interview.

13. John Jacobs, "A Rebel Sunset—Ken Meade," *California Journal,* August 1976, p. 261.

14. Joseph Williams interview. Told of the incident many years later, John Burton said, "She knew me."

15. David Looman, interview, February 23, 1987, by telephone. The story of the 1975 mayor's race and the peace between the Burton and McCarthy forces is based on more than four dozen interviews the author conducted with colleague Phil Matier in February and March of 1987 for a series of articles in the *San Francisco Examiner* about the San Francisco political era from 1975 to 1987. Among the most useful interviews were those conducted with public officials Willie Brown, March 5, 1987; Hadley Roff, February 23, 1987; Art Agnos, March 2, 1987; John Burton, March 2, 1987; Dianne Feinstein, March 2, 1987; and Quentin Kopp, February 21, 1987; political consultants Clinton Reilly, February 26, 1987; Jack Davis, February 23, 1987; David Looman, February 23, 1987; Joseph Shumate, February 24, 1987; and Dick Pabich, February 27, 1987; and political activists Agar Jaicks, February 24, 1987; Calvin Welch, February 19, 1987; Susan Bierman, February 25, 1987; Claude Everhart, February 24, 1987; Jim Foster, February 26, 1987; Vincent Courtney, February 24, 1987; Richard DeLeon, February 27, 1987; and Morris Bernstein, February 24, 1987. See also Jerry Burns, "How a Liberal City Nearly Went Conservative," *California Journal,* February 1976, pp. 54–56.

16. Interviews with Michael Berman, March 28, 1991; Agnos; Willie Brown; McCarthy; John Foran, May 10, 1991, Sacramento; John Burton, May 10, 1989.

14. ONE VOTE

1. *Congressional Quarterly Almanac,* 1976, pp. 25–30. Interviews with former Hays chief of staff Frost; Bob Woodward, November 18, 1991, by telephone; Rudy Maxa, November 22, 1991, by telephone. Woodward was working on a profile of Hays, tentatively to be titled, "The Mayor of Capitol Hill." He said he did not get far enough along with his story to interview Hays, but he and Maxa both recalled hearing Hays's line about the double-ring ceremony. Bruce I. Oppenheimer and Robert L. Peabody, "The House Majority Leader's Contest—1976," delivered at the meeting of the American Political Science Association, Washington, D.C., September 1977.

2. *Congressional Quarterly Almanac,* 1976, pp. 25–30. Interviews with Wertheimer; Cohen, December 10, 1990; Mikva, April 10, 1991; Mark Gersh, May 18, 1989, by telephone.

3. O'Neill, *Man of the House,* p. 258.

4. Mary Russell, "Hill Scandal Fallout Feared by Freshmen," *Washington Post,* July 8, 1976.

5. Mineta interview; Mary Russell, "Struggle for Power in the House," *Washington Post*, June 6, 1976.
6. Rostenkowski interview; O'Neill interview.
7. Interviews with Leo Diehl, April 8, 1991, by telephone; Wright; O'Neill; Bolling; Rostenkowski. For the visit to Staggers, see Barry, *The Ambition and the Power*, pp. 12–16; Ben Palumbo, interview, April 4, 1991, Washington, D.C.
8. Interviews with Wright; Bolling; Rostenkowski.
9. These quotes are from Oppenheimer and Peabody's impressive seventy-five page account of the race, "The House Majority Leader's Contest," p. 34.
10. Thompson interview; Mikva interview.
11. Oppenheimer and Peabody, "The House Majority Leader's Contest," p. 15.
12. Ibid., pp. 22–23, 31–37.
13. Mathis interviews, May 10, 1989 and April 10, 1991; Rose interview.
14. The Annunzio and Skelton stories are from former House members who did not want to be quoted by name. The incident with Ryan is from his former aide, Joe Holsinger.
15. Jay Power, interview, April 2, 1991, Washington, D.C.
16. Wright interview, by telephone; Barry, *The Ambition and the Power*, pp. 24–25; Peabody and Oppenheimer, "The House Majority Leader's Contest," p. 48.
17. Interviews with Wright; O'Neill; Rostenkowski.
18. Oppenheimer and Peabody, "The House Majority Leader's Contest," p. 50; interviews with John Burton, May 10, 1989, and Palumbo, who recounted the Udall story.
19. Mary Russell, "It's a Bitter 4-Man Race for House Majority Leader," *Washington Post*, November 22, 1976; Schroeder interview.
20. Phillip Burton memo, November 16, 1976, from "1976 Majority Leader Race," carton 10, PB Papers.
21. Herblock cartoon, *Washington Post*, December 2, 1976; Claybrook et al., letter to the editor, December 2, 1976; "Dear Colleague" letter, December 2, 1976. David Broder, "The Second Most Important Election of 1976," *Washington Post*, December 1, 1976; interviews with Diehl; Billie Larsen, April 2, 1991, Washington, D.C.; Mikva; Claybrook.
22. Nicholas Masters, interview, May 28, 1991, by telephone; Jack Brooks, interview, April 12, 1991, Washington, D.C.; Wright interview; Barry, *The Ambition and the Power*, pp. 25–26.
23. Michael Berman, interview, December 28, 1988, Los Angeles; Beeman, May 22, 1989.
24. Oppenheimer and Peabody, "The House Majority Leader's Contest," n. 75.
25. "Meet the Press," December 5, 1975, transcript, vol. 20, no. 49, pp. 1–4, 11, 14–15.
26. Wright interview; Barry, *The Ambition and the Power*, pp. 26–27.
27. Proceedings of House Democratic Caucus, December 6, 1976, transcript, pp. 40–83; Rostenkowski interview; Palumbo interviews, May 23, 1989 and April 4, 1991.
28. It is also possible that Burton did ask for Ashley's vote, but, faced with Rostenkowski towering over him on the House floor and badgering him to vote for Wright as a "personal" favor, the Ohio Democrat simply caved.
29. The Wilson quote is from a Larry King article in the *Washington Star*, quoted in Oppenheimer and Peabody, "The House Majority Leader's Contest." Other quotes and description of atmosphere on the floor during the balloting is from interviews

with the following: Mikva, May 18, 1989 and April 10, 1991; Rostenkowski; Wright; Bolling; Mathis, May 10, 1989 and April 10, 1991; Rose; John Burton, May 10, 1989 and August 5, 1991; Mineta; Michael Berman, December 28, 1988 and May 11, 1989; Palumbo, May 23, 1989 and April 4, 1991; Gersh, May 18, 1989 and May 31, 1991; Beeman, December 6, 1988 and May 22, 1989; former Congressman Bill Stanton, December 5, 1988; Lud Ashley, May 22, 1989, by telephone; Bill Cable, April 3, 1991, Washington, D.C.; Bob Moss, April 5, 1991, Washington, D.C.; Don Edwards, May 17, 1989, by telephone; and George Miller, April 19, 1991.

30. Oppenheimer and Peabody, "The House Majority Leader's Contest," p. 3; Barry, *The Ambition and the Power*, p. 29; Foley interview.

31. House Democratic Caucus transcript, p. 82.

32. Interviews with Jaicks; Edwards; Michael Berman, December 28, 1988; Mikva, April 10, 1991; Kraus; Waxman.

33. Mary Russell, "Burton's Rejection as Majority Leader Laid to Aggressiveness, Over-Ambition," *Washington Post*, December 8, 1976.

34. John Fogarty, *San Francisco Chronicle*, December 11, 1976. See also Fogarty, "Burton: No Relaxing, No Regrets," *Washington Post*, January 3, 1977.

35. John Burton denied that he ever called those men to apologize on his brother's behalf. John Burton interview, August 5, 1991. Interviews with Mineta; House staffer and Leo Ryan aide, both of whom requested anonymity.

36. Anthony Beilenson, interview, May 10, 1994.

37. Tobin interview.

15. COMEBACKS AND TALL TREES

1. George Kundanis, interview, August 10, 1990, Washington, D.C.

2. Frank A. Aukofer, "Zablocki Tangles with Tip O'Neill," *Milwaukee Journal*, February 28, 1977; Foreign Affairs staff consultant Peter Abbruzzese, interview, July 10, 1991, by telephone; O'Neill to Burton, carton 10, PB Papers.

3. Morris Udall, interview, December 4, 1988, Washington, D.C.; Rose interview.

4. Interviews with environmental lobbyists Douglas Scott, May 18, 1991, San Juan Islands; David Weiman, December 5, 1990, Washington, D.C.; Interior Committee staffers Lee McElvain, August 10, 1990, Washington, D.C.; Stan Scoville, August 9, 1990, Washington, D.C.

5. Interviews with Gaylord Nelson, December 2, 1991, by telephone; Dr. Haydn Williams, July 12, 1991, by telephone; Jeff Farrow, December 7 and December 10, 1990, Washington, D.C.; Burton to Bush, January 3, 1977, from "PB Kudos, Awards," carton 9, PB Papers.

6. Interviews with Wayburn, January 16, 1991; John Amodio, February 6, 1991, Sacramento; Cleve Pinnix, May 15, 1991, Olympia; John Amodio, "Lobbyist for Redwood National Park Expansion," Sierra Club Oral History Project, 1982.

7. *Congressional Record*, speech of Phillip Burton, April 22, 1975, quoting the 1971 National Park Service report.

8. Robert E. Wolf, Congressional Research Service, Environment and Natural Resources Policy Division, August 26, 1977; Amodio interview; Robert A. Jones, *Los Angeles Times*, May 8, 1977; Dick Curry, interview, May 29, 1991, by telephone.

9. Carl Irving, "Redwood Companies Stir Up Hornet's Nest," *San Francisco Examiner*, March 30, 1977; Merlo to Burton, from "Redwoods 1," carton 32, PB Papers.

10. Interviews with Amodio; Pinnix, May 15, 1991; Clausen; Amodio, "Lobbyist for Redwood National Park Expansion." See also "Harvested Lands; Clausen, Burton Sharply Disagree," "Over 2,000 against Expansion Gather in Big Demonstration," and "Consensus on Burton: Barking up Wrong Trees," *Eureka Times Standard,* April 13, 1977; Alan Cline, "Lumbermen Rebel at Redwood Park Plan," *San Francisco Examiner*, April 13, 1977; Dexter Waugh, "Redwood Park Fans Clash with Labor Here," *San Francisco Examiner*, April 15, 1977.

11. Elizabeth Wehr, "Redwoods: Critical Vote Postponed," *Congressional Quarterly*, November 12, 1977; John Fogarty, "How George Meany Stalled Park Bill," *San Francisco Chronicle*, October 19, 1977; Amodio interview; Power interview.

12. Interviews with Power; Amodio; Curry; Wayburn, January 16, 1991; Pinnix, May 15, 1991; Clausen; and Rose. See also Democratic Study Group Fact Sheet, no. 95-28, February 6, 1978, carton 32, PB Papers; "Redwood Park Expansion," *Congressional Quarterly Almanac*, 1978, pp. 678–80.

13. Jim Bierne, interviews, March 8 and April 3, 1991, by telephone and in Washington, D.C.; James Abourezk, interview, June 5, 1991, by telephone.

14. Amodio interview.

15. Burton press releases, July 27, September 23, and October 20, 1977, from "Redwoods 2," carton 32, PB Papers; "Four-Step Minimum Wage Increase Approved," *Congressional Quarterly Almanac*, 1977, pp. 138–46; Carter to Burton, carton 32, PB Papers.

16. Richard E. Cohen, "The Return of Phil Burton?" *National Journal*, February 4, 1978; Struck to Burton on discussion with Raupe from green binder "'76," carton 10, PB Papers.

17. Phillip Shabecoff, "Rep. Burton Held Likely to Seek House Leader's Post," *New York Times*, February 23, 1978.

18. Wright interview.

19. John Berthelsen, "Park Payoff . . . Abuses Reported in Redwood Workers' Program," "Timber Faller Makes It Big," *Sacramento Bee*, February 18, 1979; John Berthelsen, "A Redwood Windfall," *Washington Post*, March 2, 1979; and a rebuttal by Nat Weinberg, "Fairness for Felled Loggers," *Washington Post*, March 31, 1979.

20. Quoted in Leo Rennert, "GAO Says Loggers' Aid Bill Abused," *Sacramento Bee*, July 8, 1980; John Fogarty, "GAO Finds Abuse in Lumberjacks' 'Rescue,'" *San Francisco Chronicle*, July 8, 1979.

21. Interviews with Power; Wayburn, January 30, 1991; Curry; Burton's copy of *Eureka Times Standard* story, from "Redwood Employees Protection Plan," carton 32, PB Papers; undated Affidavit of Phillip Burton, *Local 3-98 International Woodworkers of America, AFL-CIO v. Raymond J. Donovan, Secretary of Labor and California Employment Development Department.*

16. PARK BARREL

1. "Summary National Parks Legislation, Burton Years," carton 37, PB Papers.
2. Interviews with Miller, December 6, 1988; Beeman, January 9, 1991; Pinnix, May 15, 1991; Carl Pope, July 9, 1988 and May 14, 1991, San Francisco.

3. Turnidge interview.

4. Joe interview, April 5, 1991; Joan Moody, interview, April 30, 1991; Moody, "Meeting the Needs of Tomorrow Today: NPCA Interviews Phillip Burton," *National Parks and Conservation* (May 1979): 22–26. Interviewer Moody was kind enough to send the author her copy of the tape transcript and the tapes, from which some of these previously unpublished quotes were taken.

5. Charles Hayslett, "Chattahoochee Park Bill Held 'Hostage,'" *Atlanta Journal*, March 24, 1977; Phillip Burton speech, delivered at GGNRA's Fort Mason in San Francisco, October 30, 1978, tape recording, PB Papers; Pope Barrow, interview, August 9, 1990, Washington, D.C.

6. Udall interview. See also Mo Udall, "Udall Promises to Support Location-Patent System, Fight Leasing Bill," *Pay Dirt*, no. 5, October 1977, pp. 1–3.

7. Miller interview, April 19, 1991.

8. Robert Bauman, interview, July 7, 1991, by telephone.

9. Bud Heinselman, interview, May 29, 1991, by telephone; "Boundary Waters Canoe Area," "BWCA Media" (including Phillip Shabecoff's *New York Times* article of July 27, 1977), cartons 36 and 37, PB Papers.

10. William Oscar Johnson, "Passionate Suitors for a Wild Paradise," *Sports Illustrated*, October 10, 1977, pp. 50–58. See also Harold R. Kennedy, "A Noisy Environmental Fight over a Quiet Wilderness," *U.S. News and World Report*, October 31, 1977; statement of Donald Fraser, House Subcommittee on National Parks and Insular Affairs, August 4, 1977.

11. Gil Bailey, "Phil Burton: The 'Benevolent Steamroller' of Washington," *San Jose Mercury News*, July 30, 1978.

12. Moody, "Meeting the Needs of Tomorrow Today," p. 23; Burton speech, Fort Mason.

13. Moody, "Meeting the Needs of Tomorrow Today," p. 23; Burton speech, Fort Mason.

14. John Fogarty, "Burton Is Balancing the Books, House OKs Georgia Park," *San Francisco Chronicle*, February 15, 1978; Burton speech, Fort Mason; Dale Crane, interview, May 17, 1991, Seattle.

15. Arnold Hano, *New York Times Magazine*, August 17, 1969; Barrow, interview.

16. George Baker, "House Panel Deals Blow to Mineral King Ski Plans," *Fresno Bee*, February 28, 1978. Interviews with Pinnix, May 15, 1991; Crane. The author is indebted to Pinnix and Crane, who sat for more than fifteen hours of interviews, many on the specifics of the provisions of the Omnibus Parks and Recreation Act of 1978.

17. The source on gay orgies on the Sequoia did not want his name used.

18. Thompson interview; Moss interview.

19. "The Delaware Undammed," *New York Times* editorial, July 10, 1978; Editorial, "They're Reviving Tocks, a $1 Billion Pork-Barrel," *Philadelphia Inquirer*, July 7, 1978.

20. Mary Russell, "'Park-Barrel Bill' Clears House Panel," *Washington Post*, June 22, 1978.

21. Tom Eastham, "'Park Barrel' Bill Rolls," *San Francisco Examiner*, July 9, 1978.

22. *Congressional Record*, July 10, 1978, p. H6333.

23. Ibid., p. H6342; Thompson interview.

24. Burton speech, Fort Mason; *Congressional Record*, July 12, 1978, p. H6498.

25. Paul Houston, "House Okays Parks Bill Amid Charges of Burton Pressure," *Los Angeles Times*, July 13, 1978; Dick Kirschten, "Park Barrel Politics Triumphs on Capitol Hill," *National Journal*, August 19, 1978, p. 1322; Burton speech, Fort Mason.

26. "Soft Side of a Hard-Driving Official," *San Francisco Examiner*, September 20, 1978.

27. Roberta Hornig, "Rep. Burton Out to Save Parks Bill: He's a One-Man Conference Committee," *Washington Star*, October 12, 1978; Kathy Files Lacey, interview, April 3, 1991, Washington, D.C. Lacey, formerly Senator Alan Cranston's top environmental aide now holding the same job with Senator Dianne Feinstein, spent several hours explaining just what Burton did procedurally to get his omnibus bill passed.

28. *Congressional Record*, October 4, 1978, pp. H11559–60.

29. Burton speech, Fort Mason; George Baker, "Huge Park Bill's Chances Grow," *Sacramento Bee*, October 6, 1978; Curry interview.

30. Burton speech, Fort Mason.

31. *Congressional Record*, October 12, 1978, p. S18545. See also "Omnibus Parks Bill," *Congressional Quarterly Almanac*, 1978, pp. 704–7.

32. Barrow interview.

33. Abourezk interview; Bierne interview, April 3, 1991; press release of Sen. Harry F. Byrd, Jr., October 19, 1978; "Senate Blocks Trick on Manassas Park Bill," *Washington Post*, October 20, 1978.

34. Winnett to Burton, November 17, 1978, from "Omnibus Parks Bill-HR 12536," carton 41, PB Papers.

17. PROXY FIGHTS AND MORE PARKS

1. Richard E. Cohen, "They Won't Take Jim Wright for Granted This Time," *National Journal*, May 6, 1978, pp. 713–14.

2. Richard E. Cohen, "A Rematch in the Making?" *National Journal*, November 4, 1978.

3. Barry, *The Ambition and the Power*, p. 30; John M. Barry, interview, April 3, 1991; Leo Rennert, "Burton May Delay Bid for Leadership," *Sacramento Bee*, November 11, 1978.

4. Al McConogha, "Burton Denies Oberstar's Statement on Political Deal," *Minneapolis Tribune*, November 15, 1978; "Deal for House Job Denied by Burton, *San Jose Mercury News*, November 15, 1978; Herbert Johnson, "Rep. Oberstar's Latest Excess Is Just Too Much," letter to the editor, November 17, 1978. Johnson's letter began, "To now sully Rep. Burton's name with claims of vague deals to trade the BWCA for House leadership is just too much. Character assassination is one of the lowest of crimes." Dale Crane, interview, May 16, 1991, Olympia; Pinnix interview, May 17, 1991.

5. Barbara Strong, "Californian May Oppose Wright for House Speaker," *Dallas Morning News*, December 3, 1978.

6. John Fogarty, "Phillip Burton's New Post Puts Him in a Spotlight," *San Francisco Chronicle*, December 7, 1978; "Democratic Caucus Reactivates Committee Organization Panel," *National Journal*, December 16, 1978; Foley interview. Burke lost

to Republican George Deukmejian, who served one term as attorney general and two terms as governor of California.

7. Ellen Hume and Paul Houston, "O'Neill Teaches Calif. Members Political Lesson," *Los Angeles Times*, January 17, 1979; John Fogarty, "O'Neill's Privilege," *San Francisco Chronicle*, January 19, 1979; former O'Neill staffer Billie Larsen interview.

8. Interviews with Waxman; Michael Berman, December 28, 1988; and Robert Matsui, December 12, 1990, Washington, D.C.; Richard E. Cohen, "The Mysterious Ways Congress Makes Committee Assignments," *National Journal*, February 2, 1979, pp. 183–88. See also B. Drummond Ayres, Jr., "Rep. Waxman's Donations Linked to Bid for Power," *New York Times*, reprinted in *San Diego Union*, January 16, 1979; Mary Russell, "Leadership Keeps House Budget Committee in Liberal State," *Washington Post*, January 21, 1979; Russell, "Rep. Preyer Loses Battle to Head Key Health Unit," *Washington Post*, January 31, 1979; Ellen Hume, "Waxman Wins Challenge to House System," *Los Angeles Times*, January 31, 1979; Leo Rennert, "Frustrated California Demo Bloc Plans New Strategy," *Sacramento Bee*, January 25, 1979.

9. Mary Russell, "Liberal House Democrat Contest: Loyalists vs. Independent," *Washington Post*, February 26, 1979; Ellen Hume, "Californians in the House: Clout Divided," *Los Angeles Times*, February 6, 1979.

10. Panetta to Burton, April 10, 1979, carton 6, PB Papers; Leon Panetta, interview, July 24, 1991, by telephone.

11. Spellman to Burton, October 11, 1979, from "HR 5419, Goodloe Byron (PL 96-87)," carton 40, PB Papers; Bierne interview, March 8, 1991; Paul Hodge, "Chief Is Buried in Piscataway," *Washington Post*, November 12, 1979; Phil Swann, "Chief Turkey Tayac Is Buried in Indian Ritual," *Washington Star*, November 13, 1979.

12. Phillip Burton, summary of the provisions of HR 3757, including Channel Islands National Park, February 20, 1980, carton 36, PB Papers. See also John Fogarty, "A Parks Bill That Kept Growing," *San Francisco Chronicle*, February 22, 1980; Jeff Mapes, "'Parks Barrel' Bill Clears Congress," *Petaluma Argus Courier*, February 29, 1980.

13. For a fuller discussion of the Sagebrush Rebellion, see Joe Bauman, "The 'Thirteen Western Colonies' Take on the Feds: The Sagebrush Rebellion," *Cry California* (Summer 1980): 5–9.

14. James Santini, interview, July 2, 1991, by telephone; Santini former staffer Mary Lou Cooper, interview, July 9, 1991, by telephone; Crane interview; "HR 7306: Lake Tahoe Community; '79–80 Santini-PB Bill," carton 36, PB Papers; DSG Legislative Report, "Federal Land Disposal and Acquisition in Lake Tahoe Basin Area," September 8, 1980; *Congressional Record*, September 8, 1980, pp. H8431–38. See also Ron Roach, "Jerry's Suit for Divorce from Pat's Tahoe Marriage," *California Journal*, March 1978.

15. Santini interview; Leo Rennert, "Burton's Half-Loaf," *California Journal*, January 1981. See also Al Donner, "Congress Passes Tahoe Land Acquisition Bill," *Sacramento Union*, December 6, 1980.

16. Turnidge interview; Lacey interview.

17. Harry Jaffe, "Big Sur Bill Clears Subcommittee," *San Francisco Examiner*, States News Service, July 22, 1980.

18. Pat Griffith, "Panetta Big Sur Bill Clears House by 8-Vote Margin in Political Cliff-Hanger," *Monterey Herald*, August 26, 1980; Griffith, "Hayakawa, Friends of Big Sur Vow to Block Push for Panetta Bill," *Monterey Herald*, September 22, 1980;

Ward Sinclair, "Big Sur Coastline Caught Up in a Riptide on Potomac," *Washington Post*, October 15, 1980; Panetta interview.

19. Adams to Burton, February 17, 1981, from "Ansel Adams Correspondence," carton 7, PB Papers.

20. Ward Sinclair, "Building an Empire: Burton is 'Lord' of Parks, Territories," *Washington Post*, September 8, 1980.

21. Foley interview.

22. Herbst to Udall, May 14, 1980, in House Committee on Interior and Insular Affairs, 96th Congress, 2d session, H. Report 96-1024 (to accompany HR 3), pp. 52–53, from "HR 3," carton 35, PB Papers.

23. Interviews with Sierra Club lobbyist Tim Mahoney, June 4, 1991, by telephone; Udall; Pinnix, May 17, 1991; Crane; Bauman.

24. Lemons interview, June 16, 1994.

25. *Congressional Record*, May 19, 1980, pp. H3768–82.

18. YOUR MOTHER'S ARMS

1. See Jack Citrin, introduction to *California and the American Tax Revolt: Proposition 13 Five Years Later*, by Paul Richter (principal writer), edited by Terry Schwadron (Berkeley: University of California Press, 1984), pp. 3–8.

2. See Tim Reiterman with John Jacobs, *Raven: The Untold Story of the Rev. Jim Jones and His People* (New York: E. P. Dutton, 1982), esp. ch. 28, "San Francisco in Thrall," pp. 262–72, and ch. 36, "Exodus," pp. 331–41. Despite the perception that Jones had up to two thousand Peoples Temple members on the voter roles in San Francisco, no more than two dozen voted. But Jones could move hundreds of people around on a moment's notice for a political demonstration or for campaign work.

3. *San Francisco Examiner* reporter Lynn Ludlow, interview, December 20, 1991, by telephone. See also Ludlow's brilliant five-part series on the City Hall killings, written five years after the fact, especially parts one and two: "The Dan White File: A Moment of Madness Changed San Francisco Forever," and "The Politics of Murder," *San Francisco Examiner*, September 6–7, 1983, from which many of these details are taken.

4. Cynthia Willet, "The Next Speaker? Probably Howard Berman," *California Journal*, November 1979, pp. 380–81; Robert P. Studer, "McCarthy as Speaker: Unique Ability to Persuade," *California Journal*, November 1979, pp. 382–83.

5. Willie Brown interview; McCarthy interview; Assemblyman Phil Isenberg, interview, June 1, 1991, Sacramento.

6. Interviews with Knox; Willie Brown; Isenberg; Foran; Howard Berman, April 2, 1991, Washington, D.C.; Leo McCarthy, February 12, 1991; Willie Brown oral history-in-process, begun on December 17, 1991, conducted by Gabrielle Morris, Regional Oral History Office, Bancroft Library, UC Berkeley. See also Dan Walters, "Anatomy of a Battle for the Assembly Speakership," *Sacramento Union*, February 8, 1980; Ed Salzman, "The Bitter Berman-McCarthy Struggle for Speakership Power," *California Journal*, February 1981, pp. 48–50.

7. Al Martinez, "Speakership Fight: A Study in Power, 'Smell of Blood' in Capitol," *Los Angeles Times*, February 19, 1980.

8. Ed Salzman, "And the Speaker Is . . . Berman, McCarthy, None of the Above,"

California Journal, August 1980, p. 315; Jerry Gillam, "Bitter Struggle for Speakership Spills into Assembly Campaigns," *Los Angeles Times*, October 16, 1980.

9. Brown oral history-in-process.

10. Ibid.

11. Ed Rollins, interview, December 10, 1990, Washington, D.C. Rollins said he "never dreamed" that, ten years later, Willie Brown would still be speaker and would break Jesse Unruh's record as the longest serving Speaker in California history. Indeed, as of mid-1995, Brown was *still* speaker. Also, Willie Brown interview, May 24, 1994; Ken Maddy interview, May 17, 1994; James L. Richardson, "Willie Brown: The Play for Power," *Alicia Patterson Foundation Reporter* 6, no. 1 (November 1993): 22–35. Richardson is at work on a biography of Brown. See also James Richardson, "Speaker Brown: A Career of Struggle and Style," *Sacramento Bee*, December 4, 1994.

12. Claudia Luther and Robert Fairbanks, "Willie Brown Vies for Speaker's Post," *Los Angeles Times*, November 21, 1980; Luther and Fairbanks, "Governor Joins Speaker Battle," *Los Angeles Times*, November 22, 1980.

13. Claudia Luther and Tracy Wood, "Willie Brown New Assembly Speaker," *Los Angeles Times*, December 2, 1980; Linda Breakstone, "New Speaker Willie Brown Rose from Poor to Powerful," *Los Angeles Herald Examiner*, December 7, 1980; Dan Walters, "Speaker's Feud Ended in Surprise," *Sacramento Union*, December 7, 1980.

14. Mike Qualls, "Willie Brown Tells Why He Won't Be 'Imperial' Speaker," *Los Angeles Herald Examiner*, December 4, 1980.

15. Eric Brazil, "Why the GOP turned to Willie Brown," *Marin Independent Journal*, Gannett News Service, November 26, 1980.

16. Willie Brown interview, August 21, 1991; Michael Berman interview, December 28, 1988 and March 28, 1991.

17. Interviews with former House Democratic Whip Tony Coelho, August 10, 1990, Washington, D.C.; Michael Berman, December 28, 1988 and March 28, 1991; Miller, August 20, 1991.

18. Phillip Burton press release, February 2, 1981, carton 21, PB Papers.

19. T. R. Reid, "Liberal Leaders, Foot Soldiers Gird for Battles in Reagan Era," *Washington Post*, February 6, 1981; Margot Hornblower, "Mountain Man's Turf: Perkins Stoutly Resists Reagan's Move to Cut Education, Nutrition Aid, Public Service Jobs," *Washington Post*, April 6, 1981; Marjorie Hunter, "Budget Cuts Test Easygoing Legislator," *New York Times*, May 20, 1981.

20. Fred Feinstein, interview, December 12, 1990, Washington, D.C.; Lemons interview, April 11, 1991; Subcommittee on Insular and International Affairs Staff Director Jeff Farrow, interviews, December 7 and 10, 1990; an Interior Committee staff member who spoke on background.

21. Gramm was later elected to the Senate, where he became one of the most partisan and conservative Republicans, chaired the Republican Senatorial Campaign Committee, and is considered a leading Republican candidate for president in 1996.

22. Leo Rennert, "Burton Criticizes Demo Leadership for Poor Strategy," *Sacramento Bee*, May 3, 1981; interviews with Fred Feinstein; Interior Committee budget officer Bill Anderson, August 10, 1990, Washington, D.C.; Vic Fazio, September 24, 1993, Washington, D.C.; *Congressional Record*, June 26, 1981, pp. H3813–14; *Congressional Insight* 5, no. 28 (July 10, 1981).

23. Fazio interview.

24. *Congressional Record,* May 7, 1981, p. H2006.

25. Fred Feinstein interview.

26. Had Rostenkowski chosen to take the whip's job, he likely would have been Speaker of the House. Tom Foley was elevated instead. He became majority leader in 1987 and moved up to Speaker when Jim Wright was forced to resign in 1989.

27. Leo Rennert, "Burton Criticizes Demo Leadership for Poor Strategy," *Sacramento Bee,* June 4, 1981; John Rousselot, interview, May 28, 1991, by telephone.

28. Robert Naylor, interview, May 30, 1991, by telephone; Quinn interview.

29. *San Diego Union,* February 8, 1981; *Sacramento Bee,* February 15, 1981; Robert Dornan, interview, August 14, 1988, New Orleans.

30. Naylor interview; Gorman interview. The tablecloth was later framed and hangs on the wall of GOP reapportionment consultant Tony Quinn.

31. Even so, of 180 House elections in California conducted between 1982 and 1988, the only incumbent Democrat to lose was Jerry Patterson. Bob Dornan beat him in 1984 when he moved south into Patterson's Orange County district.

32. For full details on Burton's 1981 reapportionment, see cartons 21–25, PB Papers.

33. Ed Davis, interview, April 5, 1991, Washington, D.C.; Ed Zschau, interview, February 20, 1990, Sacramento; Rose Institute, "California Redistricting: Proposition 6 Compliance," p. 14.

34. Interviews with Leroy Hardy, June 29, 1989 and March 26, 1991; Michael Berman, December 28, 1988 and March 28, 1991; Edwards; Beilenson; Fiedler; Congressman Bill Thomas, June 6, 1991. See also Ellen Hume, "Lawmaker in Powerful Role Has Colleagues on Edge: Rep. Phillip Burton is Key Redistricting Figure," *Los Angeles Times,* July 23, 1981.

35. Daniel B. Levine, acting director of Bureau of the Census, to Phillip Burton, April 9, 1981 draft, from "1980 California Census Tracts," carton 25, PB Papers.

36. John Berthelsen, "Computers For Redistricting Tilt Toward GOP, Critics Say," *Sacramento Bee,* November 30, 1980.

37. "Redistricting: Gov. Gerry's Monuments," *Congressional Quarterly,* May 9, 1981, p. 811.

38. Hume, "Lawmaker"; Jim Boren, "Reapportion Plan: 3-Way Fresno Split," *Modesto Bee,* July 26, 1981; Coelho interview; Michael Berman interview, March 28, 1991.

39. Claudia Luther, "2 Democrats' Hopes for Congress Ignite Redistricting Feud," *Los Angeles Times,* August 31, 1981; Ed Mendel, "Burton Foes Working on Remap Plan," *Sacramento Union,* August 22, 1981; Claire Cooper, "Roberti To Do Own Redistricting Map, Direct Challenge to Burton," *Sacramento Bee,* August 22, 1981.

40. Burton's September 9, 1981 press conference in Sacramento was widely covered. See Chuck Buxton, "Burton Draws State Congressional Lines in Democratic Colors," *San Jose Mercury News,* September 10, 1981; Claire Cooper, "Demo Gains Seen in Congress Remap," *Sacramento Bee,* September 19, 1981; Jeff Greer, "GOP Furor over Burton Seat," *San Rafael Independent Journal,* September 10, 1981; W. E. Barnes, "Convoluted Turns in Congressional Plan," *San Francisco Examiner,* September 10, 1981; Pete Golis, "Burton's Reapportionment Decree," *Sonoma Press Democrat,* September 13, 1981.

41. "State Politics and Redistricting, Parts I and II," carton 22, PB Papers. See California Assembly and Senate Conference Committee, September 11, 1981, transcript, p. 6.

42. Michael Berman interview, March 28, 1991. See also "'81 Reappo—Media," cartons 21 and 22, PB Papers.

43. "'81 Reappo—Media," carton 21, PB Papers. For Naylor comments, see California Assembly and Senate, p. 8.

44. "Phil Burton's Plan Is an Insult," *San Francisco Examiner* editorial, September 11, 1981; "Congressional Districts: A Classic Gerrymander," *San Jose Mercury News* editorial, September 11, 1981; "Democratic Remap a Travesty of Greed," *Sacramento Union* editorial, September 22, 1981; W. E. Barnes, "GOP Readies Redistricting Battle," *San Francisco Examiner*, September 11, 1981.

45. Declaration of Tony Quinn to the California Supreme Court, November 6, 1981, carton 22, PB Papers.

46. Jourdan to Burton, from "Reappo—Media," carton 21, PB Papers; Rian Malan, "BOSS: You Don't Want To Cross Phil Burton, the Man Who Carved Up California," *California*, November 1981, p. 90.

47. See Quinn, "Carving Up California," pp. 1–53; Claudia Luther, "Speaker's Crown Firmly Affixed: Redistricting Plan Unites Democrats, Gets Rid of GOP Coalition," *Los Angeles Times*, September 28, 1981; Claire Cooper, "Power Play: Remap Draws Feuding Democrats Together," *Sacramento Bee*, September 20, 1981.

48. Quinn, "Carving Up California," pp. 53–72. According to Quinn, the Republicans were split on the issue of at-large elections, with one lawyer, former Congressman Charles Wiggins, opposing it, while lawyers for the Republican National Committee espoused it. They argued between themselves before the California Supreme Court, six of whose seven members were appointed by Democrats.

49. Ibid., pp. 78–79. The Republican effort against Rose Bird succeeded four years later when Bird and two other Brown appointees were removed from office.

50. Huerta interview.

51. Bauman interview.

52. This is highly speculative, but according to the author's calculation, based on multiple interviews, Burton may have lost as many as thirteen votes in California in the 1976 race and won sixteen. After the 1982 elections, the California delegation might have voted 24-4 for Burton over Wright, assuming there would be such an election. Those voting for Wright likely would have been Tony Coelho, Ed Roybal, Augustus Hawkins, and Glenn Anderson. Even if Mineta had voted for Wright in 1976, sources said, there would have been little reason for him to vote for Wright again. By now, B. F. Sisk, John McFall, Bizz Johnson, Robert Leggett, James Corman, John Moss, Charles Wilson, and Jim Lloyd were all out of Congress and Ryan was dead.

19. AIN'T THAT A BITCH!

1. Interviews with John Burton, August 5, 1991; Willie Brown, August 21, 1991; George Miller, April 19, 1991.

2. *San Rafael Independent Journal*, April 22, 1981.

3. Sellers interview, August 9, 1990.

4. Miller interview, August 20, 1991.

5. Dennis J. Opatrny and Carol Pogash, "John Burton: I Just Want to Go Home," *San Francisco Examiner*, March 7, 1982.

6. Interviews with Agnos; Jack Molinari, December 13, 1991, San Francisco; Nancy

Pelosi, May 24, 1992, San Francisco. Rollins quote is from *San Rafael Independent Journal*, June 5, 1982, from "JLB Quits Congress," carton 4, PB Papers.

7. Willie Brown interview.

8. Shelley was the son of the late Mayor Jack Shelley, Burton's former rival. He had earlier applied for a job in Burton's office, but the application sat on Burton's desk for a year. In 1978, Burton ran into Shelley's mother and said, "Oh, Thelma, I'm sorry. I didn't know what to do." She replied, "Phil, you always were and still are one of the biggest bastards I've ever known." Burton laughed and said, "He's got the job." Burton became a mentor to Shelley, who idolized him. Kevin Shelley, interview, June 5, 1991, San Francisco.

9. W. E. Barnes, "Marks Deciding on a Challenge to Phil Burton," *San Francisco Examiner*, March 10, 1982; Carl Irving, *San Francisco Examiner*, March 13, 1982.

10. Martin Smith, "Stories about Burton and Marks," *Sacramento Bee*, October 10, 1982. Duane Garrett, interview, July 19, 1988, San Francisco.

11. Mike Nevin, interview, May 30, 1991, San Francisco.

12. Bob Barry, interview, May 30, 1991; Paul Chignell, interview, May 30, 1991, San Francisco.

13. Larry Liebert, "Tip O'Neill Lauds Phil Burton," *San Francisco Chronicle*, April 26, 1982.

14. John Burton interview, August 5, 1991.

15. Bill Boldenweck, "Fifth District's Eyes More on November than Primary," *San Francisco Examiner*, June 4, 1982.

16. Ellen Hume, "Godfather of California Politics May Be Mortal," *Los Angeles Times*, May 3, 1982.

17. Frances Fitzgerald, *Cities on a Hill: A Journey through Contemporary American Cultures* (New York: Simon and Schuster, 1986), esp. pp. 25–36. See also Randy Shilts, *The Mayor of Castro Street* (New York: St. Martin's Press, 1982), pp. 111–85.

18. Both the dialogue and history about Bill Kraus are from Randy Shilts, *And the Band Played On: People, Politics and the AIDS Epidemic* (New York: St. Martin's Press, 1987), pp. 13, 162, 234; Dick Pabich, interview, June 23, 1988, San Francisco.

19. Kraus to Burton, April 27, 1982, from "1981–82 PB Campaign—Gay/Lesbian," carton 4, PB Papers.

20. Accounts of Kraus's standing in the gay community, of the leather bar incident, Gay Freedom Day parade, and Gay Games are from Kevin Shelley interview; Gwen Craig, interview, June 6, 1991, by telephone; Pat Jackson, interview, August 21, 1991, by telephone.

21. Jim Lauer and Brad Bannon, "Confidential Report on a Poll Conducted in the Fifth Congressional District of California for Congressman Phil Burton," DSG Survey Research, pp. 1–75. Quotes from pp. 39, 17. Poll was made available courtesy of Michael Berman.

22. Larry Liebert, "Marks' Fundraising Letter Paints Him as Conservative," *San Francisco Chronicle*, July 9, 1982.

23. John Fogarty, "Watt Halts Buying of New Park Lands," *San Francisco Chronicle*, February 20, 1981; Robert A. Jones, "Parks Join Budget Cut Target List," *Los Angeles Times*, March 24, 1981.

24. Phillip Burton press release, March 22, 1982, from "Watt et al.," carton 43, PB Papers.

25. Carl Pope, interview, May 14, 1991; Power interview. Power observed the scene and

recounted the conversation. Pope denied that Burton threatened him or demanded the cover, but conceded that Burton had "requested" it.

26. Michael Novelli, interview, May 29, 1991, by telephone.

27. Michael Berman, "Burton Campaign Strategy Memo: Confidential," October 3, 1982, pp. 1, 10–11. The memo was made available courtesy of Michael Berman.

28. Ibid, p. 29.

29. Milton Marks press conference, transcript, August 23, 1982; Marshall Kilduff, "Marks' Ads Assail Burton the Man," *San Francisco Chronicle*, August 24, 1982; Dennis Farney, "Phil Burton Has Cut Many Political Deals; Is It One Too Many?" *Wall Street Journal*, September 28, 1982; Jenkins interview; Murphy interview.

30. Larry Liebert, *San Francisco Chronicle*, September 4, 1982; interviews with Power; Barry; Chignell.

31. Reno Rapagnani, interview, May 30, 1991, San Francisco.

32. Rich Hays, interview, May 31, 1991, San Francisco; Novelli interview; *Sun Reporter* editorial, September 16, 1982.

33. Michael Berman, "Burton Campaign Strategy," p. 28; Kraus to Burton, from "1981–82 PB Campaign—Gay/Lesbian," carton 4, PB Papers; debate quotes are from Carl Irving, "Marks Assails Burton, Who Criticizes Reagan, In Debate," *San Francisco Examiner*, September 25, 1982.

34. Carl Irving, "Poll Gives Burton a Lead of 10 Points over Marks," *San Francisco Examiner*, October 15, 1982; Jennifer Foote, "Round Two of Heavyweight Debate," *San Francisco Examiner*, October 19, 1982; "Burton: The Arrogance of Power," *San Francisco Examiner*, October 24, 1982; Shelley interview.

35. Windmiller interview.

36. Hays interview.

37. Novelli exit memo to Burton, November 23, 1982.

38. Jennifer Foote, "Burton Re-elected by 'Sticking to Issues,'" *San Francisco Examiner*, November 3, 1982.

39. Power interview.

20. THE MAN WHO WOULD BE SPEAKER

1. Novelli interview. After Burton's death, Novelli published that anecdote in an *Examiner* collection of stories about Burton. Afterwards, an irritated Barbara Boxer went up to Novelli and said, "Which was I, Attila the Hun or Winnie the Pooh?"

2. Proceedings of the House Committee on Interior and Insular Affairs, transcript, January 26, 1983, pp. 53–54.

3. Naylor interview. See also Quinn, "Carving Up California," pp. 79–94; Malan, "BOSS"; Bill Cavala, interviews, February 2, 1991 and June 1, 1994, Sacramento; Michael Berman interview, March 28, 1991. See also Tracy Wood, "Rep. Burton to Be Excluded in Remapping," *Los Angeles Times*, November 11, 1982.

4. Bruce Cain, interview, January 7, 1992, Berkeley; Cavala interviews, February 2, 1991 and June 1, 1994; Michael Berman interview, March 28, 1991; Foran interview. See also Quinn, "Carving Up California," pp. 94–98; Susan Smith, "New California Redistricting Map Approved," *Congressional Quarterly*, January 8, 1983, p. 9.

5. Howard Berman interview; interview with a Burton aide who spoke on background. See also Andy Plattner, "Democrats Set Stage for House Rules Battle," *Congressional*

Quarterly, December 11, 1982, p. 3031; John Fogarty, "Freshmen Warm Up for 98th Congress," *San Francisco Chronicle,* December 13, 1982.

6. Robert Matsui eulogy, *Phillip Burton: Memorial Addresses Delivered in Congress* (Washington, D.C.: Government Printing Office, 1983), p. 36; Matsui interview.

7. *Congressional Record,* December 17, 1982, p. H10267, and December 18, 1982, pp. H10357–58; Miller interview, April 19, 1991.

8. *Congressional Record,* December 21, 1982, p. H10731.

9. In 1987 Democrat Roemer was elected governor of Louisiana. But on the eve of his 1991 re-election campaign, Roemer switched his registration to Republican. The move did him no good. He finished third in the primary to Democrat and former Governor Edwin Edwards and former Klan and Nazi leader turned Republican David Duke.

10. Howard Berman interview; Billie Larsen interview.

11. Billie Larsen interview.

12. Laurence McQuillan, "Burton Asks $10 Million to Study AIDS Disease," *San Francisco Examiner,* March 18, 1983; Pabich interview.

13. Interviews with Mahoney; Patty Schifferle, February 1, 1991, San Francisco; Scott; Pope; Charles Cluson, June 4, 1991, by telephone; Andy Weissner, June 6, 1991, by telephone; Lacey; Clausen. See also Dennis H. Roth, "The Wilderness Movement and the National Forests, 1980–1984," Forest Service History Series, August 1988; "RARE II Bills Sail through the House, Stall in Senate," *Congressional Quarterly Almanac,* 1983, p. 342.

14. Public Lands Subcommittee, markup session of California Wilderness Bill, HR 7702, July 30, 1980, pp. 4–6. See also George Baker, "Fight for Forests; Reps. Johnson, Burton, Battle over Wilderness," *Fresno Bee,* October 19, 1979; Ellen Hume, "Huge Wilderness Area OKd by House," *Los Angeles Times,* August 19, 1980.

15. Newsom interview; Mahoney interview; the weekly newsletter is *Congressional Insight,* July 17, 1981; Chappie quote is from *Eureka Times Standard,* July 28, 1981— both are from "HR 7702—California Wilderness Bill," carton 38, PB Papers.

16. Palumbo interview, April 4, 1991.

17. Interviews with Huerta; Power; Davis; Barry.

18. Molinari interview.

19. Wayburn interview, February 13, 1991; Farber interview, December 13, 1988; Rose interview; death certificate, carton 45, PB Papers. See also editions of *San Francisco Examiner* and *Chronicle,* April 12 and 13, 1983, esp. Don Lattin and Edvins Beitiks, "Death of a Titan," *San Francisco Examiner,* April 11, 1983; Leo Rennert, "Rep. Burton, Champion of Liberal Causes, Dies," *Sacramento Bee,* April 11, 1983.

EPILOGUE

1. Sherrie Keith story is from Robert Roth, "Mourners Pay Tribute to Burton," *Sacramento Bee,* April 14, 1983; Novelli interview.

2. Agnos interview.

3. Pelosi interview. The gay candidate was a family law and women's rights attorney named Roberta Achtenberg. Several years later she was elected to the San Francisco Board of Supervisors and was an early and outspoken supporter of Bill Clinton's

presidential campaign. When President Clinton selected her as an assistant secretary of housing, she became the highest-ranking openly gay official in his young administration.

4. Interview with Willie Brown, Sacramento, January 26, 1995. For details of how Brown won back his speakership, see John Jacobs, Forum Section, *Sacramento Bee,* "The Two Secrets That Helped Willie Win," February 8, 1995.

5. Greg Lucas, *San Francisco Chronicle,* "Burton Offers Bill That Would Make Poverty a Crime," December 13, 1994.

6. Quinn interview; Barry, *The Ambition and the Power,* p. 742.

7. David Rogers, *Wall Street Journal,* "New Democratic Leadership of House Is Guided by Memories of Rival Reformers Bolling, Burton," June 22, 1989.

8. Lemons interview, May 21, 1991. See also John Jacobs, "Watch Out Agribusiness: It's Miller Time," *California Republic,* June 1991, pp. 32–33.

9. Gerald Adams, interview, November 24, 1993, San Francisco. Adams, who covers urban affairs for the *San Francisco Examiner,* has carefully followed the unfolding story of what will happen to the San Francisco Presidio.

10. For details, see the four-part series in the *Baltimore Sun,* January 22–25, 1995, "The Disabling of America," especially pt. 1, "America's Most Wanted Welfare Plan," by John B. O'Donnell and Jim Haner.

11. Fazio interview.

12. Interviews with Al From, Sacramento, January 13, 1995, and Susan Rasky, who covered Gingrich as a *New York Times* correspondent, April 4, 1994, Berkeley.

13. Interview with Lou Cannon by telephone, February 27, 1995.

14. Interview with Leo Rennert by telephone, February 20, 1995.

15. George Raine, "Phillip Burton Statue Unveiled in S.F.," *San Francisco Examiner,* June 16, 1991. See also John Jacobs, "Phil Burton Draws a Crowd—Eight Years after His Death," *San Francisco Examiner,* June 14, 1991.

BIBLIOGRAPHY

Albert, Carl, with Danny Goble. *Little Giant: The Life and Times of Speaker Carl Albert.* Norman: University of Oklahoma Press, 1990.

Ambrose, Stephen E. *Nixon: The Education of a Politician, 1913–1962.* New York: Simon and Schuster, 1987.

Barone, Michael. *Our Country: The Shaping of America from Roosevelt to Reagan.* New York: Free Press, 1990.

Barone, Michael, Grant Ujifusa, and Douglas Matthews. *The Almanac of American Politics.* Boston: Gambit, 1972–1974; Washington, D.C.: National Journal, 1975–.

Barry, John M. *The Ambition and the Power: A True Story of Washington.* New York: Penguin, 1989.

Beatty, Jack. *The Rascal King: The Life and Times of James Michael Curley, 1878–1958.* Reading, Mass.: Addison-Wesley, 1992.

Bell, Charles G., and Charles M. Price, *California Government Today: Politics of Reform?* Chicago: Dorsey Press, 1988.

Bolling, Richard. *House Out of Order.* New York: E. P. Dutton, 1966.

———. *Power in the House: A History of the Leadership of the House of Representatives.* New York: E. P. Dutton, 1968.

Broder, David. *Changing of the Guard: Power and Leadership in America.* New York: Penguin, 1980.

Bullough, William A. *The Blind Boss and His City: Christopher Augustine Buckley and Nineteenth-Century San Francisco.* Berkeley: University of California Press, 1979.

Burke, Vincent J., and Lee Burke, *Nixon's Good Deed: Welfare Reform.* New York: Columbia University Press, 1974.

Burns, James MacGregor. *Leadership.* New York: Harper and Row, 1979.

Butler, David, and Bruce Cain. *Congressional Redistricting: Comparative and Theoretical Perspectives.* New York: Macmillan, 1992.

Cain, Bruce E. *The Reapportionment Puzzle.* Berkeley: University of California Press, 1984.

Cannon, Lou. *Ronnie and Jesse: A Political Odyssey.* New York: Doubleday, 1969.

————. *Reagan.* New York: G. P. Putnam, 1982.

Caro, Robert A. *The Power Broker: Robert Moses and the Fall of New York.* New York: Alfred A. Knopf, 1974.

————. *The Years of Lyndon Johnson: The Path to Power.* New York: Alfred A. Knopf, 1982.

————. *The Years of Lyndon Johnson: Means of Ascent.* New York: Alfred A. Knopf, 1990.

Carson, Clayborne. *In Struggle: SNCC and the Black Awakening of the 1960s.* Cambridge, Mass.: Harvard University Press, 1981.

Citrin, Jack. Introduction to *California and the American Tax Revolt: Proposition 13 Five Years Later,* by Paul Richter (principal writer), edited by Terry Schwadron. Berkeley: University of California Press, 1984.

Congressional Quarterly, Inc. *Congressional Quarterly Almanac.* Washington, D.C., 1966–1983.

————. *Inside Congress: A Contemporary Affairs Report.* Washington, D.C., January 1976.

Cummings, Milton C., Jr., and Robert L. Peabody, "The Decision to Enlarge the Committee on Rules: An Analysis of the 1961 Vote." In *New Perspectives on the House of Representatives,* edited by Robert L. Peabody and Nelson W. Polsby. Chicago: Rand McNally, 1963.

Davidson, Roger H., and Walter J. Oleszek. *Congress against Itself.* Bloomington: Indiana University Press, 1979.

DeLeon, Richard Edward. *Left Coast City: Progressive Politics in San Francisco: 1975–1991.* Lawrence: University of Kansas Press, 1992.

Erie, Steven P. *Rainbow's End: Irish-Americans and the Dilemmas of Urban Machine Politics, 1840–1985.* Berkeley: University of California Press, 1988.

Farrelly, David, and Ivan Hinderaker. *The Politics of California.* New York: Ronald Press, 1951.

Fenno, Richard F. *Watching Politicians: Essays on Participant Observation.* Berkeley: Institute of Governmental Studies, University of California, 1990.

Fitzgerald, Frances. *Cities on a Hill: A Journey through Contemporary American Cultures.* New York: Simon and Schuster, 1986.

Gitlin, Todd. *The Sixties: Years of Hope, Days of Rage.* New York: Bantam, 1987.

Hardy, Leroy. "Considering the Gerrymander," *Pepperdine Law Review* 4, no. 2 (1977).

————. *The Gerrymander Origin, Conception, and Re-emergence.* Rose Institute of State and Local Government, Claremont McKenna College, 1990.

Hardy, Leroy, and Alan Heslop. *The Westside Story: A Murder in Four Acts.* Rose Institute of State and Local Government, Claremont McKenna College, 1990.

House Committee on Interior and Insular Affairs. Subcommittee on National Parks and Insular Affairs, comp. *Legislative History of the National Parks and Recreation Act of 1978 (Public Law 95-625).* Washington, D.C.: Government Printing Office, 1978.

Joe, Tom, and Cheryl Rogers. *By the Few for the Few: The Reagan Welfare Legacy.* Lexington, Mass.: Lexington Books, 1985.

Johnson, Haynes. *Sleepwalking through History: America in the Reagan Years.* New York: W. W. Norton, 1991.

King, Larry L. "The Road to Power in Congress: The Education of Mo Udall, and What

It Cost." In *Education of a Congressman: The Newsletters of Morris K. Udall*, edited by
Robert L. Peabody. New York: Bobbs-Merrill, 1972.

Kotz, Nick, and Mary Lynn. *A Passion for Equality: George Wiley and the Movement*. New
York: W. W. Norton, 1977.

Leamer, Larry. *Playing for Keeps in Washington*. New York: Dial Press, 1977.

Lee, Eugene C., and Willis D. Hawley, eds. *The Challenge of California*. Boston: Little,
Brown, 1970.

Loomis, Burdett. *The New American Politician: Ambition, Entrepreneurship and the
Changing Face of American Political Life*. New York: Basic, 1988.

Mankiewicz, Frank. *Perfectly Clear: Nixon from Whittier to Watergate*. New York: Popular
Library, 1973.

Mann, Thomas E., and Norman J. Ornstein, eds. *The New Congress*. Washington, D.C.:
American Enterprise Institute for Public Policy Research, 1981.

Matusow, Allen J. *The Unraveling of America: A History of Liberalism in the 1960s*. New
York: Harper and Row, 1984.

Mayhew, David R. *Congress: The Electoral Connection*. New Haven: Yale University Press,
1974.

Monagan, Robert T. *The Disappearance of Representative Government: A California Solution*. Grass Valley, Calif.: Comstock Bonanza, 1990.

Mellon, Carlotta Herman. "The Rise and Fall of Grassroots Politics: The California
Democratic Council, 1953–1966." Ph.D. diss., Claremont McKenna College, 1972.

Mills, James R. *A Disorderly House: The Brown-Unruh Years in Sacramento*. Berkeley:
Heyday, 1987.

Moynihan, Daniel Patrick. *The Politics of a Guaranteed Income*. New York: Random
House, 1973.

Nelson, John R., Jr. *Black Lung: A Study of Disability Compensation Policy Formation*.
Washington, D.C.: School of Social Service Administration, University of Chicago
and the Center for the Study of Social Policy, 1985.

O'Neill, Thomas P., Jr., with William Novak. *Man of the House: The Life and Political
Memoirs of Speaker Tip O'Neill*. New York: St. Martin's, 1987.

Oppenheimer, Bruce I., and Robert L. Peabody. "The House Majority Leader's Contest—1976." Delivered at the meeting of the American Political Science Association,
Washington, D.C., September 1977.

Ornstein, Norman J. "Causes and Consequences of Congressional Change: Subcommittee Reforms in the House of Representatives, 1970–1973." In *Congress in Change*,
edited by Norman J. Ornstein. New York: Praeger, 1975.

———. "The Democrats Reform Power in the House of Representatives, 1969–1975."
In *America in the Seventies*, edited by Allan P. Sindler. Boston: Little, Brown, 1977.

Papers of Phillip Burton. Forty-five cartons. Bancroft Library, University of California,
Berkeley.

Phillip Burton: Memorial Addresses Delivered in Congress. Washington, D.C.: Government
Printing Office, 1983.

Polsby, Nelson W. "Two Strategies of Influence: Choosing a Majority Leader, 1962." In
New Perspectives on the House of Representatives, edited by Robert L. Peabody and
Nelson W. Polsby, Chicago: Rand McNally, 1963.

———. *Consequences of Party Reform*. New York: Oxford University Press, 1983.

Quinn, T. Anthony. "Carving up California: A History of Redistricting, 1951–1984."

Ph.D. diss. Rose Institute of State and Local Government, Claremont McKenna College, n.d.

Reisner, Marc. *Cadillac Desert: The American West and Its Disappearing Water.* New York: Penguin, 1987.

Reiterman, Tim, with John Jacobs. *Raven: The Untold Story of the Rev. Jim Jones and His People.* New York: E. P. Dutton, 1982.

Rusco, Elmer. "Machine Politics, California Model: Arthur H. Samish and the Alcoholic Beverage Industry." Ph.D. diss., University of California, n.d.

Sala Burton: Memorial Addresses Delivered in Congress. Washington, D.C.: Government Printing Office, 1983.

Samish, Arthur H., and Bob Thomas. *The Secret Boss of California: The Life and High Times of Art Samish.* New York: Crown, 1971.

Sheppard, Burton D. *Rethinking Congressional Reform.* Cambridge, Mass.: Schenkman, 1985.

Shilts, Randy. *The Mayor of Castro Street: The Life and Times of Harvey Milk.* New York: St. Martin's Press, 1982.

———. *And the Band Played On: People, Politics and the AIDS Epidemic.* New York: St. Martin's Press, 1987.

Smith, Hedrick. *The Power Game: How Washington Works.* New York: Random House, 1988.

Stone, Chuck. *Black Political Power in America.* New York: Dell, 1970.

Stone, I. F. *In a Time of Torment, 1961–1967.* Boston: Little, Brown, 1989.

Tacheron, Donald G., and Morris K. Udall. *The Job of the Congressman: An Introduction to Service in the U.S. House of Representatives.* Indianapolis and New York: Bobbs-Merrill, 1970.

Tuchman, Barbara. *Practicing History: Selected Essays.* New York: Ballantine, 1981.

White, Theodore H. *The Making of the President, 1968.* New York: Pocket Books, 1970.

———. *The Making of the President, 1972.* New York: Atheneum, 1973.

Wilson, James Q. *The Amateur Democrat.* Chicago: University of Chicago Press, 1962.

Williams, T. Harry. *Huey Long.* New York: Alfred A. Knopf, 1969.

Wirt, Frederick M. *Power in the City: Decision Making in San Francisco.* Berkeley: Institute of Governmental Studies, University of California Press, 1974.

CONGRESSIONAL ORAL HISTORIES
Library of Congress, Washington, D.C.;
oral histories conducted for Former Members of Congress, Inc.,
as part of its project, the Modern Congress in American History

Green, Edith. Recorded by Shirley Tanzer, November 18, 1978, November 25, 1978, December 2, 1978, and March 18, 1980.

Griffiths, Martha W. Recorded by Emily George, December 1977–April 1978, and by Fern S. Ingersoll, October 1979.

Gubser, Charles. Recorded by Charles T. Morrissey, December 4, 1978.

Hansen, Julia Butler. Recorded by Shirley Tanzer, March 3, 1980.

Hillings, Patrick. Recorded by Enid H. Douglass, January 29, 1979, March 19, 1979, and January 14, 1980.

Hollifield, Chet. Recorded by Enid H. Douglass, April 25, 1975 and May 7, 1975.

Laird, Melvin. Recorded by Charles T. Morrissey, April 18, 1979 and May 14, 1979.

Mailliard, William. Recorded by Charles T. Morrissey, October 3, 1977, January 26, 1979, and June 13, 1979.

McCormack, John W. Recorded by Sheldon Stern, March 30, 1977, for the John F. Kennedy Library.

Mills, Wilbur D. Recorded by Charles T. Morrissey, April 5, 1979 and June 7, 1979.

Mink, Patsy. Recorded by Fern S. Ingersoll, March 6, 1979, March 26, 1979, and June 7, 1979.

STATE GOVERNMENT ORAL HISTORY PROGRAM
California State Archives, Sacramento, California;
also available at Regional Oral History Office,
Bancroft Library, University of California, Berkeley

Bagley, William. Interview conducted by Ann Lage, April 11, 1989.

Burton, John. Interview conducted by Julie Shearer, December 17, 1986 and March 12, 1987.

O'Connell, John. Interview conducted by Carole Hicke, February 12 and 17, 1988.

Rees, Thomas. Interview conducted by Carlos Vasquez, December 10 and 11, 1987.

Waldie, Jerome. Interview conducted by Gabrielle Morris, June 8, 18, and 26, 1987.

GOODWIN-KNIGHT-EDMUND BROWN, SR. ERA,
REGIONAL ORAL HISTORY PROJECT
Bancroft Library, University of California, Berkeley

Blease, Coleman. "A Lobbyist Views the Knight-Brown Era." 1979. Interview conducted by James Rowland, 1979, copyright 1982.

Bradley, Don. "Managing Democratic Campaigns, 1954–1966." 1982. Interview conducted by Amelia Frey, 1977–79, copyright 1982.

Brown, Edmund G., Sr. "'Pat,' Years of Growth, 1939–1966"; "Law Enforcement, Politics, and the Governor's Office." Interview conducted by Malca Chall, Amelia Frey, Gabrielle Morris, and James Rowland, 1977–81, copyright 1982.

Champion, Hale. "Communication and Problem Solving: A Journalist in State Government." Interview conducted by Amelia Frey and Gabrielle Morris, 1977–79, copyright 1981.

Coffey, Bertram. "Reflections on George Miller, Jr., Governors Pat and Jerry Brown, and the Democratic Party." Interview conducted by Gabrielle Morris, 1978, copyright 1982.

Copertini, Cyr Mullins. "Campaign Housekeeping, 1940–1965." Interview conducted by Gabrielle Morris, 1986, copyright 1987.

Dutton, Frederick. "Democratic Campaigns and Controversies, 1954–1966." Interview conducted by Amelia Frey, 1977–78, copyright 1981.

Eliaser, Ann. "From Grass Roots Politics to Top Dollar: Fundraising for Candidates and Nonprofit Agencies." Interview conducted by Malca Chall, 1976–77, copyright 1987.

Elkington, Norman. "From Adversary to Appointee: Fifty Years of Friendship with Pat Brown." Interview conducted by Julie Shearer, 1978–79, copyright 1982.

Gatov, Elizabeth. "From Grass-Roots Organizer to Treasurer of the United States. Interview conducted by Malca Chall, 1975–76, copyright 1978.

Heller, Elinor Raas. "A Volunteer Career in Politics, in Higher Education, and on Governing Boards." Two volumes. Interview conducted by Malca Chall, 1974–80, copyright 1987.

Kent, Roger. "Building the Democratic Party in California, 1954–1966." Interview conducted by Anne H. Brower and Amelia Frey, 1976–77, copyright 1981.

Leary, Mary Ellen. "A Journalist's Perspective: Government and Politics in California and the Bay Area." Interview conducted by Harriet Nathan, 1979, copyright 1981.

Malone, William. Oral history. Interview conducted by Malca Chall, 1978–.

Rattigan, Joseph. "A Judicial Look at Civil Rights, Education, and Reapportionment in the State Senate, 1959–1966." Interview conducted by James Rowland, 1978, copyright 1981.

Salinger, Pierre. "A Journalist as Democratic Campaigner and U.S. Senator." Interview conducted by Amelia Frey, 1979, copyright 1982.

Wedemeyer, John. "California State Department of Social Welfare, 1959–1966." Interview conducted by Gabrielle Morris, 1978–79, copyright 1980.

SIERRA CLUB ORAL HISTORY PROJECT

Amodio, John. "Lobbyist for Redwood National Park Expansion." Interview conducted by Carol Holleuffler, 1982.

PERSONS INTERVIEWED

signifies members and former members of Congress

Ralph Abascal, January 30, 1991, Berkeley
Peter Abbruzzese, July 10, 1991, by telephone
*James Abourezk, June 5, 1991, by telephone
Art Agnos, March 2, 1987 and June 5, 1991, San Francisco
*Carl Albert, May 24, 1989, by telephone
Joseph Alioto, November 30, 1990, San Francisco
Jodie Allen, August 8, 1991, Washington, D.C.
John Amodio, February 6, 1991, Sacramento
Bill Anderson, August 10, 1990, Washington, D.C.
Lou Angelo, February 8, 1991, Sacramento
*Thomas "Lud" Ashley, May 22, 1989, by telephone
William Bagley, December 14, 1990, San Francisco
William Below, March 29, 1991, by telephone
Pope Barrow, August 9, 1990, Washington, D.C.
Bob Barry, May 30, 1991, San Francisco
John Barry, April 3, 1991
*Robert Bauman, July 9, 1991, by telephone
Joe Beeman, December 6, 1988, May 22, 1989, Washington, D.C., January 9, 1991, San Francisco
Sue Bierman, February 25, 1987, by telephone

*Howard Berman, April 2, 1991, Washington, D.C.

Jack Berman, January 21, 1991, San Francisco

Michael Berman, December 28, 1988, May 11, 1989, March 28, 1991, Los Angeles, and December 13, 1994, by telephone

Morris Bernstein, February 24, 1987 and January 16, 1991, San Francisco

Robert Beverly, February 5, 1991, Sacramento

Jim Bierne, March 8, 1991 and April 3, 1991, Washington, D.C.

Coleman Blease, February 7, 1991, Sacramento

*Richard Bolling, April 11, 1989, Washington, D.C.

Joan Brann, January 15, 1991, Oakland

Robert Brauer, April 12, 1991, Washington, D.C.

Willard Bretz, May 14, 1991, by telephone

David Broder, April 3, 1991, Washington, D.C.

Charles Brohammer, May 13, 1991, by telephone

*Jack Brooks, April 12, 1991, Washington, D.C.

Alan Brotsky, December 19, 1990, San Francisco

Doug Brown, March 20, 1991, by telephone

Edmund G. "Pat" Brown, July 5, 1989, Los Angeles

Jerry Brown, March 19, 1991, Berkeley

Willie Brown, March 5, 1987, August 21, 1991, May 24, 1994, January 26, 1995, Sacramento

*John Burton, March 2, 1987, May 10 and 14, 1989, August 1, 2, and 5, 1991, San Francisco

Robert Burton, November 16 and 20, 1988, April 17, 1991, San Francisco

Larry Bush, May 30, 1991, by telephone

William Cable, April 3, 1991, Washington, D.C.

Lou Cannon, March 25, 1991, Santa Barbara, February 27, 1995, by telephone

Harry Carter, May 29, 1991, by telephone

William Cavala, February 8, 1991 and June 1, 1994, Sacramento

Joseph Cerrell, July 6, 1989, Los Angeles

Hale Champion, March 21, 1991, Berkeley

Paul Chignell, May 30, 1991, San Francisco

Winslow Christian, February 20, 1991, by telephone

Judd Clark, May 9, 1991, Sacramento

*Don Clausen, July 11, 1991, by telephone

Joan Claybrook, July 1, 1990, Washington, D.C.

Charles Cluson, June 4, 1991, by telephone

James Cobey, January 31, 1991, by telephone

William Coblentz, February 1, 1991, San Francisco

*Tony Coelho, August 10, 1990, Washington, D.C.

Bert Coffey, January 6, 1991, Richmond, Calif.

David Cohen, December 6 and 10, 1990, Washington, D.C.

Charles Conklin, March 8, 1991, by telephone

Al Conti, March 8, 1991, by telephone

Mary Lou Cooper, July 9, 1991, by telephone

Cyr Copertini, January 31, 1991, San Francisco

Vincent Courtney, February 21, 1987, by telephone

Gwen Craig, June 6, 1991, by telephone

Dale Crane, May 17, 1991, Seattle
Joseph Crapa, December 5, 1990, Washington, D.C.
Jack Crose, February 7, 1991, Sacramento
Richard Curry, May 29, 1991, by telephone
Ed Davis, April 4, 1991, Washington, D.C.
Jack Davis, February 23, 1987, by telephone
Richard DeLeon, February 27, 1987, by telephone
Henry Der, February 25, 1987, by telephone
Leo Diehl, April 8, 1991, by telephone
William Dietz, April 4, 1991, Washington, D.C.
Harold Dobbs, December 14, 1990, by telephone
Thomas Dooley, May 8, 1991, Sacramento
*Robert Dornan, August 14, 1988, New Orleans
David Dreyer, May 28, 1991, by telephone
Pamela Duffy, January 11, 1991, San Francisco
Thomas Dunmire, February 28, 1991, by telephone
Roy Dye, August 8, 1991, Washington, D.C.
Martin Eber, March 2, 1991, San Francisco
*Robert Eckhardt, May 28, 1991, by telephone
*Don Edwards, May 17, 1989, by telephone, and August 23, 1989, Washington, D.C.
*John Erlenborn, April 4, 1991, Washington, D.C.
Jack Ertola, January 3, 1991, San Francisco
Claude Everhart, February 24, 1987, by telephone
*Eni Faleomavenga, December 11, 1990, Washington, D.C.
Dr. Seymour Farber, December 13, 1988 and July 21, 1991, San Francisco
Jeff Farrow, December 7 and 10, 1990, Washington, D.C.
*Vic Fazio, September 24, 1993, Washington, D.C.
Dianne Feinstein, March 2, 1987, by telephone
Fred Feinstein, December 12, 1990, Washington, D.C.
Gil Ferguson, May 8, 1991, Sacramento
*Bobbi Fiedler, March 14, 1991, by telephone
Thomas Fleming, November 3, 1990, San Francisco
*Tom Foley, April 11, 1991, Washington, D.C.
John Foran, May 10, 1991, Sacramento
Walter "Buzz" Forward, May 13, 1991, by telephone
Jim Foster, February 26, 1987, by telephone
Murial Fox, March 8, 1991, by telephone
*Donald Fraser, May 4, 1994, by telephone
Al From, January 13, 1995, Sacramento
Doug Frost, April 4, 1991, Washington, D.C.
Duane Garrett, July 9, 1988, San Francisco
Matt Gately, December 19, 1988, Washington, D.C.
Mark Gersh, May 18, 1989, Washington, D.C., and May 31, 1991, by telephone,
    Washington, D.C.
Dugald Gillies, February 7, 1991, by telephone
Paul Golding, April 8, 1991, by telephone
Martha Gorman, February 5, 1991, Sacramento
Gene Goss, April 22, 1991, by telephone

George Gould, April 9, 1991, Washington, D.C.
Roy Greenaway, April 6, 1989, Washington, D.C.
William Hagen, April 8, 1991, by telephone
Dr. Steven Haig, July 1, 1991, Berkeley
Terrence Hallinan, July 1, 1991, by telephone
Vincent Hallinan, June 22, 1989, San Francisco
Jack Hanley, December 1, 1988, San Francisco
Leroy Hardy, June 29, 1989, Long Beach, and March 26, 1991, Claremont
David Harris, May 31, 1991, by telephone
Rich Hays, May 31, 1991, San Francisco
Bud Heinselman, May 29, 1991, by telephone
Jack Henning, February 7, 1991, Sacramento
James Herman, December 12, 1993, by telephone
Siegfried Hesse, April 29, 1991, Berkeley
*Patrick Hillings, April 8, 1991, by telephone
Harlan Hoffman, November 29, 1990, San Francisco
William Holayter, December 12, 1990, Washington, D.C.
Joseph Holsinger, May 8, 1991, Sacramento
*Joseph Holt, April 24, 1991, by telephone
William Houck, May 8, 1991, Sacramento
Dolores Huerta, July 12, 1991, Berkeley
Harvey Hukari, August 20, 1991, by telephone
Ellen Hume, June 4, 1991, by telephone
Charles Hurley, March 5, 1991, Berkeley
Gary Hymel, July 13, 1990, Washington, D.C.
Phil Isenberg, June 1, 1991, Concord, Calif.
Pat Jackson, August 21, 1991, by telephone
John Jacobs (no relation to author), March 14, 1991, by telephone
Agar Jaicks, February 24, 1987 and July 2 and 3, 1988, San Francisco
David Jenkins, July 9, 1988 and January 8, 1991, San Francisco
Alan Jenson, April 8, 1991, by telephone
Tom Joe, April 1, 1989, February 1, 1991, March 8, 1991, April 5, 1991, and
    September 27, 1991, Washington, D.C.
Huey Johnson, May 14, 1991, San Rafael
Linda Kamm, August 9, 1990, Washington, D.C.
Mark Kasky, December 17, 1991, by telephone
*Robert Kastenmeier, December 18, 1988, Washington, D.C., and May 4, 1994,
    by telephone
Susan Kennedy, January 14, 1991, San Francisco
Frank Kieliger, August 1, 1988, Concord
Donald King, November 29, 1990, San Francisco
John Knox, January 5, 1991, Richmond, Calif.
Don Koniewski, April 2, 1991, Washington, D.C.
Quentin Kopp, February 21, 1987, by telephone
Patricia Kraus, December 10, 1990, Washington, D.C.
Daniel Krivit, July 11, 1991, by telephone
George Kundanis, August 10, 1990, Washington, D.C.
Kathy Files Lacey, April 3, 1991, Washington, D.C.

*Robert Lagomarsino, April 11, 1991, Washington, D.C.

Billie Larsen, April 2, 1991, Washington, D.C.

Nancy Larsen, February 28, 1991, San Francisco

John Laurence, July 9, 1988 and April 4, 1991, Washington, D.C.

Mary Ellen Leary, February 18, 1991, Berkeley

Lim P. Lee, March 8, 1991, San Francisco

Judy Lemons, April 11, 1991, May 21, 1991, April 25, 1994, Washington, D.C.

David Looman, February 23, 1987 and July 8, 1988, San Francisco

Mary Louise Lovett, January 14, 1991, San Francisco

Harry Low, January 24, 1991, San Francisco

Lynn Ludlow, December 20, 1991, by telephone

Marshall Lynam, May 28, 1991, by telephone

Ken Maddy, May 16 and 17, 1994, Sacramento

Tim Mahoney, June 4, 1991, by telephone

Frank Mankiewicz, April 9, 1991, Washington, D.C.

Ellen Marcus, March 11, 1991, Washington, D.C.

Larry Margolis, February 6, 1991, Sacramento

Gene Marine, February 20, 1991, Berkeley

Nicholas Masters, May 28, 1991 and June 1, 1991, by telephone

*Dawson Mathis, May 10, 1989 and April 10, 1991, Washington, D.C.

*Robert Matsui, December 12, 1990 and April 9, 1991, Washington, D.C.

Harvey Matthews, January 3, 1991, by telephone

Rudy Maxa, November 22, 1991, by telephone

Leo McCarthy, November 29, 1990 and February 12, 1991, San Francisco

Robert McCarthy, February 24, 1987, by telephone

James McClatchy, April 20, 1994, Sacramento

Sharon McCormick, April 8, 1991, Washington, D.C.

Jack McDowell, February 18, 1991, by telephone

Lee McElvain, August 10, 1990, Washington, D.C.

Sidney McFarland, March 8, 1991, by telephone

Howard McGuigan, April 24, 1991, by telephone

Paul McKaskle, June 3, 1991, by telephone

Ken Meade, February 27, 1991, by telephone

*Lloyd Meeds, December 5, 1990, Washington, D.C.

Rick Merrill, July 10, 1990, Washington, D.C.

Amy Meyer, December 3, 1990, San Francisco

*Abner Mikva, May 18, 1989 and April 10, 1991, Washington, D.C.

*George Miller, December 6, 1988, April 19, 1991, Washington, D.C., and
    August 20, 1991, Pleasant Hill

*Wilbur Mills, April 22, 1991, by telephone

*Norman Mineta, April 11, 1991, Washington, D.C.

Jack Molinari, February 24, 1987 and December 13, 1991, San Francisco

Robert Monagan, February 2, 1991, Sacramento

Joan Moody, April 30, 1991, by telephone

Tom Moore, January 24, 1991 and March 16, 1991, San Francisco

Celia Morris, May 11, 1991, by telephone

Jack Morrison, January 22, 1991, San Francisco

Jane Morrison, January 22, 1991, San Francisco

Stanley Mosk, January 24, 1991, San Francisco
Robert Moss, April 5, 1991, Washington, D.C.
Dan Mundy, April 23, 1991, by telephone
Dick Murphy, July 11, 1990, Washington, D.C.
Ralph Nader, December 12, 1993, by telephone
Robert Naylor, May 30, 1991, by telephone
*Lucien Nedzi, July 8, 1991, by telephone
*Gaylord Nelson, December 2, 1991, by telephone
Robert Neuman, July 11, 1989, Washington, D.C.
Michael Nevin, May 30, 1991, San Francisco
Richard Nevin, March 26, 1991, Pasadena
William Newsom, January 3, 1991, San Francisco
Lee Nichols, March 4, 1991, by telephone
Martin Nolan, July 20, 1988, Boston
Rudy Nothenberg, February 24, 1987 and December 14, 1990, San Francisco
Michael Novelli, May 29, 1991, by telephone
John O'Connell, August 11, 1989, San Francisco
Bartly O'Hara, April 8, 1991, Washington, D.C.
Walter Oleszek, December 6, 1990, Washington, D.C.
*Thomas P. "Tip" O'Neill, December 18, 1988, Washington, D.C.
Norman Ornstein, July 11, 1991 and May 3, 1994, by telephone
Toby Osos, March 26, 1991, Pasadena
Dick Pabich, February 27, 1987 and June 23, 1988, San Francisco
Ben Palumbo, May 23, 1989 and April 4, 1991, Washington, D.C.
*Leon Panetta, July 24, 1991, by telephone
Dr. Robert Peck, August 7, 1991, by telephone
Nancy Pelosi, May 24, 1992, San Francisco
Ed Percell, January 3, 1991, by telephone
Stan Perkins, February 13, 1991, by telephone
Nicholas Petris, February 22, 1991, Oakland
Cleve Pinnix, May 15 and 17, 1991, Olympia
Nelson Polsby, September 15, 1991, and August 14, 1993, Berkeley
Carl Pope, July 9, 1988 and May 14, 1991, San Francisco
Sandra Powell, February 20, 1987, by telephone
Jay Power, April 2, 1991, Washington, D.C.
John Quimby, May 9, 1991, Sacramento
Reno Rapagnani, May 30, 1991, San Francisco
Susan Rasky, April 4, 1994, Berkeley
Joseph Rattigan, January 31, 1991, by telephone
*Thomas Rees, August 28, 1989, Scotts Valley
Clinton Reilly, February 26, 1987, by telephone
Leo Rennert, February 20, 1995, by telephone
Gerard Rhine, July 7, 1989, San Francisco
Rosalyn Rifkin, July 1, 1991, Berkeley
Hadley Roff, February 23, 1987, by telephone
Ed Rollins, December 12, 1990, Washington, D.C.
Paul Rosenberg, February 1, 1991, San Francisco

*Dan Rostenkowski, April 5, 1989 and June 6, 1991, Washington, D.C., and
    by telephone
*John Rousselot, May 28, 1991, by telephone
*James Santini, July 2, 1991, by telephone
 Douglas Scott, May 19, 1991, San Juan Islands
 Patricia Schifferle, February 1, 1991, San Francisco
*Patricia Schroeder, February 22, 1991, Berkeley
 Stanley Scoville, August 9, 1990, Washington, D.C.
*John Seiberling, May 18, 1989 and June 28, 1991, by telephone
 Gary Sellers, August 9 and 10, 1990, December 7, 1990, and April 6, 1991,
    Washington, D.C.
 John Sheehan, April 3, 1991, Washington, D.C.
 Kevin Shelley, June 5, 1991 and August 22, 1991, San Francisco
 Thelma Shelley, July 3, 1991, by telephone
 Joseph Shumate, February 24, 1987, by telephone
 Dr. Margaret Singer, July 22, 1991, Berkeley
*B. F. Sisk, May 19, 1989, by telephone
 Irving Sprague, August 9, 1990, by telephone
*William Stanton, December 5, 1988, Washington, D.C.
 Lionel Steinberg, January 12, 1991, by telephone
 Betty Stephens, May 15, 1989, by telephone
 Milton Stern, July 15, 1991, Berkeley
 Dr. Stephen Teale, February 13, 1991, by telephone
 Joy Temes, July 1, 1991, Berkeley
 William Thomas, December 19, 1990, San Francisco
*Frank Thompson, May 22, 1989, by telephone
 Patrick Tobin, March 9, 1991, San Francisco
 Robert Tolstad, May 13, 1991, by telephone
 Peter Trimble, March 20, 1991, by telephone
 William Turnidge, June 4, 1991, Berkeley
 Joan Tuomy, January 10, 1990, San Francisco
 Tony Turyn, May 28, 1991, by telephone
*Morris Udall, December 4, 1990, Washington, D.C.
 June Unruh, August 11, 1989, by telephone
 Robert Vagley, April 1 and 23, 1991, Washington, D.C.
 Yori Wada, January 8, 1991, San Francisco
*Jerome Waldie, February 5, 1991, Sacramento
 Charles Warren, February 7, 1991, Sacramento
 Maudelle Watson, March 26, 1991, by telephone
 Mel Wax, February 21, 1987, by telephone
*Henry Waxman, July 6, 1989, Los Angeles
 Dr. Edgar Wayburn, January 16 and 31, 1991 and March 3, 1991, San Francisco
 David Weiman, December 5, 1990, Washington, D.C.
 Andrew Weissner, June 6, 1991, by telephone
 Calvin Welch, February 19, 1987, by telephone
 Robert Welles, March 7, 1991, by telephone
 Fred Wertheimer, December 12, 1990, Washington, D.C.
 Dr. Haydn Williams, July 12, 1991, by telephone

Joseph Williams, August 10, 1989, San Francisco
Robert Williams, January 31, 1991, by telephone
Marshall Windmiller, December 30, 1990, Alameda
Adrian Winkle, April 24, 1991, by telephone
Thomas Winnett, August 10, 1989, Berkeley
Bob Woodward, November 18, 1991, by telephone
*Jim Wright, June 3, 1991, by telephone
Roz Wyman, March 8, 1991, by telephone
Ken Young, April 4, 1991, Washington, D.C.
Ed Zschau, February 20, 1990, Sacramento

INDEX

Beilenson, Tony, 326, 384; and reapportionment, 429, 433–34, 438–39
Belli, Melvin and Lia, 465
Berkeley, 81
Berman, Howard, 69, 479; "Berman-Waxman Machine," 412, 436–37; and Burton, 281–82; in House, 440, 476, 478; 1974 assembly speaker race, 288–89; 1980 assembly speaker race, 406–14, 440; and 1981 reapportionment, 415, 429, 433–34, 438, 439, 440, 473, 475
Berman, Jack, 23, 29
Berman, Michael, 69, 281, 282, 387; on Burton, 296, 416, 487–88; campaign management, 385, 408, 459–60, 461, 465–66, 467–68; and Carl D'Agostino, 460; and 1976 majority leader race, 313–14, 316, 319; and 1981 reapportionment, 415, 418, 426, 429, 431, 433, 435, 439, 473, 474, 475
Bernhard, Hubert, 168
Bernstein, Carl, 249
Bernstein, Morris, 123, 171, 326
Berry, William ("Cliff"), 21, 34, 36
Bethune, Mary McLeod, 399
Bevinetti, Peter, 378
Bible, Alan, 214, 356
Biemiller, Andrew, 145, 146, 201, 246, 305, 343
Bierman, Sue, 173
Bierne, Jim, 344–45, 380; practical jokes, 378, 390
Big Sur, 391, 395–96
Bill of Rights, 84
Billings, Linda, 340, 344
Bingham, Jonathan, 220, 246
Bird, Rose, 439
"Black Friday," 82
black lung disease, 181–85, 187, 194, 195; legislation, 184, 185, 187–88, 190–91, 193–95, 196–97, 370, 495; "rebuttable presumption," 185, 193. See also Coal mining
Blacks. See African Americans; Burton, Phillip, and the black community

Blanchard, Jim, 254
Blease, Coleman, 59, 76, 77, 79, 80, 85, 103
Blue Key, 14
Boddy, Manchester, 26
Boeing, 462
Boggs, Hale, 158, 175–77, 227, 228, 237, 239, 259, 301, 357
Boggs, Lindy, 239
Boise Cascade, 462
Boland, Ed, 228
Boldenweck, Bill, 452
"Boll weevils," 421, 422
Bolling, Richard, 137, 217, 224, 237, 252, 258, 365, 382, 385, 416; and Burton, 138, 146, 229, 244, 269–70, 278–79, 305, 312, 342, 382, 384, 386–87, 471–72; House analysis and reform, 135–36, 222–23, 225, 244–47, 251, 256, 277, 305; and 1976 majority leader race, 299–301, 303, 304, 307, 310, 313, 314, 316, 317, 319, 321; protégés, 317, 387
Book of memorial tributes, congressional, xxi
Bosco, Doug, 413, 440, 478
Boston Globe, 273, 351, 418
Boundary Waters Canoe Area, 361–63
Boxer, Barbara, 446, 451, 471, 473, 478, 479, 494, 536n1
Boyle, Father Eugene, 381
Boyle, Tony, 182, 189, 191
Braceros, 75–77
Brademas, John, 217, 222, 270, 305, 324, 416; and Burton, 146, 186, 206, 229, 230–31, 240, 246, 269, 312; and 1976 majority leader race, 300, 302, 312
Bradlee, Ben, 297, 312
Bradley, Don, 72
Bradley, Tom, 473
Brann, Frank, 165
Brann, Joan, 165–66
Brauer, Robert, 431
Brazil, Eric, 414
Bridges, Harry, 8, 46, 173
Britt, Harry, 450, 452, 454, 465, 489
Broadhead, William, 438

and the Kennedys, 156, 157, 171; Korean War, 31–32; and labor, 14, 24, 35, 46–47, 70, 91, 121, 123, 130, 165, 187, 200, 234, 253, 254, 305, 307, 339, 341, 381, 417, 419, 447, 450, 463, 469, 484; law practice, 34, 45, 125; legislation (*see* Assembly legislation; House legislation); marriage, 31–32; and media, xiv, 46, 49, 64, 70, 75, 259–60, 274–76, 382, 435, 467, *516n18*; as mentor, 68, 69, 94–95, 165–66, 200, 235, 240, 253–54, 391, 465, *535n8*; mentors, 45, 58, 59; need for acceptance, approval, 10, 42, 164, 178, 196, 198–99, 199; need for company, 10, 101, 232, 361, 419; obsession for leadership, 397, 401, 415–16, 419, 483, 484; organization memberships, 29; personal papers, xv, 42–43, 70; personality and character, xx, 13–14, 39, 59, 78, 100–101, 321, 328, 338, 345, 397, 423, 449; political skills and strategy, xv, xxi–xxv, 12, 64, 66, 70, 75, 77, 79, 80–81, 85, 90, 91, 100–113, 102, 117–18, 140, 144, 146, 151–52, 175–77, 199, 231, 241, 351, 353–55, 359, 363, 365, 422; postgraduation, 22–27; relationship with father, 1, 4, 11, 29–30, 42; social and political values, xxiv, 6, 52, 59, 74, 78, 102, 127, 129, 131, 143, 169, 186–87, 383, *509n23*; southern support, 386; and staff, 29, 93–94, 109, 138, 161, 181, 188, 189, 205, 393, 397, 420, 424–25; tributes to, xxi, 339, 485; at USC, 10–14, 311; Vietnam War, 143, 153–55, 180; WWII, 7–11

Burton, Robert (brother), 2, 3, 4, 8, 35, 68, 477

Burton, Sala Galant Lipschultz (wife), 27, 83, 163, 189, 232, 293, 360, *515n12*; after Burton, 488–89; career support, 28, 36, 37, 58, 68, 100, 131, 182, 257, 302, 310, 322, 419, 441; courtship and marriage, 27, 219, 282; daughter Joy, 27, 66, 374, 488; as wife, 27–28, 66, 233–34, 235, 420

Burton, Shirley (sister-in-law), 69, 138
Burton, Thomas (father), 2, 5–6, 8–9, 31, 52, 131, 154, 218, 295; influence on son(s), 1–4, 7, 8, 9, 29–30, 74, 264
Burton-Rattigan Act, 109
Burton-Santini Act, 495
Bush, George, 332, 462
Busterud, John, 67, 73–74
Byfield, Canon Richard, 82
Byrd, Harry, Jr., 371, 378, 383
Byrd, Robert, 376
Byrnes, John, 176–77
Byron, Beverly, 390
Byron, Goodloe, 340, 372, 389–90

Cable, Bill, 247, 319
Caen, Herb, 128, 483
Cain, Bruce, 474–75
CAL-TAX (California Taxpayer's Association), 109; *CAL-TAX News*, 112
California: Department of Employment, 77; Department of Finance, 102, 111; Department of Welfare, 101, 102
California Bankers Association, 425
California Coastal Act of 1976, 395
California Democratic Council. *See* CDC
California Farm Bureau Monthly, 112
California Institute of Social Welfare, 53
California Journal, 290, 291, 394, 406, 410, 448
California Republican Assembly, 31
California Retail Association, 65
California Rice Grower's Association, 173, 175
California Roundtable, 431
California State Federation of Teachers, 70
California Taxpayers' Association, 109
California Wilderness Act, 480, 485
Californian, xxiv
Cambodia, 273, 276
Campaign funding: dispersement, 60, 115, 252, 252–54, 281, 346, 385, 408, 456; reform, 70, 88, 92, 138, 234–35, 254–56, 274–75, 288, 313, 315, 346,

Malone, William (*continued*)
   decline, 30, 33–34, 35, 37; rise and
      power, 18–23, 24, 25–26, *503n8*
Maloney, Tommy, 39, 41; last race, 43–
   44, 45, 48, 52, 53–55, 57, 71, 131, 172
Manassas National Battlefield, 371, 378
Mankiewicz, Frank, 35, 285
Margolis, Larry, 16, 91, 93, *509n23*
Marin Headlands park, 211, 212–13
Marine Cooks and Stewards, 14, 47
Marine, Gene, 54, 55
Marks, Milton, 292; assembly and state
   senate, 94, 122, 170–71, 174, 447–48;
   and Burton, 441, 470; and Jim Jones,
   404; 1982 election, 446–47, 452, 453,
   456–57, 458, 460, 461, 462, 466, 467,
   468–70
Martin, Del, 462
Martinez, Matthew ("Marty"), 409, 415,
   436, 437, 440, 478
Masters, Nicholas, 313
Mathias, Bob, 254, 257
Mathis, Dawson, 269, 270, 306, 319, 356
Matsui, Robert, 380, 381, 382, 386, 493;
   and 1981 reapportionment, 428, 432,
   440
Matsunaga, Spark, 344, 376
Matthews, Harvey, 29
Maxa, Rudy, 297–98
Mazzoli, Roman, 476–77
Meade, Ken, 291
Meany, George, 146, 147, 341–42, 348,
   400
Measure A, 464–65, 470
Measures I and J, 464, 470
Medicare, 385
Meeds, Lloyd, 220, 221, 226, 246
Meet the Press, 315
Mello, Henry, 475
Mel's Drive-In, 125
Merlo, Harry, 336
Merrill, Rick, 206, 207
Mexican-American Legal Defense and
   Education Fund (MALDEF), 413, 436
Mexican Americans, 75, 168
Meyer, Amy, 211, 212, 214, 215

Meyers, Charlie, 21, 120
Meyers, Helen, 31
Michel, Robert, 274, 423, 496
Micronesia, 331
Middle East, 249
Mikulski, Barbara, 303, 309, 387
Mikva, Abner, 4, 155, 217, 322, 494; and
   Burton, 233, 270, 302, 312, 314, 317,
   321; on Burton, 230, 266, 272, 304,
   307, 318; in Congress, 155, 231, 241,
   257, 268, 298, 387
Milk, Harvey, 294, 404, 452, 453, 462,
   467; assassination, 405–6; Harvey
   Milk Gay Democratic Club, 450, 452,
   462, 464, 465
Milken, Michael
Miller, Cynthia, 419
Miller, George, III (congressman), 248;
   on Burton, 326, 353, 358, 380, 477,
   487; and Burton, 253–54, 261, 312, 323,
   419; and John Burton, 442, 444; Interior chairman, 494
Miller, George, Jr. (state senator), 24, 30,
   86, 254; and Burton, 22, 53, 66, 130;
   and CDC, 31, 32, 97; Finance chair-
   man, 92, 105, 107, 108, 110
Miller, George (no relation), 151
Miller, Henry, 85
Miller, John, 289–90
Mills, Jim, 90, 412
Mills, Wilbur, 217, 245, 249–50, 274;
   and Burton, 204, 218, 229, 230, 232,
   243; Tidal Basin incident, 262–64;
   Ways and Means chairman, 135, 175,
   176, 206, 207, 236, 242, 250–51
Mineta, Norman, 258, 267, 312, 316, 388,
   478; loyalty to Burton, 318, 320, 325,
   429
Minimum wage, 64; federal increase,
   180, 345–46, 495
Mink, Patsy, 68, 220
Mississippi Freedom Democratic Party,
   142, 143
Mississippi River (upper), 371
Mitchell, John, 216, *516n7*
Moakley, Joe, 372
Model Cities, 292

Power, Jay, 307–8, 341, 342, 343, 344, 349, 470, 483, *535n25*
Prescription drugs, welfare costs of, 77
Presidio, 213, 367, 495, *516n17*
"Presumptive eligibility," 106
Preyer, L. Richardson, 266, 385, 386, 387
Price, Melvin, 268
Progressive, 8
Proposition 6 (reapportionment guidelines, 1980), 430
Proposition 13 (property tax limit, 1978), 383, 403
"Proposition 13 Babies," 403
Proposition 14 (bipartisan redistricting, 1982), 472
Proposition 23 (state senate redistricting, 1962), 99
Prostitutes, use of, 89, 232, 327
Public Citizen, 312
Puerto Rico, 220

Quakers. *See* American Friends Service Committee
Quie, Albert, 274
Quimby, John, 113
Quinn, Mike, 8, 10
Quinn, Sally, 297
Quinn, Tony, 426, 438, 440, 490

Rafferty, Max, 179
"Raggedy Ass" lobby, 76, 78
Rahall, Nick Joe, 327
Ralph, Leon, 290
Randolph, A. Phillip, 167
Randolph, Jennings, 185, 193
Rangel, Charles, 150
Rapagnani, Reno, 464, 465
Rapoport, Daniel, 315
RARE II (Second Roadless Area Review and Evaluation), 480–83
Rasmussen, Donald, 184
Rattigan, Joseph, 87, 109–10
Rattigan-Burton Act, 109
Rauh, Joseph, 143
Raupe, Craig, 302, 308–9, 346–47
Ray, Elizabeth, 297–98

Rayburn, Sam, 134, 136, 137, 146, 147, 249, 251, 278, 304
Reader's Digest, 89
Reagan, Ronald: administration, 383, 416, 446, 452, 455, 456, 462, 468; economic policies, 323, 416, 417–18, 420–22; and environment, 349, 364, 394, 396, 457; as governor, 106, 151, 163, 171, 280, 281, 282, 283, 284, 286, 287; and 1981 reapportionment, 402, 438
Reapportionment: *1961*, 73, 87, 89–90, 116–22, 489–90, *507n4*, *510n5*; *1967*, 150–52; *1971*, 253, 281, 282–84, 286, 288; *1981*, 401, 402, 408, 414, 415–16, 418, 425–40, 442, 472, 475; *1991*, 494–95; Fifth Congressional District (Burton's), 117–18, 121–22, 152; gerrymandering, 117, 286, 401; Hispanic seats, 427, 436, 437, 440; state senate redistricting, (Proposition 23), 99, 150; and state supreme court, 151, 152; and U.S. Supreme Court, 99, 150
Recession, *1958*, 69; *1974–75*, 263, 276–77
Redistricting. *See* Reapportionment
Redwood Creek, 334
Redwood National Park, 141, 209, 374, 375; expansion, 209, 334–45, 347, 348–50, 355–56, 363, 364, 370; Redwood Employee Protection Plan (REPP), 339–45, 348–50
Rees, Tom, 59, 63–64, 88, 99, 233, *507n4*
Reform. *See* House issues
Reilly, Clint, 381
Reilly, George, 36, 37, 53, 54
Reilly, Jim, 37
Reinhardt, Richard, 122
Reiterman, Tim, 403
Renne, Louise, 446
Rennert, Leo, 192, 196, 383, 394, 500
Reporter, 62
REPP (Redwood Employee Protection Plan). *See* Redwood National Park
Republican Caucus. *See* Assembly
Republican National Campaign Committee, 255, 425, 447
Republican National Committee, *534n48*

San Francisco (*continued*)
    Center, 216. *See also* Chinatown; Irish
    community, San Francisco
San Francisco Call Bulletin, 49, 55, 66, 71.
    *See also San Francisco News–Call Bul-
    letin*
San Francisco Chronicle, 49, 129, 170,
    404; on Burton, 55, 114, 114–15, 132,
    139, 172, 177, 215, 324, 364, 476; and
    Examiner, 169; 1982 election, 456,
    464, 468; reporters and editors, 28, 36,
    55, 61, 73, 132, 214, 324
San Francisco Daily Commercial, 165
San Francisco Examiner, 49, 112, 128, 139,
    403, 404, *516n18*; on John Burton, 95,
    443, 444; on "Burton Machine," 168–
    69, 276; critic of Burton, 125, 140–41,
    169–70, 437–38; joint operating agree-
    ment; with *Chronicle,* 169; 1967 may-
    oral race, 167, 170, 171; 1982 election,
    452, 468, 470; obituary, 485; reporters
    and editors, 66, 124, 140–41, 168, 290
San Francisco (magazine), 122
San Francisco News, 34, 39, 55, 95
San Francisco News–Call Bulletin, 82
San Gabriel Valley Tribune, 299
San Jose Mercury News, 78, 434, 438
Sanford, Terry, 235
Santini, Jim, 254, 391–92, 393, 394, 495
Savings and loan industry, 256. *See also*
    Ahmanson, Howard
Schlackman, Rich, 466
Schmitz, John, 4
Schneider, William, 258
Schroeder, Patricia, 235, 241, 267, 311
Schwerner, Mickey, 142
Scott, Hugh, 197
Scott, William, 371, 378
Sebelius, Keith, 337, 344, 359, 363, 370,
    374–75, 398–99
"Second American Revolution," 391
Seiberling, John, 79, 313, 331, 359, 360,
    367, 370, 417, 480, 485
SEIU. *See* Service Employees Interna-
    tional Union
Sellers, Gary, 178, 180–82, 185, 188–90,

193, 196, 199–200, 201, 231; and John
    Burton, 444
Senate (state), 99, 105, 106–7, 108, 109–
    10; Finance Committee, 92, 107, 108,
    202; Governmental Efficiency Com-
    mittee, 99, 102, 105, 107, 108; Social
    Welfare Committeee, 102
Senate (U.S.), 207–8, 373–77
Senator Hotel, 61
Seniority system. *See* House issues
Sequoia (presidential yacht), 368
Sequoia–Kings Canyon National Park,
    481
Service Employees International Union
    (SEIU), 35, 180, 253, 419, 455; *See also*
    Building Service Employees
Sheehan, Jack, 187, 201, 253
Shell, Joseph, 121
Shelley, John F. ("Jack"), and Burton,
    127–29, 162, *512n10*; in Congress, 22,
    37, 47, 48, 52, 113, 117, 141, 144; mayor
    of S.F., 115, 118, 123–26, 140, 161, 162,
    166–72; union leader and state sena-
    tor, 20, 118
Shelley, Kevin, 447, 454, 455, 460, 465,
    469, *512n10, 535n8*
Shelley, Thelma, 123, 124, *512n10, 535n8*
Sheridan, John, 22
Sherrill, Robert, 183, 184
Shorenstein, Walter, 171
"Shrimp Hour," 61
Shultz, George, 195
Sierra Club, 209, 211, 334, 342, 343, 354,
    366, 457; and Burton, 333, 359, 458–
    59, 464–65, 480–81, 482; members,
    141, 210, 337
Silverthorne, Don, 162
Simon, Paul, 323
Simpson, xix, 335
Sinclair, Ward, 396
Sirica, John, 249
Sisk, B. F. ("Bernie"), 144, 227, 261, 317,
    384; and Burton, 138, 259, 260, 302,
    325, 342; and Tony Coelho, 259, 416
Siskiyou Wilderness, 342, 482
Skelton, Ike, 306, 307, 443

Skubitz, Joe, 355, 356, 363, 370
Slevin, Ed, 456, 461
Smith Act, 132
Smith, Howard Worth, 136, 137, 149
Smith, Martin, 411
Smyth, Jimmy, 33
SNCC (Student Nonviolent Coordinating Committee), 141
"Snipe," 51
Social Security Administration, 197
Solano County Central Labor Council, 428
Solarz, Stephen, 254
Southeast Asia. *See* Cambodia; Vietnam War
Southern Pacific, 19
Special interests. *See* Lobbyists, PACs, and special interests
Spellman, Gladys, 267, 390
Spinosa, Tom, 448
Spock, Benjamin, 462
Sports Illustrated, 362
Sprague, Irving, 134, 138
SPUR (San Francisco Planning and Urban Renewal), 211
SSI. *See* Supplemental Security Income
Staggers, Harley, 183, 302, 386
Stanton, Bill, 270
Stark, Fortney ("Pete"), 4, 261, 307, 432, 493
State Brewers Institute, 61
Steiger, Sam, 221
Steinberg, Lionel, 25, 30, 32, 55
Stephens, John and Betty, 238
Stevens, Ted, 342
Stevenson, Adlai, 30, 31, 51, 52, 55–56, 88, 89
Stockman, David, 349
Stone, C. Clement ("Chuck"), 147, 149
Stone, I. F., 139
Strauss, Robert, 253, 275
Struck, Myron, 346–47
Student Nonviolent Coordinating Committee (SNCC), 141
Subsidies. *See* Agribusiness
Sullivan, Jerry, 54

Sullivan, John E., 55
Sullivan, Raymond, xv, 21
Sullivan, William, 132
Sun Reporter, 23, 38, 47, 51, 127, 149, 166, 169
Supplemental Security Income (SSI), 202, 204, 208, 332, 496
Supreme court (state), 85, 151, 152, 284, 439; special masters, 286
Supreme Court (U.S.), 85, 99, 150, 249, 255
Sweeney Ridge, 400
Sweigert, William, 334
Swift, Al, 387
Swig, Ben, 171, 172
Symms, Steve, 374

Taft-Hartley Act, 28, 144; collective bargaining, 72
Tahoe Regional Planning Agency, 394
Talmadge, Herman, 207
Tayac, Billy, 390
Tayac, Chief Turkey, 389–90
Taylor, Roy, 331, 333
Teague, Charles, 284
Teague, Olin ("Tiger"), 227–28, 243, 247, 252, *517n12*
Teale, Stephen, 99, 107, 108
Teamsters, California, 419; San Francisco, 22
Temple, Arthur, 308–9
TenBroek, Jacobus, 93, 108
Third house. *See* Lobbyists, PACs, and special interests
Thomas, Doris, 138
Thomas, Norman, 167
Thomas, William (aide and reporter), 140, 175, 181, 211, 212, 214, 215, 216
Thomas, William (congressman), 426–27, 430, 433
Thompson, Frank ("Thompy"), 186, 206, 222, 252, 424; Abscam, 417; and Burton, 146, 229, 230, 246, 369, 370–71, 373, 384, 420; and Wayne Hays, 269–71, 296; and House reform, 137,

Designer:	Nola Burger
Compositor:	Terry Robinson & Co.
Text:	Adobe Garamond
Display:	Gill Sans
Printer:	Edwards Brothers, Inc.
Binder:	Edwards Brothers, Inc.